THE COMMUNIST PARTY OF CHINA
AND MARXISM, 1921–1985

Without an understanding of the Communist Party no one can understand the China in which the Party has dominated the country for nearly four decades. Marxism is the soul and inspiration of the Communist Party. What has Marxism meant to China? This book follows the development of the Communist Party and of Marxism in China from the early years. It sheds new light on themes such as Mao's own history, the rise and fall of Lin Biao, the battle between Mao and Zhou Enlai, the Cultural Revolution, the defeat of the 'Gang of Four', and Deng Xiaoping's consolidation of power. The book relies entirely on what the Communist Party has revealed about itself and for this reason is subtitled 'A Self-Portrait'.

Laszlo Ladany, born in Hungary in 1914, studied the violin at the Budapest Conservatoire and obtained the degree of *Dr Iuris Utrisque* at the University, entering the Jesuit Order in 1936. In 1940–9 he studied in China, then left for Hong Kong where, during the years 1953–82, he published a weekly newsletter, *China News Analysis*, known to all China experts. He died in 1990.

LASZLO LADANY

The Communist Party of China and Marxism

1921-1985

A Self-Portrait

With a Foreword by
ROBERT ELEGANT

HURST & COMPANY, LONDON

First published in the United Kingdom in 1988 by
C. Hurst & Co. (Publishers) Ltd.,
41 Great Russell Street, London, WC1B 3PL
© Laszlo Ladany, 2018/The Procurator in Hong Kong of the English Assistancy
of the Jesuit Order, 1992

This paperback edition published, 2018

Printed in India

The right of Laszlo Ladany to be identified as the author of this publication is
asserted by him in accordance with the Copyright, Designs and Patents Act,
1988.

A Cataloguing-in-Publication data record for this book
is available from the British Library.

ISBN: 978-1-84904-910-8

www.hurstpublishers.com

FOREWORD

by Robert Elegant

As his seventieth year approached, Laszlo Ladany decided to retire from the strenuous tasks of periodical scholarship to which he had voluntarily subordinated himself since the early 1950s. He gave up producing the newsletter *China News Analysis*, which was his own creation, in order to consider and record what he had learned in some four decades of scanning the press of the People's Republic of China. Even those who knew his tempestuous and dedicated character believed that he might then allow himself to assess in tranquility the past and present condition of the turbulent nation to which he has devoted his life. I, for one, hoped—and almost expected—that his self-imposed labours would be less strenuous in quasi-retirement.

I should have known better. Instead of complacently reviewing past accomplishments, he has been breaking new ground. Perhaps he has no choice, for he has been lured onward by the continuing revelations of the chief players in the great drama of China.

Almost an entire generation of senior Communist leaders has in the last few years been setting down its recollections of the decades from 1920 to 1949 with rare and remarkable candour. The spotlight of memory has even illuminated some obscure aspects of the landscape since the establishment of the People's Republic. Freed by the death of Chairman Mao Zedong in 1976 from his overwhelming pressure, the eminent Chinese have assuredly also felt the wind of mortality chill on their backs. Whether wishing to justify themselves or to set the historical record right, perhaps both, they have recently published extraordinarily candid reminiscences. Because of their implicit disavowal of the Communist Party's official line in so many cases, those reminiscences carry conviction.

Ladany was clearly impelled by those revelations to enlarge the scope of this work. He originally planned a judicious recollection of the information and insights already published in *China News Analysis*—with additional material assayed since he gave up the newsletter in 1983. When I first looked into these pages, I expected only a measured assessment of the past.

This book is, however, far more: a fast-moving, yet comprehensive *tour d'horizon* of China during the past nine decades, and, also, a voyage

v

of discovery. The author is not only a formidable historian, but a journalist of great distinction. Like Xenophon and Herodotus, he explores the frontier between history and immediate events.

Parts of this read like a spy thriller—and other parts like a rather grim realistic novel. Drama is inherent. The author writes of the great purges that have regularly shaken the Communist Party—and have, consequently, shaken the structure of the People's Republic which is ruled by that Party.

Yet history is not as obliging as a novel; although further explicated, some events are, of necessity, left unresolved. For example, the fall in the early 1970s of Field-Marshal Lin Biao, who was for a time—a tumultuous time—the designated successor to Chairman Mao. The definitive account of Lin Biao's defeat and death must wait until the survivors of that violent episode are free to tell the whole story—if, of course, anyone knows the whole story.

Yet Ladany's revelations are more than enough to force students of China to reassess some cherished ideas. Letting go of long-held concepts is painful since our mature judgments are integral to our intellectual and, even, our emotional being. Moreover jettisoning fundamental facts means writing off substantial portions of one's intellectual capital. I, too, am reluctant to make major revisions in my estimates of the country that has engaged much of my attention for decades. Nonetheless, Ladany's revelations and new insights will require of us all substantial revision of many basic concepts.

This book will, therefore, be attacked vigorously by part of the scholarly community. Some will instinctively resist reconsidering basic facts and, therefore, basic interpretations. Others may even feel moral outrage at the doubts cast upon beliefs they have long cherished.

Central to this book, whose tone is remarkably uncontentious, is a view of Chairman Mao Zedong that may appear highly contentious. Ladany offers a portrait of the Chairman that differs significantly from previous portraits. Yet every alteration in the familiar physiognomy is substantiated by the words of Mao's contemporaries and colleagues.

For one thing, Mao Zedong, Ladany contends, did not himself convince the Chinese Communist Party that it must base its campaign for the conquest of power on the peasantry. Neither did Mao defy the Kremlin by championing that strategy. Nor, it appears, did he become the unchallenged leader of the Party at the Cun Yi Conference in 1935—but only some time afterwards. Such details are, perhaps, of absorbing interest only to specialists—despite their profound implications.

However, Ladany's full portrait of Mao Zedong will assuredly interest—and, perhaps, horrify—a wider public. Despite consistent criticism of the Chairman by his fellow Communists since his death, the outside world is still inclined to view him as a heroic, self-sacrificing, and idealistic revolutionary leader. Ladany portrays a brilliant schemer, indeed a schemer of genius, but, nonetheless, an essentially ignoble figure.

The Mao Zedong presented here was not only an ignoramus regarding Marxism, but a mean-spirited plotter devoted to his personal safety only a whit less than to his personal advancement. He was also a petty domestic tyrant, as well as a public despot.

The story of the Communist Party is the story of China in this century. This book crowns the career of Laszlo Ladany—and lays upon all China specialists an even greater debt to him. Idiosyncratic, sometimes scathing and sometimes tender, it is unique and quite brilliant.

May 1987

AUTHOR'S PREFACE

Having lived in North China and Shanghai for nine years during and after the Japanese war, I arrived in Hong Kong in 1949, eager to know how China was about to develop. Having written jottings on the Communist press for some years for a monthly, I began in 1953 the publication of a weekly, *China News Analysis*, which covered every aspect of Chinese reality — political, economic and cultural — relying entirely on Chinese sources. (This weekly newsletter became a fortnightly in 1979, and closed down in 1982, restarting in 1984 under new editorship.)

It now seems opportune to sum up the essentials grasped in thirty years of reporting. I have therefore begun with the development, the ups and downs, of the Chinese Communist Party; for it is the Communist Party that dictates all action and shapes every aspect of the nation's life. Without an understanding of the Party, no one can understand the China of the nearly four decades in which the Party has dominated the country. Marxism is the soul and inspiration of the Communist Party. What has Marxism meant to China? The Communist Party of China and Marxism did not begin with the establishment of the People's Republic in 1949. Their history goes back to the 1920s, so what were they before the establishment of the Communist regime? So long as Mao Zedong was alive the world had a one-sided vision of the pre-1949 period. Books written about the early history of the Communist Party and Marxism in China relied necessarily on the official Maoist version of Party history. Only after Mao's death in 1976 were Chinese Party historians allowed to dig out old documents not published during the reign of Mao. The early history of the Party has therefore to be written anew.

This book follows the development of the Communist Party and of Marxism in China from the early years. Its purpose is not to accumulate historical data; what it seeks is an understanding of what Marxism and the Chinese Communist Party meant in the twentieth century and how it can have happened that China became Communist. Many details that would interest specialists have been deliberately passed over lest they should cloud the non-initiated reader's understanding of Communism in China. The Chinese background, let alone Chinese names, is confusing enough already for those not familiar with the subject. Yet this book is not abstract speculation. It is a concatenation of first-hand sources. In relating the history of the Party and Marxism in the years

1921–49 it relies mainly on revelations that appeared in the Chinese press in the early 1980s, particularly in 1979–82, the years when Chinese historians of the Party were relatively free to write. (In more recent years this freedom has been severely curtailed.) In the part of the book dealing with the period of the People's Republic, the period that began in 1949, we summarise what we reported in the *China News Analysis* week after week. In the part dealing with the years 1983–5, contemporary Chinese sources are indicated.

Since it relies entirely on what the Communist Party has revealed about itself, the book is truly, as the sub-title says, a self-portrait of Chinese Communism.

Scrutiny of the Chinese sources for thirty-six years develops in the student a sixth sense in sorting out reliable statements from mere propaganda. The Chinese press is not like its Western counterpart. Important events may be kept secret for ten or twenty years. In 1985 the head of the Communist Party, Hu Yaobang, said bluntly to journalists that up-to-date reporting is not the purpose of newspapers; important documents may not be published till years after the event. Many things that happened in the 1950s, even in the 1920s, were not revealed till thirty or sixty years later.

Twenty years from now, when all the actors in this drama have died and perhaps the archives have been thrown open, another history of the Communist Party and a more widely based interpretation of the events will have to be written. At present all that can be done is to put down as much as can be detected from the Chinese sources that are available now.

I use this occasion to express special thanks to the Revd A. Birmingham, a long-standing collaborator, whose wish to remain anonymous I could not in good conscience honour.

Hong Kong, 1987   L.L.

CONTENTS

xi

THE PEOPLE'S REPUBLIC OF CHINA

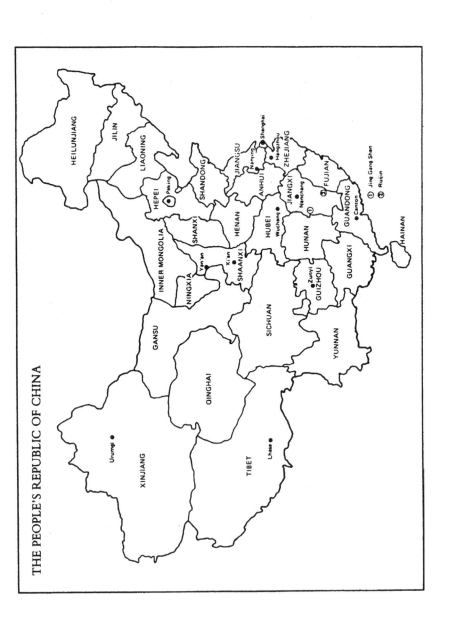

Part One: 1921 – 1949

CHAPTER I

HOW CHINA BECAME COMMUNIST

The more you study China the less you understand her. This is probably true of every country. Superficial visitors gain fleeting impressions which are often correct; but they do not acquire the whole picture, and the complicated reality of a country escapes them. Studying a Communist country presents additional complications, for the Communist Party is, in essence, a secret society: vital decisions are taken by a few behind closed doors.

For many people, China is an emotion-laden term; for some it means an earthly paradise, for others the reign of the devil. Sidney and Beatrice Webb saw paradise in Stalin's Soviet Union. Enthusiastic Americans visiting China during the reign of Mao's wife, Jiang Qing, and her associates saw paradise there. A few years later, when the Chinese press revealed the darker side of life, China experts were inclined to see nothing but squalor, corruption and spittoons. It is difficult to understand how such a vast country with such a long history came under Marxist rule.

After forty years devoted to the study of China and thirty years to the production of a weekly newsletter on China, the *China News Analysis*, I have begun to recognise how much more there is about China that I do not know.

My original intention for this book, or series of books, was to coordinate the matter contained in the weekly reports of my newsletter, each of which dealt with a single topic, and thus to sum up in a systematic form the development of the People's Republic over thirty or so years. But on looking at this period in perspective, I became aware that it would be impossible to give an adequate picture of that history without examining the prelude to those thirty years, namely the way in which China became a Communist state.

To understand China it is necessary to go back to its history, in particular to the efforts made at modernisation in the period since the shock of invasion by Western powers in the last century. As a minimum, it is necessary to grasp the early history of the Communist movement in China. It is not, indeed, necessary to have a comprehensive knowledge

1

of the sequence of events in full detail; but it is necessary to understand the convictions and the nature of the governing body and, above all, the process by which China became Marxist.

The history of the Communist Party in China is inseparable from the person of Mao Zedong (Mao Tse-tung). The Party was, and became, the Party of Mao. First, therefore, we study what the Party was like before the ascendancy of Mao (Chapter II), then the ascent of Mao (Chapter III), his rule in Yan'an (Chapter IV), the secret of his success (Chapter V), and what the Japanese war did for the Communist Party (Chapter VI) and the nature of Marxism in the years in Yan'an (Chapter VII). We then look behind the curtain, studying how the Party attempted to mould the nation's hearts and minds (Chapter VIII) and how the last phase of the civil war led to victory (Chapter IX). We end with a look at the inner-Party disorder — which was revealed only after Mao's death (Chapter X).

The fundamental question remains: how did a country like China become Marxist, indeed, how does any country become Marxist?

For a country to become Marxist it is not necessary for all the inhabitants, or even the majority of the people of that country, to become Marxists. Experience has shown that this does not happen. Lenin said that a country is called Marxist, or Communist, if the ruling élite is Marxist.[1]

Both Mussolini in Italy in 1922 and Hitler in Germany in 1933 came to power by a majority vote, elected by a misinformed public that did not know what the consequences of their votes would be. But there is no Marxist-ruled country in which Marxists came to power by a popular vote. Fidel Castro was not a Communist Party member when he squeezed out his opponents. In most of the countries which have become Marxist, or Communist, or 'socialist', as they euphemistically called themselves, there were not many Marxists before the Marxists took power. In Czechoslovakia alone, there probably was already a considerable number of Marxists; but even there the Communist regime was not established by a popular vote.

Before the Second World War the powerful German Socialist Party (SPD) was a Marxist party, but West Germany did not become a Communist state. At the end of the war East Germany did, thanks to the presence of Soviet troops.

Communism in China was not created by the presence of Soviet troops. Indeed, at the end of the Second World War the Soviet Union signed a treaty with the enemies of the Communists, the Nationalist government. Yet there too Communism was not established by a popular vote. The Communists won by military victory in a civil war. There is some parallel between the establishment of the Marxist regimes in Yugoslavia and China. In both countries, guerilla fighters won political power and established Marxist regimes. It certainly cannot be said that China first became Marxist and then the Marxists took over the government of the country. This did not happen in Russia either. The October Revolution was not a surge of majority opinion transforming Russia into a Communist country. Much less was this the case in China. Marxism in China had very shallow roots.

In Russia the roots of Marxism go back to the last century, when Marxism was hotly debated among prominent Russians, inside Russia and in Western Europe. The 1848 *Communist Manifesto* written by Marx and Engels was translated into Russian in 1860 and was discussed in the press in Russia itself. The first volume of *Das Kapital* was published in Russia in 1872. Marxist economic theories were taught in Russian universities. Marxism was hotly debated among Russian émigrés in Western Europe at the end of the last century. The influence of these émigrés in Russia itself was considerable. The great figure was Plekhanov (1856–1918), whose writings had, as Lenin said, an important influence on the Russian Revolution. For years Lenin collaborated with him, but later their ways parted. Lenin put his stamp on Russian Marxism in his book *What Is To Be Done?*, published in 1902. He outlined the role of the Party as he conceived it: it was to be an organisation of professional revolutionaries.

Lenin, according to experts on his career, learnt historical Russian conspiratorial techniques before he began to read and to understand Marx[2] — a strange parallel with Mao, who studied the history of power-covetous men in Chinese history before he learnt anything about Marxism.

The Russians of the nineteenth century knew their Marx and Engels, even if they twisted their ideas to their liking; the best brains among them were familiar Western philosophers such as Hegel and Kant. They were also deeply involved in Marxist movements in Western Europe. At the end of the nineteenth century Marxist writings and Marxist newspapers began to appear in Russia itself.

By the time of the October Revolution in 1917, Marxism had already had a long history among the Russians. Lastly, Russia is a European country, and for centuries Western trends had influenced Russian cultural circles.

The situation in China was entirely different. In the first years of this century there were some references to Marxism in the writings of the two great figures of that period, Kang Yu Wei and Liang Qichao. Nobody seems to have paid much attention to these references. A Peking quarterly on modern history published in 1983 recalled this, and mentioned that after early and sporadic mentions of Marxism, practically nothing about it appeared in Chinese from 1908 until the October Revolution (1917).[3] Mao himself wrote in 1949: 'Before the October Revolution we Chinese knew nothing about Lenin and Stalin, nothing about Marx and Engels.'[4]

Yet China had been in a revolutionary mood ever since the beginning of the century. In 1911 the Manchu dynasty was overthrown and the Republic was declared. The country was in disarray. A longing to modernise China and a rejection of all traditions were in the air. The news of the October Revolution in Russia aroused excitement. Without knowing what Marxism was, a tiny group of people, with the help of Comintern agents, established the Chinese Communist Party in 1921. Immediately, plans were drawn up for the translation of all the works of Marx and Lenin — but practically nothing happened. Leftist magazines carried inflammatory articles; that was all.

Of Hegel's works, his *Philosophy of History* was the first to appear in Chinese, years after the establishment of the Communist Party, in two translations by non-Communists, one in 1932, one in 1936. The other works of Hegel were not translated until the 1950s and 1960s.[5] The first fragments, fragments only, of the 1848 *Communist Manifesto* appeared in a Chinese magazine in 1906. The whole text was translated in 1920 and again in 1921.[6] (The first Japanese translation of the *Communist Manifesto* was published in 1904, sixteen years before the first Chinese one.)[7] The first volume of *Das Kapital* appeared in Chinese in 1930, and all three volumes in 1938.[8]

Marx's *Critique of the Gotha Programme* appeared in a magazine in 1922. Engels' *The Origin of the Family, Private Property and the State* was translated in 1929. Only one important work of Lenin's, *The State and Revolution*, appeared at an early date in China, in 1927, ten years after its first publication.[9]

The first translation of Lenin's theoretical writing appeared in the early 1930s, some copies printed in China itself, others printed in Chinese in Moscow. (The sale of Lenin's works was permitted under the Nationalist government.) New translations of *Imperialism, the Highest Stage of Capitalism* and *Materialism and Empirio-Criticism* were published in Shanghai in 1948. A year earlier, in 1947, the *Selected Works of Lenin* had been published in Chinese in Moscow. In 1953 the translation from Russian of the thirty-eight volumes of Lenin's writings began. This undertaking was finished in 1959.[10]

In 1953, four years after the establishment of the People's Republic, a Marx-Engels-Lenin-Stalin Translation Office was established in Peking. Two years later the publication of the *Complete Works of Marx and Engels* began; this took thirty years.[11]

The Party leaders did not really begin to study Marxism until the late 1930s in Yan'an, and what they studied was the Marxism of Stalin. *Methodology of the Thoughts of Marx, Engels, Lenin and Stalin* was printed in Chinese in Moscow in 1942. This was a sort of compendium of Stalinist Marxism. The introduction said it should fill the gap left by the lack of Chinese versions of Marx, Engels, Lenin and Stalin. What China learnt in those days was not Marxism but the Lenin-Stalin ideology.

Marx, it should be remembered, disliked the word 'ideology'. In his *German Ideology and the Poverty of Philosophy*, and even in the first volume of *Das Kapital*, the word meant an abstract, *a priori*, and false concept or method. However, it got the seal of approval from Lenin. From 1902 onwards, Lenin spoke of proletarian ideology, class ideology, Marxist ideology, bourgeois ideology.[12] The original meaning of ideology as something unreal, untrue, a mere product of the imagination, was transferred in the Marxist world to the word 'metaphysical'. Thus with Lenin and with Stalin, Marxism — a doctrine, perhaps even a philosophy — became an *ideology* and was openly acknowledged as such; spreading Marxism was called *propaganda*; denying it became *lèse-majesté*.

Did China become Communist by adopting Marxist ideology? In 1983, sixty-two years after the establishment of the Chinese Communist Party, the man then in charge of the propaganda department of the Party Central Committee, Deng Lichun, wrote as follows about *patriotism*: 'Many of our revolutionaries of earlier generations were led to the road of Communism by the path of patriotism. Many of them at first had no knowledge of Communism; but they saw the poverty of the country and the misery of the people, and a determination to save the country and the people surged spontaneously in their hearts. Having seen other efforts fail, they turned to Marxism-Leninism and found that it was the only way of saving China.'[13]

(This was written in 1983, at a time when everyone knew that faith in Marxism was at a low ebb. It had become necessary to encourage the young to love their country, and thus to lead them back to faith in Marxism.)

Zhou Yang was one of the early revolutionaries, and he was no ordinary person. He was a Party leader of culture in the Communist underground in Shanghai in the 1930s; he was a leading literary figure in the early years in Yan'an, and under the People's Republic he was a deputy head of the Party Central Committee's propaganda department until the Cultural Revolution swept him away. Ten years later, in 1977, he returned to public life.

In 1983, on the centenary of the death of Marx, when he himself was seventy-five, he gave the following account of the origins of Marxism in China:

We had had no theoretical preparation before the establishment of the Party. In nineteenth century Russia, Chernyshevsky and Herzen, though not Marxists, did pioneer work [both were populist revolutionary writers] and Bukharin and Lenin had published many writings well before the Russian Revolution. In China the situation was different. Chen Duxiu, the founder of the Party, was merely a radical revolutionary. Li Dazhao was one of the first propagators of Marxism, one of the founders of the Party and also its first martyr, but he wrote little.

(A study of Li Dazhao in the journal of Liaoning University said that until 1924 his writings were not really Marxist.[14] The Chinese Communist Party was founded in the early 1920s. Li was executed by Zhang Zuolin, the ruler of Manchuria, in 1927.)

'It was only when the Thoughts of Mao Zedong were formed that the Chinese Communist Party acquired a mature theory. [The term 'Thoughts of Mao Zedong' made its official appearance at the Seventh Party Congress, in 1945, four years before the establishment of the People's Republic, twenty-four years after the founding of the Party.] Indeed, one great weakness of our country's Party is the lack of a theoretical foundation of Marxism.'

The Marxism of Marx and Engels, Zhou Yang said, was born in the most developed countries of those days, England, France and Germany. Marx spent more than half his life in England, and many of his works were written there. He studied English economics, and many of his theories were illustrated by English examples. He was also influenced by French revolutionary writers such as Saint-Simon and Fourier.

German philosophy had a profound influence on Marx and Engels, both of whom were German. The greater part of Marx's work consists of refutations of German philosophers. Lenin himself in his later years studied the German philosopher Hegel, and wrote that without understanding Hegel one could not understand Marx. Early Chinese translators of Western works, in the opening decades of the twentieth century, knew no German and neglected German authors.

The trouble with Stalin, Zhou Yang continued, was that he despised German philosophy.

Copying Stalin, we, in our study of Marxism, ignored its origins in German philosophy. This had serious practical consequences in China. Stalin ignored the Hegelian concept of unity of opposites. Comrade Mao Zedong in his 'On Practice', which was written before Stalin's *Dialectical Materialism and Historical Materialism*, spoke of synthesis, but Stalin knew only antithesis, i.e. struggle, which degenerated into devastating class struggle. In the last period of his life Comrade Mao Zedong made the same mistake, which was manifest in the Great Leap in the late 1950s and in his exaggerated emphasis on class struggle in the early 1960s, which culminated in the Cultural Revolution.[15]

In the years after Mao many such soul-searching articles were published. Unyielding Party leaders like Zhou Yang, who had been Mao's 'whip' and chief persecutor of Communist writers, calmed down when they themselves felt the lash, were imprisoned and suffered hardship, and saw many of their colleagues die at the hands of Red Guard hordes during the Cultural Revolution, or in the prisons of the radicals led by Mao's wife, Jiang Qing. When others were suffering in earlier periods they did not recognise that anything had gone wrong. When it was their turn, things were different. Most of them did not give up being Marxist, but they did discover that Marxism was not what they had been taught, and that China had followed the wrong Marxism, or indeed that it had become Marxist without knowing what Marxism was.

It can perhaps be said that, paradoxical though it may seem, a country may become Communist before becoming Marxist. In the early 1920s China was ripe for change and there was revolutionary ferment in certain intellectual, or pseudo-intellectual circles. (No Communist regime has ever been set up by peasants or workers, the proletariat.) The radical changes in the Soviet Union attracted their attention. Marxism was learnt much later, in the Yan'an period in the 1930s and 1940s; but even then few books had been translated into Chinese. The bulk of Marxist literature did not appear in China till many years after the establishment of Communist rule over the whole country. (Probably the same can be said of other late-comers in the Marxist camp, such as Cuba and other Latin American and African nations. They became, or were believed to have become, Communist before they knew what Marxism was.)

It can also be said that there is not a single Marxist country in the world; there are only Leninist-Marxist regimes. Lenin had the genius to take Marxist theories, which had been designed to liberate suppressed workers living in Dickensian misery in highly developed industrialised countries, and apply them to a predominantly agrarian, non-industrialised society. Lenin's contributions were the energetic élite, the Party with a capital P, the 'vanguard of the proletariat', and the prolongation, indeed the permanence, of the dictatorship, called 'proletarian dictatorship', which in Marx's original concept was to have been a brief transitional episode. It was quickly discovered in the Soviet Union — the Tsarist regime had shown the way — that the power of the Party could not be maintained without a secret police. In the 1930s Stalin's Soviet theoreticians constructed round all this a compact edifice of Marxist theories composed of carefully chosen phrases and fragments from the writings of Marx and Engels, thus conveying an illusion of a monolithic concept of the world. The foundation of this edifice was materialism — not simple materialism but dialectical materialism, which allows human action, the action of the Party, to 'accelerate the march of history'.

All Communist regimes are based on these three factors: dialectical materialism, the power of the Party, and a secret police. No Communist regime is based on pre-Lenin Marxism.

Sources

Party history is still in many ways obscure. During Mao's lifetime there was a set version of official Party history, which, unhappily, has influenced much Western writing on Mao and on the Party. Independent scholars, however, have made a substantial contribution to the subject by making use of early texts of Party documents preserved in the United States (Hoover Institution) and Taiwanese archives and Russian-language sources.

After Mao's death a revival of writing on Party history began in China. It was now possible to say things that had been taboo during Mao's period of rule. Distortions of the official Party history were corrected. People whom Mao did not like reappeared. The early role of Mao himself was reduced to its proper, modest dimensions. Since 1979 the Academy of Social Sciences has been publishing a 300-page small-format quarterly, *Modern History Studies* — the first issue for internal circulation only, from the second issue onwards open to subscription — which has published some remarkable studies on Party history, written with the modesty of the genuine historian. One such study, to which we shall refer often, lists the names and posts of Party officials from 1921 till 1937 and goes on to explain that the work is based on a critical analysis of Party documents, reminiscences and other sources. It points out that the minutes of some important meetings — that held at Zunyi in January 1935, for instance — are nowhere to be found. Many other dates, the review admits, are uncertain.

This is an impressive study, but not all the studies are of the same calibre. The influence of the old Maoist version of Party history is still felt in a number of them. The publications of the Party Schools have to be taken with a pinch of salt: they are more 'Maoist' than those of the Academy of Social Sciences. One gains the impression — though it is not said explicitly — that the archives of the earlier years were put at the disposal of inner-Party historians, but apparently this is only true of the documents of the 1920s and 1930s.

Our ignorance is being dispelled to some extent by reminiscences published since Mao's death, which reveal hitherto unknown facts and events. All this matter is used in the following chapters to throw new light on past events and, more importantly, on the inner life of the Party and on the knowledge of Marxism in the Party. Yet everything has to be accepted with caution.

Our purpose here, as was said above, is not to present a detailed history of the Party or to get lost in meticulous detail which only interests historians. We are trying to understand what Marxism meant in China.

CHAPTER II

BEFORE MAO

The Comintern

The Chinese Communist Party was launched by the Third Communist International (Comintern) from Moscow. In no other Asian country was Moscow so interested, or so successful, as in China.

There were Marxist groups in India in the 1920s; but the Indian Communist Party was not formally established until eight years after the Chinese Party. At the end of 1928, Lenin's close ally, the Indian M.N. Roy, had lost his post on the Executive Committee of the Communist International (ECCI) — in the following year he was expelled from the Comintern itself. The Indian Communist Party followed the militant policies of Stalin, but six years after its foundation it had only 150 members. It did not begin to grow till the mid-1930s, when it was cooperating with the Congress Party.

The Communist Party of Japan, founded in 1922, was dissolved by the party itself in 1924, much to the displeasure of Moscow. When it was re-established in the following year, it was led by men critical of Moscow. In 1932 the Japanese Communists intended to overthrow the Emperor system. The Communist Party of Japan's very existence was illegal until after the Second World War. It broke with the Chinese Communist Party during the Cultural Revolution and maintained its independence from Moscow. Japan can hardly be counted among Moscow's success stories.[1] Success in Japan, the only fully industrialised country in Asia, would have proved that Marx and Engels were right, that capitalism leads to Communism.

The history of the Comintern in China was different. Not only had Moscow and the Comintern organised the Chinese Communist Party; Moscow had also had a direct hand in the reorganisation of the Nationalist Party, the Kuomintang. Originally named the T'ung Meng Hui, it had been founded in 1905 by Sun Yat Sen, who later became the President of the provisional government of China after the overthrow of the Manchu dynasty in 1911. Sun was a man of high aspirations, but he was not an organiser. When the Russian October Revolution broke out, his forces were at the southern tip of China, planning revolution and the conquest of the country. Moscow saw that the Kuomintang could serve as a Trojan horse for Chinese Communism, and Sun Yat Sen was eager to learn from the emissaries of the Comintern how to organise his party into a revolutionary force. The Kuomintang broke with the Communists in 1927. Marxism was rejected, but the principles of organisation adopted from the Soviet Communists were retained.

Even today, in Taiwan, the party is the supreme ruler, overshadowing government organisations. The essential instrument of repression, a secret police, is there, and was headed for many years by Chiang Ching Kuo. Yet the Kuomintang has never become, and never was on the mainland, a totalitarian force interfering in people's private lives. Indeed from its early years the Government of Nanking turned to the West and became a faithful ally of the West.

Before the break with the Kuomintang

The October Revolution mesmerised a group of Chinese intellectuals. In the early 1920s there was not much difference between the revolutionary Kuomintang, then active in the southern end of the country, and the few dozen Communists.

The Communists themselves knew little about Marxism. An article on the first contact with the Comintern, published in 1981 in a Shanghai newspaper, says that even Chen Duxiu, leader of the Communist Party for the first six years, 'was not really a thorough Marxist'.[2]

The newly established Soviet government in Moscow made a grand gesture towards China when, before sending the Dutchman G. Maring (H. Sneevliet) to China, it renounced the Soviet Union's rights to territories acquired by what China called the Unequal Treaties. (In those days of course the new Bolshevik government was not yet in active possession of what had been the Russian territories in the Far East under the Tsars.)

In 1922 Abram Joffe was sent to China to deal with the old-style government in Peking (Sun Yat Sen's revolutionary Kuomintang was still in the South). In 1923 he and Sun Yat Sen made a common declaration in Shanghai.[3] When Joffe arrived in Peking from Moscow in November 1922, he was entertained at a great banquet by representatives of fourteen different groups, Kuomintang members and affiliates, and some Communists. This was an indication of the enthusiasm of young Chinese intellectuals for the mirage of a new world.[4]

From the Soviet side, cooperation with the small group of Chinese Communists and with the long-established, and no less revolutionary, Kuomintang fitted well into the new tactics of a common front, decided upon by the Fourth Comintern Congress in November-December 1922.[5] Comintern advisers helped to organise both the Nationalist and the Communist parties in China.

Early in 1920 a Marxist group in Peking, led by Li Dazhao, contacted Moscow, and Moscow promptly despatched Grigori Voitinsky to China.[6] In June 1921 Maring contacted Sun Yat Sen, and was present at the establishment of the Chinese Communist Party.

How the Communist Party in China came into being had been a moot question for many years. New light was shed on this problem in 1980 when a 452-page collection of original documents was published in Peking for restricted circulation within the Party.[7] In 1984 the review *Modern History Studies* extracted some basic facts from this collection. Small groups of Communists, it was now revealed, were established in four cities, the first by Chen Duxiu in August 1920 in Shanghai. In the whole country there were some fifty Party members. July 1 used to be the traditional anniversary of the founding of the Party. The documents corrected this: the date of the First Congress was July 23.[8] The Second Chinese Communist Party Congress was held in July 1922 in Shanghai (Chen Duxiu and Zhang Guotao were present, but not Mao). Party membership had increased from 50 to 195, and the Second Congress formally decided to join the Comintern.

The Comintern in Moscow kept a close eye on China. In January 1923 the Executive Committee of the Communist International (ECCI) published a resolution which said: 'Given that there is only one revolutionary organisation in China, the Kuomintang, which is a mixed group of bourgeois nationalists, petty bourgeois, intellectuals and workers, and that the working class does not yet form an independent force . . . [the] cooperation of the young Communist Party with the Kuomintang is a necessity.' The Chinese Communist Party, however, must maintain its independence and its independent leadership, the document said.[9]

Land reform

The Fourth Congress of the ECCI, held in May 1923, instructed the Chinese comrades to support the land programme of the Kuomintang: expropriation of the land of the landlords and of temples, distribution of the land among the peasants, abolition of the land-tax system and cancellation of outstanding rents. But opposition should be offered to the Kuomintang's connections with warlords who are hostile to the Soviet Union, in particular those who are linked with Japan.[10]

The May 1923 instructions of the Comintern were addressed to the Third Chinese Party Congress, to be held in June, but they did not reach China till the second half of July, after the close of the Congress. The Third Chinese Party Congress spoke merely of a reduction in land rent.[11]

The Party in China, still only a small fragment of the Kuomintang, was neither in the mood nor in the position to advocate radical policies. A Central Committee Plenum held in July 1926 spoke about opposition to inhuman government officials and to excessive land rent, but it opposed the proposed overthrow of the landlords. An extraordinary meeting of the Central Committee held in December 1926 in Hankow adhered to this same policy.[12]

In November-December 1926 the Seventh Enlarged Meeting of the ECCI was held. Stalin spoke about the Chinese revolution. At that time Pavel Mif was the rising Soviet expert on China. A year later he became deputy director, and in 1928 director, of the Sun Yat Sen University in Moscow.[13] Stalin approved of some of Mif's statements and disapproved of others. He approved his evaluation of the Communists in China as still very weak, and he compared the Chinese situation to that of Russia in 1905 — the year of the revolution that failed. Stalin approved of the policies of Chiang Kai Shek's southern forces in Guangdong province (he did not mention Chiang by name) and their initial efforts to conquer the North. He supported them because they were opposed to 'US and Japanese imperialism'. Stalin wanted the Chinese Communists to penetrate the Chinese revolutionary army.[14]

Stalin, however, disapproved of Mif's advocacy of the establishment of rural 'soviets' in China. The cities should not be abandoned, Stalin said. In the villages, Farmers' Committees could be established. Yet Stalin was hesitant. It is wrong, he said, to oppose revolution in the villages. He approved of the report delivered by Tan Pingshan at the meeting. Tan did not propose radical reforms, but described the right, left and middle wings in the Kuomintang: the Communists should cooperate with the left wing. On agrarian reform, he mentioned the arming of the villages for self-defence, and he expanded on improving the lot of the peasants, reducing taxation, improving irrigation, restricting usury — 'not to exceed a yearly rate of 30 per cent' — and so on.[15]

Tan Pingshan himself had an extraordinary career. In 1928, two years after his report to the ECCI in Moscow, he was expelled from the Party; after the disastrous 1927 clash with the Nationalists, he had formed a third party. He opposed Chiang Kai Shek and remained on good terms with the Communists. In the early 1950s he held high government office in the People's Republic until his death in 1956.[16]

Not many of those who had been expelled from the Party attained high positions under the Communist regime. (Several biographies of Tan omit all mention of his expulsion.)

The Resolution Concerning Chinese Conditions issued by the Seventh meeting of the ECCI in November and December 1926 instructed the Chinese Communists to stay in the Kuomintang and to seek leading posts in the bodies in charge of Kuomintang agrarian policy. The Communists should promote the Canton Kuomintang Government's agrarian revolution. The landlords' armed guards should be dissolved; the poor and 'middle' peasants should be armed, and Farmers' Associations should be established. Land rents should be reduced, and the land of landlords, the gentry, the temples and the churches should be nationalised. In its early days the peasants had supported the revolution, the Resolution said, but their enthusiasm had waned. Steps should be taken to make sure that peasant support for the revolution would be permanent.[17]

This Comintern Resolution reached China at the beginning of 1927. Qu Qiubai, then leading the Party, proposed what he called 'a thorough solution of the land question'. Mao Zedong made a survey of the peasant situation in Hunan and went to Wuhan in February to report to the Party Central. Qu wrote a preface to Mao's report on the Hunan peasant movement. Liu Shaoqi agitated in Hunan province. One of the Kuomintang leaders, Sun Fo, also advocated land division, and this was urged at a Kuomintang meeting in March.[18]

A good study of the history of the Communist land policy in China, published in 1983 in a Peking review, *Historical Research*, says that until the end of 1926, the Chinese Communist Party wanted no more than a reduction in rents.[19] *Historical Research* quotes the Comintern directives calling for more radical action; it does not point out that the Chinese Communists were not carrying out the orders received from Moscow. Chen Duxiu, a highly-educated man, had no sadistic tendencies. That trait became apparent only after he was purged in 1927. Moreover as long as the Communists were weak and remained junior partners of the Nationalists, they had but limited room for manoeuvre. Among the Nationalists there were radicals ready for action, but there were others, too, who only wanted to improve the lot of the peasants with the good of the whole country in mind. The difference in temperament between the left wing of the Nationalists and the Communists was slight; but the difference in purpose and in the nature of the movements was enormous. The Nationalists were 'nationalist'; the Communists were affiliated to a foreign power and took orders, or were supposed to take orders, from the Comintern in Moscow; and Moscow's and the Comintern's intentions were, even in those days, guided by the interests of the Soviet Union.

1927

In 1927 relations between the Kuomintang and the Communists deteriorated. On January 1, the Nationalist government moved from Canton to Wuhan and the Communists were harassed in several places.[20]

The Fifth Communist Party Congress was held in Wuhan from April to May. The Congress recognised the decisions on China made at the Seventh Meeting of the ECCI of November-December 1926, and this time it decided to accept the radical measures proposed by Moscow: confiscation of the land of landowners, and the land of the temples and of 'foreign religions', but not the land of small landlords. Chen Duxiu, the General Secretary of the Party, was opposed to radical measures. Indeed he proposed that since the imperialist forces were strong in the big cities (there were still 'foreign concessions', sections of cities administered by foreigners) and the power of the high bourgeois class was strong, thought should be given to a move to the remote northwestern provinces. This was rejected — though it was to happen seven years later, when Yan'an in the northwest became the Communist headquarters.

Three Comintern representatives, Roy, Borodin and Voitinsky, were present at the Party Congress. Chen Duxiu was re-elected General Secretary, and he, together with Li Weihan, Zhang Guotao and Secretary-General Zhou Enlai, formed the Standing Committee of the Politbureau. Mao Zedong was made an alternate-member of the forty-five-man Central Committee.[21]

The break

In Party history the summer of 1927 is known as a time of defeat, and as the end of the first period of the revolution. It was a turbulent time throughout the whole of China. In March the Northern Expedition, launched in June and July 1926 in the South by Chiang Kai Shek,

reached Nanjing and Shanghai, and in April 1927 the National government was set up in Nanjing. This was in opposition to the rival Nationalist Government in Wuhan, headed by Wang Jingwei, leader of the left
wing of the Kuomintang, who was supported by the Communists. The
North was still in the hands of local warlords, but in June Yen Hsi-shan
raised the flag of the Nanjing government in Shanxi. Feng Yü-hsiang
was also sounding his way on how to cooperate with the Nationalists,
and first met Wang Jingwei in Henan and then Chiang Kai Shek in
Xuzhou (Hsüchow). Zhang Zuolin, the ruler of Manchuria, occupied
Peking, raided the archives of the Soviet embassy and arrested and killed
Chinese Communists, including Li Dazhao, the forerunner of Chinese
Communism.

On June 30, 1927, at a Central Committee enlarged meeting, it was
decided that the Party should remain loyal to the left wing of the Kuomintang. On July 12, at an *ad hoc* meeting of the Politbureau, Chen
Duxiu was deposed from the leadership of the Party and was replaced by
a five-man Provisional Politbureau (Zhang Guotao, Zhou Enlai, Li
Lisan, Li Weihan and Zhang Tailei). On July 15 came the complete
break with Wang Jingwei's Wuhan government.

In the middle of July the Comintern published a criticism of Chen
Duxiu and the Chinese Party leadership, and sent Lominadze to
Wuhan.[22] In July the ECCI issued a resolution on the situation in China,
published in *Pravda* on July 14. This resolution said that the Chinese
leadership was not carrying out the Comintern's instructions and had
failed to recognise that the Wuhan government had become a counter-
revolutionary force that would destroy the Communist Party. Party
members should resign from the Wuhan government, but should
remain in the Kuomintang and should arm workers and
peasants[23] — ambiguous and rather futile instructions. (Stalin spoke
twice about China in May; he seemed to be well informed, but his main
theme was the attack on Trotsky.)[24]

Chen Duxiu had to go. He was a 'rightist deviationist'. It is interesting to speculate what would have happened to the Communist Party,
and to China, if Chen had stayed and his policy had been accepted — if
the Communists had been led by men of his cultural standards and not
by rising but ignorant country bumpkins, savage soldiers manipulated
by a sagacious leader, Mao, and if the Chinese Communists had been
independent of the Comintern and Stalin. Communism could have
become what the Communist parties are today in Italy, France or Japan,
alive but not dominant. China would have been spared internal division

during the Japanese war, spared the ensuing civil war — and spared Mao's regime, which the Chinese Communists themselves deplored after his death.

After the Wuhan defeat in July 1927 the comrades were in complete disarray. The very nature of the Party, which until then had been the radical junior partner in the Kuomintang, had to be re-thought. Yet there was no time for thinking. There was, instead, an urgent sense of the need for a decisive show of strength.

Three days after the July 15 break with Wang Jingwei's Wuhan government, a meeting was held to plan a revolt and the occupation of Nanchang, the capital of Jiangxi province. Nanchang was taken on August 1, in combined operations by the Communists, the ultra-left Kuomintang and Ye Ting's troops. A Revolutionary Committee was set up and the arrest of Chiang Kai Shek and of Wang Jingwei was ordered; but within four days the whole affair was over. The insurgents had to retreat from Nanchang and were soon on the run.

However the Nanchang Uprising became a landmark in Party history, and August 1 the official birthday of the Red Army. Books and articles were written about the Uprising, each leader claiming that he had played the leading role in this heroic act. In Lin Biao's time in the 1960s, he was the principal claimant.

Who planned the action? This has long been a cause for debate. Fifty-three years later, it was possible to examine the whole affair more objectively, and it was admitted that no documents have been found and that it is impossible to reconstruct the course of events. It is not even certain that a regular Party meeting planned the Uprising.[25]

Violence

On August 3 some of the leaders came together — it is not known who — and elaborated a programme for a general uprising in the autumn in the four provinces of Hunan, Hubei, Guangdong and Jiangxi, a decision which, as we shall see below, gave rise to savage devastation, not unlike that of the Cultural Revolution forty years later. On August 7, another *ad hoc* emergency meeting was held, with the participation of two Comintern emissaries, Lominadze and Heinz Neumann.

This August 7 meeting, known as the 'Eight-Seven' Meeting (seventh day of the eighth month) was considered a turning-point in the history of the Party. It injected *violence* into political life in China and was to poison it for years to come. Violent acts had occurred before as

they do in every country. In China the warlords' armies were fighting
each other, but, in the traditional Chinese manner of warfare, they were
occupied with advancing and retreating rather than with bloody battles.
The Northern Expedition of the Nationalists was not a peaceful affair;
but it was a temporary action. The violence introduced at this meeting
of the Communists was an enthroned, doctrinal violence, something
unknown till then in Chinese history. This doctrine corrupted the traditional texture of Chinese life. Before and after the Communist take-
over, it spawned incessant violent earthquakes in Chinese political life.
How and when China will regain her traditional sense of balance and
graceful living — will she ever do so? — is a secret of the future.

The emergency 'Eight-Seven' Meeting prescribed armed struggle.
Mao, who was present at the meeting as alternate-member of the Politbureau, said that it was absurd for the Communists not to have an army
when the Nationalists did. Cai Hesen said that it had been a mistake for
the Communists to have taken no part in the Northern Expedition,
which was a mass struggle; in fact, the Party had restrained the masses
from taking part in that struggle. (Cai, one of the earliest Chinese Communists, was excluded from the Politbureau in November 1928.[26] He
was executed by the Nationalist Government in 1931.)

The meeting decided that workers should be trained for street-to-
street fighting, and that peasants should be led to land reform in armed
struggle. The uprising in the autumn, the Autumn Uprising as it is
called in Party history, was to be an armed struggle.

Should the Communists cooperate with the Kuomintang? Yes, the
meeting decided. They should cooperate with the leftist local organisations of the Kuomintang, win power and establish a national government, still ruled by the Kuomintang, but one in which the Communists
would form a majority. It would be a 'Government of Democratic Dictatorship of Workers and Peasants'. (This term comes from Lenin and
was used in the 1905 Russian rising.[27])

The meeting elected a Provisional Politbureau Standing Committee,
consisting of three members, Qu Qiubai, Li Weihan and Su Zhaozheng
(Su died two years later in Shanghai); Zhou Enlai became head of the
Military Department.[28] Action followed quickly. On September 9, Mao
led the peasants in Hunan in violent uprisings, and others acted similarly
in other provinces. All the uprisings failed miserably, collapsing after a
few days. The Autumn Uprising and the whole programme of the
emergency meeting — uprisings, violence, taking over power in the

Kuomintang and establishing a government — were beautiful dreams, utopias. (Such utopian planning remained a permanent feature of the Communist regime and caused havoc time after time — Great Leap, Commune, Cultural Revolution and instant modernisation.)

The frenzy did not end with the failure of the Autumn Uprising. In October some remnants of the troops from Nanchang (led by He Long and Ye Ting) occupied the southern coastal city of Swatow for five days, and in December a violent and similarly unsuccessful uprising was staged in Canton city. On September 29, Mao led the remnants of his Autumn Uprising followers to Yongxin county on the borders of Hunan and Jiangxi provinces, and in a village called Sanwan formed them into a small military troop. The Mao legend built this into a historic military event, the Sanwan Military Reorganisation.

On October 27, Mao and his men arrived at the foot of the Jing Gang Shan cliffs.[29] Mao's activity was not looked upon with favour by his colleagues. On November 9–10 (still in 1927), an Enlarged Meeting of the Provisional Politbureau was held in Shanghai — although many members were unable to attend. At this meeting the Hunan leadership and Mao in particular were condemned and Mao's defeat in the Autumn Uprising was castigated in harsh words as 'military opportunism', 'total disregard of the policy of the Party leadership' and so on. Mao lost his position as an alternate-member of the Politbureau, and Zhou Enlai also received an admonition. Nothing good was said about the unsuccessful Nanchang Uprising. Yet the fierce tone of the 'Eight-Seven' Meeting was not lowered; on the contrary, it was pitched even higher. There was to be no more cooperation of any sort with the Kuomintang; the Kuomintang must be smashed. City workers and village peasants should be led to violent revolution; there should be no talk of reduction of land rents; all land should be taken away in violent revolution; an army of workers and peasants should be formed. Revolution and violence were the leading themes. The meeting was led by the same Lominadze who had been at the 'Eight-Seven' Meeting.[30]

Who was this Georgian, Besso Lominadze? According to one student of the Soviet Union, Lominadze was one of Stalin's men. In December 1927 at the Fifteenth Russian Party Congress he became alternate-member of the All-Russian Communist Party Central Committee; in 1934 he committed suicide.[31] According to another scholar, he was a radical ultra-leftist whose arguments on China were contradicted at the same Fifteenth Russian Party Congress by Pavel Mif, Stalin's adviser on the China question. According to this author, Lominadze's suicide was in 1936.[32]

In February 1928 at its Ninth Plenum the ECCI, which kept a close eye on events in China, issued a Resolution on China. It approved the 'Eight-Seven' Meeting and the dismissal of Chen Duxiu (described as an opportunist). It praised the December 1927 uprising in Canton as an exemplary heroic act while admitting that it had failed; but it omitted all mention of the Nanchang Uprising. The ECCI praised the revolutionary actions in the provinces, but criticised leftist excesses, aimless terrorism, and the practice of forcing workers to strike. It criticised Tan Pingshan for wanting to organise a third party, his 'True Communist Party'. It also criticised others, not named, who were putting faith in the Trotskyist slogan of 'uninterrupted revolution' and who wanted to neglect the historical preparatory period of 'Bourgeois Democratic Revolution'.[33]

Two months later, on April 30, 1928, the Chinese Party leadership accepted the criticism of the February ECCI resolution and said that what was needed was not aimless struggle but well-prepared 'combined violence of workers and peasants'.[34] The 'aimless violence', however, went on unabated.

A vivid picture of how the Communists acted in those days can be found in the reminiscences of Huang Kecheng. When he wrote these down in 1980, he was seventy-eight years of age. Born in the same province as Mao, Huang joined the Communists in the 1920s. At the Seventh Party Congress in 1945 he became an alternate-member of the Central Committee. In 1959, when Chief-of-Staff, he was purged by Mao along with the minister of defence Peng Dehuai. In October 1977 he re-emerged and in December 1978 became a leading member of the Party's Disciplinary Investigation Committee. Here is what he wrote in 1980.

After the defeat at Nanchang, and the defeat of the Autumn Harvest Uprisings in 1927, the Party, headed by Qu Qiubai, held a Politbureau meeting in November 1927, which called upon the Party for the establishment of political power through violent uprisings. Zhu De and Chen Yi, leaders of the uprising at Nanchang, led their troops to the border area between Guangdong and Hunan provinces and occupied a county town there. In several counties young people, mostly secondary and primary school students, led the violence. The directive from the central organisation of the Party and from the Party committee in charge of Party members in Hunan province was: 'Kill! Kill! Kill the counter-revolutionary gentry! Burn! Burn! Burn down their nests!' Huang himself was at the head of one such violent group, peasant youngsters who wore red belts and red ties, and carried red banners — foreshadowing the Red Guards of the Cultural Revolution forty years later. They went around in groups of hundreds or thousands, killing people and burning houses. In the county of Zhenxian, a soviet government was established. The Party secretary was a student from the city of Henyang named Xia; a local peasant named Li became head of the soviet government. Then, going forward to 'bring the revolution' to other places, they got together 1,000 people and attacked another county town where there were no Kuomintang soldiers but only some local guards, and set up a Party committee there.

A student from Hengyang started the revolution in another county. 'I remember how this young man, Cao, killed a wicked landlord and how his hands were full of blood.' In another county a soviet government was established by a peasant soldier who had taken part in the uprising in Canton in December 1927.

In January 1928 I met a man who had come from Pingshi county (on the Jiangxi side of the Hunan-Jiangxi border), and he told me about a Red Army led by a man called Zhu. In those days I had not yet heard the name of comrade Zhu De. I had heard only that the Party had taken Pingshi. I got together some violent youngsters and we went into action to spread the revolution through the whole region. We beat down the gentry, divided the land and carried out land reform. In the first quarter of 1928 revolutionary violence flared up in the whole region. Government offices and houses of the gentry were set on fire. Near Pingshi all houses within a radius of 7 km. were burnt down.

This, however, aroused resentment among the masses, and the reactionary landlords induced them to take action. In Zhenxian the peasants, when ordered by the revolutionaries to burn the houses of landowners, refused to do so and turned against the revolutionaries and killed many of them. Comrade Chen Yi came to Zhenxian and suppressed this counter-revolution. The peasants also resisted in Yong Xing county and put up a white flag, but they were suppressed by Comrade Zhu De's men.

In April 1928 the Nationalist troops arrived. They destroyed the Communist bases and killed many comrades. Comrade Zhu De led his troops from Zhenxian to Jing Gang Shan. Many of the early revolutionaries of the Party sacrificed their lives. There was a secondary student, a violent revolutionary who had himself killed landlords;

later his own father killed him. Comrade Huang recollects many names, but has forgotten others. Thousands sacrificed their lives for the revolution, he sighs.

Zhu De brought 2,000 men to Jing Gang Shan [Huang goes on]. Chen Yi, when he had to abandon Zhenxian, also went there with another 2,000 men. Other groups of men defeated in neighbouring counties by government troops joined. In Jing Gang Shan 8,000 men were organised into the Red Fourth Army. Zhu De was commander, Mao Zedong was the Party representative. The army was divided into divisions and regiments. One division was commanded by Mao, one by Chen Yi, and one regiment by Huang Kecheng. Huang recited the names of all the commanders and Party representatives in each group. On May 5 they got together to celebrate the birthday of Marx.

Soon after this, the troops were reorganised and were sent back to the neighbouring counties to engage in a guerilla war. Huang Kecheng went to Yongxing county where a man called Li was to be the Party secretary of the county, but Li left with his wife, and Huang has never learned what happened to them. He[Huang] took his place. He had only a few hundred men, old and young, men and women, with no training and only twenty or so rifles. He heard that Mao Zedong was planning to establish a base; but he had not even seen Mao when he was in Jing Gang Shan. These troops were a disorderly rabble. Many grew homesick and went back to their villages. To deceive the enemy, Huang's troops raised a Nationalist flag. His men attacked the landlords and took two or three dozen rifles.

Other groups of soldiers were despatched from Jing Gang Shan to other counties. Their leaders were killed, one after the other. Huang remembers a man whose wife ran away to Nanking and joined the enemy. The husband also went to Nanking, was betrayed by his wife and was executed. Some went back to Jing Gang Shan; among these was Deng Hua. Deng Hua was to have a distinguished career. In the 1950s he was commander of the troops in the Northeast until 1959, when, having become involved in the Peng Dehuai affair, he was removed and made a vice-governor of a province, a very lowly post indeed. After Mao's death he became vice-president of the Military Science College; he died in 1980. In August 1928, Zhu De himself led a troop to Zhenxian in southern Hunan, but was defeated by the enemy; only a few men, including Xiao Ke survived. A man named Hu was killed later in 1930 or 1931, another named Li, a student from Henyang, was sent as a guerilla and was killed. Not many of the 8,000 peasant soldiers who had gathered at Jing Gang Shan survived. When they were sent down from the mountains as guerillas, they had little food, few weapons, no training and no proper leadership. In all, about 4,000 or 5,000 men perished in these actions.[35]

This is of course a devastating criticism of Mao's direction of the operation in Jing Gang Shan. Apparently, he was not so foolish as to go down the hill and expose himself to the dangers of fighting.

The Sixth Congress

Amid this chaos the Party was itself disunited and had no stable leadership. A Party Congress, the sixth, was held in June-July 1928, in Moscow.

At this Congress, the Party Charter was revised. The new version contained the following declaration: 'A Party Congress can be held only with the previous approval of the Comintern.' These words were never put into practice. The next Party Congress was not held for seventeen years, and by the time it was held, in Yan'an in 1945, the Party had changed to one that enshrined the thoughts of an absolute ruler. The Yan'an of Mao maintained close relations with Moscow and learnt Marxism in its Stalinist form; but the old subordination belonged to the past. The Comintern itself had ceased to exist in 1943: by then the Soviet Union had joined the Allies fighting against Hitler.

When the Sixth Party Congress opened in Moscow on June 18, 1928, the Party had no leader. Chen Duxiu, the leader from the earliest days (1921), had been deposed at the 'Eight-Seven' Meeting in 1927 after the ignominious clash with the Kuomintang, and for ten months Qu Qiubai was at the head of affairs. At the Sixth Congress a colourless figure, Xiang Zhongfa, a workers' leader in Wuhan city who had taken part in the last three Party Congresses, became General Secretary of the Party. The Seventh Plenum of the ECCI, in February 1928, elected him to the Praesidium of the ECCI. Obviously he had got the post of head of the Chinese Party from the Comintern, but he was very much a nominal leader.[36] The explanation may be that the Chinese comrades made a formal bow to the will of the ECCI, but did not accept him.

The Sixth Party Congress and its resolutions have been discussed and interpreted in different ways by students of Party history — though their number is small.[37] Perhaps the most significant comment is what Mao Zedong said about it in 1944 during the Party Rectification campaign in Yan'an: The Sixth Congress was right in promulgating a Ten-Point Programme, 'but it failed to point out the protracted nature of the

Chinese revolution [the Sixth Congress expected quick results] and the very great importance of rural base-areas to the revolution.'[38] The Resolution on Questions of Party History, promulgated in 1945 at the Seventh Party Congress in Yan'an expressed Mao's view more clearly: The Sixth Congress was right in defining Chinese society as semi-colonial and semi-feudal; it was correct in its Ten-Point Programme. The Sixth Congress was right in proclaiming that the main task at that time was not to organise insurrections, but to win over the masses. But the Sixth Congress 'lacked the necessary understanding of the Party's need for an orderly retreat after the defeat of the Great Revolution[the defeat in 1927], and of the importance of rural base-areas.'[39]

At the Sixth Congress in Moscow Mao, though not present — he was already at his base in Jing Gang Shan — , was made a member of the Central Committee. He may have felt gratified; but he did not think that his work, his establishment of a rural base, had received sufficient acknowledgment.

Mao's approval of the statement that China was 'semi-feudal' — nobody has ever tried to define what this means — was an act of faith in Stalin and a repudiation of Trotskyists in the Soviet Union and at home. One of the battle themes in a speech that Stalin delivered against Trotsky in May 1927, a year before the Chinese Party Congress was held in Moscow, was that Trotsky was ignorant of Chinese conditions and that there were no remnants of feudalism in the Chinese villages.[40] (Trotsky, who had played a prominent role in the Comintern, was ousted from it in May 1927 and was expelled from the Party in November that year.)

The Ten-Point Programme of the Sixth Congress, which Mao approved of, was a curious jumble of reformist and revolutionary, realist and utopian items: overthrow of imperialist rule, which meant perhaps American and Japanese influence and the foreign concessions in Chinese cities; confiscation of foreign enterprises and banks; an eight-hour working day; higher wages and unified progressive taxation — so far, not a revolutionary programme. But also among the ten points were: overthrow the Kuomintang; set up a government of councils (soviets) of workers-peasants-soldiers; take away all land from the landlords and give it to the peasants to till. The last point was: union with the proletariat of the world and with the Soviet Union.[41]

The overthrow of the government and the establishment of a Communist government were what had been proposed a year earlier at the 'Eight-Seven' Meeting immediately after the Communists' disaster at

Wuhan. Mao was, of course, right in saying that the Sixth Congress had aroused over-sanguine expectations.

According to the *List of Important Party Meetings*, published in 1982, the Sixth Congress warned against establishing scattered soviet areas. It wanted a 'worker-peasant revolutionary army, a Red Army',[42] and insisted on revolutionary work among the workers. This may have been why Xiang Zhongfa, a worker, was made General Secretary.

The Sixth Congress can hardly be called a watershed in the Party's history. The Comintern wanted to raise spirits and to recreate the Chinese Party, battered by the defeat of a year earlier. It could not find a leader who could breathe new life into the Party.

In February 1929 the ECCI sent a letter to the comrades in China — they had moved from Wuhan to Shanghai — urging the implementation of the Sixth Congress' decisions and the creation of unity among the scattered Communist forces, for each group was running its own base. The letter arrived in April. In June, Shanghai held a Central Committee Plenum, admitting the deficiencies. Moscow also urged the expulsion of Trotskyites from the Party. Trotsky's denial of the 'semi-feudal' state of China was brought up again. Stalin had won in the Soviet Union, and he won in China too. The Plenum promised intensive activity among industrial workers in the cities, land reform, and a brake on indiscriminate killing and the burning of houses. 'The focus of the revolutionary work should move from the villages to the cities.'[43] The condition of the Party was chaotic and remained so for many years to come.

The leadership crisis

The 1983 Peking study on Party leaders in 1921–37, which was based on an examination of contemporary documents, revealed that it had not been able to establish who were the leaders of the Party in certain periods.[44]

Xiang Zhongfa, made General Secretary at the Sixth Party Congress in Moscow, was a mere figurehead. From the beginning of 1930, Li Lisan, though nominally only head of the Propaganda Department, was the real ruler of the Party. How this happened has never been explained. His rule lasted for only a few months and proved disastrous. On February 26, 1930, a Party Circular said that the country was ready for an overall armed rebellion (though not in the North where the warlords were dominant). More incredibly still, another Circular, of May 22, proclaimed that the revolution in China would be the beginning of a world-wide revolution. On June 11, Li Lisan chaired a Politbureau meeting in Shanghai. The meeting predicted the victory of the revolution in at least one, possibly several provinces. Orders were given for the occupation of major cities in central and south China. A Party meeting on July 18 said that the revolution was ready to burst forth in twenty-two provinces. The Party, it was stated, had 193,422 members.[45]

The Comintern in Moscow seemed to agree with the Shanghai meeting. In July and August 1930 it issued a series of directives to China.[46] A July directive said: 'The revolutionary condition may cover some major provinces, if not the whole country . . . The Red Army . . . may be able to take over one or more key cities.'[47]

The outcome contradicted these sanguine hopes. The Communist attacks were defeated instantly everywhere, and this was the end of Li Lisan (but not of the Comintern). Party membership was said to have dropped from 190,000 to 120,000. The September 1930 Third Central Committee Plenum held in Shanghai demoted Li Lisan, but he remained one of the seven full members of the Politbureau. The meeting was opened by Qu Qiubai, who had been head of the Party for a short while before the 1928 Moscow Party Congress. It was closed by Xiang Zhongfa, still nominally General Secretary. In October the Comintern thundered against the Li Lisan line. Pavel Mif brought his protégés, Wang Ming, Bo Gu (alias Qin Bangxian) and others, to China and found the Party leadership deeply divided. Mif held the Fourth Central Committee Plenum in January 1931 in Shanghai and put his own men into leading posts. Xiang Zhongfa remained General Secretary until June, when he was arrested by the Shanghai police. He betrayed his comrades but was nevertheless executed. (His name was blotted out from Party history.) Who succeeded him as leader of the Party? In 1983 the Party historians — as we said above — were still unable to answer this question. Was it Wang Ming? (Wang Ming returned to Moscow before the end of the year.) Or was it a man called Lu Futan (alias Lu Shen)? The answer is still unclear.[48]

The situation of the Party leadership in Shanghai, living in hiding under the National government, had become more and more difficult. Zhou Enlai left Shanghai at the begining of December 1931 and arrived at Ruijin, where Mao stayed, on about December 20.[49] Wang Ming left China for Moscow months before Zhou left Shanghai, and lived in the Soviet Union until the autumn of 1937.[50] In September 1931, eight months after the Fourth Central Committee Plenum, a Provisional

Politbureau was formed in Shanghai under Bo Gu, one of the 'returned students'.[51] Whether Bo Gu had the title of General Secretary was disputed by Party historians in 1983.[52]

In January 1933 the Party leadership moved from Shanghai to Ruijin in the South.[53] In 1931, when the leadership was still in Shanghai, the Japanese occupied Manchuria. The Party thought that the national anger might serve their purpose and that the time for armed rebellion and the occupation of some major cities had come. Once again, these proved to be vain hopes.[54]

Li Lisan was condemned for having launched unsuccessful attacks on cities. (At the end of 1930 he was summoned to Moscow, where he apologised. He married a Russian girl; he was jailed during the Stalin purge, and returned to Yan'an in 1936.[55]) Li Lisan's policy was condemned, but those who led the Party after him followed the same line and aimed at the major cities. Mao himself, as we shall see below, intended to occupy the provincial cities round his base. This was the programme put forward by the Comintern in the July 1930 instruction quoted above.

The reason may well be that the Communists, both in China and in Moscow, regarded the conquest of the cities by their rival and enemy, Chiang Kai Shek, as a setback to themselves. Chiang launched what is known as the Northern Expedition in Canton in June–July 1926. In 1927 he conquered the key cities of central China, and in September 1927 the establishment of the Nanjing government was officially proclaimed. (This was the month of the Communists' abortive Autumn Uprising.)

Official Communist propaganda has always maintained that the Communist forces took a positive part in the Northern Expedition. This was stated even in the 1980 edition of the *Ci Hai* (*Tz'u Hai*) *Dictionary* in its section on modern history.[56] But the book listing important Party meetings published in 1982 says that the Party 'took a negative attitude towards the Northern Expedition', indeed 'ignored it completely'.[57]

Bases

The revolutionary turmoil that began after the break with the Kuomintang in 1927 spread to several corners of China. In the years after 1927 Mao's base was only one of several revolutionary bases round the country. The official version of Party history, published in 1945, said: 'The idea of creating rural base areas was Comrade Mao Zedong's.' It glossed over, in a few casual words, the existence of revolutionary areas other than Mao's. Some other revolutionary bases did exist, it said, and they prospered for a time until, on account of wrong guidance (i.e. through lack of a wise man like Mao), they collapsed.[58]

Some did indeed collapse; but others fared exactly as Mao's base did. The members of the bases fled from pursuing government troops and moved westward.

Post-Mao documents describe seven bases in addition to that of Zhu De and Mao, and list their leaders as they were in 1927–30. Many of the local leaders of these areas perished and have long since been forgotten. Other bases survived and their leaders later became famous figures.

Peng Pai was active in the southern province of Guangdong, years before Mao set up his base in Jing Gang Shan. This man, an early Communist Party member, organised talks in Canton in 1924 in the name of the Kuomintang Executive Committee and, with the blessing of Sun Yat Sen, trained revolutionaries for the villages. Revolutionary leaders from other southern provinces took part in these talks. A later course of talks was organised by Mao Zedong. (The site of Mao's talks became a place of pilgrimage under his regime.) Peng Pai was associated with the Kuomintang Whampoa military school, organised by Soviet emissaries, which had Chiang Kai Shek as commander and Zhou Enlai as head of the political department. Zhou apparently helped Peng Pai to gather thirty or so Canton workers under Peng's leadership. This handful went under the imposing name of the Eastern Expedition. Its task was to incite the peasants to revolt against the landlords and to organise a village militia to fight for a reduction of land rents.

Peng Pai was present at the Communist emergency meeting on August 7, 1927, in Hankou, immediately after the break with the Kuomintang, and was elected an alternate-member of the Politbureau. Obedient to the new Party line, *violence*, he agitated in his native county, Haifeng, and the neighbouring county, Lufeng, and established in November 1927 what was called the Hailufeng Workers-Peasants-Soldiers Soviet. Party history — after Mao — called this 'the first Red government'. Four months later, in February 1927, this soviet government collapsed. (Meantime in December 1927 the revolutionaries had occupied Canton city and set up the Canton soviet government, which lasted only three days.) Peng Pai lost his territory, but not his courage. Three months later, in May 1928, he organised fifteen comrades into a Violence Team, also known as a Dare-To-Die troop. In July 1928 he was elected *in absentia* to Politbureau membership at the Sixth Party Congress, held in Moscow. Peng Pai moved to Shanghai and worked in the central leadership of the Party. In August 1929 a comrade betrayed him and he was arrested and executed.[59] (For what happened to the man who betrayed Peng Pai, see Chapter X, p. 154.)

After the defeat of the Communists in 1927, revolutionary agitation began and revolutionary bases sprang up in various parts of the country. A few years later, harassed by government forces, they moved in separate 'long marches' to the west.

Peng Dehuai — commander of the Chinese forces in the Korean War, promoted to the rank of Marshal in 1955, rejected by Mao in 1959 — began his revolutionary action in the border areas of Hunan-Hubei-Jiangxi provinces. (Communist insurgents often worked at the meeting-places of several adjoining provinces, as bandits had always done in Chinese history, to avoid pursuit by the authorities of any one province.) In December 1928 he and his troops joined Mao and Zhu De at Jing Gang Shan. A month later the Mao-Zhu troops — or as they were called in the early years the 'Zhu-Mao troops' — hemmed in by government forces, abandoned Jing Gang Shan, leaving Peng behind. A few months later Peng also found the place undefendable and moved, as Mao had, to the southeast region of Jiangxi province. Peng arrived at Ruijin before Mao. The two men obviously could not get on. Peng was sent away. He went back to Jing Gang Shan and held it for a few years.[60] Peng was a man of independent character, yet he never turned against Mao and took part in the Long March with him.[61]

Where the three provinces of Hubei, Henan and Anhui meet, there was a turbulent Party base founded in 1927 and led by Xu Xiangqian (promoted to the rank of Marshal in 1955) and Zhang Guotao. In 1932 they led their troops to the West. When Mao's group arrived at the end of 1934 in what is now northern Sichuan province, these troops already had a base not far from the then borders of Sichuan and Shaanxi provinces. They joined Mao's troops. The fierce rivalry that then developed between Zhang Guotao and Mao did not end until four years later when Moscow intervened. (See next Chapter.)

Another base, also in the Hubei-Henan-Anhui borderland, was set up at the end of the 1920s by Xu Haidong. 'Under pressure from government troops he led his troops on its long march' to the north of Shaanxi province in August 1935, where he arrived two months before Mao's group.

He Long, also promoted to Marshal in 1955, established his own base in the late 1920s in the plains round Lake Honghu in the southeastern

corner of Hubei province, close to Hunan province, a flat terrain very
different from the mountainous cliffs of Mao's Jing Gang Shan. He
Long, together with Ren Bishi, who played a prominent role in the
Party until his early death in 1950, maintained their base until the great
onslaught of the government forces, which wiped out many Communist bases and forced their members to flee. In 1934 He Long began his
'long march' to the West, and set up another base at the meeting-point
of Hunan-Hubei-Guizhou-Sichuan provinces. Under enemy pressure he
had to move further to the west, where he met up with the troops of Zhu
De, Xu Xiangqian and Zhang Guotao in what is now West Sichuan.
Ultimately they arrived in Shaanxi province in October 1936, one year
after Mao, thus 'triumphantly ending the Great Long March', as one of
his biographers wrote in 1981.

Fang Zhimin had his base in the north of Jiangxi province. He died
there in July 1935. (See Chapter ·X, pp. 158–60.) Mention should be
made of the localised agitation which took place in Guangxi in 1929.
The Party leaders in Shanghai sent Deng Xiaoping to take over the
leadership; the agitation lasted for over a year. In 1931 Deng went to
Mao's base in Ruijin. Zhou Enlai, his companion from the early 1920s in
France, went there in the same year.

In the northwestern province of Shaanxi there were sporadic Communist actions led by Gao Gang (purged in 1954), Jia Tuofu (later involved
in running the economy), Xi Zhongxun (still prominent in his old age in
the 1980s) and Liu Zhidan. In official Party history, Liu Zhidan, who
died in battle in 1936, was the leading figure in this area. The obscure
story that he and his men were arrested when the first troops of the Long
March arrived in north Shaanxi and that Mao freed him has never been
clarified.[62]

These and other local insurgents and their revolutionary bases, tiny
and ephemeral as they were, kept some tenuous contact with the Party
leadership in Shanghai. Establishing local 'soviets' was the official policy
of the Party.

The official Party history of 1945 exalted Mao alone. In that history
there was only one 'Long March' to the West, Mao's Long March; the
Chinese Communist Party was Mao's creation. The others joined him
earlier or later. Those who opposed him were evil anti-Marxists. Those
who repented could be generously readmitted to the fold.

CHAPTER III
FROM JING GANG SHAN TO YAN'AN, 1927–1937

In perspective

Mao was in the Party from the start. At the First Party Congress in 1921 he was the representative of the handful of Communists in his own province, Hunan. The Third Congress in 1923 elected him to the seven-member Executive Committee.[1] After the reorganisation of the Kuomintang in accordance with the plan of the Comintern emissary Borodin, Mao became an alternate-member of the Kuomintang Executive Committee at both the First and the Second Kuomintang Congresses, in January 1924 and January 1926.[2] In the late 1920s and the early 1930s he encountered a great deal of trouble in the Communist Party. In 1925, the Fourth Party Congress removed him from the Executive Committee of the Party. The Fifth Party Congress in April 1927 made him an alternate-member of the Central Committee. The emergency meeting held on August 7, 1927, after the break with the Kuomintang, made him an alternate Politbureau member; but three months later, after his move to Jing Gang Shan, Mao was blamed for this action and removed from the Politbureau. In 1928 the Sixth Party Congress, held in Moscow, listed him, though absent, as a member of the Central Committee. In September 1930 the Third Central Committee Plenum, held in Shanghai, made him, again *in absentia*, an alternate Politbureau member.[3]

But from 1931 on, when Mao was in Ruijin, his second base, his fortunes declined rapidly. During the Long March, which began at the end of 1934, he began to intrigue in the hope of squeezing out the Party leaders, the 'returned students' (returned from Moscow). In 1938 he won this battle. In 1942 he began the great purge of his enemies. Three years later he was the supreme ruler, the Chairman of the Party (a title which had never been used before). He also became head of the Politbureau and head of the Central Committee Secretariat. All Party power was concentrated in his hands. Within another four years he was the ruler of China.

Mao had a long apprenticeship in political manoeuvring. To help understand how he gained this experience, it is useful to go back to the turbulent year 1927 and see how he conquered the cliffs of Jing Gang Shan.

31

Up to the cliffs

Gong Chu, one of the early leaders, left the ranks in 1935 and wrote his memoirs in a book entitled *The Red Army and I*. He gives a vivid picture of Jing Gang Shan and how Mao got there.

In the autumn of 1927 Mao was sent by the Party leadership to start the Autumn Harvest Revolt in east Hunan. He organised a band of ruffians who — like the revolutionaries elsewhere — took to killing landlords and setting houses on fire. The peasants were horrified; but government troops dispersed the rampaging intruders. Mao crossed over into Jiangxi province and went to Ninggang county, northwest of the mountain known as Jing Gang Shan. Jing Gang Shan's high cliffs were unscaleable. There were five mountain villages and there were some shops in the town of Ciping at the foot of Jing Gang Shan. The peasants had terraced some mountain land and lived on potatoes and millet. Jing Gang Shan was 7 km. from Ninggang at the western border of Jiangxi province. Only three paths led to this inaccessible peak, which was traditionally the home of bandits. A memorial stone there commemorates a rebel of the Ming period who, having been defeated, fled to Jing Gang Shan (the stone carries an inscription by the famous Ming philosopher Wang Yang Ming).

When Mao arrived there with his men there was already a bandit called Wang Zuo on the mountain, the leader of a bandit group of about ninety men. He was associated with another man in Ninggang, Yuan Wencai, who sold him rifles. (Both names are mentioned in the first volume of the *Selected Works of Mao Zedong*, in 'Struggle in the Ching Kang Mountains'. Mao described the bandits as 'two units of local armed forces in the vicinity of Jing Gang, each unit having sixty rifles in bad repair'.)

Gong Chu says that Jing Gang Shan was practically the private property of the two bandits, and he adds: 'Mao Zedong understood the military value of Jing Gang Shan.' To gain the bandits' favour he presented two rifles and some other presents to Yuan, who then introduced him to Wang Zuo. The three got together and, following the ancient custom, swore brotherhood. The two bandits recognised Mao's higher intelligence and accepted him as their leader. In those days people in the villages of Jing Gang Shan called him 'Commander Mao'.[4]

General Han Wei, one of those who followed Mao to Jing Gang Shan, described in 1965 how Mao talked to his followers about the bandits in Jing Gang Shan, telling them how he himself had learnt from them how to get around the enemy instead of attacking openly. He also gained the experience which he summed up in the axiom: 'If you can win, you fight; if you may lose, you move away.'

General Han also recalled how strict Mao could be. When he was leading his few hundred men after the defeat of the Autumn Harvest Uprising, one group deserted him. Mao went after them and court-martialled the leaders.[5]

The two bandits were active in Mao's troops for a time. Both died in 1930. In his 1970 confession, Marshal Peng Dehuai indignantly denied the accusation that he had ordered their deaths. He claimed that they were shot in a skirmish on a bridge and drowned in the river.[6] According to the personal testimony of a Jing Gang Shan peasant whom the present author met outside China, Mao finished them off, first one, then the other. This is possible. What is more important, however, and what shows the sagacity of the man, is that Mao, who had mixed with educated people in Peking and in Hunan and was high in the Communist Party, could sit down and establish comradeship with two bandits and learn from them. *All are Brothers* — an ancient novel describing men who, having fled from the wrath of the Emperor, took to the mountains to live as noble bandits — was one of Mao's favourite books.

For Mao, Jing Gang Shan was an experiment; the place was a remote one in which to learn the new trade of revolution. In 1928, a year after his arrival there — this was stated later by Zhou Enlai — Mao was still thinking of capturing the cities in the three neighbouring provinces. This was what the Communist Party was attempting to do in those days wherever it existed.

The speech in which Zhou made this statement was addressed to the Party School in Yan'an in March 1944, and it was reproduced in the *Selected Works of Zhou*, published in 1980. At some time before 1925, two comrades wrote to Mao proposing revolutionary work in the villages. Mao replied in a letter: 'At present we are hardly able to carry out our work among the workers in the cities; how could we have time to work in the villages?'

In 1925 Mao fell ill and retired to his village in Hunan. There he observed village life. Writing about 1928, the time of the Sixth Party Congress (held in Moscow — Mao was not present), Zhou said: 'I think that at that time Comrade Mao Zedong had not yet thought of centering the work on the villages and enabling the Party, representing the proletariat, to lead the peasants in guerilla war. He still thought that the centres of work should be in the cities.' In the early days he thought of setting up a Soviet Area where the borders of Fujian, Zhejiang and Jiangxi provinces meet, to influence and support the work in the cities. (In January 1929 Mao did move to that area, to Ruijin.) Mao's first mention of the plan for armed village bases is found in his letter to Lin Biao.

Zhou Enlai came to the conclusion that 'the development of Comrade Mao Zedong's Thought on this question also [rural revolution] went through phases.'[7]

Zhou's reference to Mao's letter to Lin Biao is inaccurate. In this letter, dated January 1930, Mao says that rural revolution is important only in that it provides support for the conquest of the cities. He meant immediate conquest, not the conquest that happened twenty years later.[8]

Mao's troubles

Documentation on the Jing Gang Shan base, which lasted from 1927 to January 1929, and the Ruijin base which lasted from 1929 to October 1934, is unsatisfactory. Even the Party history records, published fifty years later, are reticent and the role of Mao himself is not always made clear. As we saw earlier, in September 1930 the Third Central Committee Plenum held in Shanghai made Mao — who was not present, being at his base in the South — an alternate-member of the Politbureau.[9] The two meetings held at the base, one in November 1931, the other in October 1932, turned against Mao. The records say only that Mao lost his leading posts both in the Party and in the army.[10] One record says that in January 1933, when the highest Party leadership had moved from Shanghai to Ruijin, Mao became a regular member of the Politbureau and that the January 1934 Fifth Central Committee Plenum, held in Ruijin, confirmed him in his position;[11] but a parallel document says that Mao was severely attacked at this Central Committee Plenum.[12]

According to the 1982 *Record of Events*, Mao was elected 'Politbureau secretary' of the Ruijin Soviet Area Central Bureau in April 1931, and lost his post to Xiang Ying in November the same year.[13]

What was the real situation? In 1930 Mao carried out a violent purge. It is said that he eliminated 4,400 men from the Red Army on charges of being anti-Party rebels, members of what was called the A-B League. ('A-B' meant anti-Bolshevik. These two Latin letters, along with 'C.C.', the Kuomintang clique, entered the vocabulary of the Party.) In December a group in the Red Army rose up against Mao in an area called Futian. In Party history this is called the Futian Incident. The Party leadership in Shanghai was opposed to the A-B League but it had no affection for Mao, and it is said that a Ruijin Area Central Bureau was set up to keep Mao in check. This is the story that emerges from Professor Hsiao Tso-liang's painstaking commentary on contemporary sources.[14] (A 1982 inner-Party publication said that the truth behind the Futian Incident has never been made clear.[15])

Cai Hsiao-ch'ien, an ex-Communist, joined the Ruijin Area in 1932 and became chairman of its Anti-Imperialist League. What follows is his recollection of the course of events. Having observed the troubles in Ruijin, the Shanghai Party leadership decided in September 1930, at the Third Central Committee Plenum, to set up a special body called the Soviet Areas Central Bureau to guide the soviet (i.e. Communist) areas in various parts of the country. Shanghai sent Xiang Ying — the only Party leader of proletarian origin (he died in 1941) — and a little-known figure named Gu Zuolin to Ruijin. They were joined in December by Zhou Enlai.

Before Zhou arrived, Xiang held a Party conference at Ruijin on November 1–5, 1931, and accused Mao of a series of mistakes: first, he had followed the line of Li Lisan (which Mao, who wanted to attack the cities, had done); secondly, he had misled the land reform; thirdly, he did not separate the military and Party leadership of the army; and lastly, in the purge of the A-B League, he had gone to excess.

When Cai, whose book we are citing, arrived in Ruijin in June 1932, he found that Zhou Enlai was the leader, with the title of Party secretary, and that all power was in his hands.[16] What happened to Mao in Ruijin has never been fully explained in the accounts of Party history written under Mao's regime. In 1983 a distinguished Communist general, Li Zhimin, stated in his reminiscences that Mao lost his post as 'Central Committee Secretary' in November 1931, and that when the Central Committee's Military Committee was reorganised in the following month, Mao, who had been its head till then, lost this post too and was listed twelfth out of the fifteen members of the Military Committee. 'The excuse [for the removal of Mao] was that he was needed for the work of the government.'[17]

According to Cai's book, published in Taiwan, Zhou Enlai took over the leadership on his arrival in Ruijin in December 1931. No mainland Party historian would ever say that Zhou Enlai, the untarnished saint of the Party, squeezed Mao out of the leadership. The historical record of early Party posts, published after Mao's death, said merely that in January 1931 the Fourth Central Committee Plenum held in Shanghai made Zhou a member of the highest body of the Party, the Politbureau

Standing Committee, and head of the Central Committee's Military Department, and that the January 1934 Fifth Plenum of the Central Committee changed the name of the Politbureau Standing Committee to Central Committee Secretariat. This Secretariat had five members, Bo Gu, Zhang Wentian, Zhou Enlai, Xiang Ying, and one more person whom the Party historians in 1983 could not identify. The historical record does not say who was in charge of the Military Committee.[18]

How Zhou was later reconciled with Mao, becoming his subservient adjutant till the end of his life, has never been explained; it was one of the amazing facts of Zhou's supreme art.

At the January 1934 Plenum, Mao was still a member of the eleven-strong Politbureau. (Two of the eleven, Wang Ming and Kang Sheng, were residing in Moscow.[19]) Mao, though eliminated from the highest leadership of Party and army, was entrusted with the running of the Ruijin soviet government. In the Communist system, government, compared to the Party, is of secondary importance. Yet the leadership of the Ruijin government was no paltry post. It was not a local invention, but had been prescribed by Moscow in a letter from the ECCI in July 1931, which urged the setting-up of a central soviet government in a safe area, and gave detailed instructions on how to act and how the land reform was to be carried out.[20]

Moscow must have approved of Mao becoming Chairman of the soviet. The Comintern saw the situation in China in the best possible light — ignoring the fact that the government troops were menacing not only Ruijin but the other Communist bases as well — and predicted the collapse of the Nationalist government and a quick victory for the Communists. The Fifth Plenum of the Chinese Communist Party held in January 1934 shared this optimism, and the Ruijin soviet government enacted laws as if it were the government of the whole country — and not merely of a godforsaken corner of China.[21]

Eleven years later the 'Resolution on Party History' (published as part of the *Selected Works*), which was Mao's version of past events, did not mince words when speaking of the Fourth Plenum (Shanghai 1931) and the Fifth Central Committee Plenum (Ruijin 1934). The leadership of the Party, the Resolution said, ever since it had come under Bo Gu in 1931, and in particular at the Fifth Plenum, had been anti-Marxist, and had brought disaster to the Communist cause. Comrade Mao had been 'diametrically opposed' to their line from the time of the Fourth Plenum held in 1931 in Shanghai.[22]

He probably was, but during the Ruijin period kept his feelings to himself, waiting for the day of revenge. His opponents could not eliminate a man whom Moscow did not reject.

Two events, the Luo Ming Line (1932) and the Fujian Incident (1933), both well-known in Party history, which took place in Fujian province, throw doubt on Mao's opposition to the 'returned students' in Ruijin in the early 1930s, and on his veracity in Yan'an ten years later.

Luo Ming was a Communist leader in Fujian province in 1932. He did not share the optimistic view of the Party leadership that, with an expanded army, they would be able to defeat the coming onslaught of the government troops. He carried on successful guerilla resistance to the attacks of the government troops. He was accused of deviation, and a purge of those who allegedly followed the 'Luo Ming Line' was instituted by the Ruijin leadership.

Forty-nine years later when Luo Ming, who had survived all these troubles, was eighty, he gave a long interview to the Canton Party newspaper. He recalled that in 1931 the 'returned students' took over the Party leadership in Shanghai and sent representatives to all regions to purge the regional Party leadership. In February 1933, a month after the Shanghai leadership's move to Ruijin, *Struggle*, the Party newspaper, accused him of deviation. This took him by surprise. He was summoned to Ruijin and was locked in a room for interrogation. He was accused of carrying out guerilla action when he should have been preparing troops for a frontal attack. Luo said that he had never heard of that Party directive. The Luo Ming Line became a big affair, and well-known Party leaders of later years, Zhang Dingcheng, Tan Zhenlin, Deng Zihui and Deng Xiao-ping, were accused of having followed it.

In August 1932 Mao and Luo Ming were being treated in a Christian hospital that had been taken over by the Communists. Luo recalls that the two had a long talk. Mao was all for guerilla war. How right Mao was, Luo said in his 1981 article. The Yan'an Rectification in 1942–4 and its concluding Resolution on Party History justified his own actions and Mao's guerilla policy to the full.[23]

The 1945 document on Party history certainly condemned the Ruijin leadership — the enemies of Mao — and their daring policies. But Mao's own role in the Ruijin days is far from being as clear as Luo Ming makes out. The 1945 Resolution on Party history says nothing about Luo Ming and the Luo Ming Line. Moreover it refers to a July 1933 speech of Mao's, delivered in Ruijin, which defended, not Luo Ming's strategy, but that of the Ruijin Party leadership (the 'returned students'). Mao spoke of 'class struggle in villages and cities'; he believed, as Moscow and the Chinese Party leadership believed, that the coming fifth anti-Communist military campaign of the government troops would be defeated and that 'the Kuomintang government would perish'.[24]

The Fujian Incident at the end of 1933 was a revolt against Chiang Kai Shek in Fujian province by a group of Nationalists: Chen Mingshu, Li Jishen and Cai Tingkai. The revolt collapsed within two months. If the Communists in Ruijin — so Mao's faction argued — had followed Mao and collaborated with these men in Fujian and with Chen Jitang and other dissident Nationalists in Guangdong province, Chiang Kai Shek could have been defeated; there would have been no need for the Long March; the Communists would have been victorious in China.

This thesis was still supported in 1983 by Hu Yuzhi — then eighty-eight years of age — a venerated old collaborator with the Communists. He wrote about Pan Hannian (whose history we shall relate in Chapter VIII). Pan, who in those days was head of Party propaganda in Ruijin, went to Fujian and negotiated with the men there and also went to Guangdong and talked to Chen Jitang. Everything could have been arranged. But the Party leadership in Ruijin, which was following the Wang Ming line, and Li De (the Comintern's Otto Braun), but not Mao, rejected the idea.[25]

The facts are quite different. Mao Zedong, as head of the soviet government of Ruijin, spoke on three consecutive days at the second meeting of the Ruijin Congress in January 1934. He started by expressing his admiration for the Soviet Union and its marvellous achievements. He then said that the Ruijin Soviet Congress was carrying out the policy of the Party's leadership — the 'returned students' — and that it firmly believed that Chiang Kai Shek's impending fifth military campaign would fail: the Communist army would be victorious and a Soviet New China would be born. He described at length — his two reports fill eighty-five pages — the weakness of world imperialism and of Chiang Kai Shek's collapsing regime, and the strength of the Communists in the Ruijin base. Mao's government report outlined a whole range of government policies, not just for tiny Ruijin but for the whole country: the political structure (provincial soviets, city soviets), the economic policy, land reform (the radical policy as outlined in 1931 at the first session of the Ruijin Soviet Congress), the legal system (including 'suppression of counter-revolutionaries', capital punishment and re-education camps, but excluding physical torture), the fiscal system (with progressive taxation), education, family policy — everything in fact. He spoke in 1934 as if the Communists were about to rule the whole of China in the immediate future. He also spoke, twice, about what had happened in Fujian. The Kuomintang rebels in Fujian were a bunch of good-for-nothings, he said. 'One comrade has said that they are not wholly counter-revolutionaries. He is wrong . . . They are cheating the people; they hold that the soviets are their enemies; they do say the Kuomintang has rotted, but they want their own people's revolutionary government; they are cheating the people; there is not a whit of the revolutionary in them.'

These documents appeared in the ten-volume collection of Mao's speeches and writings published in Japan, but not in the *Selected Works of Mao* or in any other Chinese Communist publication.[26] When Mao came to power, he accused others, his rivals, of having failed to cooperate with the Fujian Kuomintang rebels.

In October 1934 the Ruijin base was abandoned, and the Long March began.

Land reform

We have mentioned that the Comintern prescribed land reform for Ruijin. It had been urging radical land reform ever since the 1920s, but the Chinese Communists were slow to act so long as they were collaborating with the Kuomintang. After the break with the Kuomintang, Communist action in the villages degenerated into brutal savagery.

In Ruijin a regulation on land reform was issued in December 1931 by the 'soviet government' and was signed by Mao as head of the Chinese Soviet Republic.

This document ordered confiscation of the land of landlords, kulaks ('rich peasants') and all counter-revolutionaries, but not of the land of middle-peasants. The kulaks might be given small plots, though only on poor, infertile soil. But landlords and counter-revolutionaries (enemies of the Communists) were to lose not only their land but all their property, including their houses. Land, housing and all other goods were to be distributed evenly among hired labourers, poor peasants and middle-peasants.

Common land and land owned by ancestral halls should be taken and handed over to the peasants to be used as they wished, but their religious feelings should not be hurt.

This document was reprinted in Shanghai in 1932 and in Moscow in 1933 and 1934, but it was not included in Peking's *Selected Works of*

Mao.[27] In January 1934, Mao, as Chairman of the Ruijin soviet, reiterated the policy laid down in 1931: 'Rely on the poor peasants and hired labourers, make allies of the middle-peasants, exploit the kulaks and exterminate the landlords'.[28]

These regulations had no lasting effect, for a few months after they were drawn up, Ruijin retired into the pages of history. The Communists had to flee. The Long March had begun.

A political dictionary published in 1951 in Peking said that from the time of the Long March in 1934 to the end of the war in 1945, radical land reform ceased.[29]

On the march

In official Party history the turning-point in the life of the Party came when the caravan of the Long March stopped at Zunyi, a village in Guizhou province.

The meeting of the Party leaders at Zunyi, according to the official Party history, inaugurated 'a new central leadership headed by Comrade Mao Zedong'. Is this true? In the 1980s, long after Mao was gone, Party historians began to search through early documents. One account described the meeting and what led to it. The Long March began as a disorganised flight. (The leadership itself was in disarray as a result of Party infighting. See Chapter X.) During the first forty-five days, from October 16 to November 30, the fleeing army was under pressure from the enemy and its numbers fell from 80,000 to 30,000; morale was also low. The fugitive troops were pursued by the 400,000-strong army of the Nationalist Government. It was then that Mao Zedong proposed to give up the original idea of settling in the west of Hunan province, and decided to push on west to Guizhou province, where there were fewer government troops. On January 10, 1935, a meeting was held in Zunyi, in Guizhou province. After three days of fierce discussion it was decided that a new soviet area should be established in the region where Guizhou, Sichuan and Yunnan provinces meet. The Party leadership was changed. Bo Gu and the German Otto Braun, the Comintern representative, were replaced. Zhang Wentian became the General Secretary, and Mao Zedong, Zhou Enlai and Wang Jiaxiang formed a military leading team.[30] This was one version of the story.

In 1982 a manuscript was found. Old Chen Yun recognised it as his own handwriting, but did not remember when he wrote it. According to this version, the conference was held, not on January 10–12, but on

January 15–17. No changes in personnel were made at this meeting. A few weeks later, in February, during the continued march, 'Lo Fu [alias Zhang Wentian] replaced comrade Bo Gu in general responsability.' From these obscure words the conclusion was drawn that Zhang Wentian was in charge but that he did not have the title of General Secretary. Moreover, the three-man military committee, consisting of Mao, Zhou Enlai and Wang Jiaxiang, was not set up till one month later in March.[31]

All this is still obscure. At the Politbureau meeting in December 1937 and the Central Committee's Sixth Plenum in September and October 1938, both held in Yan'an, Zhang Wentian performed the opening cere-monies. He must have been the head of the Party.[32] What is certain is that a huge deception — that Mao became the leader of the Party in January 1935 — was kept alive by Mao for forty-five years, and that none of the noble leaders of the Party present on that occasion had the guts to reveal the truth. Among them were, to mention only those alive at the time of the revelations in the 1980s, Deng Xiaoping, Chen Yun, Yang Shangkun, Liu Bocheng and Nie Rongzhen.

Profound silence was preserved about the fact that for some years Zhang Wentian, and not Mao, had been the Party boss.

In 1981 Wu Liping, who had studied in Moscow in the 1920s in com-pany with Zhang Wentian, summed up his memories of his one-time fellow-student. Zhang, he wrote, knew his Marxism well. He was an excellent student in the Sun Yat Sen University, Moscow, and in 1928 he taught Marxism in the Institute of Red Professorship in Moscow. At the Zunyi meeting he was elected General Secretary. Zhang respected the views of Mao Zedong even when others were opposing him. He was a good Communist and as General Secretary he listened to contrary opinions.

At the Lushan meeting in 1959, Wu added, when Mao was at the height of his power and was purging those who criticised his policies, Zhang Wentian put forward his own views without fear. He was to suffer for this until his death in 1976, but he remained a loyal Marxist.[33]

The caravan left Zunyi, and arrived in March 1935 at the north-western corner of what is today Sichuan province (then called Xigang province), close to the border of Shaanxi province. The stronger and more powerful troops of the Fourth Front Army, led by Zhang Guotao and Xu Xiangqian, arrived around the same time. This force had been driven by government troops from its base at the border of Sichuan and Shaanxi provinces, a few hundred miles east of where Mao's First

Front Army was stationed. United, all remained where they were for six months, discussing and quarrelling, undecided where to turn.

It was characteristic of the Communists that, even when they were in the most miserable circumstances, they never forgot their national ambitions and always spoke with an air of grandeur. In 1931, when they were in Ruijin, an obscure area in the South, they established a soviet government in accordance with the policy of Moscow, and claimed it to be a national government. When the Long March troops, sorely reduced in numbers, arrived in the godforsaken northern corner of Xigang province and found themselves locked in bitter disputes, they made the grand gesture at one of their meetings of publishing a *Letter to All Compatriots on Resisting the Japanese and Saving the Country*.[34] This letter, which was echoed in leftist circles all over the country, became known as the 'August 1 Proclamation'. It was issued at a time of national indignation against Japanese infiltration in the North.

The Red Army in those days may have been only a tiny group of men wandering aimlessly in the western wilderness, like Moses and the Jews in the desert, but they kept their sense of a saving mission and felt protected, not by the luminous clouds that protected Moses and the Jews, but by the worldwide might of the Comintern in Moscow. There were several widely scattered Communist groups and military bases in China, but only the group to which Mao belonged was recognised by international Communism as the official Communist Party of China.

The August 1 (1935) Proclamation was drawn up in Moscow with the help of Wu Yuzhang (1878–1966), a member of the Chinese group in Moscow. This is what Chinese sources said in the early 1980s.[35]

In the Xigang camps the dispute about where to go went on. Zhang Guotao, one of the founders of the Party in 1921, wanted to march on to the west, which looked like a safer haven from the continuous pressure of government troops, and to build up a base there. This was a powerful argument. But Mao's group, which was leading the militarily weaker First Front Army Group, wanted to turn to the north and establish a base at the Shaanxi-Gansu-Sichuan borders. Zhou Enlai argued that although militarily it would be more difficult to remain close to the interior of China, it would be wiser to do this than to turn to the west; the western regions were sparsely inhabited, and the population, being non-Chinese, might not welcome a Chinese army, and might even turn against them. If this happened, the army might not be able to find enough food to feed the troops. Zhang Guotao, who had a number of military leaders with him, was accused of having wanted to seize power in the Party and of having set up an alternative Party Central.

They held many meetings; Zhang Guotao was always present. In August a compromise solution was reached: the troops were to divide, taking different routes. Zhang Guotao refused to oblige. Then in September the Mao and Zhou group received news about the situation in northern Shaanxi and decided to move. They knew that a Communist base, independent of Mao's base in Ruijin, had existed there for many years. This was the base led by Liu Zhidan. They also heard of the arrival in Shaanxi of the Twenty-Fifth Army of Xu Haidong, who from 1931 onward had had his own base in central China but was forced to flee and begin his own 'long march' in November 1934. Accordingly, Mao's troops moved. In October 1935 they arrived in northern Shaanxi at a place called Wuqi, west of Yan'an.

The real motive for moving must have been a change in the political and military situation in north and northwest China. In 1935 Japanese troops, which had occupied Manchuria four years earlier, began to move into the northern and northwestern regions of China, and the government troops had to redeploy. Therefore the danger of attacks by government troops was much less than it had been a few months earlier.

That was how the Communists got to the western hills of Shaanxi, and how the myth of Yan'an, their final destination, came into being. Which of the Party leaders were on Zhang Guotao's side, i.e. against Mao, during the discussions about the direction the Long March should take? This is one of the obscure points in Party history. As Zhang Guotao was considered an enemy and a traitor to the Communist Party until his death in Canada in 1979, it was never made clear who was on his side. Possibly Zhu De, Liu Bocheng, He Long, Xu Xiangqian, Ren Bishi and Guan Xiangying — at least these are names cited in connection with Zhang.

Agnes Smedley, a great admirer and a confidant of Zhu De, says in her *Life and Times of Chu Teh*: 'Chu Teh never talked to me about the year he spent in Sikang [present-day north Sichuan] as the virtual prisoner of Chang Kuo-t'ao.'[36] Could Zhu De have been a 'virtual prisoner'?

According to an eyewitness, General Xiao Ke, when Zhang Guotao's troops parted from Mao in 1934 and took the western route to Ganzi in Xigang province, Xu Xiangqian — who had been with Zhang from his early base in Hubei — Zhu De, Liu Bocheng and He Long (all promoted to the rank of Marshal in 1955) went with them. Xiao Ke, reminiscing about this, wrote: 'Some old comrades said to me: "The Party Central [i.e. Mao] is responsible for the split with Zhang Guotao." I myself blindly believed this. I was dissatisfied with the heavy losses and the weaknesses of the First Front Army [Mao's] during the Long March.'

The official Party history has never denied Zhu De's association with Zhang Guotao, but this association has been presented as a continual fight between the two, the consequence of Zhu's effort to win Zhang over to Mao's side. Xiao Ke repeated this, in a milder form. Zhu De did not want to break with Zhang, he wrote; he wanted to influence him.[37]

Zhang was still there when Mao was in the north of Shaanxi province, in a region north of Yan'an. The generals moved around the same area, and engaged in their own battles against the government troops — the common enemy. Mao's relationship with the generals has remained a well-hidden secret of Party history. He gained supremacy in the Party only in 1938, when he overcame his arch-enemy, Wang Ming. In the same year Zhang left the ranks.

The fate of Liu Zhidan

Mao first arrived in North Shaanxi, which for years had been Liu Zhidan's base. Liu, a native of the province, launched the revolution with the help of a young friend of his, Xie Zichang, at the age of twenty-five. Both died young; but others, young men from the same province who had cooperated with them, later became important figures in the Party. These included Ma Wenrui, before the Cultural Revolution a minister of labour, and in the 1980s a provincial Party head; Yan Yongyan, 1st Party secretary of Yunnan province, who was assassinated during the Cultural Revolution; Xi Zhongxun, General Secretary of the Cabinet before the Cultural Revolution, and who held high office after it; and Gao Gang, whose name was deleted from Party history after he was purged in the 1950s. The presence of men of such importance may explain why the real story of what happened to Liu Zhidan when the Communists from other areas arrived is hard to decipher.

In 1980 there appeared in Peking an article not about Liu Zhidan, but about his companion Xie Zichang. Until his death at the age of thirty-eight (in February 1935), Xie Zichang was the leader of the Shaanxi revolutionaries. Liu Zhidan was his close friend and followed him in many revolutionary exploits.

These two were romantic figures, Party members, friends and revolutionaries since their youth, who fought, they hardly knew what for, sometimes organising a few hundred peasants and a few students, sometimes leading only a handful of men. They wandered from place to place trying to spread the sparks of revolution. Often they were battered by government troops, but they never gave up, but simply tried again. It was a disorderly, haphazard revolution, hardly distinguishable from organised banditry or Robin Hood-like outlawry. They organised guerilla groups, Communist armies or revolutionary bases as occasion offered.

They formed part of the Party's regional organisation in the Shaanxi-Gansu area, but this itself was disoriented, and was often regrouped and reorganised. Far away from the central leadership of the Party, which had moved from Wuhan to Shanghai in 1927 and from Shanghai to south Ruijin in 1933, the young revolutionaries in the primitive northwest had only the remotest contact with the centre. In 1928 their attempt to organise a regional revolt ended in failure. In 1932 they formed an 'anti-Japanese alliance', headed by Xie Zichang, with Liu Zhidan as second in command.

In September 1932 they did not have enough food to feed their men, and ultimately they had only thirty soldiers left. They then founded a Chinese Workers-Peasants Red Army Shaanxi-Gansu Guerilla Troop. They 'began to learn the methods of Mao, introducing political work into the troops, abolishing equality'. The new Party leadership in Shanghai, now under the 'returned students', accused Xie Zichang and Liu Zhidan of deviation, describing their actions as 'banditry', and summoning them to Shanghai for reform. Liu did not go. The Shanghai leadership then ordered Liu to Chahar, which came under the Party's North Bureau. When resistance to the Japanese in this region failed, Liu went back to Shaanxi. In 1934 Xie and Liu were more successful and were active in fourteen counties. They set up a North-Shaanxi soviet government and a Northwest Revolutionary Military Committee, with Xie as head and Liu as deputy. In February 1935 Xie Zichang died from wounds received a year earlier and the mantle of leadership fell on Liu Zhidan.[38]

This account of the early Communists in Shaanxi makes no mention of one important companion of Xie and Liu, Gao Gang. His name appears, however, in the list of Party leaders published in *Modern History Studies*, no. 1, 1983, from which we have quoted heavily. According to this list, in 1931 Xie Zichang was head of the Shaanxi-Gansu guerilla troops, Liu Zhidan was his deputy, and Gao Gang was political commissar. In 1933–4, Xi Zhongxun was Party secretary of the Shaanxi-Gansu Military Committee, and Gao Gang was political commissar. After the arrival of Xu Haidong's troops in the second half of 1935, Xu

Haidong was commander, Liu Zhidan was deputy, and Gao Gang was head of the political department.[39]

In 1979 Xi Zhongxun, then First Party secretary of Guangdong province, wrote about Liu Zhidan. In August 1935, he says, Xu Haidong and Cheng Zihua's troops were in the van of the Twenty-Fifth Army which, having had to leave its base at the Hubei-Henan-Anhui border region, arrived in North Shaanxi and was very well received by Liu Zhidan. The two forces united under the command of Xu Haidong, with Liu Zhidan as his deputy. However, 'some leftist opportunists falsely accused Liu Zhidan, calling him a counter-revolutionary.' They arrested all the higher cadres, including Xi Zhongxun himself, who at that time was head of the Shaanxi-Gansu border soviet government.

When Mao Zedong arrived in North Shaanxi two months later, on October 19, 1935, Xi goes on, he immediately sent Wang Shoudao, Jia Tuofu and Liu Xiangsan to liberate these men from jail. The prisoners were released. Liu Zhidan was appointed deputy head of the North-west Revolutionary Military Committee, which was headed by Zhou Enlai, and he was also appointed commander of the garrison of Wa-yao-bao. On April 1 in the following year, 1936, Liu Zhidan fell in battle.[40]

Xi Zhongxun's report does not reveal who arrested Liu Zhidan and his men. One might be excused for thinking that, if it is true that it was Mao who released him, they were probably arrested by the first troops to arrive, namely the Twenty-Fifth Army of Xu Haidong. Yet Xi Zhongxun emphasises that Xu's Twenty-Fifth Army was warmly welcomed by Liu Zhidan and that Liu became Xu Haidong's deputy. A book published in 1984, *Biographies of Generals of the Liberation Army*, contained biographies of, among others, Liu Zhidan and Xu Haidong. From September 21, 1935, onwards, this book says, a man called Zai Jiying, head of Party security in the Northwest, and a man called Zhu Lizhi, carried out a savage purge of the Party. They arrested Liu Zhidan, Xi Zhongxun and others, and subjected them to physical torture. When Mao arrived in the area in October, Xu Haidong reported this to him, and Mao saved the imperilled man.[41]

It was not made clear on whose authority the two men carried out this purge in the Party. Biographical notes say that in 1935 Zhu Lizhi was connected with Liu Zhidan and Gao Gang in North Shaanxi province, became a vice-minister and deputy head of the State Planning Committee later in the 1950s, and died in 1978.[42]

Two expeditions

The north of Shaanxi province, the centre of Communist activities and the region where Mao established himself, was a poor, sparsely inhabited region, barely able to feed the troops. In 1936, therefore, the Communists began to think about expanding their territory. At that time they were engaged in what were known as the 'two expeditions', the eastern and western expeditions. To the east, the Yellow River, flowing from north to south, separated Shaanxi from Shanxi province. Crossing the river would be difficult. It would be more difficult still to establish a foothold in Shanxi province, which was ruled by a powerful military leader, Yan Xishan. Peng Dehuai, Xu Haidong and Liu Zhidan led the troops and crossed the river, despite great difficulty, in February 1936. Chiang Kai Shek, however, sent troops to Shanxi, and the expedition failed. In April the Communists retreated, suffering heavy losses, to North Shaanxi. It was at this time that Liu Zhidan was wounded and died.[43]

In the second half of 1936 another expedition was undertaken, this time to the west. For some unexplained reason, this western expedition was never mentioned in Party histories written before the 1980s.[44]

In the 1980s the reminiscences of several old soldiers were called upon to describe the western expedition in great detail. At about the time of the expedition, Lin Biao was appointed head of the Red Army University. In May 1936 the army leaders, led by him, discussed the plan. All the major armies joined the expedition, taking separate routes. They penetrated deep into the West, suffered great losses and won many victories. The various groups met at a place called Hui-ning, some 300 km. from the western border of Shaanxi province. This was a joyous event.

A number of men who were to be major-generals in coming years took part in the western expedition: Peng Dehuai, Nie Rongzhen, He Long, Liu Bocheng, Zhu De (all five were made marshals in 1955), Yang Dezhi (Chief-of-Staff in the 1980s), Xiao Hua (elevated and then rejected by Lin Biao in the 1960s), Xie Fuzhi and Chen Xilian (both held high office during the Cultural Revolution), Wang Hongkun (an admiral in the 1960s) and Xu Haidong, a highly respected general who from the 1940s onwards suffered from tuberculosis and, after persecution during the Cultural Revolution, died in 1970. Liu Hsiao (ambassador in Moscow in the 1950s) and Ren Bishi, who died in 1950, also took part. All these were prominent leaders of the revolution. They were all young in 1936, in their late twenties or early thirties.[45]

Ultimately the western expedition failed. The failure was attributed to Zhang, who after the Hui-ning meeting went off alone, taking his troops with him. Peng Dehuai in his reminiscences in the 1980s stated his conviction that, if the troops had been kept together, the whole of the northwest, including the key city of Lanzhou and the whole of Gansu province, could have been conquered, and, as he put it, the Xi'an incident, i.e. the capture of Chiang Kai Shek, could have been carried out at an earlier date and with more significant results.[46]

The Xi'an Incident

The whole nation was shaken in December 1936, when Chiang Kai Shek, then visiting the Northwestern city of Xi'an, was seized by Yang Hucheng, the Nationalist general in charge of the region, and the Manchurian troops led by Zhang Xueliang, who had fled from the Japanese.

Good relations between the Communist troops and the latter two had developed earlier. The Communists established contact with the Nationalist General Yang Hucheng. In December 1935 Jiang Feng (in the 1950s deputy head of the United Front Department) brought him a letter from Mao.[47]

As Marshal Nie wrote in the 1980s, in those days a saying existed among the Communist troops that 'Yang Hucheng does not attack the Red Army, the Red Army does not attack Yang Hucheng.' The Red Army did attack what was then called the Northeast Army of Zhang Xueliang and captured some officers. They were treated with kindness and subjected to gentle political education. Persuaded that the Communists were also anti-Japanese, they went back and won over Zhang Xueliang. A Communist delegate was then sent to Zhang, and in April 1936 Zhou Enlai had a talk with him in Yan'an (which was not yet the Communists' headquarters.). Zhang wanted cooperation with the Nationalists, whom the Communists hated, in a common fight against the Japanese. The Communists agreed, at least in principle. Chiang Kai Shek was held in captivity for twelve days. Nation-wide indignation and, on the Communist side, a word from Moscow resulted in his release.

Peng Dehuai was perhaps right when he wrote that if the western expedition had been successful, the Xi'an incident might have had a different outcome. In the event, the expedition failed and the Communist troops were severely mauled.

The Chronological Table of CCP History, published for inner-Party use in 1981, says that the Fourth Front Army (Zhang Guotao) and the fifth regiment of Mao's First Front Army, 20,000 troops in all, crossed the Yellow River and went to North Gansu province, but were utterly routed. In March 1937, 'Li Xiannian fled with 700 men to Xinjiang and then returned to Yan'an. Of the 300,000-strong Red Army, only 30,000 remained.'[48]

During the turbulent years of the Communists' Long March and their ventures in the north of Shaanxi province, the comrades lost contact with the central Party leadership (see Chapter VIII). Wang Ming stayed in Moscow from the autumn of 1931 till 1937. Chen Yun went to Moscow in the autumn of 1935, shortly before the end of the Long March, and stayed there till 1937. Another Party man, Lin Youying (alias Zhang Jie), a member of the Chinese delegation in Moscow, had gone there in the spring of 1933. A Party magazine recalled in 1983 that the Comintern, badly informed about the state of the Party in China, sent Lin to China in 1935. He travelled disguised as a Mongol trader and reached North Shaanxi in November 1935.[49] He must have gone back to Moscow, for it was he who sent a cable to Yan'an on January 24, 1937, ordering Zhang Guotao, in the name of the Comintern, to abandon the idea of setting up a rival leadership. Two months later, in March 1937, at a Party meeting held in Yan'an, Zhang Guotao apologised. At the suggestion of Zhang Wentian, he was demoted to vice-chairman of the government of the Shaanxi-Gansu-Ningxia border area. In April 1938 Zhang resigned and left for the Nationalist area; he was promptly expelled from the Party.[50]

Summing-up, 1921–1937

Party historians, both before and after Mao, distinguish between the periods before and after the break with the Kuomintang in 1927. During the first period, 1921–7, the period of cooperation with the Kuomintang, the small Communist Party succeeded in maintaining its identity, had one leader Chen Duxiu, grew gradually and asserted its will. After the break in 1927, the Party became destabilised, had no permanent leadership, and was blown by the wind in all directions.

What, it may be asked, did Communism mean in China in those years? It meant very little indeed. Marxism, the doctrine of Communism, was not well known even among the higher Communist ranks, much less so among the illiterate peasant Party members. In the 1930s, as we shall see in Chapter VIII, through a curious mixture of half-baked Marxism and anti-Japanese patriotism, being leftist became fashionable in the intellectual circles of the larger cities. These salon Communists were worlds apart from the Communist fighters in the villages. The Communist forces, having no stable leadership, were scattered in rural bases, one of which was Mao's, and had only loose and not always friendly contact with the Politbureau (which had gone into hiding in Nationalist-ruled Shanghai). These revolutionary Communist pockets led precarious lives. At best they ruled a few counties, but none of the cities, not even the smaller cities. Their power was not comparable to that of the northern warlords, who ruled vast territories and who from time to time even ruled great cities like Peking. Communist power was even less comparable with that of the Nationalist government, which was established in 1927 in Nanjing and which gradually overcame the warlords.

In all those years Marxism and Communism were an irritant, but not a power that could decide the nation's future.

The Communist leadership had to leave Shanghai. Their major local bases in south and central China had to be abandoned. Moreover, during their flight the leadership was torn by dissension. On their arrival in the wild and remote area in the north of Shaanxi province, they tried to enlarge their bases to the east and west, but this attempt failed and their troops were decimated. They did have, however, the distant support of the Comintern, the effective work of their underground in the Nationalist-ruled big cities, and the sympathy of restive intellectuals and of some American journalists. This sympathy was fostering the myth of the heroic 'social reformers' who would create a 'New China'. The myth of Mao's Long March — ignoring the long marches of other troops who had also fled to the west — and the myth of Yan'an were born. Behind these lay the genius of a man, a brilliant strategist, who kept away from the battlefields, got rid of his enemies and imposed his personality on his brave but uneducated ruffian generals.

What really saved the Cause, however, was the Japanese war, which began in September 1937, a few months after Mao moved his headquarters to Yan'an.

CHAPTER IV

IN YAN'AN, 1937–1948

In the period following the Zunyi meeting in January 1935, Zhang Wentian presided over Party meetings, but it seems that he never imposed his will. His style was one of genuine collective leadership. At the Party conference held in Yan'an in May 1937 the report on Party organisation was drawn up not by Zhang but by Bo Gu, who had been leader of the Party in 1931–5. Mao Zedong, who was becoming ever more important, spoke of the need for a new turn in the policy of the Party, the need for cooperation with everybody in a common front against the Japanese. In this he was echoing the world-wide common-front policy of Stalin and the Comintern. Mao proposed that the Nationalist Government should abandon its anti-Communism, guarantee democracy, and grant freedom of speech, assembly and association — a daring proposal from the mouth of a Communist leader.

Mao was not yet the supreme leader. It is recorded in the *List of Important Meetings of the History of the Chinese Communist Party,* published in 1982, which we are following here, that some objected to Mao's proposal of democracy and also objected to the way in which the Party had handled the Xi'an Incident of December 1936. The release of Chiang Kai Shek after his arrest had been an error; Chiang had continued to act in his old authoritarian way.[1]

Mao's inveterate enemies were the 'returned students', Pavel Mif's protégés, who had squeezed him out of leading positions in his own territory in Ruijin. Yet he got on well with some of them, including Zhang Wentian and Bo Gu. His chief enemy, Wang Ming, was still in the Soviet Union. At the end of 1937 Wang Ming returned to China and acted as Moscow's emissary and as leader of the Party. Mao's open struggle with Wang Ming began at the Sixth Plenum of the Sixth Central Committee held from September to November 1938 in Yan'an (the Sixth Plenum after the Sixth Party Congress held in Moscow in 1928). A post-Mao account says that Zhang Wentian presided and opened the meeting — he must have still been General Secretary — and Wang Jiaxiang brought an instruction from the Comintern. (We shall see in Chapter V what this instruction may have been.) The meeting turned in favour of Mao and against Wang Ming. The holding of a Party

51

Congress, the Seventh since 1921, was decided on.[2] It was not in fact held for another seven years.

For seven years, 1938–45, the Communist Party in China had no official leader. The available sources say that at the end of 1938, i.e. immediately after the fateful Sixth Plenum, Zhang Wentian was in charge of the Central Committee's Secretariat, but that by March 1943 he was no longer in the Secretariat (the members of which were Mao, Liu Shaoqi and Ren Bishi), and that in June 1943 Zhang was head of the Propaganda Department.[3] Nowhere is there mention of Zhang, or anyone else, holding the title of General Secretary. Those were the years of Mao's ascent to power. The Seventh Party Congress of 1945 gave him the supreme title, Chairman.

This Seventh Party Congress was preceded by a Plenary meeting of the Central Committee, the Seventh Plenum since 1928, an exceptional meeting that lasted a whole year, from May 1944 to April 20, 1945. The Plenum ended the 1942–4 Yan'an Rectification Movement, a two-year period of indoctrination and purges led by Mao. On April 20 the famous, or infamous, Decision on Some Questions on History, i.e. Party history, was passed — an act of abject homage to Mao. On April 23, 1945, three days after the closing of the Plenum, came the opening of the Seventh Party Congress, which was to make Mao supreme ruler.[4]

Contemporary events proved favourable to Mao. While he was moulding the Party in Yan'an, Moscow was deeply involved in the Second World War. The Comintern itself was dissolved in 1943. According to Peter Vladimir, a Tass correspondent in Yan'an, there was visible jubilation in Yan'an when the news of the dissolution of the Comintern arrived. The 'returned students' had lost their patron.[5]

The Yan'an Academy

The Communist headquarters was established some time in the summer of 1937 in Yan'an, a tiny town, barely more than a village. For the next forty years little was known about what really happened in Yan'an. In 1957 a woman writer, Ding Ling, was condemned for writing critically about the Yan'an era. (She was rehabilitated in the 1980s.)

In 1981 a group of ageing men and women met in Peking to reminisce about their life in Yan'an forty or more years earlier. They had been brought together by Li Weihan, one of the doyens of the Communist movement from the early 1920s. In 1984 the reminiscences of these people were published as a book, with a few ancient photographs and a group photograph of the 1981 gathering comprising sixty men and ten women, most of them in their sixties, a few in their seventies or eighties. The first illustration in the book was an early photograph of Zhang Wentian with a reproduction of his handwriting from 1943. (Zhang Wentian died in July 1976.)

The outstanding article in the book was written by Li Weihan. It describes how a Marxist-Leninist college was organised in May 1938, with Zhang Wentian as its head. The vice-director of the school was Wang Xuewen, who had become a Marxist in the early 1920s when studying in Japan. He joined the Communist Party in 1927 and worked in the Communist underground in Shanghai in the 1930s. In 1937 he went to Yan'an at the age of forty-two. He was a scholar, and never became a member of the Party Central Committee. (He died in February 1985 at the age of ninety.[6]) He belonged to the older Yan'an generation. Most of those doing research in the new college were enthusiastic youngsters in their twenties who had left their families in the cities after the outbreak of the Japanese war in 1937. After adventurous journeys through the Japanese lines at great risk to their lives, they arrived in Yan'an. (In those days many youngsters left Japanese-occupied Peking, Tianjin and Shanghai as soon as they had finished their studies. The majority went to the south to join the universities that had moved from Japanese-occupied territory to cities ruled by the Nationalist Government.)

Among the prominent members of the research group were Zhang Qilong, who later took part in the battles in Hubei and led the Hubei group's long march to north Shaanxi, and Deng Liqun, in the 1960s secretary to Liu Shaoqi, and in the 1980s head of the Party Propaganda Department. Among the teachers were Wang Xuewen, Ai Siqi and Wu Liping. Chen Boda's name is left out. Chen was thirty-four when the college was founded. Before going to Yan'an he had been teaching at Shanghai University. As a leading victim of the Cultural Revolution (imprisoned in 1970), he became a nonentity. Mao Zedong, Zhou Enlai, Liu Shaoqi and Chen Yun were invited to give some talks in the college. In July 1941 its name was changed from Marxist-Leninist College to Marxist-Leninist Research Academy. Six months later it was renamed Central Research Academy. Zhang Wentian was still head and Fan Wenlan, whose career as a historian of China began there, was still vice-director. (He died in 1969.)

Living conditions were primitive, but remarkable efforts were made to adjust Chinese history and other branches of knowledge to Marxism.

Nine research bureaux were set up. The bureau of Chinese history was
headed by Fan Wenlan, that of Chinese politics by Zhang Ruxin (who
was persecuted in the Cultural Revolution, and died in 1976). The academy was divided into the following sections: economics, Chinese culture, Chinese literature, Russian language, education, journalism. A
three-year research plan was carefully drawn up. A library was established, but Yan'an was cut off from the world and there was a great
shortage of books.[7]

The 1942–1944 purge

In the meantime Mao's power had been growing. In February 1942, he
launched the Party Rectification. He succeeded in sending Zhang Wentian away from Yan'an to carry out what was called an investigation of
the villages.

— Trouble

Serious study and research soon came to an end. The three-year research
project was discarded after seven months. Throughout his life Mao
never thought much of theoretical studies. The Rectification purge of
Yan'an started in this research academy. It started among the young,
those aged between twenty and thirty who made up 80 per cent of the
research personnel, but a little later it was extended to the older members. They were sent to do manual labour. The Stalinist method of
exposing their own thoughts and criticising others was introduced. The
youngsters revolted; they put up posters not only in the school but in the
public square of Yan'an, asking for freedom and democracy, attacking in
particular Li Weihan (the writer of this report), who at that time, Zhang
Wentian having left, was in charge of the research academy. The majority of the young scholars supported the revolt, and Fan Wenlan himself, the vice-director of the academy, was on their side. The leader of the
group was a young man, Wang Shiwei. He became renowned in Party
history as the man who had revolted against Mao. At the end of March,
with help from Hu Qiaomu, Mao reacted violently. Wang was accused
of being a Trotskyite, an anti-Party reactionary. The criticism of Wang
Shiwei and his companions went on for months. The Party Rectification, the purge of Mao's enemies, was in full swing.[8]

— *The method*

The Rectification, the moulding of the Party to Mao's liking, lasted two years, 1942–4, and ended with the year-long meeting of the Central Committee that prepared the Seventh Party Congress, which was to declare Mao the supreme ruler. This Rectification was not a mere theoretical study session; it was a terrifying purge.

In Yan'an a Central Study Committee was set up. It had Mao himself at its head and Kang Sheng as deputy head. Twenty-two writings were prescribed for study, including three works by Stalin, one by Dimitrov, the Bulgarian head of the Comintern, Liu Shaoqi's *How to be a Good Communist,* and Chen Yun's *How to be a Party Member.* During the Rectification process Kang Sheng and Peng Zhen delivered important speeches.

The main items for study were three of Mao's speeches, 'Rectifying the Party's Style of Work', 'Oppose Stereotype Writing', and 'Concerning Methods of Leadership'. These speeches appeared later in vol. III of Mao's *Selected Works,* in highly stylised revisions, written in general terms or giving practical advice on how to behave. The good Party man, they say, should be like Stalin, not only a man of theory but also a man of action. He should not be a sectarian, like Zhang Guotao.[9] In writing he should follow the advice of Dimitrov and use a brisk, fresh, forceful style. He should be able to organise the masses, getting to know their views, setting up a nucleus of activists in each unit, making experiments in specified places, and guiding the masses through 'unified, centralised leadership'. This is the fulfilment of the principle 'From the masses to the masses'[10] — in which the 'masses' in the end do what the Party orders.

The Party purge was aimed, above all, at the comrades from Moscow, and in particular against Wang Ming. Wang Ming was sick and Zhang Wentian, always considerate, went to visit him, and told him that his (Wang Ming's) main fault was that he was too outspoken and thus offended many people. We all have to admit that in the past we committed many mistakes, he said. But Wang Ming refused to make a confession of his mistakes.[11] According to Wu Liping, a contemporary witness, Zhang Wentian supported Mao. Wu remembers that he himself was upset on seeing that many comrades had given up studying Marxism during the Zheng Feng Rectification in Yan'an; some even said that studying Marxism was useless.[12]

In 1981 Li Weihan, then well over eighty, wrote an article about early Party history. Li came from the same province as Mao, and held high office in the Party leadership from the early 1920s onwards. What he says about the Yan'an Rectification purge in 1942–4 contradicts Wu Liping's account. When the Moscow group, the 'returned students', took over the leadership in 1931, he himself, like Mao, was demoted. He was sent to the Soviet Union to learn some Marxism, but, he says, did not learn much. A year later he returned to China and then went to Mao's base in Ruijin.

The Rectification in Yan'an, Li Weihan says, 'was a school of ideological liberation for me, and Comrade Mao Zedong was my teacher.' It was only then that he learned from Mao how to combine Marxism and Leninism with the Chinese revolution. Oddly enough, in this article written in 1981, Li Weihan, who was purged in 1963–4, expresses unlimited admiration for Mao and for Mao's Chinese style of Marxism.[13]

The contrast between these three veteran Party members, Wu Liping, Li Weihan and Zhang Wentian, is striking. All three studied Marxism in Moscow. Wu Liping saw that Yan'an treated the subject with contempt. Li Weihan was probably not bright enough to absorb the doctrine; he became enthusiastic when he discovered that he could understand Mao's Marxism. Zhang Wentian, probably the most intelligent of the early Chinese leaders, lived his Marxist faith and fearlessly expressed his criticisms when Mao introduced his own brand of Marxism at the end of the 1950s. Zhang Wentian was dismissed by Mao. Wu Liping never got anywhere in the Party and his name was virtually forgotten in China. Li Weihan, purged in 1963–4, was again in a leading position in the 1980s.

— *Soldiers*

A book on contemporary Chinese history, produced in 1981 by three members of the Teachers' Training Colleges in China, says that 300 army and Party leaders took part in the Rectification, one-third from among the Yan'an activists, two-thirds from outside. The army sent those who held the rank of regimental commander and above. All were to study the prescribed documents, and a Central Study Committee was set up in Yan'an headed by Mao with Kang Sheng as deputy head. (The word 'study' often meant in reality the beginning of a purge.) In 1942 Zhang Wentian was sent off with a group to carry out what was described as a survey of the villages in the north of Shaanxi and Shanxi provinces. They stayed away from Yan'an for a full year. In August 1943 Zhou Enlai, who had been representing the Communists in Zhongqing, the war-time capital of the Nationalist Government, returned to Yan'an to take part in the drafting of the document on Party history. In that year, the Teachers' Training Colleges book says, Kang Sheng carried the purge to excess, and cruelly persecuted Party members suspected of deviation, extracting confessions from them under torture. On August 15, a Party resolution laid down the norm, 'Arrest few and do not kill.'[14] This book was written years after Mao's death, when all the crimes of those years were attributed to Kang Sheng. (We shall deal with this further in Chapter X.)

The trouble caused by the Rectification among the troops outside Yan'an is well illustrated in the reminiscences of General Zhang Yunyi (which were written down in 1983 by the man who had been his secretary in those years). Zhang and his secretary were not in Yan'an. They were in the Party's Central China Bureau which led the area situated at the meeting-point of three provinces: Henan, Anhui and Jiangsu. The main Communist forces, the Eighth Route Army and the New Fourth Army, were grouped closely together there. General Zhang was deputy commander of the New Fourth Army and Chen Yi was acting commander. Rao Shushi had taken the place of Liu Shaoqi as acting political commissar.

The reminiscences reveal that in 1943 the Party Rectification caused confusion and disruption among the leaders of the New Fourth Army and in the Party Bureau. There was a bitter struggle between Chen Yi and Rao Shushi. Rao instigated a smear campaign against Chen Yi, accusing him of real and imaginary defects and denouncing him to the Party leaders in Yan'an. In the autumn of 1943, Chen Yi went to Yan'an, and Zhang Yunyi became acting commander of the New Fourth Army. General Zhang Yunyi was on Chen Yi's side and, his secretary recalls, wrote a letter to the Party leaders in Yan'an. The letter, the secretary says, was altered and its meaning distorted. Chen Yi was eliminated from the command of the New Fourth Army and from the Central China Bureau; and many officers, believing the accusations, turned against Chen Yi.[15]

All this was previously unknown. It provides a rare glimpse into how widely and how violently the Yan'an Rectification affected the Party leadership.

(The conflict between Chen Yi and Rao Shushi foreshadowed later events. At the time of the Communist victory, Rao became First Party secretary of East China, and Chen Yi became Third Party secretary of the same region and boss of Shanghai. Five years later Rao was condemned together with Gao Gang. No one knows why. Chen Yi was close to Zhou Enlai and in 1958 he took over the Foreign Ministry from Zhou.)

— Converts

The 1942–4 Rectification had a lasting effect on the Party, and thus on China. It moulded a number of dedicated young men in the Stalinist way of thinking and acting. This insistent inculcation of total submission to the Party for the good of the Cause made spectacular converts.

As at an evangelical revival meeting, there was insistence on total conversion, combined with the confession of past sins. This eliminated the disbelievers — through more ruthless means than those of an evangelical meeting — and it inspired total dedication in the enthusiastic youngsters, mostly in their twenties, who had come to Yan'an not knowing what to believe in. Now they knew what to live for and what to die for. In the *Reminiscences on the Yan'an Central Research Academy*, written forty years later, several old men recalled the conversion that fixed their route through life. As one of them, Xia Guangwei, wrote:

The Yan'an Rectification taught me to reject old thoughts totally. It gave me new strength to fight, to smash the old thoughts within me and to gain new thoughts. Once this had happened, the new gained the upper hand in me. I broke through my former narrow little world. My bosom opened to a wide vision. This gave me optimism to go ahead fighting unremittingly. Later, through the battles, I reached a full Communist outlook on life (pp. 151–2).

This young man had come from a poor mining village in the Northeast. He went to Yan'an in 1938, and joined the Academy in the beginning of 1942, a month before study was suspended and the political struggle began.

— Ma Hong

The Rectification campaign, however, did not have the same effect on all the young researchers. The *Reminiscences on the Yan'an Central Research Academy* contains a contribution by Ma Hong (who in the 1980s took over from Hu Qiaomu the leadership of the newly-established Academy of Social Sciences in Peking).

Ma Hong entered the Yan'an school in 1938, when it was still called Marxism-Leninism College and was led by Zhang Wentian. The school was transformed into the Central Research Academy in May 1941 by Mao, who on that occasion delivered his speech 'Reform Our Study' (contained in the third volume of *Mao's Selected Works*).

Ma Hong's three-page contribution to the book is dedicated to the memory, not of Mao but of Zhang Wentian. He does not say that Mao sent Zhang off from the centre of power. He says merely that Zhang went with a group to make a thorough investigation of the situation in the north of Shaanxi province. 'I was a member of this investigation group.' In May 1943, after seventeen months away, the group returned to Yan'an. The Central Research Academy was then transformed into a part of the Central Party School. Zhang Wentian 'left an impression on me which will last through my life'.[16]

— Lasting effect

The Party purge, the Rectification of 1942–4, created a pattern which China was to find difficult to get rid of. It put an almost indelible stamp on China in the second half of the century. What Mao did to the Central Research Academy in 1942, his abolition of serious studies, had repercussions in the 1950s when the Party was in power and when the intellectual class was branded as reactionary and 'rightist'. It culminated in the Cultural Revolution, which made a clean sweep of all culture. Mao made a number of fanatical converts who from their earliest days had only known one way of governing the Party and the country: namely the way Mao dealt with the Rectification campaign in the 1940s. In every Party purge the same methods, Stalinist methods, have been used: study of prescribed documents, acquisition of conviction, exposure of people to extreme humiliation through criticism and self-criticism, and the elimination of those who resist. Even the Party reform of the 1980s followed the same pattern, Mao's Rectification campaign in Yan'an being held up as a model.

Revised Party history

The document on Party history known as the 'Resolution on Some Historical Questions' is a brazen readjustment of history. It starts with the words: 'Ever since its birth in 1921, the Communist Party of China has made the integration of the universal truth of Marxism-Leninism with the concrete practice of the Chinese revolution the guiding

principle of all its work, and Comrade Mao Zedong's theory and practice of the Chinese revolution represents this integration . . .' 'Comrade
Mao Zedong has creatively applied the scientific theory of Marxism-
Leninism . . .' 'The Communist Party of China . . . pushed forward
and assisted in the reorganisation of the Kuomintang and the formation
of the National Revolutionary Army. The Communist Party provided
the political backbone . . . of the Northern Expedition.' In 1927 a clique
of reactionaries in the Kuomintang defeated the revolution. In the Party
a rightist ideology was represented by Chen Duxiu, who refused to
carry out the wise directives of the Communist International and of
Comrade Stalin and to accept the correct views of Comrade Mao
Zedong.

A leftist error arose in the Central Committee in the years 1930–5,
and lasted till the Cun Yi meeting. In 1930 there was the leftist deviation
of Li Lisan, but he lasted less than four months. His error was corrected
by Mao Zedong. Qin Bangxian (Bo Gu) was in error from 1931 to 1935,
and Mao Zedong in his Jiangxi base was right. The dogmatist errors of
those comrades — the 'returned students' — were cloaked in Marxist-
Leninist theory.

The January 1935 Cun Yi meeting 'inaugurated a new central leadership headed by Comrade Mao Zedong'. Under him the Long March was
carried through victoriously, and during the Long March the erroneous
line of Zhang Guotao, who wanted to set up a second Party, was overcome. During the Japanese war the Communist Party alone held aloft
the great banner of anti-imperialism. The Communist Party created the
Red Army and set up revolutionary bases. Without the Communist
Party, resistance to the Japanese would not have been started and sus-
tained and carried through to victory. Since 1942 Comrade Mao Zedong
has been carrying out rectification of leftist and rightist errors. 'Today,
with unprecedented unanimity the whole Party recognises the correctness of Comrade Mao Zedong's line.'[17]

This document was an incredible concatenation of lies and distortion.
The Party, it proclaimed, was the Party of Mao Zedong from the
beginning; only evil men deviated from his correct line. Party history
became the history of Comrade Mao Zedong. What this document
stated was accepted for many years — and accepted by many foreign
writers — even the statements that the Party backed the Northern
Expedition and that the burden of resistance to the Japanese invasion was
borne by the Communist forces. Hitler was quite right when he said in

Mein Kampf that lies repeated many times become truth. The old comrades knew, of course, what the 1945 document on Party history was worth, and so do the younger Party historians who are working through the old files. (Have not the Russians been rewriting history in this way all the time?)

In 1980, at the time of the 'thaw' in China, the *People's Daily* published a daring article on writing Party history, under the telling title 'Keep the Original Form of Historical Documents'. When the old masters Marx, Engels, Lenin and Stalin re-edited their earlier writings, it said, they changed nothing and left their previous writings intact, even if what they had written was erroneous. The only changes they made were stylistic, they did not change the content or omit the names and views of those who later became their enemies. (The article ignores the rewriting of Soviet Party history in Stalin's *Short Course*.)

'We must admit that, for a long period, we did not treat historical documents in a scientific way.' When old writings by leading personalities were republished, major changes were made in the content; views which developed after the date of their early writings were added without explanation and without comment. Also, the words and even the names of persons who fell in disgrace were erased. 'All this is not scientific, not dignified, not proper. It gives the impression that the thoughts of a great personality [a pointer to the Thoughts of Mao] show no development with experience, as if they were beyond time and space.'

The speeches and writings of the late great leaders, Mao Zedong, Zhou Enlai, Liu Shaoqi, Zhu De, Dong Biwu and other old comrades, should be published, but in making a selection from their writings there should be no thought of 'this can stand today', or 'this is useful today', or 'this cannot stand', 'this is not useful'. The original documents should not be altered. If any change is made, an explanation should be added.[18]

In 1981, on the sixtieth anniversary of the Party, a prominent military leader, Xiao Ke, wrote openly about Party history. Xiao Ke joined the Communist forces in his teens. In the 1950s he was in charge of military training schools, and in the late 1950s he was apparently implicated in Mao's purge of Peng Dehuai, and was relegated to a minor job. After Mao's death, although he was then over seventy, he again became head of the army's military school.

One can now speak, he said, about many things that were formerly taboo. It is not true that Mao was the inventor of the peasant movement and of land reform. The Fifth Party Congress held in May 1927 had already issued several decrees on this. It should not be thought either that Mao was putting forward original thinking in 1927 in his 'Report on an Investigation of the Peasant Movement in Hunan' — the second item in the first volume of Mao's *Selected Works*. That report was inspired by a long article by Qu Quibai — who soon after writing it became head of the Party.

For many years, Xiao Ke continued, nobody dared to discuss Chen Duxiu (the first leader of the Party), and 'even now [in 1981] some hesitate to tell the whole truth. Many of the Party's early heroes have been shrouded in silence because the truth would dim the glory of Mao. There are still many questions awaiting clarification. Even today six years after Mao's death, it is not easy to write an objective history of the Party. Certain things cannot be touched because the writers are afraid that, though the persons they would write about may be dead, others still alive might seek revenge if the truth were revealed.'[19]

This 'thaw' in Party history writing did not last long. In June 1981 a meeting of the Party Central Committee produced another document on Party history, covering the years since 1949, the year of the establishment of the Communist regime. This was a continuation of the 1945 document. The earlier document was not contradicted. Mao was still the great leader, though at the end of his life he had made a great mistake, the Cultural Revolution, 'the mistake of a great leader'.

The two documents were formulated by the same person, Hu Qiaomu, who was thirty-three years old in 1945 and sixty-nine in 1981.[20] Amazing endurance!

CHAPTER V

THE SECRET OF MAO'S SUCCESS

The secret of Mao's success was composed of many elements. One was that he made Marxism seem Chinese. He could express Marxist categories in Chinese terms, in simple, straightforward, often — as the unedited version of his speeches testifies — vulgar language, applying Marxist doctrine to the problems of the day in China, using illustrations from Chinese realities and from Chinese history.

Mao's Chinese heroes were powerful, rough figures — Qin Shi Huang, the First Emperor, whom Chinese tradition condemned for having 'burnt the books and buried scholars alive'; Cao Cao, a cunning warrior in the time of the Three Kingdoms, and the noble bandits in the old novel *All Are Brothers* — men well-fitted to inspire Mao and his rough guerilla fighters. For Mao, traditional Chinese courtesy, politeness and the delicate arts were abominations.

Mao left his imprint on Chinese society. Not for years after his death did the Party leadership discover how rough and uncouth social life had become, and feel the need to introduce, in 1982, a yearly month of politeness in which people would learn how to behave in a civilised manner (as the Chinese had behaved for thousands of years).

Mao trained warrior bands, and military discipline was implanted in the nation's life. (After Mao it was discovered that all this was largely superficial and that the Chinese character had changed little.) Despite all this, in his personal relations Mao could be friendly, spontaneous, simple and humble. Gong Chu, whom we mentioned in Chapter III, has described his first meeting with Mao: how Mao sat down with him at a simple table while his bodyguards served good food, asked about Gong Chu's activities, showed a sense of simple humour, and complimented his guest on not smoking even while he himself smoked on. Mao was charm itself.

Peter Vladimir, the Russian whose memoirs were referred to earlier (Chapter IV, p. 52), described Mao's personality in similar terms. It was probably through friendly behaviour that Mao succeeded in winning Wang Jiaxiang and Zhang Wentian, two of the 'returned students', to his side for the attack on Wang Ming and the destruction of the men sent from Moscow. Mao was an adroit and far-sighted operator, not an impulsive dictator. This explains his success in breaking up the Moscow-trained group and establishing his own authority. This manoeuvre was described in detail many years later, in 1982, by an authoritative witness, Wu Xiuchuan.

Wu Xiuchuan is a man who has achieved prominence in the army, in the Party and in the government's conduct of foreign affairs — an example of the interweaving of army, Party and government in China. His memoirs of Wang Jiaxiang, a dear colleague, are unlike most memoirs, which rarely tell the whole truth and are often written only to exalt the writer himself. These are an honest statement of fact.

Wu Xiuchuan tells us that in 1925, when he was seventeen, he went to study in Moscow along with Wang Jiaxiang and others. Wang was then aged twenty. In Moscow, Wu and Zhang Wentian became good friends. In 1931 Wu returned to China, to the soviet area bordering Fujian, Guangdong and Jiangxi provinces, and was wounded in battle. He was with Wang Jiaxiang at Ruijin, where Wu was doing translation work and Wang was deputy head of the Party Military Committee. In 1941 he worked under Wang, still in the Military Committee, in Yan'an. In 1945 he and Wang were transferred to the northeast. After the establishment of the People's Republic in 1949, Wang became vice-foreign minister and ambassador in Moscow, and Wu was put in charge of the Soviet Union and Eastern Europe section of the ministry. In 1952 Wang returned to Peking to become head of the Central Committee Foreign Liaison Department and first vice-minister of the foreign ministry; Wu was one of the vice-foreign ministers. In 1955 he was made ambassador to Yugoslavia, but he disagreed with Peking's policy towards Yugoslavia, and was recalled. Wang Jiaxiang then made him deputy head of the Central Committee Foreign Liaison Department, and he remained in that post until 1966. During the Cultural Revolution both Wang and Wu were purged. Wu spent eight years in prison, and Wang, who was apparently not imprisoned, helped Wu's family.

Wu Xiuchuan was thus a close associate of Wang Jiaxiang for fifty years. Wang died in January 1974 at the age of sixty-eight. Wu's memoirs of Wang Jiaxiang explained some hitherto unknown facts, such as Mao's relations with the Moscow men and his relations with Moscow.

Wang Jiaxiang left Shanghai and went to Mao's headquarters in Ruijin, in 1931, two years before the Central Party leadership moved there from Shanghai. In Ruijin, as we said above, he was deputy head of the Party's Military Committee. He disagreed with the opinions of Bo Gu, head of the Party, and Li De (Otto Braun), the German Comintern representative, and supported Mao Zedong. When Xiao Jingguang (who after 1949 became the head of the Chinese Navy) was accused of defeatism and of having followed the heretical Luo Ming line, and condemned to five years in prison by Bo Gu and Braun, Wang Jiaxiang saved him by refusing to sign the sentence.

In the early days of the Long March, at the end of 1934, both Wang Jiaxiang and Mao were sick and were carried side-by-side on stretchers (or in sedan chairs), and spent their evenings together discussing military affairs. Wang aired his worries about Braun's leadership — worries which Mao certainly shared. Wang then talked to Zhang Wentian and lobbied among the others against Bo Gu and Braun and in favour of Mao. He won support from Zhou Enlai and from Zhu De and Nie Rongzhen (both made Marshals in later years). The upshot was that at the Cun Yi conference and its aftermath from January to March 1935, Bo Gu and Braun were demoted and Zhang Wentian was made leader of the Party. Mao Zedong, Wang Jiaxiang and Zhou Enlai formed the Military Committee. This explanation of the changes made at the Cun Yi meeting is more convincing than that given in other documents. It also indicates that during the Long March the Party leaders, carried by coolies, did not have quite the hard time that legend credits them with.

Wu's memoir of Wang Jiaxiang also reveals other important points. After the Long March, Wang Jiaxiang was sent to the Soviet Union to report to the Comintern, and stayed there for some time. He made his report to Georgi Dimitrov, the Bulgarian who had just become head of the Comintern and was to retain that post until its dissolution in 1943. Wang was full of praise for Mao Zedong, telling Dimitrov that Mao was ready to cooperate with the Kuomintang against the Japanese — this fitted into Moscow's world-wide policy in the 1930s for a common front — and that Mao would not repeat the error of Chen Duxiu and would maintain the independence of the Communist Party. Wang returned to China in 1938 and 'carried on severe struggle' against Wang Ming.

Wu says that the term 'Mao Zedong Thought' was invented by Wang Jiaxiang, who proposed it in an article written on the twenty-second anniversary of the Chinese Communist Party in 1943. 'Today and in coming times', Wang wrote, 'the correct road is the thought of Comrade Mao Zedong, what Comrade Mao Zedong has laid down in his writings and manifested in action. The Thought of Mao Zedong is Chinese Marxism-Leninism; it is Chinese Bolshevism; it is Chinese Communism.' In the same year Wang promoted the publication of the

Selected Works of Mao Zedong, compiled by Deng Tuo[1] (later to be chief-editor of the *People's Daily*, purged in 1966).

If Wu Xiuchuan's account is true — and there is no reason to doubt it — Mao owed his arrival at a position of supreme power in the Party to the great shrewdness he showed in dividing the 'returned students' who were then the leaders of the Party and winning some of them over to fight the rest. Luckily for Mao the 'Russian boys' were themselves disunited. Wang Jiaxiang, who was not a friend of Wang Ming, was given a high-ranking post in Mao's early headquarters and remained in such posts for more than thirty years. Zhang Wentian, who became head of the Party at the Cun Yi meeting, was an intellectual rather than a forceful Party leader, and did not interfere with Mao's manoeuvres. All that remained to be done was to fight Wang Ming, who was disliked by both Wang Jiaxiang and Zhang Wentian.

Meanwhile the situation in Moscow had changed. Mif, who had brought the 'returned students' to China, disappeared in Stalin's Great Purge. The Marxist mentors of the 'returned students', the men whose Marxist doctrine the 'students' had learnt in Moscow, had, as we shall see in Chapter VII, been discredited by Stalin. Moreover, Mao found a high-ranking patron in Moscow in the person of Georgi Dimitrov.

We saw earlier that Wang Jiaxiang had painted a glowing picture of Mao to Dimitrov. In 1981, six months before the publication of Wu Xiuchuan's memoir, the *People's Daily* published an article entitled 'Dimitrov and the Chinese Revolution'. It quoted a speech Dimitrov made at the Seventh Congress of the Comintern in 1935: 'The views of Comrade Mao Zedong are perfectly correct and people all over the world should learn from them.' Dimitrov said this in the presence of Wang Ming, who was a member of the Chinese delegation. When Dimitrov was bidding farewell to Wang Jiaxiang and his colleague Ren Bishi (who died in 1950), he said: 'You must tell the whole [Chinese] Party that they must support the leadership of Comrade Mao Zedong; he is a leader formed in real struggle; no one else should fight for leadership.'

The Seventh Comintern Congress, at which Dimitrov made this comment, was held from July to August 1935, when Mao was still on the Long March and Zhang Wentian was still head of the Party. Three years were to pass before Mao launched his attack on Wang Ming at the Sixth Central Committee Plenum in Yan'an in 1938. The *People's Daily* article quoted above ended by saying that Dimitrov's remarks about Mao formed one of the twenty-two texts assigned for study during the 1942–4 Rectification movement in Yan'an.[2] It is hard to say whether the words attributed to Dimitrov, head of the Comintern, are genuine or not. He delivered a seven-hour report at the Comintern Congress, but the full records of this Congress have never been published, not even in Russian.[3] In his memoir of Wang Jiaxiang, Wu Xiuchuan states, as we saw above, that after the Long March Wang went to Moscow and in conversation with Dimitrov extolled Mao's gifted leadership. (Wang went to Moscow in October 1936 and stayed till August 1938.)[4]

Yet Wu says nothing about Dimitrov having talked to Wang about Mao and nothing about what Dimitrov said at the Seventh Comintern Congress. Whatever the truth, two things seem clear. One is that Mao succeeded in splitting the 'Russian boys'. The other is that while in Yan'an, Mao was not indifferent to the reactions of Moscow and the Comintern. True, it was in Yan'an that the returned Bolsheviks were eliminated from the leadership and saw their ten-year reign over the Party come to an end. It was in Yan'an too that Mao began to manipulate the Party, moulding it in his own image. Yet all this did not lead to a break with Moscow. The flow of Chinese-language Stalinist-Marxist books printed in Moscow makes this evident. So does the presence of Soviet observers in Yan'an throughout the war years, and the continued visits paid by Chinese Party leaders to the Soviet Union.

Stalin still had a direct say in the affairs of the Chinese Communist Party. When Chiang Kai Shek was arrested in Xi'an in December 1936 — the Xi'an Incident — Zhou Enlai went to negotiate on the spot.[5] According to a collection of documents published in 1980 for internal circulation within the Party, the Moscow embassy to the Nationalist Government went into action, and Stalin sent firm instructions to Mao demanding the release of Chiang Kai Shek. Stalin was then supporting Chiang's resistance to Japanese infiltration.[6] (For more on the Xi'an Incident, see pp. 106ff.)

Mao showed a remarkable talent in handling his friends and enemies. Stalin killed his enemies; Mao honoured them, but kept them on a short leash. At the Seventh Party Congress in Yan'an, which made Mao the supreme ruler of the Party, the 'Russian boys' were admitted to the Central Committee. Wang Ming and Bo Gu were listed, though listed last, among the regular Central Committee members. Wang Jiaxiang became an alternate-member and Zhang Wentian became a member of the Politbureau.

Bo Gu died in an aeroplane accident a year after the Seventh Congress.

Wang Ming fled to the Soviet Union at the end of the 1950s and carried on a campaign writing articles against Mao. The two who had helped Mao — Wang Jiaxiang and Zhang Wentian — both became ambassadors to Moscow in the early 1950s. In 1959, however, Zhang Wentian was dismissed. He was arrested during the Cultural Revolution and died in 1976. Wang Jiaxiang, as we saw above, retained high office in the Central Committee until his fall in the Cultural Revolution. He died in 1974 and was posthumously rehabilitated in 1979.

Mao could remain loyal to his old friends and kept many of them in the same posts for twenty years. Thus Li Weihan remained head of the United Front Department, Lu Dingyi remained head of Party Propaganda, Zhou Yang remained Mao's cultural 'Grand Inquisitor', and Zhou Enlai, Mao's rival in Ruijin, became his pliant, faithful and congenial servant. Many others retained their posts for twenty years, until the upheavals of the Cultural Revolution in the second half of the 1960s. Mao had a stable staff for twenty years — a remarkable achievement for a supreme ruler.

CHAPTER VI

THE JAPANESE WAR, 1937–1945

In 1945, the year in which the Seventh Party Congress was held in Yan'an, the general situation in China was utterly different from what it had been when the Communist headquarters was set up in Yan'an ten years earlier. In 1935, the Japanese, who had already established Manchukuo (in 1931), began to encroach on North Chinese territories. In 1937 they began an open invasion of China. The Communist Party benefited immensely from the war with Japan and emerged from it in control of a large area of territory and with a vastly increased membership.

Communist propaganda held that the Communists, not the Nationalists, fought the Japanese. In 1985, forty years after the war, the tone of propaganda changed and the merits of the Nationalist troops were admitted — a concession not so much to historical truth as to the needs of psychological warfare against Taiwan.

A booklet published by the Nationalists in 1951 gave a more realistic analysis of the situation. The goal of the Japanese army was the conquest of the major strategic centres of China, indeed of the whole of East Asia. Japanese conquests extended to the Philippines, Burma and Singapore. The guerilla resistance of the Communists in the North Chinese villages was nothing more than a nuisance.

The people who lived in disputed areas in those days, as the author did, remember well those turbulent times, when a handful of Japanese soldiers living in fortified towers kept control of a whole county harassed by roving bandits, patriotic anti-Japanese guerilla troops and Communist troops. Often a village would be ruled in the daytime by the Japanese soldiers or by Nationalist guerillas, and at night by Communists. The government troops, this Nationalist account said, were unable to organise the scattered local patriotic fighters against the Japanese, whereas the Communists excelled in this work and armed the villages for self-defence.[1]

It is no exaggeration to say that the Communists were fishing in troubled waters. Their main purpose was to maintain and expand their forces. In the country as a whole, the main resistance was carried on by the Nationalist army, which had to halt the advance of a formidable enemy.

69

Lasting ties

The men who were leading the Communist troops made names for themselves, and the friendships established among them were to influence Chinese politics for many years. The groups of military leaders and army political commissars who had cooperated in controlling particular sections of the Communist troops later maintained that cooperation, and it formed the basis of rival factions in the political arena. The men who ruled the country under Lin Biao during the Cultural Revolution in the late 1960s were men who had worked with Lin for thirty years, first during the anti-Japanese war, then after the war in the Northeast, Manchuria, and ultimately in the Fourth Field Army organised in 1948. Similarly many of the leading personalities who came to power after the death of Mao under Deng Xiaoping had been together since the Japanese war and had been members of the Second Field Army organised in 1948.

This coherence of groups and cliques, which lasted for forty or fifty years, and their domination of the political life of the country are a peculiar feature of the Communist Party in China. Friendship and friendly relations have always counted for much throughout Chinese history. Such ties are stronger than both family ties and ideological Marxist convictions. The crucial factor in China is not the often-asked question, whether the Chinese leadership is primarily Communist or nationalist, but rather which group of men is on top.

The long history of early Chinese Communism has never been expounded in so many words in the Communist press. Indeed, after the take-over of power in 1949 and during the long reign of Mao, nothing was heard about the pre-1949 events in Party history, apart from rapturous praise of Mao, the Long March and the Red Army. Names other than Mao's were rarely mentioned. A discreet veil covered the pre-1949 years and students of China in the following years almost had the impression that the world was created in 1949. Within the Party leadership, however, everyone knew who was who, and the power groups, as later events have shown, guided the fate of the nation.

Party and army had been identical for many years. It could hardly be otherwise when the Communist Party was fighting a war, first to preserve its own existence, and then to win supreme power in the country.

Respectability

War and fortuitous circumstances transformed Mao's small group of ragged armed troops operating in the primitive northwestern hills of Shaanxi into a powerful party and army. Four years after the war, on October 1, 1949, Mao established the People's Republic.

Without the Japanese war the Chinese Communist Party never could have become what it did. In the crucial years, it mattered little whether the Party members were Marxist or not. They were a revolutionary force with the enthusiasm and fresh optimism of revolution and they were facing tired, disunited and demoralised government forces.

The government

The National government, having put an end to the rule of the warlords and the reign of divisiveness in China, established an effective central government in Nanjing in 1928. However, it had a difficult time. The Japanese took Manchuria in 1931, they made a bloody though unsuccessful attack on Shanghai in 1932, and they kept on penetrating further into China's Northern territories. Generals and politicians in the south were reluctant to submit to the central government. Not until 1936, a year before the Japanese war, did the Nanjing government succeed in uniting the whole country. With German military advisers, it built up a modern army; it developed the economic infrastructure rapidly, and cultural life flourished. It is a tribute to the Nanjing government that during those ten difficult years 1928–37, China, oriented towards the West, achieved as much as it did. Those years were the best China has known this century.

When the war with Japan broke out in July 1937 and the Japanese forces occupied the great North Chinese cities, Peking and Tianjin, the nation rose up in a common effort against the invaders. In August a Sino-Soviet non-aggression pact was signed.

Liaison offices

In September the Communists formed a common front with the Nationalist army. The Red Army became the Eighth Field Army of the united armed forces and the Nationalist government organised the few thousand Communist troops scattered in Central and East China into the New Fourth Army. Zhou Enlai, number three in the Communist leadership, liaised between the Nationalist and Communist forces. He received the nominal title of deputy head of the National government's Military Committee and resided in Nanjing, the seat of the National government. All this was a heavensent opportunity for the Communists to increase their power and their influence in non-Communist-controlled areas.

They were allowed to open liaison offices in the Nationalist-ruled cities that had not yet been occupied by the Japanese. After the loss of Nanjing, the Nationalist government moved, in November 1937, to Zhongqing (Chungking). The Communists also moved, and in Zhongqing, the wartime capital of China, they were allowed to open their Eighth Route Army office. Using this as a cover, the Party set up its clandestine South Bureau, under Zhou Enlai. Forty years later a comrade who had been there in 1941–3 described the Zhongqing years.

Zhou Enlai was helped by Dong Biwu, by his own wife Deng Yingchao and by others. Ye Jianying maintained secret communications with Communist Party members outside Zhongqing. When in 1939 Zhou Enlai went to the Soviet Union for medical treatment for his hand — the reason for this has never been made public — Bo Gu, Kai Feng and Dong Biwu took over responsibility for the Zhongqing office. The Communist *Xinhua Daily* (formerly based in Wuhan) was allowed to restart publication in Zhongqing, and this gave the Communists an opportunity to hold a secret Party meeting every Thursday.

The secret South Bureau conducted a wide range of activities. Its task was Communist penetration into all political and cultural organisations, even into the Christian YMCA and into the organisations of the Kuomintang itself. If possible, it was to insert its men into leading positions in all groups. Sympathisers — landlords and big capitalists included — were welcome. The best universities in China had moved from the Japanese-occupied North to the South, and in them the Bureau succeeded in winning dozens of secret Communist Party members. Some rich capitalists were ready to help them to transfer secretly large sums of money. The Zhongqing Bureau had a secret radio transmitter for maintaining contact with the Communist headquarters in Yan'an.[2] It even used the government's military radio for its own purposes. At the end of 1939 — this was revealed forty-four years later — a pretty girl went to visit somebody in the government's military radio station. She made friends, penetrated deep into the organisation and succeeded in setting up a Communist cell. She had been trained for this in Yan'an. The cell communicated to Zhou Enlai's office the secret code and the military secrets of the government's military transmitter. One day this was detected, almost by accident, and some members of the cell were arrested. One man escaped, ran to the headquarters of the South Bureau — which outwardly was the respected 'Residence of Mr

Zhou' — and was smuggled out through an air-raid shelter to Zhou Enlai's car.[3] All this was done in secret. At the same time Zhou Enlai was openly carrying on important negotiations with the National government.

Negotiations between the Nationalists and the Communists had started years before the full-scale war with the Japanese invaders. In 1932, a year after the Japanese occupation of Manchuria, the Soviet Union, feeling threatened, resumed diplomatic relations with the Chinese Nationalist government. At the end of 1935 and in 1936, after the Communists had settled in Yan'an, Chiang Kai Shek used the good offices of the Soviet Embassy in Nanjing to open negotiations with the Communists in the hope of furthering national unity. Pan Hannian (see Chapter VIII, pp. 124–7), Party historian Lu Zhenxiang, and Mao's private secretary Zhou Xiaozhou (purged in 1959, died during the Cultural Revolution) began these negotiations with the government in Nanjing. The arrest of Chiang Kai Shek in Xian in December 1936 did not end the contacts. Four months later Zhou Enlai was negotiating with Chiang. When the full-scale Japanese invasion began on July 7, 1937, Zhou, Ye Jianying and Zhu De took part in a Defence Conference in Nanjing. A month later the Communist troops in the North were organised into the Eighth Route Army and joined the Nationalist resistance to the Japanese. During the war the negotiations continued in Zhongqing, each side demanding that the other should give up attacking it. Chiang, eager for national unity, even offered the dissolution of the Kuomintang. On the Communist side, Zhou consistently refused to give up the independence of the Communist bases.[4]

United States observers

For four years China fought the invading Japanese alone, though with some help from the Soviet Union, until the outbreak of war between the Soviet Union and Nazi Germany in 1941. Pearl Harbor (1941) and the United States' entry into the war changed the picture. The Americans became involved in China in the common fight against Japan.

Contact with China turned out to be a highly emotive issue. (In the United States China has always aroused emotion.) Disappointment with Chiang Kai Shek and with the government's badly-paid, badly-fed and disunited army, caused disillusionment in Washington, and in the eyes of many the significance of Yan'an and of the Communist forces grew out of all proportion. China's fate became a burning issue in Washington circles — as if it were for Washington to decide what

China should become. In 1944, with the end of the war already in sight, Americans — at first journalists, then US Army observers — flew from Zhongqing, where they had been softened under the gentle influence of Zhou Enlai, to Yan'an.

The Americans' visit to Yan'an gave the negotiations an international dimension — and became a source of acrimonious controversy in the United States. This controversy has lingered on for forty years. Who was right and who was wrong among the American officials in charge of China policy in Washington? Was China lost to the Communists by the United States? Would the Chinese Communists have become America's allies if Washington had followed the advice given by some of those who visited Yan'an in 1944? In the McCarthy era, scapegoats were sought for what was called the 'loss of China', and some former advisers did not fare well. When good relations between Peking and Washington were established in the 1970s, the wheel had turned full circle. These advisers felt rehabilitated, and a spate of books were published justifying their past views and actions.

The American visitors to Yan'an were indeed impressed. What they believed they had seen was an ideal society, a city at war, yet with no police in sight and hardly any soldiers. This was a genuine simple life-style: even Chairman Mao travelled on foot. There were no guards and no secret service men round him, quite unlike Chiang Kai Shek's appearances in the streets of Zhongqing. In Yan'an there was a refreshing absence of show and formality. Clothing and living standards were simple, but there were no beggars and no signs of desperate poverty; morale was high; people did not bother to lock their doors; there was visible emphasis on democracy.[5]

American soldiers and political observers believed that Yan'an was a paradise of democracy, boding well for the future of China. Some American literary nonentities who were making names for themselves as witnesses of Yan'an went a great step further and nurtured the myth, widespread throughout the world in those days, that these revolutionaries in Yan'an were merely agrarian reformers, not real Communists. Edgar Snow said in 1945 that Chinese Communism was an 'agrarian reform movement'; Günther Stein said that the Chinese Communists did not intend to remain Communist; Freda Utley said: 'Chinese communists are a party of social reformers and patriots — "radicals" in the English nineteenth-century meaning of the world.' Even Walter Judd, a ferocious anti-Communist in the 1950s, admitted that in 1945 he believed the Communists were agrarian reformers.[6]

The authorities in Yan'an never issued any denial of this distortion of their real identity. Rather, they inspired such distortions, like traders selling merchandise under false labels. In some sense they knew that 'Communism' was an ugly word.

A leader of an American military group in Yan'an, David D. Barrett, looking back at those days twenty-five years later, wrote:

As I look back on my service with the Dixie Mission, I am perfectly willing to admit that in some way I was unduly impressed with the communists in Yenan. . . The communists were then very much on our side in fighting Japan. There were no police in Yenan. Police were probably unnecessary, for, as we came to know later, the whole of Chinese communist society is pervaded with spies, snoops and informers . . . I did not know when we first went to Yenan [that] a concentration camp was there not far from the area where we had our quarters.[7]

Coalition government

The Communist outlook was clear. They wanted to influence public opinion at home and abroad, to become acknowledged as an integral part of China's national life and to pave the way to power by establishing a coalition government. At the Seventh Party Congress in 1945, Mao delivered a speech entitled 'On Coalition Government'. This was one of his most typically crafty speeches. No, the Chinese Communist Party would not follow Russia's example and establish dictatorship of the proletariat, he said. The Communist Party was not opposed to the development of private capital or to private property. The Communists wanted freedom of political conviction and of religious belief. During the years of fighting the Japanese, it was not the Communists who fought brother Chinese troops; the Kuomintang government had turned against the Communists.

The Nationalists, he said, say: 'Hand over your troops and we will grant you freedom'; but 'a political party which has no armed forces has no freedom. . . . For the past eighteen years, workers, peasants and students . . . have had no armed forces and no freedom.' The Communists were ready to hand over the armed forces to a new democratic coalition government, if the Nationalist government would do the same.

Mao knew that the Communists were weak compared to the Nationalists. He therefore sought to gain power by diplomatic manoeuvre, by trying to enter a government coalition. Yet he was afraid that this might turn out badly, so he would not give up the independence of the

Communist forces. Was he able to imagine a government which would have no army, or a government under which political parties could maintain their separate armies?

In the present stage

What Mao wrote in 'On Coalition Government' about freedom, capitalism and so on, may seem like open deception. But there is a recurrent phrase in that speech that is easily overlooked — a phrase, much used by Communists, that often misleads their partners. The phrase is 'in the present stage'. In good Marxist thinking, which they call dialectical thinking, what is true today may not be true tomorrow. In this speech Mao used the words 'in the present stage' several times. In what was then the present stage, China wanted a coalition government, democratic freedoms and capitalism.

The Chinese system for the present stage is being shaped by the present stage of Chinese history. The present stage is called 'bourgeois-democratic revolution' . . . a new democratic revolution now and socialism and communism in the future. Indeed we have too little capitalism . . . From our knowledge of the Marxist laws of social development, we communists clearly understand that under the state system of new democracy in China it will be necessary in the interests of social progress to facilitate the development of the private capitalist sector of the economy.[8]

Innocent foreigners in China may not have understood the real meaning of these ironic pronouncements; the Nationalists in Zhongqing certainly did. They knew that, though the Communists were allowed to spread their ideas in Nationalist territories, the Communist-ruled areas were hermetically closed to Nationalist propaganda. They also knew that in 1944, when the Americans were making their friendly visits to Yan'an, the two-year internal purge, the Zheng Feng Rectification, was just coming to an end there. The Communists were a state within the state.

The Communists speak in one language to outsiders and another at home. During the Rectification of the Party in Yan'an, Mao gave a speech, 'On Literature and Art'. That speech was for internal consumption, and what Mao said has haunted the Party ever since. He stated without hesitation and with great force that literature and art are 'subordinate to politics' and that 'politics, whether revolutionary or counter-revolutionary, is the struggle of class against class'. There is nothing more dangerous than artistically accomplished writings with a politically erroneous content, he said. 'Some works which politically are downright reactionary may have a certain artistic quality. The more reactionary their content and the higher their artistic quality, the more poisonous they are to the people, and the more necessary it is to reject them.'[9] We shall come back to this in the next chapter.

How different Mao was when speaking to his own men and when speaking to outsiders about coalition government!

At the end of the war

Mao was a complex personality and a shrewd politician. In 1945, when Germany and Japan had collapsed and the war had come to an end, China — Nationalist China — had become one of the great powers, one of the five members of the Security Council of the United Nations. Mao knew that the Communist forces in China represented only a comparatively small part of the nation and of the armed forces, and he was ready to negotiate. On August 28, 1945, he flew to Zhongqing to negotiate with Chiang Kai Shek.

He knew the many difficulties the Nationalists faced. According to Nationalist sources, their army had lost 2.4 to 3.5 million soldiers during the war, including more than 100,000 officers, and China had suffered immense destruction of industry, railways and roads,[10] a loss from which the Nationalist government could hardly recover before 1949.

The Communists had no industries worth mentioning and no railways to maintain. They had profited from the war years. It was claimed that the number of Party members had increased from 40,000 at the beginning of the Japanese war in 1937 to 1,210,000 at the end of the war in 1945.[11] By the end of the war the Communist army was 940,000 strong, ruling ten 'liberated areas' with a total population of about 100 million people, of whom 220,000 were said to be village militia.[12] Other Communist sources gave different figures, 1.3 million in the army and 2.4 million militia.[13]

Yet, taking the country as a whole, the Communists in China were a threat, not a rival power. The Chinese people, after seven years of war, were longing for peace. Both Washington and Moscow wanted peace in China. Stalin sent a cable to the Chinese Communist Party, urging it to 'develop peace' as a means of getting a voice in the government of the country.[14] Mao arrived in Zhongqing on August 28, 1945, and left on

October 11. He was ready to grant concessions and to withdraw the Communist troops from some areas; but he was not ready to incorporate the Communist troops in the national army, and he insisted on a coalition government in which the Communists would form a respectable part. Back in Yan'an he explained that he was ready to make major concessions and to withdraw the Communist troops from south of the Yangze, but that he was not ready to 'hand over our guns to the Kuomintang'.

His stay in Zhongqing had been a powerful exercise in public relations. As he explained in Yan'an, 'When in Zhongqing, I had a profound sense of warm support given us by the broad masses of the people. They are dissatisfied with the Kuomintang government and place their hopes on us. I also met many foreigners, including Americans, who sympathise with us. The broad masses of the people in foreign countries are dissatisfied with the reactionary forces of China and sympathise with the Chinese people's forces.'[15]

On October 10, National Day, Mao and Chiang signed the agreement known as the Double Tenth Agreement. The two sides agreed to avoid civil war, to release political prisoners, to withdraw Communist troops from eight 'liberated areas' in the South, and to hold general elections for a national parliament, to be prepared by a Consultative Political Conference in which parties other than the Kuomintang and the Communists would also take part.[16] All these points, however, were viewed merely as the basis for further negotiations. Mao, who was assisted by Zhou Enlai, showed himself to be a superb diplomat, but also a stubborn defender of the Communist Cause. Washington thought it could solve China's problems.

George Marshall

Two months after Mao left Zhongqing, George Marshall, head of the combined Chiefs-of-Staff during the Second World War and a future Secretary of State, came to China to negotiate peace. Tortuous negotiations dragged on for a year. During that time three-party committees, Nationalist-Communist-American, were established in many parts of the country, and this again gave the Communists increased respectability and contact with many people around the country.

Before Marshall arrived, US marines had transported Chinese government troops to North Chinese cities, where the Japanese military had kept public order until their arrival. These troops, however, arrived in the Manchurian cities too late, after the Russians had dismantled and carried away the essentials of Manchurian industry and had allowed the Chinese Communist troops to establish themselves in various places.

The cities, which had been under Japanese rule for years, had looked forward with high hopes to the arrival of the Chinese troops, but the war-weary soldiers and their political leaders did not live up to these hopes. Corruption and financial disorder spread. Meanwhile the Communists, whom the cities had never experienced at first hand, were presenting themselves as a vision of impeccable honesty embodied in a new force.

Marshall had hardly been in China two months when the Communists began to stir up anti-American demonstrations among students, who barely knew where the agitation stemmed from. The demonstrations began in February 1946. In December 1946, a month before the end of the Marshall Mission, the students in large cities surged forth in angry protests against the alleged rape of a Chinese girl by an American soldier.[17] (These demonstrations, manoeuvred by underground Communist forces — see Chapter VIII — ,do not square with the theory that, had Washington behaved otherwise, the Chinese Communists would have turned to the United States and not to the Soviet Union.)

The negotiations and the respectability gained from the Marshall negotiations gave the Communists a chance that they would not otherwise have had to penetrate into the life of the nation. The Chinese public knew nothing about Leninist tactics, had never lived under a Communist regime, and did not know that in Marxist parlance words do not mean what they say. The Marshall Mission ended in failure and Marshall left China in January 1947.

CHAPTER VII

MARXISM IN YAN'AN

In the 1920s knowledge of Marxism in the Party was, to say the least, sketchy. Few Marxist works had been translated into Chinese. After the break with the Kuomintang in 1927, the Communists led hazardous lives, working underground in the cities and fighting for their existence in primitive rural revolutionary bases. Not until their flight and eventual regrouping in the western reaches of Shaanxi province did they have time to study Marxism. Even then they were in the midst of the Japanese war. Moscow had, indeed, provided them with Chinese-language books printed in Moscow, and in 1939 a simple printing press was brought from Shanghai to Yan'an. Some Marxist books, and Mao's 'On Protracted War' and 'On New Democracy' were printed there (but not his 'On Practice' and 'On Contradiction'). On May 16, 1941, the first issue of *Liberation Daily* appeared in printed form.[1]

Yan'an was far removed from the intellectual centres of China, and even those who knew foreign languages had no easy access to books. Nevertheless there was among them a handful of intelligent young men in their twenties who had studied Marxism and had come to Yan'an from the cities. Among these were Ai Siqi, Wu Liping and Chen Boda.

In those years Stalinist doctrine was being crystallised in the Soviet Union in that famous — or notorious — textbook, *History of the Communist Party of the Soviet Union (Bolsheviks), Short Course*, and in the works of Mitin and Yudin, two of Stalin's trusted aides. These books were quickly absorbed by Marxist theoreticians in Yan'an; but the influx of Marxism from the Soviet Union also stirred up trouble.

Mao gave three talks on Marxism to his men at the Anti-Japanese Military and Political College in Yan'an in 1937 and 1938. Soon after this the Stalinist works arrived. The publication of the three talks was halted. Two of them, Mao's famous 'two philosophical essays', 'On Practice' and 'On Contradiction', were published many years later, and were included in his *Selected Works;* the third talk has never been officially published. Twenty years later in 1957 — four years after the death of Stalin — Mao delivered a speech to a restricted Party audience in which he criticised Stalin's Marxism. Another twenty years passed before Mao's speech was published, in the fifth volume of the *Selected Works*, in 1977. Six years after this, in 1983, Peking's main philosophical review said that in those early years, 1937–8, Mao was only beginning to study Marxism, with the intention of writing a book about it later. He never did. This is the subject of this chapter.

What Marxism?

How Marxist were the Communists in the Yan'an era (1935–48)? It is hardly surprising that the many millions ruled by the Communists at the end of the Japanese war did not know much about what Marxism was. Nor could the Red Army, its numbers suddenly swollen by peasant guerillas, have become Marxist. Many soldiers, officers included, had no notion of what Marxism was. When Christian missions along the Yangze River were occupied by Communist troops, the missionaries thought that this signalled the end of their churches and perhaps the end of their own lives. In fact, it turned out that a whole troop, officers included, consisted of Christians recruited by the Red Army in the neighbouring province.

Marxism was therefore the privilege of political commissars, who were the Party representatives in the Red Army, and of a limited number of high-ranking officers. He Long, who was to be made a Marshal in 1955, was not yet a Party member on the day of the attack on Nanchang in 1927, the attack that is still commemorated as Army Day.[2] General Ye Ting was another who was not a Party member in 1927. This famous general, who had studied in the Soviet Union, commanded the Communist Fourth Route Army, which clashed with the Nationalists. He was taken prisoner and released, but died in an aeroplane accident in 1936.[3]

In Yan'an, as was mentioned earlier, Stalinist Marxism was studied: but were there any discussions on Marxism? The intellectual scene was dominated by the growing influence of Mao and the imposition of his ideas in the 1942–4 Rectification campaign.

Some discussions must have taken place. We saw earlier that though Wu Liping, looking back forty years later, had deplored the neglect of Marxism as such in the Yan'an days, Li Weihan thought that it had been the first time he had understood Marxism — Marxism in its simplified form as interpreted by Mao.

There is still little information available about those years and about what happened during Mao's purge of his enemies in the 1942–4 Rectification campaign. In the 1980s, Party historians have had some access to early documents, but not yet to those of the 1940s, the last ten years before the Communist take-over of the country. Few of those who played a role in the 1920s are alive, but some of the men of the 1940s still survive. Practically the only sources for the 1940s are Mao's *Selected Works*, his four speeches in 1942, and the rewritten *Party History*. In one of the speeches, 'Rectify the Party's Style of Work', he said: 'It is necessary to master Marxist theory and apply it, master it for the sole purpose of applying it . . . how to look at China's problems after having studied Marxism-Leninism.'[4] In another speech, 'Oppose Stereotype Party Writing', Mao wanted writings to be 'vigorous, lively, fresh and forceful'; he referred to the *History of the Communist Party of the Soviet Union (Bolsheviks), Short Course*, which describes Lenin's writing as an example of good writing. Mao also praised the style of Dimitrov,[5] his protector in the Comintern. There are also his two other speeches, 'On Literature' and 'On Art'.[6] The most important document, however, was the rewritten *Party History*, which rejected Mao's enemies, the Moscow 'returned students'.

Thus, Marxist studies in China were suffocated at the very beginning of Mao's rule, and Marxism became a tool of Mao's politics. There are no signs of anybody having challenged Mao's Stalinist Marxism and his exposition of the Stalinist-Marxist truth. Before the Rectification campaign, Mao produced what are known as his 'two philosophical essays', 'On Practice' and 'On Contradiction'. A sort of halo has shone round these over the years, the idea of Mao as a philosopher. Mao probably never claimed to be a philosopher. Neither did Marx or Engels, Lenin or Stalin. They were men whose theories were directed to action in accordance with Marx's famous dictum that one should not only know the world, one should also change it. Nevertheless we do speak of the philosophy of Marx, of Engels, of Lenin and even of Stalin — we do not speak of the philosophy of Hitler or Mussolini.

Marxism

Marxism is in fact a sort of philosophy. It grew out of Hegelianism — but so did the fascism of Mussolini. Hegel was of course one of the greatest philosophers of the modern age. It may be asked whether Marxism is not a caricature of Hegelianism. One of Marx's most famous sayings is that he took the philosophy of Hegel, which was standing on its head, and made it stand on its feet. It could as well be said that what was standing on its feet was made to stand on its head, an operation that gives a topsy-turvy view of the world.

Hegel's was a magnificent system of the 'Spirit'. Marxism was a system of 'Matter', but a 'Matter' which — absurd as it may seem — kept all the attributes of the Hegelian 'Spirit'. Marxist 'Matter' has its own internal spontaneity; it is not inert matter, reacting to external action.

In June 1982, Chinese Marxist philosophers held a conference to discuss whether the definitions of 'Matter' given by Engels and Lenin should be revised. Both were found deficient. Engels defined 'Matter' as 'the sum of all Matters'. Lenin defined it as 'objective existence perceived by the [material] senses'. The conference decided that a better definition of 'Matter' must be sought. It also said that Lenin did not explain what is meant by saying that 'Matter' is dialectical, or how dialectical materialism is distinguished from mechanistic, old-fashioned materialism. He did not even explain the difference between 'Matter' and 'Thought'.[7] Nothing like this could have been written while Mao was around.

Marxism is an agglomeration of unexplained and unproved, often contradictory and absurd statements. The material world is an economic production system, which is the basis of everything that the human spirit can create, i.e. of the 'superstructure'. A production system, in Marxism, is not created by human thinking. It is the product of the mysterious 'Matter', which, having developed to a certain grade, makes a sudden leap into a new system. A primitive society of paradisiacal happiness and simplicity in which there is no private ownership and all things are common breaks down suddenly through the sin of private ownership, and jumps to the worst state of all, that of a slave society. This in time jumps into feudalism (the concept of feudalism is never properly explained), then jumps to the capitalism of industrialised society. This, going to excess through the accumulation of capital and the ever-growing misery of the labouring class, culminates in a new revolutionary break, through a transition of dictatorship of the workers — of the proletariat — to final Communism, the abolition of private property, and of all forms of coercion, the State, the police etc. This new paradisiacal state will apparently last for ever. No wonder that many detached students of Communism have found in these theories not a caricature of Hegel but a caricature of Christian doctrine, which speaks of the original sin that broke up harmony, and a period of earthly struggle which leads to Heaven.

In good Stalinist Marxism, all these are affirmations: the only proof is that Marx or Engels, Lenin or Stalin said so. The appropriate passages, perhaps from a preface to a book or from a private letter, are quoted.

When, after the death of Mao, the study of Marxism was taken up in the inner Marxist philosophical circles in China by minds uninhibited by the shackles of Stalin and Mao, it was discovered, with quite a bang, that neither Marx nor Engels nor Lenin, but only Stalin, had spoken of the five stages of human economy and human social history from primitive society to slavery, and so on.[8] It was discovered also that Marxism was far from being as simple as had been believed and preached for some forty years in China, that Dialectical Materialism and Historical Materialism stand on weak foundations, and that Marx himself was much less clear and less definite than had been thought for a long time.

There had been various Marxist schools and thinkers since the nineteenth century — the schools and thinkers condemned by Stalin — in Western countries, even in Poland; but under the rule of Mao these were forbidden in China.

In Yan'an the Communist Party was only beginning to study Marxism seriously, in its Stalinist form. There was only one authoritative Marxist teacher, Mao himself. He had learnt the Stalinist brand of Marxism and was assisted by a group of highly intelligent Chinese, including such well-known figures as Ai Siqi and Chen Boda. It was in this way that the philosophy of Mao, if it should be called that, was created. It is best known through 'On Practice' and 'On Contradiction'.

It is usual to add to these 'two philosophical essays' Mao's speech of February 1957, 'On the Correct Handling of Contradictions within the People', and his 1963 two-page article on the theory of knowledge. The first is a long political document that led to fierce struggles in the Party and outside; it deals with 'antagonistic contradiction', a euphemism for beating down Mao's enemies. The two-page article on the theory of knowledge is a concatenation of Stalinist jargon with special emphasis on the theory of the Great Leap. It was written in 1963, and so must have evoked unpleasant memories of the failure of the Great Leap five years earlier. Mao repeated that the purpose of knowing the world is to change the world — but change the world into what? Truth, he said, is recognised in success, and falsehood in failure. He emphasised the influence of the Spirit, 'Spirit that becomes Matter' — a doctrine that Stalin had emphasised earlier. It meant simply that the Party knows the truth and guides events.

All these unconnected and unproved theses of 1957 and 1963 were contained in the earlier 'two philosophical essays', about which so much has been written in China and which have been taken perhaps too seriously by students of China abroad.

The great question, discussed not in China but abroad, is whether the two essays, officially published after 1949, were really written or delivered in Yan'an in 1937 as indicated in the *Selected Works of Mao*.

This question has been discussed in several issues of the *China Quarterly*, London. In a joint article, two scholars, one from Stanford University, the other from Harvard University, have sought to prove that 'On Contradiction' as it stands cannot have been written in 1937 but was composed at a much later date, and that it copied the theses of Stalin and Zhdanov. Their argument is that the essay had not been quoted until it appeared in the official edition of the *Selected Works*, published in the 1950s.

It was not even mentioned in the official Party history by Hu Qiaomu, *Thirty Years of the Chinese Communist Party*, published in 1951, and there had been no mention of it in earlier writings. There is, for example, no reference to its use in the 1942–4 Rectification campaign in Yan'an. It simply cannot be found anywhere.

Part of another, never officially published essay by Mao, 'On Dialectical Materialism', has been found in a Chinese review of 1940. Although it was written after the official date of the writing of 'On Practice' and 'On Contradiction', it is a much less mature exposition of the thesis, containing few true Marxist elements. (An English translation has been published.) It deals mainly with the sharp distinction between idealism and materialism.[9] (We shall come back to this essay of Mao's.) The article in the *China Quarterly* refers to *The Political Thought of Mao Tse-tung* by Stuart R. Schram. Schram does give in detail the content of this third essay of Mao's, followed by a similar treatment of 'On Practice' and 'On Contradiction', which were supposed to have been written in 1937; but he does not discuss the problem of the dates.[10]

Professor Wylie, in a long study of Mao's 'two philosophical essays', claims that they were originally delivered in 1937 and were later polished for publication in the *Selected Works*. He discussed at length the influence of Chen Boda on Mao's thinking, particularly on the 'sinification' of Marxism. (Mao's two essays contain many references to Chinese realities and some references to Chinese history. We shall discuss later whether this amounts to a 'sinification' of Marxism.) Professor Wylie says that Chen arrived in Yan'an in mid-1937, and that by September he was close to the master. Chen, he says, knew his Marxism and Leninism, and so did Mao. 'Both men were good Marxists in that they firmly believed in union of theory and practice.'

The *China Quarterly* article quotes in a note the far-fetched theory of Professor John E. Rue, published in the May 1967 issue of the *Journal of*

Asian Studies, that Mao's 'Dialectical Materialism' was forged by Mao's enemies to discredit him as a theorist. [11]

Another study, by a professor in Australia, holds that the two philosophical essays of Mao are genuine. The argument is that 'On Contradiction' has been found as a concluding section in a volume published before 1949. [12] The argument is not wholly convincing; the book it relies on, found in Dalian, bears no date and it is merely assumed that it was published between 1946 and 1948 — ten years after 1937.

The controversy will continue until Chinese Marxist Party historians have been allowed to delve more deeply into the archives. The fact remains that for over ten years, even in writings which the Party must have considered important, there were no quotations from the two essays, and no reference was made to them. This silence was certainly not due to political reasons. It is true that in 1937 Mao was not yet head of the Party. His great battle was fought at the Sixth Central Committee Plenum in 1938. But after 1944, as we saw earlier, Mao's position was firmly established and his Thoughts were being put on a pedestal. Why then did a deep silence cover the sublime Marxist thoughts of the Master?

Wu Liping, who was in Yan'an in those years, wrote in 1982 that Mao devoted himself there to the study of Marxist philosophy, and that in 1937 he produced two philosophical essays, 'On Practice' and 'On Contradiction'. He also says that when Ai Siqi arrived in Yan'an in 1937, Mao, knowing that he was the author of a popular book on Marxism, gave him mimeographed copies of the two essays and asked for his opinion. [13] Ai Siqi (who is discussed on p. 100) was then in his twenties and like Mao was not yet a full-blooded Marxist scholar.

Wu is probably right. Mao did write two Marxist essays in 1937, but their relation to the canonical 'On Practice' and 'On Contradiction' remains obscure. The obscurity is lessened if, before studying the 'two philosophical writings', we examine the third, 'On Dialectical Materialism', which has remained in its original 1938 form. It was printed in the Communist-ruled Shanxi-Chahar-Hebei Border Area, but on Mao's orders it was withdrawn from circulation. [14]

The unpublished essay

Parts of the essay 'On Dialectical Materialism' were found in a 1940 edition of the magazine *Min Zhu* (Democracy), published in Shanghai. They were translated and analysed in the aforementioned article in the

China Quarterly by the 'grandmaster' of Marxism, Professor Karl A. Wittfogel, with the assistance of S.C. Chao, and published in 1963 in *Studies in Soviet Thought*.[15] The whole text was published in Japan in Chinese in vol. VI of the ten-volume *Collected Works of Mao Zedong* edited by Takeuchi Minoru, in that admirable collection of Mao's writings from 1917–49, published with an *apparatus criticus*. The text of Mao's speech 'On Dialectical Materialism' is taken from handwritten volumes from the Yan'an Resistance University, dated 1938. It fills thirty-eight pages in the book.

The essay is less primitive than first appears from the fragments found in the 1940 *Min Zhu* magazines and translated into English. In the fragments Mao explains the emergence of Materialism, saying that when the oppressed classes find the correct plan (the plan that will improve their situation) they discover that they have found the law of matter and of the objective world. 'This makes man realise that religion and idealistic illusions are useless; hence they reach a materialistic conclusion.'

The full text of the essay is better than this passage, though not much better. The essay is divided into short sections. We learn, under 'Difference between Idealism and Materialism', that idealism believes that the world is an illusion, while materialism believes that it is real and is matter. The section on 'Sources of Idealism and its Development' says that idealism is the philosophy of the exploiting class and that Communism will put an end to it. In other sections we hear that in China in the early 1920s there was great interest in Marxism, but a lack of understanding of what it is. Ordinary, mechanistic materialism and the influence of the Russian philosopher Deborin did harm, but 'under the influence of the recent purge of philosophy in the Soviet Union a mighty movement of dialectical materialism is visible in China. This comes not from traditional Chinese philosophy but from learning Marxism-Leninism.'

Mao then explains. The world is Matter; it is infinite; dialectical materialism applies in the same way to nature and to society; Matter has its inner force and moves in spiral lines of development; knowledge is not a secretion of the brain, but is the product of Matter; Absolute Truth can be known, but this is the sum of many relative truths. To expound all this, Mao sometimes quotes Marx, more frequently Engels and Lenin; but never Stalin. He mentions negation of negation, which was not in Stalin's vocabulary. Mao did not use this phrase when his two other essays came to light in later years.[16] Neither the tricky Marxist doctrine that the Spirit, a superstructure, can influence Matter, nor the intricacies of contradiction are discussed.

Unlike the two other essays, 'On Dialectical Materialism' is not decorated with picturesque examples from Chinese history. The only reference to ancient China comes when Mao says that ancient Chinese
philosophy was idealist. In 1938 Mao, though undoubtedly a keen and
intelligent reader of Engels and Lenin, was still a beginner.

An article in *Philosophical Research*, Peking, written forty-five years
later said:

Comrade Mao Zedong was never of the view that he had explained all the
aspects of Dialectical Materialism. On the contrary, in the lecture notes he
wrote in Yan'an entitled 'Outline of Dialectical Materialism', written not long
after his 'On Practice' and 'On Contradiction', he said that he was just
beginning to study Dialectics and intended to write, after further study, a book
on Dialectics. After the establishment of the new China, he said, not once, that
he would want to study and improve the correct philosophical system. It is
regrettable that this desire could not become reality before he left us.[17]

What was said about Mao's 'On Dialectical Materialism', written in
1983, could undoubtedly be said about his two essays, the texts of two
speeches he had delivered one year earlier, in 1937. Mao was brave
enough to impart what he knew of Marxism to his élite audience. But
the ink on his 'On Dialectical Materialism' was hardly dry when trouble
arose in Lenin's homeland.

Stalin's Short Course

In 1938 the Stalinist *History of the Communist Party of the Soviet Union (Bolsheviks), Short Course*, the Bible of the Soviet Union till the death of
Stalin, was first published in Moscow after serialisation in *Pravda* and
other newspapers in the Soviet Union.[18] It dealt with the history of
Communism in the Soviet Union and with the victory of Stalin over his
opponents. It was a rewriting of Party history in the Soviet
Union — much in the same way as a few years later, in 1945, the history
of the Chinese Communist Party was rewritten to glorify Mao. The
fourth chapter of the *Short Course* summed up Marxism as seen by Stalin,
a brand of Marxism that became compulsory in the Soviet Union and all
its dependencies.

Important Marxist discussions were being held in Moscow throughout the 1920s. Bukharin was the leading authority until 1927–8, but he
opposed Stalin's radical plans and was executed in the Great Purge in
1937. Bukharin had learnt his economics in the West. His Marxism
emphasised the conflicts and the dialectical opposition between various

social forces, not the mythical force hidden within 'Matter'. He stressed the influence of environment. His theory was ridiculed as 'mechanised' because it implied that 'Matter' reacts to outside impulses. In a speech delivered in 1929, Stalin attacked this theory for not keeping pace with the practical problems of the Soviet Union. In that year Bukharin's opponents, Deborin and his followers, were rewarded with all the leading positions in Marxist circles. They dubbed the Bukharinists 'vulgar materialists' who paid too much attention to positive sciences. Deborin saw materialist dialectics as the inner force of 'Matter', operating in the same way in nature and society. Consciousness is a development of 'Matter', a development reached by sudden dialectical leaps.

Stalin adopted much of this. Yet he, or rather his men Mitin and Yudin, turned against Deborin, accusing him of keeping philosophy apart from the work of the Party. Philosophy must support the Party line.[19] The young Chinese who studied in Moscow were there in the days of Bukharin and Deborin. Bukharin was head of the Comintern in 1927 – 8.

Reaction in Yan'an

The *Short Course* was translated[20] and was published in Yan'an in 1939. (Mrs Fu-mei Chen of the Hoover Institution found two copies of it in the library there.) How the men in Yan'an, and Mao himself, received the *Short Course* is not known. At that time, Mao's sole ambition was to oust the Moscow boys, the 'returned students', from the Party leadership and to establish himself.

One can only speculate about the reception of the *Short Course* in Yan'an. The 'returned students' who had studied Marxism in Moscow in the late 1920s must have been shocked to learn that their old Marxist mentors were being held up as counter-revolutionaries. Mao may have been pleased. Yan'an was certainly quick to adapt itself to the new Moscow line. In 1939 Mitin's *Dictionary of Dialectical Materialism* was translated into Chinese. (We have the fourth edition, published in Shanghai in 1947 with a preface dated 1939.)

In the same year, a 268-page book, written jointly by Wu Liping and Ai Siqi, which quoted at length from the *Short Course*, was printed in Yan'an to help explain Marxism in China. It was Wu Liping who expressed regret that the study of Marxism had been belittled during the 1942−4 Rectification. Ai Siqi was a much better known figure. We shall return to him later (pp. 100−1).

Their book, so Wu Liping wrote in 1982, was first printed in Yan'an with the title *Historical Materialism*. In the edition published outside the Communist area (probably in Shanghai) the title was changed to *Textbook of the Scientific View of History*[21] (we have the fifth edition, published in 1946. It indicates that the first edition was published in 1939, but the place of publication is not given). This was a propagandist work, skillfully urging the Chinese public during the dark days of the Japanese war to believe that the Communist Party and Marxism would save the country and would fulfil all the people's expectations. It started, in a rather un-Marxist way, by showing that human beings differ from animals. It then went on to say that humans would need a scientific outlook on history, i.e. historical materialism, if they were to defeat the Japanese and the Chinese traitors. In imitation of the *Short Course*, it condemned Bukharin — whom the Chinese masses hardly knew — and Tao Xisheng, a theoretician of the Nationalist party, the Kuomintang. In this way the book, full of quotations from Marx, Lenin and the *Short Course*, made Communist ideals palatable to the Chinese public.

What happened to Mao's 1937 writings, 'On Practice' and 'On Contradiction'? The original texts, as we know, have not yet been found. How do the final editions, published many years later, compare with the Soviet *Short Course*? A comparison with the fourth chapter of the *Short Course*, which deals with Marxist theories, may be instructive.

'On Practice'

'On Practice' is a sort of theory of knowledge used to help carry out the revolution properly. Its contents run as follows. Marx found out that knowledge is gained from material production. In a class society, different classes have different roles in production, and these roles generate different kinds of knowledge. Perfect knowledge lies with the proletariat of industrial society and is learnt in class struggle. 'Social practice alone is the criterion of the truth of knowledge of the external world.' Marx, Engels, Lenin and Stalin worked out their theories through class struggle and scientific experimentation.

Man's knowledge of the world comes from perceptions gained in the course of practice. Through a sudden leap these perceptions are formed into concepts. This is the dialectical materialist theory of knowledge. Knowledge is not an end in itself. Its purpose is to change the world. Lenin said: 'Without revolutionary theory there can be no revolutionary movements.' If thinking lags behind reality, political deviations appear, rightist opportunism or leftist excess. Absolute truth is formed from innumerable relative truths. 'The movement of change in the world of objective reality is never-ending and so is man's cognition of truth through practice.' Only the proletariat and its party know the world correctly and know how to change it: thus 'On Practice'.

The idea that knowledge comes from 'praxis' has haunted Marxists ever since Marx. Philosophically this can be given an intelligible meaning by using the analogy of a new-born baby, which has an aptitude to know, but only acquires knowledge through the senses. However, to assert that knowledge is gained through practical productive activity, as if such activity did not presuppose knowledge, is a philosophical blunder. That 'consciousness is only the reflection of being, at best an approximately true reflection of it', comes from Lenin and is quoted in the *Short Course*. The qualitative leap to a higher stage — which in turn justifies revolution — is as old as Marxism and is found in the *Short Course*.

The *Short Course* says: 'How immensely important is the application of these principles to the history of society and to the practical activities of the party of the proletariat.'[22]

Marxist philosophy is not a detached search for truth; it is a justification of action, a pliant tool in the hands of the Party. The Party is the vanguard of the proletariat, the proletariat which possesses the truth. Philosophically all this is nonsense, but it is convenient for arguing that the Party is right, and for expressing this in abstract philosophical language. Chinese writers, ever since, have loved to play with such terms as 'idealism', 'materialism', 'dialectics', and 'historical materialism'. Bombastic and meaningless phrases of this kind fill the pages of the *People's Daily* and official pronouncements.

Mao had the knack of sweetening dry Marxist language with lively references to Chinese realities; this was also evident in Wu Liping and Ai Siqi's *Historical Materialism*. Thus, as an example of the progress from perception of the outside world to the formation of concepts, 'On Practice' cites the superior knowledge of the situation gained during the Japanese war, when the Communist Party advocated a united front against Japan. It asserts that the failure of the Taiping Rebellion in the middle of the nineteenth century and the failure of the Boxer rising at the turn of the century were due to the fact that the Chinese people had not yet reached 'the stage of rational knowledge', i.e. knowledge of Marxism.

'On Contradiction'

This juggling with colourful local examples is found also in Mao's 'On Contradiction', published, like 'On Practice', in 1951 in the first volume of the Chinese edition of Mao's *Selected Works*, and in volume I of the Peking English edition of 1965.

'On Contradiction', a longer work, is divided into six sections:

1. Contradiction is within the thing and is not due to such outside circumstances as geography or climate. (The *Short Course* explained this at length, against Bukharin.)

2. Contradiction is universal. Marx, Engels, Lenin and Stalin successfully applied it 'to analyse in many aspects human history and natural history and to change in many aspects society and nature'. Lenin defined the law of the 'unity of opposites' as 'the recognition of the contradictory, mutually exclusive, opposite tendencies in all phenomena . . .' In war, Mao explains, 'offence and defence, advance and retreat, victory and defeat, are all mutually contradictory phenomena'. (Did anyone need Marxism to discover this?) Mao adds that opposition and struggle exist within the Party: 'If there were no contradictions in the Party and no ideological struggles to resolve them, the Party's life would come to an end.' Deborin, Mao says, did not understand that although there was contradiction between workers and peasants in the Soviet Union, this was not antagonistic contradiction.

3. There is contradiction between positive and negative numbers in mathematics, between action and reaction in mechanics, between positive and negative charges in electricity, and so on. There is also contradiction between forces of production and relations of production, between classes, and between idealism and materialism. In different conditions, contradiction must be solved in different ways. In the historical Chinese novel *All are Brothers*, the hero failed to conquer a village until he had familiarised himself with the circumstances, broken his alliance with former friends, and sent his men in disguise to explore the enemy position. This was materialist dialectics. There was dialectic in the Communists' relations with the Nationalist Kuomintang — at first, close cooperation, then the break in 1927 and then renewed cooperation, a united front, during the Japanese war. Yet even at that time, contradic-

tion between the Kuomintang and Communists persisted in a 'complicated state of simultaneous alliance and struggle'.

The way to handle such situations, Mao says, is learnt from Marx and Engels, who 'applied the law of contradiction in things to the study of socio-historical process'.

'Stalin's genius showed itself in applying the doctrine of contradiction to the situation in the Soviet Union,' Mao said.

All this is far away from what is usually called philosophy. The Chinese reader might not have learnt much Marxism, but he could be shown that the subtle methods of warfare in ancient China — action through ruse and subterfuge — fitted perfectly, according to Mao, into the Marxist doctrine. Mao does not say that China had discovered the subtle principles of Marxism ages ago. No Marxist could have said that explicitly.

4. There are, Mao says, many contradictions, but at each specific time there is one principal contradiction. When imperialism launches a war of aggression against a country, that becomes the principal contradiction; other contradictions — between the feudal class, the bourgeoisie, the proletariat, and so on — become secondary contradictions. (If this is true, then when a country is in danger, patriotism should prevail above Marxism.) Then there are occasions, Mao continues, when the enemy wants to split the revolutionary front, as the capitalist countries wished to do at the time of the October Revolution in Russia, and as Chiang Kai Shek wished to do in China in 1927. The situation then changes and another contradiction may become the principal contradiction. In 1911 the Manchu dynasty was overthrown. In 1927 the Communist Party, having suffered from attacks by the Kuomintang, eliminated opportunists within its own ranks and grew in force again.

Then there is the question of production force and production relations. The production force is the base upon which all else — the superstructure, and thus production relations — is based. Yet production relations may become the principal and decisive factor. Politics and culture, which are superstructures, may become the leading factors. To prove this, he quotes from Lenin's *What is to be Done?*: 'Without revolutionary theory there can be no revolutionary movement'. (Therefore, theories and political aims are more, not less, important than 'Matter', with all its mythical attributes inherited from Hegel. When a Marxist is reminded of this, the answer given is: Truth is dialectic — it changes with the political purpose.)

5. Identity and struggle. Everywhere there is an inter-penetration of

opposites, and contradictory aspects are transformed into their opposites. 'No contradictory aspect can exist in isolation . . . Without life, there would be no death; without death there would be no life. Without "above" there would be no "below"; without "below", there would be no "above". . . without the bourgeoisie, there would be no proletariat; without the proletariat, there would be no bourgeoisie . . . This is what Lenin means when he says that dialectics studies "how opposites can be . . . identical".'

'By means of revolution the proletariat, at one time the ruled, is transformed into the ruler, while the bourgeois, the erstwhile ruler, is transformed into the ruled . . . . The Kuomintang . . . became a counter-revolutionary party after 1927.' The landlords who owned the land are transformed into a class that has lost its land; this has already taken place in the Soviet Union.

War and peace transform themselves into each other. 'All contradictory things are inter-connected . . . This is the full meaning of Lenin's "identity of opposites".' Mao, rather awkwardly, refers to ancient Chinese legends, even to old stories of ghosts and foxes who change into human beings to seduce innocent women.

He finds it appropriate here to explain something that both Russian and Chinese Communists have always found embarrassing: how Marxism can become victorious in a country without a working class, without going through the capitalist stage. With Marx, it was the culmination of the evils of capitalism that was to lead to the break and to the change of system. Mao poses the question: 'Why is it that the Chinese revolution can avoid a capitalist future and be directly linked with Socialism without taking the old historical road of Western countries, without passing through a period of bourgeois dictatorship?' The way the question is put enables the Chinese reader to imagine that the transition towards Communism has been carried out in China in a way superior to that predicted by Marx for Western countries.

Mao quotes Lenin's saying: 'The unity of opposites is temporary. The struggle is . . . absolute.' He repeats these words twice and adds: 'Struggle is inherent in identity, and without struggle there can be no identity.' Mao liked struggle.

The same doctrine is found in the *Short Course*: 'Dialectics holds that internal contradictions are inherent in all things and all phenomena of nature, for they all have their negative and positive sides . . . Something dying always and something developing . . . The struggle between these opposites . . . transformation of quantitative changes into qualitative changes.' The *Short Course* quotes Lenin as saying 'Contradiction is the very essence of things', and 'Development is the struggle of opposites'. This, which is already in nature, is applicable to the history of society and 'to the practical activities of the party of the proletariat'.[23]

Mao's doctrine was the same, but he used a different formulation of Lenin's 'unity of opposites' taken from Lenin's obscure and short 'Dialectics', found in both volume 38 of the Soviet 1958 edition of *Collected Works*, and in the Chinese translation of *Stalin's Collected Works*, published in 1959. Neither the *Short Course* nor Mao himself uses the Marxist term, derived from Hegel, 'negation of negation'. Stalin omitted the Hegelian category of negation of negation. Once the Communist system had been established in the Soviet Union there was no room for its negation.

Philosophically, all this stands on weak ground. Nature and human society are said to follow the same law. This would have fitted well into ancient Chinese philosophy, according to which nature and human behaviour were so connected that the evil behaviour of the Emperor could bring about natural disasters; the two were one. But Mao does not refer to ancient Chinese thought. For the Communists the old Confucian philosophy was an abomination.

Marxism, in spite of this principle of unity of nature and human society, believes, and Mao here follows Marxism faithfully, that human acts, the acts of the Party, which is a superstructure, built not upon nature but upon the productive activity of man, can re-enact and transform nature and human society in struggle. All this is a hotchpotch of apparently philosophical notions used in the service of the Communist Party.

6. This section goes a step beyond the *Short Course*. It speaks of 'antagonistic contradiction'. Contradiction is difference in opinion, a dispute between friends or colleagues, but antagonism is the devil, the irreconcilable enemy whose existence must not be tolerated.

The term 'antagonism' was new in China. The 1939 Chinese translation of Mitin's *Dictionary of Dialectical Materialism* equivocated and gave two possible translations — '*fandui*', which means opposition, or '*chongtu*' which means conflict — and explained that it is 'a special form of contradiction; it is struggle against opponent forces'. It quoted Lenin: 'Antagonism and contradiction are not the same; the first has disappeared; the second is still found under socialism.'[24]

What translation Mao used in 1937, if he used the term at all, is not known. When Mao's 'On Contradiction' appeared officially in his

Selected Works, a new term, '*dui kang*', was used for antagonism. He cannot have used this term in 1937.

If there is anything that Mao added to Marxist 'philosophy' it is his doctrine on antagonism under socialism — which he amplified later in his devastating 1957 speech, 'On Proper Handling of Contradictions within the People'. In the Soviet Union the theory was that once the enemies of true Marxism had been beaten down, there was no longer room for antagonistic contradiction, though there were, according to Stalin, leaps in social development, exemplified by the Stakhanov movement and the collectivisation of agriculture. Not even the latter, in which millions of people perished, was called antagonistic.[25] According to Stalin, antagonistic contradiction within the Party in the Soviet Union was unthinkable. But in 1926, at the Seventh Plenum of the Comintern Executive Committee, Stalin — not yet fully in power — said: 'I can say without exaggeration that the history of our Party is the history of struggles of contradiction within the Party.'[26] In the Great Purge of 1935–8, Stalin executed the cream of the Party leaders: Zinovyev, Kamenev, Bukharin, the head of the NKVD Yagoda, Radek and many others.

In this sixth section of 'On Contradiction', Mao states — and his words have been repeated many times since — that 'contradictions which were originally non-antagonistic may develop into antagonistic ones . . .', and that 'contradictions between correct and incorrect ideas in the Communist Party . . . with the development of class struggle may grow and become antagonistic.' Mao justifiably cites the example of the history of the Communist Party of the Soviet Union. 'The history of the Communist Party of the Soviet Union shows that the contradictions between the correct thinking of Lenin and Stalin and the fallacious thinking of Trotsky, Bukharin and others did not at first manifest themselves in an antagonistic form, but that later they did develop into antagonism.' And so it was in the Chinese Communist Party also, with 'Chen Duxiu, Zhang Guotao and others'.

Towards the end of this section Mao quotes Lenin's statement that 'antagonism and contradiction are not at all one and the same. Under socialism the first will disappear, the second will remain.' Mao himself concludes: 'The formula of antagonism cannot be arbitrarily applied everywhere.'

In the *Selected Works* of Mao a note was added: 'The ideas contained in this essay were presented by Comrade Mao Zedong in a lecture at the Anti-Japanese Military and Political College in Yan'an.'

Comparison of the final version of Mao's 'two philosophical essays' with the doctrine of Stalin uncovers nothing specifically Maoist except this insistence on antagonism.

Throughout the years Mao has been extolled, even long after his death, for having developed Marxism creatively, particularly in two ways, through his doctrine on antagonistic contradiction within the people, which he hinted at in his 'On Contradiction' and developed in his speech in 1957, and through his application of Marxism to Chinese reality. He probably deserved his fame, but not on the philosophical plane; his contribution was that he served trite Stalinist Marxism to the Chinese public on a plate garnished with Chinese frills that the average Communist Party leaders could understand, and that he explained to them that what the Communist Party was doing in Yan'an was exactly what Marxism was teaching.

In 1957

What Mao really thought about Stalin's *Short Course* he revealed much later, to inner-Party circles only, in 1957, four years after the death of Stalin and one year after Khrushchev's denunciation of Stalin. Mao expressed his feelings about the *Short Course* in an address to a group of regional Party secretaries. At the time, this address was not published. It was published only in the fifth volume of Mao's *Selected Works* in 1977. (In China one has to wait for a long time for news, even about philosophical questions.)

According to this, in 1957 Mao said: 'Stalin had a fair amount of metaphysics in him. [Metaphysics is a very bad word in Marxist parlance, see p. 5.] 'In the *History of the Communist Party of the Soviet Union (Bolsheviks), Short Course*, Stalin spoke of internal contradiction in all things, but he then dealt only with the struggle of opposites, without mentioning their unity . . . According to the basic law of dialectics, there is at once struggle and unity between opposites, which are both mutually exclusive and interconnected and which under given conditions transform themselves into each other.'

Mao goes further:

Stalin's viewpoint is reflected in the entry 'Identity' in the *Short Dictionary of Philosophy*, fourth edition, compiled in the Soviet Union. It is said there: 'There can be no identity between war and peace, between the bourgeoisie and the proletariat, between life and death and other such phenomena, because they are fundamentally opposed to each other and mutually exclusive.' In other words, between these fundamentally opposed phenomena there is no identity in the Marxist sense . . . This interpretation is utterly wrong . . . Lenin did quote Clausewitz's famous saying, that 'war is the continuation of politics by other means' . . . War and peace are both mutually exclusive and interconnected . . . Stalin failed to see the connection between the struggle of opposites and the unity of opposites.[27]

The *Short Course*, as we saw above, was published in Russian in the Soviet Union in 1938 and translated into Chinese in 1939. The *Short Dictionary of Philosophy*, by Rozenthal and Yudin, first appeared in Russia in 1939 when Mao was still in Yan'an. Mao, however, when speaking in 1957, referred explicitly to the fourth edition, a revised and amplified edition published in Russian in 1955, two years after the death of Stalin, and translated into Chinese in the same year.

From what he said in 1957 it is clear that Mao did not like the Soviet *Short Course* and the *Short Dictionary of Philosophy*: but he kept his mouth shut until after the death of Stalin.

Human nature

In 1942 Mao delivered a speech in Yan'an, which is not considered a philosophical essay, but which is no less important as a source of information on the kinds of Marxism prevalent in the Yan'an era. This was his speech on literature and art, delivered during the Rectification purge (actually two speeches, both delivered in May 1942).

In the meetings at which he made these speeches, Mao was intent on remoulding the minds of men of literature and culture who had come to Yan'an, imposing iron discipline on them and demanding their total submission. Moreover in Yan'an Liu Shaoqi wrote his *How to be a Good Communist* and Chen Yun his similar *How to be a Communist Party Member*, both demanding total subjection to the Party.

Mao referred to a short work that Lenin wrote in 1905, *Party Organisation and Party Literature*, which was an uncompromising demand that literature should follow the Party line, become organised and form part of the Party organisation.

Mao based his doctrine, if doctrine it should be called, on the Marxist doctrine on classes. Every culture and every type of literature and art, he said, belongs to a definite class and adheres to a definite political line. 'Proletarian literature and art . . ., as Lenin said, are "cogs and wheels" in the whole revolutionary machine. Literature and art are subordinate to politics . . . It is a struggle of class against class.'

Mao went a little further than Lenin and radicalised the notion of class more completely. He took up the discussion of human nature. He was speaking, he said, to 'writers and artists who come from the ranks of the intellectuals', and who 'believe that the fundamental point of literature is the artist's love of humanity'. There is no such thing as love of humanity, Mao said:

There has been no such love since humanity was divided into classes . . . So-called sages and wise men advocated it, but nobody ever practised it, because it is impossible in class society . . . Classes have split society into many antagonistic groupings; there will be love of all humanity when classes are eliminated, but not now. We cannot love our enemies, we cannot love social evils; our aim is to destroy them. This is common sense; can it be that some of our writers and artists still do not understand this? There is no human nature above classes. [28]

These words of Mao's reverberated through the history of the People's Republic and did immense damage. Writers were banned from writing, and nationwide campaigns condemned prominent writers, including prominent Party members, and sent them to jail or to toil in labour camps. In all Communist countries freedom of literature has been a sensitive point and all have seen prominent writers excluded from writers' organisations. In China this went much further than elsewhere. On this point Mao took the Marxist doctrine seriously.

His doctrinal condemnation of humanism, his statement that only the proletariat, i.e. those who support the Communist Party, have full human nature, is unparalleled in the Communist countries of the world. Stalin was never a humanist, quite the contrary; yet even under Stalin the doctrine of human nature was not defined as Mao defined it in Yan'an.

Not until years after Mao's death was the question of the Communist attitude towards humanism, whether Communists are for it or against it, discussed in China in Marxist circles. Even then Mao's 'Talk on Literature and Art' was not repudiated. In 1981 on the anniversary of Mao's second 1942 speech, the Chinese Writers' Association held a meeting at which Zhou Yang — before the Cultural Revolution the Party boss of literature — encouraged the audience to study Mao's 'Ya'nan Talk on Literature and Art'. [29]

Dictatorship over people's minds has been considerably more intense in China than in the Soviet Union. Remoulding the minds, brainwashing as it is usually called, stems from the Yan'an brand of Marxism. Life in the concentration camps of Siberia was physically more terrifying than life in many camps in China; but the mental pressure was much less severe. In the Siberian camps people felt mentally free; the daily control of words and thoughts in the Chinese camps made life more inhuman. Lenin introduced the discipline of the Party, in many ways an external discipline. Mao learnt the total subjection of minds. This has not transformed the Chinese, as he may have expected, into 'New Men'. After thirty years, long-suppressed aspirations reappeared. That, however, is a story for later pages of this narration.

Ai Siqi

No treatment of Marxism in the Yan'an era can fail to mention Ai Siqi and his book *The Philosophy of the Masses*. Ai Siqi was a bright young man living in Shanghai, who at the age of twenty-three — they were all young in those days — wrote a popular exposition of Marxism. It met with immense success. The first edition appeared in January 1936, and the thirty-first in 1947. Astutely, the permit for publication granted by the Interior Ministry of the Nationalist government was reproduced on the first page.

This book did more than any other publication to win the sympathy of the Chinese public. No Nationalist propaganda could penetrate the Communist-controlled areas, but the Nationalist government was naive enough to let Communist propaganda penetrate everywhere. The Communists won power in China partly by military action, but much more importantly by the use of underground, or in some cases open, propaganda.

The Philosophy of the Masses was a youthful, cleverly written book that could be understood by anybody who could read. It was full of fun, and abounded in popular stories and images from real life. Long descriptions of Charlie Chaplin and his dress and his gait were used to explain that inspection of the exterior does not give understanding of the inner meaning. The theory of knowledge and practice was explained by the example of a nut, which seems hard and tasteless until it is cracked and the kernel is relished. Idealism was ridiculed through a story taken from Buddhist literature. The Marxist idea of the transformation of quantity into quality was illustrated by the story of a tower in Hangzhou from which stones were stolen until at last the tower collapsed. Negation of negation was exemplified by the 'chicken-egg-chicken' story. All this taught that materialism is right, that knowledge comes from practice, that mechanistic materialism is faulty, that matter itself has an inner dynamism.

Ai Siqi went to Yan'an in 1937 and remained active in Marxist circles until his death in March 1966. Not until 1981 was it revealed that in 1953 Chen Boda, another great authority on Marxism from the Yan'an era, had severely criticised Ai's *The Philosophy of the Masses*, saying that every page contained errors in Marxist theory, and that it presented a mechanistic materialism. In a speech made to Marxist circles in 1953, Ai said: 'The Chinese revolution must have a leader, this is a necessity. But that the leader should be Chairman Mao is accidental.' Ai was condemned and made a confession, but this was not publicised and he was not purged. His confession was kept in the Party archives. However *The Philosophy of the Masses* was proscribed for twenty-five years, and even after his death and after the death of Mao, when Ai's book had been rehabilitated, the argument about his confession still raged on. In 1981 it was said that the condemnation of the book was regrettable, since it had had such immense influence on the masses.[30]

In 1982 Ai Siqi's writings were published, including the text of the first edition of *The Philosophy of the Masses*. The preface was written by no less a person than Zhou Yang, who had survived all the troubles and had again become a leading personality in cultural questions.[31]

CHAPTER VIII

UNDERGROUND PARTY WORKERS

An ancient Chinese saying says: 'Attack hearts first, then attack the cities.' Ai Siqi's *The Philosophy of the Masses* was an attack on hearts, presenting Marxism, in a popular style, as the only way of solving the country's urgent problems. It had widespread influence.

This was an 'attack on the hearts'. The Communists, and this is not confined to China alone, have other approaches too, less obvious, more hidden, more deceptive. Hiding their identity, they create illusions. They penetrate into the ranks of the enemy and, much in the manner of a nation at war, plant spies wherever they can to gather information and do everything possible to undermine the enemy's resistance.

The Chinese Communists have never rivalled anywhere the success the Russians enjoyed in Great Britain, where their agents held strategic posts in British intelligence. But agents were planted everywhere, and, as we saw earlier (Chapter VI), Zhou Enlai himself, while openly leading negotiations with the government, was secretly directing underground operations. Zhou, as we shall see in the following pages, was the mastermind of the Communist penetration of cultural circles, and of others besides.

This was a subtle, all-pervading operation, mobilising masses of students for patriotic demonstrations against the Japanese or against the Americans, and sending theatrical troupes to rove through the country, performing plays discreetly propagandist in tone. The film industry was thoroughly infiltrated. Hatred of the social system and disenchantment with the government of Chiang Kai Shek was spread everywhere. Last but not least, some army generals were won over. The people's consciousness of national unity was sapped and undermined. What the Communists planned to do with China was never revealed at the time. It was, one may say, a gigantic deception.

There was no precedent in Chinese history for such systematic deception being used to prepare the way for a new political regime. Secret societies had existed for centuries, but these recruited their adherents from among ignorant peasants, not by deceiving them but by zealous propaganda based on obscurantist magic doctrines. At the end of the last century, such societies were used by the xenophobic Manchu court in what is called the Boxer Rebellion.

The activities of the Communist underground were different. They succeeded in deceiving and winning over a large section of the intellectual élite of the nation, without revealing their own identity. The Communist Party — as all students of Communist affairs know — is by definition a secret society. It reveals only what it wants to reveal at any given moment, and not its ultimate aims.

The underground work of the Party in the White Areas — the regions ruled by the government — remained a closely-guarded secret for many years. The veil began to lift only forty or fifty years later, when the whole operation was past history and many of the participants were dead. Many such revelations appeared in the reminiscences and obituaries of persons whom nobody had suspected of having been secret Party members for decades.

It was revealed in 1979 that at the time of the Communist take-over in 1949, the Party members in Peking numbered a mere 3,000,[1] and that Shanghai, a city of 9 million people, had only 8,000 Party members. In 1979 a Shanghai newspaper mentioned that at that time the Party, though small in size, had had many supporters in the political parties, in the business world and among religious leaders, and that even some members of the police and gendarmerie had been won over. 'Comrade Zhou Enlai was in charge, entrusted by the Party leadership with the underground work of the Party.'[2]

Clandestine work in the White Areas had a long history. An article in 1980 referred to a 1928 Comintern instruction to China, outlining a threefold policy: establishment of local soviet territories, organisation of a Red Army, and 'mass movement in the White Areas'.[3] Another article in 1980 recalled Mao's words: 'Lie low, act with caution, remain covered for a long time, waiting for the occasion [to act]; do not rush, do not reveal your identity.'[4]

The left wing of the Kuomintang

In the early 1920s, when the Kuomintang was an unruly revolutionary party in the south of China, it would have been hard to differentiate between the Communists — small in number but very active — and the Kuomintang, especially its radical left wing. The Kuomintang, Soviet advisers and Communists worked hand in hand. There was not much visible difference between Sun Yat Sen, Mao Zedong, Chiang Kai Shek and Zhou Enlai and the rest. They were all preparing for the victory of the revolution in China, whatever that might mean.

The first Communist to become an official member of the Kuomintang was a man called Li Shizhang. So we were told in a press article written in his memory after his death at the age of eighty-three, in 1983. Li Shizhang was a young correspondent, first in Peking later in Shanghai, for *Shen Pao*, then the leading newspaper in China. In 1925 the Party sent him to Canton, where he joined the left wing of the Kuomintang. After the 1927 break with the Kuomintang, the left wing formed a Kuomintang Action Committee, with this man as one of its leading members — ostensibly simply one of the Kuomintang men who were dissatisfied with Chiang Kai Shek. In 1928 he found it safer to retire to Japan for a year. Having come back to China in 1929, he continued to work against Chiang, and became associated with the famous northern warlord Feng Yuxiang, with Zhang Xueliang (who was to kidnap Chiang Kai Shek in 1936), and with General Cai Tinggai (who heroically defended Shanghai against a sudden Japanese attack in 1932 and turned against the Nanjing government in Fujian in 1933). Li Shizhang certainly knew how to choose his friends. During the Second World War, in 1943, he was in Zhongqing, the war-time capital of the Nationalist government, and there joined some enemies of Chiang in forming the San Min Zhu Yi Comrades Association, which maintained secret contacts with the Communist Party. This organisation was the forerunner of the Revolutionary Committee of the Kuomintang, of which he remained vice-chairman until his death in 1983.[5]

The Revolutionary Committee of the Kuomintang was one of the 'democratic parties' which were satellites of the Communist Party. It was formed and led by clandestine Party members.

Regional offices

From the earliest days, clandestine Party committees were set up in various regions. According to the list of Party officials in the early years, published in 1983, the Party — its central leadership residing in secrecy in Shanghai — had three regional bureaux in 1930, the North Bureau, the Yangze Bureau covering the centre of China, and the South Bureau. The head of the North Bureau was the twenty-four-year-old He Chang, a member of the Central Committee, who died in a guerilla battle five years later. The successive heads of the Yangze Bureau were the thirty-two-year-old Xiang Ying, a Central Committee member who died in battle with government troops in 1941, and the twenty-six-year-old Guan Xiangying, also a Central Committee member, who died in

Yan'an in 1946. The head of the South Bureau was the twenty-five-year-old Luo Dengxian, who two years later was captured and executed in Nanjing. Sixteen provinces, practically all the provinces in the interior of China, and five cities (Peking, Tianjin, Hankow, Qingdao and British Hong Kong) had their underground Party committees. The regional bureau heads were all young men.

In those turbulent years the clandestine regional and provincial Party organisations went through many changes. In 1931 Mao's headquarters was called the Soviet Area Central Bureau, although the Party leadership was still in Shanghai. In 1935 the North Bureau and in the following year the South Bureau were reorganised. At that time twelve provinces, parts of three other provinces and twelve cities had their own Party organisations. In the northeast there was a Manchurian Party committee, dissolved in 1935 and replaced by Party committees of the three Manchurian provinces. There was also a Northeast Special Committee.

These facts, made public in 1983, are said to have been collected from various documents, and it is thus difficult to put together a chronological history of the clandestine regional organisations.

The roll of leaders of the regional organisations contains many names which have long since fallen into oblivion, but there are also names of persons who became prominent in later periods. For example in Chapter VI we discussed the activities of the South Bureau under Zhou Enlai, and at one time Liu Shaoqi was a secretary of the North Bureau. Peng Zhen, Chen Boda, Ke Qingshi, Lin Feng and Nan Hanzhen also worked in this bureau.[6]

The North in the 1930s

As we saw earlier (Chapter III), following the violent break with the Kuomintang in 1927 and in the subsequent confusion, radical action was engineered. In Peking, then known as Peiping, street demonstrations were held in 1931, ostensibly against the Japanese occupation of Manchuria. Huang Yifeng, an economist (in 1979 head of the Social Sciences Academy of Shanghai), took part in the 1931 demonstrations and recalled them in 1980. In those days, he wrote, there was national indignation against the Japanese occupation of Manchuria; but we were wrong to organise demonstrations as we did, not merely against the Japanese but in support of the Soviet Union, then threatened by the Japanese occupation of Manchuria, and in the interest of the Ruijin Communist base. (The nation as a whole was indignant at the Japanese action, but it was not concerned about the interests of the Soviet Union or of Mao's small Communist base lost somewhere in the southern end of China.) The result, Huang recalled, was disaster. Communist activity was suppressed, some Communists lost their lives, and it became publicly known how weak our forces were.[7]

Chen Yi, propaganda head of Shanghai in the 1980s (not to be confused with Marshal Chen Yi), recalls that in 1931, at the age of eighteen, he worked for the Party in Peking. Using a spurious dinner meeting as cover, the Federation of Leftist Writers was established in Peking, in February 1931, a year after its establishment in Shanghai. The young Chen, who was from Shanghai, was asked to speak about the Shanghai Federation.

In the summer the government clamped down on the Communists. The underground Hebei provincial committee and the Peking city Party committee disappeared, and with them the Writers Federation. In the wave of national indignation following the Japanese occupation of Manchuria in September, the Peking Federation was reborn. In the following year, 1932, Lu Xun, a celebrated writer, came from Shanghai on a personal visit to Peking, and Chen was given the task of guiding him (he was touched by Lu Xun's kindness to so young a Communist as himself).

Chen recalls that the Peking Federation organised a street demonstration. It marched to the house of Zhang Xueliang, protesting that he was listening to Chiang Kai Shek and abandoning the three provinces of Manchuria to the Japanese.[8] Four years later this same Zhang Xueliang arrested Chiang Kai Shek, then on a visit to Xi'an. No details on how this was achieved were made public until 1983, when they appeared in a tribute by Hu Yuzhi to the memory of 'martyr Du Zhongyuan'. Few people in China had heard of Du before the 1980s, but Hu Yuzhi was a well-known figure in the People's Republic. In the 1940s he was the organiser of Communist dailies in Hong Kong and in Singapore, and he was the first editor of the *Guang Ming Daily*, Peking, which was aimed at the educated classes. He had probably been a Party member since the early years and he always acted as a leader of the small political parties. In the 1950s Hu was the head of China's Publication Administration; in 1983, he was eighty-seven years of age.[9]

Du Zhongyuan and the Xi'an Incident

Du Zhongyuan, now little known, was not a Party member, but he had an extraordinary history. Born in Manchuria, he moved to Shanghai after the Japanese occupation and became a close friend of Zou Taofen (a leftist writer who died in 1944 and was posthumously honoured with Party membership). In Shanghai, Du published several leftist magazines but remained friendly with the Nationalist leaders. In May 1935 he wrote an insulting article about the Emperor of Japan. Japan protested and demanded that Du be punished; the Chinese government reluctantly put him in prison for a year. In prison Du, who hated Chiang Kai Shek, contacted Communist agents serving in the army of Zhang Xueliang, whose troops had moved from Manchuria to North China. Du also managed — while still in prison — to get in contact with the Communist leadership in Yan'an, and succeeded in bringing Zhang Xueliang and Mao's men together.

After his release from prison, Du described to Hu Yuzhi how he had achieved this feat of bringing Zhang Xueliang (son of the former lord of Manchuria, Zhang Zuolin) and the Communists together, and how Zhang Xueliang had come to Shanghai in April 1936 to see him and had talked about his agreement with the Communists — asking him to keep this secret. In December 1936 the Xi'an Incident took place, when Zhang Xueliang's troops and those of a Nationalist general, Yang Hucheng, arrested Chiang Kai Shek in the Northwestern city of Xi'an. There followed a national outcry and Chiang was released. Du Zhongyuan was not happy about this turn of events.

Du Zhongyuan's life ended unhappily. In 1938 Zhou Enlai sent him to Xinjiang. Sheng Shicai, governor of Xinjiang and a former schoolmate of Du in Japan, was then cooperating with the Soviet and Chinese Communists. Du arrived in Xinjiang in 1939 and became president of the University College of Xinjiang. Mao Zemin, brother of Mao Zedong, Chen Tanqui, one of the founders of the Chinese Communist Party, and other Communists all went to Xinjiang at that time and got high government posts there. In 1940, Governor Sheng changed sides, turning to the Nationalists. He arrested Du Zhongyuan and the other Communist leaders and executed them.[10] (According to other sources, Mao Zemin was executed in 1942 and Du in 1943.[11])

Peking University

In 1980 another old man who had been active in the Communist underground in Peking in the 1930s, Xu Deheng, then aged ninety, gave his account of events in Peking in 1931. (In 1983 Xu still held high office in the government, having the title of deputy head of the People's

Congress.) In 1935 all China was raging against the Japanese advance into the regions north of Peking. Xu, then a young teacher in Peking University, and a small number of fellow teachers responded enthusiastically to an anti-Japanese manifesto issued by the Communists. The demonstrations were organised by a Communist, Xu Bing (alias Xing Xibing, who in later years was a leader of the United Front Department of the Central Committee, and died in prison during the Cultural Revolution). Among the Peking University professors were Yang Xiufeng (in the 1950s minister of education, died in 1983), Qi Yanming (worked in the Cabinet in the 1950s, died in 1978), and Zhang Youyu (in the 1950s vice-mayor of Peking, legal expert, still active in the 1980s). The leader of the Peking University students was Yu Qiwei — who, under the name of Huang Jing, became Party head and mayor of Tianjin after 1949 and died in 1959.

A Students' Federation was organised in Peking and big demonstrations were held on December 16. The student body, Xu recalls, was divided between those who supported the demonstrations organised by the Communist North Bureau and its man Xu Bing, and those on the Nationalist side. In 1936 the government — Xu describes it as 'the reactionary authorities' — arrested a number of rioting students and two professors, and the students' leftist organisation disappeared.

Liu Shaoqi then arrived, representing the Party's central authority. He condemned the radical activities and brought a new directive from the Party: stop adventurism, stop fighting one another, unite against the Japanese. (This was the new Yan'an policy, modelled on the world-wide Common Front tactics of Moscow.) Xu Bing and the North Bureau promptly obeyed and purged the 'ultra-leftists'. (As always, those who had followed the Party's directives heroically were purged as soon as the line changed.)

Acting on Liu Shaoqi's instruction the leftist Peking students issued a declaration on May 4, nominally dissolving the previous association, but in fact merely changing its name to the Peiping Students Federation for Saving the Country. After this, similar federations were established in other cities in North China, and a National Salvation Association, comprising organisations in various professions, was set up in Shanghai.

In the summer of 1936 Jiang Mengling, President of Peking University, dismissed three professors, including Xu Deheng, the writer of the article we are discussing, and Ma Shulun — who became minister of education under the People's Republic and died in 1970. The leftist students protested, and a college of the University re-employed the three professors. On December 12 the leftist Peking students took to the streets to demonstrate against Chiang Kai Shek. This happened to be the day of the Xi'an Incident.

The comrades in Peking were surprised by the nationwide support for Chiang Kai Shek, or, as Xu put it, were surprised to find that many people did not understand the policy of the Communist Party. To explain the Communist position, two of the leading Communists in the North Bureau, both working underground, Xu Bing and Peng Zhen — then known as 'Comrade Lao Gao' — entertained distinguished people at dinners to explain in a friendly atmosphere why the Communist Party had acted as it had done in Xi'an — which reveals something that has not always been evident, that the Communists played their part in the arrest of Chiang Kai Shek in December 1936. (Most leaders like Peng Zhen, 'Lao Gao' — including Mao, 'Li Desheng' — used pseudonyms in their clandestine operations.)

The aged Xu Deheng's relation of things that had happened forty-five years earlier shows that either he had a fabulous memory or, more probably, that he was helped by Party historians. He has another interesting story to tell about Liu Shaoqi and the change of Party policy. In 1937, after the Xi'an Incident, the pro-Nationalist Peiping Students Federation, the rival to the leftist federation, relying on the support of a group of Nationalist professors at Peking University, started a brawl with the leftists, and the pro-Communist professors were accused by their colleagues of having incited the leftist students to wild demonstrations. The leftist students did not knuckle under. They put up posters against the commander of the Twenty-Ninth Government Army, Song Zheyuan, whose troops were stationed in Peking.

Liu Shaoqi reprimanded the leftist students. General Song, he told them, was anti-Japanese, and everybody should collaborate with him. At that time General Song was on the point of resigning from his post in Peking and transferring elsewhere. Liu succeeded in sending him a message saying that the students supported him and Song stayed on. The leftist students made a complete volte-face and put up new posters saying: 'We support the anti-Japanese stance of Song Zheyuan.' This happened in May and June 1937, and on July 7 the Japanese started open war against China.[12]

Liu Shaoqi

Liu Shaoqi, as we have seen, played an important role in the work of the

North Chinese underground, and became a powerful figure in White Area operations. He had been a Party member since 1921, had agitated among workers in the 1920s, and in 1931 he became head of the Workers Department of the Party in Shanghai. In the following year he joined Mao and Zhu De at the Ruijin base and became the underground Party leader in Fujian province. After the Long March, in 1936, he was head of the underground North Bureau. In March 1936 he wrote a letter to the Party leader (Zhang Wentian) on Party work in the White Area, and he spoke about this work at a meeting in Yan'an. In the 1930s, the problem of how to act in government-ruled (White Area) territories was much disputed: should the underground instigate direct resistance and act openly? Or should it infiltrate the 'enemy' ranks? Liu defended the second position.[13]

Shanghai in the 1930s

Shanghai in those days was not merely the business centre of China; it was also a pulsating cultural centre, open to the world, open to new ideas and new initiatives. In the years 1927–33 the central leadership of the Communist Party was based there, living in secret. The intensity of cultural life in Shanghai in the 1920s and 1930s, with its new trends and its prominent writers, playwrights and journalists, was unprecedented in modern China — and there has been nothing like it since. Towards the end of the 1930s this came to an end. Then came the war with Japan, followed by the Second World War, and then, before the city had time to breathe again, the Communist regime, under which even writers who were accepted by the new regime became sterile.

In the 1920s and 1930s Shanghai was a free society, with all possible cultural and political currents criss-crossing. The cultural figures of those days were familiar with Chinese classical literature; they had been reared on it. Many of them knew foreign languages and translated the European classics. They created a new Chinese literature. They were men of wide aspirations; they were free.

The dominant cultural trend in the Shanghai of the 1930s was leftist — in particular the discussion of radical ideas — and at the same time intensely nationalistic, particularly in face of Japanese aggression: in 1932 Japan carried out a bloody, and unsuccessful, attack on the city. The Communists had a wonderful opportunity for winning over many of the best brains, not among down-to-earth businessmen, or lawyers or scientists, but among writers and religious leaders, who were more open to romantic new ideas. Throughout the history of the People's Republic, the most prominent writers have been those who matured in the literary world of Shanghai in the 1930s. Not all were won over. Politically, the Shanghai literary world was divided.

The history of the Party underground in the 1930s in Shanghai is a story of extreme complexity. It is more than an illustration of the complexity of Party life in those days: the inner-Party conflicts of the 1930s were to have serious repercussions twenty, thirty, even fifty years later. The passions aroused by the events of the 1930s have not yet been extinguished in the 1980s.

The most celebrated writer, a man whom the Party adopted, quite unjustifiably, as its own hero, was Lu Xun, a very cultured man, a master of words, and a publicist with a vitriolic pen, an independent thinker who hit out at both right and left as he saw fit.

Lu Xun, born into a family which played an important role in the cultural life of Zhejiang province, was one of three highly talented brothers. His family name was Zhou; his personal name was Shuren. Lu Xun was his literary name; his two brothers were Zhou Zuoren and Zhou Jianren. During the war Zuoren, the eldest of the three and a brilliant writer, remained in Peking and collaborated with the Japanese. Mao called him a traitor. The third, Jianren, born in 1890, nine years after Lu Xun, collaborated with the Communists and under the People's Republic became minister of higher education and governor of his native province of Zhejiang. He died in 1984.

Lu Xun died in October 1936 at the age of fifty-five, a mature writer of many years standing. In the late 1920s the Communists in Shanghai — mostly young men, barely thirty years old — launched a fierce intellectual attack on him, until the Party line changed. After that they were all out to win him to their side. By then, in the 1930s, the Communists themselves were divided, suspecting a leftist writer, Hu Feng, a confidant of Lu Xun's, of being a Nationalist agent. Mao, at that time far away in Yan'an, had never met Lu Xun, but he was aware of his nationwide prestige. After Lu Xun's death, Mao held him up as a model for Communist admiration and in 1938 a Lu Xun Academy of Art was founded in Yan'an. Lu Xun remained the Party's 'model writer'. Nevertheless internal Party disagreements about his reputation never died away. This wrangling had begun in the 1930s and it flared up in the late 1950s, one group taking revenge for what had happened in Shanghai twenty years earlier. Ten years later those who had triumphed in the 1950s were silenced during the Cultural Revolution. Even in the 1980s, forty-five years after his death, the memory of these struggles still stirs deep feelings; Lu Xun certainly left his mark on the Party. We are not dealing here with the literary achievements of Lu Xun or with his literary friends or adversaries — much has been written about them — but with the activities of the Communist underground in the intellectual life of Shanghai in the late 1920s and 1930s; it is a complex story. A first-hand description of the initial battles against Lu Xun was written by Yang Hansheng, an early member of the Party, and leading figure in cultural circles, purged in the Cultural Revolution, but active again in the 1980s. In an article which he wrote in 1980, at the age of seventy-eight, Yang recalled those far-off days. In 1927 Yang was sick and Zhou Enlai sent him to Hong Kong to seek a cure. From there he went to Shanghai, then to Japan, then back to Shanghai. He was invited by the distinguished writer Guo Moruo to join the Creative Society — a move encouraged by Zhou Enlai, who wanted more Party-member writers in this society.

The Creative Society was founded in 1921 by three young writers, Guo Moruo, Yu Dafu and Cheng Fangwu. It turned Marxist, and was shut down by the government in February 1929.[14] Guo Moruo, Yang recalls, joined the Party shortly after the attack on Nanchang in 1927, although he did not join publicly till 1958 (died 1978).[15] Cheng Fangwu (born 1898) was not yet a member of the Party. (Under the People's Republic he was president of several universities. In the 1980s he was still active.[16]) The Creative Society published several magazines, cautiously propagating Marxist ideas. There was in the Society at this time a small Party cell consisting of Pan Hannian, Li Yimeng and Yang himself. All of them (Lu Xun too) lived in a district of Shanghai inhabited by many Japanese. This provided them with good cover. Guo Moruo spoke fluent Japanese and, Yang says, could himself be taken for a Japanese.

Yang has some special words of praise for Pan Hannian (Pan, condemned in 1955 as a traitor, died in prison in 1977 — see below, pp. 124–5). Whatever his later history, Yang says, Pan Hannian made a remarkable contribution to the cause during the Shanghai era. In the period of Communist cooperation with the Nationalist government, before 1927, he worked in the Political Department of the government in Wuhan, under Guo Moruo. (The Political Department was a Marxist bird's nest on the Nationalist tree.)

In the late 1920s the Party cell of the Creative Society came under the authority of the clandestine Party Committee of Jiangsu province. The head of the propaganda department of the provincial Party Committee was Li Fuchun (a leading figure, head of the Economic Planning Committee under the People's Republic; he died in 1975). Other members of the Creative Society joined the Party in the 1920s, including Xu Dixin (born in 1901, a leading writer on the economy, in 1983 president of Amoy University).

For two years the Creative Society's magazines published bitter attacks on Lu Xun — and he answered in kind. In the eyes of the comrades Lu Xun was not a Marxist, but a despicable 'democratic radical' (which in fact he was).

In the autumn of 1929, Li Fuchun met Yang in a café in Avenue Joffre (in the old French Concession). They spoke about Lu Xun, who at that time was translating the works of Bukharin and Lunacharsky. He is an important person, Li Fuchun said, and instead of writing against him we should get round him. Soon after this, the nine Party members in the Society held a meeting, again in a café, under the chairmanship of Pan Hannian, and decided to carry out the instructions of 'Hua Han' — as Li Fuchun was called in those days. Three men were sent to visit Lu Xun: Feng Xuefeng, Xia Yan and Feng Naichao (died 1983).

At the end of 1929 the Party members in the Society were trying to organise a writers' Leftist Federation (Zuo Lian); ostensibly a neutral organisation, it was in fact led by them. They had the full support of Lu Xun, Yang says.

The full truth, even after fifty years, has not been revealed by Yang. He argues that it was not Li Lisan (the heretic), propaganda head of the Central Committee, but Li Fuchun, propaganda head of the provincial committee, who ordered the reconciliation with Lu Xun. But he also says that the Party nucleus of the Leftist Federation came directly under the Central Committee. He enumerates the subsequent leaders of the writers' Party nucleus: Pan Hannian, Zhu Jingwo, Feng Xuefeng, Zhou Yang and himself.[17] When Yang's article appeared in 1980, another former member of the Leftist Federation, eighty-five-year-old Wang Xuewen, felt hurt, and protested. Yang had neglected to say that he, Wang Xuewen, had also been head of the Party nucleus, even if for only three months. In this post he followed Zhu Jingwo (died 1941), who had been transferred to the Propaganda Department of the Central Committee, and he was followed by Feng Xuefeng. The nucleus used to meet in Feng's home, a quiet inconspicuous spot.[18]

The veteran Yang Hansheng's statement that the approach to Lu Xun was not ordered by the Central Committee is contradicted in an article written by the octogenarian Xia Yan, another leading Party writer of the time. Towards the end of 1929, Xia Yan says, the Party Central proposed that the Creative Society and the Sun Society (another undercover literary organisation) and Lu Xun should come together and form the Writers' Leftist Federation. Lu Xun agreed. The Leftist Federation was set up in October 1929 and was formally established in March 1930. It was led directly by Li Lisan, of the Provisional Central Committee (as it was called in those days) — not by Li Fuchun, as Yang claims. The Party leadership at that time consisted of Zhou Enlai, Chen Yun, Li Fuchun, Wang Jiaxiang and Li Weihan. (Chen Yun and Li Weihan were still alive and active in the 1980s.)

It should not be thought, Xia Yan says, that after the establishment of the Leftist Federation all was sweet harmony between Lu Xun and us. We were young, inexperienced striplings, under thirty years of age, and we did not look up to Lu Xun as an immortal master. There was a great deal of friction. Yet it is not true either to say that the whole Shanghai Communist underground opposed Lu Xun, though this allegation was levelled against us during the Cultural Revolution. In fact, Lu Xun treated us younger writers with a sort of benevolence, pointing out our defects in a good-humoured way.

Xia Yan then turns to praise of Qu Qiubai, the man who in 1930–1 was, for less than a year, head of the Party. In the first two years of the Leftist Federation, we ardent youngsters provoked and offended many people and got into a lot of trouble. The government clamped down and arrested many of us, but in 1932 there was a turn for the better. This was due to Qu, himself a man of literature with excellent contacts with literary authorities and with Lu Xun himself. Qu was in charge of the Party's cultural activities in the years 1931–3. It was in those years that the underground Party members penetrated into the Shanghai theatre and film world — Shanghai films were shown throughout the country. (Though he himself does not say so, it is known that Xia Yan did the lion's share of this work.) Party members were in leading positions in most of the film studios, even in those run by the government. They were also composers, and their patriotic songs sung at mass concerts influenced many throughout the country. It was a highly successful covert operation. (It shows also how difficult it is to detect Communist agents pulling strings behind apparently innocuous cultural activities.)

Then came another crisis, a Party crisis, the nature of which a non-Communist finds difficult to understand.

In 1933 the Central Committee quit Shanghai and joined Zhu De and Mao at Ruijin in the south, and the Shanghai underground was put under the authority of the clandestine provincial committee of Jiangsu province. A year later the Ruijin Communists, harrassed by government troops, began the flight known as the Long March. 'We could not get instructions from the Party Central' — and, apparently, if a good Communist does not get orders from above, he does not know what to do.

Ultimately they got news from Paris, where a Chinese Communist magazine, *National Salvation Journal (Jiu-guo shi-bao)*, was being published. From this unlikely source came the news of the Seventh Congress of the Communist International held (in 1935) in Moscow, and Dimitrov's report on the China question. In this way Shanghai learnt about the new policy, the 'Common Front' policy ordered by the Comintern. They interpreted this as meaning that all forces were to be united against Chiang Kai Shek and the Japanese. They also got a letter sent by Xiao San from Moscow and delivered through the agency of Agnes Smedley, the enthusiastic American journalist who died in 1950 and wanted her ashes to be sent to Zhu De in China. Xiao San, a writer and a Hunanese, a contemporary of Mao's, represented the Leftist Federation in Moscow. Xiao San recommended a new policy to the Chinese cultural underground, the dissolution of the Leftist Federation and the founding of a wider national movement in the spirit of the united front. (Xiao San was a member of the Soviet Communist Party and of the Soviet Writers' Federation. He died in 1983.[19])

At the end of his article, Xia Yan answers a question which, he says, numerous people have asked: How many members — apart from the handful of underground Party members — did the Leftist Federation have? It is impossible, he says, to give exact figures, but undoubtedly many were exposed to its influence. Comrade Gu Mu (prominent in the 1980s in directing foreign trade) sprang from the Leftist Federation, and so did Comrade Li Kenong (who became deputy Chief-of-Staff under the People's Republic).[20]

The issue of the *People's Daily* containing Xia Yan's reminiscences also contained a shorter article written by Wu Taichang. What he says illustrates admirably how the Party underground worked. People wonder nowadays (in 1980), he says, why some prominent leftist writers did not join the Leftist Federation. One of them was Ye Shengtao, a well-known teacher and man of letters, who was to play an important part in the cultural life of the People's Republic and was still active in the 1980s.

Last year (1979), the author of the article says, Ye Shengtao was asked: why did he not join? He answered that in those days Feng

Xuefeng, a leader of the Leftist Federation Party-nucleus, told Ye that it would be better for the Cause if Ye and some other well-known writers did not join. By not being members, yet showing sympathy for the movement, they might exercise wider influence.[21]

This is typical Communist practice. Notable persons were told to remain apparently outside the Party so that they might attract others to the Party line. Thus Shen Yanping, alias Mao Dun, a well-known novelist widely read from the 1920s onwards, entered the Party in 1921 but left it in 1928. Yet he held important government posts under the People's Republic (he was minister of culture till the Cultural Revolution). He was readmitted to the Party shortly before his death in March 1981.[22] The only convincing explanation of this devious way of acting is that the Party knows that 'Marxist' and 'Communist' are not appealing epithets, even under a Communist regime, and that if others are to be attracted it is better to conceal the Communist convictions of some influential persons.

The Party's involvement with Lu Xun did not end with the dissolution of the Leftist Federation in 1935. A critical year followed. This was a year of bitter division among the Party men themselves. The ashes of that fiery conflict were still warm half a century later.

Vivid testimony to this can be found in a long article that Xia Yan wrote in 1980 for a Peking literary magazine. What he said explains many things previously unknown, including the origin of the purging, twenty or thirty years later, of leading Communist cultural leaders, which developed into terrifying political campaigns that brought woe to many. In 1954 a nationwide campaign was waged against Hu Feng. In 1957 Feng Xuefeng, the editor of the leading literary magazine — in China this is a political post — was purged, obviously by Zhou Yang, deputy head of the Central Committee's Propaganda Department, the man in charge of literature. In 1966 it was the turn of Zhou Yang himself. He was violently attacked and purged. Under Jiang Qing's rule the whole Shanghai Party underground of the 1930s was purged. And all these purges revolved round the name of Lu Xun, who had died in 1936. The criterion in each purge was: who had been for Lu Xun and who had been against him?

Xia Yan's article lays bare the deep roots of these purges. Writing forty or so years after the events, he did not pose as an objective observer. He had been one of the main actors in the drama of the 1930s, and even after so many years he was still unable to hide his indignation and anger as he lashed out at the dead Feng Xuefeng, and defended Zhou Yang (still active in the 1980s) and himself.

The Party underground in Shanghai, the article tells us, was deeply divided. Lu Xun did not have unquestioning admiration for the comrades. Much older than these young men, he sometimes treated them with hostility or sarcasm. Moreover, he lent his full support to Hu Feng.

When writing his memoirs, Xia Yan becomes so deeply involved in ancient grievances that, though normally a lucid writer, he tells the story in a confused manner, getting lost in small details, jumping from the mid-1930s to earlier years. The following is the gist of what he wrote.

Xia Yan had known Comrade Feng Xuefeng since 1928, when Feng was making translations from Japanese, and the two met often. They were also cooperating in preparing the Leftist Federation. In 1933 Feng left Shanghai with the whole Party leadership and went to Ruijin. He took part in the Long March.

In 1935–6 the underground Party men in Shanghai were, as we saw earlier, hard-pressed. In 1935, Xia Yan recalls, the clandestine Party Committee of Jiangsu province was suppressed by the government, and five comrades, including Yang Hansheng, Xu Dixin and the playwright Tian Han, were arrested. The rest, other underground Communists, lost contact with the highest Party leadership and became disoriented. Xia Yan and other members of the Shanghai underground heard that the Party leadership had sent Feng to take over the leadership in Shanghai and that Feng had arrived; yet he did not look them up. Xia Yan sent Feng an angry letter and ultimately they met. Feng, all smiles, talked about life during the Long March and said that he had been despatched to Shanghai, first to set up a secret radio station to maintain contact with Yan'an, and secondly, to meet Shen Junru, a founder of the Salvation Association (Shen, already sixty-one years old in 1936, remained a close collaborator with the Party till his death in 1963; in the 1950s he was head of the Supreme Court), and thirdly, to explain the policy of the Party to Lu Xun. He had not been sent — and this shocked Xia Yan — to lead the Shanghai literary underground.

The root of the trouble, however, lay not in this disclosure, but in the person of Hu Feng. In 1933, on the day before his departure from Shanghai for Ruijin, Feng Xuefeng had asked Xia Yan to co-sponsor the entry of Hu Feng into the Party; Xia refused. He refused because he had heard from various sources that Hu Feng was on the pay-roll of the Kuomintang. One of his sources was an important figure in the Nationalist government, Shao Lizi. (Shao was a high official in the Kuomintang. In the negotiations with the Communists on the final collapse of the Nanjing Government in 1949, Shao Lizi represented the Nationalist Government. Nevertheless he was a secret collaborator: when the Communist regime was established a few months later, he assumed important positions within the People's Republic. He died in 1967.)

The trouble was that Lu Xun had placed full confidence in Hu Feng.

In 1934, when Feng Xuefeng was no longer in Shanghai, Zhou Yang asked Xia Yan to make an appointment with Lu Xun. Zhou and Xia, joined by Yang Hansheng and Tian Han, went to see Lu Xun at his favourite rendezvous, the Japanese Nei-shan (Uchiyama) bookstore. Unfortunately, as it turned out, Tian Han joined them: he was then aged thirty-six; the other three were barely thirty. Tian Han, asserting his seniority, caused trouble by his straight talk. While the three young men were trying to explain gently to Lu Xun that they, the Communists, were now taking a more liberal attitude towards other writers and were no longer following their previous 'closed door' policy (a policy obviously unpalatable to Lu Xun), Tian Han brought up the question of Hu Feng, saying that his political stance was not beyond suspicion. On hearing this Lu Xun grew very angry and refused to hear any more criticism of Hu Feng. Xia Yan believes that Lu Xun's unlimited confidence in Hu Feng can be traced to the influence of Feng Xuefeng.

In 1935, when the time came for the dissolution of the Leftist Federation, Hu Feng indulged in unremitting attacks on Zhou Yang and Xia Yan. 'Everyone knew that Hu Feng and Zhou Yang were on bad terms.'

The year 1935 was a difficult one — only about 110 people remained in the Party in Shanghai and reorganisation had become necessary. At the request of Zhou Yang and myself (Xia Yan), Mao Dun explained the new policy to Lu Xun, namely the closing of the Leftist Federation. Lu Xun thought this was only another tactical move by the comrades. Sun Wu Kong — the Monkey King of the old legend — would not give up his magic golden club (with which he smashed his enemies), Lu Xun said. By this he meant, Xia Yan says, that we were using the Leftist Federation to club people. In the end, however, Mao Dun succeeded in convincing Lu Xun that the comrades meant what they said.

Then came the question of choosing a new motto, a slogan for the new policy of uniting all good patriots. (This wrangle over choosing mottoes was to agitate and divide the comrades throughout the ensuing thirty or forty years.) The new motto, decided on between February and March 1936, was 'Defence Literature' *(Guofang Wenxue)*.

When Feng Xuefeng arrived in Shanghai in April he gave his support to another motto, 'Masses Literature of National Revolutionary Struggle'. This motto had originated from Hu Feng and had the support of Lu Xun. This was in June and July 1936 — only a few months before the death of Lu Xun.

Feng, armed with the authority of the Party leadership, wanted to get rid of Zhou Yang. First he proposed that Zhou should go to Japan, but he refused to go. Then Feng wanted him to accompany a foreign guest (name not revealed) to Shaanxi, but Zhou did not go.

In this long article Xia Yan often refers — not in very good taste — to a secret document that Feng Xuefeng wrote in 1966, when Zhou Yang was under fire. In that document, Feng accused Zhou Yang and Xia Yan of having spread vilifying rumours about him in Shanghai. In fact, it was Hu Feng and company who were spreading rumours, going so far as to say that Zhou Yang, Zhou Lipo and Sha Ting — well-known writers — intended to beat up Mao Dun.

In his 1966 document Feng also asserted that Zhou Yang's motto 'Defence Literature' had originated from Wang Ming; however, in 1980 Xia Yan wrote that Feng's claim was a lie. (Wang Ming has always been the black sheep in the history of the Party.)

This fight over the two mottoes remained the source of bitter controversy for many years. Many protagonists referred to a letter from Lu Xun to a writer, Xu Maoyong (alias Yu Yangling), which defended the 'Masses Literature' motto, the choice of Hu Feng and Feng Xuefeng. Even today, Xia Yan wrote in 1980, some people still allege that the motto he and his friends favoured, 'Defence Literature', came from Wang Ming. No, no, Xia Yan protests. In 1938 Xu Maoyong (who had gone to Yan'an) asked Mao Zedong about the two Shanghai mottoes of 1936, and Mao said, diplomatically, that both were unexceptionable, both were revolutionary. The (unpublished) record of this conversation is verified by Comrade Chen Yun, Xia Yan wrote. Xu Maoyong is dead, but his memory was rehabilitated recently. (Obviously Xia Yan, even after forty-four years, wanted to clear himself from persistent accusations.)

In those days, the octogenarian Xia Yan admits, he was an impetuous young man and he did once say to Wang Xuewen, if he remembers correctly, that when he met Feng Xuefeng, he would start a serious quarrel; but that was said in the anger of the moment.

Feng Xuefeng was dead. Xia Yan ended his diatribe by remarking that one must admit he had his good points. He set up a clandestine radio station in Shanghai. After his condemnation in 1957 he led a fairly miserable life, but he still wanted to be received back into the Party.[23]

To complement Xia Yan's emotional relation of the history of the two mottoes — which twice, in 1957 and again in 1966, became a political issue that rocked the intellectual classes — here is the judgment given in a 1978 issue of *Literary Criticism*, which devoted three essays to that 1936 dispute.

In flat contradiction to what Xia Yan was to write two years later, the *Literary Criticism* essayist said that the motto 'Defence Literature' came from Wang Ming who, at the Seventh Congress of the Comintern in 1935, spoke about the need for a Defence Government in China — i.e. a combined Nationalist and Communist effort. The letter the comrades in Shanghai received from Xiao San in Moscow — instructing them to dissolve the Leftist Federation for being too narrow an organisation that did not take in others in the spirit of the common front — was written on the orders of Wang Ming. Lu Xun objected to the use of the motto, on the grounds that it was not appropriate to the word literature (it dealt with 'defence').

Zhou Yang, in obedience to Moscow, dissolved the Leftist Federation and set up instead an Association of Writers, but he did not explain the change properly to Lu Xun. The new organisation should have been larger, attracting more figures from outside. In fact the most outstanding writers, Ba Jin, Cao Yu and Lu Xun himself, were not members. Consequently the Party was unable to create a widely-based association of writers during the war.

The 1978 magazine did not mention Hu Feng's name. Hu Feng was still out of favour in 1978; he had not yet been rehabilitated. But this 1978 review of past events did express regret that when the *Complete Works of Lu Xun* were published, in 1958, the notes contained sharp criticism of Feng Xuefeng, which was equivalent to criticism of Lu Xun.[24]

These disputes in the Shanghai literary underground had indeed split the comrades; but in those days few outside the Party knew about it. Communist influence over the general public was wide and profound, and it was not entirely undeserved. They had some men of outstanding talent whose names have entered the roll of modern Chinese literature. These men succeeded to a great extent in concealing the fact that they were Party members. In 1948 the well-known female writer Su Xuelin wrote on 'Present Day Fiction and Drama in China'. Under the heading 'A Word on Communist Propaganda', she listed only nine authors — and not even one of the Shanghai comrades was included in the nine.[25]

Xia Yan's angry article, mentioned earlier, was published in January

1980. In October 1981 the Chinese Writers' Association held a meeting under the chairmanship of Ba Jin (aged seventy-six), and decided to re-admit Hu Feng (aged seventy-seven) to membership.[26] It is unlikely that Xia Yan, who in that year was aged eighty-two, can have welcomed this news.

The Salvation Association

National indignation at Japanese encroachment on North Chinese terri-tories in 1935 gave rise to the National Salvation Association. This was launched, not by the Communists, but by a ninety-five-year-old man named Ma Xiangbo. Ma, born in 1840, was ordained as a Jesuit priest in 1870, but left the priesthood and along with his two brothers became active in political and diplomatic life. At the end of the century he returned to the Church. By that time he was a nationally-known figure, a pioneer in modern education, and founder of the Aurora and Fudan Universities.[27]

The National Salvation Association, inspired by Ma and fostered by student demonstrations in Peking and Shanghai, was founded in December 1935 with a committee of thirty, including the pro-Communist Shen Junru, Zhang Naiqi and Zuo Taofen. A month later Song Qingling, Sun Yat Sen's widow, joined and was destined to play a prominent role. The Communist underground tried to turn the Associa-tion into an anti-Chiang Kai Shek movement.

In February 1936 the Kuomintang leadership declared that the National Salvation Association was a cover for Communist activity. A Shanghai newspaper said retrospectively in 1980: 'The National Salva-tion Association used legal forms in dealing with the enemy [the Kuomintang], and the comrades kept under cover while engaged in public activities. This was useful United Front work.'

In November 1936 seven pro-Communist leaders of the National Salvation Association were arrested. The Communist underground con-ducted a widespread protest against the arrest of the seven, the 'Seven Gentlemen' as they were called. Tao Xingzhi and other friends who were outside China wrote to Chiang Kai Shek and asked John Dewey, Albert Einstein and other prominent international figures to intervene. Inside China, Sun Yat Sen's widow, Song Qingling, led the protest. She was then a distinguished member of the Kuomintang. In February 1937 she took part in the plenary meeting of the Kuomintang, which dis-cussed relations with the Communists.

On July 7, 1937, the full-scale Japanese attack began. On July 17 Zhou Enlai and other Communist leaders held a discussion at Lushan with Chiang Kai Shek about common defence. On the way to Lushan, Zhou Enlai discussed the Party underground situation in Shanghai with Pan Hannian and his companion, Liu Xiao (Chinese ambassador in Moscow in the 1950s). On the last day of the month the seven were released.[28]

Song Qingling

Song Qingling's father was one of the few Chinese to study in the United States in the last century — after his return to China he would not even eat Chinese food. His three daughters, all Americanised, made history. The first, Hayling, married T.V. Soong; the second, Qingling, married Sun Yat Sen; and the third, Meiling, married Chiang Kai Shek. Perhaps the best of the many books that have been written about them is Emily Hahn's *The Soong Sisters*, published in 1941. By the time the book was written the sisters had parted ways. Qingling's husband, Sun Yat Sen, the founder of the Republic, died in 1925. She always considered herself the First Lady of China, but once Chiang Kai Shek had become head of the government in Nanjing in 1928, his wife became the First Lady, and she could shine only among the Communists.

Qingling was at Sun Yat Sen's side in the early 1920s when he was flirting with the Comintern emissaries. In 1927, at the time of the break between the Communists and the Kuomintang in Wuhan, she refused to follow Chiang Kai Shek (and his wife, her sister), and left with Borodin and some Chinese Communists for the Soviet Union, saying that she was continuing her late husband's pro-Soviet policy. She was back in China when Xu Deheng, then a professor at Peking University, was arrested in 1931. Song Qingling sent a cable from Shanghai to the government in Nanjing, and Xu was released from jail.[29] Qingling saved several other people in a similar way.

She was not an underground Party member, but she was a great help to the underground. At the end of 1936, around the time of the Xi'an Incident, she was in permanent contact with Pan Hannian, and he became the channel through which the detail of the Party's policy was conveyed to her. Chiang Kai Shek was arrested by the Communists in Xi'an and Chiang's wife Meiling, in despair, asked her elder sister to intervene with his captors. Qingling conveyed the message to Pan

Hannian.[30] During the war she succeeded in providing substantial material aid to the Communists, under the aegis of the Chinese Industrial Cooperatives, the head of which was the Nationalist minister of finance, H.H. Kung.[31]

In May 1981, when Song Qingling lay dying at the age of ninety, Xu Deheng wrote that she was 'a great fighter for patriotism, democracy, internationalism and communism'.[32] This description was used in the official announcement of her death by the Party and government leadership.

Under the People's Republic, Song Qingling was one of the vice-presidents of the Republic for six years, 1959–65. Two weeks before she died, she was saluted as a 'great fighter for patriotism . . .', and was given the title of Honorary President of the People's Republic. On the preceding day, the Politbureau, using the same encomium, had made her a Party member. Qingling was then very ill, with a high fever and heart trouble.[33] She was probably unaware of what was going on around her.

Why was Party membership delayed so long? Did she not want to be a Party member? Or had she been told that it would be more helpful if she remained what she was? She was the wife of the Father of the Republic, and all doors were open to her. Often nobody else could help imprisoned Communists, but she could. Was she a convinced Marxist, or was she driven by her feelings towards Chiang Kai Shek, who had made her younger sister First Lady? This question remains unanswered. If she was a woman of principle, she must have resented the fluctuations in Sun Yat Sen's reputation as the mood changed in Peking throughout the first thirty or so years of the People's Republic. In some years Sun was regarded as a bourgeois to be ignored; in others his name was extolled as an enticement to Sun's old followers in Taiwan.

After her death several distinguished persons wrote eulogies on Qingling. One of these eulogists was Wang Guangmei, widow of Liu Shaoqi — also a First Lady in her time. All that Wang Guangmei had to say about Song Qingling's early life was that when Qingling and Liu Shaoqi met they had no common language. She spoke the Shanghai dialect but preferred to speak English, while Liu's speech was a mixture of Hunanese, Mandarin and Russian.[34] Song Qingling always remained an American-Chinese.

The master-spy

We came across Pan Hannian as the confidant of Song Qingling. Pan was the tragic star of the Party underground.

The underground, in spite of internal friction, worked effectively among the educated classes in the cities. In their early years the underground organisations were uncovered several times by the government. They then learned to act more subtly, rarely revealing their identities and penetrating the body of the nation with unobtrusive skill. Zhou Enlai, the mastermind of the operation, was shrewd enough not to expose himself to direct danger. Pan Hannian, a man no less subtle and versatile, did so expose himself, though never to unnecessary danger. He was never caught by the enemy and was an accomplished master-spy.

He rose to prominence from the Leftist Federation of Shanghai. In the 1930s he was in charge of cultural work in the Party Central Committee's Propaganda Department in Shanghai. In 1933 he, like many others, left Shanghai to join the Jiangxi Soviet Area of Ruijin, and he became the head of Party propaganda there. In 1934, as we saw in Chapter III, he negotiated with Cai Tinggai, the Nationalist general who revolted against Chiang Kai-shek in Fujian, and with Chen Jitang, governor of Guangdong in the south, who in those days was on bad terms with Chiang Kai-shek. (Chen died in 1967 in Taiwan.) The Ruijin base was hard-pressed by government troops and Pan wanted to get help from Fujian and Guangdong, but the Party leadership, notably Wang Ming and the German Comintern adviser Otto Braun, are said to have opposed this. If he had succeeded, the flight from Ruijin — the Long March — would not have been necessary. How the Long March could have been prevented was not a topic discussed in the earlier years. It was presented, not as a flight, but as a glorious accomplishment (see Chapter III).

Pan went with the Long March, but after the Cun Yi meeting in January 1935, he was sent to Moscow to report to the Comintern, and took part in the Seventh Congress of the Comintern in July the same year. While in Moscow he entered into secret negotiations with the military attaché of the Embassy of the Nationalist government. In 1936 Pan was in Hong Kong, running the Hong Kong underground and publishing a daily paper. In Hong Kong, he and some other comrades composed a Letter to the Nation, a cleverly formulated epistle which concealed the political affiliation of the authors. It proposed that the government should stop persecuting the Communists, and that the Communists should give up their army in a grand national union. The letter evoked little response and hardly any newspapers reproduced it in China.

Pan moved freely in Nationalist circles, and even wrote articles praising the Nationalists. In consequence many Party members avoided him, not knowing where his loyalties lay. Very few knew that he had a mission from the highest Party authorities to act in this way.

He was authorised by the Comintern itself to talk with Kuomintang leaders about the cessation of hostilities. (The Comintern wanted unity in China against the Japanese. This would have been to the Soviet Union's advantage.) Pan held discussions with two well-known anti-Communist brothers who were members of the Kuomintang, Chen Lifu and Chen Guofu. At the time nobody knew about this, not even his best friends; only the leadership in Yan'an were kept informed of his activities. In the second half of 1936 Pan was in Si'an, working in secret to win over Zhang Xueliang.

Before the outbreak of the Japanese war in 1937, Pan was sent by the Party leadership to carry on secret negotiations with the Nationalist government in Nanjing. In Nanjing he was the guest of T.V. Soong, Chiang Kai Shek's powerful brother-in-law, and lived in Soong's house. In the first years of the war he was in Shanghai as head of the publicly-run office of the Eighth Route Army, all the while sending intelligence reports to Yan'an.

After the Communist take-over, Pan became deputy mayor of Shanghai under General, later Marshal, Chen Yi.

Then in April 1955 came a terrible shock. Pan was in Peking at the yearly session of the People's Congress, where he met many of his old friends. His friends were thunderstruck to hear Chen Yi, the Party boss and mayor of Shanghai, announcing that Pan Hannian had been arrested for a treacherous act committed in 1943. Chen Yi himself seemed genuinely shocked.

The nature of the treacherous act in 1943 was not revealed. (It may have been, as often was the case, an act of personal revenge.) Pan was condemned to fifteen years in prison. He was released in 1963, but was condemned again during the Cultural Revolution, this time for life. He was sent with his wife, a Party member, to a labour camp in Hunan province, where he died in 1977.

All this was related in the *People's Daily* in 1983, after his posthumous rehabilitation by Hu Yuzhi, whose reminiscences about Du Zhongyuan we quoted earlier.[35]

In 1980, three years before Hu Yuzhi's article, Pan Hannian, though not yet officially rehabilitated, was, as we saw above, highly praised by Yang Hansheng. Yet the first volume of the *Selected Works of Zhou Enlai*, published in December 1980, called Pan a traitor, and said that he had been a traitorous Nationalist agent since 1936.[36] Chen Yi, the boss of Shanghai, as we saw above, declared in 1955 that he had been a Nationalist agent since 1943. This is an odd discrepancy that is hard to explain. Three years later, in 1983, all the accusations against Pan were declared false. The man spent fifteen years in the prison of his former comrades and died in prison — for nothing.

Posthumous rehabilitation has been granted to many dead leaders, but the rehabilitation of Pan Hannian was carried out in a unique way. He was rehabilitated by an act of the Party Central on August 23, 1982,[37] but this was not announced at the time in the newspapers. It was announced to the members of the Congress on the first day of the Twelfth Party Congress in September 1982, but the public heard nothing of this until it was revealed five months later in an article by Xu Dixin, the old Party member and economist whom we came across earlier in Shanghai.

After Pan's rehabilitation, many of his friends hurried to publish articles expressing their superabundant esteem for the man who had done so much during the revolution and who had been so badly treated. The accusation that Pan was a traitor could not be true, Xu wrote. When Pan was in Shanghai in 1946 and Hong Kong in 1947–9, he could have betrayed the Party's underground to the enemy, but he did not do so. The accusation against Pan was fabricated, Xu wrote in 1983; he did not say by whom.

Xu Dixin pointed out that Pan's wife was the daughter of a rich Hong Kong banker (Dong Zhongwei) and that this fact had provided Pan with useful cover. When Party members all over the country were checked in a Party purge early in 1948, somebody brought up against Pan the fact that in Hong Kong he dressed in Western clothes and did not look like a Party member. How else could Pan have worked in Hong Kong?[38]

The Hong Kong banker's daughter was carried away by revolutionary fervour in her student days — as often happens to children of rich parents. She joined the Communist Party and took part in the December street demonstration in 1935 in Peking. When her husband was doing clandestine work in Hong Kong, she resumed the lifestyle of a rich banker's daughter, thus providing useful cover for Pan.[39]

She and her husband spent years in a labour camp, but, being higher Party cadres, they led a more comfortable life than their ordinary campmates. Few in the camp knew who they were, but it was known that they were 'special criminals'. They had books to read; they had a television set. She did not know how to cook, so the family of a cadre served them. She even had her pet dog with her. Another Party member camp inmate who knew them once asked the man in charge why they had not been executed. The answer was: 'We do not kill people like Hu Feng and Pan Hannian — not that their guilt does not deserve it, but killing them would not be useful. To cap that, Pan Hannian was Chen Yi's right hand.'[40] (Mao once said: 'We kill little Chiang Kai Sheks but we do not kill the big ones.')

The story of Pan Hannian, as published by his friends in the newspapers after his rehabilitation, raises more questions than it answers. None of the reminiscences tells us what Pan was doing in the 1940s, when he was supposed to have behaved so treacherously. Who accused him, and on what grounds? This has never been revealed. How is it that his immediate superior, Chen Yi, high as he was in the Party ranks, could not defend him? The Communist Party, and especially those who worked underground, remained, even forty years later, shrouded in silence.

When a man of Pan Hannian's calibre is condemned, a number of his colleagues and friends are inevitably accused of complicity. Not much is said about this in the reminiscences. It is known, however, that in 1955 Sha Wenhan, an old Party member who as early as 1937 was the propaganda head of the Shanghai underground Party organisation and in the 1950s a leading figure in his native Zhejiang province, fell under suspicion of involvement in the Pan Hannian affair. In 1957 he was expelled from the Party. In 1958 he was condemned to forced labour, and he died, still in forced labour, in 1964, at the age of sixty-four.[41]

An old Shanghai journalist who had worked in the Shanghai Party underground since the 1930s became implicated in the Pan affair. He was arrested in 1955 and spent ten years in jail.[42]

In the same year, 1955, another old and highly intelligent Party man, Hua Kang, editor in 1938 of the Communist *Xinhua Daily* in Zhongqing, was thrown in jail, where he died in 1972.[43]

The banker

Ji Chaoding, who gained a Ph.D. in economics at Columbia University in the 1920s, had a distinguished career in China. During the Japanese war he was head of the foreign currency administration in the

Nationalist Government and head of the economic research bureau of the Central Bank. For a long time he lived in the house of H.H. Kung, the minister of finance. Under the Communist government he was in 1951 the first Chinese financial expert invited to lecture at Cambridge University, England, and he led delegations to a number of West European countries. In 1963 he died of a heart attack while preparing to lead a Chinese trade exhibition to Algeria. In 1984 his memory was commemorated in Peking. It was revealed then that he had been a clandestine Party member since the 1920s and a spy in the very heart of the financial establishment of the Nationalist government.

On one occasion, it was revealed, his activities aroused suspicion. H.H. Kung confronted him, saying, 'Are you a Communist'? He replied jokingly, 'Do I look like one'? Kung said 'no', and that was the end of the matter.

In the first half of January 1949, three weeks before the Communist troops entered Peking, Zhou Enlai sent him a message, asking him to go to Peking. At that time communications between the two cities were difficult. General Fu Zuoyi, the Nationalist defender of Peking, invited him to handle the finances of his defence against the Communists and brought him and his wife to Peking in a special plane.[44]

In the North in the 1940s

As we said earlier, some of the Party archives of the 1920s and 1930s are open to Party historians, but not yet those of the 1940s. Little information is therefore available about Party underground work in the 1940s. One gets however a fair picture of what went on in North China, particularly in Peking and Tianjin, from Marshal Nie Rongzhen's reminiscences of Liu Ren, published in 1979. Liu Ren was the leader of the Party underground in Peking and Tianjin during and after the Japanese war. After the Communist victory he was second Party secretary of Peking city for many years.

At the outbreak of the Japanese war in 1937, the underground Party workers were withdrawn from Peking and Tianjin, and only a few Communists remained in these two cities. In 1942 the Shanxi-Zhahar-Hebei Bureau of the Party, situated not far from these two cities, established the City Work Committee, later renamed the City Work Department. Its head was Liu Ren, then aged thirty, who had joined the Red Army in 1927 at the age of fifteen. Liu Ren recruited youngsters who had left the two cities, trained them in underground work and sent them back to the cities. He taught them how to recruit collaborators and how to keep their own identities secret. Winning over a single other person, he told them, is like putting a bomb into the heart of the enemy. When Liu Ren's trainees went back to the cities they won over many sympathisers and established special committees for students, for workers, for railway workers, for the cultured and for ordinary people. This was a successful operation.

(Marshal Nie neglects to say that when the two cities were under Japanese rule, the Nationalist government also had secret members in all fields, and that many leading personalities were helping it out of patriotism. The author of these lines was living in Peking and Tianjin at that time.)

When the war ended in 1945, some of the Communist underground members expressed the view that they should emerge and work in the open; Liu Ren opposed this.

At the end of 1946 big anti-American demonstrations caused by the alleged rape of a Chinese girl by an American soldier were launched in Peking and spread throughout the whole country. (This was mentioned earlier in connection with the Marshall Mission, in Chapter VI.) These 1946 demonstrations, Marshal Nie says, were organised behind the scenes by the Communist underground. (When American soldiers appeared in Chinese cities in the post-war period and moved around freely in the streets, there were no signs of anti-American feeling among the people.) Other student demonstrations were staged in May 1947, with the motto: 'Against hunger, against civil war, against oppression'. These were anti-Chiang Kai Shek activities fomented by *agents provocateurs*, and there were more demonstrations in 1948 which used similar slogans. In August the same year the police began rounding up secret agents, but the Party underground succeeded in sending many of their agents away to Communist-ruled territories.

In October 1948, when the fighting was raging in southern Manchuria, Mao had set up his Communist headquarters at Pingshan near the city of Shi-jia-zhuang, about 240 km. from Peking. Chiang Kai Shek flew to Peking with a secret plan for organising shock troops to destroy the Communist headquarters. On the very day on which this was decided upon in Peking, the Communist underground learnt about the plan and sent a secret radio message to Pingshan. Zhou Enlai went three times to report to Mao that night, Marshal Nie says. All the necessary military preparations were made, and the Communist Xinhua

News Agency made the secret plan public. Chiang Kai Shek's planned military operation came to nothing.

After the Communist take-over, Liu Ren became, as we said above, second Party secretary of Peking city. Marshal Nie says that he was successful in organising the police force and suppressing counter-revolutionaries. (Liu Ren knew, of course, from earlier years who in Peking were opposed to, or did not welcome, the Communists; they were 'suppressed'.)

At the very beginning of the Cultural Revolution in 1966, Liu Ren was caught. He was kept handcuffed for a long time, and died, Marshal Nie says, 'quite miserably in the prison we ourselves had built for the suppression of counter-revolutionaries'. The Marshal reveals that at the moment of the Communist take-over of Peking, in the last days of January 1949, there were only 3,000 Party members and 5,000 collaborators in the whole of that great city.[45] And we saw at the beginning of this chapter that at the time of the takeover of Shanghai the total number of Party members in that still larger city was only 8,000. The moral is that it takes very few people, less than 0.1 per cent of the population, to launch emotional appeals, to win over disoriented intellectuals, to mobilise tens of thousands of students, and to represent the 'people's will'. This is not particular to Communism, but it is an answer to questions about how China became Communist.

In 1981 the *Peking Daily* added something to the story of Liu Ren. This account also says that the Shanxi-Zhahar-Hebei Bureau was charged with the organisation of the Peking underground. In 1945, immediately after the war, a clandestine Peking city Party Committee founded by Liu Ren sent 100 Party members and collaborators to the city. In a single night they covered the city walls with posters announcing the liberation of the city by the Eighth Route Army. They were to gather weapons and organise an underground army to prepare for the liberation; but the liberation of Peking did not come about at that time, and the Peking City Party Committee was dissolved. Liu Ren, however, remained in the City Work Department of the Party's Shanxi-Zhahar-Hebei Bureau, and his men stirred up anti-Chiang Kai Shek feeling in the city.[46]

This quite astonishing story was not told by Marshal Nie. One would like to know more details about it. Who can have conceived the plan of taking over Peking immediately after the war, and who called it off? This had never been revealed earlier.

Shanghai in the 1940s

After 1945, with the war ended, the Party sent new men to lead the underground work in Shanghai. Among these were Liu Xiao, whom we met earlier as a close ally of Pan Hannian, and who was later ambassador to Moscow; Liu Changsheng, a labour leader, who in the 1950s was prominent in Chinese international trade union activities (died 1967); and Zhang Zhiyi, under the People's Republic deputy head of the United Front Department (died 1983).

The Shanghai of the 1940s was very different from the Shanghai of the 1930s. The intellectual battle was over and the leading personalities had left. Through the war years it was occupied by the Japanese and came under Wang Ching Wei's government in Nanjing. When the Nationalist government returned after the war, Communist propaganda efforts were renewed.

One of the centres of the underground was the house which is today no. 916 Yan'an Road, Central. It was the home of an important rice merchant, himself an underground Party member; the Communists had a secret radio transmitter which they operated from there. Shortly before the Communist occupation of Shanghai, the rice merchant was arrested and executed: he was thirty-six years old. A month later Shanghai was 'liberated'.[47]

The underground Party workers organised large street demonstrations, beginning on June 23, 1946. The 8,000 underground Party-members of Shanghai could mobilise tens of thousands of people when needed.[48] As in other cities, the underground put agents into every major organisation, and when the new regime was established these men promptly took over the leadership. The day after the Communist takeover, many banks, offices and schools were surprised to see an insignificant clerk standing up and declaring that he or she was the boss.

In the army

The deepest and most dangerous penetration achieved by the Communist underground was in the government army. On the whole, the Nationalist generals stood out against temptations, but a few were entrapped, and the damage done was immense.

When Chiang Kai Shek was held captive for a week in Xi'an in December 1936, he knew that he was in the hands of Zhang Xueliang

and the Communists, but up to the last minute he did not suspect that
his own man, General Yang Hucheng, would come out against him.[49]
After the Xi'an Incident, Yang fled abroad, but he returned and was
killed in 1949.[50]

A spectacular example of an undercover agent in the Nationalist army
was He Jifeng. He was an officer stationed near Peking when the
Japanese offensive began in July 1937. He became commander of a regiment in the Twenty-Ninth Army and fought the invading Japanese cou-
rageously. Early in 1938 he met Zhou Enlai in Wuhan. (By that time the
Communists had been legalised and had an Eighth Route Army office in
Wuhan.) Zhou Enlai's charm and praise of his bravery apparently dis-
armed He. He went secretly to Yan'an and stayed there for a month.
There he was complimented by Mao, by Liu Shaoqi and by Zhu De, and
he applied for Communist Party membership. This was not mere youthful folly; he was forty years of age. He was sent back to his original post
in the Nationalist army. A few months later he was promoted to be
deputy commander of the government's Seventy-Seventh Army. In
1939 he was made head of a special Exploratory Team, which he packed
with Party members. The team carried on guerilla warfare against the
Japanese, and secretly protected the Communists in their territory in the
northwest of Hubei province.

A clandestine Communist regional Bureau was established in 1938
and was led by Liu Shaoqi. Its theatre of operations included parts of
Henan, Hubei, Anhui and Jiangsu provinces. When the leaders of this
Bureau went to Yan'an to take part in the Seventh Party Congress in
1945, He Jifeng's troops protected them on their journey. His men also
helped the New Fourth Army, the Communist army then collaborating
with the government, by sending them weapons and money.

When relations between the Nationalists and Communist troops
deteriorated, He went through the motions of attacking the Communists. At the end of 1938 a Communist comrade revealed the Communist presence in the troops. He Jifeng helped those under suspicion to
escape. In the following year he was summoned to Zhongqing for
retraining; he was interrogated rigorously but he passed the test and was
a guest at a dinner held by Chiang Kai Shek before eventually being sent
back to his post. He became commander of the Seventy-Seventh Army.
Next he was transferred to the deputy commandership of the 'Third
Pacification Area', which had been set up to check the Communist
advance. He was in a dilemma. In September 1946 he went to

Peking for the funeral of his father, and there he met the Communist leader Ye Jianying who, as a member of the Marshall Mission, was taking part in the peace talks with the Nationalists. Ye encouraged him to stay where he was in the Northwest.

On November 8, 1948 — a major part of North China being already in Communist hands — he and another Nationalist officer, Zhang Kexia, also a secret Party member, led a revolt in the Xuzhou area on the instruction of Chen Yi, the Communist commander of the New Fourth Army. This happened on the very day before the start of the long battle at Xuzhou, the greatest battle of the civil war.

He Jifeng, according to a 1983 commemorative article, 'wrote a glorious chapter in the history of the liberation of the Chinese people'. By February 1949 he was fighting on the Communist side and took part in the occupation of Nanjing. Under the People's Republic he first was deputy commander of the Nanjing garrison, and then vice-minister in the Cabinet. He died in January 1980.[51]

Not all were as lucky as He Jifeng. In 1947 the government discovered a Communist group in the armed forces. They were rounded up and executed. An impressive group statue in Nanjing perpetuates their memory.[52]

Two distinguished old comrades, Liu Lantao and Yang Xianzhen, revived in 1981 the memory of a colleague, Zhang Youqing, who died in the Nationalist government's prisoner of war camp in 1942 and had been nearly forgotten in the interval. Their memories of him remained vivid on account of an earlier incident. In 1931, the two writers of the memoir and nine other Communists were arrested by the government along with Zhang and were condemned to death. They were saved only because Japanese military activity in Tianjin drove their guards away.

Zhang Youqing, the article says, worked in the North Bureau of the Party and his most praiseworthy act was that in 1939 he succeeded in persuading a battalion of government troops to desert and join the Communist troops.[53]

Such attempts did not always work out as planned. A certain regimental commander in the government forces was an underground Party member. In 1941 his troops were in Anhui province, close to units of the Communist New Fourth Army. There were recurrent skirmishes between the two forces — though this was during the war when both were supposed to be fighting the Japanese. Senior Communist Party authorities, wishing to teach the government troops a lesson, ordered their man to bring his troops, government troops, over to the

Communists. He gave the appropriate orders, but both his officers and his men revolted and he himself was severely wounded. (This incident is described in a story about a kindly general who cared for him when he was wounded, namely Zhang Yunyi, deputy commander of the New Fourth Army, who died in Peking in 1974.[54])

In June 1983 another underground Communist army officer died in Canton at the age of eighty-eight. His personal history was briefly outlined at his funeral service. He had been a soldier from a very early age and he joined the Communist Party in 1937 but was told to keep this secret. He carried out the Party's instructions faithfully and protected many Party members. In 1948 he took part in the battle of Xuzhou. Whether or when he revolted was not revealed. Under the People's Republic he held minor provincial posts.[55]

More sensational still was the revelation of how the Party got round General Fu Zuoyi, who held out in Peking until the end. The 200,000-strong forces of Fu Zuoyi surrendered on January 31, 1949. The story of Fu's surrender is found in an article written by Marshal Nie Rongzhen about Liu Ren. General Fu was not a Communist collaborator, but his daughter was a member of Liu Ren's underground Party organisation. Liu Ren taught her and other underground Party members how to approach General Fu and how to deal with him. They reported almost daily on every step Fu was taking. Fu Zuoyi kept on hesitating about what he should do until the neighbouring city of Tianjin was taken and the Communist troops began their approach on Peking. Then he surrendered. The peaceful occupation of Peking was regarded by Mao as a great achievement, an example for the 'liberation' of the provinces in the southwest which were not yet under Communist rule.[56] (When the People's Republic was established eight months later, Fu Zuoyi became minister of water conservancy. He died in 1974.)

On the whole, the Communists were not notably successful in winning over high-ranking army leaders. Old comrades, now ready to dilate on the events of forty years ago, have been able to remember only a few Nationalist officers who worked underground for them. Several Nationalist generals fought to the last and were killed in action (Commanders Hung Ho-tao and Chiu Ching-chuan, for example, who died in the battle of Xuzhou in 1948).[57] Others surrendered only when there was no longer any hope of survival for their troops. Few were opportunists who betrayed their cause.

What happened in later years to the men who had lived the dangerous life of the clandestine underground in the cities? The few military men — we have seen the case of He Jifeng — were rewarded with posts in the Liberation Army. The generals who were taken prisoner spent fifteen or twenty years in labour camps, underwent political re-education, and were released in their old age. Thousands of Nationalist army soldiers captured in 1949–50 were rehabilitated — that is, those still alive — thirty-five years later.[58]

Civilians fared worse. There was an unbridgeable gap between the guerilla fighters and the city workers. The guerilla comrades had lived in the wild areas of Yan'an, or had moved round in the 'liberated areas', always in primitive villages. They themselves were uneducated rustics who had been separated from their wives and children. The underground Party workers in the big modern cities however lived in an environment dominated by electricity, running water, restaurants, theatres and cinemas, schools, bookshops and libraries. Many of those working in the cities were highly-educated men who fitted naturally into a sophisticated urban society. They had to live a normal city life and to use all the amenities of the cities if they were to avoid being suspected and caught by the police.

A chasm opened up between these two types of men. The educated city men did not have a high opinion of the new arrivals from the country-side. It became a standing joke that when the former guerillas entered the cities in 1949, they did not know how to use a water closet, had never sat on a sofa, and their only thought on entering the cities was to look for city wives. The brave fighters of guerilla wars could not under-stand their city brethren, who looked and behaved as all the bourgeoisie looked and behaved. Mao himself took pride in his generals, rough and coarse, but brave soldiers.

The Yan'an brigade won. That is why there are spittoons everywhere in the People's Republic. To be an 'intellectual', i.e. to have been at school, remained for many years an ill-omened stigma. We have seen what happened to Pan Hannian in 1955. Two years later it was the turn of the Party intellectual underground writers, Feng Xuefeng and a score of others. Ten years later during the Cultural Revolution purge, former underground workers were condemned *en bloc*. In Shanghai ninety-nine former underground Party workers were dismissed from their jobs, sixty-five were detained for interrogation, and four died under duress.[59] In other places they fared no better. Those who had worked in the Party underground in Guangxi, in South China, were not rehabilitated till 1983.[60]

CHAPTER IX

CONQUEST OF THE COUNTRY, 1947–1949

In 1945, at the end of the Second World War, the Communists announced (as we noted in Chapter VI) that their rule extended over territory containing 100 million inhabitants, and that they had 910,000 regular troops and 2.2 million men organised in local militias. These figures were greatly exaggerated. The truth was that only a single city, and a small one at that, Yan'an — if that big village could be counted as a city — was under Communist rule. In the countryside they held large expanses of North China and some territories in Central China, but even in these areas their presence was spasmodic and it would have been difficult, nay impossible, to make a firm estimate of the area or the population under their control or to count the numbers of men in the village militia. The Communists, confident as they were, cannot have dreamt in 1945 that in four years the country would be theirs.

They were fully aware of the weakness of their situation. Otherwise Mao Zedong would not have gone to Zhongqing to negotiate with the arch-enemy, Chiang Kai Shek. Obviously he hoped that if the Communists could form a coalition government with the Nationalists they could in time manoeuvre the Nationalists out of the government — as their fellow Communists had done after the war in Eastern European countries.

The Communists stubbornly maintained their independence and they were not willing to incorporate their troops into the national army. It was clear therefore that civil war must come, or rather that the fight against the government forces would continue. The Marshall Mission — under which the Communists, with American assistance, dealt with the Nationalist government on an equal footing, out of all proportion to their real power in the country — helped the Communists to enhance their prestige throughout the nation.

Their underground Party work was very effective; but not effective enough to win the country over to Communism. The street demonstrations, the tens and hundreds of thousands involved in protest marches, produced very few Marxists. (How many of the Communist troops themselves were Marxist?) It was easy to enkindle mob passion against the government, which was exhausted after the long war and had had no breathing space in which to rebuild the state; but these mobs had no idea of what Marxism was, no suspicion of what the rigour of a Marxist state would be. The reason that the Communists stirred up the mobs was not to convert the demonstrators to Marxism, but to destroy the credibility of the Nationalist government. Yet even this was a far cry from any possibility of overthrowing the government and establishing a Communist regime. That could be done only by the 'barrel of the gun', the only thing, as Mao said, that can win political power.

The collapse of the Nationalist government was largely due to the economic and financial deterioration of the country. After the war there was a pressing need for long years of peaceful reconstruction. Civil war made this impossible. The civil war did not merely hinder reconstruction; it disrupted the economy still further. It is probably true to say that it did more damage to the country than the Japanese war had done. The most advanced industries were those in Manchuria which had been developed by the Japanese. When the Russians entered after the war they stripped the industries of the Northeast (Manchuria) and let the Chinese Communists take over from them. The Japanese had maintained the lines of communication and had kept the economy intact. The Communist guerillas mined the railways, the main transport arteries of the country. Operating in the countryside, they made it difficult to feed the cities, which were in government hands. The government had the burden of keeping the national economy in normal running order, and this was made impossible by the civil war.

A remarkably objective book was published in Taiwan in 1964, with the title *Why was the Mainland Lost?* A section of this book deals with the economy between 1945 and 1949.

The currency had been unified, it says, and a good start had been made. But expenditure rose along with the civil war. By 1948, 64 per cent of the budget was being spent on the armed forces. Inflation spiralled and so did the budget deficit. In 1945 banknotes for a billion dollars were issued; about the same amount was collected in taxes. In 1947 banknotes for 33 billion dollars were in circulation and 14 billion were collected in tax. In 1948 the circulation had reached 374 billion dollars and taxation had reached 320 billion. With inflation, the black market and rising prices, government employees were becoming ever poorer and more dissatisfied, and the farmers were burdened with intolerable taxation. In 1947 a more conservative financial policy was discussed but the newly-appointed minister of finance O.K. Yui opposed it, and the economy deteriorated still further. From January

1948 onward, inflation was at a monthly level of 100 per cent. In August a radical step was taken. A new paper currency, called Gold Yuan, was introduced with an exchange rate of 3 million of the old dollars to one Gold Yuan. People were called upon to hand in their gold and silver in exchange for the new paper currency. The result was disaster. The author of *Why was the Mainland Lost?* believes that the treasury had enough bullion and foreign currency reserves to maintain the convertibility of the paper money; but this was not done, and the economy collapsed completely.[1] That book does not mention that one of the government's chief financial advisers was an underground Communist Party member who had never been detected (cf. Chapter VIII, pp. 127–8).

The Communists' financial burden was considerably lighter. They were operating in primitive villages and did not have to pay for public utilities or for running the cities. They were fed by the local population. They only had to pay for rifles, bullets and artillery.

There was corruption in the government, but not enough corruption to explain the collapse of the economy. (There could hardly be any corruption among the Communist forces, which, operating in primitive villages, had no access to wealth.) The real causes of the government's economic collapse were the expense of the civil war and the disruption of national life.

Popular dissatisfaction with the government was fanned by underground Communist propaganda. But this dissatisfaction was not equivalent to a vote for a Communist government. When the rough and ragged Communist troops entered Peking on January 31, 1949, people lined both sides of the streets, looking either resigned or cynical, and showing no signs of enthusiasm.

Nor was there any visible sign among the peasants that they would welcome the new regime. The Communists made an incredible blunder when they introduced radical land reform in some parts of North China during the civil war. Not only landowners but all suspected enemies were treated brutally; one could walk about in the North Chinese plains and see hands sticking out from the ground, the hands of people buried alive. The Communists themselves became aware of the blunder and began to blame what they called the 'leftist deviation' of local leaders; but, as we shall see below, the blame lay with the policy ordained by the Party's highest leadership.

Luckily for the Communists, government propaganda was so poorly organised that people living in regions not occupied by the Communists knew nothing of such atrocities.

The military achievement of taking over the country with forces inferior in numbers and greatly inferior in equipment to the government troops has been described with admiration by several Western military specialists. It was indeed an astounding achievement. The Communists were a newly-emerging force and as such they were better disciplined. Moreover they looked after their men better than the government's army, in which the rank and file were neglected and poorly treated, and the wounded were not properly cared for. On the whole, the government forces were on the defensive, which is demoralising for any army. Military experts blame Chiang Kai Shek for having spread his forces too wide, thus diminishing their effectiveness. Yet it is far from true to say that the government's army collapsed like a pack of cards. The Communist narrative of the years 1945–9 makes the opposite clear. A number of Nationalist generals died in action. This may of course mean that they — unlike the Communist generals — were not prudent enough to protect their own persons; but the patriotism and dedication of the generals cannot be denied. Those few who had been secret Communist Party members for years surrendered, in the belief that their example would be followed by others. But the other generals fought to the end, and those who ultimately surrendered did so only when the final outcome was inevitable.

The military conquest was rapid, perhaps too rapid for Communist convenience. The Party leadership was not prepared for taking over the administration of the state machinery. It was only at the last minute that the Party leadership began to discuss what should be done after the takeover. Discussions began only in March 1949, a few weeks after the first Communist troops marched into Peking and only a month before Mao and his comrades moved into the city.

War chronicle

In 1961 a remarkable book appeared in Peking on the Third Revolutionary Struggle. (The First Revolutionary Struggle was the period of cooperation with the Nationalists, 1921–7; the Second ran from the rupture with the Kuomintang to the Japanese war, 1928–37; the Third from that time to the 'Liberation' in 1949.)

This booklet gives a month by month account of military and political events on both sides, Communist and government, in the years 1945–9. It is a fairly objective account, except that the numbers of government casualties are exaggerated — this happens in every war

report. Here are some of the salient events from the book for the years
1947–9.

— *1947*

In *January* the Liberation Army annihilated 16,000 Kuomintang troops
in the west of Shandong province and 'caught alive' [took prisoner] a
brigade commander. In south Shanxi 52,000 government troops were
defeated and a regimental commander was caught alive.

On January 7, George Marshall, who 'under the cover of mediation
helped the Kuomintang reactionary government', left China.

Chiang Kai Shek wished to send Zhang Zhizhong to Yan'an for peace
negotiations, but this was not acceptable to Yan'an.

In *February*, an inner-Party instruction encouraged the troops to fight.
9,000 enemy troops were annihilated in the east of Henan province.
Kuomintang troops occupied the East Shandong Liberated Areas.

Ye Jianying, who had been the Communist representative in Peking
for the Marshall negotiations, returned to Yan'an. Other liaison groups
were withdrawn from Nanjing, Shanghai and Zhongqing. The Kuomintang police in Zhongqing shut down the [Communist] *Xinhua
Daily*.

In *March* a Kuomintang regiment was annihilated near Changchun in
the Northeast [Manchuria]. On the 19th the Kuomintang troops occupied Yan'an. After this Comrade Mao Zedong directed the war from the
borders of Shaanxi-Gansu-Ningxia provinces. [Who would have
thought that only two years later the Communist troops would be in
Peking?] On the 23rd the [Communist] Inner Mongolia self-governing
government was established.

In *April*, 35,000 enemy troops were annihilated and victories were
recorded around Shi-jia-zhuang, Hebei province, and in the north of
Shaanxi province, where a brigade commander was 'caught alive'.

On the 18th Chiang Kai Shek reorganised his government and Chang
Ch'ün took the place of T.V. Soong as head of the Executive Yuan
[Premier].

In *May* students and workers demonstrated against the Kuomintang
in several cities.

In *June*, 16,000 enemy [Nationalist] troops were annihilated in the
Northeast in a twelve-day battle.

The deputy chairman of the Kuomintang, Sun Fo, complained about
Washington's neglect of China.

In *July* the Liberation Army in the northeast occupied fourteen county towns, thus making communications easier for the Communist troops.

The Kuomintang held a government meeting with the participation of some members of the Youth Party and the Democratic Party [other members of these small parties were on the Communist side] and adopted Chiang Kai Shek's proposal to 'pacify the Communist-bandit-ridden land and prepare the way for democracy and for constitutional government'. 'Thus [the Kuomintang] showed the people their reactionary face.'

In *September* Mao Zedong issued an inner-Party instruction ordering attacks against Nationalist troops.

The Kuomintang General Pai Chung Hsi complained that some people believed that the Communists could not be completely exterminated — though in the past the government had overthrown the Manchu dynasty, carried out the Northern Expedition and resisted the Japanese. We shall win this struggle, General Pai said.

In the northwest of Shandong province the Liberation Army annihilated the enemy's Fifty-Seventh Regiment and took its commander prisoner. In the Northeast a large-scale attack was made outside the main cities.

In *October* victorious battles were fought in the countryside around Luoyang, Henan, in Shandong, in the west of Anhui province, and in the east of Hubei province. On the 10th, a proclamation drawn up by Mao Zedong was published calling upon all Chinese to overthrow Chiang Kai Shek and to liberate China. On the same day the *Outline of the Chinese Land Law* was published.

In *November*, for the first time, a city, Shi Jia Zhuang, was occupied.

In *December* the Party leadership held a meeting in Mizhi county in northern Shaanxi at which Mao reported on the war situation.

— *1948*

In *January* the Democratic League — the biggest of the small political parties — was revived in Hong Kong under the leadership of Shen Junru. In the same month a Kuomintang Revolutionary Committee was founded, also in Hong Kong. [Both were pro-Communist and anti-Chiang Kai Shek groups.] The Communist Party issued an inner-Party instruction, asking for respect for industrial and commercial activities and repudiating the excessive radicalism that had revealed itself in the land reform. 'The enemy', Mao wrote, 'is isolated but this does not yet mean victory.' In the same month Communist sympathisers in New York held a meeting in an effort to persuade the American dock-workers to refuse to load arms for Chiang Kai Shek.

In *February* the Communists scored military successes in the countryside in the Northeast. On the 26th, Ying-kou, in the Northeast, was liberated and Wang Chia-shan, commander of a regiment of the Kuomintang army, surrendered.

In *March* there was a great victory in the north of Shaanxi. A Nationalist army commander was killed.

The Liberation Army published a document written by Mao ordering 'three surveys': a survey of the family origins of the men, a survey of their work, and a survey of their fighting spirit.

President Truman spoke about China, expressing the hope that all liberal elements, but not the Communists, would join the Nationalist government.

The Liberation Army took the town of Si-ping-kai in the Northeast, annihilating 19,000 enemy troops. Luoyang in Henan was taken and the regiment's commander was taken prisoner.

This battle in the northeast isolated the Nationalist-held cities of Shenyang and Zhangchun.

On the 20th the Party Central issued a situation report, written by Mao, which said that at the current rate the Nationalist army would be completely defeated by 1951, and asked the Party to make allies of the 'democratic gentlemen' and to prepare for the establishment of a central government.

15,000 enemies were annihilated in the Northwest and 12,000 in Shandong province.

The Nationalist government established a special criminal court to punish Communist collaborators. It also convoked a parliament which elected Chiang Kai Shek as President and Li Zongren as Vice-President. This was done to win the support of public opinion in the United States. Li Zongren declared that his election would help towards the destruction of the 'bandits'. The American government was orchestrating support for Li Zongren so that when Chiang Kai Shek had to step down, another reactionary, Li, would take his place. On the 30th, the city of Wei-hai-wei, in Shandong province, was taken by the Liberation Army.

In *April* the American Congress voted 460 million dollars in aid for the

Kuomintang reactionary government in the year 1948. Chiang Kai Shek told the so-called parliament that within three to six months the 'bandits' [the Communists] would be cleared from south of the Yellow River.

On the 22nd the Liberation Army recaptured Yan'an. Four days later it took [temporarily] the city of Baoji in north Shaanxi province.

In Shandong 25,000 enemies were annihilated and the commander of the army was taken prisoner.

In *May* Mao called upon all democratic parties and organisations to hold consultative conferences and to discuss the convocation of a People's Congress. Eight small political parties expressed their support. Seventeen towns in Shandong, east of the railway line, were taken, but not the major cities of Qingdao and Yantai. 21,000 enemy troops were annihilated in central Shaanxi province and 25,000 in Shanxi, where a deputy commander was taken prisoner.

In Shanghai and in other major cities, students demonstrated against the United States and Japan.

In the middle of the month two Liberated Areas were united into the North-China Liberated Area. The North-Chinese Military Area was established.

In *June* 11,000 troops were annihilated in Henan province and 39,000 around Kaifeng city in the same province.

24.5 per cent of Chinese territory and 35 per cent of the population were in Communist hands, so also were 586 towns and cities, 29 per cent of the 2,009 towns and cities of China. The number of Kuomintang troops had shrunk to 3.6 million, and the Liberation Army had grown to 2.8 million.

More demonstrations were held in Shanghai and Peking, and hundreds of professors in Peking universities protested against United States aid to the Nationalist government.

In *July* an agreement on economic aid between the United States and China was signed.

The Nationalist army used poison gas. More Nationalist troops were annihilated. Student demonstrations in the cities were brutally suppressed by the government.

Vice-President Li and Premier Wang Wen Hao spoke in public about eventual peace negotiations. When this caused alarm in the Nationalist army, their words were dismissed as rumours and were withdrawn.

In *August* a [Communist] National Labour Congress was held in Harbin [in the Northeast], the first since 1929.

Chiang Kai Shek swore that he would continue to fight to extirpate the 'bandits'.

A People's Congress was held in the North-China Liberated Area. It elected a North Chinese government.

American sailors were accused of abusing Chinese women. This caused national indignation. The Kuomintang government arrested a number of students and 'democratic gentlemen'. The Kuomintang government, in the midst of growing inflation, issued a new paper currency, the Gold Yuan.

In *September* the Nationalist Li Zongren and General Ho Ying-Ch'in, urged by American imperialists, made peace proposals.

In the Northeast the battle for Shenyang, the first great battle of the civil war, began. The Kuomintang troops were isolated in the cities of Shenyang, Changchun and Jinzhou.

On the 20th, Mao's report on land reform in the Liberated Areas was published and stricter discipline in the army was ordered.

The Liberation Army attacked Jinan, capital of Shandong province, and took the provincial governor and a commander prisoner; one army commander surrendered.

The Party Central held a meeting at Pingshan county in Hebei province: the Kuomintang would be overthrown by 1951, it proclaimed.

In *October* Jinzhou and Changchun in the Northeast were taken and one of the army generals surrendered. After that, Baotou in Mongolia and Kaifeng in Henan fell.

Chiang Kai Shek flew to Peking and negotiated with General Fu Zuoyi. Plans were laid to attack the Communist headquarters south of Peking.

In *November* the Liberation Army was reorganised into field armies, local armies and guerillas.

In the Northeast 149,000 Nationalist troops were defeated and Shenyang fell to the Communists; this meant that the Northeast was now in their hands.

There was heavy fighting at Xuzhou [known as the battle of Huai-Hai], the second great battle in the civil war. The Nationalist generals Liu Shih and Du Yuming were defeated. Generals He Jifeng and Zhang Kexia surrendered. [These were the two underground Communist Party members mentioned in Chapter VII.]

Mao Zedong declared that it would take about a year to defeat the Kuomintang reactionary forces.

Speaking in Peking, Hu Shih [the celebrated initiator of the cultural modernisation of China in the 1920s] said that any compromise with the Communists would be illusory.

Fall of the city of Baoding, Hebei province. A regimental commander surrendered in a battle in East China. Fall of two cities, Shanhaiguan and Qinhuangdao on the east coast of North China.

In *December* Lin Biao's troops came south from the northeast and, joined by Generals Luo Ronghuan and Nie Rongzhen, approached Peking. Fall of Xuzhou in Central China. General Du Yuming flees. On the 20th Sun Fo, speaking in Nanjing, asserted the government's determination to fight. Zhang-jia-kuo in Hebei was taken by the Communists.

— 1949

On *January 1*, Chiang Kai Shek made peace proposals based on the existing government structure. On the 5th Mao wrote an article about [Kuomintang] war criminals.

The US Government abruptly turned down a request from the Chinese government for aid, with the comment: 'It might not be of any use.'

West of Xuzhou two military corps led by Du Yuming, the general who had used gas at the Xuzhou battle, were defeated. One commander was killed and another escaped.

On the 14th Mao Zedong declared that he was ready for peace talks with the government on the basis of eight conditions, including punishment of war criminals, confiscation of major properties and the establishment of a coalition government which excluded all reactionaries — in other words, total surrender.

Fall of the city of Tianjin and of two cities in Anhui province, Bengbu and Hefei.

On the 21st Chiang Kai Shek retired and Li Zongren became acting President. Li declared that he was ready to talk and nominated five delegates, Shao Lizi, Zhang Zhizhong, Huang Shaohong, Peng Zhaoxian and Zhong Tianxin. The Communist spokesman declared that, since the reactionary Nanjing government still had some military power, they [the Communists] would be ready to talk after the liberation of Peking, but they would not accept Peng Zhaoxian, who was a criminal. [The Communists were well aware of who was who: as soon as their government was established, the first three of the five Kuomintang delegates joined them.]

Mao Zedong protested against the acquittal of a Japanese general named Okamura by a National government military court.

On the 31st the Liberation Army entered Peking.

In *February* a Nationalist army commander was taken prisoner in Hubei province. On the 5th the Executive Yuan of the government moved to Canton. The Liberation Army occupied five towns in central Shaanxi province.

Thirty-five 'democratic gentlemen', including Guo Moruo, Ma Shulun, Shen Junru and Li Jishen [who were all to play leading roles in the People's Republic] came from the Northeast to Peking and were solemnly received.

In *March* the Communist Party held a Central Committee Plenum in Pingshan county, south of Peking. On the 25th the Central Committee moved to Peking.

The Communists nominated a six-man team, headed by Zhou Enlai, for talks with the Kuomintang.

In *April* the Kuomintang reactionary government sent six men, headed by Zhang Zhizhong, to Peking, but the Kuomintang turned down the Communists' eight conditions.

The [Communist] Youth Corps [League] held its first national conference in Peking.

The United States Congress decided that the portion of the 1948 aid budget not yet transferred to China should be delivered to the 'Kuomintang reactionary government'.

On the 16th Huang Shaohong and Qu Wu, who had represented the Kuomintang at the negotiations, flew to Nanjing with the Communists' proposals. The proposals were turned down.

Mao and Zhu De ordered the guerillas in South China, the Second Field Army led by Liu Bocheng and Deng Xiaoping, and the Third Field Army led by Chen Yi, to prepare to go on the offensive.

The administration of the Kuomintang government moved from Nanjing to Shanghai and Canton. On the 23rd the Liberation Army entered Nanjing. The next day Taiyuan city, capital of Shanxi province, was occupied and the commander was taken prisoner. On the 27th Suzhou was taken.

In *May* Xi'an, the capital of Shaanxi province, was taken and the Fourth Field Army of Lin Biao and Luo Ronghuan liberated Wuhan.

In *June* the cities of Yulin, in north Shaanxi, and Qingdao, in Shandong, were occupied. On the 15th a preparatory meeting of the Political Consultative Conference was held in Peking. It elected Mao Zedong as Chairman and Zhou Enlai, Li Jishen, Shen Junru, Guo Moruo and Chen Shutong as Vice-Chairmen.

In *July* Baoji city in Shaanxi was taken [for the second time] and 43,000 enemy troops were annihilated. A preparatory committee of the Sino-Soviet Friendship Association was founded.

In *August* two cities, Tianshui in the northwestern province of Gansu, and Zhuzhou in Hunan province, were taken, and the commander of the Hunan troops, Chen Mingren, and the governor of Hunan, Cheng Qian, surrendered. The capital of Gansu province, Lanzhou, and the capital of Fujian, Fuzhou, were liberated.

In *September* the capital of Qinghai province, Sining, and the capital of Ningxia province, Yinchuan, were taken, and the Nationalist governor of Xinjiang, Tao Shiyueh, and the head of the Xinjiang government, Burhan, telegraphed their surrender to the Communists.

On the 30th the Chinese People's Political Consultative Conference was opened in Peking, and Mao was elected head of the government. On *October 1*, the Chinese People's Republic was officially established.

In April 1950, Hainan Island was occupied. In October 1951 the Liberation Army entered Lhasa.

Between July 1946 and June 1950, 8 million Kuomintang troops had been defeated. 4.5 million were taken prisoner, 1.7 million were killed and 290,000 were absorbed into the Liberation Army.[2]

The above summing-up of events in the period 1947–9 reveals how the Communists saw those events, and in that context is instructive. It shows deep hatred of the United States, though it is admitted that Washington was reluctant to give aid, even economic aid, to the Chinese government in its fight against the Communists. It shows even greater hatred of Chiang Kai Shek and his regime. The nation's legitimate government is consistently called the 'reactionary Kuomintang government'.

Politically aware intellectuals were divided. Some were loyal to the Nationalists, others to the Communists. Those who supported the Communists were referred to as the 'democratic gentlemen'. They fared well in the first few years of the People's Republic, but were later rejected.

From these Communist accounts it is clear that, as we said earlier, the Nationalist generals were brave soldiers. Many of them fought to the end and either fell in battle or were taken prisoner.

An interesting point in the account is that Communist activities and victories were all in the North. But even there Shaanxi (where the Communist base of Yan'an was located) resisted, and the city of Baoji had to be 'liberated' twice. The South — the immense territories south of the Yangze — and West and Southwest China were in the hands of the government.

Why was it that the Nationalist government could not form a line of defence, as it had done in the Southwest against the mighty Japanese army? The answer can only be a matter for speculation. History seems to prove that those who control the Northeast (Manchuria), being unimpeded by geographical barriers, can penetrate into the wide North Chinese plains and cross the Yellow River in winter when the water level is low. After that, there are no more natural obstacles until the Yangze is reached, which cuts China in two. This was what happened in the middle of the seventeenth century when the Manchus poured out of Manchuria and overthrew the Ming dynasty. Three hundred years later the Japanese invasion also started from Manchuria. The Manchus were halted in the South for many years. It is true to say, of course, that the Manchus were a foreign race whose only advantage was their military prowess. The Communists were Chinese and their propaganda, spread by the underground Party apparatus, portrayed the Nationalist regime in a very bad light and promised all manner of good things in the future. Communism was to mean 'liberation' from all social evils.

The Japanese invasion was halted when the Nationalist government, the same government that was to collapse under the Communist attack, became part of a worldwide anti-fascist bloc in the Second World War. China received help from the Allies, but after the war, when facing the Communist threat, the Nationalist government did not get similar outside support; disappointment with the Chiang Kai Shek regime had had a paralysing effect on Washington. The Communist propaganda was not less but perhaps more effective outside China than inside.

Mao was a far-sighted politician. Already in his remote headquarters in Yan'an, he spoke as if he ruled China, inspiring optimism, whereas the Nationalist government was on the defensive. But the Communists themselves, as can be seen from the list of events mentioned earlier, did not expect victory in 1949. They were busy consolidating the territories they had gained, by introducing land reform.

Land reform

Land reform lay dormant for several years during the Japanese war. It was re-introduced after the war, and was carried out with growing intensity. Its purpose can hardly have been the reform of agriculture in the turbulent days of the civil war — when normal economic reform was hardly practicable. The political purpose, winning over peasants by giving them land and eliminating hostile elements in the villages, was more important.

On May 4, 1946, the 'Party Central' — whatever this may mean — published an instruction entitled 'Reduction of Rent and the Question of Land', which in the Party was referred to later simply as the May 4th Instruction. The implementation of this instruction was called a 'struggle', and a struggle it turned out to be.

In July 1947 a Party meeting expressed disappointment that in some regions the policy had not been implemented. This meeting, led by Liu Shaoqi, published an 'Outline of Chinese Land Law', which was not less but more radical than the May 4th Instruction. Going beyond a mere reduction of rents, it decreed that all landlords' properties and all temple lands and ancestral halls were to be confiscated. The land was to be divided evenly among the poor peasants. Poor Peasants' Committees were to be established. People's Courts, with no laws other than this rude charter, were established to decide the fate of the landowners. Simultaneously a purge of the Party was ordered; all those who belonged to landlord or rich peasant families were to be expelled.

In October 1947 a Party Central Committee Decision pressed for executions, and executions, in the literal sense, were carried out on a large scale. Three months later, in January 1948, urgent inner-Party instructions were issued in an effort to put an end to the excesses and to restore normal agricultural production, which was being disrupted by the prevailing violence.[3]

In February 1948 Mao himself felt it necessary to put the brakes on the brutality, which he called an 'ultra-left' trend. Too much power had been given to the local peasants. They had turned on landlords (and of this Mao did not disapprove) but they had also turned on what he called 'middle peasants' and on those engaged in local manufacture and trade. Such excesses had been deliberately, and in Mao's view wrongly, encouraged by the Party's own newspapers and radio stations.[4]

We Communists are opposed to killing people, Ren Bishi, Mao's close collaborator, wrote in the Party magazine *Masses* in February 1948; but this does not apply to wicked landlords and counter-revolutionaries. Sentences on these, however, should be passed by the People's Courts.[5]

The Party leadership was against indiscriminate killing, but not against the execution of the Party's enemies or of landlords. 'Landlord' was an elastic term. In the northern and northwestern regions of China, where the Communists had power, there were no *latifundia* with absentee landowners. If there had been any, they would have been living in the cities beyond the reach of the Communists. The land reform — as carried out during the civil war in the Communist-ruled territories, and after 1949 everywhere — was a reign of terror, designed to impose the political will of the Party on the villages.

The last Party meetings

After the July 1947 Party meeting on land reform, mentioned earlier, the Party leaders held three more meetings before entering Peking.

The first was held in December the same year in Mizhi county in the north of Shaanxi province. At that time there was no serious consideration of the possibility of a quick take-over of the administration of the whole country. Decisions were taken on the land reform, on military affairs, on the United Front policy and on the economy.

On military affairs: caution was prescribed; the small towns should be taken first, and then the middle-sized ones, before the large ones were tackled; battle should not be launched without due preparation and a prospect of success; small towns should be attacked only when they were poorly defended.

On United Front Policy: all possible people outside the Party, particularly 'democratic gentlemen', should be brought into alliance, but all should be under the guidance of the Communist Party.

Only in the deliberations on economic policy was much thought given to the future. The property of large owners was to be expropriated but not the property of others; small capitalists were to be tolerated for a long time. The structure of the economy was to consist of the state economy, leading the whole economy; a gradually collectivised rural economy; and a middle-sized capitalist economy — small factories and shops.

The next meeting, this time a meeting of the Politbureau, was held in September 1948 at a village called Xi-bai-po in Ping-shan county. The meeting discussed the problem of how to find enough men to administer the greatly enlarged territories ruled by the Communists, the population of which was estimated at '50–100 million'. (In the fluid military and political situation, no exact computation of area or population was possible.)

In territories where power had already been consolidated, Party congresses were to be held. The widely-scattered liberated areas should all obey the 'Party Central'. A Decision was published on the 'Method of Asking Permissions from and Reporting to the Party Central', by all central bureaux, branch bureaux, military areas and branches of the (central) military committee. Criteria were given for deciding which actions needed prior approval by the highest leaders and which should be reported after the fact. Moreover, 'the greatest effort should be made to overcome lax discipline and anarchic attitudes and to end regionalism and guerilla-ism, thus concentrating power in the Central and the organs representing the Central.' Obviously the widely-scattered 'liberated areas' did not always report their activities to Mao and did not always ask for approval of major actions.

The meeting was attended by Mao Zedong, Zhou Enlai, Liu Shaoqi, Zhu De, Ren Bishi, Peng Zhen and Dong Biwu (all Politbureau members), and by Deng Yingchao, Liao Chengzhi, Nie Rongzhen, Teng Taiyuan, Chen Yi, Rao Shushi, Zeng Shan, Deng Xiaoping, Xu Xiangzhen, Bo Yibo, Ye Jianying, Liu Lantao, Zhang Dingcheng and He Long (all Central Committee members). In addition, Hu Yaobang, Li Weihan, Yang Shangkun, Hu Qiaomu and six others were present.

The third Party meeting was again held in the village of Xi-bai-po, Ping-shan county, in March 1949. This was the second Central Committee Plenum. The first had been held four years earlier, immediately after the Seventh Party Congress in Yan'an. Thirty-four Central Committee members were present at this second Plenum. Mao Zedong, Liu Shaoqi, Zhou Enlai and Zhu De headed the list.

The Liberation Army was already in Peking and Tianjin at this time, though it had not yet taken Shanghai or several other large cities. It was only at this Party meeting — the quick victory had come as a surprise — that policies for running the country were first discussed. Hitherto, it was said, our work has been done in the villages. Now the Party 'will have to make the greatest efforts to learn how to administer the cities. There will be struggle in the cities against imperialism, against the Kuomintang, against the bourgeois class, struggle in politics, in the economy, in the fields of culture and foreign relations. There must be open struggle as well as secret struggle . . . step by step.'

(Other new governments promise peace. The Communists promised 'struggle'.) It will be necessary to bring all people, including the 'democratic gentlemen' into alliance; 'make allies of them through criticism and struggle'.

The capital of bureaucrats was to be confiscated, the meeting decided. Individual farmers and artisans were to be left as they were for a long time (this was to mean three or four years), but they were to be led to collectivisation and modernisation. There was to be a state economy and a collective economy and a gradual transition from New Democracy to Socialism.

The private business of the 'national bourgeoisie' was to survive for a long time (in fact for six years), but was to be directed for the benefit of the national economy, to be restricted by tax and price policies and labour discipline, and to be restrained from further capital development.

International obligations assumed by the Kuomintang (the outgoing government) were not to be recognised, but foreign relations were to be established with all countries on the principle of equality, and trade was to be carried on with both socialist and capitalist countries. Foreigners in China were to be protected.

The austere spirit of the Party would have to be maintained. Party members would be exposed in the cities to 'sugar-coated shells', i.e. to corruption by the bourgeoisie. They must be cautious and humble.

A special recommendation of the meeting was the prohibition of any cult of leadership: Mao Zedong proposed that in order to prevent the exaltation of persons — he must have been thinking of Stalin — the birthdays of leaders should not be celebrated, and no city, street or enterprise should be named after a leader.[6]

CHAPTER X

DIRTY LINEN

No city, street or enterprise was named after any leader, but on October 1, 1949, Mao and the other leaders appeared on the balcony above the main gate of the Imperial Palace — something that no Emperor had ever done. Mao and his colleagues took up their quarters in the Forbidden City of the Emperors, and postage stamps were issued bearing a picture of the triumphant leader.

The People's Republic was called New China. A few months after the take-over — the Liberation, as it was called — an English-language booklet was published by the Foreign Language Press in Peking: it was called *A Guide to New China*.

The Party leaders were displayed as mirrors of devotion and honesty: they were the immaculate leaders of the New China. One of the most peculiar features of the day, and of the years that followed, was the complete silence about the past life of the Party. Only the military glories were written about — usually without the names of the participants — and of course the Long March. Both inside China and outside, the Long March was celebrated as an epic event in the history of mankind.

There was much to keep silent about in the early history of the Party — mutual jealousies, persecutions, imprisonments, betrayals and executions. The new men were guerilla fighters, not 'democratic gentlemen'. Only a few did not have blood on their hands.

Old enmities did not cease with the entry into Peking. Behind the immaculate facade of the New Heaven and New Earth there were smouldering ashes, ready to burst into flames. There were Mao's old enemies. There was Gao Gang, supported by the Russians. There were high military leaders who dared to speak their minds. There were the 'democratic gentlemen' who, a few years later, when they had learnt what the regime was really like, came out in a chorus of disapproval. There were those who knew the private life of the second-rate Shanghai film actress who had become Mao's fourth wife in Yan'an. These are but a few examples. We have already discussed the Communist master-spy, Pan Hannian (see pp.124–7), who was imprisoned a few years after the establishment of the People's Republic. His sad fate was not made public for thirty years.

During his lifetime, Mao was the only star. Only after his death were the merits of past Party leaders proclaimed in print; as long as Mao was alive their names could not be mentioned. To understand the People's Republic, to find out who its leaders were, one must look back and dig up old scores. As with Party history in general, information about these internal struggles is now available for the earlier decades, the 1920s and 1930s, published after a delay of half a century. About periods closer to the present, however, little is known.

Death of a traitor

We have already come across one of the earliest Communists, Peng Pai, who established a rural revolutionary base before Mao did, situated on the southern borders of China. At the end of 1927, after the futile attempt to capture the city of Nanchang, Peng Pai's village base provided a refuge for the demoralised troops. At the Sixth Chinese Communist Party Congress, held in Moscow in September 1928, he was elected to the Politbureau, though he himself did not go to Moscow. In the following month Peng Pai was betrayed to the Kuomintang, arrested and executed. He was thirty-two.[1]

Fifty-three years later, in 1981, a provincial newspaper wrote about the man who had betrayed Peng Pai. His name was Bai Xin and he worked in the Military Committee of the Party leadership. He betrayed Peng Pai and three other Communist leaders. After the betrayal, 'Bai Xin, knowing that the underground Party organisation deals mercilessly with traitors', intended to flee to Europe; but though he was guarded by government police, he was killed by Chen Geng at the last moment. Chen Geng had kept him under surveillance. Bai Xin got an attack of malaria and went to one Dr Ke Lin for treatment, not knowing that the doctor was a secret underground Party member. Dr Ke Lin then told Chen Geng where Bai Xin, the betrayer of Peng Pai, was staying, and Chen Geng went there and killed him.[2]

Chen Geng and Dr Ke Lin were honorable gentlemen. Chen Geng was born in 1904, and was in the Kuomintang military academy at Whampoa in the 1920s. He had a distinguished career in the Red Army, and under the People's Republic he was governor of Yunnan province; he died in 1961. Ke Lin, born in 1901, became a distinguished doctor under the People's Republic. Before the Cultural Revolution he was President and 1st Party secretary of Zhong Shan Medical College in Canton, one of the leading medical schools in China. During the Cultural Revolution he was denounced as a counter-revolutionary. After Mao's death he was rehabilitated and became a consultant in the Ministry for Public Health.

The Longhua 'martyrs'

In 1931 Lu Xun, the celebrated writer, wrote an emotion-laden article glorifying 'the blood of proletarian revolutionary writers'. Zhou Enlai also wrote commemorating the 'martyrs'. On January 17, 1931, these martyrs, twenty-three young Communists, members of the underground Communist literary movement, were executed by the government at a place called Longhua on the outskirts of Shanghai. Among the twenty-three were four who had studied in Moscow in the years 1924–6.

January 1931 was a turbulent month in Party history. A few days before the execution of the twenty-three, the Fourth Central Committee Plenum was held in Shanghai. This was the meeting at which the 'returned students', the students of Mif (who did not himself take part in the meeting), asserted their authority. The leadership was sharply divided, and two lists of candidates deemed suitable for membership of the Politbureau were presented, one by Luo Zhanglong and one by Wang Ming. What Wang Ming presented was the list approved by the Far Eastern Bureau of the Comintern; Luo Zhanglong was expelled from the Party.[3]

In 1980 a long article in a Peking magazine described how the twenty-three martyrs were betrayed by their comrades. How could the twenty-three be betrayed simultaneously? it asked. Party members, divided into small cells, did not know one another. Only the highest leadership knew all the cells: they must have been betrayed by Wang Ming.[4]

It is impossible to say whether this is the whole story. Wang Ming was not the head of the Party; he had just been elected to the Politbureau. Others, including Zhou Enlai, also knew about the Party's organisational structure. The whole truth about how the twenty-three were betrayed may never be revealed. What is certain is that a large number of the Party's intellectual élite were sent to their death by someone in the very heart of the Party.

Luo Zhanglong

Luo Zhanglong, one of Mao's earliest companions, attended the Eighth

Party Congress in Moscow. After his expulsion from the Party in 1931 he was heavily criticised in the 1945 'Resolution on Some Historical Problems', contained in the third volume of Mao's *Selected Works*. Forty-eight years after his condemnation, the elderly Luo, then aged eighty-three, reappeared, was elected to the Chinese People's Political Consultative Council, and became a consultant to the Chinese Museum of Revolution.[5] In 1980 he published reminiscences dealing not with his troubled years, but with the early 1920s.[6]

Luo Zhanglong opposed the 'returned students' and was therefore expelled from the Party. It may seem odd that he, who had opposed Mao's enemies, was condemned by Mao in 1945. But he had also opposed Stalin's emissaries. The Chinese Communists could not afford to oppose Stalin. Luo was even accused of having been a Trotskyite.[7]

Trotskyites in Moscow

The influence of Trotsky on young Chinese Communists who studied in Moscow in the mid-1920s had been greater than had previously been admitted. In 1983 an article on an unknown Communist 'martyr', Yu Xiusong, who went to Moscow in November 1925, said that the Chinese students in Moscow were sharply divided, and that a group called the 'Jiangsu-Zhejiang Association' was ostracised by Wang Ming and other students of Mif in 1927 — the year when Stalin defeated Trotsky. The 'Jiangsu-Zhejiang Association' was labelled counter-revolutionary, and Yu Xiusong and his companions were branded as Trotskyists. Yu Xiusong, who was working in Xinjiang in June 1938, was sent to the Soviet Union, and was executed there in the Great Purge at the age of thirty-nine. In 1959 a military court in the Far East Military Region of the Soviet Union rehabilitated him posthumously. In 1962 the Chinese Communist Party gave him the title of 'martyr', but this Party decision was not made public. Indeed his name, the 1983 article said, never appeared in Party history.[8] A very odd story indeed!

This article does not mention the name of Luo Zhanglong, the old companion of Mao who opposed the Stalinist group of 'returned students' led by Mif and Wang Ming at the January 1931 Party meeting. In the Soviet Union, in the period before Stalin came to full power, there was, one may conclude, an important group of young Chinese Communists who followed the doctrine of Trotsky and were opposed to the Chinese Communist Party's taking orders from Stalin. They could well have been described as Chinese Communist nationalists who rejected Soviet Stalinist influence. Compared with them, Mao Zedong was a practitioner of *realpolitik*. He was opposed to Wang Ming but not to the Soviet Union and not to Stalin.

The Chinese Trotskyites were never numerous, but for many years they constituted an irritant in Mao's Party. When they came back from Moscow in 1929, they divided into tiny groups. In the early 1930s they were imprisoned by the Nationalist government. They were released in 1937, and in the following year, under the direct influence of Trotsky (who was to be assassinated in 1940), they held a congress; but they split again. Scarcely any of the Trotskyite groups had more than a hundred members.[9] Yet as late as 1980, some Trotskyites in Hong Kong — so Deng Liqun, head of Party propaganda, said in 1981 — established contact with, and sent money to, some restless elements in China.[10]

Gu Shunzhang

On December 10, 1931, the 'Soviet Provisional Central Government People's Committee' in Ruijin ordered the arrest of a counter-revolutionary, Gu Shunzhang.[11] A political party has no authority to order arrests; but the Communist Party has always acted as a state within a state.

The indignation that spurred the Party to move against Gu Shunzhang was understandable. Gu was the head of the 'Special Affairs Unit' of the Party — in other words, head of the Party's secret police. He was arrested by the Nationalist government in April 1931, and disclosed the names of many Party members.[12] As a result of Gu's information, Xiang Zhongfa, who had been made head of the Party at the Sixth Party Congress in Moscow, was arrested and executed. So also was another well-known Communist, Yun Daying. Chen Geng, who had killed a renegade Party member with his own hands, was also arrested, but he escaped. Gu revealed the underground addresses of Zhou Enlai and Li Weihan in Shanghai, but they too escaped.[13] When in Hong Kong, Gu revealed the identity of Cai Hesen, one of Mao's earliest companions and an active leader of the Party. The Hong Kong authorities handed Cai over to the authorities in Canton, and he was executed there at the age of thirty-six.[14]

Li Qiang, vice-minister of foreign trade in the 1950s and minister in the late 1970s, recalled in 1978 the events to which he had been an eyewitness. The traitor Gu Shunzhang, he wrote, was arrested by the Nationalist government in April 1931. He sent a secret telegram to Nanjing asking for an interview with Chiang Kai Shek. The telegram was addressed to Xu Enzeng, who was related to Yao Wenyuan (one of the 'Gang of Four' of the Cultural Revolution), but it was seen in transit by an underground Communist agent working in the Nanjing government 'and this man came immediately to Shanghai to inform us. That evening Zhou Enlai, Chen Geng and I myself moved house and thus we were not arrested. To avoid further danger, I was sent to Moscow.'

Gu Shunzhang joined the Kuomintang secret agency, the Blue Shirts, but he caused trouble there too, and he was executed on the orders of Chen Lifu (an important Kuomintang leader).

Zhou Enlai

In the same article Li Qiang recalls the story of a workers' uprising in April 1927 in Shanghai, which he calls a 'successful liberation of the city of Shanghai, planned, organised and led by Zhou Enlai, a glorious feat that will always be remembered'. The uprising was bloodily suppressed by the government. One of the victims was Chen Yannian, the eldest son of Chen Duxiu. Zhou Enlai escaped unharmed; he was shrewd enough to leave Shanghai in time.

Li Qiang wrote this in criticism of the 'Gang of Four', who during the Cultural Revolution accused Zhou Enlai of having caused the deaths of Party members.[15]

Fang Zhimin

Another well-known figure in Party history is Fang Zhimin of Jiangxi province, the province in which Mao established his headquarters, first in Jing Gang Shan in the southwest, and then at Ruijin on the southeastern border of the province. Fang Zhimin was a revolutionary in Jiangxi years before Mao arrived. It is quite probable that the two were rivals, but party historians take great pains to dispel such suspicions. After Fang's death in 1935, Mao praised his memory on several occasions. His activities had been carried on in the north of the province, hundreds of kilometres away from Mao's headquarters. In those days there were several military bases in Southeast China independent from Mao. The true situation between the two men is not known.

Party historians have since described conflicts, bloody conflicts, that took place not between Fang and Mao, but between Fang and the emissaries of the central leadership of the Party. However, they do not explain who constituted the 'central leadership'. In that period, 1931–5, the Party leadership was in a state of flux. Some of the leaders, such as Zhou Enlai and Wang Jiaxiang, as we saw earlier, had left Shanghai, the seat of the Party leadership, and gone to Ruijin in 1931; the others followed in 1933.

What is certain is that internecine strife was raging among the Communist guerilla forces.

Fang Zhimin's brother, Fang Zhichun, who under the People's Republic was governor of his native province of Jiangxi, recounted what had happened to his brother half a century after the events took place. Obviously he is not an impartial observer.

In 1931, he says, the 'leftist opportunist Party Central of Wang Ming' sent a plenipotentiary in the person of Zeng Hongyi to the northeast of Jiangxi province. This man summoned a Party congress there and came out strongly against Fang Zhimin, calling him an adventurist. He started a purge (*Sufan*) and 'arrested and killed many "masses" and leading cadres who were opposed to him'. Comrade Fang Zhimin offered stiff resistance, and Zeng accused him of resisting the purge. Fang was put under arrest, forced to confess, and deprived of his leading Party and military responsiblities.

Early in 1933 when the government troops were pressing the Communists, Fang again collected some troops, but Zeng frustrated his efforts. Ultimately Fang turned to the Party leadership (then in Ruijin) and Zeng was removed from the area.

Another account, written a year later by the same Fang Zhichun, says that at the end of 1932 Fang Zhimin, then at the height of his power, had an army of 30,000 and established a 'soviet government' ruling dozens of counties in Jiangxi, Anhui, Zhejiang and Fujian provinces, a territory containing 1 million inhabitants.

Fang again found himself in trouble when the decisions of the Central Committee's Fifth Plenum reached northeast Jiangxi early in 1934. No further elucidation of this is given. The Fifth Plenum was held in January 1934 in Ruijin, under the leadership of men who had come from Shanghai and were opposed to Mao. It is said that in October 1934, on the instructions of the Party leadership, Fang moved with his troops to Anhui. We are not told who constituted the 'Party leadership'. The Long March had started from Ruijin two months earlier, in August 1934. Fang's troops were routed in

Anhui and he returned to northeast Jiangxi, where he was betrayed and arrested in January 1935; a few months later he died. In prison he produced some remarkable revolutionary writings which were later published and had a great influence on the Party.[16]

Why the Long March?

For forty-eight years the official Party history maintained that the base at Ruijin, which had been held for five and a half years, had to be abandoned because of the overwhelming strength of the government forces, and that the Communist forces' inability to resist was due to the fact that the defence at Ruijin was led by the wrong men, not by Mao.[17] In 1982 another and very different reason was put forward in a book written by two teachers at Amoy University. The Peking quarterly *Modern History Studies* has summed up a section of their book as follows:

Why could the Red Army not resist the [government forces'] Fifth Extermination Campaign; why had it to abandon the terrain and flee to the far west? For a long time this question has agitated minds. In a word, it was the result of the wrong leftist Wang Ming Line. [Wang Ming was in Moscow, but traditionally all actions directed against Mao have been attributed to the 'Wang Ming Line'.] There were more important reasons, however: *a.* the huge enemy force; *b.* the incorrectness of our Line; and *c.* the internecine feuds in our ranks. That the Line was incorrect, that our forces were weak, are common knowledge. But mention of internecine feuds was taboo in Party history and was shunned like the plague. This book reveals the grave error committed in the purge in the west Fujian base. The purge in west Fujian, which lasted a year and two months and raged throughout the whole soviet area, began in December 1930 with the Futian Incident. A great number of Party cadres and masses were accused of belonging to the Social-Democratic Party and lost their lives. The number reached 4,000 to 5,000. In fact no Social-Democratic Party at all existed in west Fujian, and there were no Party members of that kind. This purge weakened our forces severely and led to collapse and military defeat: the soviet area shrank rapidly. That west Fujian purge was a great tragedy. Many years have passed and one may now reflect on what happened.

If the Party had drawn a lesson from the purges of those years, which occurred in every base, if it had learnt a lesson from the errors of the 'Saving Campaign' of later years [in Yan'an in 1943, see below under 'Kang Shang'], then it would have been possible to avoid the errors committed after the Party had gained power in the country [in 1949] and the murderous tragedies of the great ten-year disorder [the Cultural Revolution].[18]

Party history has many secrets, including what happened in the Ruijin base. We saw earlier (Chapter II) that the Party leadership in Shanghai charged Mao with committing excesses in the purges and sent men to Ruijin to take over the running of affairs.

The revolutionary base in west Fujian, the 1982 book says, began well before Mao went to Ruijin (which is in Jiangxi on the Fujian border). The first to start agitation in Fujian was Deng Zihui (head of village works in the 1950s, who died in 1972). In 1929 and 1930 Mao and Zhu De's troops went to west Fujian with the intention of setting up a base there. In September 1931 that area of west Fujian was incorporated into the Ruijin base. Thus the Ruijin base controlled twenty-one counties with a population of 2.5 million people. When the Long March began, the leaders in west Fujian (Deng Zihui and the others) were left behind, and they kept up guerilla fighting for three more years. [19]

All this is still obscure, and leaves many questions unanswered. How could inner-Party violence continue after the Shanghai leadership had moved to Ruijin in 1933? Who was pursuing whom? One thing is clear, though it was not revealed until forty-eight years after the event: comrades were killing comrades, not in tens or hundreds but in thousands, and this was kept secret — although the Party leaders must have known it — for many years.

The book in question draws the melancholy conclusion: inner-Party violence has never ended.

He Long

He Long was one of the military heroes of the war against the Japanese and of the civil war. In 1955 he was promoted to Marshal. In 1966, at the beginning of the Cultural Revolution, he stood next to Mao in a moving jeep, surveying the millions of jubilant Red Guards at the Tian An Men Square. A few months later the waves of the Cultural Revolution swept over him. He was arrested by the Red Guards — this could not have happened without Mao's consent. He suffered from diabetes, but was neglected while imprisoned, and died on June 9, 1969.

In 1974, while Mao was still alive, he was posthumously rehabilitated and on the sixth anniversary of his death, June 9, 1975, a funeral service, at which Zhou Enlai spoke, was held in his honour. His fame was proclaimed in many articles, books and plays; he is now a national hero.

He Long was one of the most colourful figures in the history of the People's Republic. The following is derived from two articles written about him. One was written in 1978 by General Liao Hansheng, a

follower of He Long since his youth and an outstanding political commissar in the army before and after the Cultural Revolution. The other
account was published in the book *Biographies of Personalities in Party History*, published in 1981.

He Long was born in Hunan in 1896. At the age of fourteen, joining
some companions armed with a few rifles, he took up the life of a bandit.
He never had any chance of going to school. He was, as Party history
says, a revolutionary, indeed a born revolutionary. In 1924, when he
was twenty-eight, he was a member of Sun Yat Sen's revolutionary
army. He took part in the abortive uprising on August 1, 1927, at Nanchang, along with Zhou Enlai, Zhu De and Ye Ting. After Nanchang,
he became a Party member, recruited by Zhou. In November he went to
Hong Kong and from there to Shanghai.

The Party wanted to send him to study in the Soviet Union, but he
objected: 'I scarcely know Chinese; how could I learn Russian?'[20]

He Long was not the only semi-literate top military leader. Mao, it is
said, took pride in the fact that some of his best generals had never been
to school, and he would assert that China's best emperors had been illiterate.[21] He had a deep-rooted disdain for people who came from families
with a long cultural tradition of refinement and civilised manners. He
felt at home with semi-literate ruffians who, like himself, sat at table
with their caps on, spat on the floor and used coarse language, but were
intrepid Party fighters. They were loyal to their comrades and merciless
to their enemies.

He Long was a tough man. In 1931 the Party leadership in Shanghai,
which was under the influence of the 'returned students', sent one of
their number, Xia Xi, to check on He Long's movements in the west of
Hubei province.

Xia Xi was named head of the Central Committee's Hunan-West-
Hubei Party Bureau. He reorganised He Long's troops completely, took
over command and started a purge. All the chief officers were arrested
and a dozen of them were executed. According to the accounts, thou-
sands of people were killed. Thanks to the energetic intervention of He
Long, some of the officers escaped, including Wang Shangrong and
Huang Xinting, who later became leading figures in the Liberation
Army.

In 1932 and 1933 the troops had to move from place to place under
pressure from hostile government forces. Nevertheless Xia Xi continued
his purge, suspended the whole Party organisation in the army and went
on executing those opposed to him.

This is the account given by General Liao Hansheng, a relative of He Long, who was there on the spot. Another general, General Xiao Ke, who was fighting in the same region, whitewashed Xia Xi, saying that he merely carried out the mistaken orders of the pro-Moscow Party leadership then residing in Shanghai. Xiao Ke and Wang Zhen — another general with a long army career — had great respect for Xia Xi. (Xia Xi was drowned when crossing a river in 1936.)

In December 1933 when the Communist troops and He Long in particular were hard-pressed by the Nationalist forces, Chiang Kai Shek employed a former friend of He Long's to contact him. He Long reported this to the Hunan-West-Hubei Party Bureau, which gave him permission to meet the emissary. The man arrived, but He Long lost his temper and ordered his execution.[22]

The killing of a peace envoy was not an act of gallantry, but it was not this aspect of the meeting that was held against him. The *Biographies of Personalities in Party History*, written in 1981, recalls that when He Long was arrested in 1967 the Red Guards accused him of having betrayed the Party and asked him what he had talked about with Chiang's envoy in 1933 and what agreement he had made with him. He Long again lost his temper, banged the table and said, 'Beat the devil of your mother! That man was killed by me.' (The words may not be authentic, but that was probably the kind of language He Long used.) This 1981 account does not blame He Long for having killed a peace envoy. On the contrary, this is regarded as a laudable act that proved that He Long was not negotiating with the enemy. In fact He Long had the permission of the Party authorities to kill the man. The relevant document is still in the Party archives.

It seems to have occurred to nobody in the Communist Party, either in 1933 or in 1981, that killing an officially accepted peace envoy from the enemy is not a proper thing to do.

In the *Biographies of Personalities in Party History* it is recalled that He Long and his men began their Long March in October 1935, the month in which Mao finished his. He's journey is also called a Long March. In July 1936 he and his men joined the troops of Zhang Guotao and Zhu De. However, it is not alleged that He Long and Zhu De cooperated with Zhang, who was not a friend of Mao's. On the contrary, to exonerate Zhu De and He Long, all Party historians assert that they both opposed Zhang Guotao. In October 1936, a year after Mao, He Long arrived in north Shaanxi, where Mao was then stationed.[23]

Zhou Enlai was noted for his loyalty to his comrades, and he saved

many of them during the Cultural Revolution; but his loyalty had its
limits. When He Long was in trouble during the Cultural Revolution,
Zhou let him and his wife stay in his own house, but only for a few days.
When resentment against He Long grew stronger, he sent them to live
by themselves in a house in the western hills of Peking. There they were
caught by the Red Guards. Nevertheless, at the funeral service for He
Long in 1975, as was mentioned earlier, it was Zhou Enlai who delivered
the eulogy.

Suspicions: Chen Yi

Fang Zhichun, brother of the Fang Zhimin whom we discussed before,
has recalled a conversation he had with Marshal Chen Yi. He told Chen
Yi a story about him that he had heard from Zhou Enlai when he met
Zhou in Moscow in 1939. Zhou told him that when Chen Yi reported to
a comrade named Tan Yubao that the Communists would have to
cooperate with the Nationalist troops in fighting the Japanese invaders
and that Tan and his troops would have to leave the mountains and come
down to fight the Japanese, Tan, thinking that Chen Yi had turned
traitor, arrested him. (Tan Yubao was a Hunanese who before the Cultural Revolution was a member of the provincial Party committee of
Hunan.[24]) In the same period the Party sent a man called Guan Ying to
bring the same message to a Communist commander, Yang Wenhan.
Yang remembered that Guan Ying had deserted the Communist ranks
at an earlier period. Not trusting the man, and afraid of falling into a
trap, he took his revolver and shot him. Fang Zhichun asked Marshal
Chen Yi whether these stories were true and Chen Yi replied that they
were. It should be remembered that there were in fact cases in which
Party members had been cheated by traitors — 'were called down from
the mountains and were sacrificed'.[25]

It was dangerous to be a Party fighter, and the danger did not come
from the enemy alone; it could come from trigger-happy guerilla comrades too.

Yang Yong

Yang Yong, a distinguished general and a close ally of Deng Xiaoping's
in the 1980s, died in January 1983. In an article published in his memory,
it was recalled that at the end of 1949, after the establishment of the
People's Republic in Peking, Yang Yong's Communist troops were still

striving to conquer the Southwest of China. A government troop in Guizhou province surrendered and joined the Communist forces, but some of the surrendered troop killed Communist officials. In revenge, Yang Yong 'exterminated these bandits to the last man'.[26]

Going too far

After the rehabilitation of Liu Shaoqi in May 1980, many articles appeared honouring his memory, telling, for example, how he corrected deviations that occurred after the *Decision on the Thorough Fight Against Traitors* was published by the Party leadership in Yan'an in September 1939. In West Hunan — the territory where He Long had been active eight years earlier — under the pretext of pursuing traitors, 'many Party members and cadres were arrested and killed, and this caused great confusion among the ranks.' Comrade (later Marshal) Luo Ronghuan (died 1963) noticed these abuses when passing through the region and reported them to the Party leadership. The abuses did not stop. In the following year, 1940, they spread to Shandong province, where an inner-Party fight was being waged under the pretext of pursuing 'Trotskyist bandits'. Liu Shaoqi, in conjunction with Luo Ronghuan, stopped the abuses, ordering that 'confessions under torture should not be permitted and people should not be killed for no reason'.[27]

Kang Sheng in Yan'an

After the arrest of the 'Gang of Four' in 1976, Kang Sheng (died December 1975), who had been a leader of the Cultural Revolution team that condemned many Party leaders, was described as the devil, the persecutor and torturer of numerous Party members ever since the Yan'an days. One of his crimes was that he had distorted Mao's 1942 speech 'On Literature and Art' and had persecuted intellectuals, the educated, and literary and artistic comrades in the army. This was stated in 1980 by a group of leading army generals, among them Zhang Aiping, who in the 1980s was minister of defence. They were writing in memory of a little-known soldier, Xiao Xiangrong, who had been the head of the Eighth Route Army's Propaganda Department in 1938 and deputy secretary-general of the Party's Military Cor·mittee in the 1950s, and died in 1976 as a result of persecution by the 'Gang of Four'.

In 1942 Xiao organised a propaganda theatre group in Yan'an. Kang

Sheng denounced them as enemy agents, and many of them suffered physical injury.[28]

This is an obscure story, but since Kang Sheng could not have acted without Mao's authorisation, it seems to show that Mao's speech 'On Literature and Art' was not an academic exercise. It was already known that some notable Communist writers had been ostracised; but it was not known that Party propagandists within the Red Army had been treated so brutally.

According to a Peking press article published in 1980, Kang Sheng was the head of security in 1943 — during the Yan'an Rectification Campaign. Under the pretext of a salvaging operation, he brutally persecuted underground Party members when they came to the headquarters in Yan'an. Many were branded as counter-revolutionaries and accused of having formed their own Red Flag Party. Kang Sheng was quoted as having said that it was better to kill them than to let them get away.[29] That year (1943) was the time of the Yan'an Rectification campaign, of which so little is known. Kang Sheng (as we saw in Chapter IV), was second in seniority to Mao on the Central Study Committee in Yan'an, which led the Rectification. The Rectification was not a mere mental exercise; Mao imposed his will on the Party, and at the Seventh Party Congress in 1945, when it was over, all acclaimed Mao as the supreme leader.

The same story, the persecution by Kang Sheng of the alleged anti-Mao group called the Red Flag Party, was recorded in an article written in 1983 by Yang Xianzhen, for years the Party's leading philosopher; Wu Xiuquan, a very powerful figure both in the army and in the foreign ministry; and two other comrades. The article was written to commemorate a little-known Party member, Luo Yangshi, who died at the age of sixty-two in 1982, at which time he held the post of Party secretary of the Central Academy of Industrial Art.

Luo Yangshi, one learns, was from his very early days a fervent Party propagandist in Lanzhou, capital of Gansu province, in the Northwest. He converted his own family, and his home became a haven for underground Party activists. He was transferred to Yan'an, and there in 1943 Kang Sheng invented the story that he was running a secret anti-Party organisation, called the Gansu Red Flag Party. The whole Party organisation in and around Lanzhou was disbanded and Luo was imprisoned for three years.

Beginning with the Great Leap in 1958 and the persecution of 'rightists', Kang Sheng turned against the Party School (which explains why

Yang Xianzhen, leader of the Party School, signed the article). Luo Yangshi had the courage to stand up and criticise Kang Sheng by name. During the Cultural Revolution Kang Sheng turned against Luo, who was again arrested and spent two years in prison.[30]

Kang Sheng probably did nothing more than carry out Mao's wishes. After Mao's death, in the Deng Xiaoping era, it was admitted that Mao had made errors in 1958 and still greater errors during the Cultural Revolution. Yet Mao's early reputation remained intact. All his crimes were laid at the door of Kang Sheng, who, as everyone knew, was a Soviet-trained secret police chief.

A good security agent

In 1980 a man called Liang Guobin died, whose name few had heard, either inside China or outside. His life was described in a press announcement written in praise of his memory. One cannot read it without a sense of revulsion. Liang was a dedicated killer, typical of the Party's internal security forces.

He joined the revolution in 1927 and took part in fierce guerilla fighting. In 1939 he was in charge of security under Liu Shaoqi. Liu — who, we have been told, stopped excesses of brutality — instructed the security men to deal harshly with the Nationalists (with whom in those years the Communists were supposed to be cooperating).

In July 1940 the people of eight counties north of the Huai River revolted against Communist rule. Liang and his security men went into action and killed the leaders of the movement. Several times he protected and saved the Party leaders of the New Fourth Army. Always on the lookout for traitors in the Party, in 1942 he was made the deputy head of a department of the New Fourth Army, the Department for the Extirpation of Traitors. In 1949 when the Communist troops crossed the Yangze River, he was deputy head of the Social Department of the East China Bureau (the Social Department was the Chinese equivalent of the KGB). He took part in the Communist take-over of Shanghai and did excellent work in suppressing the Party's enemies, i.e. members of the Nationalist army, government and police. Sent to Fujian province, he became head of the security office of the Fujian provincial Party committee. There also, in two cities, Fuzhou and Xiamen, 'implementing the policy of the Party and Chairman Mao, he suppressed the counter-revolutionaries efficiently and finished off landlords, enemy agents and reactionary religious leaders.' People's masses, the report said, were happy and said that since the Communist Party was suppressing the counter-revolution, they would follow the Communist Party. In the ensuing years Liang acted similarly during the land reform and at the time of the Korean war. He received praise from Luo Ruiqing, the then minister of security in Peking.

During the Cultural Revolution Liang himself had a taste of what he had imposed on so many people. He was arrested and spent eight years in prison. However, unlike his victims, he was not 'suppressed', i.e. executed, and after the Cultural Revolution he continued to work for security in Shanghai. This Party butcher died heaped with honours.[31]

Part Two: 1949 – 1976

CHAPTER XI

RULING THE COUNTRY

The Communist troops entered Peking at the end of January 1949. Two months later the Party Central Committee moved there, and Mao and General Zhu De inspected a simple military parade at the airport. The city was not yet the capital of China and was called Peking (Beijing), 'northern capital'. It was still known as Peiping, 'northern peace'. The Nationalist government was still in Nanking (Nanjing, 'southern capital'). Yet the country's fate was sealed. The year 1949 was not one of victory for Marxism though it was the year ending military conquest by the Communist forces. This was not a Marxist conquest of the minds: there was no question of a popular vote or anything equivalent; nor was it a victory for the penetration of Marxist ideas into the Nationalist troops who had surrendered. It was the last stage of conquest by a newly-emerging force, a force which the Nationalist army in many important parts of the country resisted to the end. In April the Communists offered to negotiate with the Nationalists, but only under the most humiliating conditions. The Nationalists rejected this offer. At the end of April the Communist troops crossed the Yangze southwest of Nanjing. The government forces left the city and on the following day, April 24, the Communist troops entered it. On the same day they occupied the city of Taiyuan, capital of Shanxi in the Northwest; by May they were in Wuhan.

In the summer the Nationalist government was in Canton, in such complete disorder that — to speak from personal experience — one ministry did not know in what parts of the city other ministries were to be found. On June 30, Mao Zedong published his *On the People's Democratic Dictatorship*. In August the capitals of Hunan and Fujian provinces were taken.

The Communists, now assured of victory, held a constituent assembly, the People's Political Consultative Conference, in Peking, from

September 21–30, and on October 1 at the Tian An Men Square, Mao Zedong announced the establishment of the People's Republic with its capital in Peking. One day later, the Soviet Union recognised the new regime. Its ambassador to the Nationalist government had left Canton for the Soviet Union only four months earlier, and this same man, R.N. Roschin, arrived in Peking on October 10 as ambassador to the Communist regime. Two days later the Nationalist government moved from Canton to Zhongqing, and from there to Taiwan. On October 14, Communist troops entered Canton. In November and December other southern cities and Chengdu in the Southwest were occupied. Xinjiang surrendered in September but Tibet had not yet been taken.[1]

China thus entered a new phase of its history. The Nationalist government had been defeated, though the South had not yet been 'liberated'. In March 1949 the Communists held a National Women's Congress in Peking, and in April they held a Youth Congress there. In June they invited members of small pro-Communist political parties, 134 people in all, to a conference held to prepare the September constituent assembly. In July there was a conference on literature and art.

The country had been conquered very quickly. The various Communist generals were now in charge of the places taken over by their troops. They and their troops had long experience of waging guerilla war and of radical land reforms, but now they had entered the large cities. How were they to run the administration of the whole country? They had to rely on educated people outside the Party — and on the Soviet Union: they imported the Soviet system of administration wholesale.

The cities were a new world to the Communist troops. In China the distance between city and village cannot be counted in miles. The distance is more like 2,000 years. The Communist soldiers and most of their officers had never seen asphalted roads, electricity, piped water, barber shops or grocers, cars or buses, schools or displays of newspapers, or well-dressed men and women — the characteristic sights of large Chinese cities in those days. The guerilla fighters and the rustic Party men fitted poorly into their new setting.

On December 16, 1949, two and a half months after the establishment of the People's Republic, Mao Zedong went to Moscow to visit Stalin and stayed there for two months. This was an extraordinarily long visit, Mao's first time abroad. The negotiations were carried on by Zhou Enlai. Wu Xiuchuan, a vice foreign minister for many years, acted as his interpreter, and in 1983 published in his memoirs a detailed story of the friendly reception Mao received from Stalin. He also recalled that five months before Mao left for Moscow, Liu Shaoqi had an interview with Stalin in Moscow at which Stalin apologised for his lack of support for the Chinese Communists.

Stalin and Mao had a long history of friendly and less than friendly relations behind them. The comrades, many of whom had learnt something about Marxism for the first time in Yan'an, had been taught the Stalinist form of Marxism. Yet Moscow had maintained diplomatic relations with the Nationalist government and had been taken by surprise by the Communists' quick victory. Mao himself, at his most optimistic moment, had predicted that victory would take a few more years to achieve.[2]

In his *On the People's Democratic Dictatorship*, published in June 1949, Mao wrote: 'It was through the Russians that the Chinese found Marxism', and he said categorically that China was 'leaning on one side'. That side was the side of the Soviet Union.

A long period followed in which China seemed to be a faithful follower of the Soviet Union in everything. The Russian language was taught everywhere and Soviet experts were received with honour. The army was adjusted to the Soviet model. The Soviet pattern of the economy was adopted and the first Five Year Plan was written with Soviet aid, and served Soviet interests. Even the courts, the legal system and the accounting system followed the Soviet example, and the 1954 State Constitution was a copy of the 1936 Stalinist Constitution, although by that time Stalin was dead. Russian literature was translated wholesale into Chinese, and the only Western writers allowed were those whose works were approved reading in the Soviet Union. The adoption of the Soviet system seemed complete, and everything Western, in particular everything American, was rejected. The Communists were radical revolutionaries and they wanted a new start.

A change of dynasty in China had often been a violent affair, but as soon as a new regime had established itself it would quickly lay down a fixed rule of life and publish a new legal code, thus setting a comprehensive norm for behaviour. The new code of a new dynasty would differ little from the preceding code. In spite of the change of rulers the old system would not be disrupted. The first really radical change came with the establishment of the Republic in 1911 and the years following, when everything old was rejected and China made a violent about-turn, attempting to adopt Western ways in legislation, business life, the educational system, art, literature and everything else. The Nationalist government employed Western advisers, had Western science taught, ran Western-style universities. Until the Japanese invasion, it was unable to rid itself of Western intrusion in the foreign concessions in the major cities, but it made use of years of the fight against old-fashioned landlords and ultra-radical Communists.

When the Communists took power in 1949 they also organised themselves on a Western model — but now the model was Western Marxism in its Soviet garb. Professor Karl A. Wittfogel, probably the greatest authority on Marxism in the Western world, has called the system 'Oriental Despotism'. Whether his thesis of hydraulic society is accepted or not, his descriptive term 'Oriental Despotism' for Marxism as applied in the Soviet Union and China, cannot be dismissed as inept.

Good people, highly-educated people, who for many years had collaborated with the Communists and been honoured at the time of the establishment of the Communist regime, may well have thought, as many did, that when this foreign importation, Marxism, had been planted in Chinese soil, it would be transformed and civilised, as had happened to other importations in the past, even the novelties brought by barbarian invaders. The Mongol hordes who established the Yuan dynasty in the thirteenth century, though not themselves assimilated, ruled China in the traditional Chinese manner. Some of the abler Manchu emperors became notable Chinese scholars. In Chinese historiography it had become proverbial that Chinese civilisation conquers and civilises its conquerors. It was therefore expected that the Yan'an barbarians, themselves not even of a foreign race, would become Chinese in the traditional meaning of the word. This had not happened. Most of the men from Yan'an, above all the military leaders, were men of little if any education. They knew little about traditional Chinese civilisation and culture. Their readiness to accept the cooperation of highly-educated non-Party members was but a temporary expedient.

Cleansing the country

The first few years of the new regime were turbulent. A violent campaign of land reform and the 'suppression of counter-revolutionaries' began a few months after the take-over. These moves were made at the time when the Chinese army, nominally a 'volunteer army', was entering Korea to fight the American and South Korean armies. A nationwide pro-war campaign was started in support of this warlike effort. In the summer of 1951 a new purge, a purge against corruption, was begun. At first this purge was confined to the Party itself, but it was soon extended to the business world outside the Party. The land reform, the suppression of counter-revolutionaries and the anti-corruption campaign were violent affairs that affected the whole social fabric of the nation. Many perished, not only the obvious enemies of the new regime but, as we shall see, millions who, if left alone, would have willingly adjusted their lives to the new conditions.

The Communists did not understand their own people. The Chinese are a stoical and patient people, who traditionally accept a new regime with indifference or resignation. If left undisturbed, they continue their daily life and care little who is running the country. The Communists could have consolidated their regime without the furore they unleashed.

There are few parallels in history for what the Communists did. The French Revolution had many victims, but it did not institute a lasting political system. The October Revolution in the Soviet Union was not a peaceful affair, but the mass killings did not come till years later, during Stalin's collectivisation. Ayatollah Khomeini did launch a bloody campaign of suppression in Iran in 1979, but there has been no talk of millions of executions. There were mass executions in 1965 in Indonesia when the Communists were exterminated, but this was due to widespread vengeance in the villages rather than to a well-planned action.

In China, the terror — what else can one call it? — was widespread and saw the beginning of a lasting system. Official Party history divides the twenty-seven years of Mao's rule into periods named after the political campaigns, which, in spite of their civilised titles, were violent purges that shook the whole nation, from the largest city to the smallest village. This created in Communist China a system different from that of the Soviet Union.

Since the collectivisation and Great Purge in the 1930s major political changes have happened at the top in the Soviet Union, but these have not convulsed the whole population. However, this is what they have done in China. In the Soviet Union people have lived in monotonous drabness; in China periods of relative calm have been followed by waves of terrifying campaigns. These abrupt campaigns have deprived the Chinese system of stability. In the Soviet Union the official doctrine is that there is no longer any 'antagonistic contradiction', though Konstantin Chernenko, thinking no doubt of Dubček's 'Prague Spring' in 1968 and the effects of the Solidarity movement in Poland in 1980, did warn in 1982 that a major uprising may occur if the people are discontented.[3] For thirty years or more China was in a continuous state of 'antagonistic contradiction', i.e. fear of inner opposition and revolt.

This fear was groundless. Had the country been ruled with some moderation, without the political upheaval of the campaigns, the leaders would have had little to fear from organised opposition and the country would have benefited in every way. Many of Mao's companions knew this. Their opposition to Mao's policies of upheaval became visible at the Eighth Party Congress in 1956 and again in the early 1960s — we shall come to this later. However Mao was the supreme ruler. He dictated the course of events, and he was supported by a certain number of the old guerilla fighters who had learnt only to fight and for whom human life and human welfare counted for little.

The campaigns of upheaval came one after another: suppression of counter-revolutionaries, anti-corruption campaigns, the *Sufan* purge in 1955, the anti-rightist purge in 1957, the Commune and the Great Leap in 1958, the Cultural Revolution in 1966, and in the following years the purge of Lin Biao's followers, the purge of the followers of the 'Gang of Four', the purge of opponents of Deng Xiaoping — a never-ending series. There is hardly a family in China that does not bear scars from the wounds received during these violent events.

Land reform

All this began soon after the establishment of the People's Republic. In June 1950 a Land Reform Law was published and was explained by Liu Shaoqi, the most important man in the Party after Mao. Land reform meant redistributing the land, he said. According to Liu, landowners and kulaks, though forming only 10 per cent of the population, owned 70–80 per cent of the land. This was a bold statement, one that he did not try to prove.

The earlier land reform of 1946–7, carried out in the Communist-occupied territories in North China, had been incomplete, he said, because it was carried out in the middle of the civil war. Now, under Communist rule, things were different. The land reform should be a 'violent struggle', mobilising the poor peasants, establishing peasant associations, destroying the old feudal system, suppressing all land-owner opponents of the regime. An emergency court, called the People's Court, would deal with the cases. The land and all the property of landlords was to be confiscated and redistributed; but there was to be no land reform among national minorities or in the cities.[4]

In those days China was still divided into Great MilitaryAreas run by Military-Political Committees. Each published its own instructions on how to carry out the land reform.

The procedure was the same everywhere. The first step was to rouse the masses against the landlords. It might have been thought that the peasants, if given a free hand, would seize the land, but this did not happen. The peasants obviously became suspicious when they saw that huge numbers of Party cadres and even soldiers had been sent to stir up anger against the landlords. In Guangdong province alone, 62,000 Party officials and soldiers were sent to the villages to mobilise the peasants. This was done on the instructions of the Party Central Committee's South China Bureau. The peasants had to be disciplined into discontent and revolt against the landowners.[5]

A report presented to the Military-Political Committee of Central-South China described the difficulty of 'arousing the masses'. Many peasants were reluctant to act; in some places they sympathised with the persecuted landowners.

Land reform was a violent activity; it was not a mere redistribution of the land. 'Land reform is a struggle; it is not a peaceful reform. The land reform must be combined with the campaign for the suppression of counter-revolutionaries and with the nation's support of the Korean war, the Resist-US-Aid-Korea campaign.'[6] That land reform was not a mere redistribution of land was repeated everywhere. The land reform and the suppression of counter-revolutionaries were to be inextricably linked. The purpose of the land reform was not merely economic reform. Its main purpose was the elimination of genuine or potential enemies of Communist rule. It was bloody. Landowners were beaten and lynched; and those who survived became outcasts from society, 'landlord elements', a title that was to be inherited by their children and grandchildren for the following thirty years, until the end of the 1970s when this ignominious title was abolished.

Academics, both professors and students, were despatched from the cities to the villages to take part in the land reform so that they might see the violence and learn what class struggle is. This was considered the proper way of learning Marxism. A professor from Peking University described in the *People's Daily* what he had heard and seen. There were regions, he said, in which the landlords were beaten and cow-dung was thrown at them, or they were left to freeze to death or were simply killed. The professor, writing in the *People's Daily*, defended this violence. It was merely revenge for what the peasants had suffered under the landlords in earlier years. The local cadres, he wrote, tried to restrain the anger of the masses, telling them not to kill the landlords but to let them be judged by the popular court which would condemn them to death anyway. This, the professor wrote, curbed the excesses of the land reform.[7]

The land reform was indeed much more than a reform of ownership of the land. It was designed not only as a way of eliminating the enemies of the Party in the villages throughout China, but also as a lesson to all, a lesson in the way the Communist Party would rule the country. It was meant, a contemporary newspaper said, to train the cadres and government officials, and to serve as a reform of people in all walks of life. That was why thousands of university professors and students and members of smaller political parties were sent to the villages to help in the land reform and to see what was going on.[8]

It was a lesson in terror. At the end of 1951, Liu Ruilong, then fifty years of age, was in charge of agriculture in the East China Party Bureau. (Later he became vice-minister of agriculture, and after the Cultural Revolution, at the age of eighty, he returned to this post.) In that year, 1951, he reported on the land reform in East China. It was, he said, 'the first manifestation after the Liberation [1949] of the wisdom and power of the peasants, under the leadership of the Communist Party. The land reform was combined with the Resist-US-Aid-Korea campaign and with the suppression of counter-revolutionaries movement . . . First the landlords and the counter-revolutionaries [there was hardly any distinction between the two] were arrested, and then the anti-feudal struggle went ahead. The land reform was an extremely violent struggle which reached every corner of the country.' In East China 33 million peasants were organised, 27 per cent of the inhabitants of the villages; among them were 2.9 million militiamen and 15 million women. Every village produced 100 or 200 activists. 'The political power of the peasants [and of the Party] had been established.'[9]

The land reform did not change the agricultural system radically. There was only a change of ownership. As soon as this had been completed, the first step was taken towards the collectivisation of land, which was to mean taking the land away from everybody.

The land reform was above all a political move. Typically, in the publication containing the month's major reports, the *Xinhua Monthly*, land reform was dealt with not under economy or agriculture but under politics. This was an open admission of the true purpose and nature of the land reform.

The land reform was not demanded by the peasants; it was dictated from above. The villagers themselves were often reluctant to take the land and houses of others, fearing that Heaven would punish them for the injustice. Thirty years later, in the 1980s, the Party leadership regretted neither the land reform, with its accompanying brutalities, nor the killing of the enemies of the regime, but the collectivisation, which had taken the land away from the farmers and with it their spirit of initiative and their willingness to work. As a result agriculture stagnated for thirty years.

Thirty years later, therefore, the land was given back to the peasants (not the ownership but the use of the land). The question then arose: could former landlords claim the land, houses, gardens and woods that had belonged to their families thirty years earlier? Even after a generation the families knew which areas of land belonged to whom, and even the local cadres were conscious of the injustices done so long before.[10]

Having looked at the land reform and how it was carried out in combination with the 'suppression of counter-revolutionaries', one can understand how Peking could boast in the following years that the collectivisation of the land in 1955–6 had been accomplished without the bloodshed of the collectivisation in the Soviet Union. There the suppression of the enemies was carried out simultaneously with collectivisation. In China it had been carried out years earlier. All the Party's potential enemies in the villages had been exterminated in the early stage of the revolution, during the land reform.

Suppression of counter-revolutionaries

The timing of the suppression may have been different in China and in the Soviet Union, but the method was the same. The *People's Daily*, and after it other newspapers, quoted sayings from Lenin and Stalin about the 'suppression of counter-revolutionaries'. Lenin said that all enemies should be arrested and some executed. Stalin went further, and long passages were quoted from his March 3, 1937, report delivered after the conclusion of the bloody purge which began with the assassination of Kirov in January 1935. Stalin explained how right he had been in suppressing both his public and secret enemies, and how wrong were those who had wanted to spare their lives. He also quoted a report in which Molotov spoke against Trotskyites. Stalin said clearly what should be done to them.[11]

Mao and his companions were good students of Lenin and Stalin.

The extermination of the class enemies came immediately after the establishment of the People's Republic. Between January and October 1950, 13,812 persons were arrested on charges of being agents of the enemies of the Communists. On July 23, the Cabinet issued a joint instruction (signed by Zhou Enlai), ordering a stepping-up of the pursuit of counter-revolutionaries. In December 1950 the *People's Daily* referred once more in an editorial to Stalin's 1937 speech with its demand for merciless pursuit of the enemy. Many of those who adjudicate on the cases, it said, are still under the influence of the old legal system of the Nationalist government and are not severe enough. They speak in legal terms of the old law, of 'attempted crime', of 'crime committed in self-defence'. They do not follow the instructions of Chairman Mao. Chairman Mao wants to defend the interests of the masses of the people and not to apply spurious notions from the old law. Some comrades say that such severity is in contradiction to the United Front policy of the Party, which seeks to embrace the whole population; but this is a sophism. US imperialism is threatening our country and there are many latent reactionary elements — they must be suppressed.[12]

This was done: 80 per cent of the Chinese population were said to have taken part in mass accusation meetings of counter-revolutionaries in the first half of 1951. This was combined with the Resist-US-Aid-Korea and land reform campaigns.[13]

On February 21, 1951, a *Regulation on Suppression of Counter-Revolutionaries* was published, signed by Mao Zedong as head of the government. The aim of the suppression of counter-revolutionaries, the *Regulation* said, was to strengthen the People's Democratic Dictatorship. The *Regulation* recognised only death sentences, life sentences and prison sentences with minimum terms of five years. Among those aimed at were people who had opposed the Communists before the Communist take-over and had not gained merit after it ('gaining merit' meant denouncing friends and comrades, saboteurs in factories, mines and agriculture, and those who disturbed the market).[14]

This legislative act, if it may be given that name, was published months after executions had become the order of the day.

The *Regulation* was explained by Peng Zhen, Politbureau member, secretary of the Peking city Party Committee, mayor of Peking and first deputy head of the Political-Legal Commission of the Cabinet. He rebutted the opinion current in the Party, that excesses were being committed. The power is already in the hands of the People (i.e. of the Party), these objectors argued, so why not be lenient? Will not such radical repression arouse a general feeling of terror? Will this not harm the Common Front policy of the Party? Peng Zhen disagreed; the policy of broad generosity must be corrected and evil people must be exterminated.[15]

At the time, the minister of justice was a woman, Shi Liang, who was not publicly a member of the Communist Party. Her ferocity mirrored Peng Zhen's, and she blamed the courts for not being severe enough. As an example, she described a court in the north of Shaanxi province where a counter-revolutionary was not condemned to death but only to ten years in prison, on the grounds that he was already over sixty years of age. She also blamed prison administrators who insisted too strongly on the educational function of the prisons. A prison is not a school, she said. (This appears to contradict the much publicised 'reform of thoughts' effect of the prisons. In those days, that consideration was conveniently shelved.) The lady minister of justice complained indignantly that people still judged crimes according to the legal codes of the Nationalist government, using such bourgeois legal terms as 'first offender' or 'habitual criminal' and distinguishing between the intention and the deed. Judges who refuse to hand out the death sentence fail to draw a line between the enemy and us, she said; instead of strengthening the people's democratic dictatorship, they weaken it.[16]

What has just been reported may give the impression that the suppression of counter-revolutionaries was carried out through courts which had been instructed to act brutally. In fact, it was a mass movement, the worst of its kind. In April 1951 the *People's Daily* reported that in all the cities — and in the land reform campaign in all the villages — people had been organised to terrorise those who were 'latent counter-revolutionary elements'. The *People's Daily* boasted that in Xinxiang, a small town in Hebei province, latent counter-revolutionaries had been executed at mass meetings. In another provincial town every street held mass accusation meetings. In Nanjing 400,000 people gathered for a similar meeting, which was broadcast. In Zhongqing, counter-revolutionaries were paraded through the streets and people were obliged to leave their houses and line up to watch the parade and express approval. Here too the mass executions were broadcast.[17]

People were obliged to denounce counter-revolutionaries. A report from Shanghai said that everywhere, in factories, government organs, schools and street organisations, Cleansing of Counter-Revolutionaries Committees had been set up, to help the security forces and the police.[18]

The newspapers were filled with articles under such headlines as

'Tianjin Executes a Bunch of Counter-Revolutionary Criminals' and 'Three US Spies Arrested' (the three were French Jesuit professors in a Catholic university in Tianjin).[19]

On March 24, 5,000 people were assembled for a mass execution meeting in Peking. Among the condemned were workers, peasants, secondary school students and members of a Taoist secret society known as *Hui Dao Men*. The meeting was led by Peng Zhen, who described the crimes of those to be executed. The press reported the meeting thus. Peng Zhen: 'What should we do with them? [All the representatives unanimously shouted 'Shoot them!'] What you people say is correct. They must be shot. [Fervent applause.] Should anyone be generous to them? [All the representatives unanimously said 'no!'] Indeed, no one should be generous. If generosity were shown to them the People's Government would be making a mistake indeed. It would be a crime.' Peng Zhen went on: 'Would shooting these agents, tyrants, bandits, reactionary heads of the *Hui Dao Men*, would that be excessively cruel? [All responded 'It would not be cruel!'] Indeed, it is not cruel. It is the greatest of mercies. If a counter-revolutionary killed a thousand people, would that not be cruel? Would not that be horrible? . . . Comrades! Who is right? Are they right or are we right?' (All the representatives shouted 'We are right! Support for the People's Government! Suppress counter-revolutionaries! Support Mayor Peng!')

Peng Zhen then shouted 'Hail Chairman Mao!', and explained that the executions would take place in accordance with the legal norms of the *Regulation on Suppression of Counter-Revolutionaries*. 'According to this *Regulation*', he said, 'those who should be killed are condemned to death, those who should not be killed are not condemned to death. We do not kill those who may or may not be killed; but those who should be killed we certainly kill, and we do not let one of them get away with it.'[20]

The *People's Daily* in an editorial on this event said that the mass meeting had been broadcast live to Peking and broadcast in the evening to the whole country, and that on the following day the counter-revolutionaries were shot at another mass meeting. The neighbouring city of Tianjin had acted similarly, in imitation of Peking. Thus 'good examples were set for the whole country.'[21]

In May 1951 the second Peking mass execution took place, led by Peng Zhen and Luo Ruiqing, head of security in Peking city and minister of security for the central government. As on previous occasions, Peng Zhen shouted: 'What should be done to these beasts?' (The public shouted, 'Shoot them!') This time they were not all executed. Some were given death sentences suspended for two years. This, Peng Zhen explained, 'is a new method; the aim is still the total extermination of the counter-revolutionaries; it is not a weakening of the struggle against the counter-revolutionaries. A suspension of execution for two years does not mean that the state is wasting millet [the staple food in North China] on them. The People's Government will organise them for forced labour and production. They will not eat millet for nothing. By forcing them to produce and to labour, the state will save millet and they will produce millet for the country. They will thus be punished, and they may be reformed. Their labour will be useful on some state construction works.'[22]

Luo Ruiqing addressed the same mass meeting. Since the last meeting a month earlier, he said, 199 counter-revolutionaries had been executed in Peking. This was a great service to the people.

The suppression of counter-revolutionaries had produced good results, he went on:

A great number of people have denounced counter-revolutionaries. Wives have denounced their counter-revolutionary husbands; children have denounced their fathers. Young students have caught counter-revolutionaries and brought them to the security offices. This shows that the great propaganda has moved the masses to struggle against the counter-revolutionaries and that the People's Government and the people struggle together. Accusation meetings have been held in many quarters of Peking, and a total of 200,000 people have taken part in them. Many have written letters to the police. Many, however, have not dared to sign their letters in fear of revenge. The masses have nothing to fear. The government will eradicate the counter-revolutionaries totally. In recent days we have examined the cases of 500 persons. Most of them were denounced by others; 221 will be executed.[23]

The killings continued for months. On July 10, 1951, 277 counter-revolutionaries were executed in Tianjin city, and fifty-six were condemned to death with two years' suspension of execution. Among the executed were *Hui Dao Men* members and leaders and members of a Buddhist association called the New Buddhist World Association.[24]

On August 22, at another mass meeting, 237 were executed in Peking; twenty-five got death sentences with two-year suspensions; another twenty-five got life sentences. Among the executed were former Nationalist soldiers and policemen and twenty-seven *Hui Dao Men* leaders.[25]

On National Day, October 1, 1951, Luo Ruiqing wrote that the suppression of counter-revolutionaries was a magnificent act of the people's democratic dictatorship. Its February 1951 *Regulation* had been implemented in cities and also in villages. Masses had been mobilised, accusation meetings had been held in every corner of the country. Many people had been denounced as counter-revolutionaries. Exhibitions, books, films, songs and pamphlets had spread the policy. It was estimated that, taking the country as a whole, about 330 million people took part in the mass meetings. In Shanghai, in the course of the campaign, 2.4 million copies of the *Regulation on Suppression of Counter-revolutionaries* were printed, 29,000 persons were denounced as counter-revolutionaries, and large numbers of activists devoted themselves to the search for evil people. Similar action took place in other cities; in Tianjin the campaign mobilised 12,000 activists.

When speaking of the suppression of counter-revolutionaries, Luo Ruiqing did not distinguish between cities and villages. The land reform was part of the suppression. Some peasants, he said, were reluctant to take the landowners' land and houses. They were afraid of what they called 'change of heaven', i.e. a change of the regime, or a reversal of policy. There are still places, he said, particularly in the newly-liberated areas, where the suppression and the land reform have not yet been carried out or not carried out properly. In East China only 73.5 per cent of those who should have been executed have in fact been finished off. (This surprisingly precise figure seems to defy explanation unless the number of people to be dealt with in these campaigns had been laid down in advance.) In a number of places the leadership is slow to act through fear of revenge. The mobilisation of the masses and the violent struggle must continue, and the suppression of the counter-revolutionaries must be brought to a satisfactory end.

(In those days there were still some foreign missionaries in the villages of China. They reported that executions were taking place almost daily in the villages, as part of the land reform and of the suppression of counter-revolutionaries.)

Not all counter-revolutionaries are executed, Luo said. Many get prison sentences or are sent to 'correction by labour' — a system, inherited from the Russians, which became a permanent feature of life in China. Luo expounded the doctrine that corrective labour will change a counter-revolutionary and turn him into a New Man. Corrective labour, he added, also has an economic function. (As in the Soviet Union, a number of public works were built by people condemned to forced labour.)[26]

Luo's report mentioned activists, in Chinese called 'positive elements', produced by the campaign to suppress counter-revolutionaries. These were people who had shown that the Party could rely on them. They were helpful in finding and condemning the counter-revolutionaries. The most 'positive' were those who were ready to betray their best friends or members of their families, men whom the civilised world would call ruthless, bloodthirsty scoundrels. They were an asset to the omnipotent Party because they put Party interests above all human feelings, and above their own consciences. The most zealous of them were good candidates for acceptance into the Party. A few years later a report on Party membership said: 'The land reform, the suppression of counter-revolutionaries and the Resist-US-Aid-Korea campaign raised the political consciousness of the masses and many people joined the Communist Party. In the three years, 1950–3, Party membership grew by more than 500,000.'[27] The Party purge did not decrease Party membership. It rejected those unworthy of membership and accepted many who had shown that they were not afraid to shed blood, the blood of others, to promote Party interests.

Peng Zhen and Luo Ruiqing were, and remained for years, outstanding leaders of the People's Republic. Four years later, as we shall see below, Luo Ruiqing was to lead a similar terrifying campaign. In 1959 he became Chief-of-Staff. During the Cultural Revolution he was tortured severely, but after Mao's death he regained power, becoming secretary-general of the Central Committee's Military Committee. He died in 1978.

Peng Zhen's star kept on rising until the Cultural Revolution, when Mao rejected him; but in the 1980s, as we shall see later, he once again led the suppression of the regime's enemies. He was then over eighty years old. Peng Zhen had not changed.

These men, even the civilised Zhou Enlai who signed the 1950 Instruction on the punishment of counter-revolutionaries, were the products of twenty years of war and civil war, in which human life counted for little. Behind them all was the august figure of Mao, who orchestrated the purge.

Compared with these men, Chiang Kai Shek, whom they accused of many crimes, was an amateur. Some of Chiang's political enemies were arrested and executed, but these were selected deadly political enemies. Under the Nationalist government there was no suggestion of mass hysteria and there were no mass executions.

The violence of the first year set the tone for the coming thirty years, till the post-Mao leadership discovered how much damage the political campaigns had done. They discovered it during the Cultural Revolution when they themselves became the targets of a campaign.

Who was regarded as a counter-revolutionary in the early 1950s? *Current Affairs Handbook*, a tract for the indoctrination of Party members, gave a definition: 'A counter-revolutionary is a person who is an enemy of the People and endangers the Fatherland.' What was the distinction between a common criminal and a counter-revolutionary? 'All counter-revolutionary crimes are criminal acts; but not all criminal acts are counter-revolutionary crimes. If the criminal intends to act against the People [i.e. against the Party] and the Fatherland, he is a counter-revolutionary.' To the question 'Were all former Kuomintang members counter-revolutionaries?', the answer was 'Not all, but many.' To the question, 'Were all members of the *Hui Dao Men* counter-revolutionaries?', the answer was 'Not all, but most of them.' To the question 'Were the members of a counter-revolutionary's family in the same category?', the answer was 'No, except such members as knew about the counter-revolutionary and did not denounce him.' To the question 'Why were so many people suppressed as counter-revolutionaries?', the answer was that 'it was necessary to clear the air; the counter-revolutionaries were numerous.' Could it not be the case that innocent people were condemned? The answer was that 'the police and the People's Government acted carefully and did not punish innocent people.' Were all counter-revolutionaries to be killed? The answer was 'No, some of them might be sent to prison; some of them might be kept under surveillance, their movements restricted. Those who confessed spontaneously and denounced others and thus "established merit" would be treated mildly.'[28]

Even children were incited to look for counter-revolutionaries, and stories were published about ten-year-olds spying on people in parks, listening to their conversations, and denouncing them to the police. They were praised as fine young heroes.[29]

All walks of life were affected by the purge. The leaders of the small democratic parties, whose support had been of considerable importance before the take-over and who had been honoured when the People's Republic was established, now had to join the pursuit of counter-revolutionaries, searching them out even from within their own ranks. A leader of the Kuomintang Revolutionary Committee (which had cooperated with the Communists) expressed satisfaction that some of its members had been executed as Kuomintang spies. Zhang Bojun, head of the Chinese Peasants-Workers Democratic Party, and Zhang Naiqi, one of the leaders of the Chinese Democratic National Construction Association, both denounced counter-revolutionaries in their own organisations. The latter spoke of counter-revolutionaries among private businessmen, and expressed satisfaction that twenty-two of them had been executed.[30] These two Zhangs both became Cabinet ministers, but six years later, in 1957, both were condemned. By that time the Party did not need the services of such 'democratic gentlemen'.

The two Zhangs could not have paid careful attention to Mao's *On the People's Democratic Dictatorship*, published in 1949, just before the establishment of the People's Republic. 'The State apparatus', Mao wrote, 'including the armed police and the courts, is the instrument by which one class oppresses the other. [This is the classical Leninist formula.] It is an instrument for the oppression of antagonistic classes; it is violence and not benevolence . . . Our policy of benevolence is applied only within the ranks of the People. Who are the People? At the present stage in China they are the working class, the peasantry, the urban petty bourgeoisie and the national bourgeoisie. These classes, led by the working class and the Communist Party, . . . enforce their dictatorship over the running dogs of imperialism, the landlord class, the bureaucratic bourgeoisie . . . the Kuomintang reactionaries — suppress them, let them behave properly and not be unruly in word or deed.'[31]

Mao made it clear that the Communist Party would not tolerate its enemies; it would suppress them. The significance of the words 'at the present stage', often used by Mao, was not understood: it meant that at any time Communist policy may change and a new stage begin. What he said was frightening enough in 1949, at that stage; but Mao's friendly handshakes and the gentlemanly demeanour of Zhou Enlai blinded those who had entrusted the future of China into their hands.

Anti-corruption campaigns

The suppression of the counter-revolutionaries and the land reform were not yet over when another double bomb was hurled, the 'three-anti' (*san-fan*) and 'five-anti' (*wu-fan*) corruption campaigns. The 'three-anti' was directed at Party members, the 'five-anti' at private businessmen. These anti-corruption campaigns were designed to streamline the economy, and formed part of what was called the More-Production-and-Thrift Campaign. This last was meant to restore the economy after the civil war to a normal footing. But in the mind of the Party, this, like everything else, was to be carried out in the manner of the guerilla fighting of earlier days. It did not occur to these guerilla fighters that the economy could be re-established by less ruthless, though still severe means.

When did the 'three-anti' campaign start? In January 1952, Zhou Enlai stated that it had been launched by Mao Zedong in December 1951. The campaign, Zhou said, was then, in January 1952, at its very beginning, and it was meant to intensify and cover the whole country.[32]

On New Year's Day 1952, Mao, as head of the government, published his New Year resolution : 'Victory to the Resist-US-Aid-Korea frontline! Victory to the land-reform frontline! Victory to the suppression of counter-revolutionaries frontline! Victory to the economic and financial frontline! Victory to the cultural and educational frontline!' He then added: 'The struggle against corruption, waste and bureaucracy [the 'three-anti'] must be carried out, like the other campaigns, with flags and drums in array, with thunderlike violence and windlike swiftness.'[33] (The phrase 'with flags and drums . . .' was constantly repeated in every campaign up to the Cultural Revolution. It is not found in post-Mao Peking dictionaries.)

The campaign among Party members started in the highest offices of the Party, government and army. Hardly a month had passed when, on January 9, 1952, the man in charge of the campaign at the highest levels, Bo Yibo (thirty years later, in the 1980s, once again in charge of the Party reform), reported that 1,670 people had been found guilty of corruption. Among them, he said, were the head of the administrative office for public security, who had embezzled a large sum of money, and a deputy department head in the ministry for railways, who had transported opium and morphine. Inefficiency also was punished — for instance, a man who had ordered 300 tons of anti-foot-and-mouth disease drugs from the Soviet Union, instead of three tons, and engineers who had delayed by a year the building of a stretch of railway in the west. The campaign, like all campaigns, was characterised by accusations and self-accusations. In the high Party and government offices, 823 persons accused others, and 250 spontaneously confessed their crimes. This, Bo Yibo said, was only the beginning.[34]

The minister of security, Luo Ruiqing, carried out a major purge in his ministry, aimed principally at those who had been retained from the previous administration and, as he put it, 'pretended to be progressive to win our confidence'. The purge also swept away some newly-recruited members of the police force, men of weak character who had been bribed by businessmen, received presents, helped the businessmen to evade taxes and taken part in clandestine business.[35]

Zhou Enlai was speaking inaccurately when he said that the campaign started in December 1951. In fact it started months earlier in the Northeast, in what was Manchuria, where Gao Gang was the Party boss. Major actions in the first few years of the People's Republic started not in Peking but in the Northeast under this man, Gao Gang, Vice-Chairman of the Central Government and boss of the Northeast. This area, being close to the Soviet Union, was under strong Soviet influence. In December 1951 the *People's Daily* published a document which was to form the basis of the whole campaign, a speech by Stalin on thrift, delivered in 1926.[36]

Gao Gang began to seek out corruption in August 1951, four months before Peking made its first move. He quoted Stalin and upbraided his own men in the Northeast. He purged a minister in his Northeast regional government who was employing sixteen evil persons, among them four traitor Communist Party members and two former landlords. He also purged a department head in Shenyang city who had defended the reputation of an engineer of the former Kuomintang regime, a man already executed as a counter-revolutionary. Local Party leaders were being corrupted by the new environment, he said. Gao Gang quoted some as saying that on moving from the villages to the cities one has to adapt oneself to the new conditions.[37]

A famous case, publicised throughout the country in those days, was that of two high Party officials in the city of Tianjin — Liu Jingshan and Zhang Zishan. In the middle of 1951 they appropriated huge sums of money, funds destined for flood regulation and for a special flood-relief fund for Party cadres, and invested the money via local businessmen in the hope of earning large profits. They also transported timber from the Northeast to sell it at a higher price in Tianjin.[38] Both were condemned to death and immediately executed at a public trial on February 10.[39]

As was often the case, regulations and legislation did not precede drastic action, but rather followed it.

It was not until March 1952 that a Regulation on the 'three-anti' was issued by Zhou Enlai's Cabinet. Those involved in corruption below the million yuan (the old yuan) level were not to be punished if they confessed and paid back the money. (A million yuan of the old currency was equivalent to 100 yuan of the new currency introduced in 1955 — about US$60.) Cases involving between 1 and 10 million yuan were subject to administrative sanctions only. Those accused of corruption involving amounts above 10 million yuan were subject to criminal prosecution unless they repented, denounced others and thus 'established merit'. Administrative sanctions might range from admonition to dismissal. Court sanctions were as follows: supervision in the place of work for one or two years, forced labour from two to four years, prison, a life sentence, and ultimately, the death penalty.

These sanctions applied to cases of corruption. For the two other delinquencies covered by the 'three-anti' — waste and bureaucracy — only administrative, not penal, sanctions were to be imposed. Party members living above the appropriate standard were to correct their way of living; in flagrant cases the offender was to be exposed to public criticism. All cases not involving corruption were to be settled before March 20. For cases of corruption a popular court was to be established and was to settle the cases before the end of April.[40]

On March 30, 1952, three weeks after the publication of this Cabinet Regulation, a Cabinet Order signed by Zhou Enlai established Popular Courts to deal with cases of corruption. The sanctions to be imposed were those indicated in the earlier Cabinet document: supervision, reform by labour, prison, life sentences and the death penalty. The sentences of these courts needed the approval of government organs. Death sentences needed the approval of the Cabinet or the Revolutionary Military Committee of the Great Administrative Areas.[41]

Like the counter-revolutionaries, the culprits of the 'three-anti' were condemned at broadcast mass meetings. One such mass meeting was held in a Peking park by a Provisional Court organised by the Supreme Court. The mass trial was led by the president of the Supreme Court himself, Shen Junru, and among the speakers were Luo Ruiqing, minister of security, and Yao Yilin, in those days vice-minister of commerce (a Cabinet Councillor in the 1980s).

At that mass meeting seven handcuffed persons were exposed to the masses. A former industrialist who had held a high position in state commerce under the new government and the head of the administrative bureau of the ministry of security were condemned to death and executed. A third, working in the ministry of agriculture, was condemned to fifteen years in prison. The mass trial ended with a speech by Bo Yibo.[42]

In the 'three-anti' campaign, as in all other campaigns, everybody was mobilised. A *People's Daily* editorial was addressed to members of corrupt officials' families. Family members, it said, had an obligation to denounce corrupt members of their family. Wives, it pointed out, were reluctant to denounce the offences of their husbands, being afraid that family life would become difficult, that good feelings between husband

and wife would be destroyed and that denouncing the husband might involve the wife too. The wives should therefore be instructed and convinced about their duty. To accomplish this task teachers and students of girls' schools in Peking and associations of working women were sent in teams to the homes to instruct the wives.[43]

Propagandists

For the further implementation of the campaigns, more people were needed. So as early as January 1, 1951, the Party leadership issued a Decision on the establishment of a mass propagandist network by the Communist Party.[44] They were to help in all three campaigns, the land reform, the suppression and the 'three-anti', and were called 'the spokesmen of Chairman Mao'. At that time about 20 per cent of local Party branches had not yet enlisted propagandists. The goal was that one per cent of the whole population of China should become propagandists.[45]

Results

In February 1953 An Ziwen, at that time deputy head of the organisation department of the Central Committee and head of the government personnel bureau, reported on the results of the 'three-anti' campaign.

The campaign was completed, he said, in October 1952 — six months after the date set by Premier Zhou Enlai. It had investigated 3.8 million Party members at county level and above, and found that 150,000 officials, 2.7 per cent of those investigated, had been involved in corruption amounting to more than 10 million yuan. (He calculated wrongly: the figure should have been 4 per cent). Corruption cases involving smaller amounts were not counted. The anti-corruption campaign instigated among Party members in the villages, An Ziwen said, caused consternation. He did not point out that this was the time of the land reform, when the county Party leaders were leading mass trials of landowners: now they had to face their own purge. Things became so bad, An reported, that when the 'three-anti' campaign was tried in the countryside, all work stopped, and the campaign had to be suspended. Later it was restarted after careful preparation, though it was now combined with the Party purge.[46] (The anti-corruption campaign and the Party reform were two different activities.)

A report published in 1957 in the *People's Daily* said bluntly that the 'three-anti' campaign had a pre-arranged target of 25 per cent of Party members to be purged;[47] there is little doubt that this figure was attained.

Cleansing the Party

Ever since the Communists took over power, one of the major preoccupations of the new leaders had been the adjustment of the Party to its new role in the country. How was this to be done? They could have started crash courses in education, to teach illiterate Party cadres to read, and to teach educated Party men basic notions of twentieth-century national administration. Instead, they started with a Party purge.

On June 6–9, 1950, a Third Central Committee Plenum was held, the third since the Seventh Congress in 1945. It was the first Central Committee Plenum held after the Communists entered the cities. The Plenum decided on a Party purge. The main report was delivered by Mao; other reports were delivered by Liu Shaoqi (on land reform), Zhou Enlai (on foreign relations), Chen Yun (on finance) and Nie Rongzhen (on the army).[48]

This was the third purge of the Party. The first was the grea: purge in Yan'an that confirmed Mao as Leader. The second was launched in September 1947, in conjunction with a violent land reform campaign in the areas occupied by the Communists. It came in a time of turmoil, in the middle of the civil war, and it miscarried. It had been excessive; whole Party branches had been wiped out. The purge, the Rectification campaign, had to be halted in the spring of 1948.[49]

The Third Plenum found that Party membership had grown too quickly. In 1937, before the outbreak of the Japanese war, there were 40,000 Party members; in 1945, at the end of the Japanese war, there were 1.2 million. By the end of 1949 the figure was 4.5 million, and at the time of the Third Plenum, in June 1950, there were 5 million Party members. Of these, 3.65 million were civilians and 1.2 million were soldiers. In 1949 and the first half of 1950, 2 million new members joined the Party. The most important decision was that the admission of peasants to the Party should stop. The purge was to be finished before the spring of 1951.[50]

When dealing with Party membership figures it should be kept in mind that the statistics have to be taken with a pinch of salt. On March 8, 1951, the *People's Daily* said that owing to the ignorance and the low educational level of a number of Party members, many inexact and contradictory figures had entered the Party registers. In some regions nonexistent village Party branches had been reported, and in many places there were considerable discrepancies between different reports. The figures for earlier years, the years of the guerilla war, could claim even less accuracy and were mere guesswork.

The intention of the Third Plenum was to reduce the number of illiterate peasant Party members: a Communist Party is by definition a party of the industrial proletariat. Peng Zhen, mayor of Peking and a member of the Politbureau, used contorted argument to show that the Chinese Communist Party was an orthodox Communist Party: it had always professed dialectical materialism, and, although the majority of its members were poor peasants, most of them had left their villages and joined the Red Army, where they received the true Communist stamp.[51]

By the end of 1950, i.e. six months after the announcement of the Party purge, the number of Party members, instead of decreasing, had grown to 5.8 million.[52] New members were being enrolled in the newly-conquered regions. The majority of the Party members were still to be found in the areas ruled for years by the Communists, in the Northeast and in parts of North China and of East China. Of the 5.8 million Party members, only 1.4 million belonged to the vast areas of Central, South and Southwest China.[53]

The Party purge followed the usual Soviet pattern. In addition to compulsory reading and discussion of texts by Marx and Lenin, there were public accusations and self-accusations designed to uncover unworthy Party members. The avowed purposes of the purge were the better execution of the land reform campaign, winning the support of people outside the Party, reducing the number of peasant Party members and recruiting Party members among industrial workers. The Party reform started in the highest levels of the Party (though none of the highest leaders were sacked) and went down step by step to the lower grades. The purge was instituted in March 1950 and was meant to end in the spring of 1951. What it achieved is not clear.

In March 1951 at its first national meeting the Central Committee's Organisation launched the purge in the lowest Party branches. It was decreed that this purge, the Party Rectification, was to last three years.

In the first phase, up to the end of 1952, 40,000 village Party branches were processed and 10 per cent of the Party members were purged. Of these 30 per cent were found to be counter-revolutionaries or something similar, and the remaining 70 per cent were judged not to be up to the standard and were advised to leave. There were, in all, 180,000 village Party branches, and the remaining 140,000 were to be checked before the spring of 1954.[54]

New recruits

In every political campaign, those who unscrupulously denounce friends and relatives are praised. They are the 'positive elements', the 'activists', from among whom Party members can be selected. This is precisely what the Party Central Committee's Central-South Bureau said towards the end of the 'three-anti' movement. The land reform, it said, had helped to find the good men in the villages; the 'three-anti' had done the same in the cities. 'From the campaign there emerged activists and positive elements who could be promoted to responsible positions, to become the inner core of all works.'[55]

In October the highest Party leadership, the *Zhong Yang* or Party Central, as it was called, issued an order for the admission of new members, and in May 1952 a new instruction said that those who had shown merit in the 'three-anti' campaign should be admitted to the Party.[56]

The Central-South area was ruled by Lin Biao. His first deputy, Deng Zihui, said that five qualities were required for Party membership:
1. Proper family origin (proletarian).
2. Clean personal history (i.e. past fidelity to the Party Line).
3. 'Positiveness' in work and determination in struggle.
4. Progressive thinking and class consciousness (i.e. fidelity to the Marxist doctrine of the Party).
5. Close connection with the masses and trust by the masses. 'The "three-anti" campaign was very useful in producing such persons.'[57]

The Communist press did not hide the fact that there was little eagerness to join the Party either among the peasants or among the workers.

Peasants

The answers to a sort of questionnaire in the villages reflected the peasants' attachment to private property. A rhyming motto quoted in the press summed up the peasants' wishes: 'Children, wife, land, a stove for the night, and cattle'. Among industrial workers, the newly organised trade unions with their violent accusation-and-self-accusation meetings, the strict labour discipline, and the use of the newly-introduced labour insurance for the segregation of the politically reliable, did not serve as enticements to join the Party. People had not yet been conditioned to the new regime.[58]

The majority of Party members were peasants, often illiterate, who had little or no idea about what being a Party member meant. As soon as they got land in the land reform campaign, they were satisfied. The good peasant philosophy of their attitude was described in the *People's Daily*: 'Should one continue to be a Party member? Party member or not, one has to eat. Indeed to be a Party member is much more inconvenient than to belong to the masses.' 'Masses' means non-Party members. These men were told that the revolution was for life and that giving up Party membership was a disgrace.

What did the peasants know and what were they supposed to learn about Marxism? 'Some Party members know that the Communist Party is the political party of the workers; but they do not understand it. Most of the [village] Party members know nothing about the working class. They say: "We carried out the land reform in accordance with the instruction of Chairman Mao, but we have never seen a worker." '

What were they told about Marxism? First, the quality of life in the Soviet Union was explained to them. Secondly, they were told that in the coming socialist society there would be no exploitation, but there would be an abundance of products; in Communism 'all will work according to their capacity and receive according to their needs' and 'there will be no poverty and no misfortune.' The peasants' answer, quoted in the press, was: 'That would be wonderful but we are still far from it. We have just finished the land reform and we are satisfied.' The third lesson was about the Party's history, the great struggle of the Party during past years; first the defeat in the 1920s, then the turn to the villages, the revolution leading the peasants' struggle and the villages surrounding and conquering the cities. The memory of the early Communist heroes who died for the Cause was presented to the audiences to encourage them to follow their example.[59]

Obviously many peasants had supported the Communists in order to become small landowners. But this hope had barely been realised when the first step towards collectivisation was taken through the formation of mutual-aid groups. The village Party members were told that 'only through mutual-aid cooperation can Socialism and Communism be attained.' They were expected to study the March 26, 1953, Decision of the Party on agricultural mutual-aid cooperation.

Some hotheads went too far and organised collective farms, grouping hundreds of peasant households and taking away land and livestock from the individual peasants. This was wrong and the local leaders were told to act with restraint and advance step by step.[60] These misguided local Party leaders had taken the Marxist doctrine of transition towards Socialism and to Communism too seriously — or perhaps they simply wanted to impose their own power on their localities.

The time for collectivisation had not yet come, but the individual peasant household economy was to go. Lin Feng, the first deputy Party secretary of the Northeast Bureau of the Central Committee, explained that there were two possibilities: either capitalism, which was bound to develop from small-scale ownership, or cooperation. As the peasants were not familiar with cooperation, it should be introduced under the guidance of the working class and the Communist Party. Lin Feng, quoting from Engels, Lenin and Stalin and from Mao, said that the old traditional individual household economy was a feudal system under which the peasants would remain poor for ever; that was why collectivisation would have to be introduced, though gradually.

This was the doctrine, Lin Feng said, that must be explained to the peasants.[61]

Workers

To counterbalance the overwhelming majority of ignorant peasants in the Party, recruitment of workers began. The Party became more and more city-minded. Party leaders lived in the cities, and the Soviet-style first Five Year Plan was on the way. The anti-corruption campaign was carried out mainly in the cities and, like other campaigns, was a preparation for taking in Party members. In some cases, however, the anti-corruption campaign backfired. Party members in the economic departments who had come under suspicion during the campaign lost much of their enthusiasm for the new regime. They had to be re-indoctrinated.[62]

The recruitment of workers to the Party moved slowly. City people were still treated with mistrust. A *People's Daily* editorial said at the end of 1953: 'The focus of work has turned from the villages to the cities . . . The Party Central has decided to take a number of reliable village Party leaders, whose political stance can be trusted, and transfer them to responsible positions in the state-owned industries.' In the years 1952 and 1953, 70,000 county cadres, 10 per cent of all county cadres, were transferred to industries to become managers, directors, Party secretaries or heads of trade unions in factories.[63]

This may have seemed like a sensible way of ensuring Party control in the industries. But sending these admirable but semi-literate village Party men to run industries in the cities could not do much to help economic development. This was not mentioned, perhaps not even noticed, in those days.

Some efforts were made to induce engineers and technicians to enter the Party. But the old Party men, who were uneducated and had no notion of technology, were unhappy about admitting them to their ranks: 'They may have technical knowledge, but their political level is not high. They come from a different society and their personal history is not clear. Most of them come from bourgeois "exploiting" families.' The old Party members could not see how such men could be accepted into the Party. The Party leadership itself held that the political standard of Party membership should not be lowered; for acceptance into the Party more was needed than being an engineer or a good factory foreman. These people should be helped to transform their minds, and thus become ready to enter the Party.[64]

The number of workers and technicians in the Party grew slowly. In the second half of 1953 only 11,000 workers joined in the greatest industrial city, Shanghai.[65] In a whole year 6,200 workers joined in Zhongqing city, Sichuan province. In Shaanxi province, 800 joined.[66] In the big modern city of Tianjin 8,600 joined.[67]

These were very small numbers compared with the millions of peasant Party members. Tens of thousands of semi-literate county Party leaders who had been sent to the cities were running the industries. This situation did not change throughout the years ahead.[68]

Intellectuals

In his 1952 New Year greetings Mao wished 'victory to the cultural and educational frontline'. In a Communist-ruled country everyone has to be a Marxist and to be under the control of the Party. The terrifying campaigns did much to achieve this by imposing, if not conviction, at least submission.

The word 'intellectual' has to be taken in its broadest sense in China, for it includes people who have finished their secondary education, or perhaps only their primary education. In the universities the Soviet system was introduced and textbooks were translated from Russian. In

Peking and Tianjin 3,000 teachers from twenty schools were obliged to attend indoctrination courses, introduced by Zhou Enlai in a five-hour speech on September 29, 1951. Senior professors, including experts of world repute, had to listen to Party philosophers from the caves of Yan'an so that they might learn about Marxism and so change their minds. Those who resisted, like Zhang Dongsun, a professor of philosophy, were put under house-arrest. Many of them disappeared without trace. Many others, however, said they were doing their best to get rid of bourgeois ideas acquired when studying abroad.[69]

Not long after the establishment of the new regime the genuine 'intellectuals' experienced what Marxist Party control meant. In 1951 a film entitled *Wu Xun Zhuan*, the story of a village teacher who taught everyone without class distinction — he had no class-consciousness —, was condemned in a thunderous nationwide campaign. The condemnation of this excellent film exerted a paralysing influence on the film industry. This influence lasted for years — for thirty years, in fact. In the 1950s Russian films were shown in the theatres.[70] In 1953 the classic historical novel, the *Red Chamber Dream*, was condemned.[71] More important still was the condemnation of the writer Hu Feng, which began in 1952 and led to his branding as 'counter-revolutionary' in 1955. This was not so much a struggle for Marxist purity as a battle between the writers who had come from Yan'an, and the Marxist writers of the 'White Area' who had been influenced by Mao, Communist Party men who had worked in the Nationalist-ruled cities.[72]

The Hu Feng case grew into a nationwide witch-hunt. Supporters of Hu Feng, dubbed 'Hu Feng elements', were found in many universities.[73] Lu Dingyi, the Party's propaganda boss, reported to the 1955 meeting of the People's Congress that many 'Hu Feng elements, forming counter-revolutionary cliques' were to be found in the country. Hu's name was associated with that of Pan Hannian, of whom little was known in those days.[74] Hu Feng survived the troubles and was rehabilitated after Mao's death.

The nature of campaigns

The pattern of Party action was clear: all sectors of the population were to be submitted to the almighty Party. The brutal handling of peasants, the suppression of all opposition, and the anti-corruption campaign all followed the same pattern: intimidation; pressure for the denunciation of neighbours, friends and even one's own family; government regulations published not before but during the action; public executions of numerous culprits; elimination from the Party of those whom these actions repelled; and recruitment of those who were ready to take part in the violence. The power of the Party was to be made unassailable. Yet the rulers never felt safe. Such violence could intimidate people, but it could not create spontaneous support.

It was deemed necessary to repeat campaigns on this pattern periodically in the ensuing years, even after the death of Mao. In the 1980s, in what seemed to be a liberal period, the labour camps were not dissolved; only the type of inmates changed. Disorderly youngsters filled the camps. The years 1981–3 saw the return of mass executions, said to be executions of criminals only, but then all counter-revolutionaries, all who are opposed to the regime, are criminals.

This terrifying aspect of life under the People's Republic is beyond the understanding of those who have never lived under similar conditions or those who read only foreign-language Peking publications and the reports of travellers and of China experts who are worrying about their next entry permit to China. It is impossible to put oneself into the frame of mind of people who have been flung off their own land and out of their houses, members of whose family have been executed, and whose lives have never been free from constant fear.

The first storm at the top

The local Party cadres who were enthusiastically killing the enemies of the Party and recruiting new members can hardly have known what was brewing at the top.

Until 1954 the highest Party leaders did not live together in Peking. The Central Committee had six regional bureaux, each ruling several provinces. The government administration was similarly divided into six regional administrations, Northeast, North China, Central China, Central-South, Northwest and Southwest. The top Party leaders, most of them military men, were living in the major cities of their regions. There were no visible divergencies of policy between the regions — except that many new reforms were first introduced in the Northeast before being adopted for the whole country by the Central Government in Peking. This changed in 1954–5. In 1954 the regions were abolished, and their leaders were summoned to Peking.

General Peng Dehuai, the former head of the Northwest, became minister of defence; General Liu Bocheng, from the Southwest, became head of training in the Liberation Army; Liu Lantao, from North China, became deputy secretary of the Central Committee, General Lin Biao of the Central-South became vice-premier and, in 1955, a member of the Politbureau. Two others, Gao Gang of the Northeast and Rao Shushi of East China, two out of six, were purged.[75]

To all appearances, Mao's rule had been consolidated and the possibility of rivalry had been precluded. In 1953 the first Five Year Plan went into force, though the Plan itself was announced only in 1955. It was in all its aspects a Soviet plan, emphasising the development of regions close to the Soviet Union and neglecting those far away.

There were, however, clear signs that the concentration of the top leaders in Peking had not brought about greater cohesion among the leaders, and that not all agreed with Mao.

The purge of Gao Gang was decided upon, not by a Party Congress but by a Party Conference, an *ad hoc* gathering. The collectivisation of the land was introduced by Mao at a casual meeting of provincial Party leaders, not even at a Party Conference or a Central Committee Plenum. Would Mao have done this if he had had the support of his partners in the leadership?

Gao Gang became head of the State Planning Committee in November 1952. Fifteen months later he was already a finished man, though at that time his condemnation had not yet been made known to the public. It has never been stated, but it was only too obvious, that Gao Gang and his Northeast region were leading the nation in economic transformation on the Soviet model. The Soviet presence was more extensive in Manchuria than in other parts of the country. Gao Gang was not touched during Stalin's lifetime, but Stalin died in March 1953, and eleven months later his fate was sealed.

On National Day, October 1, 1954, Khrushchev and his colleagues were at the Peking parade. The Soviet Union agreed to return to China the port city of Port Arthur. China had to assert her independence, and the Soviet Union obviously had to make some concessions. But China was still following the Soviet example closely. With the Soviet Union building up China's economy, she could hardly have done otherwise.

What went on within the highest leadership in those years was not revealed until September 1956, when at last a Party Congress, the eighth since 1921, was held. It was held shortly after the sensational Twentieth Party Congress in the Soviet Union at which Khrushchev revealed Stalin's crime of 'cult of personality'. The Eighth Chinese Party Congress, ostensibly adhering servilely to the Russian model, spoke against the 'cult of personality', which in China meant the cult of Mao. Mao remained Chairman of the Party, but he had to give up his other leading posts in the Party. This cannot have been the result of a sudden move. Opposition to the overwhelming power of Mao must have been brewing during the years preceding 1956. Mao may have regretted having gathered in his chief lieutenants from the regions to Peking. In 1957–8 he reacted violently against the 1956 Party Congress, as we shall see later.

The years 1954–6 were a sort of watershed in the history of Communist rule in China. Let us look at the details.

Gao Gang

According to the decisions of the Seventh Party Congress held in Yan'an in 1945, a Party Congress should have been convoked every three years and a Central Committee Plenum every six months. No Party Congress had been held since 1945. The first Central Committee Plenum was held in 1945, the second in March 1949 and the third in June 1950.[76]

The Fourth Plenum of the Seventh Party Central Committee was held on February 6–10, 1954. The announcement that it had been held was not made till eight days later. Mao was conspicuously absent; he was 'on holiday'. The Plenum unanimously passed a Resolution 'proposed by Mao' on Strengthening Party Unity. It decided that a Party Conference was to be held in the same year, 1954. Liu Shaoqi presided over the Plenum. He extolled Mao's virtues and gave high praise to land reform, the suppression of counter-revolutionaries, the anti-corruption campaign and the mental reform of the intellectuals.

Liu announced that the new 'democratic revolution' was coming to an end and that now was the time for the 'socialist transformation'. This was to be a threefold process involving the socialisation of agriculture, handicrafts and private business. It was not to be a peaceful process but a 'complex struggle'. Social classes were doomed to extinction; but they would not expire peaceably. They would resist, and would conspire with foreign imperialism to overthrow the Party.

'The enemy knows as well as we do the truth that a fortress can most easily be destroyed from within,' Liu said. The enemy wants to make use of factions inside the Party exploiting them for their own purposes.

Historic lessons have been taught by Chen Duxiu and Zhang Guotao in China and by Beria in the Soviet Union.

Chen Duxiu and Zhang Guotao were the old heretics in the Party. Beria disappeared suddenly following the elevation of Khrushchev.

Liu announced that the Party then had 6.5 million members but he said that the ideological and political attitudes of many were still confused.

Even in high circles, he said, there was a lack of understanding of

1. Party cohesion.
2. Collective leadership.
3. The importance of the prestige of the Central Committee.

He pointed out what he saw to be the main defects of the Party: emphasis on personal prestige, vindictiveness against those who criticised, divisions and factions within the Party and, last but not least, regarding one's own region or department as personal property or as an 'independent kingdom'.

Liu prescribed the Stalinist remedy, criticism and self-criticism. Those whose faults were of little importance or who sincerely made amends should be cured but not expelled. Those who caused dissension and stirred up factionalism would be 'fought mercilessly' and expelled from the Party.[77]

The Party's National Conference was convoked in March 1955, but news of the meeting was released only after the event. A Party Conference, as we said earlier, is not a Congress. Neither the frequency of its meetings nor the number of representatives to be present was determined in the 1945 Party Constitution. A Conference is supposed to represent more than half of the provincial Party committees; at a Congress half of the members of the Party should be represented.

Mao Zedong presided at this March 1955 Party Conference. Three points were discussed: the Five Year Plan, the establishment of a Party Control organ, and the expulsion of Gao Gang and Rao Shushi from the Party.

Why Rao Shushi was included with Gao Gang has never been explained. Did he die, or did he linger on somewhere in obscurity? That too has never been made clear. The elimination of Rao may have been an act of revenge by Chen Yi and his friend Zhou Enlai. The rivalry between Rao and Chen Yi went back to 1943, the time of the Party reform in Yan'an (see Chapter III). During the Japanese war and the civil war, General Chen Yi was commander of the powerful Fourth Route Army and he remained its commander when it was renamed the Third Field Army before the take-over of the country. At the time of the 'liberation', he became mayor of Shanghai, but in the Party he remained the number two man in the Central Committee's East China Regional Bureau, after Rao Shushi. Chen Yi was promoted to the rank of Marshal in 1955. In 1958 he took over the post of foreign minister from Zhou Enlai; obviously he was one of Zhou Enlai's men.

The case of Gao Gang was very different and had much wider implications. He was not one of Mao's early companions. Mao met him only at the time of his own arrival with his troop in the north of Shaanxi province in 1935, after the Long March. Gao Gang had been a revolutionary Party leader in that area before Mao arrived (see Chapter X).

After the Japanese war Gao Gang was sent to Manchuria with Lin Biao, Lin Feng, Chen Yun and Li Fuchun. Lin Biao was the military leader and Lin Feng was the head of the Northeast Government Council. Gao Gang took over the leadership, military and political, of the Northeast at the end of 1948 when the Nationalist army, then in Manchuria, collapsed and Lin Biao led his troops south to conquer the country.

It should be remembered that the first troops to enter Manchuria in 1945 were Soviet troops. The Soviet Union had always regarded Manchuria as lying within its own sphere of interest. In the first years of the People's Republic, after 1949, when the Communists were still struggling to subdue the South and even many parts of North China, Communist rule had already been consolidated in Manchuria, known as the Northeast. In August, a month before the establishment of the People's Republic, the Communist labour organisation held its national conference at Harbin in the Northeast. In 1950 the Communist-organised trade union had a total membership of 5 million, and 1 million of these were in the Northeast. Labour insurance started there in 1949; it was extended to the whole country in 1951. Party propagandists were organised in 1950. There were tens of thousands of them in every province in the Northeast; but there were only 3,000 in the whole of Central-South China and only a few hundred in Peking. The 'more production and thrift' campaign, organised on the Soviet model as a prelude to the anti-corruption campaign, began in the Northeast and was subsequently extended to other parts of the country. Even the railway administration of China was modelled on that of Manchuria — on the Harbin railway, which was Soviet-administered until the end of 1952. The regional Communist currencies were unified a year before the takeover of the whole country; the Manchurian currency was maintained until 1951. The development of heavy industry was started under Soviet direction in Manchuria. The Soviet-style economic reforms and institutions introduced in the Northeast served as models for the whole country.

When, on November 15, 1952, the State Planning Committee was established in Peking, its first head was Gao Gang. This Committee was parallel to, not subject to, the Cabinet, and it included some of the highest leaders: Chen Yun, Peng Dehuai, Lin Biao, Deng Xiaoping and Lu Fuchun. Six weeks after the establishment of the Committee, the first Five Year Plan period started. A major item in the first Five Year Plan was the steelworks of Anshan in the Northeast, built by the Soviet Union. When three large new factories were opened there in December 1953, the Soviet minister of metallurgy attended in person, and the Peking government was represented by Gao Gang — as Vice-Chairman of the Peking Government Council. The Soviet guests proceeded to Peking, and Zhou Enlai, the prime minister, gave a banquet in their honour. Gao Gang's name was at the head of the list of Chinese guests; it was his last public act.

Three months later at the Fourth Plenum of the Central Committee, Liu Shaoqi thundered against those who were leading 'independent kingdoms'. To implement the decisions of the Fourth Plenum, the Central Committee sent a special envoy to the Northeast — and nowhere else — and subjected the Party leadership there to sharp criticism.

In June 1954 a Government Council meeting, attended by Mao and all the Vice-Chairmen except Gao Gang, decided upon the suppression of the Great Administrative Areas. In September 1954 the First People's Congress reorganised the structure of the government. The State Planning Committee lost its independent position, becoming an organ of Zhou Enlai's Cabinet, and was given a new head in the person of Li Fuchun. Perhaps at this time Gao Gang was no longer alive.

None of the speeches delivered at the March 1955 Party Conference was published; only the final resolution. Some of the key passages are worth quoting:

'From 1949 Gao Gang engaged in conspiratorial activities, aimed at seizing the power of leadership in the Party and in the state.'

'In Northeast China and other places, he created and spread many rumours slandering the Central Committee of the Party, and lauding himself . . . undermined Party unity and solidarity and made the Northeast Area an independent kingdom of Gao Gang.'

'He even tried to instigate Party members in the army to support his conspiracy against the Central Committee of the Party.'

'For this purpose, he raised the utterly absurd "theory" that our Party consisted of two parties — one, the so-called "party of the revolutionary bases and the army", the other, the so-called "party of white areas" [the areas which before 1949 were under the rule of the Nationalist Government].'

'Jao Shushi was Gao Gang's chief ally in his anti-Party conspiratorial activities. In 1953 he thought that Gao Gang was on the point of success in his activities to seize power in the Central Committee.'

'Gao Gang, Rao Shushi and others formed an anti-Party alliance . . . against the Central Political Bureau of the Central Committee of the Party headed by Comrade Mao Zedong.'

'The characteristics of the Gao-Rao anti-Party alliance was that they never openly put forward any programme opposed to the Central Committee of the Party in any Party organisation or at any Party meetings or among the public . . . They did their utmost to cover up their true character . . .'

'The National Conference of the Communist Party of China unanimously decided to expel from the Party Gao Gang and Rao Shushi.'

'Rao Shushi has never shown any signs of repentance, and now persists in an attitude of attacking the Party [a scarcely credible statement].'

'Gao Gang not only did not admit his guilt to the Party but even committed suicide as an expression of his ultimate betrayal of the Party. [Suicide, as in the days of the old Empire, was looked upon as a protest against the regime.]'

With these two, seven other leading Party members, all associated with Gao Gang, were censured.

Thirty years have passed. The memory of Gao Gang has never been rehabilitated, but some of the men condemned with him reached high positions in later years. The most prominent of these is Ma Hong, who during Gao Gang's time was director of the Secretariat of the Party's Northeast Bureau. In 1979 he became deputy head of the Academy of Social Sciences, and in August 1982 its head. Guo Feng was deputy director of the Northeast Bureau's organisation department under Gao Gang. After Mao's death in 1979 he became a Party secretary and in 1980 First Party secretary of Liaoning province in the Northeast. Zhang Mingyuan was Third Party secretary of the Northeast Bureau under Gao Gang. Years later under Lin Biao he was military representative in a ministry in Peking. When Lin Biao fell in 1971, he disappeared. Zhao Dezun was the head of the village department in the Northeast. After Mao's time, in 1979, he became Party secretary and head of the provincial People's Congress in Heilongjiang province in the Northeast. Zhang Xiushan was chairman of the Northeast Control Committee under Gao Gang. In the 1970s he took up an overseas posting as a military attaché. In the 1980s he was a member of the Central Committee's Advisory Board and of the Party Reform Committee.

The true reason for the purge of Gao Gang has never been revealed. There are two possibilities. Moscow may have thought that the Peking government was solidly established and that it was accepting fully the guidance of the Soviet advisory groups, which were to be found in all ministries of the central government. Sovietisation, under Russian guidance, was going ahead in all directions. Accordingly, a special Russian stronghold in the Northeast was no longer essential: Russian influence had spread over the whole country. This is possible but is not a sufficient explanation of the thunderous purge of Gao Gang. He could have been moved quietly from the Northeast to Peking. It is more probable that Mao Zedong wished to assert his sole leadership *vis-à-vis* the Soviet Union. Mao's oldest companions supported his action, since Gao Gang did not belong to their group. If we accept this interpretation, the purge of Gao Gang was the first attempt at asserting the independence of China from Moscow.[78]

The Sufan purge

By 1955 there were not many foreigners left in China apart from a few diplomats and technical experts from the Soviet Union and other Communist countries. It had become possible to carry out a huge nationwide purge without the outside world knowing anything of it.

Purges, unlike the Cultural Revolution, were not carried out in the streets. A foreign diplomat could stay in Peking without having an inkling of what was going on in the factories or in Party and government offices. He could travel by train without knowing that the person sitting next to him had been sent to interrogate someone suspected of having had anti-Party private conversations with a friend in another part of the country. Large amounts of money and manpower were devoted to the purges, and huge numbers of people were engaged in such investigations.

In 1955 we hardly knew that a purge was going on. Only in 1956 did we learn that one had been started in 1955, and that it had not yet ended. In June 1956 the minister of security, Luo Ruiqing, reported to the yearly meeting of the People's Congress that even after the campaign of Suppression of Counter-Revolutionaries there were still latent counter-revolutionaries in the Party, in the army and among intellectuals, and that the fight against them had been going on since 1955. This fight, he said, was also being waged against those who had resisted the collectivisation of the land. The purge would be over by the following year, 1957, he said.[79]

Three months later, at the September 1956 Party Congress, he repeated that a purge of latent counter-revolutionaries was going on. This *Sufan* purge, he said, had been ordered by Chairman Mao, because political control had become lax in 1954 and early 1955. Mao, Luo said, had forbidden the extortion of confessions under torture; he had expressed regret that such things had happened and that some innocent persons had been executed. On the other hand, some security men, among them the head of security of Shanghai city, were too indulgent and had protected some evil men. The Shanghai offender had been removed from office.

Luo took pains to be very correct. He expressed regret that some of his men had arrested people without notifying the procuratorate and the courts, and had not notified the families of the persons arrested.[80]

What the *Sufans* — the word '*Sufan*' means 'purge' — really meant and their extent were not revealed until January 1958 when, the *Sufan* having come to an end, Luo's report appeared in the January 1958 issue of *Xue Xi* (Learning), the official Party magazine of those days. In this report Luo was less scrupulous about legal niceties. He criticised the leaders of the 1956 People's Congress and Party Congress for having wanted to damp down the vigour of the purge. (The political climate in China in 1958 was very different from that of two years earlier.)

Luo's January 1958 report on the *Sufan* is worth quoting:

The purge started in June 1955 and was carried out under the guidance of the Party Central Committee and of Chairman Mao, he said.

Why was this purge launched? Luo said merely that it had started with the purge of Hu Feng's counter-revolutionary group. (For the Hu Feng case of 1955 and the purge of intellectuals, see pp. 195–6.) Why was the Hu Feng case built up into a huge nationwide purge? Luo did not explain.

The purge lasted two and half years and ended in October 1957. According to the Central Committee instruction, 5 per cent of the people in Party, government, army, government organs, social organisations, economic enterprises and schools were to be regarded as 'counter-revolutionaries or other bad elements'. 'This was only an approximate estimate and not an executive order,' Luo said. Each Party committee set up a committee of five persons to lead the *Sufan*. They were to decide who should be investigated or arrested.

Eighteen million people took part in the campaign, listening to political reports and taking an active part in self-accusation and mutual-accusation meetings; 1,770,000 people were investigated; 750,000 people were engaged in full-time investigation. The number of documents denouncing counter-revolutionaries reached 2 million.

It was a mammoth purge. No stone was left unturned in the attempt to find out who was unreliable: 130,000 were under grave suspicion, 100,000 counter-revolutionaries and bad elements were discovered (more than the prescribed 5 per cent), among them 5,000 Party members and 3,000 Youth Corps members. Of them, 220 were in the central government offices — which means that the majority of those purged were non-Party member cadres. Another campaign parallel with the *Sufan* — Luo did not explain — for the suppression of counter-revolutionaries 'in society' found 370,000 such persons.

The purge had its ups and downs, Luo said. In August 1955 people were beaten and innocent people were condemned. In 1956 there was a reaction and the 'bourgeois rightists at the People's Congress' cried out that the suppression of counter-revolutionaries was all wrong and that families were being destroyed and people were perishing. They wanted to organise a commission for rehabilitation. This meant, Luo said, that they wanted to overthrow the people's democratic dictatorship. In the spring of 1956 the *Sufan* was at its low point: those who should have been arrested were not being arrested and those who should have been given severe sentences were being given light ones. This was corrected in 1957.

Luo had a low opinion of the 1956 Party Congress, at least of those at the Congress who argued that the stormy revolutionary period was over and that crimes should be dealt with through proper legal channels. This was an error, Luo said. The masses should investigate the counter-revolutionaries; punishment is measured by legal procedure.[81]

CHAPTER XII

MAO AND THE PARTY, 1956–1958

The invisible rupture

As the Party in the Soviet Union was the Party of Stalin, so, ever since 1945 when Mao (then in Yan'an) became the undisputed leader of the Party, the Chinese Communist Party had been the Party of Mao. It can be said that for thirty years Mao and the Chinese Communist Party were synonymous terms. This does not mean that Mao did not have his ups and downs: there was a tug-of-war between him and the Party leaders in his immediate entourage. For many years, however, indeed until the Cultural Revolution, this was hardly visible. Now, in the vista of the intervening years, the dissension and the tug-of-war have become clear.

In the years 1956–7, indeed from as early as 1954, the Party was pulling in two opposite directions. There was a strong though barely visible trend towards diminishing Mao's power. Mao was patient but resilient; he always won.

1955: Mao riding high

In September 1954 the first State Constitution of the Republic was passed by the People's Congress. It was a faithful copy of the 1936 Soviet Constitution. It introduced, along with many other legislative innovations, a sort of rule of law, even if this was the Soviet rule of law. This was the opposite of the way the country had been governed up to that time, by rhapsodic political campaigns without rules or regulations.

According to the 1954 State Constitution, the Head of the State, the President, called Chairman, is hardly more than a figurehead. Mao was the Chairman. The Chairman had no special powers. He could not veto the decisions of the Congress. He did indeed retain the title of commander of the armed forces, but he could not declare war. However Mao was also the Chairman of the Party, and the Party Chairman was the supreme leader.

Since his visit to Moscow in the winter of 1949/50, Mao had not made an important speech. His public statements had been short and jejune. With the passing of the years his old flow of words seemed to have dwindled down to a trickle of after-dinner speeches and short opening addresses at official meetings. Was this because he was under the shadow of Stalin, or was it because the Party and government administration of China was still divided between Peking and the regional leaders of the Great Administrative Areas, two of whom he distrusted, Gao Gang and Rao Shushi? In 1953 Stalin died. In 1954, on Mao's orders but not in his presence, the elimination of Gao Gang was launched.

After the disappearance of Stalin the Soviet Union and the whole communist world began to breathe more freely, and the leaders around Mao were using this opportunity to introduce the State Constitution and to try — as we shall see below — to curtail Mao's power in the Party. They failed.

On July 31, 1955, Mao summoned to an *ad hoc* meeting not the Politbureau, or the Party Central Committee, but some regional Party leaders. The holding of this meeting and the speech Mao made were not revealed to the public till three months later. It was a true Mao speech. He started with the story of an old-fashioned woman, hobbling along on bound feet, lurching from side to side, and angry with the bystanders who urged her to walk faster. Many of our comrades, like this woman, are terrified, he said. Mao wanted a faster rate of economic development. Obviously he did not have the unanimous support of his companions in the highest Party leadership. There are comrades, he said, who lecture us about the perils of this speedy advance. They do not see that the cleavage between the poor and the rich villages is growing even wider.

Mao got what he wanted. Two and half months later, on October 4–11, 1955, the Central Committee held its Sixth Plenum, which formulated the decision on collective farms. This was explained by Chen Boda, a close confidant of Mao's since Yan'an days. It was also decided that a Party Congress, the eighth, should he held.[1]

Mao's banner was flying high. In September 1955, the Youth Corps organised a mass meeting in the lavishly decorated Congress Hall, with a huge statue of Mao Zedong standing on view. The Congress was addressed by Deng Xiaoping and Hu Yaobang, and also by Luo Ruiqing, the man whose job was the pursuit of 'latent counter-revolutionaries' in all walks of life.[2]

That was the year of Luo Ruiqing, the year of the *Sufan* purge, which was carried out under Mao's direction.

Hu Yaobang, the boss of the Party in the 1980s and in those days head of the Youth Corps, belonged to the same fellowship. In August 1955 he decorated members of the Youth Corps who were denouncing latent counter-revolutionaries. All this — the *Sufan* purge and Hu Yaobang's decoration of informers — happened only a year after the publication of a regulation on arrest and detention: 'No citizen may be placed under arrest except by decision of the People's Court or with a permit from a people's procurator.' A jury system and legal counsellors had been established.[3] No scruples about such legal niceties were felt during the *Sufan* purge and the pursuit of the Hu Feng clique, two events which shook the country.

1956: Cultural freedom

In the following year, 1956, the *Sufan* pursuit of the enemy slowed down and, as we saw above, Luo Ruiqing complained that the slowing down was the work of the People's Congress and the Party Congress, which wanted moderation and the rule of law.

This was an odd year. In February the Twentieth Congress, at which Khrushchev denounced Stalin, was held in the Soviet Union. A month before that, Zhou Enlai, the number three man in the Party and prime minister of the government, delivered a subtle speech addressed to intellectuals.

Zhou Enlai was one of those men who never tell the truth and never tell a lie. For them there is no distinction between the two. The speaker says what is appropriate to the circumstances. Zhou Enlai was a perfect gentleman; he was also a perfect Communist.

His speech, delivered in January 1956 and remembered to this day, dealt with 'high intellectuals'. He admitted that this was a vague term. There may be 100,000 in this category, he said. He was speaking at a ten-day conference, convoked not by the government but by the Party and attended by members of the Central Committee and of Party committees in the provinces, and by Party secretaries from universities, scientific institutes, major factories, mines, hospitals, literary and artistic organisations and the army. It was a solemn occasion expressing the official view at the time on highly educated people.

Zhou divided the 100,000 or so 'high intellectuals' into three categories, according to their conformity to the Party Line: 40 per cent he believed, were 'progressive elements' who supported the Communist Party actively; 20 per cent were backward, some being counter-revolutionaries; in between were 40 per cent who did their duty but were indifferent to politics.

Zhou pointed out that since 1949 the intellectuals had been receiving what he called a sound education in the school of class struggle. They had had to take part in the land reform, in the suppression of the counter-revolutionaries, and in the anti-corruption campaign.

He did not say that that had been enough to put the fear of the gods into these educated people, so different from the tough Party men, the former guerilla fighters. Even in Zhou Enlai's opinion, the majority would not even pretend that they had become Marxist.

They had good reason not to become Marxist. As Zhou himself said, the Party comrades did not trust these educated people. In the name of guarding state secrets, all such people had been denied access to even the most innocuous documents, or even to libraries. They were told to relearn science from the Soviet Union.

Zhou made no secret of the fact that the purge of counter-revolutionaries among the intellectuals, the *Sufan* purge, was still going on and would not end until the following year, 1957. He hoped that education in Marxism would bring the intellectuals closer to the Party, and predicted that by 1962 the proportion of the present 20 per cent of 'backward intellectuals' would have been reduced to 5 per cent.[4]

At the end of May 1956, Lu Dingyi, head of Party propaganda, delivered an epoch-making speech to scientists, doctors, writers and artists, under the title 'Let a Hundred Flowers Blossom and a Hundred Schools of Thought Contend'. 'A Hundred Schools', a phrase taken from ancient China, signified the divergent philosophical schools of the time of Confucius. Lu said that in using this phrase he was quoting Mao.

The Hundred Flowers policy meant a relaxation of discipline and a liberal tolerance of varying opinions. Lu said that this liberal policy was modelled on the Soviet practice, although, he said, learning from the Soviet Union did not mean mechanical imitation. In the Soviet Union many restrictions had been relaxed after Stalin's death, and even criticism of Lysenko's theories was allowed.

Scientific theories, Lu said, should not be labelled feudal, bourgeois or socialist. It should not be said that Pavlov's theory was socialist and Morgan's hereditary theory capitalist. Yet neither Pavlov nor Michurin should be rejected simply because they were Russians; that would be a political deviation. Liberalism did not mean that counter-revolutionaries would not be pursued, or that in philosophy idealism might be defended instead of materialism. In religious matters there was freedom of propaganda, but only within the churches and temples; anti-religious propaganda should not be carried on inside the churches and temples. Literature was of course intended to hymn the new society and its heroes, but this was not to be done in a stereotyped way. 'A strict distinction must be drawn between the ideological struggle within the ranks of the People and the struggle against counter-revolutionaries.'

Lu proposed that, to help people understand the new liberal policy, four documents should be studied — the four writings issued by Mao during the great and terrifying Yan'an purge of 1942–4.[4] This should have been enough to warn people of the limits of the blooming of the Hundred Flowers.

The question of Stalin

At that time the Communist world was stirred up by Khrushchev's report on Stalin. The Chinese comrades had learned all their Marxism from Stalin; they were disinclined to rock the boat. Two months after Khrushchev's revelations, Peking's Politbureau published a document called *The Historic Experience of the Dictatorship of the Proletariat*. 'Stalin made certain serious mistakes in the latter part of his life,' it said (twenty-six years later the same thing was to be said about Mao Zedong). 'Marxism-Leninism acknowledges that leaders play an important part in history . . . But when any leader of the Party or of the state places himself above the Party and the Masses, he alienates himself from the Masses.' The Chinese Communist Party, the document proudly stated, has always followed 'the Line of the Masses'. The Chinese Party has, of course, had its troubles, beginning with Chen Duxiu in the 1920s to Gao Gang in recent years. 'The great camp of Peace and Socialism, headed by the Soviet Union, will be stronger.'

This was written at the time when only a single picture hung above Tian An Men, that of Mao, and when pictures of Mao were taking the place of old Buddhist shrines in private houses.

Khrushchev's repudiation of Stalin was not altogether a bolt from the blue. After Stalin's death *Pravda* had written about the need for collective leadership.

Works of Stalin's — *Dialectical and Historical Materialism* and his speech on linguistics — had been criticised. At the Twentieth Congress the *History of the Communist Party in the Soviet Union (Bolshevik), Short Course*, the bible of the Stalin era, was rejected by Khrushchev, to the consternation of the Chinese Communist Party, which had learned its Marxism from that book.

In China timid steps had been taken towards independence from the Soviet Union. In 1956 a Chinese economist aired the complaint that since 1949 most books on the economy had dealt with the Soviet economy. Another wrote that of the 279 books published by the Academy of Science, 271 were translations from Russian, and that it was difficult to get books by Chinese authors published. It was even alleged that many scientists did not dare to breathe a word that was not a quotation from Marx, Engels, Lenin or Stalin.[5]

These were faltering steps towards liberalisation and detachment from the Soviet model. China could not do much more. The industrialisation of China during the Five Year Plan of 1953–7 was entirely in the hands of the Soviet Union. In April 1956, during a visit to Peking, Anastas Mikoyan signed an agreement increasing the number of Soviet-aided projects from 156 to 211.[6] Moreover in the spring of 1956, when the Chinese Cabinet was preparing a twelve-year plan for the development of science, seven Soviet scientists were invited to help in drawing up the plan. About the same time Yudin, Stalin's Marxist philosopher who was ambassador to China, and eight other Soviet experts on Marxism were lecturing in Peking, explaining the development of Marxism in the Soviet Union since Stalin's death (for this they were thanked profusely by Guo Moruo, President of the Academy of Science).[7]

Marxism as philosophy was in a rather poor state in China. The Academy of Science had a Department of Philosophy and Social Sciences, headed by Pan Zinian, a brother, obviously not a 'friend', of the 'traitor' Pan Hannian who had been imprisoned in 1955 (see p. 124). Nothing, however, was being produced by the department, not even textbooks on Marxism; the members were too busy writing in support of the political campaigns, the condemnation of the film *The Story of Wu Xun* and the condemnation of Hu Feng. A Philosophy Research Bureau was still at the planning stage, and only one single school of higher education, Peking University, had a department of philosophy.[8] All had of course to study the 'philosophical essays' of Mao 'On Contradiction' and 'On Practice'. It was a period of astonishing intellectual poverty in philosophy and in Marxism.

Party membership

Through the years the Chinese Communist Party had become the biggest single party in the world. At the Fourth Central Committee Plenum in February 1954, Liu Shaoqi spoke of 6.5 million members. This implied a 2.5 million increase within two years. There was certainly intense recruitment of Party members going on in the villages, particularly in the vast regions of the South and Southwest and in other regions that had not been under Communist rule before 1949.[9]

Peasants

In 1954, 700,000 'activists among peasants' entered the Party. This was a welcome development, since the Party's agrarian policy could not be implemented without the basic Party organisations in the villages. It was important that only reliable people should be admitted. The authorities in some regions were rebuked for having admitted people without letters of recommendation from Party members or without discussion and approval by the higher Party committee. For this reason some evil counter-revolutionary people did manage to sneak into the Party. On the whole, however, things were going well.[10]

During the first half of 1955 in the country as a whole, 480,000 peasants joined the Party, yet in November there were still 20,000 villages without a Party branch. In March 1955 the total of peasants in the Party was 4 million. Who were the others, the non-peasants? In 1955 no overall figures were given for worker Party members, and only fragmentary data about a few cities were available, e.g. by the end of 1954, 20,000 workers had joined in Shanghai, and 40,000 in Wuhan.[11]

A *People's Daily* editorial published in January 1956 said that in Tianjin, for long one of the most modern and industrialised cities in China, there were only 870 Party members among the 84,000 employees of 7,900 private factories, and only 344 Party members among the 32,000 employees of the 9,000 private commerical firms there. This was the sum total yielded by the great purges, the anti-corruption purge and the taking over of private firms — a poor result![12]

Educated people were also taken into the Party, but according to a report for the year 1956, only 500 or 600 'higher intellectuals' and a few thousand 'lower intellectuals' joined in that year. As for the 'lower intellectuals', it was said that the rural Party branches despised the village teachers, because they had not come from proletarian families. In March 1956 the *People's Daily* said that an immaculate personal history was required for joining the Party. 'Undoubtedly many of the intellectuals and especially many of the high intellectuals, being descended from landlords and capitalists, have had a complex political, economic and social background.'[13]

At the Eighth Party Congress, in September 1956, Deng said that the Party had 10.7 million members, of whom 69 per cent (7.38 million) were peasants, 14 per cent (1.5 million) workers and 11.7 per cent (1.25 million) intellectuals. (The remaining 5.3 per cent, 587,000, were classed as 'others'.)

The great increase in the number of peasants — if the figures are correct — from 4 million in November 1955 to 7.38 million in September 1956 could be explained only by the sudden collectivisation of the agrarian world. The figure for workers, 1.5 million, was 6.25 per cent of all 'workers and other employees', and 17 per cent of 'industrial workers'. The higher number, 1.25 million, of intellectuals must have included many low-grade intellectuals with minimum education. In January 1956 Zhou Enlai put the number of 'higher intellectuals' at 100,000. Few of them were Party members.[14]

The Eighth Party Congress, 1956

The Congress was carefully prepared. Its convocation was decided upon at the Seventh Central Committee Plenum in October 1955. In April 1956 the Party leaders of the provinces held a meeting in Peking. In May the draft documents of the forthcoming Congress were discussed in the provinces and in the Party committees of the army and of the Party in government central offices (40,000 Party members), and representatives to the National Congress were elected. In August and September the Central Committee and provincial leaders were working out the final texts to be presented to the Congress.[15]

The results of their deliberations are not without interest. They show that a wide range of Party leaders were unaware of what was to come at the Congress. From the documents alone, who could have foreseen what was to happen?

The Congress itself, held on September 15–27, with sixty-one foreign Communist parties represented, looked like a great demonstration of unity.

The Congress documents were published in two volumes totalling 1,300 pages, with the speeches of 112 Chinese representatives and with speeches or greetings from sixty-one foreign Communist parties. The main reports were delivered by Liu Shaoqi, Deng Xiaoping and Zhou Enlai, with an introductory address by Mao Zedong. Never before or since has a Chinese Party Congress produced anything like this.

Mao complimented the 'brotherly parties', mentioning the great Soviet Union six times. All he said about the Soviet Union's Twentieth Party Congress was that it had 'formulated correct policies and criticised shortcomings'. The Chinese Communist Party with, so he said, its 10 million members was studying Marxism-Leninism eagerly. It had also had some defects — 'subjectivism, bureaucracy, sectarianism'.

Liu Shaoqi in his long report spoke mainly about the economy, and failed to mention the second Five Year Plan (1958–62). Turning next to the Party, he said that it had made the right decision at the Cun Yi conference in January 1935 which had made Mao the leader. (This, as Party documents were to reveal thirty years later, was not true — see pp. 55ff.)

The Rectification campaign in Yan'an (1942–4) combatted subjectivism and sectarianism, Liu said. He mentioned briefly the need for collective leadership on all levels of the Party organisation. Collective leadership, he said, does not mean negation of the role of the leader. 'The leader of our Party, Comrade Mao Zedong, has played the great role of helmsman in our revolution . . . He steadfastly upholds the Party's principles of democracy and collective leadership.' Comrade Deng Xiaoping, Liu said, would explain the new Party Charter.

Democratic Centralism, Deng Xiaoping said, was a principle learnt from Lenin. No Party Congress had been held for eleven years and Party democracy had suffered accordingly. However, many minor Party meetings had been held. Inner-Party democracy should not weaken centralisation. 'We do not advocate the strengthening of collective leadership in order to reduce the role of the individual. In Lenin's famous words, the leaders are those who are "the most authoritative, influential and experienced".' But the leaders, he said, must maintain close contact with the Masses, obey the Party organisations and observe Party discipline. The Twentieth Congress of the Communist Party of the Soviet Union showed us 'what serious consequences can follow from the deification of the individual . . . Our Party abhors the deification of the individual . . . A decision in 1949, at the suggestion of Comrade Mao Zedong, prohibited the use of Party leaders' names to designate places, streets or enterprises . . .' The Party was also opposed to exaggerating the role of leaders in art and literature.

There was nothing particularly striking in Deng Xiaoping's speaking against the cult of personality. The most prominent foreign speaker at the Congress was Mikoyan, representing the Soviet Union, who spoke about the Twentieth Soviet Party Congress which had condemned the cult of personality. That condemnation, he said, was supported by other Communist parties.

In those days the Chinese Communist Party was in the Soviet camp and everything seemed to be following the Soviet line. It would have been odd if Peking had disagreed on this point. The cult of personality, the deification of a leader, had been condemned; yet, as we saw earlier, both Liu Shaoqi and Deng Xiaoping paid tribute to Mao's leadership. Mikoyan himself spoke of 'the outstanding Marxist – Leninist comrade Mao Zedong, who has made a great contribution to the theory of Marxism – Leninism'.

Deng explained the changes introduced by the new Party Charter in the structure of the central leadership of the Party, but said that the new Party Charter did not 'differ in fundamental principles from the Charter adopted by the Seventh Congress' of 1945. At the end he paid special tribute to 'the leader of our Party, Comrade Mao Zedong'.

When explaining the Charter he did not touch the most sensitive point, the changes that had curtailed Mao's power.

The 1945 Party Charter laid down that 'the Chairman of the Central Committee (C.C.) is Chairman of the C.C. Politbureau, and Chairman of the C.C. Secretariat.' In those days there were no Vice-Chairmen, no Central Committee Standing Committee,[16] nothing to limit Mao's power.

In the 1956 Party Charter: 'The C.C. elects the Politbureau, the Standing Committee of the Politbureau, the Secretariat, the Chairman, Vice-Chairmen and the Secretary-General of the C.C. The Chairman and Vice-Chairmen are concurrently Chairman and Vice-Chairmen of the Politbureau. The Secretariat is under the direction of the Politbureau and its Standing Committee.'

The Charter did not say that the Secretary-General was a member of the Politbureau Standing Committee and that the C.C.'s Chairman (Mao) was not Chairman of the Standing Committee. Deng did not point out, and many of those present at the Congress may not have noticed, that a substantial change had been introduced. They may even not have noticed that in the new Party Charter there was no mention of the Party Conference, an *ad hoc* forum convoked at Mao's pleasure.

What Deng had not explained became clear at the first C.C. Plenum held immediately after the Congress. According to the prescribed procedure, the first Plenum after a Congress elects the holders of the leading posts. Mao was elected Chairman and four Vice-Chairmen were also elected, Liu Shaoqi, Zhou Enlai, Zhu De and Chen Yun. (Till then, there had been no Vice-Chairmen.) Deng Xiaoping was elected Secretary-General. The Standing Committee consisted of the Chairman, four Vice-Chairmen and the Secretary-General, all on an equal footing.

The Plenum elected seventeen regular and six alternate-members to the Politbureau. The Secretariat had seven regular and three alternate-members; the C.C. Chairman (Mao) was not a member.

The most important man in the Secretariat was the Secretary-General, Deng Xiaoping.

The members of a Control Commission were elected, with Dong Biwu as secretary.[17] The Control Commission, with Dong Biwu as head, had been set up at the 1955 Party conference, taking the place of the earlier Disciplinary Investigation Commission which, being subject to the local Party committees, was found to be too weak.[18]

Hitherto, Mao had been the head of all the highest organisations; now he was not even a member of the Secretariat. A top-level policy-making body, the Standing Committee of the Politbureau, was set up. Mao was not its Chairman; all five members were on an equal footing.

The bitter medicine administered to Mao was so sweetly coated that the curtailment of his power was barely noticeable. He remained Chairman of the Party and to all appearances was still the supreme boss. Some of the Central Committee organisations may have been run by others, but he was Chairman.

Naturally Mao knew that his wings had been clipped. (He knew also that the Party Charter, like many regulations and laws, was only a scrap of paper.) To add insult to injury, the Congress documents did not mention his Thoughts. The Thoughts of Mao Zedong had been officially proclaimed at the Seventh Party Congress by Liu Shaoqi, the very man who now presented the main report at this new Congress without a word about the Thoughts. Mao certainly understood that the criticism of the cult of the individual in Deng Xiaoping's report was not a mere compliment to, or a mere repetition of, the Soviet doctrine of the day. Ten years later, during the Cultural Revolution, Red Guard tabloids were to say that in opposing the cult of the individual at the Eighth Congress, Deng had opposed Chairman Mao.[19]

The last straw was the article in the 1956 Party Charter that said: 'The Central Committee may, when it deems necessary, have an Honorary Chairman.' Mao and everybody else knew that only he could become Honorary Chairman. Was provision being made for his old age? He was over sixty while the other Party leaders were around fifty. Mao, however, as subsequent events were to prove, had no intention of retiring from power. From that moment on, and probably from even earlier, he was planning his counter-attack, planning his rise to supreme power. The events that followed that 1956 Eighth Party Congress were, we now know with hindsight, Mao's revenge for what had been done to him at the Congress.

Mao's name did not appear in the 1956 Party Charter. At the next

Party Congress, the Ninth, held in 1969, two names were included in the Party Charter, Mao's and Lin Biao's. As that Charter said, 'Comrade Lin Biao always raised high the great banner of the Thoughts of Mao Zedong.'[20]

It should not be thought that Mao sought his own deification. What happened after the 1969 Party Congress showed that this was not the case; on the contrary, he was afraid of being pushed by Lin Biao up into heaven, out of the sphere of the realities of power on this earth. But the 1956 Eighth Party Congress deprived him of direct rule over all the works of the Central Committee. Moreover, the Congress adopted a project for the Second Five Year Plan that was not to his liking. Two years later Mao rejected it.

Changes had occurred in the Politbureau between 1945 and 1956. Of the thirteen who had been members in 1945, nine were still members in 1956. Of the other four, one, Ren Bishi, had died in 1950; Gao Gang had committed suicide, and Zhang Wentian and Kang Sheng had become merely alternate-members (with no right to vote). The places of Ren Bishi and Gao Gang were taken in 1955 by Lin Biao and Deng Xiaoping. At the Eighth Congress in 1956 the Politbureau got six new regular members, four Marshals (in addition to Zhu De and Lin Biao), Luo Ronghuan, Chen Yi, Liu Bocheng, He Long, and two leaders of the economy, Li Fuchun and Li Xiannian.[21] In 1956, the Politbureau members and candidate members were the following:

FULL MEMBERS

Mao Zedong, *Central Committee Chairman*
Liu Shaoqi, *Central Committee Vice-Chairman*
Zhou Enlai, *Central Committee Vice-Chairman*
Zhu De, *Marshal, Central Committee Vice-Chairman*
Chen Yun, *Central Committee Vice-Chairman*
Deng Xiaoping, *Secretary-General*
Lin Biao, *Marshal*
Lin Boqu
Dong Biwu
Peng Zhen
Luo Ronghuan, *Marshal*
Chen Yi, *Marshal*

Li Fuchun
Peng Dehuai, *Marshal*
Liu Bocheng, *Marshal*
He Long, *Marshal*
Li Xiannian

CANDIDATE MEMBERS

Ulanfu
Zhang Wentian
Lu Dingyi
Chen Boda
Kang Sheng
Bo Yibo

Of the ninety-seven regular members of the Central Committee, sixty-four had been full or candidate Central Committee members since 1945. Thirty-two were new members, and of the seventy-three alternate-members seventy were new. (Twenty-eight years later, in March 1984, fifty-five of these ninety-seven regular Central Committee members were dead, seventeen of them victims of the Cultural Revolution. Twenty-four of the seventy-three alternate-members were dead, eight of them victims of the Cultural Revolution.)[22]

Moscow – Peking

The Eighth Party Congress was held at a time when the world Communist camp was in ferment, demanding, after the Soviet Twentieth Congress, greater freedom from Moscow. Mikoyan himself, speaking at the Congress in Peking, said that 'undoubtedly, every country has its own peculiarities in the way of Transition to Socialism, but this, as Lenin said, should not go beyond the essentials.' He did not mention the June 1956 workers' riot in Poznan in Poland, which had been suppressed by the Polish army and had introduced the leadership of Gomulka.

In October 1956, a month after the Chinese Party Congress, came the revolt in Hungary, suppressed by Russian tanks on November 4. On October 30, 1956, the Moscow press admitted mistakes in the treatment of other Communist countries. With extraordinary rapidity, Peking, on November 1, issued a declaration supporting the statement of the Soviet government.

The Peking declaration was ambiguous. It supported the suppression of what it called Polish counter-revolution, but it also spoke of 'large-country chauvinism', a term till then unknown in the Chinese Communist vocabulary. On November 5, one day after the suppression of the Hungarian revolt, the *People's Daily* greeted the Soviet army 'which has liberated the Hungarian people twice'.[23]

On December 28, 1956, the Peking news agency published an important article entitled 'Once Again on the Historical Experience of the Proletarian Dictatorship', and on the following day the *People's Daily* reproduced this article. Stalin was wrong, it said. He monopolised power and treated people harshly. He did help other Communist countries, but Russians working abroad interfered in the internal affairs of those countries. The Soviet Declaration of October 30 and Moscow's November negotiations with Poland show that the Soviet Union is determined to abandon past mistakes in its relations with other Communist countries.

Stalin, however, was right in exterminating counter-revolutionaries, collectivising the land, abrogating private ownership and working for world peace. Under Stalin the Soviet Union wrought victory in the war against Hitler. (Khrushchev, at the Twentieth Party Congress, was most scornful of Stalin's role in the war.) Stalin must be understood properly, the Peking article said. Guidance of the state was a new experiment for the Party; the tense internal and external struggles limited the possibilities of developing democracy; the victories and the plaudits and the praise turned Stalin's head. Yet from beginning to end he directed the struggle, steering it according to the historical trend. Stalin's and other comrades' faults are not enemies' faults; they are fellow-Communists' faults. Even when our fellows make mistakes they should not be treated as enemies (a direct reference to Khrushchev's Twentieth Congress speech); otherwise there will be confusion between the mistakes in our own ranks and antagonisms between the enemy and us.

Turning to Hungary, Peking said that it was startling to find that some Communist intellectuals in some countries, instead of upholding proletarian dictatorship, had attacked the Soviet Union's righteous defence of Hungarian socialism and dubbed the Hungarian counter-revolution a 'revolution'.

Next the Peking article deprecated servile imitation of the Soviet Union. Marxism-Leninism is the universal truth, it said, but each nation applies it in its own way. In Marxist parlance, servile imitation is called dogmatism. The Peking article said that in China dogmatism had been eliminated in 1935, when Mao had become ruler of the Party. 'We fully appreciate the greatness of the Polish and Hungarian comrades who are correcting the past errors of dogmatism', it went on, but nobody should fall into the opposite error, revisionism, which means abandoning the common ground, the universal truth. Solidarity among all socialist countries must be maintained and must centre on the Soviet Union for common defence against the imperialists, headed by the United States.[24]

This was a subtle document. To all appearances it defended the Soviet Union and its leadership of other Communist parties. 'Following the peculiarities of each country' was a popular phrase in Moscow too in those days. It was striking, however, that Peking spoke with the authority of a leader of the Communist world.

Mao in Moscow

A year later, in November 1957, Mao Zedong went to Moscow to take part in the celebrations for the fortieth anniversary of the October Revolution and to attend a meeting of all Communist parties.[25] It was his second trip to Moscow and, as he never went anywhere else in the outside world, it was his second and last trip abroad. Why did he go? China needed further Russian financial loans, and was seeking nuclear expertise.

In July 1957 at the People's Congress, Li Xiannian, then minister of finance, had reported a budget deficit for 1956.[26] Li accompanied Mao to Moscow. The Chinese Academy of Science sent a huge delegation to the Moscow celebrations to discuss further 'scientific cooperation' with the Soviet Union. The foreign press was at that time discussing the possibility of a new US$2 billion Soviet loan to China; Peking said nothing.[27]

On October 15, 1957, two weeks before Mao left for Moscow, a secret agreement was made between Peking and Moscow on 'new technology for national defence, . . . to provide China with a sample of an atomic bomb and technical data for its manufacture'. (This was revealed by Peking in an exchange of polemical letters six years later).[28] Just on the eve of the Moscow celebrations, Chinese military leaders were suddenly summoned to Moscow.[29] Mao in Moscow was as humble as he could be, though he made the incredible blunder of saying that in an atomic war only half of the human race would perish (reported in the Chinese press in 1963[30]). He congratulated the Russian Twentieth Party Congress on 'having overcome the cult of personality', and he expressed his admiration for Khrushchev's policies in agriculture, regional decentralisation and the reform of industrial management.

At home shameless adulation of things Soviet was reintroduced in the press. Deep gratitude was expressed for the construction by the Russians of a chemical fertiliser plant in the Northeast.[31] Gratitude was also expressed to those Russians working in Chinese art organisations, in theatre, film, music and ballet.

Soviet advisers to the ministry of education in Peking issued directives on how to teach in schools. The Soviet General Adviser to the Chinese Cabinet, Ivan Arkhipov, on his own initiative, organised a six-month series of lectures to Chinese higher intellectuals in a dozen Chinese cities, and it was a Russian adviser to the Weights and Measures Office of the Cabinet who urged the introduction of standards for precision machinery. All criticism of the Soviet Union was condemned and the critics were rebuked.[32]

In 1956, after the Twentieth Soviet Congress and after the events in Poland and Hungary, Peking had been addressing Moscow in arrogant tones with an air of superiority, pointing out the mistakes the Russians had made in China. Now, a year later, all was sweetness and flattery in Moscow and at home.

In that year, 1957, Mao at home was a different man. This was the year in which he first solicited free criticism of the Party, and then, in June put an abrupt stop to it. Six weeks before he left for Moscow he thundered against the Third Central Committee Plenum for the way in which the Eighth Party Congress in 1956 had dealt with his ambitious economic plans. Critics of his regime, inside the Party and outside, were sent to labour camps. A few months after his return from Moscow he launched the Communes and the Great Leap.

At the time when Mao was in Moscow the Russians could not have known that the communes were coming. No one in China knew it either. But everybody did know that the free speech and criticism that Mao had solicited had been a gigantic fraud. Khrushchev can hardly have shed tears over the fate of educated people in China, but he was puzzled by the personality of the Chinese leader. He wrote in his *Memoirs*: 'He [Mao] deceived us for several years before we saw through his tricks. . . . He is not — as some claim — a madman . . . Mao is very intelligent and very cunning.'[33]

CHAPTER XIII

1957: THE TRAP

Call to speak up

Six months after the Eighth Party Congress, on February 27, 1957, Mao delivered one of his major speeches. This was the famous 'On the Correct Handling of Contradictions among the People'. It dealt with contradictions within the People, and with contradictions with the Enemy — not the external enemy but the enemy inside the country: contradictions with the enemy within are called 'antagonistic contradictions'. The 'enemy' is to be treated harshly and to suffer the blows of dictatorship. (All this was not Mao's invention. It was the old Marxist sorting out of friends and enemies.)

This speech of Mao's, though made in February, was not published until June. This was Mao's established way of acting. Twelve years earlier his Yan'an speech on 'Literature and Art', declaring that there was no human nature, only class nature, did not appear in print in the Yan'an *Liberation Daily* until seventeen months later. The 1957 speech was published four months after delivery, when the critics had become too vociferous and free speech was to be halted.

Mao's speeches were not delivered at secret meetings, whether in 1942 in Yan'an or in 1957 in Peking. In Peking, 1,800 people listened to him, and the speech was recorded and listened to by people all over the country. (Khrushchev's 'secret' speech at the Twentieth Congress of the Soviet Union was treated in the same way.) Yet, as no less a person than Ba Jin, a famous pre-Communist writer, pointed out, Mao's speech was hard to understand. The reason may have been faulty recording, or it may have been Mao's diction. Mao spoke a dialect of a kind that few Chinese could understand. When he spoke in Moscow in 1957, his speech was transmitted by radio in China, but after a few sentences the lady announcer in Peking took over because of Mao's dialect.

The most likely reason, however, is that what Mao said in February was altered in the published text in June.

Mao's February speech was welcomed as a relaxation of discipline, and an invitation to free criticism of the Party. 'The storm-like class struggles of the masses have ended,' he said. 'There are still counter-revolutionaries though there are not many of them . . . The class struggle has not yet ended.' (Twenty years later Deng said the same.) 'Can criticism of Marxism be allowed? Of course Marxism may be criticised, Marxism is not afraid of criticism.'[1]

Shortly after Mao's February 1957 speech, Lu Dingyi, head of Party propaganda, delivered a speech on the impending Party purge. It will not, he said, be a rough pursuit of enemies. Since the Party took over the government, many abuses have crept into the Party ranks — bureaucracy, factionalism and the like. All these are 'contradictions within the People and are not questions between us and the enemy. Such problems should be solved by patient and meticulous persuasion, not by rough administrative methods. What is needed is the Hundred Flowers and the Hundred Schools policy. This will continue for a long time. Party members and non-Party members will supervise each other.' He hoped that people from outside the Party would put forward suggestions for solving the Party's problems. That was how the problems brought up at the Eighth Party Congress could be solved.

Lu said that Party membership had reached 12 million, of whom 60 per cent had entered the Party after 1949; these members were not yet properly trained. He recalled the Party Rectification campaign in 1942.[2]

On April 27, an official instruction was issued about a forthcoming Party reform. It was as mild and deceptive as the speeches of Mao and Lu Dingyi. Referring to Mao's February speech, it said that the Party reform would be an exercise in Hundred Flowers discussion. It would start — unlike previous purges — from below, from the counties. There would be no 'struggle meetings', public criticisms or anything of that sort, and those who were criticised would be free not to accept the criticism. Even if great mistakes were revealed, unless these were enormous irregularities, no sanctions would be imposed. Criticism of people from outside the Party would be welcome.[3]

Many fell into the trap. There was an atmosphere of easygoing freedom — not unlike that of twenty-one years later, when Deng Xiaoping took over power.

Ever since the announcement of the Hundred Flowers policy in 1956, university students had been taking things easy. They were not turning up for compulsory exercises, much less for political indoctrination. Moreover, events in Eastern Europe were having a great influence on Chinese youth. The Party was quick to react, and stricter discipline was reintroduced in the schools.[4] However, the wave of freedom could not be halted. On May 23, 1957, a woman law student at the People's University went to Peking University, the leading university in the country, and made a fiery speech about the injustices of the *Sufan* purge and the lack of freedom, and about socialism being nothing other than feudalism. Her speech was reported only later when the repression had set in.[5] (This law student, Lin Xiling, disappeared and was not to reappear until twenty-five years later in 1983, when she was allowed to leave the country.)

For two months, in April and May 1957, freedom and liberalism flourished ever more abundantly. This was the period of Free Speech. In April, Zhou Enlai, talking to the visiting Russian, Voroshilov, spoke with approval of the student protests. Zhou Yang, deputy head of Party propaganda, told foreign correspondents that workers' strikes were acceptable. 'The Chinese people have the right to strike just as they have the right to free speech and free meetings,' he said.[6]

The educated adult population was more cautious than the students. The chief librarian of a Shanghai university, who was not a Party member, was quoted as having said that Chairman Mao's proposing free expression of opinion was very welcome. 'Yet doubt remains. Today I may speak as I will, but after a period, after a year or two, will not a written record of my words be brought up against me? I am not the only one who thinks this way. Everyone I meet thinks similarly. Today there is a reform movement inside the Party. Many are wondering whether this will not hit us too.'

These intellectuals, a Shanghai newspaper pointed out in April, had already undergone much. They had had juvenile Party cadres coming to visit them, saying 'I have come to reform you'; they had gone through the purge of the intellectuals and through the anti-corruption campaign. One of them had said that when he heard the words 'mental reform' the picture of a forced labour camp rose in his mind. Their caution was well-judged. Luo Ruiqing's ministry for public security had just opened an exhibition of evidence gathered to prove the guilt of counter-revolutionaries in Peking.

A Shanghai professor said that ever since the Communists came to power it had been necessary to take great care even in private conversation: 'You said something without meaning what you said, in the excitement of the moment or as a joke. The cadres recorded the words they heard in private conversations, and, later on when a new campaign started, quoted these words, holding you by them as if by a pigtail. You did not know whether to laugh or to cry. No wonder we learned not to talk. Many learned to be hypocritical in order to win the confidence of the officials.'

Even daring to say this was itself an expression of free speech, and was not without danger. Another Shanghai professor said that there was an invisible wall between people in the Party and those outside it: our words may be recorded and quoted later during a purge. Even Party members are afraid to mix with people, lest they be accused of mixing with politically suspect persons.

Some criticised the educational system. Thus a professor in Peking University said that among teachers there was no scholarly atmosphere; nothing but daily quarrels about housing and living conditions and meetings for planning teaching and for the transmission of higher orders. Minor grievances were also brought up; for example, that members of professors' families living in the University were not allowed to pass through the gate without identification cards. A famous old professor of philosophy, Feng Youlan, said that a review which was supposed to publish his articles had had to ask the permission of the Cabinet. Another professor said that first-class experts on education had been sent to teach in remote villages and that professors of foreign literature had been despatched to primitive border areas to teach elementary Chinese. This professor added very justly that making this statement was the most courageous act of his life. Another professor complained that the *People's Daily* had condemned a book about evolution which he had written in 1950 because it was Darwinist and did not follow Michurin. In 1955 it was condemned again. Ultimately, he wrote an apology, but this was turned down. His university dismissed him and even his best friends began to avoid him. Now, however, the spirit of the Hundred Schools was encouraging him to rewrite the book and publish it.

Another professor said that he was unable to write about the Chinese economy as he could not get any statistics. Statistics were state secrets. 'The ridiculous thing is that one can find in foreign books and magazines information about China which cannot be found here.'[7]

And so the criticism of the Party, solicited by the authorities from the intellectuals, went on. It was the pale criticism of people who had already been intimidated by past purges. They could not foresee what was to happen ten years later in the Cultural Revolution! They all said the same things, what they thought they were allowed to say: there was a wall between the Party and outsiders; there was not much scholarship in the schools; non-Party members were being discriminated against, and so on.

The *People's Daily* quoted one professor as saying: 'Although we are now being given a chance to talk, our anxiety has not yet been completely dispelled. If I say everything now, will it all go unpunished for ever? Shall I not be branded a ''self-made counter-revolutionary element''? Last time, during the *Sufan* purge, some were called ''self-made counter-revolutionary elements'', a phrase the meaning of which was never made clear. A Party secretary has told me that he guarantees that nothing will happen; but I have my doubts. Can it be guaranteed that no citizen will later be sent to a mock trial or to mob denunciation for a crime that has not been proved against him?'[8]

Clampdown

How right these fears were! Early in June there was a sudden turn of events. The flood of criticism was halted. On June 8 a *People's Daily* editorial said that rightist elements, under the pretext of helping the Communist Party to reform, were challenging the Communist Party, and even wanted to overthrow the Party and turn back history to the dictatorship of the bourgeoisie.[9]

On June 19 the text, the revised text, of Mao's February speech was published. Six criteria were laid down for distinguishing 'fragrant flowers from poisonous weeds'.

The six points were that words and deeds should:
1. Promote unity between the nationalities in China.
2. Be beneficial to socialist transformation.
3. Consolidate and not undermine the People's Democratic Dictatorship.
4. Consolidate and not undermine Democratic Centralism.
5. Strengthen the leadership of the Communist Party.
6. Be beneficial to international socialist unity.

Of these, Point 5 was the most important. The six points had not been mentioned before nor had they been included in Mao's February speech. This was the trap.

Mao ascribed the untoward events to the influence of the Hungarian revolt. 'There is no reason why we should not examine the effects the events in Hungary have had in our country. A section of our intellectuals has been disturbed . . . What happened in Hungary was a bad thing to begin with, but it turned out to be a good thing in the end; every country in the socialist camp learnt its lesson.' Mao admitted that 'whether among the population as a whole or among the intellectuals, Marxists are still in the minority . . . Throughout history no new thing has been acknowledged by the majority from the start.'

This was Mao's famous speech about 'contradictions within the
People', and 'antagonistic contradictions', the latter also called contradiction 'between the enemy and us'. The 'enemy' were 'counter-
revolutionaries'. It was up to the leaders to decide who were the enemy.

Stalin had declared that there were no longer any antagonistic contradictions in the Soviet Union. Mao was of a different opinion about
China.[10]

The people who had been urged to express their criticism of the Party
became the enemy. When the fury of the Party is unleashed, it has no
limits. On August 3, a Cabinet decision, signed by Zhou Enlai, established a new type of forced labour camp. The camps set up in the early
1950s imposed what was called 'corrective labour'; the new ones
imposed 'labour education', which was defined as 'one form of implementing forced educational reform'. Corrective labour was imposed by
the courts, and labour education by administrative measures. It was
designed primarily for the 'rightists', those who had criticised the
Party.[11] Much of what the critics of the Party had said was published only
after the speakers had been branded enemies of the Party. The professors
quoted above as expressing their anxieties were right. Mao had it down
in his Six Points that words count as much as deeds — even words that
went unspoken.

It is hardly possible to separate what the 'rightists' really said from the
accusations, false accusations, raised against them.

A teacher at the People's University in Peking named Ge Peiqi was
supposed to have said: 'You Party members say "We are the State". If
you act wrongly, the masses may overthrow you; they may kill the
Communists. This should not be called unpatriotic, for the Communist
Party is not serving the people. Though the Communist Party should
perish, China will not perish.'[12]

Twenty-five years later, in 1982, Ge Peiqi's name was cleared. He had
never said the words for which he was condemned. In 1982 he told his
story to a visiting journalist.

As a student of physics at Peking University in 1935, he took part in
demonstrations and was twice arrested but was later released. He later
joined the Nationalist army to resist the Japanese. Then he joined the
Communist Party, which told him to remain in the Nationalist army as
an underground Party worker. After the war in 1946 he served under the
Nationalist General Du Yuming and organised underground Party
work. Under the People's Republic in 1950 he became a teacher of
physics in the People's University in Peking. At the very beginning of

the repression of free speech, on June 8, 1956, the *People's Daily* published the incriminating words we quoted above. On the following day he wrote a letter to the newspaper, asking it to publish a correction. His letter was not published. Twenty-odd years later the letter was still in the Party dossier. All he had said was in fact that if errors in the Party were not corrected the Party's existence might be in jeopardy — an opinion usually put forward during a Party reform.

He was condemned to life imprisonment. In 1975 he was released under an amnesty for war criminals, but he was still detained in a labour camp. In 1978 when the rehabilitation of rightists began, his case was re-examined but even then he was not fully rehabilitated. At the end of the year he went to the office of Hu Yaobang, who was then the head of the Party's organisation department. A further review of his case was promised. In April 1980 he went to Hu Yaobang's home. With Hu's approval his case was ultimately settled.

By then he was an old man. He told the interviewer, however, that his health was unimpaired. He did not suffer during the Cultural Revolution. (He was safely locked away.) In this he was luckier than Liu Shaoqi and Marshal Peng Dehuai, who lost their lives during the Cultural Revolution.[13]

His story exemplifies what may happen even to an old Party membei who had been an underground Communist agent among the Nationalists. He was condemned in 1957, not for what he had done but for words which had been misquoted in the Peking press. He was not rehabilitated till after he had spent eighteen years in prison. He was not the only underground Party worker of the early days who had to undergo such treatment.

The 'rightists' included three Cabinet ministers, non-Party members: Zhang Bojun, minister for communications, Luo Longji, minister for forest industry, and Zhang Naiqi, minister for food. All three were members of small satellite political parties. Zhang Bojun was accused of having said that the ministry was never consulted on major construction works — the roads to Tibet, the construction of ports etc. — and that all decisions were taken within the Party. He was also accused of having said: 'During this Party Reform people outside the Communist Party were asked to express their opinions. Master Mao [*sic*] must have calculated the effect of this. The democratic parties [the small satellite parties], however, miscalculated badly. The situation that has now arisen is something that escaped all our calculations. Today we are awkwardly placed: we cannot take any step, whether forward or backward.'

It was obvious to all that this was exactly what was happening. These men were caught in a trap laid by Mao.

He (Zhang Bojun) confessed his sins and apologised. Zhang Naiqi, minister for food, had the guts to say that capitalist enterprises were more efficient than the present ones, and that the Party was treating the former owners badly. He refused to apologise.

Luo Longji, minister for forest industry, wanted to rehabilitate those wrongly condemned in previous purges. He was a 'bourgeois', educated in Britain and the United States. He wrote an abject confession, recalling that thirty years earlier when editing a monthly he had criticised the Communists. To clear himself he turned against Zhang Bojun. Much of the early history of these men was dug up. Luo Longji was accused of having disobeyed the Shanghai Party underground in 1948.

Two leading newspapers were also in trouble. The editor-in-chief of the *Guang Ming Daily* of Peking, Chu Anping, was accused in an article in the *People's Daily* of having written against the higher Party leadership by asking: 'Have the leaders of the Party Central Committee no responsibility for the general shortage?' He was also upbraided for having written that since 1954 all the twelve Vice-Premiers had been Party leaders, and that every office, even the lowest, was headed by a Party member. In the Shanghai *Wen Hui Bao*, Pu Xixiu, Luo Longji's wife, was accused of having been responsible for the many erroneous articles in the paper.[14] Two years later, however, Pu Xixiu was rehabilitated (she died in 1970).

(Pu Xixiu had two sisters. One, Pu Anxiu, was the wife of Marshal Peng Dehuai. The other, Pu Jiexiu, was the leader of one of the small satellite political parties. Their brother was vice-minister for education in 1978. All four have been working for the Communists for many years. A remarkable family.)

A great many people who worked with or were acquainted with the condemned ministers had to accuse them, and these accusations were printed prominently in the newspapers. A man called Pan Dakui, for example, wrote against the minister for forest industry, Luo Longji. Pan returned from study in the United States in 1930 at the age of twenty-seven. He taught law in Shanghai and during the war joined the Democratic League founded by Luo Longji. He was a follower of Luo for more than twenty years. He accused Luo of having said in 1950 what Zhang Dongsun, a famous Peking professor of philosophy, had said: that the Korean war was started by the North Koreans. In the preceding year,

1956, Pan said, Luo Longji had become a minister, yet he remained dissatisfied. He opposed the Party and the People and the Soviet Union. He believed that the Russians should not have interfered in Hungary. Worse still, Luo Longji used to read American magazines even after the Liberation![15]

On July 1, 1957, the *People's Daily* published an editorial that was reprinted long afterwards in the sixth volume of the *Selected Works of Mao Zedong*, published in 1977. Thus it was not till twenty years later that the authorship of that editorial was acknowledged. It was by Mao himself. This article, written against two newspapers, the *Guang Ming Daily* and the *Wen Hui Bao*, was revealing in many ways. It admitted — what by that time was common knowledge — that the trap had been laid deliberately:

For a period the newspapers refrained from publishing the correct view [i.e. the Party view] and no reply was made to the wild attacks of the bourgeois rightists. The Party-reform organs and the Party organisations in the schools were told not to counter-attack. All this was done so that the Masses [or rather the Party] might see which criticisms were benevolent and which were malicious. The criticisms were allowed to develop their own momentum until the time for the counter-attack was ripe. Some people say that this was a plot. I say it was indeed a plot. We told our enemies beforehand that it is only when the wicked ghosts and evil spirits have come out from their cages that one can destroy them.

Turning to the two newspapers, Mao said that the *Guang Ming*, its publisher Zhang Bojun and the editor-in-chief Chu Anping had changed quickly and the paper had improved. Not so the Shanghai *Wen Hui Bao*! Luo Longji and Pu Xixiu and their rightist group in the Democratic League had planned organised action against the Communist Party, against Socialism; and the members of another small political party, the Democratic Party of Farmers and Workers, had acted similarly. On June 14, the *Wen Hui Bao* published a self-criticism, but it was a mere pretence. These people are bourgeois rightists. 'Who are the bourgeois rightists? They are reactionary groups who oppose the Communist Party, the People and Socialism.' Among them are people from the small parties, intellectuals, capitalists, young students and even Party members and Youth Corps members.[16]

Many of these rightists, who according to Mao were enemies of the Communist Party, were the very people whom the Communist Party had flattered and whose cooperation the Party had solicited before it came to power. After the establishment of the Communist government, they were honoured with high titles and were made members of the highest government establishment. They were intellectuals, members of small political parties which had supported the Communists in difficult times under the Nationalist regime. When the Party thought they were of no more use, they were rejected. For 'Party' read 'Mao'.

The trap prepared for these unfortunates and the sudden action that seized and condemned them all emanated from Mao. The whole gigantic pretence, which had started with the introduction of the Hundred Flowers in 1956 and culminated in the two-month Free Speech in April-May 1957, was an introduction to a new Party purge, Mao's reaction to the Eighth Party Congress.

The purge swept through the Party and through all walks of life. It hit the legal profession hard. The pre-1949 judges and lawyers had been eliminated in 1951–2 and replaced by proletarians. In 1957 the minister of justice, Madame Shi Liang, quoted the 'bourgeois enemy' as describing these uneducated proletarian judges, workers and farmers, as 'legal ignoramuses'. She replied that in judging 7,000 cases in Shanghai they had not made a single mistake. An adviser to the Supreme Court was condemned for having said that 'many of the lawyers of the old regime were now working as coolies in hospitals and crematoria.' Members in the ministry of justice were condemned for having said that 'there is only policy today; there is no law.'[17]

The purge went through the provinces and many leading Party members lost their jobs, among them the 1st Party secretary of Henan province, Pan Fusheng. His successor Wu Zhipu led the accusations against him and against other leaders of the province. Pan was accused of having supported the rightists in the first half of 1957, of having opposed class struggle, of having held that there were no longer enemy classes in China, of having opposed violence in the land reform, of having opposed the State monopoly of the purchase and sale of grain, and of having said that after the collectivisation the economy had receded and the peasants were not happy. Pan was an anti-Marxist![18]

(During the Cultural Revolution Pan Fusheng became the first Party secretary of Heilongjiang province and first political commissar of the army in the Northeast. After the fall of Lin Biao in 1971, he disappeared.)

The search for rightists was carried out in the army too, particularly among army writers, artists and musicians. One of the chief targets was Chen Yi — not the Marshal but a man whose name sounds similar — who was the head of the cultural section of the army's political department. He, like Pan Fusheng, was accused of having denied class struggle, and of having said that 'there was not more than one counter-revolutionary in 10,000 in the country', and that 'it does not matter what kind of family one comes from'. Chen Yi, one writer said, had turned against the Party, saying that there was a wall between the Party and the people. During the purge and the pursuit of rightists he supported those who criticised the Party. A very bad man indeed![19] (Twenty-two years later Chen Yi was the propaganda head of the Shanghai city Party Committee.)

At the Third Central Committee Plenum, September 30–October 9, 1957, the third since the Eighth Party Congress, Mao spoke. His speech was published ten years later in the fifth volume of his *Selected Works*. He stated clearly what he thought about the Eighth Party Congress, held a year earlier. That Congress, he said, had slowed down economic development and abandoned his slogan 'more, faster, better, cheaper'.

He referred to the 'free speech' period. In the second half of last year [1956], he said, we gave the green light to the bourgeoisie to attack us; this year that attack was made. We, however, kept the initiative and launched the anti-rightist struggle and the Party reform. The Party reform is to go on until May 1958; then in 1959 there will be another Party reform.[20]

Deng Xiaoping

At that same Central Committee Plenum, Deng Xiaoping presented a long speech on the Party and the Party reform. In September 1957, he said, there were 12,720,000 Party members (including 2.8 million candidate-members) — 1,740,000 workers, 8,500,000 peasants, 1,880,000 intellectuals, and 600,000 'others'. He added that the majority of the intellectual Party members had not gone through the experience of manual labour and class struggle (i.e. were not proper, rough Party fighters).

These figures meant an increase of two million Party members since September 1956, when the same Deng reported at the Party Congress. The increase was made up of 1.1 million peasants, 200,000 workers and 55,000 'intellectuals'.

Deng spoke about the revolt of the rightists. He had a poor opinion of the intellectuals (he was to hold the opposite opinion in the 1980s):

Most of the intellectuals come from families of the bourgeois or petty bourgeois classes and they have had a bourgeois education; they belong therefore to the bourgeois class. Rightist elements have been found, mostly among intellectuals, in schools of higher education, in government offices, in newspapers and publishing houses, in literature and art, among politico-legal workers, among scientists, engineers, doctors and pharmacists. Among the rightists, those of the democratic parties had a privileged position from which to recruit people . . . Some of them did become leftist in earlier periods, but the majority have never abandoned their bourgeois class stance. The rightists said that 'amateurs should not lead experts' . . . they wanted independence and freedom, freedom of the press, freedom of publication, and freedom of literature and art. The Party has decided now to train intellectuals from among the working class. These will be both 'red and expert'. We must raise up cadres from among able workers and peasants. We must also get them from among able intellectuals, but these will have to go through the experience of production [hard physical labour] and struggle.[21]

(In 1983 the *Selected Writings of Deng Xiaoping, 1975–82* were published, and revered as Mao's *Selected Works* had been in earlier days. Tactfully, Deng's earlier writings were not published.)

The Mao broom

Mao was successful in Yan'an in 1942–4. He purged his enemies in a slow, carefully premeditated two-year process of *Zheng Feng*, Party Rectification. He now repeated that process. He saw clouds on the horizon: his lieutenants were opposing his radical policies — a movement that culminated in the Eighth Party Congress, which sought to elevate him to Honorary Chairmanship. He went into action, relying on the few who were unswervingly loyal to him. Lu Dingyi launched the Hundred Flowers in May 1956. In September the Eighth Party Congress was held, squeezing out Mao from several leading positions and outlining a moderate economic programme, contrary to his desires. In February 1957 Mao's speech 'On Contradiction' seemed to be a call to purge the Party by expressing liberal thoughts. Next, Lu Dingyi spoke in a way designed to dispel anxieties, promising that free expression of opinion would have no sinister consequences. The promised liberalising purge within the Party was to start in May 1957. In June free speech was abruptly halted and the dreaded broom began its work. People were condemned, inside the Party and outside, not for deeds, but for words, some times for words they had never spoken.

A Peking newspaper accused the 'rightists' of having raised the following questions: 'Is the present regime red terror? Is it the old feudal dictatorship? Is it medieval absolutism? Is Marxism-Leninism stifling oppression?' The answer to all these questions was: 'Comrade Mao Zedong has written: "Revolution is not an invitation to a banquet . . . it is a violent action". Supreme authority and even terrorism are necessary.'[22]

Why, one may ask, did the Party reveal its repulsive face? Why did it take off the smiling mask that in the past had won over many good men to the Cause? Was it that the Party leadership felt menaced, that their influence was being undermined? Or did it come from the will of one single man at the top? The answer probably is that Mao felt his authority threatened. His own men had turned against him at the 1956 Party Congress. Those outside the Party no longer counted for anything.

The magnitude of the anti-rightist campaign became clear twenty years later, when some rightists, but by no means all, were rehabilitated. In one county alone (there are 2,000 counties) there were 245 rightists. In one province (out of twenty-six) in Henan, 40,000 were rehabilitated (the total number of rightists was not revealed). In Shanghai there were 16,328 rightists. In May 1978 it was reported that by that time in all 400,000 rightists had been rehabilitated. In the early 1960s there was a period of rehabilitation involving 16,000 rightists.[23] The total number of those condemned in 1957 is still unknown.

On October 29, 1982, the *People's Daily* gave some figures for those rehabilitated, excluding 'rightists'. The figures were: 2.8 million former landlords and kulaks, 700,000 artisans and 4.2 million former members of the Kuomintang.

Six well-known Peking professors condemned in 1957 were rehabilitated in August 1980. In January 1984 four of them were still alive. One was the world-famous sociologist Fei Xiaotong, in 1957 Vice-President of the Nationalities College. After his rehabilitation he was made deputy head of the Nationalities Research Institute of the Chinese Academy of Social Sciences. Another was Qian Weichang, in 1957 Vice-President of Qinghua University. After his rehabilitation, he became a professor in the same school.[24]

CHAPTER XIV

SHOCK TO MARXISM

The Free Speech and the reaction to it, the way the intellectuals were handled, the condemnation of 'rightists' added to the condemnation of Stalin in the Soviet Union, jolted Marxist philosophy and Marxist philosophers severely in China — and not only in China. The universities were ordered to study Mao's 'On Practice' and 'On Contradiction' and his February 1957 speech 'On the Correct Handling of Contradictions among the People'. In Peking University the whole school was summoned to public criticism of the theories of two professors, Feng Youlan and Zhu Qianzhi, and in particular the population theory of a third professor, Ma Yinchu.[1]

It took the professional Marxist philosophers some time even to begin to absorb the shock. In the review *Philosophical Research*, the first articles about Mao's February 1957 speech, which was to be treated as a milestone in Marxism, were not published until the third issue in the following year, June 1958. What was said then was altogether proper; Mao's speech 'was a development of, and a great and creative contribution to, Marxism-Leninism'.[2]

This was not how *Philosophical Research* had been speaking six months earlier. In its last issue in 1957 an article, translated from Russian, on forty years of Marxist-Leninist philosophy in the Soviet Union, said merely that 'the works of Stalin, of Comrade Mao Zedong and of the leaders of other Communist parties, conveyed and explained the theories of Marxism-Leninism and thus fulfilled an important historical function.'[3] This was a far cry from Mao's 'development of and contribution to Marxism'. The Russian article on Soviet philosophy, translated into Chinese, said that the Twentieth Soviet Party Congress (at which Khrushchev exposed the errors of Stalin) had been a turning-point in Soviet philosophy. Till then the cult of Stalin had hindered philosophical research. Marxism had now to confront new and still unsolved problems posed by modern science such as matter and energy.[4]

For years Marxists in China had followed the Russian model servilely, discussing only questions that were discussed in the Soviet Union. In 1957 Ren Jiyu, a professor of philosophy, wrote a report on the status of Marxist philosophy in China. The first thing that strikes one, he wrote, is the uniformity of the two countries in the choice of questions for discussion. Logic, neglected for a time in the Soviet Union, is now being discussed there. The same thing is happening in China. Similarly in the Soviet Union it is being asked whether dialectics, epistemology and logic are three branches of philosophy, or are three aspects of a single branch; this also is being discussed in China. In the Soviet Union the philosophical categories — quantity and quality, probability and so on — and the problem of the Marxist theory on 'foundation' and 'superstructure' are being discussed; they too are being discussed in China. In 1947 Zhdanov laid down, in opposition to Aleksandrov, that the history of philosophy is a history of struggle between materialism and idealism; today, however, in the Soviet Union this is being disputed; it is being disputed in China too. There is, however, one philosophical problem that is being widely discussed in the Soviet Union but not yet in China, the problem of the relation of natural sciences to Marxist philosophy. In the Soviet Union there are two schools of thought, one which would relegate dialectics to natural science, and the other holding that dialectics belongs to philosophy. Marxists in the Soviet Union admit that they have not yet found adequate answers to Western idealist philosophical interpretations of science. No such studies have yet been undertaken in China. 'There is much in the Soviet Union from which we can learn.' Ethics, Ren Jiyu regrets to say, have been neglected in the Soviet Union, and have thus been neglected in China too. In China today (1957) Marxist books on ethics — for instance, Deng Chumin's booklet *How to Develop Communist Moral Virtue in the Youth* — are superficial works, which do not take into account the deep-rooted traditional Chinese teaching on ethics.

Under Stalin, negation of negation, a fundamental category of Marxist philosophy inherited from Hegel, was ignored. Since the death of Stalin it has returned. The discussion moves around the question of whether through negation of negation a higher development is reached in a spiral ascent. Discussion of this question began in China, and a controversy developed round the problem whether the process of negation of negation is a return to the original position in a more perfect form. Some said yes; others said no, pointing to the development of nature, which is a forward development and not a return to the past in a higher form. The controversy was launched by Peng Pu, then a young man aged twenty-six. (In 1981 he was deputy editor of *Historical Research*.[5])

The people involved in this controversy were trained philosophers, and their reasoning was clear and remained strictly on the philosophical level — in stark contrast with numerous other writers who argued merely by quoting from Marx, Engels and Lenin. A participant in the controversy, Zhen Zhangshu, wrote: 'We want to argue not from quotations from the canons, but from the total development of objective reality.' Peng Pu agreed, but said that Zhen was merely repeating arguments proposed by some philosophers at Leningrad University.

Many articles claiming to deal with Marxist philosophy dealt merely with political events. The great event of those days was the Hungarian revolt, and it was discussed whether this was caused by internal contradictions in Hungary, by external imperialism, or by circumstances in the Soviet Union.[6]

Mao the philosopher

The professional Chinese Marxist philosophers were, as we said above, slow to discover Marxist philosophy in Mao's February 1957 speech 'On Contradiction'. What kind of Marxist philosophy was it? Was it anything more than a description of Mao's shrewd political strategy expressed in Marxist terms?

'We are confronted', Mao wrote, 'with social contradictions of two types, contradictions among ourselves and contradictions between the Enemy and us. The two are totally different in nature.'

Mao explained what he meant by People and what he meant by Enemy. 'To understand these two different types of contradiction correctly, we must first be clear about what is meant by "People" and what is meant by "Enemy". The concept of People varies in content in different countries and in different periods of history in a given country.' Throughout the history of the Communist Party in China, at least since the Japanese war, there have been, he said, three variations in the meaning of People. 'During the Japanese war all classes and social groups opposing the Japanese invasion were People; Chinese collaborators with the Japanese were the Enemy. During the war of liberation [1945–9], US imperialists and their running dogs [the Kuomintang *et al.*] were the Enemy, those opposed to them were the People. In the present stage the social groups which favour the cause of socialist construction [i.e. Party direction] are the People, and those who resist are the Enemy.'

Contradictions between ourselves and the enemy are antagonistic contradictions. The distinction between the two contradictions, Mao wrote, is not new. 'In my article "On the People's Democratic Dictatorship", written in 1949, I said: "The combination of these two aspects, democracy for the people and dictatorship over the reactionaries, is the People's Democratic Dictatorship''.'

Mao and all good Marxists explain their politics in philosophical terms. 'Marxist philosophy holds that the law of the unity of opposites is the fundamental law of the universe. The law operates universally, whether in the natural world, in human society, or in man's thinking. Contradictions exist everywhere, but their nature differs in accordance with the different natures of different things. In any given thing, the unity of opposites is conditional, temporary and transitory and hence relative, while the struggle of opposites is absolute.'

This is how Marxists can use philosophy as a tool to change their policies and make friends out of enemies or enemies out of friends. That is exactly what happened during the days of the Hundred Flowers and of the Free Speech launched in 1956–7 by Mao and his satraps. Men who had helped the Communist Party to gain power, and who were the People during the civil war, were cast out from the People and became the Enemy when it was judged that they were no longer of use.

Mao also spoke about the Hungarian incident which, he said, had caused some people in China to waver. 'These people think that there is too little freedom under our People's Democracy and that there is more freedom under a Western parliamentary democracy. They want a two-party system as in the West, with one party in office and the other in opposition. But this so-called two-party system is nothing but a device for maintaining the dictatorship of the bourgeoisie.'

There is, Mao said, democracy and freedom within the People; there are also contradictions within the People, contradictions between workers and peasants on one hand and the intellectuals on the other, certain contradictions between the government and the people, contradictions between the interests of the state and the interests of the collective and of the individual, between democracy and centralism, between the leaders and the led, contradictions arising from the bureaucratic style of work of some of the state personnel in their relations with the masses. 'All these are contradictions within the people.'

There is especially 'the basic contradiction between the production relations and the productive forces and between the superstructure and the economic base'.

This contradiction between production forces and production relations dominated Mao's thinking and led in the following year, 1958, to the establishment of the communes, in the belief that once the form of organisation — 'production relations' — had changed, output — 'production force' — would grow. In his February 1957 speech he was not yet speaking of that, but he did predict: 'There will no longer be poor peasants in the countryside, and the standard of living of the entire peasantry will reach or surpass the middle-peasants' level.'[7]

Marxism out of tune

The persecution of the intellectuals did great harm to Marxism. Marxist philosophers were intimidated. Chinese Marxism, already so jejune, received from Mao's speech 'On Contradiction' a shock from which it has never recovered. It lost contact even with the mother-country, the Soviet Union. Soviet philosophers continued to discuss important Marxist philosophical problems, trying to reconcile Marxism with modern science; in China the terror imposed by the pursuit of rightists and the imposition of the unique authority — the authority of Mao — froze all initiative.

Marxism could have been highly successful in China. There was no massive intellectual opposition to its acceptance. Confucianism had been dead for many years. There was no religious opposition. Buddhism had not been a living force for centuries. The Christians were few in number and they did not constitute a social force in the country. Materialism under the influence of the American pragmatist, John Dewey, had been an accepted doctrine since the early 1920s. Marxism could have been highly successful. But the way in which it was handled did not make it attractive. The violent political campaigns followed one after another. Terror and intimidation were imposed upon the nation. All this, while it inspired fear, did not inspire spontaneous acceptance of the Marxist doctrine. The peasants were incited to kill the landowners, but no sooner had they received their own land than they saw themselves organised, first into mutual-aid groups and then into the collectives. This was followed by total regimentation in the communes.

Industrial workers, a small fraction of the population, were well treated, but were no less firmly subjected to regimentation. We have seen what happened to the educated classes.

Marxism, which could have become a unifying force in China and generated popular support for the government, degenerated into an instrument of terror.

The youth were at first enchanted by the heroic stories found in Communist literature translated from Russian and by Marxism itself, which seemed able to give direction to their lives. That enthusiasm disappeared. In their disillusionment, the youth held mass protest meetings at the universities.

By the end of the 1950s the young generation had had enough of austerity. In January 1958 the Peking press was writing, disapprovingly, of the loose morals of the young:

Everywhere in large and small cities, in dance-halls, hotels, public gardens, even in bureaux, in railway coaches and schools, the yellow music [i.e. forbidden sub-moral music] of hypnotic songs is heard. Many illegal peddlers are selling songs sung by actresses in the old days. Workers' centres, offices and shops are letting their loudspeakers blare these songs from dawn to dusk. Even radio stations, under cover of the freedom of the Hundred Flowers, have broadcast such songs . . . The effects are evident: the youth have lost their ardour, and working discipline has relaxed. Life has become slack; low morals and disorderly conduct are everywhere prevalent. One shop in Peking has made 340,000 records of such songs and the buyers are young workers, students, city people and soldiers. These songs are anti-revolutionary, reactionary, capitalist, bourgeois, indecent, obscene, decadent. One such popular song is entitled 'When will you be back, sir?' Then there are the letters written to broadcasting stations. One listener wrote: 'On listening to these songs which we have not heard for years, I was deeply moved and felt very happy.'[8]

Marxism had lost its appeal.

Very young children absorbed the Marxist doctrine in their schools because neither the teacher nor the parents dared to talk to them openly. But as soon as they reached adolescence their eyes were opened, and they turned into the protesting youth of the late 1950s. Those who were small children in the mid-1950s became murderous youngsters ten years later during the Cultural Revolution.

CHAPTER XV

1958–1959: THE LEAP

Mao in action

1957 was a rough year. The scene was set for Mao's grand act. The following year, 1958, was a year of feverish activity for him. The man who in the first four years of the 1950s had not made a single public pronouncement spent that year travelling, holding meetings and giving directives in all parts of the country.

Much of what happened in that year was not reported in the contemporary press, and was only made public many years later, in 1981. In that year, five years after his death, Mao's radical acts in 1958 were subjected to critical exposure.

On January 11–22, 1958, Mao was holding a meeting in South China in Nanning, the capital of Guangxi, with the participation of the Party leaders of nine southern provinces. He explained that the economic plans drawn up at the Party Congress in 1956 had been bad plans and he proposed the 'Great Leap' — which this 1981 booklet describes as an unrealistic plan. He spoke also of the need for being both 'red and expert', rebuffing what many intellectuals had alleged a year earlier, that ignorant 'red' comrades were guiding 'experts' in the educational and scientific institutes. At this meeting a document known as 'Sixty Articles of Working Methods' was drafted, prescribing 'uninterrupted revolution'.[1]

On February 3, 1958, a *People's Daily* editorial summed up Mao's doctrine on the Great Leap: 'Anyone who does not make a Great Leap is a rightist conservative.' Some people think that a Leap is too adventurous. It is new, it may not be perfect, but it is not an adventure. All must have 'revolutionary optimism and revolutionary heroism'. This is the proper quality of a Party member. Our country is 'poor and blank'. The editorial explained this phrase of Mao's, which became famous over the years. It means 'very poor in our economy, and in the cultural field in many ways backward, almost blank'. (This was an odd thing for a Chinese to say about Chinese culture, one of the richest cultures in the world.) We must aim, Mao said, at accomplishing in three years what was planned for ten. There will be 'three bitter years of struggle'.[2]

In March 1958, Mao held another informal meeting, this time in Chengdu, the capital of Sichuan province. He again declared that the

1956 economic plans were 'un-Marxist', and he expanded an old phrase that was to become a slogan: 'Stir up all energy, aim high, build socialism, more, faster, better, cheaper.'[3]

Party Congress, 1958

In May a second session of the Eighth Party Congress was summoned. To hold a second session of a Party Congress was unheard-of in the Party's history. A more extraordinary innovation still: this session was called a *Zheng Feng*, Party Rectification, session. The 1956 session had been a grand and solemn occasion graced by representatives of the Communist parties of the whole world. This second session lasted eighteen days, May 5–23, and was held in secret. That it had been held at all was announced only after it had closed. A brief communiqué announced that Mao's proposal 'Stir up all energy . . .' had been unanimously approved, and that it had been decided that the Party reform should be continued — it was to have ended that month, in May. It had also been decided that within fifteen years China's industry should equal and surpass that of Great Britain.

This was an incredible meeting. The gentle but determined opposition to Mao and his policies of the first session had been smashed to pieces. The speakers at the Congress supported all Mao's new policies. Liu Shaoqi presented a long report praising the fight against rightists and the admirable results of the Party reform. As Comrade Mao Zedong had said, Liu echoed, the industry of China will equal and surpass that of England in fifteen years. Again echoing Mao, he said that the economic development should be speeded up, 'more, faster, better, cheaper'. In 1956, Liu went on, the economy developed in a leap, but at the time this was looked upon as an adventurous advance. (He did not say that this criticism had been made at the first session of the Eighth Congress in 1956.) Liu praised Mao's 'uninterrupted revolution', and his slogan 'Stir up all energy . . .' He praised the Nanning and Chengdu meetings, but he mentioned the Great Leap only once. Liu refuted the objections to the Leap. Some people (did they include himself?) say that its excessive speed will cause tension and waste, and will upset the balanced development of the economy. Some do not believe that agrarian production can be whipped up to such a speed. Liu supported Mao's theory about China being poor and blank. He made no self-criticism of what he had said two years earlier. It was enough for him to say that the whole Party leadership was behind Mao.

At this 1958 session of the Eighth Party Congress, Deng Xiaoping reported on the November 1957 meeting of representatives of sixty-five Communist parties in Moscow, to which he himself had accompanied Mao. Deng praised the meeting, which had acknowledged the world leadership of the Soviet Union and condemned the Yugoslavs. This second session of the Eighth Congress, in unison with the international Communist movement, condemned Yugoslav revisionism. China was still in the Moscow camp.

The Congress session approved a revised edition of the 1956–67 Twelve-year Outline of Agrarian Development. It raised the targets of the original plan drawn up in 1956, projecting a higher speed of development (which was never reached). The speakers at this Congress session, including Politbureau members Zhou Enlai, Zhu De, Chen Yun, Chen Yi and Li Xiannian, all approved of Comrade Mao Zedong's speech, and 'all particularly emphasised the need to learn from Comrade Mao Zedong.' The Congress confirmed the expulsion of the Party leaders of seven provinces from the Party, and condemned Pan Fusheng, the 1st Party secretary of Henan province, as we saw above.[4]

Lin Biao

Perhaps the most momentous event was the election of Lin Biao to the post of Vice-Chairman of the Party, which took place at a brief afternoon meeting of the Central Committee on May 25, 1958, immediately after the Congress. He became the fifth Vice-Chairman, after Liu Shaoqi, Zhou Enlai, Zhu De and Chen Yun (the four had been elected in 1956 at the first session of the Eighth Congress).[5]

Lin Biao's nomination foreshadowed a new era. A year later he became minister of defence. In 1961 he introduced the *Little Red Book* in the army. In 1966 he stood next to Mao at the Red Guard manifestations in Peking. In 1969 he was named in the revised Party Constitution as Mao's heir. In 1971 he died in mysterious circumstances.

Communes and the Leap

After the second session of the Eighth Party Congress in May 1958, Mao's radical reforms were introduced with precipitate speed. A month earlier, in April, the first commune was established in Henan province. This contained 9,300 families, totalling 40,000 persons. There were common kitchens, and there was payment of wages instead of the previous system of marking of labour points. The Communist Party directed everything. The peasants' private plots were taken away, as were their little orchards. The marketing and supply cooperatives were taken over by the State Commerce. By the end of August the 38,000 collectives of the province, with an average household membership of 260, had been pooled into 1,378 communes, with an average household membership of 7,200. The idea of establishing large agricultural units, though not the name 'commune', had been emerging for some time. In 1956 large collective farms were set up in Liaoning province in the Northeast. They broke down in 1957, and were re-established in 1958.[6]

In the spring of 1958 Mao and some other top leaders roved about the country, obviously to see for themselves what could be done. In January and February, Mao visited Hangzhou in Central China and Changchun in the Northeast. In March he was in Sichuan in the Southwest. In March also, Liu Shaoqi and Zhou Enlai visited Sichuan.[7] In August Mao visited villages in Henan accompanied by Wu Zhipu, the First Party secretary of the province, who had squeezed out his predecessor. Mao visited a commune and a ball-bearing factory. He was told that the factory was run not in modern style but by craftsmen using primitive local methods, and that one commune was producing 500 kg. of cotton on a *mow* of land (0.6 acre), with a future target of 1,000 kg. per *mow*. Mao turned, all smiles, to Wu Zhipu and said: 'Secretary Wu, we have hope!'

Mao then went to Hebei province and visited the common dining hall of a Home of Happiness, the house in which old people were housed in the new commune. The Party secretary of the county Mao visited said that the county would harvest 220,000 tons of grain in the autumn. Mao, delighted to hear this, said: 'The population of this county is 310,000. How will you be able to eat so much? What will you do with the surplus?' The county secretary said modestly that he had not yet had time to think about that.

Mao was in Henan on August 6–8. On August 9 he was in Shandong province accompanied by Tan Qilong, Second Party secretary of the province and a member of the Central Committee. Here Mao was shown yet more miracles. In one place he was told that, although they had formerly grown only 100–150 kg. of grain per *mow*, they were now getting 400 kg. Throughout the tour he was wreathed in smiles. People would line up on both sides of the streets to shout 'Hail Chairman Mao! Hail the Communist Party!' (Tan Qilong became First Party secretary of this province in 1961, and First Party secretary of Qinghai province in

1972 and of Sichuan province in 1980 — obviously an able Party leader.)

Mao was exposed to a gigantic deception. He was told what he wanted to hear, and he believed what he heard about miracles. He swallowed without thinking the pleasing suggestion that the yield of grain and cotton could be increased by 300–500 per cent. It might have been expected that Mao, who had spent much of his life in villages, could not be duped in this way, but apparently he knew nothing about agriculture. He had been a revolutionary ever since his young days; he had read books and written articles, and his whole life had been spent in political agitation.

Apparently Liu Shaoqi was no wiser. He visited Shandong on July 14–18, accompanied by Shu Tong, First Party secretary of the province, and Bai Rubing, a Party secretary, who later, from 1974 to 1982, was to be First Party secretary of the same province. They inspected schools, factories and villages. Liu said that every factory should produce iron and steel. Having been told of miraculous increases in agricultural output, he said that the explanation was that the scientists had been kicked out and people now dared to do things.[9]

Were all Party leaders such ignoramuses, or had all become actors in the magician's show?

The first peasant reaction to the new moves was astonishing. A letter to a newspaper said: 'My sister has written to say that we now have a people's commune in the village. Food is served in common and everything belongs to the commune. Everybody is smiling. Comrade editor, can you tell me whether this means that Communist society is already here?' The editor answered, 'No, not yet. The accomplishment of full common ownership will take three to four, or five to six years, and not even then will there be full Communism.' The editor was referring to a Decision made by the Politbureau in the second half of August at a meeting in Beidaihe (Peitaiho), Hebei province. The Decision said that within three or four, or five or six years everything was to be owned by 'the whole-people', as the state-owned industries were already. Even that, however, would not yet be full Communism. The transition to Communism demands tremendously developed production, the disappearance of differences between industry and agriculture, between city and village and between mental and physical labour, the disappearance of unequal bourgeois rights, and the creation of the New Man of full Communist consciousness and of an elevated moral character. When all that has come, each will work according to his ability and receive goods according to his needs. According to this Politbureau Decision, by 1962–3 everything was to be centrally owned by the state, by 'the whole-people'.[10]

The August 1958 Politbureau meeting in Beidaihe foresaw a Great Leap in 1958, almost doubling the amount of grain and producing 10 million tons of steel, double the 1957 output. There was to be a further Leap in 1959. Although there would be an abundance of food, there would have to be three years of 'bitter struggle' if the high targets were to be reached.[11] In October two national conferences discussed steel. The experts said that iron and steel could not be produced in tiny mud and brick hearths, an objection which was rejected.[12]

Although everybody knew it at the time, twenty-one years were to pass before an open admission was made in the *People's Daily* that the Great Leap and the attempt to make iron in primitive furnaces had been a colossal waste.[13]

The communes were established almost instantaneously over the whole country. Then trouble began. At the beginning of November 1958, Mao held an informal meeting with Party leaders in Zhengzhou, Henan province, and on November 21–27 he held a similar meeting in Wuchang, Hubei. The day after the close of this second meeting, the Central Committee opened its Sixth Plenum in Wuchang, which lasted until December 10. Mao was not present. It was an odd meeting. It accepted Mao's proposal that he should no longer be Head of State. 'He will remain head of the Party . . . and he will have more time to give to theoretical work on Marxism-Leninism.' It trimmed the over-ambitious plans for the communes. It declared that the transition to final Communism was not imminent. Nevertheless it supported the communes fully and produced even more fantastic economic targets for 1959.

The inner story of this historic meeting has never been published. A long decision of the Plenum, 'About Some Questions on the People's Commune', said that 99 per cent of the peasantry, 120 million households, had been organised into 26,000 communes, an average of 4,615 peasant households to each commune.

While the August meeting of the Politbureau had looked forward to total nationalisation in three to four or five to six years, this Plenum could only foresee the realisation of state ownership in '15, 20 or more years'. Full development, it repeated, would demand a highly developed industry, a mechanised and electrified agriculture, and development in education and science. It was therefore not true, as some were saying, that 'we are entering immediately into Communism'. The time of 'from each according to his capacity, and distribution to each according to his need' had not yet come, and there could be no question yet of abolishing commerce, money and prices. Houses, clothes, domestic tools and bank deposits should belong to the individual, and members of the commune might still own scattered trees and fowls and other small livestock. The common kitchens were to be maintained, and new villages were to be built gradually, with common dining-rooms, nurseries, schools and homes for the aged — the name for the last was changed from 'Home of Happiness' to 'Home to Honour the Aged'. The commune became the lowest administrative grade of the government. Under it were the 'great production brigades', and under these were the 'production brigades', formerly known as 'small brigades'. A countywide Federation of Communes was to be in charge of manpower. The discipline of the commune was to be maintained by the militia. Leadership was to be with the Party organisations.

Sudden transition to the ideal Communist wonderland had therefore been postponed; but the fantastic economic targets of the wonderland remained. The Plenum announced that the output of steel, 5.3 million tons in 1957, had reached 11 million tons in 1958 and that it would reach 18 million tons in 1959. Similar fantastic claims were made for other items in 1958 and similar projections for 1959. Thus grain output, 175 million tons in 1957, had been 375 million tons in 1958 and would be 500 million tons in 1959.[14]

Outside observers believed that the Central Committee Plenum had censured Mao and forced him to resign the chairmanship of the Republic. Perhaps it had. Yet how can one explain the credulity with which this illustrious body, the Central Committee of the Party, believed the fantastic output figures of 1958 and planned even more fantastic targets for 1959?

Mao was still supreme. Five months later, in April 1959, the Central Committee held its Seventh Plenum in Shanghai, this time under the chairmanship of Mao, who was still Chairman of the Party. The Plenum fully confirmed the statements on the economic achievements of 1958 and the targets for 1959 as laid down at the Sixth Plenum in December 1958.[15] This Seventh Plenum prepared the agenda of the People's Congress, at which Mao officially resigned the state chairmanship and was replaced by Liu Shaoqi. As usual, the Prime Minister Zhou Enlai presented the Government Report. He repeated, and supported, the fantastic economic figures and announced that the targets laid down in the second Five Year Plan (1958–62) had been reached in the plan's first year. All the top leaders applauded this nonsense. Li Fuchun (died in 1975), then head of the State Planning Committee, and Li Xiannian, then minister of finance, poured out Leap statistics to the People's Congress. These statistics were simply lies. Li Xiannian said that the fiscal year of 1958 had ended with a surplus.[16]

What had happened to the common sense of these prominent leaders? Twenty-one years later Deng Xiaoping, talking informally to some leading comrades, said, as was published in his *Selected Writings* in 1983: 'It should not be said that Comrade Mao Zedong was the only one who erred. Many comrades in the Party leadership were also wrong. The Great Leap was the overheated idea of Comrade Mao Zedong, but were not we too overheated? Comrade Liu Shaoqi, Comrade Zhou Enlai and myself did not oppose it. Comrade Chen Yun kept silent . . . The error of the Party leadership was not the error of one person; it was our collective responsibility.'[17]

The answer probably is that these great men were in deadly fear of Mao, although Mao was no longer the Head of State. That change mattered little. Chen Yun was the only one who dared to say nothing. These were the same men who, three years earlier at the 1956 Party Congress, had defied Mao, deprived him of most of his leading posts, and voted for an economic programme which he disliked. Deng Xiaoping had even spoken boldly against the cult of the individual. Why had their courage evaporated during these three intervening years?

'Fanatical petty-bourgeois'

Four months after the Seventh Central Committee Plenum, Peng Dehuai, minister of defence, and his friends dared to challenge Mao at the Eighth Plenum, held in August 1959 at Lushan, a summer mountain resort in Jiangxi province. This was a momentous meeting. It still proclaimed the Great Leap, but it corrected the inflated 1958 output figures and lowered the targets for 1959. To explain the appalling shortage of commodity goods, it was said that this was caused by 'the greatly increased purchasing power of the people', and that owing to the lack of experience of the statistical bureaux, the 1958 figures had been set too high. New figures were published. The increase was given as 20–30 per cent instead of the earlier allegations of increase by several hundred per cent. The earlier figures showed 11 million tons of steel produced in 1958. In fact, 3 million tons of this had been produced by village methods; in other words, it was not steel. In future such 'steel' was not to be included in the state plan. In spite of all this, 1959 was still to be a year of Leap; steel output was to be increased by 50 per cent, coal by 24 per cent, and so on. The second part of the communiqué of this Plenum said that 'some people call the Great Leap and the people's commune a fanatical petty-bourgeois movement. Such erroneous rightist opportunist ideas must be overcome.'

On August 26, ten days after the end of the Plenum, Zhou Enlai explained the correction of output figures to the People's Congress Standing Committee. He defended the Leap — 'The masses showed boundless enthusiasm' — and he rebutted the criticism that described it as a 'forced labour depriving people of their freedom'.[18] The communiqué of the Plenum did not say who had called the commune and Leap policies a 'fanatical bourgeois movement'. But a month later, on September 17, the minister of defence, Peng Dehuai, lost his post and was replaced by Lin Biao. A day earlier the Chief-of-Staff, Huang Kecheng, had been replaced by Luo Ruiqing, and two vice foreign ministers, Zhang Wentian and Wang Jiaxiang, had also lost their posts.[19]

The official history of the 1956 Lushan Plenum was not published till 1967, when an official account said that the Politbureau had held a meeting in July 1959, before the Central Committee Plenum. At this Politbureau meeting, Peng Dehuai presented to Mao a memorandum ostensibly supporting him; in fact, however, Peng was a 'rightist opportunist infiltrated into the Party'. The memorandum opposed the Great Leap, the steel production and the People's Commune, dismissing them as 'petty-bourgeois fanaticism'. Peng worked in collusion with Huang Kecheng, Zhang Wentian and Zhou Xiaozhou (Zhou was First Party secretary of Hunan province). The Lushan meeting condemned all four. It declared that Peng had been an evil man from the start: he had associated with all Mao's enemies, with Li Lisan, Wang Ming and Gao Gang. In spite of these wild accusations, the four were not expelled from the Party, nor even from the Central Committee, but were given the Party sanction of being put under observation, and removed from their posts.

As soon as this was published in 1967 a spate of press articles poured over Peng. One writer said that Peng had intended to organise a secret 'military club' to overthrow Mao.[20] The four 'culprits' were given insignificant jobs in distant provinces. Peng spent some years near Peking, writing his confessions, and in 1965 he was sent to Sichuan province as deputy head of a construction work.[21] He was caught by the Red Guards during the Cultural Revolution. This man, who had been the commander of the Chinese troops in Korea and later minister of defence, died in ignominy in November 1974. Two years after the death of Mao, at the end of 1978, he was rehabilitated and a solemn memorial ceremony was held in his honour.[22]

In 1979, twenty years after the event, the Peking press began to reveal what had really happened. 'The "communisation wind", the "eating from a big common pot", was pseudo-Communism and brought great danger to the revolution . . . The attempt to introduce the system of ownership by "the whole-people", which was to lead to final Communism, had eroded the spontaneous cooperation of the peasants.' However, 'Comrade Mao Zedong quickly noticed this leftist error and led the Party to correct it. [Did he?] The heavy investment in useless small steel furnaces in 1958 sucked up rural manpower, and the excessive targets assigned to agriculture and the excessive quotas for crop delivery in 1958–61 led to a very serious shortage of food in the villages, which had a physically debilitating effect on the people' — in other words, there was a famine.[23]

In 1981 Peking published in book form what Peng Dehuai had written when in disgrace, an 80,000-word account of his life, presented to Mao in 1962, and another confession written in 1970. According to the preface, gaps in Peng's memory have been filled in or corrected in this book. His style, that of a totally uneducated man, is retained. He described what happened in Lushan. Before the Plenum opened, he discussed with some colleagues the appalling situation brought about by the communes. Huang Kecheng spoke of famine in some provinces. Zhou Xiaozhou spoke of the appalling situation and the false statistics in his own province, Hunan. Zhang Wentian was not opposed to the village steel-making; 'Mao', he said, 'is a wise man. Chairman Mao is the only one of us who knows Chinese history.' Bo Yibo, Chairman of the State Economic Commission, encouraged Peng to write to Mao to expose the situation. Peng wrote a confidential memo for Mao on July 14, hoping that Mao would rectify the abuses. He did not expect that his memo would be printed three days later and distributed at the meeting. On July 23 Mao publicly called the memo 'rightist-opportunist'. That night, Peng wrote, 'I could not sleep. I kept on thinking: although I came to know Chairman Mao relatively late [he had not been among Mao's first companions], I have spent more than thirty years with him. If he had something against me, why could he not talk to me personally?'

After the Central Committee Plenum, the Military Committee of the Party held a meeting in Peking. There Peng was accused of having got together a secret military clique, a 'military club'. He was asked to reveal the list of members and all their secrets. There were ugly scenes. Some shouted: 'Confess quickly, don't cheat us!' An appendix to the book describes an interview between Peng and Mao in 1965, in the presence of Liu Shaoqi, Deng Xiaoping and Peng Zhen. Mao said: 'It is right for you to be working in the Southwest. Perhaps later an occasion will come for restoring your reputation.' Peng said: 'I promise three things.' Mao: 'What three?' Peng: 'I will never be a counter-revolutionary; I will never commit suicide [a crime in the Party]; I will work with my hands.'[24] On September 17, not only was Lin Biao named minister of defence in place of Peng Dehuai; he also took over the direction of the work of the Military Committee of the Party (Mao was Chairman).[25]

Peng Dehuai was known as an honest, straightforward man. Zhou Enlai was different. When the backyard furnaces were supposed to be turning out iron and steel, Zhou asked Lu Dingyi, head of Party propaganda, to inspect the mushrooming small furnaces. Lu went with an expert, and reported to Zhou on the uselessness of the operation. Zhou 'listened carefully but expressed no opinion'. At the Lushan Plenum, Peng Dehuai was condemned and Lu almost got into trouble because his opinion had been included in Peng's Memorandum. Zhou Enlai remained at the top.[26]

Peng Dehuai did not oppose Mao. His memo was an effort to call Mao's attention to anomalies. On August 3, 1959, Zhou Xiaozhou, the First Party secretary of Hunan province, said that Peng had told him that Mao's long-term policies were always right, even when he did not at the time see Mao's point. In Jing Gang Shan and in the Japanese war — as he realised after the events — Mao had been right. Peng had great respect for Chairman Mao.[27] These men around Mao saw that the Party, by following his policies, had succeeded against all odds in conquering the country and winning the war against powerful forces. They thus developed a sacred awe and admiration for him. It was not only fear of the man at the top that led them to consent to his most irrational moves; it was an almost superstitious belief that in the long run Mao was always right.

Zhou Xiaozhou himself had great confidence in Mao, whose private secretary he had been in the 1930s. He had seen the devastation caused by the communisation in his own province of Hunan — less grain produced, the 50,000 village furnaces producing nothing, many village houses demolished in order to build new villages that never materialised. Nevertheless Zhou Xiaozhou told his friends that they could trust Mao and talk to him freely. After he, with the three others, had been condemned, he fell into a state of despondency, and when the attacks of the Red Guards were launched in 1966, he committed suicide.

The appendix we have been quoting was written by Li Rui, a trained engineer who was vice-minister of the ministry of power before and after the Cultural Revolution. He was present at the Lushan conference, and says that at the start, when the Party leaders gathered, they were in a happy mood. Mao himself wrote two poems, one dedicated to Zhou Xiaozhou (the other to Hu Qiaomu). However, on July 23, when Mao denounced what he thought was a plot against himself, the atmosphere became sombre.[28]

What happened at Lushan changed the political atmosphere. Two months later, in November, a blackout was imposed on the outflow of news from China. In the early 1950s it was possible for foreigners to subscribe even to provincial newspapers; from November 1959 onwards only one newspaper, the *People's Daily*, and one magazine, *Red Flag*, were allowed to leave the country.

Why communes?

One question demands an answer. What was at the origin of the radical change Mao introduced in 1958? Where did he get the idea for such innovations?

It may be thought that Mao was in revolt against his Soviet masters, that what may be called the Soviet Era had come to an end, and he was introducing his own brand of Communism. We saw above that when the Communists took over the country in 1949 they were totally inexperienced in the administration of a Communist state. As Mao said, they had to 'lean on one side'. Soviet experts were pouring into China. The first Five Year Plan, for 1953–7, was drawn up with Russian help, and in all fields, from police to accounting, from law to theatre, the Soviet system was adopted. Chinese pride could not tolerate this for long. Mao broke away from the Soviet doctrine and introduced his own system. This explanation has been held widely by China scholars. Emmanuel C.Y. Hsü, in his *The Rise of Modern China* (1970, 2nd edn 1975), says that Mao was influenced by the utopia of the great order of the universe put forward in the *Da Tong Shu*, The Book of Great Unity, written by the great statesman of the beginning of the century, Kang Yu Wei. (Hsü, like many other writers of the 1970s, believed that the Great Leap, despite some defects, was beneficial to China.)

All this is a misconception. Peking did indeed have misgivings about Soviet politics, about Khrushchev, about the way the Russians were acting in China, but Peking did not turn away from the Soviet model. Transition to Communism, the fundamental theme of communisation, ran parallel to similar trends in the Soviet Union. The only difference was that Peking took the idea more seriously and rushed into doing it better and faster. Relations with the Soviet Union suffered serious jolts in 1958–9, but the whole matter of communes and the Great Leap was very much a side issue.

Mao visited Moscow at the end of 1957 (see above, pp. 221–2). From July 31 to August 3, 1958, Khrushchev was in Peking. The communiqué signed by Mao and Khrushchev spoke of 'unshakeable eternal unity between the two Marxist-Leninist parties'. It spoke of the need for world peace, but also of readiness for war.[29] There was no mention of Communes or the Leap. On September 27, 1958, a Soviet-built atomic reactor was inaugurated outside Peking in the presence of Soviet and Chinese notables, at the very time when orders were being given that scrap-iron and copper were to be collected all over the country and thrown into primitive furnaces to make iron and steel.[30]

A year later Khrushchev was again in Peking, from September 30 till October 4, 1959. He was now in a different mood, having come from the United States where he had met President Eisenhower. Khrushchev believed that the Cold War was over, but this belief was not echoed in Peking. On September 14, 1959, the international Communist review *Problems of Peace and Socialism* printed a long article by Liu Shaoqi explaining Peking's position on the communes and the Great Leap, and on the condemnation of the rightist-opportunists. Liu spoke also of indestructible friendship with the Soviet Union and other socialist countries, saying that although the revolution might take different shapes in different countries, 'no country can go any other way than the common historical road of Marxism.'[31]

As we have already mentioned, the crucial point of disagreement with Soviet Russia was not the commune or the Leap. At the Twenty-first Party Congress of the Soviet Union in January 1959, Khrushchev denied the Yugoslav allegation that there was friction between the Soviet and Chinese Communist parties. China, he said, had her own peculiarities, but the Chinese Communist Party stands firm on class struggle and Marxism-Leninism.[32]

The divergence arose over war and nuclear policy. During his visit to China in 1958, Khrushchev refused to support China in an attack on

Quemoy Island. In 1962 Mao revealed that when Khrushchev paid his visit to China in 1958, he wanted to set up a combined Soviet-Chinese fleet in order to prevent China from attacking the Taiwanese-held islands — and so prevent confrontation with the United States. In 1959 Khrushchev came to China after his visit to Washington. He was then ready to make peace with the United States. Before leaving for the United States, Khrushchev had withdrawn his promise to provide China with nuclear know-how. Peking revealed this years later, in 1963:

On October 15, 1957, there was an agreement between the Soviet Union and China on new technology for national defence, but on June 20, 1959, the Soviet government unilaterally tore up the agreement . . . and refused to provide China with a sample of an atomic bomb and technical data concerning its manufacture. This was a presentation gift to Eisenhower at the time, in September, when the Soviet leader went to the United States to conduct talks.[33]

Transition to final Communism was a cherished idea of Khrushchev's in those days. In 1958 leading Soviet theoreticians, including M.B. Mitin, who was well known in China, were writing about the coming of Communism. An article by 'N. Anisimov', editor of the Soviet review *Agronomy*, was specially written for the July 17, 1958, issue of the Chinese review *Economic Research*. It dealt with the amalgamation of collective farms — but not before modernisation of the rural areas.[34]

In January 1959, at the Twenty-first Party Congress of the Soviet Union, Khrushchev devoted a long section to the Building of Communism. Transition to Communism had already begun in the Soviet Union, he said, and it was now necessary to create the requisite material and spiritual conditions for final Communism, in which there would be ownership by the nation. He explained that, because of outside enemies, a strong state would be maintained during the transition. He mentioned common dining-rooms as a feature of transition to Communism.[35] The myth of final Communism goes back to the *Communist Manifesto* of 1848, which spoke of abolishing private property, capital, money, social classes, the distinction between town and country, and the bourgeois family.

In his *Critique of the Gotha Programme*, written in 1875 against Lassalle and the German Workers' Party, Marx predicted two phases of Communism. In the first stage, 'bourgeois rights' would still exist. The second phase — full Communism — would come when production had grown, the difference between physical and mental labour had disappeared, and people were working not for wages but out of '*Lebensbe-*

dürfnis' (spontaneous desire). Then, 'each [will work] according to his ability and [receive goods] according to his needs.' Between the capitalist and the Communist society there would be a 'transitory period, the revolutionary dictatorship of the proletariat'.[36] Lenin, in his *State and Revolution*, called the first stage 'dictatorship of the proletariat'. In that first period, he said, remnants of the bourgeois system — commerce, money etc. ('the bourgeois rights', as he called them) — would still be there, but later the whole society would become 'a single office, a single factory, with equality of labour and equality of pay'.[37] In 1936 Stalin declared that the Soviet Union had achieved Socialism. In 1939, at the Eighteenth Party Congress, he spoke of 'gradual transition from Socialism to Communism'. In the early 1950s Marxist theoreticians in the Soviet Union, including P.F. Yudin, a future ambassador to China, started work on a *Textbook on Political Economy*, which appeared in 1954.[38] In 1952, Stalin published his *Economic Problems of Socialism in the USSR*, in which he said that the transition to Communism requires continual expansion of production, taking the collective farms into public ownership, centralised control of commodity circulation, and a transformation of man himself. He explained that the taking of collective farms into public ownership is not simply nationalisation; it would come about, he said, when 'the state has died away and the economy is directed by a central directing economic body'.

At the Twenty-first Party Congress Khrushchev, as we saw above, spoke of transition to Communism, and not as a far-away ideal: Communism was on the doorstep. Zhou Enlai was present at this Party Congress of the CPSU, and spoke. He had high praise for the achievement of the Soviet Union in 'constructing Communism' and forming the new type of Communist man. In China, he said, great progress had been made in 1958. He quoted, without blinking, the fantastic economic figures for that year, the eleven million tons of steel, and so on, and said that in China the mass movement of the communes was combining government with the management of its economy in a transition to ownership by the whole people, a transition towards Communism. Speaking a month after the Eighth Central Committee Plenum in China, he said that it would take fifteen to twenty years, or a little longer, for China to have modern industry, modern agriculture and modern science. He then read a letter from Mao to the Soviet Congress praising the Soviet plan of constructing Communism, and saying that China was doing the same.[39]

At home, however, Party theoreticians were beginning to have their doubts. Ai Siqi, Mao's adviser on Marxism in Yan'an, praised the Leap but said that the laws of nature could not be defied. Feng Ding, the Marxist philosopher at Peking University, wrote in the same vein: 'We are opposed to aimless actions which do not take objective conditions into account.' However, Li Da, president of Wuhan University and one of the earliest Marxist theoreticians, believed that the Great Leap was a great push towards more production, that differences between city and village, and between physical and mental labour, would disappear and that the gradual transition to Communism would follow.[40] Chen Yun wrote an article for the March 1, 1959, issue of *Red Flag* (his last public pronouncement, followed by years of silence); he disapproved of the conservative rightists, but he warned against excessive speed.[41] By the early 1960s all the Eastern bloc countries were professing support for the theory of preparation for final Communism, although they were doing nothing about it. The Twenty-second Congress of the CPSU, held in October 1961, dealt at length with the construction of a Communist society, to be achieved by 1980. However, after the fall of Khrushchev in October 1964, the subject fell into oblivion. Brezhnev followed a more pragmatic policy.[42]

It is clear, therefore, that Mao's radical reform in 1958–9 was not a revolt against the Soviet Union, but that Mao's inspiration came rather from Khrushchev. The difference was that in the Soviet Union the 'building of Communism' meant merely fostering economic achievement. The only organisational change Khrushchev wanted — in opposition to Stalin's policy — was that the tractor stations should belong to the collective farms; and even that became a controversial issue.[43] In China Mao wanted to change the whole political, economic and social structure, to produce instantaneously the mirage of Communist society, a Communist society of equality, without any of the bourgeois trappings of commerce and money. The theory was the same in the Soviet Union and in China, but the ways of proceeding were entirely different.

The first edition of the Russian *Textbook on Political Economy* (Moscow, 1954) spoke of 'agrarian communes', to be erected as soon as a high grade of production had been reached in the collective farms. In the book's third (1958) revised edition, the word 'commune' no longer appeared. This was probably a tacit reaction from Moscow to the policy of Peking.[44]

CHAPTER XVI

THE YEARS 1960–1965

Overview

The economic disaster caused by the communes and Great Leap forced the Party to retreat. Nominally, at least, both the communes and the Great Leap were retained; but the Party had been boxed into a corner. Between 1959 and 1962 was a time of considerable freedom. The peasants resumed work with little interference from the authorities, and in many parts of the country they began cultivating their land. The paramount question was how to produce enough food to eat after years of famine.

Cultural life revived. The cat was away and the mice played freely. Old Confucianist ethics returned and were honoured in the major universities throughout the country on the pretence that Confucian universal benevolence fitted neatly into the Communist doctrine.

The prestige of the Party was ruined, perhaps for ever. The Communist Party never again became what it had been before. Mao apologised, although his apology was not published till sixteen years later, in 1978, when Deng Xiaoping cited it as proof that Mao was not infallible. Yet even when he was apologising in 1962, Mao was reasserting his authority, but this was no longer the authority of the Party; it was the authority of a single man.

As soon as Mao had reasserted his power, 'acid rain' began to fall everywhere. A purge was launched in the villages, but it operated not in the usual single, firmly imposed direction, but in two directions at once. Apparently it was being dictated from two differing central headquarters. The 'acid rain' put a stop to cultural freedom. Jiang Qing, Mao's wife, a vindictive ex-film actress, imposed her will on the theatre. Mao himself reformed Marxism with a heavy hand. The head of the leading Party school, the depository of orthodox Marxism, was exposed to nationwide defamation. Cultural magazines published grovelling apologies for the heresies they had dared to publish.

In those years, under Mao's patronage, a new power emerged, — that of Lin Biao, who in 1958 became one of the Vice-Chairmen of the Party and in 1959 minister of defence and a dominant voice in the highest military command, the Military Committee of the Party Central Committee. The ascent of Lin Biao happened almost imperceptibly. In 1961 he published the collection of Mao's sayings that was to become known throughout the world in later years as the *Little Red Book*, the 'Sayings of Chairman Mao'. In the years that followed, the military under Lin Biao's command did their utmost to take over the direction of Party and government organisations by establishing Political Departments in ministries and elsewhere, with ignorant soldiers dictating to experienced administrators. It was not all plain sailing, however. The men around Liu Shaoqi, who was still the number two man in the Party and President of the Republic, resisted. Confusion was visible.

Mao used Lin Biao, and Lin Biao used Mao. Marxism paled before the cult of Mao, which was developed to frightening dimensions. Mao was not only the infallible leader; he was glorified as the Saviour of Mankind. A gigantic nationwide pageant was staged to show him in his new role. Zhou Enlai collaborated, in his subtle way, travelling round the world and organising what were called the 'emerging forces of Asia, Africa and Latin America' in the hope of establishing an anti-United Nations. With the failure of the coup in Indonesia in 1965 and the fall of Ben Bella in Algeria, this plan collapsed.

With Mao's China claiming world leadership, relations with the Soviet Union deteriorated. A fierce public controversy developed between Moscow and Peking; China featured as the true Marxist country and the Soviet Union as a renegade revisionist regime. The fall of Khrushchev and his replacement by Brezhnev in 1964 did not change the situation. Yet there was no complete break with the Soviet Union. Even as late as 1965, despite earlier acrimonious debates, an attempt at conciliation was made — though in vain. Mao's paranoic sense of grandeur, fostered by Lin Biao, could not be dimmed. The Cultural Revolution was coming. At the end of 1966 the whole Communist Party was smashed to pieces and disappeared. What remained was the army and the Party organisations within the armed forces. This, however, belongs to the next period.

It is interesting to speculate how this can have happened. The answer, perhaps, is that Marxism had never put down deep roots in China, and the Communist Party itself was merely a tool of power. Marxism was not learnt until the Yan'an days, fourteen years after the establishment of the Chinese Communist Party, and what was learnt then was the Stalinist brand of Marxism. Stalin's death and the collapse of his regime dealt a fatal blow to the Party in China, and prepared the way for Mao's unique type of rule. The idea of 'Transition to Communism', learnt from Khrushchev, went to his head and reawakened old revolutionary dreams. Mao had grown up in the revolutionary and nihilistic period at the beginning of the century when emperors were being deposed and traditional Chinese culture was being discarded. He wanted to create a new China and to make utopia a reality. He worked through shock treatment, in the form of terrifying political campaigns. When his own men opposed him in the later 1950s, he reasserted his power, but in the 1960s, after the failure of his radical reforms, his old companions were still resisting. Mao reviled them as bourgeois anti-Marxists within the Party. Ultimately, with the help of Lin Biao's military power, he swept them aside, and with them went the Party itself.

In many ways Mao is a tragic figure in the history of China. He was shrewd in dealing with men, but his ignorance ruined China. He had no idea how iron and steel are produced; he thought that the closer you sow, the more grain you harvest; he betrayed ignorance of elementary science; he destroyed the Communist Party itself.

It may well be said that Marxism and the Communist regime existed in China only in the 1950s when the Russian model was being imitated. Party members believed that Communism would bring prosperity to China, and enthusiasm for the new ideals carried the young along. After 1957, and in particular after the famine that followed the Leap and the communes, the Communist system, as known in other Communist countries, collapsed. There followed the ascent of Lin Biao's military, the upheaval of the Cultural Revolution and the internal wrangles after Lin Biao's death in 1971 and after Mao's death in 1976. Two years later came the regime of Deng Xiaoping, seeking new ways for China. One may well say that Communist China, as such, existed only for the eight years between 1949 and 1957.

In this chapter we deal with the retreat of the Party after the failure of the Leap and the communes, Mao's reassertion of his authority and the emergence of Lin Biao. We also examine what Marxism was in China in those years.

The Party in retreat

The communes had disastrous consequences. For many years the word famine was not breathed. In 1960, however, when sad realities brought people back to their senses, some dared to write: 'What is to be sown and how the land is to be cultivated are not subject to change by man.' 'The nature of the soil was disregarded, and systems and methods of cultivation did not suit the conditions.' 'Undoubtedly we are revolution-

aries, but revolution must have a purpose. This purpose must be condu-
cive to production and to the betterment of people's lives.' 'No one can
order the land to bring forth two or three harvests per year when neither
manpower nor fertiliser is available.' 'It is better to make no change if
the result of change may be a fall in production.'[1] In October 1959 the
ministry of food admitted that in some areas 'food supply was sparse',
but it ascribed this to natural disaster.[2] At the end of 1960 fear was
expressed that the grain harvested would not last until the following
spring, and in some provinces stringent food rationing was imposed on
those who ate from the common kitchens.

Signs that something had gone wrong were visible in Hong Kong,
where all, rich and poor, were sending food parcels and medicines to
relatives inside China, and receiving innumerable letters complaining
about beri-beri and liver diseases.[3] The Chinese press itself spoke of epi-
demics in the villages caused by the food in the common dining-halls and
by unhygienic public latrines.[4] What could not be said in plain words
was conveyed through historical allegory. On December 22, 1961, the
Guang Ming Daily, Peking, had an article about an ancient book, *Liu Zi*,
by an unknown author. The article quoted the following on agriculture:
'There is not enough grain because the number of loafers [the ruling
class] is large, and the number of peasants is small,' and 'To kindle a fire
but to wish not to have a flame, to throw water but wish it to remain at
rest, is to wish for the impossible.' The reader could understand: the
misery had come, not from natural calamities, but from irrational orders
from above.[5]

China experts round the world could not believe that there was
famine in China. A BBC commentator — giving the opinion general
among China experts — declared that widespread famine in such a well-
organised country was unthinkable. Chinese coming out from China
told gruesome stories. In 1961 *China News Analysis* published some of
these reports by Chinese travellers from all parts of China. All spoke of
food shortage and hunger; swollen bellies, lack of protein and liver
diseases were common. Many babies were stillborn because of their
mothers' deficient nutrition. Few babies were being born. As some
workers put it, their food barely sufficed to keep them standing on their
feet, let alone allowing them to have thoughts of sex. Peasants lacked the
strength to work, and some collapsed in the fields and died. City government organisations and schools sent people to the villages by night to
buy food, bartering clothes and furniture for it. In Shenyang the newspaper reported cannibalism. Desperate mothers strangled children who

cried for food. Many reported that villagers were flocking into the cities in search of food; many villages were left empty, only the old people who were not strong enough to go to the cities being left behind. It was also said that peasants were digging underground pits to hide their food. Others spoke of places where the population had been decimated by starvation.[6]

Many years have passed since then, but there are few people in China who, when asked, cannot recall the horrors of those days. In the 1980s these disasters were discussed openly. Xue Muqiao, a leading economist and for many years head of the State Statistical Office, declared in 1981 that in those years 'people in the cities had not enough to eat, and in the villages there was serious famine.' The Peking *Guang Ming Daily* declared on April 27, 1980, that in the Northwest the peasants, in their struggle to grow some food, had destroyed grassland and forests. Half of the grassland and a third of the forests went between 1959 and 1962, and this damaged the region permanently as a place for human habitation. On May 14, 1980, the *People's Daily* said that in many regions agrarian production had remained stagnant since those years of disaster, and that this had affected the lives of 100 million people.[7] On April 3, 1979, the *People's Daily* said: 'The serious shortage of food in the villages had a physically devastating effect on the people. . . . Now we know that the memorandum of Comrade Peng Dehuai, presented at the 1959 Lushan conference, was right and that the man who opposed it [Mao's name was not used] was wrong.'[8]

The famine of those years was reflected in the 1982 census figures. An analysis of the figures for the aged, published in Shanghai in 1984, said: 'Between 1953 and 1964, the ratio of those in the 60-or-higher age bracket, compared to the total population, declined from 7.32 to 6.08 per cent. This was caused by the growth of the number of the young and the high proportion of deaths of the aged in the three difficult years. The change in population figures reflected the effect of the economic conditions in that difficult period.' (By 1982 the ratio of the aged had risen again to 7.64 per cent.) The figures are:

Total population: 1953, 567.4 million; 1964, 694.6 million.
Sixty or more years old: 1953, 41.5 million; 1964, 42.2 million.[9]

If the 1953 ratio of 7.32 per cent had been maintained in 1964, the absolute figure of those aged sixty and over would have been 50 million. There were 8 million less, owing partly, as the commentary said, to the 'difficult years'.

The Statistical Bureau's population figures show a steady growth through the years and a sudden decline in the years of famine. Those for overall population and the 1:1,000 birth and death rates are as follows:

	Population	Birth rate %	Death rate %
1958	660 m.	29.2	12
1959	672 m.	24.8	14.6
1960	662 m.	20.8	25.4
1961	658 m.	18	14.2
1962	672 m.	37	10^{10}

Source: Compiled by the author.

These figures illustrate the scale of the disaster caused by the Commune and Leap policy. These disasters, and the shock Mao suffered from what he considered open opposition by Peng Dehuai and others, were too much to bear. In 1960 the Party leadership retired into its shell.

Central Committee meeting in 1961

A Central Committee Plenum, the ninth since 1956, was held in January 1961 under Mao's chairmanship. It dealt with the economic situation, and was a meeting of retreat. A policy of 'readjustment, consolidation, completion and further advance' was announced. The short communiqué that followed did not mention the economic disaster or the famine; it said rather that 'the problem awaiting urgent solution is the temporary difficulty in supplying the market owing to shortage of raw materials caused by deficient harvests.' Reactivation of village markets was ordered and, instead of a further Leap, improvement in the quality of products was prescribed. Economists explained, discreetly, what had happened and what was needed. They insisted that true statistics, not fantasies, were essential, and that the real situation must be made known. Some defended what had happened with the Marxist theory that the world develops in spiral movements: the great quantitative development of the preceding three years would be followed by a qualitative uplift, which would lay the foundation for a renewed quantitative leap. Even such discreet apologies reveal incidentally the blunders of the Leap.[11]

The Central Committee Plenum blamed the stupidity of local

Party leaders who had not grasped the Party's policy. There were some, the communiqué said, still hankering after rapid transition to Communism.[12] The communiqué spoke also of hostile elements who 'carry on destructive activities, exploiting the hardships imposed by natural disaster and of some defects in work at the lowest echelons'.[13]

A collection of Mao's *Unedited Speeches*, published during the Cultural Revolution in 1967 — a collection which has on the whole proved reliable — reproduced the speech Mao made at this Ninth Central Committee Plenum. Although the newspapers reporting the Plenum carried a picture of a radiant Chairman, it was an angry speech. In it Mao accused class enemies, counter-revolutionary former landlords and stupid bureaucrats of having blown 'the communisation wind' in order to restore their power. Thus it had happened that in Henan province — where Mao had started the communes — 'the high ambitions for a fabulous output and an overflow of grain had turned into very low output; vegetables had taken the place of grain.' At the Lushan meeting, Mao said, the rightists blamed the leadership for having made mistakes. He admitted that mistakes had been made. 'They say: you also made mistakes. This is true. Everybody makes mistakes, great or small. The Party Central authorities and the regional leaders also make mistakes.' He added that in 1960 the Party leadership were busy with the conflict with Khrushchev, thus diverting attention from the plight at home. 'In 1960 the Soviets attacked us at the Party conference in Bucharest. Nevertheless', Mao said, 'we should be united with the Soviet Union and with the eighty-seven Communist parties of the world, and should accept ill-treatment.'[14]

A major change was introduced in the Party structure. The Plenum announced the re-establishment of six regional bureaux of the Central Committee, which had disappeared in 1954 when they were suppressed along with the government's Great Administrative Areas. These were the remnants of the army-ruled regional bases of the Party during the civil war. After the Gao Gang incident, both party and government regional administrations were scrapped and the central authority of Peking was strengthened. It was significant that it was the Central Committee's regional bureaux that were re-established, whereas the regional government administration was not. The rationale of this new movement was not explained. The re-establishment of the regional bureaux was bound to weaken centralised authority, and particularly the power of Mao and of Lin Biao. The new heads of the regional bureaux were not active military men; moreover, they were not Lin Biao's men.

(The army's regional divisions did not coincide geographically with the Central Committee's regional bureaux.[15])

Material conditions were bad and the State Budget showed a deficit.[16] The deficit was highest in 1960, when it amounted to 12.5 per cent of expenditure.[17]

Culture revived

One sector of life in China, however, flourished, and this was the world of culture — history, literature and art — whose denizens felt for the first time that they could breathe freely. In the 1950s their world had been frozen by a series of condemnations — the condemnation of a film on a philanthropic educator, of a book on an ancient novel, of the writings of Hu Feng and of Feng Xuefeng, editor of the Party's literary magazine. All these condemnations were expanded into national campaigns of slander. That was the period when servile imitation of the Soviet model was mandatory.

Friction with the Russians and the withdrawal of Party control, owing to the economic blunders of the Leap, allowed the intellectuals to feel free. Things were written which could not have been written earlier. Confucianism, discarded in the early 1920s but revived in the 1930s by the Nationalists, had been rejected by the new regime; now, startlingly, it reappeared and was discussed with passion in the major universities. Ancient Sung dynasty idealist philosophy was also revived. One writer said that the rapid end of the Ch'in dynasty, founded by the first Emperor 2,000 years ago, was attributable to the 'excessive power given to the Emperor, severity without clemency'. A leading architect said that in the early 1950s architects, later condemned, wanted to retain the architectural harmony of Peking city, including the original shape of the square in front of the Imperial Palace as it had come down from the Ming dynasty, and that they had opposed the demolition of the three gates leading to the Tian An Men and of the city walls. One philosopher went so far as to ask: 'If materialism and idealism can change into one another, does this mean that Marxist philosophy also will change into idealism?'[18]

This relative freedom of culture received a sort of approval from the Party leadership when Chen Yi, minister of foreign affairs and a close associate of Zhou Enlai, spoke on August 10, 1961, to university graduates in Peking. It was perhaps the most heterodox pronouncement ever made by a high authority. He spoke of 'red and expert', 'red' standing for Communist convictions and 'expert' for expert knowledge.

Chen Yi said that Party schools were meant to train for political work — to be red; ordinary schools should train for the professions. In the universities politics must be studied and the newspapers must be read, but this should not absorb too much time. Those who study should not be called 'white experts'. 'For myself, my own mind is very complex,' he said. 'In my head there are Communist ideas, there are also ideas derived from Confucius, and there are bourgeois thoughts. I cannot say that I am thoroughly red.' No one should judge a person according to the family he comes from, whether proletarian or bourgeois. However, he added, a person like Lin Xiling — the girl student who spoke at Peking University against the Party committee in the schools — is an enemy.[19]

What he said was a half-hearted concession to reality. The Party was lying so low that the newspapers, even including the sacred *People's Daily*, were publishing unpolitical jokes. The president of a university asked for good writing instead of Party jargon. An article in the *People's Daily* said that it was outlandish to 'take isolated passages from the works of the Marxist canons to prove theses'.[20] In that atmosphere, a good word from a Party leader, not necessarily Mao, was essential.

Mao up again — Central Committee in 1962

The distinctions drawn between red and expert did not last long. In September 1962 the Central Committee met for its Tenth Plenum under Mao — and he was the tough Mao again. For many years the message of this Plenum was to be condensed into a single phrase, 'Never forget class struggle.' Mao spoke of class struggle in the period of transition to Communism which he now judged might last several decades: class struggle between the proletarian class and the bourgeois class, between socialism and capitalism, between the purity of Marxism-Leninism on the one hand and, on the other, reactionaries in the country itself and modern revisionists — this last being a label designating the regime in the Soviet Union. Class struggle, the communiqué of this Plenum said, exists within the Party itself. Never forget class struggle!

There was indeed struggle within the Party. The Plenum dismissed from the Party Secretariat Huang Kecheng, army Chief-of-Staff in 1958–9, and Tan Zheng, head of the political department of the armed forces, and it elected three new members to the Secretariat: Lu Dingyi, head of Party propaganda, who had purged the literary world in 1957; Kang Sheng, Mao's henchman in Yan'an days; and Luo Ruiqing, his henchman during the 1955–7 *Sufan* purge. (Lu Dingyi and Luo Ruiqing were both purged during the Cultural Revolution.) The communiqué was modestly optimistic about the economy, saying that some improvement was visible. It maintained with emphasis the institution of the Commune and the programme of the Leap, although these had hardly maintained themselves in the deeply wounded economy.[21]

On the first day of the Plenum, September 24, 1962, Mao delivered a speech which was not published till years later, and then only in a collection of his speeches published in 1969 during the Cultural Revolution. In it he was preoccupied with conflicts both with the Soviet Union and with his political opponents in China. His main theme was the method of dealing with Khrushchev and with his own enemies inside his Party. He did not mention the Commune or the Leap. 'Some mistakes were made in 1959 and 1960,' he said; 'primarily, too much grain was requisitioned and both agriculture and industry were guided blindly. In the second half of 1960, however, a beginning was made in correcting these errors . . . We did not pay much attention to this,' he went on, because 'revisionism arrived and our attention was focused on opposing Khrushchev, . . . I said last year that you must allow me to make mistakes. You must welcome me when I correct my mistakes. Those who make mistakes and correct them, for instance Li Weihan [the head of the Central Committee's United Front Department, who a year later disappeared from the scene], are welcome, but not the enemies of the Party. This does not mean that all the enemies must be killed. There were several Nationalist generals whom we did not kill. We did not kill the counter-revolutionaries Pan Hannian, Hu Feng and Rao Shushi. But we struggle against revisionism. This is the struggle of Marxism-Leninism against revisionism.'

Mao appeared as the lord of life and death, but in this speech he was preoccupied with China's relations with the Soviet Union rather than with the misery caused at home by the Commune and the Leap. He recalled his troubles with Khrushchev: 'In 1958 Khrushchev wanted to set up a Soviet-Chinese combined fleet in order to seal us off [from attacking the islands held by Taiwan]. In 1959, at the time of the border dispute with India, he supported Nehru. At the dinner on our National Day he attacked us [a fact not recorded elsewhere]. The trouble with the Soviet Union', Mao went on, 'began early. [In 1945, at the end of the war] Stalin wanted to halt the Chinese revolution. He said we should not start a civil war but should cooperate with Chiang Kai Shek, otherwise the Chinese people would perish. We did not follow him, and we won. After the victory he was afraid that we should become like the Yugoslavs and that I should become a second Tito. When I was in Moscow [1949–50] he did not want to sign a Sino-Soviet alliance and mutual aid treaty. He signed only after two months of struggle. When did Stalin begin to trust us? At the time of the Korean War. In the winter of 1950 he believed that we were not Tito and not Yugoslavs. Today, however, we are called ''adventurists, nationalists, dogmatists, factionalists'', while the Yugoslavs are called Marxist-Leninists.' This was now 'the struggle of Marxism-Leninism against anti-Marxism-Leninism and against revisionism'.

Mao was more interested in his dispute with the Russians than in the sufferings of people in China. He had begun to see himself as the leader of world revolution. 'We support the people's liberation movements; we support the people's masses in the three continents of Asia, Africa and Latin America.'[22] This was the first announcement of an ambitious plan for a grand alliance of the 'A-A-A' — Asia, Africa and (Latin) America — with Mao as the leader of the revolutionary new world. The execution of the plan was entrusted to Zhou Enlai.

Since 1956 the highest leaders of the Party had been Mao, the four Vice-Chairmen Liu Shaoqi, Zhou Enlai, Zhu De and Chen Yun — Lin Biao was added as a fifth Vice-Chairman in 1958 — and Secretary-General Deng Xiaoping. These seven formed the Standing Committee of the Politbureau. As we saw above, Chen Yun fell into the background after his expression of reservations about the Leap policy in *Red Flag* in 1959, and he no longer appeared. Neither Chen Yun nor Lin Biao attended the Tenth Plenum in September 1962.[23] Lin Biao was absent from numerous public functions, and many observers believed him to be sick. He was in fact busy, as we shall see, remoulding the army to his image. Chen Yun apparently had not yet been fully accepted by Mao, although two months earlier, on July 1, Party Day, two Peking newspapers (not the *People's Daily*) had published a photograph which caused a sensation. It showed all seven members of the Standing Committee with Chen Yun and Mao in the centre reaching out their hands for a handshake, the other five looking on with curious embarrassed smiles. No comment accompanied this photograph. The impression given to the reader was that Mao had become reconciled with Chen Yun.[24]

Chen Yun, one of the earliest Party leaders, enjoyed immense prestige in the Party, probably because he had kept aloof from political fighting within it. He was the acknowledged authority on economic matters, though not a trained economist. He vanished from public sight during the years of Mao's onslaught on the economic edifice, but what had happened to him at that time remained for many years a mystery. In the 1980s — when he himself was aged nearly eighty — he became an outstanding figure, second only to Deng Xiaoping. His 1926–56 writings were published, in two volumes, in 1984; his writings and pronouncements of the critical years 1956–62, when he seemed to be in obscure retirement, had been published in 1980 in a 214-page volume of which 250,000 copies were printed; although this edition was meant for innerParty circulation only, it was also made available to the general public. This volume contains a short letter which he wrote to Mao in May 1959, warning him against irrational pushing of steel production with inadequate equipment. Obviously, Chen Yun was silenced. There is no document in the book dated between May 1959 and May 1961. By the latter date the catastrophic results of the Leap were unmistakable, and after that Chen Yun was again consulted. In May 1961 he summoned a meeting to discuss fertilisers. He spoke of exhausted food reserves and the food crisis in the cities, the consequence of the influx of the rural population. (In the cities the state was feeding the population, using food-ration coupons; in the villages the harvested grain was distributed by the local authorities.) He also mentioned the shortage of coal and steel. In February and March 1962, he spoke of inflation and proposed some remedies for the food situation in the cities, for example selling three catties of soyabean per month per head. He also recommended the opening of expensive restaurants to suck up floating money.[25]

Mao and Moscow

At the end of 1962 a new feature was introduced into national life: the *Internationale* was broadcast before the news.[26] This was a symbol of a new era, of Mao the leader of world revolution.

World revolution and the dispute with Moscow had become obsessions with Mao. It may be wondered whether his purpose in resigning as Head of State in 1959 was not in fact, as was alleged in those days, 'to have more time to pursue theoretical work in Marxism-Leninism'. Liu Shaoqi, who had become Head of State in his place, was purged seven years later by the Cultural Revolution; but perhaps in those earlier days Mao was not yet contemplating his suppression.

In Moscow on October 23, 1961, Zhou Enlai ostentatiously walked out of the Twenty-second CPSU Party Congress, which had decided on the removal of Stalin's body from the Lenin Mausoleum and the condemnation of Albania. A few days earlier, in a speech at the assembly, Zhou had condemned 'one-sided criticism of one of the brother parties'. Nevertheless he thanked the Russians for their support and aid — though a year earlier Soviet experts had been recalled from China.[27]

At the end of 1962 the Italian Communist Party and the many representatives of Communist parties present at the Czechoslovak Communist Party's Congress condemned Albania, but not Yugoslavia. The low-ranking Chinese delegates at the Congress protested against the expulsion of Albania and criticised what they called Yugoslav revisionism. On December 31, 1962, the *People's Daily* published a long and bitter attack on Togliatti, the head of the Italian Communist Party, for having condemned nuclear war and minimised the threat of US imperialism.[28] In 1963 there began an exchange of controversial letters between the Party leaders of Peking and Moscow. A Chinese letter, divided into twenty-five points and dated June 14, 1963, revealed Peking's views on Marxism and revisionism, peace and war, revolution in Asia, Africa and Latin America, and Soviet domination of Comecon, the organ for economic cooperation between Communist countries. 'Certain persons interfere in the internal affairs of other fraternal parties and countries, forcing changes of leadership of other fraternal parties.'[29] Three years later, on August 14, 1966, the *People's Daily* revealed that this letter had been written under Mao's personal direction,[30] and it may well be assumed that all the shells fired at Moscow were aimed by Mao. Nevertheless relations with Moscow were not cut. On July 5, 1963, Deng Xiaoping, Peng Zhen, Kang Sheng and three others left for a week-long negotiation in Moscow. After this the *People's Daily* predicted: 'The differences between the CCP and the CPSU will eventually be settled if the fundamental principles of Marxism-Leninism are truly followed.'[31]

In November 1964 Zhou Enlai went to Moscow ostensibly for the celebration of the October Revolution, but really to sound out the new Soviet leader, Brezhnev. This visit was inconclusive — on his return to Peking Mao greeted him at the airport.[32] In February 1965 Kosygin visited Peking twice, on his way to and from Vietnam. In the middle of February Chen Yi, at a reception held by Chervonenko, the Soviet ambassador, spoke of Mao's desire to preserve Sino-Soviet unity. In May Li Xiannian, at a reception held by the newly-arrived ambassador, Sergei Lapin, spoke of cooperation between the Soviet Union and China in the Vietnam war. In the same year, however, a booklet in which Ponomarev criticised Mao's invention of the 'intermediate zone' as a term for Western Europe was rejected with contempt.[33]

The Chinese leaders did not seem to be divided on the dispute with Moscow, and perhaps this indeed reflected the true state of affairs. But while Mao was busy asserting his power in the Communist world at large, the other Party leaders were engaged in heavy in-fighting in China itself.

Mission failed

The implementation of Mao's ambitious plans for becoming the leader of the revolutionary world was entrusted to Zhou Enlai who, with his foreign minister Chen Yi, spent a great deal of time travelling around Asia and Africa. In this way the ever-cautious Zhou kept clear of the internal fight brewing in the Party, undoubtedly watching carefully to see how the pendulum was swinging.

Between December 1963 and March 1964, Zhou Enlai with Chen Yi visited fourteen countries in Asia and Africa. In November 1963 China took part in the sports festival of the Newly Emerging Forces, organised by that ambitious friend of Peking, President Sukarno of Indonesia. In July 1964 Zhou visited Burma. Towards the end of the year Chen Yi visited Algeria, Egypt, Pakistan, Cambodia, Burma and Indonesia.[34] But in 1965 the great 'A-A-A' plan collapsed. In the spring of that year a second Afro-Asian Conference (the first had been held in 1961) was under preparation, and Zhou told a Middle East news agency that its purpose was to unite revolutionary nations and 'to help Afro-Asian nations in the UN in their struggle to radically reorganise the UN'. This was in March. In April he was in Jakarta talking to Sukarno, Prince Sihanouk, Kim Il Sung of North Korea, Pham Van Dong of North Vietnam, and ministers from Afghanistan, Somalia and Zambia. In June Zhou was in Zambia, then in Cairo, in preparation for the great international conference in Algeria, but at that very time Ben Bella, the leader of Algeria, fell. Zhou waited in Egypt for twelve days, but on June 30 he left for China. His great project had come to grief.[35] A second setback came in Indonesia. For months a stream of Peking leaders had been visiting Indonesia, and vice versa; Chen Yi himself went there to take part in the celebration for the twentieth anniversary of Indonesia's independence on August 17. Two weeks later, on September 30, the pro-Peking coup was staged in Jakarta. It failed, and Peking was stunned. Not till October 18 was the news broken to Chinese readers.[36]

Peking was also doing badly in the international Communist front organisations of lawyers, trade unions, students, journalists and women and in the World Peace Council, all of which took the Russian side.[37] However, a brave man is not dismayed by failure. Early in 1966 a highfalutin article in the *People's Daily* quoted a poem by Mao: 'The Four Seas are in movement, the waters roll; the five continents are shaking; wind and thunder.' The *People's Daily* explained: 'When the ancient Roman Empire was crumbling, the slaves broke down the gates and the rule of slave-masters came to an end. The collapse of feudalism took 200 years of violent agitation. Now is the period of the extinction of capitalism, of acute international struggle, and of the rise of Asian-African-Latin American revolution.' A second article, headed 'Setback and Progress', spoke of the Yellow River with its bends and curves: this was the law of revolution. A third article referred to Hitler, the Japanese and Chiang Kai Shek: violent efforts by the wicked enemy are the prelude to his defeat.[38]

Zhou Enlai had not succeeded in bringing Mao's worldwide ambitions to fulfilment. When the Cultural Revolution came in 1966, China folded up like leaves of the Praying Hands. All Chinese ambassadors except one, Huang Hua in Egypt, were recalled. China had turned in on herself.

Lin Biao emerges

Despite this, the myth of Mao continued to grow, carefully fostered by Lin Biao. In 1959 Lin took over the army, which in 1960 he called upon 'to raise high the great red banner of the Thoughts of Mao Zedong'. He also launched the slogan which was to reverberate down the years: 'Read the books of Chairman Mao, listen to Chairman Mao, act according to the instructions of Chairman Mao, be a good soldier of Chairman Mao.' Lin Biao aimed high: 'Troops', he said, 'are to serve politics. They should not forget politics. They should not neglect politics.'[39] In 1961 he called on the military leaders to write down their experiences showing how they had applied the Thoughts of Mao in the military field. Regulations on socialist education instructed the army to study the Thoughts of Mao.[40]

On National Day, October 1, 1964, a monumental theatre show, *The East is Red*, was staged by the army. The press described it as 'a hymn to the Thoughts of Mao Zedong'. Monster choirs and ballet girls in military uniform fired rifles and danced *jeté passé* steps. All this symbolised the victory of Mao throughout the preceding forty years. The show ended with apotheosis; an immense gold flag adorned with a huge figure of Mao fluttered on the heights and the chorus sang: 'Chairman Mao, the sun in our hearts.' Two weeks later China exploded its first atomic bomb.[41] This was a double manifestation of the might of the military and Lin Biao, and of the new role of Mao — all very different from anything that had been thought of in the 1950s.

Political departments

The years 1964–5 saw a gradual penetration of the army into the civilian party and government organisations. This was the prelude to the final showdown between Lin Biao and Liu Shaoqi's men.

Political departments were to be added to all major Party and government organisations. The purpose of this duplication of organisation was that the political departments should take over control to ensure that the organisations should 'learn from the People's Liberation Army'. A national conference of political workers was held in March 1964 with the participation of the provinces and the major economic enterprises. This meeting was organised by the political department of the Party Central Committee's Industry and Communications Department. The head of the political department, at the very heart of the Central Committee, was not a soldier but Gu Mu, who held prominent posts in several state organs dealing with the economy. The meeting was presided over by Bo Yibo, the head of the State Economic Committee.[42] Apparently the military under Lin Biao tried to penetrate the highest Party organs, and so make them imitate the army; but for the moment they were unable to push aside the civilian leaders of the economy. During the Cultural Revolution, both Gu Mu and Bo Yibo were purged. Gu Mu reappeared in 1972, a year after the fall of Lin Biao, once again as a leader of the economy. Bo Yibo did not reappear till December 1978.

Gradually political departments were established in the sections of the Central Committee dealing with agriculture and forestry, industry and communications, finance and commerce. Political departments were also established in the bureaux dealing with the economy in the provinces and the major cities. Demobilised soldiers were sent to commerce, food and foreign trade departments and to the marketing and supply cooperatives to introduce the 'First-in-Four things'. This concept, which had already been introduced in the army, was an invention of Lin Biao's. It emphasised the importance (*a*) of the human elements, (*b*) of political work, (c) of ideological work, and (d) of ideology put into practice. These were the First-in-Four. It was admitted that 'demobilised comrades would feel that this was a new world to them', but they would learn. All this was a startling development. It should be recalled that after the rebuffing of 'rightist' non-Party members in 1957, the Party organisations in provinces and counties had pushed aside the government organisations; the Party committees themselves were running the country. The fundamental law of a Communist Party — dictation to the government from behind the scenes — was ignored. The plan now was for army men to push the Party administration aside and take over the direction of the work of government and introduce the 'First-in-Four'.

In February 1965 a second national conference of political departments was convened by Li Xiannian, member of the Politbureau and minister of finance. This meeting was run by the Party Central Committee's Finance and Commerce Political Department. It was not made clear whether or not Li Xiannian was the head of this political department, but the name of a deputy head of the political department was published: Yang Shugen, a former military commander of Canton. He explained the desirable policy to the meeting: 'Shoot politics up, seize and fulfil the First-in-Four, politics should take command' — all phrases of Lin Biao's. Comrade Lin Biao, he said, wants the shooting upwards of politics, and he insists that all must study the writings of Chairman Mao. Bad thoughts — i.e. disobedience and hesitation — must be seized right from the start. Not only deeds but thoughts too should be checked. This was the work of the political departments. In Peking itself 1,400 men from the armed forces, and in Shanghai 8,000 joined the city finance and commerce departments. Gradually, political departments were established in smaller cities and in a number of counties.

In those days the newspapers were not yet in the hands of Lin Biao's men, and much grumbling about the new moves, and resistance to them, became public through newspaper reports. 'When commodities are waiting to be loaded at the port or when cabbage is waiting to be put into trucks, should one sit down and hold political meetings before loading?' The answer given was that to load goods properly one needs sound political thoughts. The Peking newspaper specialising in economic affairs, *Da Gong Bao*, said in an ambiguous editorial that millions of employees in finance and commerce were welcoming the comrades from the army, but the latter, having changed their occupation, did not know much about trade. Everything was new to them, and what they had learned earlier was useless. But they had the Thoughts of Mao Zedong. In reality they had not changed their occupation, but had merely gone to new posts. Now they had to work in commerce and finance and study financial policies. They would learn. It would not be too difficult.

Another article in the same paper quoted some people as saying: 'Shoot politics up! Lay hold of the First-in-Four!' Does this mean that work in trade is not important? Another editorial in the same newspaper said: 'It must be clear that the finance and commerce departments have not yet had much time to study the Liberation Army. The foundations of political work have not yet been well laid. Politics have not yet shot upwards. The First-in-Four has not yet become a reality.' It added: 'There are many regions and counties which have not yet established finance and commerce political departments.' Yet another article in the same paper, speaking of the city of Shenyang, said that many political meetings had been held, but 'apart from talk, nothing had been done about the First-in-Four. Politics have not shot up.'[43] It was obvious that the Party committees in charge of finance and commerce were resisting the entry of ignorant soldiers; it could not have been otherwise. At the higher level this meant a tug-of-war between the Lin Biao men and the civilian Party administrators of the economy. Before 1949 all had been comrades in the army; but in the intervening sixteen years a system had been established which was now threatened by the irruption of ignorant soldiers — and by uncertainty over what Lin Biao had in mind.

The striking point in the whole operation of establishing political departments was that they were established in the finance and commerce network of the country. Obviously Lin Biao was out to gain control over money. This was the only occasion in the whole history of the People's Republic when the question of who held the purse-strings became visible. Yearly budget allocations were published many times; but neither before nor after the Cultural Revolution was it ever revealed which organ decided how much money was to be spent on what. This was indeed the only occasion when a particular body, in this case the men of Lin Biao, was seen to want to grab the purse.

Yet it was much more even than that. The battle was one of persons. It was also a battle of ideas, the battle to decide what Marxism meant.

Marxism

In the early years of the regime the Chinese youth learnt the elements of

Marxism from Comrade Feng Ding's book *The Ordinary Truth* (written in 1949, revised in 1955 and reprinted ten times). Feng Ding joined the Party in 1926, and studied in Moscow. After his return to China he taught Marxism, and in the 1950s was a professor at Peking University. When the wind changed in 1964, *Red Flag*, the organ of the Central Committee, began to criticise *The Ordinary Truth*, and gradually a nationwide smear campaign developed. The argument was subtle. In the book's 1956 edition Feng Ding, following the trend prevalent both in the Soviet Union and at home, criticised the cult of the individual. Yet the writer of one of the articles written against him was able to pick out the following passage: 'If happiness means normal life, then it means peace and no war, good food and fine clothes, clean housing . . .' How, the critic asked, can a revolutionary write such stuff? A revolutionary speaks first of the happiness of the class, of the collective, of struggle, of liberation, of labour. All must imitate Lei Feng — the young soldier who in 1963 was set up as the ideal of sacrifice for the Cause. Feng Ding, on the contrary, said in *The Ordinary Truth* that 'every man is infected by some sort of individualism'. *The Ordinary Truth* was wrong. Young people had to confess that they had been infected by his poisonous doctrine.

A short feature in the *Chinese Youth Daily* of December 10, 1964, quoted a dialogue between two young men: 'Have you read Feng Ding?' 'No.' 'This book has been condemned.' 'Luckily I have not read it.' The article added that young people were congratulating themselves on not having read Marxist books. They were reading little for fear that their reading might affect them.[44] (After the Cultural Revolution Feng Ding returned to Peking University. In 1981, when aged about eighty, he retired and became an adviser of the University.)

In May 1963 Mao drew up a document about Marxism, in particular about the Marxist theory of knowledge. Where does knowledge come from? What is truth, what is error? This was a brief, two-page introduction — not to a philosophical treatise, but to a regulation on agrarian organisation. What Mao wrote about 'philosophy' had a certain relevance to agrarian organisation, to the almost defunct communes.

His brief venture into epistemology was included in the *Selected Readings of the Works of Mao Zedong*, published by Lin Biao's army in 1965. 'Where does correct knowledge come from?' Mao asked. 'Does it come from heaven? No. Is it produced by the brain? No. Man's correct knowledge comes from social experience. It comes from three things:

production struggle, class struggle and scientific experiment.' It is the 'correct knowledge of the advanced class [the Communists], which, once accepted by the masses, becomes a material force that can transform society and can transform the world.' He then explained the process of knowledge: impressions gained by the senses go through a leap and become ideas. This is a leap from matter to spirit. The ideas, the spirit — which includes theories, policy, plans and methods — can influence the world.

Mao then turned to the question of how truth is to be distinguished from error. Success, he proclaimed, is the sign of correct knowledge; failure is the sign of error. He added a caveat: 'In social struggle, failure does not always mean that the idea is not correct. It may mean that in the struggle the advanced forces are weaker than the reactionary forces. That may cause temporary defeat. But [the correct ideas] will succeed later.' He continued this 'philosophical' errantry: 'A man's knowledge, tested by practice, may produce another leap, and this leap may be greater than the previous one. This second leap can show whether the idea — theories, policy, plans and methods — was correct or was an error.'

The word 'Leap' in Marxist philosophy can be from quantity to quality; or it can be a progress from material to spiritual knowledge. In 1963 the very word was bound to evoke memories of the attempted leap of 1958, which had failed. Obviously Mao was thinking of that; he still believed he had been right and that a new leap would come.

Mao ended his short philosophical treatise by saying that most of the comrades knew little about Marxist philosophy and felt 'that the thesis that matter changes into spirit and spirit changes into matter — that leap so evident in daily events — is unintelligible.' It must therefore be explained and taught.[45]

The booklet *Selected Readings of Mao's Works*, which included this essay, was published for the public at large in 1964–5. An article in the *People's Daily* of September 1966, when the Cultural Revolution was already raging, revealed that the *Selected Readings* had been published in 1961 for the army only — on Lin Biao's orders.[46] In 1961 the press had noted the existence of this first edition of the *Selected Readings*,[47] but nothing was then said about its having been published on the orders of Lin Biao. An inner-Party document published in 1969 said that the *Sayings of Chairman Mao* — in other words, the *Little Red Book* consisting of short quotations from Mao, to be learnt by heart, — had also been published in 1961 for the army only.[48] This too was published for the general public in 1964, as stated in the preface, on the orders of Lin Biao.

Mao's statements on the process of knowledge and on truth and error led to discussion of these questions among Marxist theoreticians and in the pages of the newspapers. This was still a fairly free discussion — within the narrow limits of Marxism. Lin Biao's authority was not yet as oppressive as it was to be a few years later, and people did not pay a great deal of attention to the *Little Red Book*.

The discussion was started in a light style by a journalist, Wang Ruoshui. Writing in dialogue form in the *People's Daily* on 'The Philosophy of the Table', he asked:

Which came first, the table or the idea of the table? If I say the table, this is materialism; if I say the idea of the table, this is idealism.

Does not a carpenter begin with the idea of the table? Where does this idea come from?

It was not born with man. It comes from the objective world.

But how did the first table come into being? Perhaps from the impression of a stone, used as a 'table'.

The human mind is complicated and dynamic, and it discovers new things, cars, planes and so on. Matter and spirit have mutual influence.

Can an idea turn into matter?

Chairman Mao said in his 'On Practice' that a subjective thing can become an objective thing. How can an idea become an object? Knowledge does not merely mirror reality. It sees the internal relations of things. Knowledge may be erroneous. Correct knowledge and error are tested by experience.

Now I understand better. Dialectical materialism says that thought and spirit originate from matter, but it does not deny the process from spirit to matter.

Wang Ruoshui's article aroused controversy. One objection to it was that Wang Ruoshui had neglected Engels' dictum that knowledge comes from labour, that is, labour of the hands and not labour of the brain. Engels explained that man had developed from the monkey by labouring with his hands. Another writer objected to this, saying that invention cannot be an unconscious process. Yet another asked some pertinent questions: 'If things are invented by man, can it be said that matter precedes idea? If a thing is made by conscious planning, does not the plan belong to the realm of ideas? Thus idea precedes existence, contradicting materialism.'[49]

The good comrades found this turning of matter into spirit and spirit into matter beyond their comprehension. If man is mere matter, as Marxism proclaims, how can he produce spiritual thoughts that change matter? But this doctrine had not been invented by Mao; it was proclaimed by Engels, and amplified by Lenin, to prove that the world can be changed by human acts, by revolution. Marxists assert that their materialism is not simple materialism but dialectical materialism. The nature of this dialectic has never been explained satisfactorily. As Mao put it, the temporary failure of the Commune and the Leap proved, not that he had been wrong, but only that for the time being the dark reactionary forces were stronger than the truth. The truth — Mao's ideas — would win in the end. Mao, the Thoughts of Mao, became the absolute truth, and the guide for a better understanding of Marx.

In that year, 1963, Mao saw struggle all around. He was involved with the Soviet Union, and was calling Moscow revisionist; at home he saw ghosts everywhere. Lin Biao's military were striving to make their way into the political scene and into the mysterious realm of Marxist philosophy. Many army leaders, it was said, had no inkling of what Marxism was. They would have to learn, but learn in a special way. They would have to learn various theses of Marx, Engels, Lenin and Stalin, helped by the writings of Chairman Mao. As a *People's Daily* article said on May 5, 1964: 'After study of a problem or of a chapter in Marx, Engels, Lenin or Stalin, the parallel treatment of the same question by Chairman Mao must be carefully considered, in order to arrive at an understanding of how Chairman Mao has developed Marxism-Leninism creatively.' The next day, the *People's Daily* said that studying Marxism-Leninism in the light of the Thoughts of Mao 'will help towards a deeper understanding of how Comrade Mao Zedong applied Marxism-Leninism and developed it creatively in the Chinese revolution'. One could therefore say that it was a matter no longer of Mao explaining the Marxist classics, but of Marxist classics explaining Mao.[50]

Then things went much further. A press article about the dialectical materialism of Chairman Mao appeared under the odd headline 'One-divided-into-two' and 'Two-combined-into-one'. These were popularisations of Hegelian-Marxist philosophical terms. The 'One-divided-into-two' was the Hegelian 'antithesis', and the 'Two-combined-into-one' was 'synthesis'. Antithesis meant fight, and synthesis meant reconciliation. The first shot against synthesis was fired by two unknown writers — that is how political campaigns begin.

Six weeks later Li Ming, a teacher in the Central Committee's Higher

Party School, was bitterly criticised. At a time, the criticism said, when the 'division of one into two' was being propagated among the masses and had become a sharp weapon in the class struggle, Li Ming — who lectured on Hegel in the school — was teaching the combining of the two into one.

Before long it was revealed that the origin of all evil teaching was to be found in Comrade Yang Xianzhen. Comrade Yang, then sixty-five years of age, had been up till three years earlier head of the Central Committee's Higher Party School, which trained leading Party officials. He was still teaching and writing about Marxism. Yang, who in his young days had studied in Moscow and Germany, was an authority on Marxism. In 1953 he was vice-president of the Central Committee's School for Marxism-Leninism, the earlier name of the Central Committee's Higher Party School. He became an alternate-member of the Central Committee and advanced to full membership in 1958, when he also became head of the Higher Party School. He held this post only till September 1961, when he was replaced by another Party veteran Wang Congwu, an old-timer trained in the 1930s in Moscow. Two years later Wang was replaced by Lin Feng. Both Wang and Lin had been members of the Central Committee since 1945. (Lin Feng died in 1977, but Wang Congwu and Yang Xianzhen were still active in the 1980s, and Yang was still carrying on a public controversy in 1981–2.) A nationwide smear campaign was started against Yang Xianzhen.

An article published in both the *People's Daily* and the magazine *Red Flag* said that 'those who profess the combining of two into one are opposing dialectical materialism . . . Everybody is aware of the present international trouble [with the Soviet Union] and of the internal class struggle. All Party papers emphasise propaganda for the "one-divided-into-two" . . . The international workers' movement [i.e. the Communist world] is divided into two. Our Party is criticising modern revisionism. The 'one-divided-into-two' is a powerful weapon in the present class struggle against errors both outside the country and inside. Yet at this very time, Yang Xianzhen dares to raise his voice in the Central Committee's Higher Party School to teach "combining the two into one". '

The July 1964 issue of *Philosophical Research* had four articles on the question. Two of them called the 'combining the two into one' metaphysics — a dirty word in the Communist vocabulary. The other two were conciliatory, saying that combining and dividing do not exclude each other; on the contrary, between them they form dialectical materialism. A press article attacking Yang said that those who were defending him and saying that this was not a political question but a scholarly discussion on the nature of Marxism were talking nonsense. The theory of Comrade Yang was metaphysics. 'Philosophy has a Party character and a class character; philosophy is a reflection of class struggle.'[51]

What the whole thing was all about was quite clear. Mao was in a fighting mood. He was putting a lot of energy into arguing against Moscow. Marxism in the Soviet Union was revisionism. China had preserved the purity of the Marxist doctrine. In other words, Hegel and Marx mattered little; this was not Marxist philosophising — it was a political struggle. Mao always liked struggle. In his 1937 'On Contradiction', he was still talking about unity of opposites, but the emphasis was on struggle. His February 1957 speech 'On Contradiction' was no different. The struggle was raging in China still, between the upcoming military and the civilian old guard of Liu Shaoqi. The condemnation of the 'two-combined-into-one' served to prepare the ground for the great battle of the Cultural Revolution.

Blows against culture

The Cultural Revolution did not begin till 1966, but already in July 1964 Mao had set up a Cultural Revolution Team. The members were Peng Zhen, member of the Politbureau; Lu Dingyi, head of Party propaganda and Politbureau alternate-member; Kang Sheng, Politbureau alternate-member; Zhou Yang, deputy head of propaganda in charge of literature and art; and Wu Lengxi, another deputy head of propaganda and editor-in-chief of the *People's Daily*.[52] Two years later, in the spring of 1966, this team was noisily dissolved and a more radical Cultural Revolution Team was formed. We shall return to this later.

In December 1963 (this was not made public till three years later) Mao declared that many departments of culture, theatre, song, music, art, literature and cinema were being 'guided by the dead', and that Party members were promoting feudalist and capitalist art. In June 1964 he said that for fifteen years the majority of literature and art associations and their publications had not been carrying out Party policy and had not reached workers, peasants and soldiers. In recent years they had come to the verge of revisionism, and if they were not corrected they would become like the Petöfy Club (in Hungary before the revolt in 1956).[53]

In August 1963, Qi Benyu — then an unknown writer, but in 1966–7 one of the leaders of the Cultural Revolution — wrote an article on an historical figure, Li Xiu Cheng, a hero of the Taiping Rebellion in the middle of the nineteenth century, who had confessed when caught by the enemy. Qi wrote that Li Xiu Cheng was a traitor. A month later his article was reprinted in the *People's Daily* and it was imitated in many other press articles. This sounded like a smear campaign — against a figure in the nineteenth century. Four years later, during the Cultural Revolution, it was explained that the story about the man who had confessed in prison during the Taiping Rebellion was meant to refer to the Party leaders who, in 1935, had confessed in prison after being arrested by the Nationalist government. They had done so on the orders of Liu Shaoqi, who wanted to get them out of prison. During the Cultural Revolution a *People's Daily* article on August 21, 1967, said that at the Seventh Party Congress in Yan'an in 1945, Liu Shaoqi had succeeded, without Mao's knowledge, in bringing these persons into the Central Committee. Red Guard tabloids poured out names, including those of people high in the Party.

To complicate matters, accusations were brought against Yang Hansheng, a well-known playwright, who in 1937 had written a play about that nineteenth-century Taiping hero. When he wrote it, the Japanese invasion was in full swing and his purpose was to portray a hero facing an overwhelming enemy. The play remained on the stage under the Communist regime and was performed on National Day, October 1, 1963, in defiance of Qi Benyu's article which had appeared two months earlier. In 1967 this was treated as a plot inspired by Zhou Yang, deputy head of propaganda, and two Party historians, Jian Bozan and Liu Danian.[54]

In 1963–4, when the purge of the cultural world was beginning, the battle between Mao's top radicals and the old guard was still a doubtful one. Highly venerated old historians were attacked in numerous articles for not writing in Marxist terms about Chinese history. They write about culture and not about the 'masses', the critics complained; they do not say that the determining factors in history are the economy and production methods. In 1963 Yao Wenyuan, a young man who was to play a prominent role in the Cultural Revolution, attacked Zhou Gucheng, a professor of history then in his sixties, who had known Mao when in his teens and was a Marxist though not a Party man. *Red Flag*, the organ of the Central Committee, said in 1964 that Zhou Gucheng 'supports Marxism in words, but in reality he has abandoned Marxism . . . Pro-

fessor Zhou opposes the theories of Comrade Mao Zedong.' Nevertheless Professor Zhou was elected to the National People's Congress at the
end of 1964.[55]

In 1964 a long and bitter campaign of criticism was waged against the
Central Music College in Peking, which had refused to give up teaching
Western classical music. Four hundred teachers and students were sent
to work in the villages. The conductor of the Central Music Ensemble
was criticised for having praised Beethoven's Ninth Symphony. The
magazine *Literature* published self-criticisms for things it had published
earlier, and made a bitter attack on prominent Party literary men and on
films it had itself praised a few years earlier. The monthly magazine
Theatre carried in October 1964 a confession by the editorial board of
'having been suffering from bourgeois ideology'.[56]

Western culture was treated very oddly. Since 1963 a campaign had
been going on against the music of Debussy — decadent music, it was
said, not unlike an Impressionist painting showing a naked woman
under the shade of a tree by the side of a formally-dressed gentleman. Yet
some articles still defended Debussy. Tchaikovsky was deplorable. Local
Chinese folk music was excellent. Romain Rolland's *Jean-Christophe*,
praised in the Soviet Union, was rejected. He was as bad as Bernard
Shaw.[57]

The most radical reform was carried out in the theatre by 'a leading
comrade of the Party'. This leading comrade was in fact Jiang Qing,
Mao's wife, but in those days her name was not yet mentioned. It was
she who in 1963–4 reformed the ancient art of Peking Opera, bringing
to the stage a new military style and Communist heroes. In June–July
1964 the new plays, produced under her direction, were performed at a
festival in Peking. Mao, Zhou Enlai, Peng Zhen and Kang Sheng
applauded. The famous old Peking Opera actors were stunned. Some
newspapers dared to criticise these plays (two years later it was revealed
that the critical articles had been inspired by Zhou Yang, one of the
members of the first Cultural Revolution team). Jiang Qing's Peking
Opera reform was, however, supported enthusiastically by Ke Qingshi,
First Party secretary of the Central Committee's East China Bureau. In
1965 Zhou Yang changed tack and wrote in high praise of the reform of
the Peking Opera, but it was too late. A year later he was condemned.
Red Flag published an article by Yao Wenyuan, with the ominous title
'The counter-revolutionary double-faced Zhou Yang'. The editorial in
the April 1965 issue of *Theatre* said that Lin Biao had been promoting
revolution in literature and art among the troops since 1960.[58]

In 1964 and 1965 the Party radicals were engaged in an obscure, obstinate struggle. Lin Biao had gained the support of that powerful lady, a second-rate film actress from the old days in Shanghai who had succeeded in winning Mao's heart in Yan'an. Mao, probably to the disgust of his colleagues, had dismissed his former wife He Zizhen, a revolutionary leader of women in her own right. Twenty years after her marriage to Mao, Jiang Qing used the ambitions of Lin Biao to take revenge for the raised eyebrows of twenty years earlier in Yan'an.

In the years 1963–5 a great battle was brewing among the Party leaders.

In the Party

For four years no meeting of the Central Committee was convened. No Central Committee Plenum could be convoked, for the Party leadership was in pieces. The most recent Plenum, the Tenth, had been held, as we saw above, in September 1962. The Eleventh was not held till August 1966, when the Cultural Revolution was already in full swing.

The United Front Department, which dealt with everything outside the Party organisation such as the small political parties, the national minorities, religions and the overseas Chinese, was purged. Li Weihan, one of Mao's earliest companions, disappeared mysteriously from the political scene sometime around 1963, and the whole department was hit hard. The Party changed its policy towards the national minorities. In the middle of 1964 Liu Chun, a deputy of the United Front Department, said in *Red Flag* that the problem of the national minorities had not yet been solved; feudal classes and slave-masters could still be found among them. The right policy towards the nationalities was class struggle, as Mao Zedong had pointed out. A radical reform, including reform of religions, would have to be carried through. The purpose of the reform would be the merging of nationalities and disappearance of their peculiarities. Liu Chun announced these harsh measures as a programme for a remote future. At that time, in 1964, the nationalities were still being treated gently. Land and livestock had been handed back to their former owners and were still in their hands. When the Cultural Revolution brought harsher men to the fore in 1966, Liu Chun and his colleagues disappeared.[59]

The purge of the United Front Department and the disappearance of its head, Li Weihan, were not made known to the public till fifteen years later when, after Mao's death, the political wind changed again and Li

Weihan and the Department were rehabilitated. In March 1979 Ulanhu, then the head of the United Front Department, declared that 'with the permission of the Party Central, the cap of shame put on the United Front Department and the government departments dealing with nationalities and religious affairs, branding them ''followers of defeatism and religionism'', had been removed.' Ulanhu also revealed that Li Weihan had been under a heavy cloud of suspicion in 1962, and had been condemned in 1964. In the 1980s Li Weihan became adviser of the United Front Department.[60] In 1981 his speeches and writings appeared in book form.[61]

Socialist education

For years, as was said above, the Central Committee held no meetings. However, the Party Central, whatever this nebulous term may cover, was active — in a rather confused manner. In March 1963 the Party Central ordered an anti-corruption campaign — a repetition of a similar campaign of the 1950s. In May class struggle was prescribed, particularly in the villages. This was at first called a Socialist Education Campaign; later it received a new name, the Four-Cleansing Campaign. The Tenth Central Committee Plenum of September 1962, the last before the Cultural Revolution, had resurrected the theme of 'Transition to Communism', and Mao ordered class struggle in the villages, relying on what were then called the poor and lower-middle peasants, the 'vanguard of the revolution'. The enemy, the upper-middle and rich peasants, were those who had made use of the 'little freedoms' at the time when the communes collapsed. The abler peasants had cultivated their plots of land and engaged in commerce, disregarding the collectives. Socialist Education was needed in the villages and the poor and lower-middle peasants would have to be organised. The upper-middle peasants should not be allowed to become rich, for that could lead to the ending of collective economy. Party cadres, who lived better than the rest, were not to be classed with upper-middle peasants. The class enemy, counter-revolutionaries and 'bad elements', were to be 'isolated and attacked'. The children of former landlords and rich peasants belonged to the enemy class; they were still 'landlord elements'. The newspapers, films and theatrical productions of that time breathed hatred and preached class struggle. A *People's Daily* article of December 15, 1963, said: 'We hope that the amateur troupes and clubs in the villages, factories and mines will produce musical entertainments and plays of all kinds, reflecting class struggle.'

The nation was stirred up again in a political campaign, but, in contrast with previous campaigns, it was hard to find out what was going on. There was no agreement among the highest Party leaders, and the strings were being pulled in different directions.[62] In his report to the People's Congress held from December 1964 till June 1965, Zhou Enlai said:

In September 1962, at the Tenth Plenary session of the Party's Eighth Central Committee, Chairman Mao called on the whole Party and the entire people never to forget classes and class struggle . . . The landlord class, bourgeoisie and other exploiting classes which had been overthrown remain strong and powerful . . . These new bourgeois elements invariably try to find protectors and agents in the higher leading organisations.' Quite a few people advocate the expansion of plots for private use and free markets. They encourage small enterprises responsible for profits and losses. This is a restoration of individual economy . . . The socialist education campaign now going on in the countryside and in the cities has a great revolutionary and historical significance . . . The socialist education campaign is a revolutionary movement embracing hundreds and millions of people.[63]

Two years later, during the Cultural Revolution, Liu Shaoqi was condemned and made three confessions, the texts of which were smuggled out and published in Japanese newspapers and in Taiwan. In the first confession, on October 23, 1966, he said that in February 1962 he had presided over the work session of the Party Central which discussed how to deal with the deficit that had been plaguing the state finances since 1960. The meeting accepted the proposals of Comrade Chen Yun, who was then working in the Cabinet, and, Liu Shaoqi said, 'encouraged the working of land by individual rural households. Since I wished to make Chen Yun head of the Central Committee's Finance Team, I introduced him to the Party Central and to the Chairman. I learnt later that the Chairman did not agree with my appreciation of the situation.' At the February 1962 Work Session, Deng Xiaoping and Deng Zihui, head of the Central Committee's Village Work Department, proposed the system of 'responsibility fields'.[64] This was another term for private farming, farming households being responsible for the working of the fields. (Twenty years later, after Mao had gone, Deng Xiaoping reintroduced the system and even the name 'responsibility fields'.)

Mao was displeased and in May 1963 a Regulation on Village Work and Socialist Education was published in ten articles. In September the same year, a thoroughly revised version of this Regulation was published, which repeated that within the coming three years the economy was to be 'readjusted, consolidated, completed and advanced'.[65] The programme put forward in the revised version was the same as that which had been decided upon by the 'Party Central', when the Party leaders were trying to rebuild the shattered economy. The September 1963 revision was, to all appearances, a reaction of a group of high Party leaders against the ten points Mao had published in May. Mao's points had asked for radical class struggle and the socialist education campaign. In his confession Liu Shaoqi said that the September revised 10-point Regulation was drawn up by 'some comrades'; he denied having known anything about it. In the following summer, he said, 'I saw that the revised 10-point Regulation was not appropriate for mobilising the masses and needed revision.' In September 1964 another revision was prepared. Comrade Wang Guangmei (Liu's wife) was at that time making a careful study of conditions in the villages, and on her return to Peking she made a speech, the text of which was circulated throughout the country. Liu confessed that this had been a mistake.[66]

In May 1964 the 'Party Central' held a discussion in Peking about work in the villages, and in December the Politbureau issued a new Regulation which contained 23 articles.[67] This was a Maoist document throughout; it was wholly opposed to capitalist development in cities and villages, and it added the ominous statement that there were 'people on the capitalist road' inside the Party. The socialist education campaign was intensified and a new organisation, the Congress of Poor and Lower-Middle Peasants, was set to work. This developed into the biggest campaign in the villages since the time of the land reform.[68]

The role of Liu's wife Wang Gungmei added to the confusion. Early in 1965 persistent rumours were spread about her. These appeared in various forms, but the gist of them was that she had investigated villages and written a report for Mao on the corruption of village Party leaders and the need to send investigative teams to the villages.[69] During the Cultural Revolution, Liu and Wang Guangmei were exposed to bitter attacks on account of her exploits in the villages.[70] The fact that two women were engaged in politics simultaneously, Jiang Qing, wife of Mao, and Wang Guangmei, wife of Liu, added a new tinge to the rivalry within the Party leadership.

In 1969, at the Ninth Party Congress which declared him heir-designate of Mao, Lin Biao spoke of the socialist education campaign of 1963–4. He said that the first 10-point Regulation of May 1963 and the

23-point Regulation of December 1964 contained Mao's orders, but that they had been distorted in the course of being implemented. He quoted Mao as having said in February 1967 that the socialist education campaign had been unsuccessful.[71]

CHAPTER XVII

THE CULTURAL REVOLUTION AND LIN BIAO, 1966–1971

Overview

The inner convulsion in the Party began years before the outbreak of the Cultural Revolution. When that great upheaval came, it was a revolution in culture — but not in culture alone. Bourgeois culture was proclaimed to be the target, but those who suffered were not the bourgeois; they were veteran Party members or people who had collaborated loyally with the Communist regime for decades. Party authorities on Marxism were purged on accusations of revisionism. The Motherland, the Soviet Union, was accused of having abandoned true Marxism and become revisionist. The United Front Department, which had charge of minorities and religion, was purged for having been too indulgent towards national minorities and religious practices. The inner wrangle in the Party became visible. The situation before 1966 should be remembered. Lin Biao, whom Mao had promoted after the dismissal of Marshal Peng Dehuai in 1959, was elbowing for power, but was meeting with strong resistance.

Then came those incredible scenes of the Cultural Revolution. In August 1966, millions of Red Guards went forth chanting slogans — as the Nazis had gone forth under Hitler — with Mao and Lin Biao taking the salute on the balcony of the Imperial Palace and looking down on an ocean of jubilant youngsters. The 'revolutionary young generals', as they were called, were launched to destroy what was bourgeois — historic monuments, Buddhist temples, Christian churches. They burst in upon middle-class families, destroying books and furniture, and tying up and beating people. Behind them were the military, pointing out which families were to be destroyed and which were to be spared. At the end of the year they were launched in hordes, with orders to surround and drag away Party leaders, enemies of Lin Biao. Millions of Red Guards were allowed to travel on trains free of charge. They went into schools about which they knew nothing, and brutalised, and often killed, the teachers — 'dirty bourgeoisie'. The disorder was complete. Province-wide rival mass organisations of Red Guards grew from the confusion, with heavy gang fighting in the streets. In February 1967 the army was sent in to restore order, but the disorder only grew worse.

The mass organisations of Red Guards destroyed both the Party and the government organisations. For four years Communist China had no Communist Party, except that which existed within the military. Proud youngsters with 'Red Guard' bands on their arms and pistols in their belts entered any office they wished. Schools came to a halt. They looted the libraries, taking away many books: later, when millions of former Red Guards were sent to remote villages, the better ones had something to read. Others simply continued their vandalism. The worst and cruellest were those aged fifteen or sixteen, and among these the worst were girls. As one of them said, the first sight of a person being killed is shocking; later you get used to it. These rampaging youngsters felt they were on top of the world.

Party leaders, including some who had been promoted in the early days of the Cultural Revolution and then rejected, organised their own Red Guard hordes. These were harassed violently by the opposing groups run by Lin Biao's army.

The Red Guard groups went through many transformations. At first the dominant groups were those formed by children of Party leaders. When their fathers were rejected and victimised, they turned into terrorist groups. Against them were large groups of children from the despised middle-class families which had no 'proletarian origin'. Often, however, the division cut through a family, brothers and sisters finding themselves in fiercely opposed camps. The official voice in Peking said that the revolutionary youths should rise up against their 'bourgeois' parents.

In 1967 an unavailing attempt was made to bring the fighting groups together. To restore some order out of the complete chaos that reigned, a 'triple alliance' of soldiers, 'revolutionary small generals' and selected former Party cadres, was formed: it was to become the Revolutionary Committee, taking the place of the old Party and government organisations. The military became predominant but they could not bring peace. They were divided, and in some provinces military forces were fighting military forces. All, however, were united in adoring Mao; 'rebel' organisations fighting one another to the death all swore by him. Posters and pamphlets were headed with 'the Highest Instruction', one of Mao's phrases. All bore badges with a picture of Mao and all carried copies of the *Little Red Book* in their hands. Every mass organisation professed itself composed of true followers of Mao, the 'Sun in our hearts', and all held that they were fighting heretical enemy groups.

The army introduced daily worship, to be observed in factories and offices, and even in private homes. Sayings of Mao were recited in the morning before his picture along with a plea for inspiration for the day. In the evening there was a parallel report of the day's events — morning and evening prayers in front of the Divinity. Children were told that Chairman Mao was looking at them all the time wherever they were. To have met the great leader in person was a high privilege. A hand shaken by Mao was venerated by others. A newspaper with his picture might not be used for any utilitarian purpose. The slightest word expressing less than the greatest respect for Mao aroused indignation and condemned the speaker to forced labour.

Labour camps were no longer run solely by the police, who had been taken over by the military. Prisons and labour camps were set up by the rebel groups for captured members of the opposing groups. China became a chaotic world, a world of violence.

The economy, despite all the turmoil, did not come to a complete stop. Nor did China fall apart. Inter-group fighting was widespread, but all were fighting in the name of the Great Helmsman. There were periods when things calmed down and the military seemed to be imposing their rule upon the country, but then new disorders would erupt and other groups would infiltrate the revolutionary committees and take power. 'Take power' was the universal cry. The rival groups were fighting for positions of power. In time, military men took a firm hold on the positions of power everywhere, and the youth were sent 'down to the villages, up to the mountains', to disappear into the ocean of primitive villages — city youngsters separated from their homes and deprived of the comforts of city life.

Gradually talk began to be heard of reorganising the Communist Party under the permanent leadership of the military. In April 1969 a Party Congress named Lin Biao successor-designate to Mao. A year later conflict between the two men erupted, and in September 1971 Lin Biao died under mysterious circumstances.

These are the facts in rough outline. The rationale of the Cultural Revolution is open to speculation, but that Mao was the initiator of the upheaval is beyond doubt. He gave the first orders; he stood at the Tian An Men for the huge Red Guard parades; and it was under his orders that the army was sent into the battle.

He had been profoundly disillusioned with his own men ever since the Eighth Party Congress, which had squeezed him out of many of his leading posts in the Party in 1956. He reconvoked that Congress two years later, in 1958, and imposed his own will. In the same year he promoted Lin Biao, who a year later took over the army and began to mould it to his own image, and to the worship of Mao. Mao was using Lin Biao to take revenge on his enemies, and Lin Biao was using Mao to win power. In the first half of the 1960s, before the Cultural Revolution, Lin Biao's manoeuvre failed, so he resorted to violence.

Mao may have persuaded himself that he was acting not out of selfish motives — to maintain his power — but because he had to do something, something radical, to create a new, powerful, revolutionary China. This had been his dream ever since his young days: it was not a Marxist dream, otherwise he would not have destroyed the Party itself. Mao grew up amid the revolutionary effervescence of the early years of the century. The Manchu dynasty had been overthrown; the early Nationalists were ready to destroy the old Chinese culture and create a new China; Western powers still held sway over parts of the major cities in what were called foreign concessions. The vindication of China's rights through the creation of an independent proud revolutionary China was in the air. The revolution in Russia showed the way.

Mao succeeded in climbing to the leadership of the Party and then within fourteen years, counting from his early Yan'an days, he led the revolution to victory. After that triumph he began to feel that his partners in the revolution had lost their old spirit. He needed a new generation trained in bloody battles, as his 'young devils' had been trained in the early years. He regarded Lin Biao, who had joined him at the age of seventeen and led the military conquest of China in 1948–9, as a man of unswerving loyalty, whereas Liu Shaoqi, the number two man in the Party who in 1959 became Head of State, had married a woman from a rich capitalist family and was in Mao's eyes a degenerate bourgeois.

At the outbreak of the Cultural Revolution, both Mao and Liu were over seventy. Mao's wife was for him a revolutionary inspiration. Although her early career in the Shanghai film world had been conventional, it was she who carried through the purge of the theatre and cinema from their decadent bourgeois trends. She was much younger than Mao and had considerable influence over him. Lin Biao was shrewd enough to win her over to his side. What Mao did not realise, much as he liked reading ancient Chinese political history, was that many dynasties had declined after glorious beginnings, when generals and women, or the wives or mothers of emperors, took over the reins.

Chinese history repeats itself. The cultural devastation of the late 1960s was not the first 'cultural revolution' in Chinese history. The proverbial long endurance of the Chinese has been interrupted from time to time by the staccato of violent eruptions. One result of this is that in China few historical monuments remain above ground. Ancient buildings such as pagodas are sometimes found, but only in remote villages. The historical Peking was built a mere 500 years ago. The fabulous capitals of ancient dynasties were pillaged and destroyed time and again. In Chinese cities one finds no buildings comparable to the early churches of Europe. Even the last 150 years have seen four waves of devastating iconoclasm: the Taiping Rebellion in the middle of the nineteenth century, the Boxer Rebellion at the turn of the century, the Northern Expedition of the Nationalist troops in 1927 which destroyed Buddhist temples in the North Chinese plains, and the Cultural Revolution of 1966. Ancient Chinese history is known only from stone steles and from scrupulously conserved books. The last Cultural Revolution did not spare even the books.

To say that a nation after long periods of endurance may explode into vandalism is not to give a full answer to those who ask why such things happen. There is no full answer to the questions posed by violence. Why do terrorists kill innocent people? Why do nations go to war? Why are the tools for the great holocaust being prepared today? What is it in the human mind that opts for evil, paving the way for destruction?

The startling thing about this last Cultural Revolution in China was, as we saw above, that the powerful gangs fighting each other all swore by Mao. Some of them were sincere, others may have used his name as a shield. But Mao's authority was undisputed till his death, and for two years after it. Then at last the new regime declared that the Cultural Revolution had been a devastating error of the Master. Yet even then the decision on Party history of June 27, 1981, described it as the fatal error of a great revolutionary. Apparently Mao's is the only name that can hold Marxists together in China.

In this book we are writing about the Communist Party and Marxism. Perhaps, in logic, we should have omitted the years of the Cultural Revolution, when there was no Communist Party, and when the selected and often distorted, Thoughts of Mao replaced Marxism. Yet it is necessary to see what happened to this country which called itself Marxist, and what happened to the Party leaders: to those arrested, to those set aside, to those still at the top, to those who became leaders at the beginning of the Cultural Revolution but soon went into opposition, and to younger men brought to the highest leadership and toppled a year later. It is necessary to examine what happened then to Marxism in China.

Preliminaries

— The play

In November 1965 the first salvo of the Cultural Revolution was fired, although it was not yet recognised as such at the time. It took the form of criticism in a Shanghai newspaper of a historical play, *The Dismissal of Hai Rui*, written by Wu Han, a historian who was also Party secretary and vice-mayor of Peking. The play's hero, Hai Rui, was an honest minister dismissed by his Emperor. Was this an allusion to Mao's dismissal of Marshal Peng Dehuai in 1959? This was not stated at that time. The criticism was written by Yao Wenyuan, the scribe of Jiang Qing, Mao's wife. In 1963 this same Yao had daringly challenged another well-respected historian Zhou Gucheng.[1]

— Men of culture

In the first few months of 1966 the anti-intellectual craze reached enormous proportions. The evening paper of Canton reported that the scientific laboratories were empty. The scientists had been sent to the countryside to take part in the socialist education campaign and in class struggle. The head of the Guangdong Provincial Science Committee told a Chinese reporter 'with a smile' that no such massive shifting of research staff to villages and factories had ever been carried out before. On January 16 the *People's Daily* editorial had the heading: 'Philosophers, pack your bundles and go into the midst of workers, peasants and soldiers' masses.' In March it was reported that a number of economists had already spent a year in the villages doing manual labour and learning the Thoughts of Mao.[2]

An intense campaign was mounted against the sixty-nine-year-old Jian Bozan, one of the pro-Marxist historians of the early days. The whole Marxist intellectual world was in confusion. A well-known Marxist literary figure, He Qifang, wrote against a well-known Marxist playwright, Xia Yan. Another playwright, Tian Han, composer of the words for the People's Republic National Anthem, was branded a bourgeois.[3] (Those who had to criticise their colleagues later fell victims to the Cultural Revolution.)

On June 1, 1966, the heading of the *People's Daily* editorial was 'Clean Sweep of All Wicked Ghosts and Evil Devils', and the editorial itself said: 'The fundamental question is political power. In all fields of superstructure — ideology, religion, art, law and political power — the centre is political power . . . The person who has political power has everything.' It called for the extirpation of 'old culture, old customs, old habits', and for the mobilisation of the masses.

— Economists

In the second half of 1965 many economists were still at their posts. In September-October 1965, the Party leaders dealing with economic planning held a three-week-long meeting. At that conference Mao asked the ominous question: 'What is to be done if the Party leadership turns revisionist?'[4]

The economists seem not to have understood the threat contained in Mao's words. They were still advocating liberal policies. The November 1965 issue of the monthly *Economic Research* reported that in August the ministry of finance had held a conference to discuss the need for a measure of mobility in the enterprises, limitation of central planning, a price policy and attention to the market;[5] but the general trend was already towards stricter all-embracing unified economic planning. At the beginning of 1966 the tone changed and the review, like all other journals, switched to radical lines. In the summer of 1966 all reviews and magazines, except *Red Flag*, stopped publication — not to reappear till ten years later.

— Leaders replaced

In November 1965, Yang Shangkun, a Party member since the 1920s, a member of the Central Committee since 1956 and head of the important Office of the Central Committee, was replaced by Wang Dongxing, the head of Mao's personal guard and of Mao's personal intelligence network. This man was to become a sinister figure in the Cultural Revolution.[6]

On December 8–15, 1965, Lin Biao, his wife Ye Qun and two of Lin Biao's generals, Wu Faxian, head of the air force, and Li Zuopeng, deputy commander of the navy, attended a Politbureau meeting held in Shanghai. (When they became Politbureau members was not revealed.) The meeting condemned and dismissed Luo Ruiqing, who had been leading the bloody campaigns ordered by Mao since the establishment of the People's Republic and who had become chief of the general staff in the army in 1959, at the time when Lin Biao became minister of defence.[7]

In February 1966 Lin Biao, in a shrewd move, entrusted literary and art work in the armed forces to Jiang Qing.[8] He had eliminated his rival in the army, the formidable Luo Ruiqing, and had won the favour of Mao's wife.

— the team

In July 1964 (see above), Mao set up a Cultural Revolution team, headed by Peng Zhen, to purge culture. On February 3, 1966, the team held a discussion in which its five members and others took part. One member of the team was Wang Li (a young man who was to become a radical leader of the Cultural Revolution and to disappear a year later). Another was Hu Sheng, the deputy chief editor of the Party magazine *Red Flag* (he was purged in the Cultural Revolution, but reappeared many years later as a leading Party ideologue).

The team's report, presented on February 12, was communicated to the whole Party. It was a savage report, speaking of 'annihilation of the bourgeois' and of the struggle between the socialist and the bourgeois lines. Nevertheless it asked for moderation in criticism and declared that 'in face of truth all are equal'.[9] All this remained unpublished until a year later, in 1967, when it was announced that on May 16, 1966, Mao had abolished that Cultural Revolution team and set up a new one. The head of the new team was Chen Boda, Mao's secretary since the Yan'an days. The deputy heads were Jiang Qing and Zhang Chunqiao. The members were Wang Li, Guan Feng, Qi Benyu and Yao Wenyuan — four writers who followed Jiang Qing. There was also an adviser named Kang Sheng, who had been trained in intelligence work in Moscow.[10] Two days later Peng Zhen was replaced as First Party secretary of Peking city by Li Xuefeng, who had served under Lin Biao in the Central-South military-political government in the 1950s, and at the time of his appointment in 1966 was First Party secretary of the North China Bureau of the Central Committee. Wu De, First Party secretary of Jilin province, became his deputy.

A year after the event, a Peking press article, commenting on Mao's order of May 16, 1966, said that Mao was superior to Stalin. Stalin, like Mao, eliminated his enemies — Radek, Bukharin and others. But Stalin had done so with no theoretical foundation. Mao had a theory.[11] In May 1966 it was not yet clear what that 'theory' was and what the new Cultural Revolution team was meant to do, whether indeed the change was anything more than a mere shuffle of persons at the highest level of the Party. Discrediting Peng Zhen, a member of the Politbureau, and Luo Ruiqing, chief of the general staff and concurrently vice-minister of defence, was a major step; but it did not mean a general nationwide upheaval.

— Let them loose

On May 25, 1966, seven philosophy students of Peking University, led by a woman called Nie Yuanzi, put up a large poster in the school attacking the president of the University, Lu Ping. The president reacted energetically, apparently unaware that the leadership of the city had already been changed. Mao kept away from Peking.[12]

This poster was a signal for schools around the country. At some universities, the organisation of revolutionary students had begun as early as April. On June 2, a week after the appearance of the poster at Peking University, posters appeared in Nanjing University demanding the dismissal of its president. Four days later students in a middle school in Peking wrote to Mao asking him to change the educational system and telling him that they had no fear of anything. A week later, admission to higher schools of education was suspended for six months and proletarian education was promised. On July 3, the *People's Daily* carried the ominous words: 'Let loose the masses.'

Students of the middle school of Qinghua University, Peking, issued a leaflet written by the sons and daughters of Party cadres and containing a vitriolic attack on students from bourgeois families. On June 23 the newspaper of the Youth Corps said: 'Leftist students are being steeled in struggle. They dare to think, to speak, to attack, to act, to carry on the revolution.' Nevertheless the Youth Corps itself was to disappear. Its Peking branch held a meeting as late as early July, but Hu Yaobang, head of the All-China Youth Corps, was no longer there (he had been removed early in 1965 to become acting Party head of a poor province in the Northwest). Before long the Youth Corps Central Committee was accused of being revisionist.[13]

On July 16 (as it was reported eight days later) Mao went for a swim in the Yangze, in Hubei province, accompanied by Wang Renzhong, First Party secretary of the province. While swimming, it was said, Wang reported on the condition of his province. Mao may have had a dip, but the elaborate story was a fairy tale. The account of Mao's swim in the Yangze was treated as an epic for many years. On July 18, Mao returned to Peking. He took the side of the revolutionary Red Guards in the universities and opposed Liu Shaoqi, who was trying to suppress the revolt in the schools.

Central Committee Plenum

On August 1–12 the Party Central Committee held its Eleventh Plenum. When it was in the middle of its business, Mao himself put up a ten-line poster under the heading 'Bombard the headquarters'. The poster, having first praised Nie Yuanzi's Peking University poster, the first poster of the Cultural Revolution, said that for fifty days the Party leaders, reactionary bourgeois, had been resisting the Cultural Revolution and setting up a 'white terror'. This was published in *Red Flag* in 1967, a year after the event.[14]

On August 8, 1966, the Decision on the Great Proletarian Cultural Revolution, the charter of the Cultural Revolution, was published. The bourgeoisie, it said, had infiltrated the Party, so let the masses act! Many schools and other organisations already had Cultural Revolution teams — similar teams should be set up in factories, mines, enterprises, street organisations and villages, and should be as revolutionary as the Paris Commune of 1871. (Ever since it was written up by Marx, the Paris Commune has haunted the Marxist imagination.) The revolutionary students should not fight each other, and they should not attack anyone without permission from the Party committees. Scientists and technicians should be protected and the economy should be promoted. On the following day *Red Flag* explained the Decision, but it added that anonymous heroes should not be hindered and that the Party committees should let them act.[15]

The reality was more terrifying than the regulation. Foreign correspondents reported from Peking that private homes were being ransacked and that professors were being dragged around the streets bearing round their necks placards with the inscription 'Anti-Party Intellectual'.

Red Guards

No list of those who took part in that fatal Central Committee Plenum has ever been published. The Plenum closed on August 12, and six days later the first mass meeting of Red Guards was held in the centre of Peking, at the Tian An Men ('Gate of Heavenly Peace'). Mao in military uniform and Lin Biao presided. The Red Guards, a million of them, were greeted by Chen Boda. Lin Biao then spoke. He referred to Mao, who did not speak, as the 'Generalissimo'. The Cultural Revolution, he said, would bring in 'new culture, new customs, new habits, a new era in Marxism-Leninism'. All that was needed was the courage to let loose the masses. They would conquer and crush the reactionary powers. Zhou Enlai was present. So were Tao Zhu (formerly Party leader of the Central-South Bureau of the Central Committee, who had taken the place of Lu Dingyi as head of propaganda), Deng Xiaoping, Kang Sheng, Liu Shaoqi, Zhu De and so on. Liu Shaoqi was there, but he was no longer the man standing next to Mao. Jiang Qing was there too.[16]

Another mass demonstration was held in Peking on August 31. Again Mao was silent. Lin Biao encouraged the Red Guards to 'daring struggle' but forbade violence and beating up — things they were doing without the slightest hindrance. Zhou Enlai in his address to the crowd said that they should imitate the army and that a great exchange of students should be made, students from Peking going to the provinces and students from the provinces coming to Peking.

There was one curious incident. A group of Red Guards calling themselves 'Red Guard Investigators from the Western District of Peking' offered labels signifying their status as 'investigators' to some leaders — to Lin Biao, to Marshal He Long whom they asked to be their Chief-of-Staff, to Zhou Enlai who said 'I will be your adviser', and to Jiang Qing who thanked them.[17] The 'investigators' were ardent sons of Party leaders who, a few months later when their fathers were purged, conducted a campaign of terror in opposition to the leaders of the Cultural Revolution. A year later a Red Guard pamphlet accused Yu Qiuli, minister of petroleum, of a variety of crimes. He was bribing the Red Guard students, it said, and was behind this Peking Western District Investigators Team.[18]

The Red Guards, according to an August 1966 *People's Daily* editorial, were being sent out to purge the Party committees all over China and bring down those who resisted. They were not yet able to do that, but they smashed old-style signboards, broke curios, cut the hair of Hong Kong visitors and took off their leather shoes, and made professors march in the streets with posters around their necks recording their bourgeois sins. Street-names were changed. In Peking one street was renamed East Is Red Road; a street in the former Legation Quarters became Anti-Imperialist Road; the street housing the Soviet Embassy became the Anti-Revisionist Road. The old East Peace Market became the East Wind Market, and the old Rockefeller Institute became the Anti-Imperialist Hospital.[19] Foreign visitors witnessed bloody fights and other scenes of horror. People rushed to the banks to withdraw their deposits. In Canton the price of rice on the black market shot up. In Shanghai many houses were ransacked.

On October 9, General Xiao Hua, for years the spokesman for Lin Biao, said that in this new stage of Cultural Revolution, the Thoughts of Mao must be put into practice. On November 28, Jiang Qing did put them into practice. After Zhou Enlai had expressed his compliments to her, she herself spoke to Red Guards about theatrical and music schools. The Red Guards in the Drama College, the Film College and the Music College began to spread leaflets attacking Liu Shaoqi and Deng Xiaoping.[20] Many years later a booklet on the history of China said that Liu and Deng had been criticised by Lin Biao by name at the August 1966 meeting (not reported publicly at the time).[21] At the end of 1966 many posters were to be found in the streets of Peking criticising Liu Shaoqui, Deng and Wang Guangmei, Liu's wife.

Red Guards in the provinces were attacking provincial Party leaders but not yet the provincial First Party secretaries.[22] On December 19, at a 100,000-strong meeting of Red Guards, Xiao Hua, Jiang Qing, Chen Boda and Zhou Enlai spoke. Zhou led the singing, as he had done at the first mass rally of the Red Guards on August 18. Tao Zhu, the new head of Party propaganda, was present.

A few days later wall-posters gave the text of Liu Shaoqi's first self-criticism, made at a Party meeting in October. At the end of 1966, *Red Flag*, no. 15, said that although six months had elapsed since the start of the proletarian Cultural Revolution, profound resistance could still be felt, and evil people were organising and deceiving the masses. 'Certain persons are making use of the slogan of "oppose the bourgeois reactionary line" to deceive and confuse people. They are in fact bombarding the proletarian headquarters.'[23]

Confusion

Towards the end of 1966 the inner convulsion in the Party took a very serious turn. On January 7, Japanese correspondents in Peking read wall-posters reporting bloody clashes in Nanjing and attributing them to the supporters of Tao Zhu, who had been taken into the highest leadership at the beginning of the Cultural Revolution. There were reports also that Tao Zhu himself, Zhang Pinghua, the former First Party secretary of Hunan province who had been summoned to Peking in the summer of 1966 to assist Tao Zhu, and Wang Renzhong, the First Party secretary of Hubei province who in July had swum in the Yangze with Mao, had been condemned. (Tao Zhu died in November 1969.) The men who had come to power with Lin Biao were being pushed aside. Apparently the highest Party leadership itself was in turmoil.

There was obstinate resistance to the irruption of rowdy Red Guards into the factories. On January 11 the *People's Daily* reported revolts in factories in several major cities. In Shanghai the Party Committee was overthrown; Red Guard groups surged; chaos reigned. In the villages, the *Fujian Daily* said on January 23; 'Big and small men in power, landlords, kulaks, counter-revolutionaries, bad and rightist elements made trouble, distributing money, grain and other resources . . . They incited the peasants to quit their working posts and rush into the cities . . . their aim was to wreck the great Cultural Revolution.' Much the same things were said about the villages around Shanghai in a Shanghai newspaper published on January 15. In Jiangxi province, the local radio said, workers went on strike and took to beating students who had been sent to the factories. Many stopped work. Revolutionary groups — the 'Nanchang Workers Scarlet Group's General Command', the 'East Is Red Fighting Troops', and a group of demobilised soldiers known as the 'August 1 Fighting Troop' — began organising peasants against the Red Guards.[24]

There was grave trouble among the armed troops. On January 11, 1967, the army's Cultural Revolution team was reorganised, with Marshal Xu Xiangqian as its new head. Xiao Hua was the first among his deputies, and Jiang Qing was the adviser. (A similar army team was established at the beginning of the Cultural Revolution, but at that time no names were published.) The day after the formation of the new team, the *Liberation Army Daily* said that capitalists within the armed forces were creating confusion and that 'a new stage of the great proletarian Cultural Revolution of the army was about to start'.

Peking was full of Red Guard posters, pamphlets and photographs. One photograph showed Luo Ruiqing, who had been thrashed, with his leg in plaster. Another showed the former Party leaders Peng Zhen, Lu Dingyi, Luo Ruiqing, Yang Shangkun and Zhou Yang tied up as criminals with heavy placards hanging from their necks. A Red Guard pamphlet accused Yang Shangkun, then aged sixty-four, of having placed a hidden microphone in Mao's residence. (Yang re-emerged after the fall of Lin Biao, and in the 1980s he became a top leader of the army.) Other posters attacked Marshal He Long, who at the inauguration of the Cultural Revolution had ridden triumphantly in a jeep with Mao through the millions of Red Guards. He was accused of having associated with those condemned (Yang Shangkun was his nephew) and of having attempted a *coup d'état*. Liu Zhijian, deputy head of the army's political department and deputy to Xiao Hua, was accused of having been behind people who had attempted to break into the Zhong Nan Hai, part of the Forbidden City where Mao and his men lived. Some posters said that Liu Shaoqi was still in Zhong Nan Hai. Even Marshal Zhu De was accused of being a 'warlord, infiltrated into the Party'.[25] Xiao Hua was still around, but a few months later he too, although he had been so close to Lin Biao ever since 1959, disappeared from the political scene.[26] (After Mao's death, he was once more in a leading regional military post.)

Many odd things happened. In 1966 the list of those who appeared on National Day, October 1, was published. Among them were Tao Zhu, He Long, Liu Zhijian and others who were to be purged soon after. When the film of the parade was shown to the public in April 1967, after a six-month delay, these men were no longer visible. The only personages to be seen were Mao, Lin Biao, Jiang Qing and Zhou Enlai.[27] (Ten years later, after the arrest of Jiang Qing, the same process was again applied to the pictures of the 1966 National Day. Jiang Qing and her followers were cut out.)

The army to act

In January 1967, soon after the reorganisation of the Cultural Revolution team of the army, Mao ordered the army to enter the sphere of the Cultural Revolution. The army, according to the January 24, 1967, issue of the *People's Daily*, swore 'to be the powerful shield of the proletarian revolution rebels'. On the following day, the *Liberation Army Daily* said: 'We must act according to the instructions of Comrade Lin Biao, ardently support Chairman Mao and the revolutionary rebels and beat down the "small clique of capitalist-road men in power" [the regular formula for those in the Party who resisted].'[28]

This was a great escalation of Lin Biao's bid for power. When he had tried to infiltrate the Party before 1966, he failed. The mobilisation of youngsters was his next step, and a violent step it was. The Party machinery stood firm, although many of its highest leaders were arrested. The Red Guards themselves, an unruly mob, were deeply divided on the lines of the family origins of the youngsters, children of fallen or menaced Party leaders forming their own violent groups. As a last resort Lin Biao's military had to be thrown into the battle.

There is no other example in the Communist world of an army being ordered to destroy the Party. This, however, was the strange country of Mao, in which all the opposing gangs that were killing one another were fighting in his name. The soldiers, so the army's newspaper said in April, found themselves in a difficult situation, not knowing how to distinguish genuine leftist fighting gangs from those defending the 'men on the capitalist road'. 'We are faced with mass organisations of all kinds. Formerly we had no contact with them. We do not understand their positions. What should we do?' The soldiers were told to make thorough investigations and find out who was who, and who stood for what.[29]

The entry of the military did not end the turbulence. Red Guards and rebel organisations sprang up everywhere, in offices, schools and factories. They grew in number, split, changed alliances, fought Peking Red Guard groups, and spread through the country. They themselves were divided and spread division, generating both heated discussion and physical fights.

Shanghai

In Peking there were three large groups, the 'Universities and Colleges Red Guard First Headquarters', the 'Second Headquarters' Revolutionary Rebel Liaison Station', and the 'Capital's Red Guards' Third Headquarters', each one grouping Red Guard groups from schools in Peking. Not much is known of the Second Headquarters. According to a January 1967 poster, the First Headquarters turned against Zhou Enlai. The most important was the Third Headquarters, which grew from the group in Peking University led by that fierce lady Nie Yuanzi. In November 1966 she led her followers to Shanghai to make a frontal attack on Cao Diqiu, the city's mayor. In February the *Guang Ming Daily*, Peking, had an article written by the Third Headquarters against two enemy organisations, *Rong Fu Jun*, a group of demobilised soldiers, and *Lien Dong* (United Action Committee). In February Zhou Enlai succeeded in uniting the Peking Red Guards, but their alliance broke again into hostile factions.

On January 31, *Red Flag* and the *People's Daily* published an article against factions and divisions supplied by the Third Headquarters. The editorial in the third issue of *Red Flag* in 1967 said: 'There are organisations which are deliberately turning the fight against the Central

Cultural Revolution team.' These organisations, it said, were supported by the Party committee of Shanghai. The Shanghai city government had its own revolutionary rebel groups, made up from the staff of the Shanghai municipality. A Shanghai newspaper complained that Shanghai cadres were being arrested and beaten up, and that furniture, windows and telephones were being smashed.

The Peking Red Guard groups made havoc of the Shanghai newspapers. In December, after an eight-day attack, these newspapers were taken over by two Peking Red Guard groups, the First Headquarters' Peking Aviation College Red Flag Organisation, and the Qinghua University Jing Gang Shan Red Guards. In January an exhibition was mounted to show the crimes of the *Liberation Daily*, the official Party paper of Shanghai, and its resistance to the Cultural Revolution. A number of local Shanghai rebel groups were organised and took to fighting in the streets against the organisation of the local party and government cadres. The Shanghai *Wen Hui Bao* on February 14 quoted a cadre as saying: 'At home my wife grumbles and says: "You have always worked for the community and neglected your family. We have had a hard time for more than ten years. Now you have become a counter-revolutionary!" '

Many Shanghai homes were ransacked by Red Guards of every variety, and many people were driven to suicide. Shanghai youngsters who had been sent to the border area of Xinjiang boarded trains and returned to Shanghai. They were ordered back to Xinjiang, but did not go. The original Shanghai authorities, now dubbed the 'Small Clique of men on the Capitalist Road', were accused of having summoned the youngsters back from Xinjiang. Then on February 5, Zhang Chunqiao and Yao Wenyuan, two Shanghai protégés of Jiang Qing, both members of the Central Cultural Revolution team in Peking, announced that the whole of Shanghai had become one commune, in imitation of the Paris Commune of 1871. A Shanghai newspaper explained that the Paris Commune meant two things, revolution and violence. The establishment of the Shanghai Commune was supported by one of the Peking Red Guard groups, that of Qinghua University, founded by Kuai Dafu, but not by the Peking Red Guards' Third Headquarters. In Peking, Mao did not approve of the name Shanghai Commune, so it was changed to Shanghai Revolutionary Committee. Peace did not return to the city. Revolutionary groups broke into offices and burnt documents. The former city authorities were accused of having induced medical doctors to stop work. The doctors were harassed by rebel groups who arrested the heads of medical departments.

In February and March the Shanghai daily *Wen Hui Bao* thundered against counter-revolutionary organisations that pretended to be rebel organisations. One was named the Shanghai General Department of what was known for short as the Red Flag Army — its full name was All-China Workers', Peasants', Meritorious Demobilised Revolutionary Soldiers' Red Flag Army for the Protection of the Thoughts of Mao Zedong. The Red Flag Army, the Shanghai paper said, was founded in Peking in November 1966 and was said to consist of former bandits and hooligans. In Peking the press, and even the wallposters, said nothing about this Red Flag Army.[30]

In the middle of February, Tan Zhenlin (since 1958 a member of the Politbureau), two leaders of the economy, Li Fuchun and Li Xiannian, and four marshals, Chen Yi, Ye Jianying, Xu Xiangqian and Nie Rongzhen, criticised the excesses of the Cultural Revolution. Their criticism achieved nothing, and the critics' effort was branded the 'February counter-current'. Marshal Nie Rongzhen recalled many years later a violent discussion on February 16, 1967, at a meeting presided over by Zhou Enlai. On one side were the four marshals, Chen Yi, Ye Jianying, Xu Xiangqian and himself, sitting with five leaders of the economy, Li Fuchun, Li Xiannian, Tan Zhenlin, Yu Qiuli and Gu Mu. On the other side were the leaders of the Cultural Revolution. There was a heated argument. Many leaders had already been arrested by the Red Guards (Marshal Nie, writing in 1984, did not mention Liu Shaoqi among them). The most violent speaker was Tan Zhenlin, who was promptly expelled from the Party and put into prison. Marshal Nie did not say how Zhou Enlai behaved at this meeting.[31]

On March 16, 1967, the 'Party Central' published a document containing the alleged confessions of sixty-one leading Party men, including Bo Yibo, head of the State Economic Commission; Liu Lantao, Party boss of the Central Committee's Northwest Bureau; and An Ziwen, head of the Central Committee Organisation Department (they were rehabilitated eleven years later, in December 1978).[32] On July 24, 1967, a *People's Daily* editorial acknowledged that the old Party leaders were hard nuts to crack. 'Even when they are beaten down they are not dead, and when they apparently confess their crimes, what they write is a counter-revolutionary manifesto. Some organisations and masses are still deceived by them.'[33]

Wuhan

Then in July 1967 there came the shock at Wuhan, the most important city on the Yangze River in the centre of China. There were two major rebel organisations there, one of which was called the One Million Fighters. The two organisations had been fighting one another for months. On June 17 the One Million occupied the important Yangze bridge. The other group asked the military for help, but the military did nothing. Peking despatched Xie Fuzhi, whom the *People's Daily* identified as deputy head of the Cultural Revolution team in the army, and Wang Li, first deputy chief editor of *Red Flag*. They arrived in Wuhan on July 16, but met with resistance from General Chen Zaidao, the military commander of the Wuhan Great Military Area, which ruled two provinces. According to some reports, Lin Biao ordered five warships to sail for Wuhan and some parachute units to enter the city. Xie and Wang, humiliated, left for Peking on July 25. A huge crowd, led by Lin Biao, welcomed them at the Tian An Men, Peking, on their return. On July 30 the *People's Daily* said that the groups in Wuhan were still fighting. On July 29 a newspaper in Shanghai said that Tao Zhu, who had already been ousted, was behind the trouble.[34] (Chen Zaidao returned to power after the fall of Lin Biao.)

Canton

The Wuhan incident had wide repercussions, particularly in Guangdong province, where General Wen Yucheng — a year later to become deputy Chief-of-Staff in Peking — blamed Tao Zhu, who had been the Party boss of the Central Committee's Central South Bureau, and whose many thousands of local Party leaders were still around. In Guangdong railway workers went on strike, train communication with Hong Kong was interrupted, newspapers stopped publication, and the inhabitants of Canton lived in fear. Even the September 1967 international trade fair, a half-yearly event, was postponed for a month.

The mainstay of the Cultural Revolution leadership in Guangdong was General Huang Yongsheng, who in the following year became chief of the general staff. He was supported by a strong group of Red Guards, children of senior army officers. These were vigorously opposed by a large organisation called Red Flag, which consisted mainly of children of the despised middle class.[35]

Zhao Ziyang (prime minister in the 1980s) was First Party secretary of Guangdong province. His role in those days is not easy to reconstruct from the turbulent Red Guard tabloids. Some accused him of having been a follower of the wicked Tao Zhu. Others said that he had been blamed by Zhou Enlai, who had visited Canton in April 1967.[36] He disappeared in 1967, to reappear in Inner Mongolia in 1971 and in Guangdong once more in 1972.[37]

In November 1967, Tao Zhu's name was still feared. An editorial in the *Hunan Daily* declared that some old cadres should be brought back to work, but that caution was needed because Tao Zhu's men, like Peng Dehuai's men — landlords, kulaks, counter-revolutionaries, bad elements, rightists—, were still causing trouble.[38]

'Lian Dong'

The fiercest fighters, children of terror, were the *Lian Dong* the United Action Group. This had sprung from the capital's Red Guards Investigation Team, which had appeared at the first mass manifestation of Red Guards on August 18, 1966. Some wallposters said that the *Lian Dong* was established on October 1, 1966, in the very centre of the Party leadership at Zhong Nan Hai. Its members were children of higher Party cadres, and their motto was 'father hero, son good; father reactionary, son bad egg'.

When their fathers were arrested, the sons changed with the changing wind. The February 3, 1967, issue of *Red Flag*, Peking, listed United Action and the *Rong Fu Jun*, the group of demobilised soldiers, among the reactionary, conservative organisations that were deceiving the masses and attacking the 'headquarters of the proletarian Cultural Revolution'. They deceive the masses, cause strikes, cut communication lines and damage state property. They are under the direction of men on the capitalist road.[39] The United Action defended the ousted Party leaders.

When the old guard ousted by Mao returned to power three years after his death, their offspring were rehabilitated. The *People's Daily* deplored the Cultural Revolution and the suffering of Party leaders — among them the three marshals, Ye Jianying, Nie Rongzhen and Xu Xiangqian, all of whom were still alive — and said that the United Action had been unjustly persecuted by Lin Biao.[40]

'May 16'

Another powerful organisation not on the side of Lin Biao and Jiang

Qing was the 'May 16 Troop', named after the May 16, 1966, order which abolished the first Cultural Revolution team of Peng Zhen. On September 8, 1967, Yao Wenyuan, in a vitriolic article against Tao Zhu and Wang Renzhong (both already dismissed), condemned the May 16 Troop. 'Comrades,' Yao wrote, 'you should recognise that today there are counter-revolutionary extreme leftists. The organisers and instigators of the May 16 are such counter-revolutionaries. They want to split the Party leadership and the army. It is a counter-revolutionary organisation active in the underground in Peking. Many of the members and leaders are not yet known, but they will be detected.'[41]

On September 1, a week before the appearance of Yao Wenyuan's article against Tao Zhu and the May 16, an important meeting was held in Peking, and was reported on the front page of the People's Daily. Present were the Premier, Zhou Enlai, the head of the Economic Commission, Li Fuchun, and several leaders of the Cultural Revolution — Chen Boda, Jiang Qing, Kang Sheng, Zhang Chunqiao 'and others'. The meeting was held to condemn the May 16 Troop, 'that counter-revolutionary organisation'.[42]

Some Red Guard tabloids said that the head of the Peking group of the May 16 had been arrested on August 20, 1967, and that the May 16 was supported by Lin Jie, assistant editor of Red Flag, and by Guan Feng and Wang Li, both members of the Central Cultural Revolution team. Wang Li was the man who had gone to Wuhan with Xie Fuzhi. Guan Feng and Wang Li were not present at the September 1 meeting. They had disappeared from the scene.[43] A broadcast on Hunan provincial radio said in October 1967 that the May 16 was still active, in the silence of the night, in Peking, spreading leaflets and putting up posters; in Zhangsha, the capital of Hunan, it was acting in broad daylight.[44]

The secret of the May 16 organisation and why it was condemned by Zhou Enlai and the others is to be found in a publication written by a Red Guard group opposed to the May 16. The May 16, this booklet says, was opposed to Zhou Enlai! It was saying: Liu Shaoqi and Deng Xiaoping were demoted at the Eleventh Plenum of the Central Committee in August 1966; why was Zhou Enlai not touched? The May 16 also opposed Li Xiannian, Li Fuchun and Yu Qiuli — three leaders of the economy. It defended General Chen Zaidao, who defied the Peking envoys in Wuhan. In August a Party leader (unnamed) condemned the May 16, but the group ignored the condemnation and expanded its activities to the whole country. The booklet says that the May 16 had been started in the Department of Philosophy and Social Sciences of the

Academy of Science by Pan Zinian and an associate of his called Wu Chuanqi. It was formally established as a group in May 1967, and on July 1 it held its first congress in Peking. It was opposed to Nie Yuanzi — the lady who put up the first Cultural Revolution poster in May 1966 and was later praised by Mao.[45]

Pan Zinian was a leading Marxist theoretician, the founder and publisher of the Communist daily, *Xinhua Daily*, in Wuhan from January 1938 — transferred to Zhongqing in October that year — until its closure in February 1947, when he retired to Yan'an. In 1955 he was the founder and head of the Department of Philosophy and Social Sciences, established in 1955. In April 1967 an article by him, 'Hail the Red Guards', appeared in the *People's Daily*. This article was a passionate defence of the Cultural Revolution; Jiang Qing herself could not have done better. The Red Guards 'dare to think, dare to act, dare to rebel. Their irresistible revolutionary stream washes away the dirty remains of the old society and cleanses the garbage piled up through thousands of years . . . They read the writings of Chairman Mao, listen to the words of Chairman Mao, act according to the instructions of Chairman Mao [phrases taken from Lin Biao] . . . They seize power from the small clique of power-holders on the capitalist road in the Party.' There are people who hate the Red Guards, spread rumours and cause confusion: 'There are class enemies who seem to be big personalities, but their blood is degenerate; they are corpses ready to be put into coffins.' He ended by wishing millions of 'Hails to Chairman Mao'.[46] Were the words 'big personalities' pointed at Zhou Enlai and his companions?

Pan Zinian, it is odd to remember, was the brother of Pan Hannian, the famous underground Party worker who, after the establishment of the Peking regime, was accused of having been a double agent, was arrested and died in prison in 1977. No suspicion clouded the name of the other brother, Pan Zinian, an ardent exponent of Marxism, until the middle of 1967, when he disappeared. He may have shared the fate of his brother. Unlike the *Lian Dong*, which had defended the old leaders, the May 16 and Pan Zinian were never pardoned and never rehabilitated.

What exactly the May 16 was has never been made clear. The facts given above create the impression that it comprised genuine ultra-radical and fanatical Marxists, Guan Feng, Wang Li and Pan Zinian — men who wanted to oust the whole old guard, the leaders of the economy, Li Xiannian, Li Fuchun and Yu Qiuli, the remaining marshals, and above all the man at the top, Zhou Enlai, and start all over again.

In 1971, when Lin Biao met his bloody end and Zhou Enlai emerged as the top man next to Mao, the pursuit of the May 16 restarted. In early November 1971, posters denouncing it were seen in the city of Canton. On November 1, the radio of Zhejiang province had a long diatribe against the May 16 which, it said, had been active since the beginning of the Cultural Revolution. Later it launched the 'Extreme-Left Trend', which wanted to overthrow everything. 'All plotters [words which at that time pointed at Lin Biao] put themselves above the masses and believed that the earth could not go round without them. The march of history has not spared them, men of ambition as they were . . . Chairman Mao has said [during his August–September 1971 tour of the province] that cunning men who follow their own ambitions and believe that they are very clever, although they are in fact stupid, will not fare well.'[47]

The May 16 wanted to destroy Zhou and apparently it continued to exist till the death of Lin Biao. One cannot dismiss the suspicion that, however remotely, it was protected by Lin Biao.

Bogged down

The Cultural Revolution, launched in the summer of 1966, became bogged down in confusion. All parties, radicals, ultra-conservatives, those for and those against Lin Biao, jumped into the fray and pulled in different directions. Had Lin Biao, had Mao himself a blueprint when they launched the movement? Lin Biao obviously wanted to eliminate his rivals, starting with Luo Ruiqing in the army and first Peng Zhen and then Liu Shaoqi in the Party. Did he and Mao know at the start whom they wanted to purge and whom to retain? In 1967 there was total confusion among the leaders of the Cultural Revolution in the provinces. In July, Zhou Enlai ordered the Red Guards to stop roaming round.[48] A few days later, on July 22, Jiang Qing launched a new slogan, telling the Red Guards to 'attack by words, defend by arms'. This added fuel to the flames.[49] Members of the top leadership of the Cultural Revolution were popping up and falling down again like figures in a puppet show. Four of the five radical civilian members of the Central Cultural Revolution team had gone. Two soldiers, Xiao Hua and Liu Zhijian, were dismissed (both re-emerged after the fall of Lin Biao).

According to wallposters, Marshal Xu Xiangqian himself was dismissed by Jiang Qing from his post as head of the army's Cultural Revolution team. Tang Pingzhu, the military man who in 1966 had taken over the chief editorship of the *People's Daily* from Wu Lengxi, was accused of having published a picture of the head of Deng Xiaoping on the body of Chen Yi. This story, though without mention of names, was contained in Yao Wenyuan's article against Tao Zhu.[50]

Revolutionary Committees

In the provinces and cities the revolutionary rebel organisations were told to unite in Great Alliances and then prepare for the establishment of Revolutionary Committees, which were to form the new government. According to this plan, the Revolutionary Committees were to be led by the military, with the participation of some leaders of the 'rebel' groups and some former Party leaders. By the end of 1967, however, only six of the twenty-six provinces had established their Revolutionary Committees. Another six provinces had preparatory teams, and fourteen were under direct military administration. In December 1967 six provinces stopped broadcasting provincial news, a sign of great internal disorder. With one exception, all provincial revolutionary committees or preparatory teams were headed by military men. Some of the regional military leaders were dismissed; others were summoned to Peking for indoctrination. Yang Yong, the military commander of the Peking Great Military Area, was purged and replaced by Zheng Weishan. (He reappeared after the death of Lin Biao, and in 1982 was the only soldier to be a member of the Central Committee Secretariat. He died in January 1983. Zheng Weishan was never purged, and seven years after Mao's death, when he was already aged seventy-two, he became commander of the Lanzhou Great Military Area.)

On November 29, 1967, Lin Biao produced a sentence which became a sacred saying: 'Sailing the great sea, we rely on the helmsman; in the revolution, we rely on the Thoughts of Mao Zedong.' The newspapers carried facsimiles of this slogan in the handwriting of Lin Biao, and commented: 'These words express the infinite love, infinite faith, infinite worship, infinite loyalty of revolutionary fighters for the great leader Chairman Mao.'[51]

Friends of Deng

Much of what we know about the events of the Cultural Revolution comes from rapidly written lithographed Red Guard tabloids or from hand-written wallposters, diligently photographed or copied by

Japanese newsmen and reproduced in newspapers in Tokyo. Caution is needed in using such sources. All were written, in hatred, by 'rebel groups' against their enemies. It was a time of passion. The official newspapers were no less passionate.

What the tabloids and posters affirmed was often confirmed by subsequent events. When, for example, in the late summer of 1967, they spoke of the fall of the ultra-radicals Wang Li and Guan Feng, these men's names disappeared for ever from the public eye. The posters had been right. One might be inclined to discredit the violent attacks by wallposters on Party leaders, with their revelations of their private lives. Yet many of these have turned out to be important sources of information and have been confirmed by later events.

Picturesque examples of this may be found in the portrayal of Deng Xiaoping in two Red Guard tabloids, the *Red Guard Combat Paper* of November 1966 and *The East is Red* of February 1967. Deng, they both said, liked playing cards. His partners were Hu Yaobang, Wan Li, Yang Shangkun, Bo Yibo, Wang Hanbin and Wu Han. In 1964 he went to the Northeast with Yang Shangkun and Bo Yibo, ostensibly on a tour of inspection, but in fact they went to have a good time and stayed at the summer palace of the Qing Emperors at Cheng De, north of Peking. Deng, the tabloids said, always addressed Wu Han, the historian, as 'Professor'. When Wu Han got into trouble in November 1965 over his theatre play *The Dismissal of Hai Rui*, which was interpreted as criticism of Emperor Mao, he kept away from the card-parties, but Wan Li told Deng that the Wu Han case would be settled and that he would again join in the card-playing. During the card games Deng said without disguise what he thought about Jiang Qing and her reform of the Peking Opera.[52]

(In fact, Wu Han died in prison in October 1969, and his wife died in a labour camp the same month. Many years later, after the emergence of Deng, his other card-partners were promoted. Hu Yaobang became the head of the Party, Wan Li became the most active of the vice-premiers, Yang Shangkun became Deng's right hand in the Military Committee, Bo Yibo was put in charge of Party reform, and Wang Hanbin was made secretary-general of the People's Congress.)

A Red Guard tabloid prepared by the 'Jing Gang Shan Commune in the Peking Teachers' Training University' exposed the private life of Yu Qiuli, who was in charge of petroleum production. Yu lived in a house of twenty-one rooms. His wife had a high position in the ministry, and drew a salary but never went to work. His children treated their servants like animals. He bought up rebel organisations to defend him. He drank, womanised and played cards with Hu Yaobang. (In the 1980s Yu was head of the army's political department.)[53]

Zhou Enlai

Zhou Enlai had manoeuvred through many difficult situations in the course of his varied life. In his young days at the end of the 1920s, he squeezed Mao out of his post in the revolutionary base at Ruijin. How they became reconciled has never been put on record. Many of his colleagues began to sink in the marshes of the Cultural Revolution. At first he would hold out a hand to help; but when they went on sinking he let go. He could not have done otherwise. He protected Tan Zhenlin as long as he could, but dropped him when it was no longer safe to do so. (Tan was up again in 1973, and died in 1983.) Many Party and government officials were similarly supported by him at first, and then dropped.

When angry delegates from rival provincial rebel groups came to Peking, he was the only one who could talk to them. He talked to protesting railwaymen in Peking. In the summer of 1967, at the height of the disorder, he was the trouble-shooter in Wuhan. He performed the same function in the autumn in Canton.[54] Zhou Enlai's masterly skill was demonstrated in April 1968 in his dealings with rebel delegates who wanted to purge Yu Qiuli (minister of petroleum in the 1950s, head of the army's political department in the 1980s). First he described the general situation of the country. It was not yet at peace, he said, but more and more provincial revolutionary committees were being established. The Cultural Revolution had been going on for two years already, and there had been many mistakes. 'My own mistakes would fill a book . . . It is possible to oppose some things but it is impossible to oppose everything. The representative of the military would help. The Chairman [Mao] is a great man, without equal in the world. Yet he is very humble and he does not exaggerate. Comrade Lin Biao raised the red flag of the Thoughts of Mao Zedong on high and has followed Mao Zedong since Jing Gang Shan [1927], and composed the precious red book [*The Sayings of Chairman Mao*]. However, some in the May 16 and those who put up posters in the foreign office had gone wrong. I rang up those at the foreign office and defended Chen Yi's position. There had indeed been evil people in the Party. There was An Ziwen [former head of the Party organisation department], who was a follower of Gao Gang [purged in 1954]. There must be some others, still undetected.'

Only after all this did Zhou turn to the case of Yu Qiuli. 'Comrade Yu Qiuli has his defects and has made mistakes,' he said, 'and these must be pointed out. But criticising him is not your task; he will criticise himself. You should not think you are always right. Chairman Mao is always right, yet he is very humble. How much humbler we should be. I agree with you people in wanting to criticise Yu Qiuli. But there is hardly anyone else who could do Yu Qiuli's work. We criticise him; nevertheless we retain him. You may criticise him three times a week, but he does not have good health. He was wounded [in the war] and he has heart trouble. All must be loyal to Chairman Mao and loyal to Vice-Chairman Lin Biao. You may shout that you want to overthrow Yu Qiuli; I will not join you.'[55]

A Red Guard tabloid, published in Canton on October 1, 1967, quoted Zhou Enlai as saying in a speech on September 17 that he knew that the May 16 counter-revolutionary secret organisation was directed against himself — and against the Central Cultural Revolution team. Zhou was to all appearances an ardent supporter of Jiang Qing and Lin Biao, and that saved him.[56] At the mass Red Guard rallies he spoke after Lin Biao. The *Little Red Book*, Lin Biao's *Sayings of Chairman Mao*, never left his hands. On November 28, 1966, when the cultural achievements of Jiang Qing were being glorified, Zhou Enlai joined the flatterers and said that the new stage of the Cultural Revolution 'could not be separated from the leading role of Comrade Jiang Qing'.[57]

Liu Shaoqi was degraded in August 1966, but Zhou still remained the number three man in the Party hierarchy. Up till then he had stood third after Mao and Liu Shaoqi; now he stood third after Mao and Lin Biao. With Liu Shaoqi, the Head of State, gone, it was Zhou Enlai who received foreign presidents, and who summoned conferences on the economy.[58]

Zhou Enlai was in a difficult position in his own particular field, foreign policy. The great dreams of the 'A-A-A' (Afro-Asian-Latin American) alliance had been ended by the failure of the coup in Jakarta in 1965. During the Cultural Revolution all ambassadors except one were recalled, and chargés d'affaires took their places. The man in charge of the embassy in Jakarta, Yao Dengshan, a bulky and ferocious-looking man, returned to Peking and, with the help of ultra-radicals, took possession of the foreign office. On August 22, 1967, the office of the British chargé d'affaires in Peking was burnt down by an angry mob;

this was an anti-British move coinciding with the riots in Hong Kong. Zhou Enlai, however, manoeuvred and saved Chen Yi, who resumed his post as foreign minister.[59] (It could scarcely have been imagined in those days that within four years Zhou Enlai, with Mao's blessing, would be inviting American table-tennis players to Peking and talking with them.[60] By that time Lin Biao's star was declining and Zhou was the winner. A few years later he denounced those 'whose hands never left the *Little Red Book*'.) Zhou Enlai succeeded in ousting the ultra-radicals in the second half of 1967, and with this the leftist uprising in Hong Kong, which had never gained popular support, came to an abrupt end.

An extraordinary aspect of the chaotic conditions in 1967 was that though the ambassadors were recalled, foreign trade, though hurt, was not disrupted. In the first half of 1967 the economy was still functioning fairly normally. Trouble started in the second half of the year when the Cultural Revolution reached the workers. There were then nationwide strikes and bloody clashes between workers and Red Guards. Many factories were shut down because there was no power, and there was no power because there was no coal.[61] Exports declined, but the overall trade figures were slightly higher than those of 1966.[62]

1968

The third calendar year of the Cultural Revolution, 1968, was yet another turbulent year — but with a difference. Lin Biao's military men, having gained some experience, were striving to restore order and impose their own overall authority. In the opposition a new trend appeared, a demand for a total rethinking of the future of China. It was an interesting year.

The soldiers

On January 8 a *People's Daily* headline said 'Support the Left but not Factions'. Evil leaders of revolutionary groups should be treated as enemies, the article said, but others should be won over, and should be invited to common study of the writings of the Chairman. Instead of the thousands of Red Guard and rebel groups, three kinds of 'representative assemblies' should be formed in provinces and cities — assemblies of Red Guards, workers and peasants. All three should be represented in the Revolutionary Committees, to be established on all levels. These were described as temporary organs of authority, but nothing was said about what should come after them. However, it was stated with emphasis that the representatives in the Revolutionary Committees represented not their own factions but the whole people. This was well said, but it could not be achieved. The Revolutionary Committees were torn asunder by the opposing groups that were within them.[63]

In the spring of 1968 the military took over the leadership of the police — that is the security organs — and of the public prosecutor's offices and courts. Great numbers of government and Party cadres were sent to be re-educated in what were called the May 7 Cadre Schools. They were concentrated in various places and set to do manual labour. The military took over the leadership of government offices, mass organisations, factories and villages. The military were to run everything.[64]

On February 19 the Peking garrison held a day-and-night celebration, singing such songs as 'Chairman Mao is dearer to us than father and mother.' An act of loyalty was read out by the commander of the Peking garrison, Fu Chongbi. A month later, on March 26, crowds were shouting 'Down with Yang Chengwu, down with Yu Lijin, down with Fu Zhongbi!'[65] (Yang Chengwu had been acting Chief-of-Staff since the downfall of Luo Ruiqing in 1966 and Yu Lijin was political commissar of the air force, the body that appeared most loyal in support of Lin Biao.) How can these three have fallen? Two days earlier, on March 24, Lin Biao had spoken to the army, telling them that the affair of the three was being discussed with Mao. The three were dismissed because they had opposed other generals. It was decided that Huang Yongsheng should be Chief-of-Staff, with Wen Yucheng as second-in-command and, concurrently, commander of the Peking garrison.[66] (After the death of Lin Biao, the three ousted generals got back their old posts, but Yang only as deputy Chief-of-Staff. Yu died at the end of 1978.)

In 1984 Marshal Nie Rongzhen recalled the events of 1968. On March 22, 1968, a military order dismissed Yang Chengwu, Yu Lijin and Fu Zhongbi, and they were arrested the same day. Two days later, at a large meeting in the People's Hall in Peking, Lin Biao denounced them, saying among other things that General Fu had gone with four armed vehicles to attack the seat of the Central Cultural Revolution team and arrest some people. Kang Sheng also spoke, saying that the three had behaved badly even before 1949 when they were leading officers of a liberated area in the North, and insinuating that there was a wicked man behind them. The author of this account, Marshal Nie, said that at that time he himself was in bed with heart trouble and did not attend the meeting, but Marshal Ye Jianying reported to him all that had happened. He knew that the talk about 'the man behind the three' was aimed at him, for he had been the leader of that liberation area. On April 6 he telephoned Ye Qun, Lin Biao's wife, but she gave him an evasive answer. Posters accusing him began to appear in the streets. On April 7 he wrote a letter to Mao in defence of Yang Chengwu. Three days later Zhou Enlai's secretary telephoned him to convey a message from Mao asking him to take care of his health. On April 16 he went to see Lin Biao, but again got no satisfactory answer. Three years later, at the beginning of 1971, Jiang Qing accused him by name, saying that in 1937 he was already a bad man. Two years later, in December 1973 (Lin Biao had gone by then), Mao declared that the condemnation of the three generals had been an error. In July 1974, all three were released from prison and resumed work. In March 1979 they were publicly rehabilitated. This was Marshal Nie's recollection of what had happened.[67]

From the spring of 1968 it was clear that the military were running the administration on all levels, in the communes, in the counties, in the special districts and in the provinces. They were giving indoctrination courses, trying to bring rival groups together, consolidate the 'great alliance' and strengthen the revolutionary committees. They were pursuing the 'enemy' and holding public trials of political culprits, and at the same time seeing to it that work in factories and farms should not stop.[68]

On September 7 the front page of the *People's Daily* announced, in letters printed in red, 'an overall victory of the Proletarian Cultural Revolution'. The establishment of revolutionary committees was given festive greeting in all the provinces. It seemed that what Lin Biao had laid down in 1966, that there should be only One Thought in the country, was coming true. On August 13 the *People's Daily* proclaimed 'One Will, One Step, One Action'. On August 5 it announced that only one centre existed, headed by Chairman Mao; there were no other centres, there were no 'multi-centres'. In October some provinces, but not all, announced that the mass organisations had been dissolved. To prevent trouble, 'Mao-Thought Propaganda Teams' were formed in the army, and these had as auxiliary organisations the 'Workers' Mao-Thought Propaganda Teams'. These made their way into all schools, universities, middle schools and primary schools and ran them. The students were to return to the schools, though no regular teaching had yet begun.[69] In December 1968 Mao ordered that 'the educated youth must go to the villages'. This only confirmed what was already being done. What was new was that the children of army officers were also to be sent off. The

People's Daily extended this order to the adult city population: 'It is hoped that non-labouring citizens in cities and towns . . . will go to the first line of agrarian production.'[70]

This year, 1968, was that in which the full strength of the military was imposed upon the nation. The task was a complex one for which the soldiers were not prepared. A year after they had been thrown into the political arena, they were still finding it hard to distinguish true leftist groups from fakes, and they were criticised and often intimidated from various quarters. Some groups asked for military assistance against others. As a broadcast from Anhui province said on March 5, 1968: 'The soldiers became impatient and rough with the revolutionary masses which were exerting pressure upon the troops, and hatred of factionalism was transformed into hatred of the people.' In another province, Jiangsu, the provincial Revolutionary Committee was established in March, but peace did not return. Some groups were deceiving the soldiers, 'seeking to prevent the aid-left troops specially sent to the province from carrying out the instructions of the central authorities'. These trouble-makers were described as scoundrels and cunning counter-revolutionary double-dealers who wanted to break down the good relations between the army and the people. Similar trouble was described in reports from many other provinces. Li Desheng, the new commander of the troops sent to Anhui province (he later rose to important posts), said: 'The evil enemy, the bad eggs who have already been demoted from power, are back again. They are committing murders and robberies, dividing the land and encouraging gambling in public. They are dividing and upsetting the unity of the Chinese People's Liberation Army and of the new-born revolutionary committees.' An editorial in the newspaper of Sichuan province said that the enemy 'were creating rumours and divisions to destroy good relations between the army and the people in an effort to split the army'.[71] The army — troops sent to 'help the left' — was often treated as the enemy. The provincial daily paper of Zhejiang province reported in July that violent groups had burst into military barracks, broken open prisons, cut communications and set up their own broadcasting station.[72]

These and similar reports from the provinces were not idle fancies. The action of the military was rough, and it had a lasting effect. It lessened the army's popularity for many years to come. Fifteen years later the *People's Daily* reported (February 8, 1983) that relations between the armed forces and local government members were strained.[73] In 1984, the question of the Cultural Revolution and its adverse influence on relations between the army and the people was still being widely discussed.[74] The friction was not confined to the army and the mass organisations which the soldiers were supposed to unite; the provincial radios of Hunan, Guizhou, Zhejiang and Jiangxi provinces spoke of cleavages among the troops themselves.[75] These may have amounted to no more than minor clashes or divergences of opinion over which mass organisation the army was to aid. However, there was a deeper division in the army. Lin Biao's men came from a single branch of the army, the Fourth Route Army, the history of which went back, under various names, to the early years. As soon as Lin Biao fell in 1971, the Fourth Route Army was rejected. Years later, when Deng Xiaoping came to the top, his army, the Second Route Army of the early days, took the first place in the country.

The Cultural Revolution left a deep mark on the subsequent history of China, but that belongs to a future chapter.

The Trend

From the turbulent events of the prolonged Cultural Revolution, there emerged what the official press called the Trend *(si-chao)* — and it was considered an inimical trend. It was much more significant than the widespread agitation of rival Red Guard groups in 1966 and 1967; it was a new line of thought that emerged at the end of 1967 and in 1968.

A Hunan Red Guard group published a manifesto which declared that 'at this turning-point intensive theoretical studies are important.' The group criticised not only the Cultural Revolution but the whole Communist movement of the preceding decades. It also referred to an open letter written by the May 16 Troop in Peking. The Hunanese manifesto, like the May 16, said that the source of evil was Zhou Enlai. China should have revolutionary élan without bureaucratic shackles. This, it said, was Mao's original idea. On June 1, 1966, the Chairman called Nie Yuanzi's wallposter in Peking University 'the manifesto of the Peking People's Commune'. The Hunanese interpreted this as: 'Chairman Mao brilliantly foresaw that the organs of our state would appear in an entirely new form.' (But why did Mao object seven months later to the 'Shanghai Commune'?)

In Shanghai, the Eastern Association, an organisation that was regarded as illegal, published a manifesto which proved by quotations from Marx, Engels and Mao that the whole system should be smashed. 'Hail universal scepticism!' 'Smash the shackles of the proletarian dictatorship.' 'Irrespective of social classes, all the oppressed are revolutionaries.' The manifesto condemned the Communist Party and said that non-Party members were better than Party members. It extolled Wang Ming, a deadly enemy of Mao's in the 1930s. (When all this was happening, Wang Ming was already in the Soviet Union, writing and broadcasting against the Chinese Communist Party.)

In Zhejiang province the Trend asked for democratic elections. 'There are no rebels or conservatives, no men on the capitalist road.' It wanted universal suffrage.[76] In Zhejiang this was not a mere theory. In the Choushan Islands, part of Zhejiang province, the established revolutionary committees had been demolished and everybody had been registered for participation in a general election.[77]

The manifestos of the Trend were not the fruit of scholarly thinking about the future of China. They were born from the angry turbulence of the Cultural Revolution, but they represented the ferment of a new orientation. Some used quotations from Marx, Lenin and Mao, but they gave new meanings to the words they used. Others rejected Marxism with its division of society into privileged and non-privileged, rulers and ruled, and wanted equality, freedom and democratic elections. This Trend did not start with the Cultural Revolution and did not die with it. It was the subdued murmur of Chinese who were worrying about the fate of China. It was to be found in the early 1950s in the Chinese publications in Hong Kong, of what in those days was called the Third Force (between the Kuomintang and the Communist party), and it reappeared in the 1980s in a group of young people from the mainland who published in the United States a review called *The Spring of China*.

Inside China the dissidents did not last long. Lin Biao's army was effective, and gradually, after years of suspension, the rebuilding of the Communist Party began.

The 1969 Party Congress

In October 1968 the Twelfth Plenum of the Central Committee (the twelfth since the 1956 Party Congress) was convened. No announcement was made of the number of Party Central members present — a large number had already been purged. Only two persons were named, Mao and Lin Biao. The convening of a Party Congress was decided upon, but no date was fixed. The Plenum discussed the draft of a new revised Party Charter, and it was reiterated that in the country there must be 'One Thought, One Step, One Action'. Liu Shaoqi was condemned and officially expelled from the Party as a 'Renegade, Traitor and Scab'.[78]

Towards the end of the year, the provinces began to hold their Party congresses, although these were in fact Party congresses only in name: only the military and other members of the provincial or regional revolutionary committees were summoned. The Congress in Hubei province promised that it would exterminate the Reactionary Trend, which was still causing trouble, but it ordered that there should be no aimless beatings or forced confessions.[79] The National Party Congress, the Ninth, opened on April 1, 1969, and lasted till the 24th. Its convocation had not been announced in advance, and no representatives of foreign Communist parties were present. Lin Biao spoke. A new Party Charter was approved, and a new Central Committee was elected.

In contrast with the Eighth Party Congress in 1956, when all the speeches were published, Lin Biao's was the only speech made at this 1969 Ninth Congress to see the light. He started by enumerating the crimes of Liu Shaoqi. Then he exalted the Cultural Revolution and spoke of Jiang Qing's reform of the Chinese theatre — though without mentioning her by name. He spoke of Mao's January 1967 order which sent the army into action. Lin Biao called the army 'the forceful column of the proletarian dictatorship', 'the main element in the state'. He also mentioned the establishment of the revolutionary committees which were run by the 'military representatives'. He said little about the economy, except that it should not be harmed by the revolution. Revolution should promote production — 'more, faster, better, cheaper'. On war and peace he repeated Mao's formula that a third world war would promote revolution and dig the graves of imperialism (the United States) and revisionism (the Soviet Union). 'We must be ready for a conventional war and also for an atomic war,' he said; 'both the United States and the Soviet Union are paper tigers.' He did not think much of the United States President Richard Nixon. Negotiations with the Soviet Union, he said, broke down in 1964; in March of the current year (1969) the Soviet government had expressed a wish for negotiations. About the border, he repeated China's stand that the present border could be made the basis of negotiation, but that the Soviet Union would have to admit that the historical border treaties were 'unequal treaties'. Lin Biao admitted that there was still much opposition to be overcome. At the end of his long speech, he quoted what Mao had said in 1962, Mao's great prophecy that within fifty to 100 years the world would go

through a great transformation.[80] Mao had not said what the transformation would bring about.

The new Party Charter was a document of military brevity, consisting
of twelve articles. (The previous Party Charter, that of 1956, had sixty
articles.) All power was concentrated in the hands of the five members of
the Politbureau Standing Committee, Mao and Lin Biao, whose names
were printed separately, and Chen Boda, Zhou Enlai and Kang Sheng,
whose names were printed according to the number of strokes in the
Chinese characters — the Chinese equivalent of alphabetical order —,
thus not revealing priorities. Earlier Party Charters had established a Secretariat in charge of daily work. There was no Secretariat in the new
Constitution. The Charter did, however, say: 'A certain number of
organs will be set up to deal with the day-to-day work of the Party,
government and army, under the leadership of the Chairman, the Vice-
Chairmen and the Standing Committee of the Politbureau.' (Of the
thirteen members of the preceding Secretariat, ten regular and three
alternate, nine had been purged by the Cultural Revolution.)

The prime feature of the document was put in the preamble: 'Comrade Lin Biao has always raised high the great banner of the Thoughts of
Mao Zedong. He has been the most faithful and the firmest in carrying
on and defending the proletarian revolutionary line of Comrade Mao
Zedong. Comrade Lin Biao is the intimate comrade-in-arms of Comrade
Mao Zedong and is his successor.'[81] It is unusual to find personal names
in a Party Charter. Mao's name was in the 1945 Charter, drawn up at
the Seventh Party Congress in Yan'an, but did not appear in that of
1956. It was an innovation to put not only Mao's but also his successor's
name into such a document.

The new Politbureau consisted of twenty-five members (twenty-one
full and four alternate). Of the twenty-six members of the previous
Politbureau, eleven had been swept away by the Cultural Revolution,
including Liu Shaoqi, Deng Xiaoping and Peng Zhen. Two who had
been alternate-members in 1966, Chen Boda and Kang Sheng, both
champions of the Cultural Revolution, now became regular Politbureau
members. The foreign minister, Chen Yi, and two leaders of the
economy, Chen Yun and Li Fuchun, all Politbureau members in 1966,
were not re-elected. Li Xiannian remained in the Politbureau. Two
women were added, Jiang Qing, the wife of Mao, and Ye Qun, the wife
of Lin Biao.

Thirteen of the twenty-five Politbureau members were active military
men. Three of these, Lin Biao, Zhu De and Liu Bocheng, had been in the

previous Politbureau; the other ten were new arrivals. Among these were Wu Faxian, commander of the air force, Li Zuopeng, first political commissar of the navy, and Qiu Huizuo, commander of logistics — all three perished along with Lin Biao two years later. Xu Xiangqian, who in 1967 was the head of the army's Cultural Revolution team, was not in the Politbureau. Nor was Marshal Nie Rongzhen, head of the scientific work of the army; he had been accused in Red Guard newspapers of having ambitions — something that Lin Biao could not tolerate. There was a noticeable preponderance of men originating from Hubei, Lin Biao's province, whereas till then Hunan, Mao's province, had been strongly represented.[82]

Lin Biao had succeeded in holding a Party Congress after a lapse of thirteen years, or at least, if the extraordinary second session of that Congress in 1958 is counted, eleven years. The way ahead to the future was paved. The new leaders were on the spot, many of them younger men. A successor had been designated, who to all appearances was Mao's own choice. The succession of the revolution, discussed for many years, had been settled. In the provinces too, younger men were taking over the leadership. (It could not have been foreseen that ten years later the old men, then ten years older, would return to power and the process of rejuvenating the leadership would have to start all over again.)

A film of the Party Congress was shown to the public. To watch it was a unique experience. The incessant hysterical cries of 'Hail Chairman Mao!' by the 1,500 delegates suggested the mass Red Guard meetings in 1966 rather than a Party meeting. Everybody, except Mao, was holding and waving a *Little Red Book*, and everyone except Mao wore a Mao badge. Zhou Enlai looked worn out. Jiang Qing smiled a happy contented smile. Lin Biao looked, as he looked in his photographs, pale and sickly. His wife Ye Qun was the only one who looked like a civilised lady from a well-to-do family. Mao looked triumphant, enjoying the incredible noise of the incessant ovations. Behind him was a huge picture, the only picture in the hall, that of himself. Yet Mao did not behave like a Hitler. Indeed he looked quite human. Several times he was seen cracking jokes, although his voice was not heard. His voice was heard only after the crowd had voted and held up their *Little Red Books*. Mao then announced the result, saying with impish glee the simple word 'Passed'. During the Congress Lin Biao and Zhou Enlai, on either side of him, kept throwing quick reverential anxious looks to see whether the master was satisfied. The film lasted an hour. It was deafening and monotonous, yet worth seeing.[83]

A woman's heart

Most of the new leaders, particularly in the regions, were soldiers, but it must have been expected that they would learn the trade of ruling, as soldiers had done when they entered the cities in 1949 after the civil war.

There was however one ominous, but at the time hardly noticeable, incident at the 1969 Party Congress. After Lin Biao's long speech, Zhou Enlai, Chen Boda and Kang Sheng also spoke, and after them General Huang Yongsheng, Wang Hongwen and four more. Their speeches were not published. All that was announced was that they expressed support for Mao's unpublished opening words, and for Lin Biao's report. This was all routine; but Jiang Qing did not stand up to express support for Lin Biao. Neither did her faithful followers, the Shanghai pair, Zhang Chunqiao and Yao Wenyuan, nor did Xie Fuzhi.[84] Why?

Many minds must have gone back seven months to the celebration on September 7, 1968, of the victory of the Cultural Revolution through the establishment of revolutionary committees in every province. On that occasion Jiang Qing started her speech very oddly. 'Only this morning, at the last minute', she said, 'did I hear about the holding of this great meeting of congratulation on the establishment of the revolutionary committees in all provinces, cities and autonomous areas. I will say a few words.' She then went on to speak about her 'Red Guard small generals' — who at that very meeting were ordered to halt and to dissolve their groups. 'The Red Guards have indeed committed errors,' she said. 'The bad ones must be purged, and all must obey the workers, backed by the army. But the workers must protect the Red Guard small generals.' Jiang Qing's short speech was interrupted frequently by hysterical shouts of 'We must learn from Comrade Jiang Qing!', an exclamation that became a set ritual whenever she spoke.

What happened behind the scenes was not disclosed. A few months earlier, in the summer of 1968, Jiang Qing had been acclaimed several times for her achievements in the theatre. That was the time when the military were preparing to overthrow the rebel Red Guards, Jiang Qing's sole mass support. In March 1968, a month before the Party Congress, Lin Biao's March 1966 letter entrusting literature and art in the army to Jiang Qing was published. Her achievements on the stage, her eight revolutionary Model Plays, and so on, were extolled and acclaimed as the opening of a new period in proletarian literature and art. Yet Jiang Qing got this recognition only for her proletarian culture. The days when she could give orders to masses of youngsters and to the army were over. Even her achievements in art were attributed to the patronage of Lin Biao. At the Party Congress the Red Guards, the mass of organisations which still existed but were now considered illegal, were not represented. Only two former Red Guards were to be found in the Congress Praesidium.[85] A woman of Jiang Qing's ambition must have felt hurt. Moreover, the fuss made about Lin Biao's letter gave the impression that it was Lin Biao who had created her. This must have angered her. Lin Biao had arrived. He no longer needed Jiang Qing. Yet he may have miscalculated in ignoring Jiang Qing's influence on her husband. Could she have given orders to Red Guards and to the army without the support of Mao?

The Party Congress had nominated Lin Biao in the Party Charter as Mao's successor; sixteen months later his political career was in shreds and before the end of the following year he was dead. The links between events in the highest quarters of the Party are never very clear; but it is certain that the dissolving of the Red Guards, Jiang Qing's protégés, without her consent was an insult to her. She expressed her feelings by her refusal to acclaim Lin Biao at the Party Congress in April 1979. She and her acolytes survived his fall and went on to become the rulers of the country. After Lin Biao's death they instituted the denigration of him in a nationwide campaign. Is it not reasonable to suggest that it was Jiang Qing who whispered in Mao's ear — Mao was an old man — that Lin Biao, assured of the succession, was plotting against him? That Mao had an open ear for Jiang Qing had been clear for years. The *People's Daily* reported in March 1969 just before the Party Congress that in 1944 Mao, already married to Jiang Qing, had expressed a wish for reformation of the old theatrical plays. Considerable reforms were carried out in the 1950s, but real proletarian plays appeared only under the direction of Jiang Qing. Mao was always present to applaud at the premiers of her theatrical creations.[86]

For five years after the death of Lin Biao in 1971, Jiang Qing was on top of the world and Lin Biao was treated as the enemy ghost. However, after Mao's death in 1976, when Jiang Qing had been arrested and (in 1981) brought to trial, Peking wanted to prove that she and Lin Biao had pulled together. The Peking press carried the story that in September 1971, four days before Lin Biao's death, his wife Ye Qun telephoned Jiang Qing to say that he was sending her some watermelons with his best regards. On the afternoon of September 12 — the day of Lin Biao's flight on his doomed plane — Jiang Qing, according to the story, ate a watermelon in the Summer Palace and told an attendant that it had been sent by Vice-Chairman Lin. Thus it was not true, the article concluded, that there was any conflict between Jiang Qing and Lin Biao.[87] This story may have been concocted ten years after the events, but if it is true, all it proves is that Lin Biao and Ye Qun wanted to camouflage their escape.

After the Congress

The Ninth Party Congress, which exalted Mao and established Lin Biao as his successor, turned out to have been the beginning of Lin Biao's decline. Immediately after the Party Congress the adulation of Mao stopped. All signs of religious worship of his person disappeared from the press and from radio broadcasts.[88] The exclamation 'Mao is the red sun in our hearts' was rarely heard.

Before the Congress, Mao-worship had grown to gigantic dimensions. In Hunan, his native province, a hundred places, twenty-four of them in Zhangsha, the provincial capital, were chosen as sites for memorials. Shaoshan, Mao's birthplace, had already become a centre of worship to which pilgrims went from all over the country. A special railway line was built and a 6-metre statue of Mao on a 26-metre pedestal was unveiled on the top of a hill in December 1967. A year later another railway line was built leading direct to Zhangsha. A 10-metre statue of Mao was set up in Nanchang, the capital of Jiangxi province, and an exhibition hall was built beside it. Monumental statues of Mao were erected in several other provinces.[89] After the Congress, nothing more was heard of monuments to Mao.

Subsequent events disproved the suspicion that Lin Biao, after his election as successor, had put a stop to the worship of Mao. Mao himself had woken to the fact that he was being pushed into heaven, away from earthly realities.

Contrasting voices

In the summer of 1970 a curious article on the Communist Party and Marxism appeared on the front page of the People's Daily (July 24). Unlike most documents of this kind, it was not reprinted in any other paper, and no reference was made to it anywhere. The article dealt with the nature of the Chinese Communist Party and was filled with quotations from old writings of Mao. It quoted, for example, a 1926 saying: 'The industrial proletariat [not the army] is the primary force in our revolution.' It also touched on earlier deviations of men who did not understand Mao's correct leadership. It cited some major events from early Party history and emphasised that the Party and not the army should run the country. It made no mention of any of Lin Biao's innovations, much talked about in those days — nothing, for instance, about the 'four-good movements' introduced by Lin Biao in 1960, nothing about the 'aid-left' (the army leading the politics of the country), nothing about the presence of 'military representatives' in every organisation. It said nothing at all about the political role of the army. This article stood alone in those years. Indeed writing about the early history of the Communist Party was not the fashion of the day. The world had begun with the Cultural Revolution. The article spoke of 'continued revolution under proletarian dictatorship', but did not attribute the phrase to Mao. It looked like an insertion into the article.[90] Lin Biao, in his report to the Ninth Party Congress, also spoke of 'continued revolution under the dictatorship of the proletariat' and attributed the phrase to Mao, but it did not get the quotation marks usually accorded to Mao words. The phrase, which smacks of Trotsky, was in fact first used in China in a 1958 Resolution on the communes, drawn up at the Sixth Plenum of the Eighth Central Committee. The Resolution referred to 'permanent revolution' and 'stages of the revolution'.[91]

In spite of the appearance in this strange article of Lin Biao's favourite phrase, it seemed clear that there was a deep divergence between the tone of the article and the general tone of the day. Around the time that it was written, the country was extolling the memory of two military conferences, one held by Mao in 1929 at Gutian and the other held by Lin Biao in 1960.[92] The article spoke with emphasis of the 1929 conference and did not refer to that of 1960. This was a slight on Lin Biao.

Around the country the army, which was in charge of everything, was still extolling Lin Biao in extravagant terms. The navy in Zhejiang province said: 'Vice-Chairman Lin Biao listens best to the voice of Chairman Mao. Vice-Chairman Lin is the best, the best in learning the Thoughts of Mao Zedong. His understanding is the deepest. Therefore he is our shining example. Through every word of his there shines the Thoughts of Mao Zedong . . . It may happen that when we first hear the instructions of Chairman Mao we do not understand them fully. But when Vice-Chairman Lin explains them, then they are easy to understand, and all understand them more deeply.' The military in the provinces were talking of nothing but the 'four-good', the 'two-decisions' (1929 and 1960) and the shining example of Lin Biao.

They went on talking in this way in September 1970, unaware of the significance of an important Party meeting held in August-September 1970.[93]

Angry Mao: The Lushan meeting

That Party meeting was the Second Central Committee Plenum after the Ninth Party Congress, held on August 23 – September 6, 1970, at the summer resort of Lushan. The Communist Party is a secret society. 'Rightist opportunists' were condemned in 1959, but it took years for the individuals to be identified. This time, too, years were to pass before the significance of the meeting came to light.

The official communiqué of the Central Committee Plenum was not exciting; such documents rarely are. It seemed merely routine for it to say that 'the whole Party must study the philosophical works of Chairman Mao carefully, with emphasis on dialectical materialism and historical materialism'. Second thoughts showed that these words were a rejection of a current Lin Biao doctrine. The communiqué did not mention Lin Biao's revolutionary slogans; it did not even say that the essence of philosophy is the 'one divided into two'; it did not say that all should study the *Three Short Stories* by Mao — *The Man who Moved the Mountain* etc. — as prescribed by Lin Biao. The communiqué spoke only of dialectical materialism and historical materialism as the bases of Marxism.[94]

That meeting in August–September 1970, just over a year after the Ninth Party Congress which had made Lin Biao heir-designate to Mao, was the beginning of the final break between the two. It seems that many of those who were present at the Lushan meeting of the Central Committee were unaware of what was happening. The military members went home and continued as before to hymn the praises of Lin Biao. In the months that followed the only surprising thing was the non-appearance of Chen Boda, one of the five members of the highest government body, the Standing Committee of the Politbureau. Yet there was another member of the same committee, Kang Sheng, who made no public appearances for months. He did not reappear till June 3, 1971, when Nicolae Ceausescu, the head of the Rumanian Communist Party, visited China and was received by Mao and Lin Biao. Chen Boda did not reappear.

All knew that a campaign of articles was being directed against what were called 'sham Marxist political swindlers'. A short leading article in

Red Flag in February 1971 attacked these 'swindlers', but the only ones to be named were Wang Ming, Mao's opponent in the 1930s, and Liu Shaoqi, who had been knocked out four years earlier. On Party Day in 1971, July 1, a joint editorial in the Peking papers described former enemies of Mao, and then incidentally gave the advice: 'Do not pretend to be little, little ordinary persons.' This stirred memories of a speech of April 12, 1967, in which Jiang Qing, speaking of Chen Boda, used his own modest description of himself and called him 'the little, little ordinary person'.

Chen Boda was the head of the Central Cultural Revolution Team. He had been prominent in Mao's writers' team since Yan'an days, and his pamphlets on Mao were the authoritative interpretation of Mao's Thoughts. In 1958 he was the founder and editor-in-chief of *Red Flag*, the organ of the Central Committee. In 1959, in an attack on the 'rightists' in *Red Flag*, he wrote that in 1957 'some bourgeois rightists had raised the flag of Liberty, Equality and Fraternity in order to oppose Socialism'. Now this very accusation — of the crime of liberty, equality and fraternity — was directed at Chen Boda himself. In July 1971 the *People's Daily*, in a long article written ostensibly against Confucianism, said that the sham Marxists extolled Liberty, Equality and Fraternity.

For those in the know, Chen Boda was clearly identified, but Lin Biao's name was still shining bright. The August 1, 1971 (Army Day), joint editorial of the Peking papers had the reassuring words: 'Chairman Mao created and guides, and Vice-Chairman Lin commands the army.'[95] Not till the following year, 1972, was the whole story of the August–September 1970 Central Committee meeting revealed, as we shall see later. Chen Boda's fate was sealed. When the 'Gang of Four' were being tried in January 1981, Chen, then seventy-seven years old, was condemned to eighteen years in prison, including the ten years he had already spent there.[96]

Mao's rejection of Lin Biao was not announced, not even in such flowery language as 'little, little man'. Removing him was a risky business. His military followers still dominated the country, and the leading posts in the newly re-established regional Party committees were filled by his men. The generals were unaware of what had happened in the highest circles at the Lushan meeting. Even as late as March 1971 a joint editorial of the three Peking papers said that 'according to the Marxist theory of the State the army is the chief component of the State power.' These words were taken from Mao's 1938 writing on war and strategy. Significantly, the editorial omitted the sentence which, in the original, had preceded these words: 'Our principle is that the Party commands the guns; the guns must never be allowed to command the Party.'[97] Evidently not even the editorial boards of the three Peking papers — People's Daily, Liberation Army Daily and Red Flag — were aware of how the wind was changing.

The wind did change. In the spring of 1971 the military's grip on the peasants was suddenly relaxed. It was still being asserted that peasants work 'for the revolution'; but remuneration in proportion to labour was now introduced. Up till then side occupations of peasants had been blamed; now they were encouraged. The private plots of peasant households had been barely tolerated; now they became respectable. Having poultry for personal consumption had been regarded as capitalism; now it was allowed. Formerly all had to be treated as equal; now differences between rich and poor were accepted.[98] All this was a considerable departure from the preceding system of military discipline. Zhou Enlai knew that Lin Biao's days were numbered. In July 1971 Henry Kissinger paid his first visit to Peking and Zhou invited President Nixon to visit China.

The end of Lin Biao

In the summer of 1971 there was a spectacular non-event: the non-celebration of the fiftieth anniversary of the birth of the Chinese Communist Party. The thirtieth anniversary in 1951 had been the occasion of a great celebration. On the fortieth anniversary in 1961 — the year of economic disaster — there was less glamour and fanfare, but a major meeting was held in Peking, a memorial postage stamp was issued, and at the Peking meeting Liu Shaoqi delivered an important speech.[99] On the fiftieth anniversary there was nothing more than a long press article and a newspaper photo of Mao with Lin Biao. The long article contained the words: 'Chairman Mao created and guides, and Vice-Chairman Lin commands the army.'[100] On the day itself, July 1, not a single personage appeared in public. A few days later preparations began for the celebration of Army Day, August 1, and on that day the People's Daily published a long list of army men, and the provinces also held big celebrations.[101] Obviously the military leaders still knew nothing of Lin Biao's troubles.

All that had happened at the August–September 1970 Second Plenum and the subsequent events was covered in a deep fog. Lin Biao made his last public appearance on June 3, 1971, with Nicolae Ceausescu.[102] Early in September, preparations began for the celebration of National Day, October 1, at the Tian An Men in Peking. In the middle of the month these preparations were stopped abruptly.

Lin Biao perished on the night of September 12–13. Nothing was announced. Foreign embassies in Peking were indeed informed that the parade, the National Day celebration and the usual dinner for foreign guests had been cancelled, but there was no sign of the great change. An album of fifty photographs was published on September 12, the very day of Lin Biao's death, as a delayed commemoration of the fiftieth anniversary of the Party. The *People's Daily*, commenting that day on the album, pointed out that some of the photographs showed Chairman Mao with Vice-Chairman Lin, 'conveying the feeling that comrade Lin Biao has always lifted high the red flag of the Thoughts of Mao Zedong' and that he, Lin Biao, 'has always been a shining example to the whole Party, to the whole army and to the people of the whole country.' At this point, an order was issued that the whole country should sing two songs, the *Internationale* and an old military song, *Three Great Rules and Eight Points to be Observed.* These songs are regularly prescribed at critical moments of political change. The *Three Great Rules* had been sung in November 1966, at a critical stage of the Cultural Revolution. The *Internationale* means world revolution, and the *Three Great Rules* is a song of military discipline. At the end of October the *People's Daily* called the singing of the two songs 'a serious political work'.[103]

In the newspapers in China there was silence. Outside the country news began to trickle through. At the end of September a Japanese newspaper reported that the Japanese government had picked up an uncoded Chinese cable ordering the cancellation of military leave 'because of an unexpected accident, and to prevent turmoil'. On October 14 Admiral John S. McCain, Jr., the US Commander in the Pacific, told Washington newsmen that military and civil air activity on the Chinese mainland had been very noticeably reduced for five weeks. The news agency of the Mongolian Republic reported on September 30 that a Chinese military plane had crashed close to the Mongolian-Soviet border on the night of September 12–13 and that the bodies of nine passengers had been found. Neither the Mongolians nor the Russians, who must have known, said anything more.[104]

Inside China, on September 18, hardly a week after the event, a brief secret notification informed the highest leaders of what had happened. On September 12, it said, Lin Biao, using the occasion of Chairman Mao's inspection of South China, had planned to shell the train in which

Chairman Mao was supposed to be travelling when it was near Shanghai, his purpose being to kill Chairman Mao. After the failure of his plot, he left Peking hurriedly in the afternoon and, having taken a Trident fighting plane, fled, thus betraying his country. When he had passed over the frontier, the plane crashed near Under-Khan (in Chinese Wen-tor-kan) in Mongolia. The bodies of Lin Biao, Ye Qun, Lin Liguo and one pilot were completely burnt (the Mongolians, as we have seen, reported nine bodies found). Lin Biao had stolen a great mass of secret documents and foreign currency, and had shot and wounded a guard who had been with him for many years. Three of his followers (lower officials) intended to flee the country in two military helicopters, but they were intercepted near the border by the Chinese air force. Two of them killed the pilot and killed themselves. The third, Chen Liyun, was wounded and arrested. Lin Biao's daughter notified Premier Zhou Enlai in good time and revealed her father's plot. This was an act of great merit, which had served the Party and the country and helped the Party Central to smash the grave counter-revolutionary coup.[105] (Nothing has ever been heard of Lin Biao's daughter since that announcement.)

The communication of the news five days after the event inclined people to assume that the story of the crashed plane and of Lin Biao's death was authentic. Yet even now it is not known for certain how he died and whether he was alive or dead when he boarded the plane. It is not known how the plane came down. The Chinese air force brought down the two helicopters. Did it also pursue the vital plane? Or was the plane shot down by Mongolian or Soviet forces? It is not even certain that Lin Biao wanted to flee to the Soviet Union. In 1981 the *Chronology of Major Events of the History of the Chinese Communist Party*, a 194-page book published for inner-Party circulation only, described what had happened in the following terms. On the 11th (September 1971) Mao Zedong took the train from Shanghai ahead of time. Thus the plot of the Lin Biao clique to assassinate Mao Zedong failed. On the 12th Lin Biao prepared to lead Huang Yongsheng, Wu Faxian, Li Zuopeng and Qiu Huizuo (his main generals) in flight to the south to Canton, intending to establish another Party leadership there and thus divide the country. He ordered a special plane, no. 256, to fly secretly to Shanghaiguan for his own use and the use of his Red Army company staying in Beidaihe. That evening, Mao Zedong arrived in Peking. Zhou Enlai found out that the no. 256 special plane had flown without prior notice to Shanghaiguan (Lin Biao's daughter is not mentioned). Lin Biao, Ye Qun and Lin Liguo, seeing that they had lost, boarded the plane early in the morning of the 13th and fled the country. The plane crashed and he perished in Under-Khan in Mongolia. (Why would Lin Biao have wanted to flee to the Soviet Union if he was planning to set up a separate headquarters in the south of China?)

Inside China the tone of mass propaganda changed. The phrases used by Lin Biao disappeared without trace. There had been the 'Two Decisions', those of 1929 and 1960, but all mention of Lin Biao's 1960 Decision was dropped. There was no longer any 1960 Decision, only Mao's Decision of 1929. On the provincial radios the old Lin Biao vocabulary was still being used in September, but after the first week of October, it was no longer heard. The report of the Ninth Party Congress, which had named Lin Biao as successor to Mao, was withdrawn from circulation.[106]

Provincial radios made strange statements about the 'self-destruction of political swindlers', without mentioning Lin Biao. Such men, Anhui radio said in November, ' do not escape their self-destructive fate'. A broadcast from Hainan island said: 'Anyone who dares to oppose the revolutionary line of Chairman Mao . . . will have his body and bones scattered and he will die without finding a place for burial.' On December 1, 1971, the joint editorial of the Peking newspapers said, without mentioning Lin Biao's name, that 'intriguers, men with foreign connections, cannot avoid losing their lives in the end, ruining their reputations and seeking their own destruction.' (These words were taken from the September 18 notification addressed to the highest leaders.)

Peking explains

What really happened in the two years between the Ninth Party Congress in May 1969 and the fall of Lin Biao in September 1971 is not really known, and it would be impossible to give any account of it that could claim even an approximation to certainty. The official Peking version of the story was revealed after long delay early in 1972 in inner-Party documents acquired by Taiwan's agents on the mainland and published in Taiwan. These were never published for the public at large in China, although everyone knew about them. Phrases from the documents were quoted in 1972 on local radio stations. The authenticity of the documents was confirmed when Zhou Enlai, in his report to the Tenth Party Congress in 1973, reiterated things said in those documents.[107]

The two major inner-Party documents were dated, respectively, January 13 and March 17, 1972. Chronologically the latter comes first since it begins its story with the Lushan Plenum of the Central Committee, August 23–September 6, 1970, allegedly as Mao related it to provincial leaders during an inspection tour of several provinces.

This document bears Mao's stamp. As in his unedited speeches — unlike the polished pieces in the five *Selected Works of Mao* — his wording is disorderly, direct and colloquial.

Lushan

During the 1970 Lushan meeting, the document says, Lin Biao, Chen Boda, Lin Biao's wife Ye Qun, four of Lin Biao's generals and the two Peking leaders, Li Xuefeng and Zheng Weishan, plotted against Mao. Mao did not give details of the plot. He alleged only two things, both seemingly innocuous. They wanted to set up a Chairmanship of the State, with Mao himself as Chairman, and they called him a genius. Mao was highly indignant. 'By speaking of genius, they opposed me. I am not a genius. For six years I studied the works of Confucius; for seven more years I studied bourgeois books. It was only in 1918 that I read Marxism-Leninism. Is this genius?'

(Since the fall of Liu Shaoqi in 1966, China has had no President or, to use the customary title, Chairman of the State. Already circulating in the country was a draft for a new State Constitution (drawn up at a Central Committee meeting in September 1970), which designated Mao Head of State for life and Lin Biao as his successor.[108] The authenticity of this draft, which came to us via Taiwan, was confirmed by a February 4, 1970 editorial of the Shandong province newspaper, which called Mao 'the highest leader of the Party and of the State'.[109] No draft of the State Constitution could have been circulated without Mao's consent, yet this newspaper was published before the August–September 1970 Party meeting.

'I said that there should be no Chairman of the Republic and that I would not be Chairman of the Republic,' Mao said. However, the attribution of genius agitated him. 'Lin Biao', he went on, 'said that it had taken the world hundreds of years to produce a genius, and that it had taken China thousands of years. This is nonsense.' There were matters even more important than disowning genius. 'What is this talk' — Mao asked — 'about the People's Liberation Army being created and led by me but commanded by Lin? Can the one who created it not command it? Created? I was not the only one.'

This was a delicate point. For years there had been a confusing variety of ways of speaking about the direction of the army. Before October 1969 Lin Biao was said to be in direct command. On October 1, 1969, National Day, the formula was changed to 'Mao-and-Lin Biao command the army'. On August 1, 1970, the Lin-Biao-alone formula returned; it was used in a circular issued by the State Council, headed by Zhou Enlai, in January 1971, therefore after the critical August–September 1970 Party meeting. Several pronouncements used the Mao-Lin formula, others spoke of Lin Biao alone. Some referred to the army 'founded personally and led by Chairman Mao and directly commanded by Chairman Mao and Vice-Chairman Lin'. There was unmistakable confusion about this not unimportant matter.[110] It all seems to have irritated Mao immensely.

Next Mao told the provincial leaders how he had reacted to the meeting. It was a typical Mao reaction. 'After the Lushan meeting, I took three measures. One was to throw stones. The second was to mix in sand. The third was to dig out the corner-stone from below the walls.' The stones, he explained, were the critical remarks he added to reports from some military areas. This was throwing stones. Next he added his own men to the Military Committee which till then had been dominated by Lin Biao. This was mixing sand. Finally he reorganised the Peking Military Area Command (he changed Li Xuefeng and Zheng Weishan). This was the 'digging out the corner-stone from below the walls'.[111] The 'mixing of sand' was done by Zhou Enlai, who in the spring of 1971 held a North China Party meeting at which he removed the old leaders and launched a new campaign called 'criticism of Chen Boda, and rectification'. In April 1971 new members were added to the Military Committee of the Party Central Committee. Lin Biao's monopoly of leadership had been broken.[112]

Lin Biao's wings had been clipped, but did his generals in the provinces know about it? According to this document, Mao informed them during his travels round the country in August–September 1971, just before Lin Biao fell. Why then was it said later that the fall of Lin Biao had taken his men in the provinces by surprise? The provincial military leaders kept on acclaiming Lin Biao for weeks after his disappearance. Half a year after his death, nationwide propaganda had to explain why Lin Biao's treachery had not been discovered earlier. On December 4, 1971, *Red Flag*, the organ of the Central Committee, went to the trouble of explaining that 'the unmasking of the counter-revolutionary double-dealers takes time'. Yet, 'however much artifice they use to camouflage themselves and however many ruses they try, they do not ultimately escape from the far-sighted penetrating investigation of Chairman Mao.'[113] The conclusion is therefore that the document quoted above is a later fabrication and that Mao did not explain in the course of his tour of the country that the end of Lin Biao, at least his political end, was near.

This document does not explain what really happened at the Lushan meeting in August–September 1970, and why Mao turned against Lin Biao. Was it merely because he had been called a genius, or because of the effort to make him Head of State, or because it had been asserted that Lin Biao was directing the army? People had been saying all these things for years without any reaction from Mao. Thus Zhou Enlai called Mao a genius in April 1966,[114] and Lin Biao did the same at the first meeting of the Red Guards on August 18, 1966. In September 1966 Zhou said that meeting Mao was the highest felicity.[115] Mao allowed Lin Biao to be named in the Party Charter and in the draft State Constitution as his successor. Did Mao think then that Lin Biao wanted to kill him in order to advance the date of his own succession? This was alleged, as we shall see later. But Lin Biao did not plot against Mao's life until after Mao had turned against him and so aroused fears of what might happen to him. From the time of the Party Congress of May 1969 Mao was suspicious of Lin Biao and, in the end, wished to remove him. The explanation may well be, as we said above, that Lin Biao snubbed Jiang Qing, and Jiang Qing, probably influenced by subtle insinuations from Zhou Enlai, then turned Mao against Lin Biao — Zhou would have been well cast to play the part of Iago.

The other inner-Party document, dated January 13, 1972, put forward a quite fantastic tale of how Lin Biao plotted against Mao and how he died. This is contained in a series of published documents, some of them confessions by people of minor rank who are supposed to have taken part in the plot. In February 1971, so this story goes, Lin Biao, his wife Ye Qun and his son Lin Liguo, who had a high post in the air force, began to discuss a counter-revolutionary *coup*. In March, Lin Liguo talked this over with Chen Liyun, a leader of the air force in Zhejiang province and an alternate-member of the Central Committee, and they worked out a plan which Lin Liguo called '571'. The Chinese words for 5–7–1, *wu-qi-yi*, have the same sounds as the words 'armed uprising'. The text of '571' is a fantastic document:

The sufferings of the people have become intolerable. The present change of policy [not explained], B-52's strategy [B-52 stands for Mao], this 'peaceful transformation', must be prevented by violence; otherwise the Chinese revolution will be set back by many years and many heads will fall. There are two possibilities: seize power over the whole country, or divide the country.

The Trotskyites with their busy pens are distorting Marxism-Leninism and are serving their own private interests. Their 'theory of continued revolution' is in fact Trotsky's 'uninterrupted revolution'. He [Mao] is not a true Marxist-Leninist. He is the supreme feudal tyrant emperor, using the weapons of the First Emperor [2nd century BC] and following the paths of Confucius and Mengzi, though clad in a skin of Marxism-Leninism.

Cadres who had had a long history in the Party's struggle were discarded and badly hit during the Cultural Revolution. Now they are angry, but they dare not talk. The peasants have not enough food or clothing. The despatch of young students 'up to the mountains and down to the villages' is camouflaged forced labour. The Red Guards were first deceived, next made use of, and then turned into cannon-fodder, to become scapegoats in the later period. The sending of a number of government cadres to the 'May 7 Cadre Schools' was camouflaged unemployment. The freezing of workers' wages was a form of exploitation.

The Soviet Union is being opposed and attacked. What we are about to do will be supported by the Soviet Union.

Our difficulties are that our forces are not yet well prepared; the masses still have deep, blind faith in B-52; on account of B-52's divide-and-rule tactics there are complex contradictions within the army and it is difficult for us to create a united force; B-52 rarely appears; his movements are hidden and treacherous and tight security surrounds him, and this makes our action really difficult.

Both we and the enemy are in a dilemma ('he who rides a tiger cannot get off'). The present apparent equilibrium cannot last long . . . This is a struggle of life and death. Either we devour them or they devour us.

There are two possible strategies. Either we get ready and devour them, or [we wait till] the enemy opens his mouth to devour us. In such immediate danger we must act whether we are ready or not.

Tactical timing and ways of acting: If B-52 falls into our hands, the enemy battleship [the major leaders] will also be in our hands; they will fall into the trap on their own. Use a high-level meeting to catch them; or cut off his right-hand men — this would do it — or force B-52 to give in; or do it in the form of a palace revolt; or use special methods such as gas or germ warfare, bombing, an arranged car accident, assassination, kidnapping, or city guerilla troops.

Then comes the enumeration of the forces that may be used. Three air force men and two armies are named. 'Outside the country the Soviet Union (secret negotiations). Using the forces of the Soviet Union as a pincer force in and outside the country.'

Then come the slogans: 'Mobilise the masses', 'Unity'; 'Overthrow the feudal dynasty of the contemporary Qin Shi Huang [the First Emperor], B-52'; 'Establish a true proletarian socialist country'; 'Unity

of world proletariat'; 'The five principles of peaceful coexistence';
'Acknowledge diplomatic relations with countries we have relations
with at present and establish them with all countries.'

'The slogan "*min fu guo qiang*" ["when the people are rich the state is
strong"] should replace "*guo fu min qiong*" ["the state is rich but the
people are poor"]. Satisfy the people with enough food and clothing
. . . We should have true Socialism, not the feudalism of B-52.'

The attack was to start when liaison had been firmly established.
'Zhang Chunqiao must be caught and his traitorous crimes must be proclaimed on the mass media . . . Shanghai must be held at all costs; radio
and cable stations and communications must be taken over, so that
Shanghai may be cut off from the outside world. Neutralise Nanjing. If
this cannot be done, prepare defence. Paratroopers and all transport in
Zhejiang and Jiangxi [two provinces] must be firmly held. A showdown on the upper level. Take over mass media and begin political offensive. Expansion of organisation. Rallying the armed forces. Liaison on
all sides.' Wide-ranging cooperation was to be ensured, in contrast with
'the policy of B-52 who uses one group to attack another group today,
and the other group to attack this group tomorrow. He lets cadres fight
cadres, masses fight masses, and military troops fight other troops.'

Look at the history of past decades; where is there a man whom he lifted high
and did not later sentence to political death? What political force could work
with him permanently? Among his past secretaries, some committed suicide,
some were arrested. His few comrades-in-arms and intimate friends have been
sent to jail. His own son was driven to madness by him. He is suspicious and
cruel. When he deals with a person he does not rest until that man is finished
and then he puts the blame on other people. It is the naked truth that one man
after another falls at his hands; all serve as his scapegoats.

Formerly, propaganda for B-52 was a historical necessity for the uniting of
the people; it was useful for resisting foreign enemies. Some of it was spread
under his fascist pressure, and much because people did not know the inside
story surrounding him.

We will protect those comrades and we will liberate all who have suffered
under the oppression of B-52.

The conclusion, only a few lines, orders that the plan be kept secret.[116]

True?

What should one think of this document? It is a Peking document, explaining how this wicked Lin Biao planned his plot and what he thought of the situation. The savagery of the accusations against Mao and the system may make the reader wonder whether these passages were not inserted in Taiwan. The answer is probably No. Mao's prestige was so high — did the Red Guard groups not kill each other to defend him? — that whatever he wanted, however irrational, even making people poor, was considered the infallible truth. Proof of this may be found in the way in which *Red Flag*, the Central Committee's official organ (therefore this is not a secret inner-Party document smuggled out of the country), dealt with the accusation that Mao wanted the state to be strong and the people poor.

In its January 1972 issue, *Red Flag*, still wrestling with Lin Biao a few months after his fall, said — this is an incidental proof of the authenticity of the document — that the Liu-type swindler (as Lin Biao was called in those days) wanted to turn China into a welfare state. China, *Red Flag* said, condemns with all severity what is called egalitarianism. Landlords, kulaks, counter-revolutionaries, bad elements and rightists must be made poor. The Liu-type swindlers took their side. When *Red Flag* said this, Party meetings were being held all over the country to prove how wrong and how anti-Marxist Lin Biao had been. He was compared with Liu Shaoqi, 'the traitor' who wanted people to get better pay. He was like Soviet revisionists who were talking about welfare-ism.[117]

The compiler of '571', whoever he may have been, blundered badly. Those who read it must have felt that the Lin Biao it portrayed had been right. Seven months later *Red Flag* found it necessary to explain: 'Our living standard is still not very high . . . We must undertake a bitter struggle for the distant goal of the proletarian revolution and for the liberation of the oppressed people of the world. The proletarian class will be able to liberate itself only when it has liberated all mankind . . . Are there not people who say, "The real standard of living has fallen"? There are. These are the small cliques of landlords, kulaks and reactionary capitalists . . . The Liu-type swindlers spoke on behalf of these people.'[118] (When Deng Xiaoping came to power seven years later, he launched the motto that people should become rich.)

There are many incomprehensible statements in this '571' project. According to that document, it was not Lin Biao but Mao who first organised the Red Guards and then discarded them when they were no longer of any use; it was Mao who sent the government cadres to the punitive May 7 Cadre Schools.

What about the anti-Mao plot? It is not unlikely that Lin Biao, pushed into a corner, did think out a plot. But it seems unlikely that months of preparation would not have enabled him to muster wider support among his provincial generals, since even after his death they still continued to express enthusiastic loyalty to him.

Lin Biao on history

Perhaps the best way of coming to an understanding of the mind of Lin Biao and the violent events in 1971 is to turn back to the speech he delivered at an enlarged meeting of the Politbureau on May 18, 1966, at the very time when the Cultural Revolution was brewing. He talked of Chinese history, which he described as a long series of revolts and acts of violence:

Throughout the history of our country, there have been changes of government every ten, twenty, thirty or fifty years. In the spring and autumn periods, 600 BC, the small states kept on fighting one another. People killed one another. The son of a king told his father to kill himself; the father obeyed. The Prince of the State of Wu killed the king's minister and seized power. The ministers of the State of Qin fought and killed one another in a struggle for power. People seized power not only by murder but also by ruses and intrigues. The son of the First Emperor killed his brothers and sisters; in all he killed twenty-six persons. After the twelve-year rule of the founder of the Han dynasty, Empress Lu seized power; then two ministers overthrew the Lu family. Emperor Wen of the Sui dynasty was killed by his own son, who became Emperor Yang. Yang killed his brother. The First Emperor of the Tang dynasty killed his two brothers. After the death of the First Emperor of the Ming dynasty, who had ruled for thirty-one years, his fourth son revolted against the old Emperor's grandsons; the two parties kept up their mutual slaughter for three years, and the palace at Nanjing was burnt down. Emperor Kang Xi wanted his fourteenth son to inherit the throne, but he was cheated by Prince Yong, the fourth son, who killed many of his brothers. When the Republic was established, Sun Yat Sen became President, but three months later Yuan Shih Kai seized power. Four months later he made himself Emperor. He was overthrown. Years of internal struggle followed. Chiang Kai Shek seized power and killed many of his enemies.

This was a ghastly outline of China's history. Lin Biao applied the lesson of history to the contemporary world:

In the Soviet Union, the system was overthrown by Khrushchev. In Yugoslavia the change took place earlier. In Hungary there was a revolt in 1956. In China there had been many signs of an impending counter-revolutionary upheaval. Luo Ruiqing held power over the army, and Peng Zhen over the Party, and Lu Dingyi was directing culture and creating public opinion. In combination these men could have generated a counter-revolution. If we are not careful, an occasion for a similar concentration of power may arise again some day. If we are vigilant, however, it will not succeed. They want to kill us, but if they make a move and seek to start a counter-revolutionary conspiracy, we will kill them.[119]

If this was the mind of Lin Biao, then he was a man who, hard-pressed as he was in the first half of 1971, would have been ready to take violent action — although it is hardly possible that he would not have planned something more sensible than the hazardous bombing of a train.

Foreign connections

A puzzling question presents itself. If Lin Biao was in fact on that plane that crashed in Mongolia, why was he fleeing to the Soviet Union? Why not, for example, to Japan? According to the documents, he flew from Weihai, which is on the coast opposite Japan.

There are no indications of his having had russophile leanings. He did say at the Ninth Party Congress of May 1969 that two months earlier the Soviet government had expressed a wish for negotiations, and that the reply was under consideration. But he also spoke of the longing of all good Communists throughout the world to overthrow the Soviet revisionists.[120] This speech does not tell us much about Lin Biao. In foreign policy the only ideas he was free to express were those of Mao. What it does prove is that in those days, in May 1969, Mao was not yet thinking of a change in foreign policy and of rapprochement with the United States.

As is well known, Peking's policy towards the United States changed radically as soon as voices coming from the Pentagon seemed to be saying that Taiwan was not within the US defence line, and secret diplomatic messages began to come from President Nixon.

On April 10, 1971, American table-tennis players arrived in Peking and with them were invited US journalists and television men[121] — this led to Kissinger's first visit two months later and to President Nixon's visit to China in 1972.

It was certainly not Lin Biao who introduced this new foreign policy. It was not Lin Biao who changed Mao's thinking. It can only have been Zhou Enlai, who after the decline and fall of Lin Biao — possibly manipulated by him — became the central figure in China. The swing towards the United States, which was visible in Peking in the spring of 1971, may explain why Lin Biao, if he wanted to flee, could not choose a different direction and take refuge in, say, pro-US Japan.

There is another unanswered question. Was the change of foreign policy orientation a cause of the estrangement between Mao and Lin Biao? A positive answer would imply that rapprochement with the United States was thought out immediately after the Ninth Party Congress held in May 1969, the time when Mao seemed to have turned against Lin Biao. This is unlikely: Mao's distrust of Lin Biao was not caused by foreign policy. But the decline of Lin Biao's authority, after the August–September 1970 Lushan meeting, offered a chance for Zhou Enlai, the mastermind of Chinese diplomacy, to exert his influence.

Through all these turbulent years even major events, internal or external, seemed to leave the internal wrangle between the leaders unaffected. There was the military confrontation with the Soviet Union along the northern Ussuri River in March 1969, and the first Chinese satellite was launched in April 1970 (the military were in charge of the nuclear programme). Yet these things did not strengthen Lin Biao's position. The Ninth Party Congress was held two months after the Ussuri incident; the Lushan meeting was held four months after the launching of the satellite. Military achievements could not save Lin Biao.

Reconstruction of the Party

When the Ninth Party Congress was held in April 1959, the Party organisation around the country had not yet been reconstituted. Towards the end of 1967 some provinces began to talk about reorganising the Party,[122] but there was too much disorder in the country to allow this. The men of the Reactionary Trend, the radio of Zhejiang province said, 'want neither rebels nor conservatives, nor men on the capitalist road; they want elections by all.'[123]

The first Party committee was established in a county in Hunan province in November 1969, seven months after the Party Congress.[124] A year later about sixty of the 2,000 counties had their Party committees.

Between December 1970 and March 1971, nine of the twenty-six provinces or equivalent Autonomous Areas established their Party committees. In the other provinces, initial 'Party nuclei' had been formed in preparation for the establishment of provincial Party committees.

The re-establishment of the Party was led by the no. 8341 military troop, stationed in Peking. This was Mao's intelligence organisation and his personal guard. It was led by Wang Dongxing, who at the Ninth Party Congress became an alternate-member of the Politbureau. In the first issue of *Red Flag* in 1970, an article by the 8341 troop, without mention of Wang's name, spoke of opposition to the reorganisation of the Party coming from the 'rebels' of the Cultural Revolution — the Red Guard bands — who were boasting that they were the pioneers of the revolution and that the Party reconstruction must be led by them: 'We must be its foundation stones.' *Red Flag* called this 'reactionary anarchism', and referred to Lin Biao's speech at the Party Congress in which he said that the political power must lie with the proletariat (for him the proletariat meant the army).[125]

Army generals became leaders of the new Party organs, but not all generals were ardent supporters of Lin Biao. To find the right candidates for the new Party organs, provincial 'activist' congresses and provincial 'Four-Good' congresses were held. By the end of January 1971 activist congresses had been held in all provinces. Only a few provinces held 'Four-Good' congresses. The 'Four-Good' was Lin Biao's formula, and had its origin in the army in the early 1960s. During the Cultural Revolution it was extended to the civilian population. Nevertheless, not all provinces hastened to hold 'Four-Good' congresses.

The holding of these congresses was reported only in the provinces. The *People's Daily* omitted all mention of them, thus avoiding the embarrassment of having the public see that things were not proceeding uniformly in the provinces, and that only seven provinces had held 'Four-Good' congresses.[126]

All the provinces had their Party committees established by August 1971[127] — a few weeks before the disappearance of Lin Biao. In twenty of the twenty-six provinces the First Party secretary was a soldier. In the other six the number two figure was a military man. Of the twenty Party leaders who were military men, six were concurrently commanders and three were political commissars of regions wider than provincial military areas.[128] Apparently the regional military men were not yet aware that after the August–September 1970 Lushan meeting, Lin Biao's fate was sealed.

Marxism

To the many victims of the Cultural Revolution one special figure should be added, Marx himself.

In the brand of Marxism produced during the Cultural Revolution,

Marx, Engels, Lenin and Stalin were approved only because they were the forerunners of the sole genuine Marxist, Mao. Mao had already been glorified as a world leader before the Cultural Revolution in a huge theatrical performance produced on National Day in 1964. On the stage, all the nations of the world paid homage to an image of Mao high in the sky.

On November 6, 1967, the fiftieth anniversary of the Russian October Revolution was celebrated. No Russians were present, nor was Mao. The speaker was Lin Biao, who expressed regret that revisionists who had abandoned genuine Marxism had seized power in the Soviet Union and other Communist countries. The highest standard of Marxism-Leninism had been reached in China in the Thoughts of Mao, he said.

On the same day the joint editorial of Peking papers said: 'We shall never forget the Bolshevik party and the October Revolution. Unfortunately, a small clique of men on the capitalist road seized power in Party and government in the Soviet Union. Khrushchev of putrid memory and his successors Brezhnev and Kosygin introduced free competition and profit under a cloak of building Communism, and turned ownership by the whole people and collective farming into capitalist institutions and kulak farms. They brought in Western bourgeois culture and put the Communist morality of Lenin and Stalin on ice. They plead "peaceful coexistence" when they kneel at the feet of US imperialism, and form a "holy alliance" with all the reactionaries of the world against China.'

They are not genuine Marxists. 'Comrade Mao Zedong's development of Marxist-Leninist doctrine on proletarian dictatorship is epoch-making. In the history of Marxism this is the third great monument.' (The first was Marx's, the second Lenin's, the third Mao's.) The revolutionary people of the world have come to recognise ever more clearly that Comrade Mao Zedong is the greatest teacher and the most outstanding leader. Chairman Mao is the Lenin of the present age. The Thoughts of Mao Zedong are the perfection of Marxism-Leninism. By means of the Thoughts of Mao Zedong one can distinguish genuine Marxism from revisionism. At the end of the eighteenth century the centre of revolution was in France, in the middle of the nineteenth it was in Germany. The proletarian class stepped on the political stage and Marxism was produced. In the early years of the twentieth century, the centre of revolution was transferred to Russia, and Leninism was produced. Subsequently the centre of world revolution moved gradually to

China and the Thoughts of Mao Zedong were produced. With the great proletarian Cultural Revolution, China, this centre of world revolution, became firmer and stronger.

The content of Mao's brand of Marxism was described thus: It means continued (not 'permanent') revolution under proletarian dictatorship. There are antagonistic and non-antagonistic contradictions (as Mao had said in his 1957 speech); there is class struggle; dictatorship must be exercised over the bourgeois class in cultural fields; those in the Party on the capitalist road must be beaten down; the Cultural Revolution should touch the souls of people and form their world outlook.[129]

In other words, genuine Marxism is found only in China: it is the Thought of Mao. It should be noted, however, that these words were not said by Mao; Mao was absent from the celebration.

Permanent Revolution

The Trotskyite Permanent Revolution had a curious history in China. When Trotsky was still a power in the Communist International in the 1920s, he had several followers among Chinese students in Moscow. They returned to China in the late 1920s — Trotsky by then had been expelled from the Party in the Soviet Union. In China they formed a small group and held two congresses in Shanghai in 1929, but they were unable to create a mass movement. In the 1930s only a few individual followers of Trotsky's theories remained. Nevertheless the official Communist Party, followers of Stalin, branded all their enemies 'Trotskyites'.[130]

After the establishment of the People's Republic, Trotsky's Permanent Revolution was still considered a heresy. The 1953 *Shanghai Dictionary of New Terms* described Trotskyism as an anti-Communist doctrine. In 1958, no one knows how or why, Permanent Revolution became the official thesis of the Chinese Communist Party. In January 1958 Mao held a meeting of Party secretaries of southern provinces and expounded the idea of Permanent Revolution.[131] In May 1958, at the second session of the Eighth Party Congress, Liu Shaoqi said: 'For a long period the Party Central and Mao Zedong have used the Marxist-Leninist doctrine on Permanent Revolution to lead the revolution in China . . . We are arriving now at a new stage in the uninterrupted development of the revolution.'[132]

The editorial in the November 1968 issue of *Red Flag* said that the foundations of this doctrine had been laid by Mao in March 1949 (a few months before he entered Peking) at the Second Central Committee Plenum (the second since 1945). Later, it had been 'enriched and developed into the doctrine of Continued Revolution under Proletarian Dictatorship'. In the same issue of *Red Flag* the text of this 1949 report by Mao was published. The term Continued Revolution is not found in it. In those days — Stalin was still alive — Trotsky and his theories were anathema.

At the Ninth Party Congress, held in April 1969, Lin Biao said that Chairman Mao had put forward the doctrine of Continuing the Revolution under the Dictatorship of the Proletariat', but these words were not dignified with the quotation marks usually accorded to Mao's words. Lin Biao made no mention of Stalin, for the simple reason that Stalin had spoken of Socialism in One Country whereas Trotsky had said the revolution would succeed after world revolution. Lin Biao said at the Congress that 'the final victory of a socialist country depends on the victory of world revolution'.

Three months after the Party Congress, on July 5, 1969, the *People's Daily* published a full-page article about Trotsky and the Permanent (Uninterrupted) Revolution. Trotsky, it said, deviated from genuine Marxism. He was followed in China by all the enemies of the Party, from Zhen Duxiu to Li Lisan and Wang Ming (all enemies of Mao). Chairman Mao proposed not Permanent Revolution but Continued Revolution, which is the Cultural Revolution.

Marx, the *People's Daily* said, spoke of proletarian class dictatorship which would extinguish the distinction between the classes. Lenin developed this doctrine and spoke of 'class struggle under proletarian dictatorship'. Lenin, however, died early and did not solve this problem. Chairman Mao applied the theory of Permanent Revolution creatively to the transition period from Socialism to Communism. 'He was the first to state clearly that when the means of production have been socialised, there will still be class struggle and the proletariat will still have to continue the revolution.'

This theory is an immense contribution to world Communism. It offers to the proletariat of all countries a weapon for taking back power from the revisionists (in the Soviet Union and elsewhere). This theory of Chairman Mao's 'organically combines the theory of Permanent Revolution and the theory of stages or revolution'. The article referred to the Sixth Plenum of the Eighth Central Committee held in November –December 1958, which said: 'We follow the theory of Permanent

Revolution. We follow the theory of stages of revolution. The stage of Socialism must precede the stage of Communism. This is 'the theory of continued revolution in stages' — the theory of Trotsky.[133]

Stuart R. Schram, an expert on this matter, was puzzled by Peking's use of the term 'Continued Revolution'.[134] The solution probably is that Mao followed Trotsky's theory but used a modified term to fend off accusations of Trotskyism.

How this change, this acceptance of Trotsky's theories, came about has never been explained. It fitted into Mao's grandiose ambitions for world revolution. Did he adopt the new line under the influence of Lin Biao, or did Lin Biao accept Mao's new way of speaking? It seems very odd to find the 1972 inner-Party document quoting Lin Biao saying that those who propose the theory of Continued Revolution merely use a different term for Trotsky's Uninterrupted Revolution. The document added that Mao was not a true Marxist-Leninist.

Who then were the Trotskyites, Mao, the scribbling satellites of Jiang Qing, Zhang Chunqiao and Yao Wenyuan, or Lin Biao? Lin Biao undoubtedly spoke at the Party Congress of Continued Revolution and of World Revolution as a precondition for success at home. These are pure Trotskyite theses.

Will

The most peculiar feature of the brand of Marxism developed during the Cultural Revolution was its voluntarism, the assertion that determination, willpower, the force of the spirit — if fed on the Thoughts of Mao —, can achieve anything. In February 1966, a few months before the eruption of the Cultural Revolution violence, the army newspaper said: 'In discussing the relation of Spirit and Matter, one must say that Matter is primary and Spirit is secondary. [This is correct Marxism.] It is only of the genesis of thought that it is said that Matter comes first, then Spirit. It is not true of the strength of the two. The strength of Spirit is much greater than that of Matter . . . Once the masses see correct thoughts, there then emerges a great material force. Therefore we must pay great attention to ideological work. The Thoughts of Mao Zedong are the sun in our hearts, the root of our lives, the source of all our strength. Through them, man becomes unselfish, daring, intelligent, able to do anything . . . The Thoughts of Mao Zedong transform man's ideology, transform the Fatherland . . . Through them the oppressed people of the world will rise.' *Red Flag* in discussing this idea in June of the same year said: 'This is a great truth, a great development of Marxism-Leninism.'[135]

Even a year earlier, in 1965, Xiao Hua, then Lin Biao's spokesman, said that Lin Biao 'applied Chairman Mao's pattern of military thought creatively'. Without the Spirit how could we, with primitive equipment, have triumphed over Chiang Kai Shek and the Japanese, and the Americans in Korea?[136]

In 1964 the army published the *Selected Readings of Mao Zedong's Writings*. This volume contained Mao's short note 'Where Do Correct Ideas Come From?' in which Mao explained the Marxist theory of process from Matter to Spirit and then from Spirit to Matter.[137] This was the theory that Lin Biao picked up and amplified. Marx was replaced by the Thoughts of Mao, and the subtle interaction between matter and spirit — excogitated by Engels in the nineteenth century — became the all-dominant theory of the power of the Spirit.

This was the basis of many of Lin Biao's utterances which became guiding mottoes during the Cultural Revolution. The 'Four-Good Company campaign' was launched as early as 1960 at the famous meeting of the military committee. Six years later during the Cultural Revolution it was extended to the civilian population, to factories, villages and schools. The 'first of the four' was to shape the other three. The 'Four-Good' were: correct political ideology, military spirit, military training and care for livelihood. The first was the most important.[138]

What would the Marxist forefathers have said of this doctrine of the predominance of spiritual forces? In China too, some people wondered.

As the newspaper of Jiangxi province said in 1969: 'Some may say that political thought is not visible and tangible, whereas doing a job is something tangible. They forget that the Thoughts of Mao paint a man's thoughts red and make him ready not to fear hardship, not to fear death. A man who has this has no insurmountable obstacles, no invincible enemies. Politics [i.e. ideology] may not be visible, but its effects are visible in material accomplishments.'

Not to fear death is a typical military term. The phrase 'One, not to fear hardship; Two, not to fear death' smacked of the barrack-room. The phrase became a sacred axiom. The July 1 Army Day 1969 editorial of the joint Peking newspapers (written four months after the Ussuri border incident with the Soviet Union) extolled the heroic soldiers who did not fear hardship or death. That was not all; inspiring stories were written about soldiers who, when wounded and dying, invoked Mao or looked at his picture. And not only soldiers. Mao-gazing heroes were pictured dying in fires or trying to save people from under the wheels of oncoming trains. There was a man, an ordinary local Party leader, who was found dead with his eyes still fixed on the *Sayings of Mao* — heroes, soldiers, proletarians not afraid of hardship, not afraid of death. (There was not a single educated member of the middle classes among these heroes.)[139]

This was the Marxism of Lin Biao. It was the Marxism of the barracks. In those years there was no longer a single genuine Marxist scholar in evidence. Li Da, perhaps the only independent Marxist scholar China ever had, died in August 1966 at the age of seventy-seven in the first onslaught of the Red Guards. Ai Siqi, the author of The *Philosophy of the Masses*, died, some say was killed, a few months before the outbreak of the Cultural Revolution. Pan Zinian disappeared during the Cultural Revolution. Feng Ding, professor of Marxism at Peking University, had his famous book, *The Ordinary Truth*, condemned. Of the old guard, only Chen Boda remained, serving Jiang Qing and Lin Biao until he fell from power at the August–September 1970 Party meeting. There remained only Lin Biao's second-rate scribblers, exalters of the glory of the Spirit.

When did the Cultural Revolution end?

It may be asked, when did the Cultural Revolution end? If the Cultural Revolution means the general disorder, the launching of the Red Guards, the *Little Red Book*, the 'Hail Mao', 'Chairman Mao the Sun in our Hearts', and the like, it can be said that it ended with the Ninth Party Congress in 1969. The army took control, hesitantly in 1967, decisively in 1968. The Red Guards, Jiang Qing's revolutionary small generals, were submerged in the ocean of China's villages. Lin Biao's military were taking over power in the provinces and were leading the revolutionary committees everywhere. The Cultural Revolution, in the form in which it was greeted with worldwide enthusiasm, had ended.

There was never any formal announcement of the day on which the Cultural Revolution ended; but in 1969 references were often made to 'the three years of Cultural Revolution', which meant from the middle of 1966 to the Ninth Party Congress in April 1969.[140] It can be said, with good reason, that the Cultural Revolution ended with the death of Lin Biao. The whole Cultural Revolution, its prelude, its drama, the Ninth Party Congress itself, had one aim: to push aside all who opposed Lin Biao and to make him Mao's successor. This was achieved — at a fantastic price — but after so many had died, the hero of the drama met a tragic end. The great play was over.

After Deng Xiaoping had taken over the direction of affairs in 1979, it became routine to say that the Cultural Revolution had lasted ten years, from 1966 to the death of Mao in 1976. One could perhaps say that it had not ended even in the 1980s. In 1984 Deng Xiaoping's regime started a fierce campaign to eradicate the remnants of the Cultural Revolution. It was found that the 'rebel' groups formed during those years were still in existence sixteen years later, and that many men in responsible positions still felt solidarity with those with whom they had fought side-by-side in the heady days of the Red Guards. Moreover, the wounds inflicted by the Cultural Revolution on millions of families did not heal easily. The years of the Cultural Revolution are bound to have a lasting effect on the history of China in this century.

CHAPTER XVIII

THE LAST YEARS OF MAO, 1972–1976

The Chinese Communist Party was led to success by Mao Zedong. This can hardly be denied. The Party was his party. After 1949 not only the Communist Party but the whole nation was moulded to his image; even after he had gone and when his colossal mistakes could not be denied, he still dominated China. When alive he ruled the nation by abrupt political campaigns. After his death the leadership swore that there would be no more political campaigns, but the country was in fact still ruled in the same old way. Reforms were launched from the top and were echoed everywhere.

Mao wanted to abandon the traditional Chinese way of writing, and this ambition persisted though nobody knew how to bring it to fruition. His language, the terms he used, entered into the common speech and writing of the people. Even his enemies could hardly think in any terms but Mao's. His poems — all Chinese leaders write poems — were known by heart.

The man who ruled the Party for thirty years and the country for twenty-seven years ended his life weak and in physical decline, but he still controlled the country and he kept on trying desperately to ensure that his style of regime should endure.

A vacuum: The army

The disappearance of Lin Biao stunned the military, who were the dominant power in the newly-established Party committees and the regional and local governments, or revolutionary committees, as they were called. The highest posts in the army, vacated through the disappearance of Lin Biao's men in September 1971, were not filled for years. China had no minister of defence, no Chief-of-Staff, no head of logistics, no political commissars of the navy, no commander of the air force.[1] Marshal Ye Jianying, who had played a modest role during the Cultural Revolution and did not seem to be close to Lin Biao, became the leading figure in the army, with the title of Deputy Chairman of the C.C.'s Military Committee (Mao was Chairman).[2] Several of the regional commanders (Lin Biao's men) had disappeared or been transferred to other regions, and their posts were filled by a transfer of generals from the Northeast and from the Nanjing Great Military Area, the two military commands which had been led by Chen Xilian and Xu Shiyou, neither of whom had supported Lin Biao. However, not all of Lin Biao's men were dismissed. Han Xianchu, for example, who was commanding the troops in the two provinces facing Taiwan, remained.[3]

Some of Lin Biao's early followers, men who had been with him in the Northeast from where he had started his military conquest of the country, were not touched. A joint editorial of the Peking newspapers gave an explanation of sorts. Lin Biao, it said, had been a failure in the Northeast. It was not he but Mao who won the military victory. Moreover, there were in the region some troops and some generals who had resisted the manipulations of the Liu-type swindler — Lin Biao's sobriquet — and retained their good spirit. This was 'the story of the apple'. In autumn when the apples were ripe in the Northeast, the article explained, these good soldiers kept discipline and never touched an apple.[4]

Lin Biao, some press articles averred, had been wicked from the beginning, from the days in Jing Gang Shan, Mao's bastion at the end of the 1920s. Even then Lin Biao 'raised the Red Flag to oppose the Red Flag'. He was a pessimist, and was reprimanded by Mao. (Once you are condemned you are black all through.)[5]

The Party

Lin Biao's disappearance left the highest Party leadership in complete disarray. The top leadership, the Standing Committee of the Politbureau, was only a shadow of its former self. Of its five members, Lin Biao and Chen Boda had gone; only three, Mao, Zhou Enlai and Kang Sheng, remained. Kang Sheng found it wiser at that time to appear only rarely in public.

The Politbureau, set up two years earlier at the Ninth Party Congress, consisted of twenty-one full and four alternate-members. Of the twenty-five, eight had been ousted: Lin Biao and his wife Ye Qun; Chen Boda, who had been arrested after the Lushan meeting; and Lin Biao's chief generals Huang Yongsheng, the Chief-of-Staff, Wu Faxian, head of the air force, Li Xuefeng, political commissar of the navy, and Qiu Huizuo, commander of logistics. (Qiu was still visible in September, and then was no longer to be seen.) When the North China leadership was purged after the Lushan meeting, Li Xuefeng went. Three members of the Politbureau, Dong Biwu and the two marshals, Zhu De and Liu Bocheng, were too old to count. It was a truncated Politbureau.[6]

No list of precedence for the leaders was published, but in public appearances Jiang Qing came immediately after the three Politbureau Standing Committee members, Mao, Zhou Enlai and Kang Sheng.

Ye Jianying, as was said above, quietly took over the difficult task of leading a badly battered army. Another prominent figure was General Li Desheng, who, though still First Party secretary and commander of Anhui province, stayed in Peking where he had been the head of the General Political Department of the army since the summer of 1970. Another was Wang Dongxing, a cloak-and-dagger figure, head of the guards and Mao's secret intelligence network. During the Cultural Revolution he became the head of the General Office of the Party Central Committee. In the summer of 1971, when the conflict between Mao and Lin Biao was reaching its climax, Wang disappeared from the public eye for six months, probably too busy with intrigue to appear. However, at the end of 1971, three months after the death of Lin Biao, it was he who presided over the traditional New Year's Eve dinner for foreign experts in China.[7]

After the disappearance of Lin Biao, two persons stood out, Zhou Enlai and Jiang Qing. The history of the next few years is the history of the struggle between these two, not only between the two personalities but also between the two systems they represented. Mao could still feel that he was in supreme command. As Lin Biao put it in his Project 571, Mao had always enjoyed playing one group against another. Now he found the two groups particularly useful. One, led by Zhou Enlai, made a success of the new venture in foreign policy; the other might bring his old revolutionary dreams true.

Zhou Enlai

Zhou Enlai's position at home was difficult. The leaders of the Great Military Areas, who still exercised great power over the provinces, and most of the new leaders of the provincial Party committees, were military men.[8]

When dealing with foreign policy, his field *par excellence*, Zhou was in his element. Six years earlier he had failed in his efforts to establish an 'A-A-A' (Asian-African-Latin American) axis, and so torpedo the United Nations. This time he succeeded brilliantly in winning China a seat in the UN Security Council and in bringing the President of the United States to China.

In February 1972 President Nixon himself came to pay his homage to the Chinese 'court', and this visit was followed by an avalanche of diplomatic recognitions of the People's Republic. It was Zhou Enlai who shared with Nixon the signing of the famous Shanghai Declaration. The Taiwan question appeared to be coming near to solution. The Sino-US rapprochement changed the political configuration of the whole world. This was Zhou Enlai's supreme achievement.[9]

Jiang Qing

Meanwhile Jiang Qing was keeping alive Mao's old dream of a revolutionary new China. In 1971 she rarely appeared in public, except on very important occasions. Jiang Qing had been humiliated by Lin Biao, but she had snubbed him at the Ninth Party Congress, and now she was once again on top.

The indicator of Jiang Qing's importance was the treatment given to the performance of her theatrical creations, the famous *Model Plays*. They were highly praised every May (on the anniversary of Mao's 1942 'Speech on Literature and Art'). Months ahead it became clear that the 1972 performance would be a major occasion. Several provinces began their preparations at the end of 1971 for the May 1972 celebration of the '*Eight Revolutionary Model Plays* created and chiselled with exquisite care under the personal leadership of Comrade Jiang Qing', as a broadcast from Xinjiang put it.

On May 23, 1972, the joint editorial of the Peking newspapers, when heralding the thirtieth anniversary of Mao's 'Speech on Literature and Art', lavished high praise on Jiang Qing's plays. Various provincial newspapers followed suit. Hubei province said that Jiang Qing's *Model Plays* were 'the best weapons for criticism of Lin Biao'.

Her revolutionary plays, the Hubei province newspaper said, train people to become revolutionary, to hit and destroy the class enemy, to demolish the old morality and establish the new; they teach the fundamentals of economy and promote learning from Dazhai, the model village where people work out of enthusiasm, not for money. When Jiang Qing's Peking Opera troupe arrived in Anhui province, the Party leaders lined up at the railway station to receive them. Li Desheng, the boss of Anhui, outdid all others in bombastic praise of Jiang Qing. In 1969, when Jiang Qing was overshadowed by Lin Biao and had to retreat, Anhui's enthusiasm faded away, but as soon as Lin Biao was dead, its praise of the lady returned *fortissimo*. Li Desheng was a careerist.[10]

Yet not everyone joined in the chorus. The thirtieth anniversary of Mao's talk was celebrated everywhere, but the provincial First Party secretaries remained silent.[11]

1972: China's year

The growth of Jiang Qing's prestige made life ever more difficult for Zhou Enlai. On October 14, 1972, a whole page of the *People's Daily* was occupied by three articles about anarchism, which levelled accusations of every kind against Lin Biao. Ten years were to pass before the public learnt from a book published in Shanghai, *Records of Major Events of Modern and Contemporary Chinese History*, that these articles had been written on the instruction of Zhou Enlai and with his approval. Lin Biao, the 'Liu-type swindler' as the articles called him, was described as an unscrupulous deceiver of people who thought only of extolling himself. He was an anarchist who defied all authority, sought the abolition of the Party, and rejected government and all discipline. During the Cultural Revolution, wanting to smash everything, he launched an ultra-left trend. All he wanted was to seize power, absolute power.[12]

A book published in Shanghai ten years later revealed that this article had been attacked in an inner-Party paper, written by Zhang Chunqiao and Yao Wenyuan, Jiang Qing's two writers. The article, they said, denied the value of the Cultural Revolution.

However, 1972 belonged to Zhou Enlai rather than to Jiang Qing's radicals. There was a slight relaxation of cultural policy and some books on ancient history were reprinted. The theatre became more lively. All songs and plays still had to echo the heroes and the evil men in Jiang Qing's operas, but the provincial theatrical styles, with singing in local dialects, re-emerged in great variety. Under Lin Biao the national peculiarities of the minorities had been disregarded. After his fall more attention was paid to the languages of the nationalities, and their way of life was recognised. Even Jiang Qing's *Model Plays* were sung in the languages of the minorities. In Inner Mongolia, Mongolian musicians were allowed for the first time to reappear in public, singing in their own language. The Nationality Colleges, one in Tibet and one in Yunnan, had disappeared during the Cultural Revolution; in 1972 they were reopened. Family clans revived. A slight relaxation in agricultural policy, introduced in 1971, continued. In the villages the area of private

plots expanded and the peasants turned to profitable activities, trans-
porting goods in handcarts and doing anything that would bring in
money. Even the local Party secretaries promoted money-earning
occupations. The provincial authorities, still mostly soldiers, were in an
embarrassing situation. An editorial of the Shaanxi provincial Party
paper blamed those who said that 'if production develops, deviation in
policy matters little.' Others, reported the *Inner Mongolian Daily*, con-
soled themselves with the thought that, in this uninterrupted revolution, the march towards Communism is made in stages. They were torn
between the relaxation of policy coming from one quarter in Peking,
Zhou Enlai's quarter, and the radicalism they were used to.

Zhou Enlai succeeded in rehabilitating a great number of ex-Party
leaders on all levels. The soldier who had emerged during the Cultural
Revolution and become the leader of Zhejiang province, now disappeared and his post was given to Tan Qilong, a former First Party
secretary of another province. Three or four similar changes took place
in other provinces. In Hunan, Mao's own province, Hua Guofeng had
the title of First Party secretary, but he was living in Peking, and at that
time it was not yet known in what capacity. A soldier called Bu Zhanya
was running the province (later this man was sent back to the army).

On August 21, 1972, the army's role in the civilian administration
was curtailed. An instruction was issued that in all places where the
Party committees had been established, the army's 'aid-left' organs were
to be dissolved.[13] This instruction was not published in the press, and
even years later the aid-left function of the army was still being praised
highly.[14]

In October, Zhou Peiyuan, a well-known scientist and vice-president
of a major university in Peking, published an article containing what in
those days ranked as a sensational novelty, a plea for educational reform
and for the re-introduction of the teaching of theoretical basic science.
Nine years later an inner-Party publication said that this article was
written on Zhou Enlai's instructions. Zhou Peiyuan's article did not
appear in the *People's Daily*, the official paper of the C.C.[15]

1973

The underlying tension between Zhou Enlai and the radicals was real but
it was scarcely visible. In the following year, 1973, the conflict came to
the surface. Under the influence of Jiang Qing's radicals, Mao declared
in December 1972, though this was not made public at the time, that Lin

Biao, contrary to all appearances, was not an extreme leftist but an extreme rightist. Propaganda was to be orchestrated to this change.[16]

Under Marxist regimes the concept of left and right is of paramount importance. A Marxist regime confesses itself to be on the left, which means progressive, but not on the extreme left, which means ultra-radicalism; and certainly not on the right, which means retrograde, reactionary, conservative. As became clear later, it was at the time when Zhou Enlai was being called a Confucianist that Jiang Qing and her followers asserted that they were the genuine radicals, the genuine leftists, whereas Zhou was a conservative, just as Lin Biao had been.

The description of Lin Biao as a conservative rightist was hard to swallow. The January 1973 issue of *Red Flag* introduced the theme timidly, saying that the main stream and side streams, the essence and appearances, should be distinguished. The provinces, which had already received the order from Peking, began to call Lin Biao a 'rightist'. When the ground had been prepared, the March 1973 issue of *Red Flag* put the question: 'Was the essence of the Liu-type swindlers's [Lin Biao's] aberration extreme-left or extreme-right?' The answer was: 'The Liu-type swindler was extremely cunning and seemed to be leftist, but the essence of his error was extreme rightist.' No one should be misled by the way Lin Biao and his men acted; they seemed to be leftists but they were rightists. They broke the unity between politics and the economy. They opposed the overall leadership of politics, yet they also said that politics can sweep everything away and they held that military matters are the highest politics. They defended the bourgeois class, and the landlords, kulaks, counter-revolutionaries, bad elements and rightists. In the international field they represented the interests of the revisionists and surrendered to Soviet imperialism. Their extreme leftism was only a pretence, not the essence. It was only a means, not the end. The Liu-type swindlers changed white into black and denied the value of the great Cultural Revolution.[17]

Accusing Lin Biao of being a conservative rightist who opposed the revolutionary acts of the Cultural Revolution may have sounded absurd, but once Peking had said anything, everyone had to repeat what had been said.

In Peking only two people besides Mao really counted, Zhou Enlai and Jiang Qing. Zhou had tried, without much success, to moderate the radicals during the Cultural Revolution; Jiang Qing had inflamed them. Zhou Enlai represented the old guard; Jiang Qing was the radical future. Zhou Enlai was the symbol of reason; Jiang Qing was the dashing revolutionary. It is impossible that Zhou Enlai can have wished to attribute to Lin Biao the conservatism which he himself represented above all. Only Jiang Qing can have wished that.

The Tenth Party Congress

In August 24, 1973, a Party Congress, the Tenth, was held, four years after the Ninth, which had made Lin Biao Mao's heir-designate. This Tenth Party Congress lasted only four days and ended on August 28. The first official announcement of even the fact that it had been held was not made till a day after it had ended. In China it is possible to gather over a thousand people for such an important meeting as this without the public knowing anything about it. The Congress was not announced in advance and there was no sign of provincial Party organisations having held regional congresses to elect representatives to the national congress.

The Congress deliberated nothing. Those who filled the first seats of the Praesidium of this Congress session were those who were to become Vice-Chairmen of the C.C. Everything had been neatly fixed in advance; the Congress was a mere formality. During the Congress, Zhou Enlai and a group of Party leaders found time to take part in the opening of an Asian-African table-tennis tournament. Sitting on either side of Mao at the Praesidium were Zhou Enlai, a young man named Wang Hongwen, Kang Sheng, Marshal Ye Jianying and General Li Desheng. Immediately after the Congress, these five were 'elected' by the Central Committee as the five Vice-Chairmen of the Party.

The Seventh Congress in 1945 in Yan'an did not elect Vice-Chairmen. The Eighth in 1956 elected four, Liu Shaoqi, Zhou Enlai, Zhu De and Chen Yun (two years later Lin Biao became the fifth Vice-Chairman). The Ninth Congress in 1969 elected only one Vice-Chairman, Lin Biao.

In the Standing Committee of the Politbureau were Mao, the five Vice-Chairmen plus two very old men, Zhu De and Dong Biwu (both died within the next three years), and Zhang Chunqiao. Wang Hongwen, Vice-Chairman, a young man in his thirties, and Zhang Chunqiao, in his fifties, were from Shanghai and were the radical acolytes of Jiang Qing. General Li Desheng, though still the leader of Anhui province, was resident in Peking, and was the head of the General Political Department of the army. He was an ambitious man, who in his province, Anhui, year after year announced widely publicised spectacular achievements. The Seventh Congress in 1945 elected a C.C. Secretariat, headed by Mao himself. Deng Xiaoping was head of the Secretariat of the Eighth Congress. The Ninth Congress of 1969 and the Tenth Congress did not set up a Secretariat at all.

The Politbureau consisted of twenty-one regular members, including the seven members of the Politbureau's Standing Committee, and four alternate-members. The Politbureau members included Wang Dongxing, whom we discussed earlier, Hua Guofeng, the First Party secretary of Hunan province, and Wu De, in 1956–65 First Party secretary of Jilin province, Manchuria, and now First Party secretary of Peking city. There was also Chen Yonggui, the famous peasant leader of Dazhai. Among the four Politbureau candidate-members was Ni Zhifu, a young worker who later became head of the official Trade Union and survived the changes after the death of Mao. There was also a woman worker, Wu Guixian, who later disappeared from the scene. Jiang Qing was a regular member of the Politbureau. She was not a member of the Politbureau Standing Committee, but was first in rank after the Standing Committee members.

The Congress formally expelled Lin Biao and Chen Boda from the Party. It was asserted, as had been asserted in earlier days about Liu Shaoqi, that Chen Boda — Mao's faithful scriptwriter for thirty years — had been a Kuomintang agent from the beginning. Chen Boda was deprived of all his offices in the Party and outside. It was not asserted whether Lin Biao had been a Kuomintang agent or not. Lin Biao was dead. The Congress condemned the 'other principal members of the anti-Party Lin Biao clique', but did not name them. It prescribed nationwide criticism of Lin Biao, study of Marxism-Leninism and of the Thoughts of Mao, and a 'struggle-criticism-change' campaign in the cultural field. The slogan 'Continued Revolution under Proletarian Dictatorship' was reaffirmed. The Three Basic Principles (also called 'Three Must, Three Must Not') were launched: 'Follow Marxism, not revisionism; be united and do not split ranks; walk along the great bright road and do not engage in conspiratorial treachery.'

The Congress communiqué, when speaking about foreign policy, did not start as communiqués had always started on such occasions by saying that the situation was excellent. It began with the words: 'At present the international situation is particularly confused, but this confusion is not a bad thing but a good thing.' It went on to say that the two superpowers, the United States and the Soviet Union, must be opposed and that the whole country must be vigilant, particularly in watching for a sudden attack by Social Imperialism. Social Imperialism meant the Soviet Union — this made it clear who the main enemy was.

The communiqué announced that the Party had 28 million members. The last official announcement, made in 1961 by Liu Shaoqi, had given a figure of 17 million. The 28 million may have been a fictitious figure. The Party had not yet been reorganised among the peasants, and without them so large a number as 28 million seems improbable. Two reports were presented at the Congress, the usual Political Report, presented by Zhou Enlai, and the report on the new revision of the Party Constitution, presented by Wang Hongwen.[18]

Zhou Enlai

Zhou Enlai said that a Draft of the Political Report presented to the last Ninth Congress in 1969 had been drawn up by Lin Biao with the collaboration of Chen Boda. It was totally wrong. It opposed the 'continued revolution under the dictatorship of the proletariat'. Indeed it was 'a refurbished version under new conditions [in 1969] of the same revisionist trash that Liu Shaoqi and Chen Boda had smuggled into the Resolution of the Eighth Party Congress [1956]'. That 1956 Resolution alleged that 'the major contradiction in our country was not the contradiction between the proletariat and the bourgeoisie, but that between the advanced socialist system and the backward productive forces of society.' The Lin Biao/Chen Boda draft in 1969 said the same things. It held that the main task of the Party was to develop production. Mao rejected that Draft Political Report.

The Eighth Party Congress in 1956, led by Liu Shaoqi, Zhou Enlai and Deng Xiaoping, did in fact prescribe normal economic development. Mao reacted by convoking a secret second session of the Congress in 1958, and in the same year he introduced his radical policies, the Communes and the Great Leap. He promoted Lin Biao in that year and later, along with Lin Biao, launched the ultra-radical Cultural Revolution, which was crowned by the Ninth Party Congress in 1969.

The assertion that the evil Lin Biao opposed the 'Continued Revolution' in 1969 solves the puzzle of certain words in the '571 Project' document. According to that document, discussed above, Lin Biao opposed 'Continued Revolution'. That passage must have been inserted in the '571' by Lin Biao's enemies to compromise him, to show that he had opposed Mao's radical policies. Lin Biao had done this, according to Zhou, as early as 1969. Zhou was never fanatical about the truth; he rarely said what he thought. Two years after making this report, he proposed at the People's Congress what was later to be called the programme of Four Modernisations, for the economic advancement of the country. That expressed his inner convictions more accurately.

Zhou had this to say about Lin Biao and his men: 'The Sayings [the *Little Red Book*] never left their hands, and *Wan Sui* [Hail!] never left their mouths. To your face they spoke good words, but they stabbed you in the back' — no mention of the fact that he, Zhou Enlai, used to wave the *Little Red Book* even when receiving foreign guests at the airport. Zhou then brought the usual exaggerated charges against Lin Biao: he was a revisionist, a fascist, one who wanted to reinstate the landlords and bourgeois class and capitulate to the revisionists and Social Imperialism, a man who acted under the baton of Soviet revisionism. Zhou paid an indirect compliment to Jiang Qing by praising the 'newly emerging things', the usual name for Jiang Qing's revolutionary creations. Zhou next ventured into the mysteries of Marxist futurology: 'In the future, even when classes have disappeared [therefore in the last stage of Communism] there will still be contradictions between the superstructure and the economic base, between the relations of production and production forces . . . struggle between the two lines, between right and wrong lines. [Therefore even in the remote period of final Communism, in a classless society, the dream of all good Marxists, there will still be struggle and there will still be two lines, and therefore counter-revolutionaries and purges.] Within the period of socialism', Zhou went on, 'there will be ten, twenty or thirty inner-Party struggles and ruffians like Lin Biao, Wang Ming, Liu Shaoqi, Peng Dehuai and Gao Gang will appear. This is something that cannot be changed by human will [i.e. it is a necessity of the "March of History"].'

'Chairman Mao', Zhou said, 'has always taught us that a deviation may be non-manifest for the time being. One deviation may cover another. In the old days when Wang Ming's leftist deviation was under attack, that same Wang Ming's rightist-opportunism was not visible. In the same way Lin Biao's opposition to Liu Shaoqi's revisionism covered Lin Biao's own revisionism. When a wrong tide comes, many follow it and only a few see through it and dare to withstand it. All should "oppose the tide". As Chairman Mao has said: "Going against the tide is a Marxist-Leninist principle.'' Chairman Mao dared to stand up against the tide in the ten struggles within the Party. Chairman Mao said: ''Our Party has already had fifty years of history and ten struggles of the Line.'' ' The ten were his fights against his enemies Chen Duxiu, Qu Qiubai, Li Lisan, Luo Zhanglong, Wang Ming and Zhang Guotao in the old days, and Gao Gang, Peng Dehuai, Liu Shaoqi and Lin Biao after 1949.

'As Chairman Mao predicted in 1966,' Zhou said, 'if an anti-Communist rightist political coup should happen in China, I am sure that there would be no peace. Almost certainly peace would be short-lived, because it would not be tolerated by the revolutionaries who represent the interests of over 90 per cent of the people.'

Zhou Enlai did not cite the source of Mao's words, although those present at the Congress knew that they came from a letter from Mao to his wife Jiang Qing, dated July 8, 1966. The letter as such was never published, but was circulated within the Party, and was obtained by Taiwanese agents in 1972. Some doubts remained, however, about the authenticity of the date, for the letter seemed to be a retrospective justification of Mao's opposition to Lin Biao. Without mentioning Lin Biao's name, the 1966 letter to Jiang Qing said that Mao had never believed that the *Little Red Book* could have any magical effect and that he disliked the way he was divinised. With his typical humour, Mao wrote: 'When there is no tiger in a mountain, the monkey is king. I am such a great king. I am not, however, a compromiser. There is in me the spirit of a tiger, and this is my dominant characteristic; but there is also accompanying it the spirit of a monkey. At the April meeting [1966] at Hangzhou I made it clear that I did not agree with my friend [Lin Biao]. But what could I do? At the May meeting in Peking he was still talking in the same way . . . What I wanted to say I could not say in public. It would only have helped the right wing in the Party [Liu Shaoqi]. For the moment the right wing must be beaten down.'[19] After that come the words quoted by Zhou Enlai in his Party Congress Report.

In his letter to Jiang Qing, Mao also said that 'the great disorder will turn into great order,' and he predicted that in seven or eight years there would be another great disorder, followed by order — another Cultural Revolution.

Zhou also spoke about foreign policy. Eighteen months had passed since Nixon's visit to China. The European Security Conference (held in Helsinki in 1975) proves, Zhou said, that the Soviet revisionists are 'making a feint in the East while attacking in the West'. (In those years China was warning Western Europe that it should become more anti-Soviet.)

Wang Hongwen

Wang Hongwen explained the revision of the Party Charter. He produced one striking passage. 'A genuine Communist', he said, 'is not afraid of being dismissed from his job, of being expelled from the Party, of being in prison or killed, nor is he afraid of divorce.' He certainly did not mean to be facetious, though the words as they stand imply that a good Communist is not less afraid of leaving his wife than he is afraid of prison or death. Perhaps Wang was thinking about Lin Biao, who had been under the influence of his wife Ye Qun. He cannot have dreamt of referring to Mao and his wife, for Wang was a devotee of Jiang Qing's. This passage was not included in the Party Charter. Wang also spoke of 'training millions of successors for the cause of proletarian revolution'. These words were included in the Charter; Wang explained that by this he meant that the old, the middle-aged and the young should be in the leadership. This had already been said in 1970–1 at the time of the re-establishment of the provincial Party committees.[20]

Deng Xiaoping

The long list of the 195 regular members of the Central Committee created by the Tenth Party Congress in August 1973 contained the name of Deng Xiaoping, the man whom since 1966 inner-Party documents and a great number of Red Guard tabloids had been calling the 'number two man [after Liu Shaoqi] on the capitalist road in the Party'. Deng, however, was never condemned openly in the public press. He reappeared in March 1973, five months before the Party Congress, and had become one of Zhou Enlai's Vice-Premiers. In December 1973 at a Politbureau meeting Mao proposed the nomination of Deng Xiaoping as Chief-of-Staff. This was not made public at the time and only foreigners visiting Peking knew of the appointment.[21] There has never been any explanation of how this happened, on whose recommendation Mao appointed Deng to a military post, although he had never been a commander but only a Party man, a political commissar, in the armed forces. The general impression was that Deng had been rehabilitated and promoted by Zhou Enlai.

This, however, is contradicted by an account of the Deng family's fortunes during the Cultural Revolution, written by Deng's daughter in August 1984. After two years of incarceration, Deng and his wife were transported by plane to a small village in Jiangxi province. They had been allowed to take books with them, and they worked a half-day in a neighbouring factory, but they were completely isolated from the outside world. News of the fall of Lin Biao (September 13, 1971) did not reach Deng until early November. He wrote a letter to the Party leaders in Peking, but it was not till after Wang Zhen had interceded with Mao that at long last Deng and his family were allowed to move to Peking in February 1973. His daughter's account says nothing about Zhou Enlai. His name is not even mentioned.[22]

General Wang Zhen, the organiser of the army in Xinjiang in the early 1950s, and later the commander of the railway troops, became a C.C. member at the 1969 Party Congress and retained his membership at this 1973 Congress. He had not been purged by the Cultural Revolution, and later, in 1975, he became one of the Vice-Premiers. Understandably, when Deng Xiaoping became leader, Wang became a very important person. It is possible that it was through him that Zhou Enlai succeeded in bringing Deng to Peking (where Deng remained a close associate of Zhou until Zhou's death). Yet Deng's daughter certainly did not feel under any obligation to Zhou Enlai for her father's return to power.

Radical craze

In 1973 the position of both Zhou Enlai and Deng was precarious. The power of the First Lady, Jiang Qing, had grown steadily, and she was nurturing the old man's peculiarities. Mao had never thought highly of formal education. In the summer of 1973 a young man called Zhang Tiesheng, in a protest against formal education, became a national hero by handing in a blank paper at an examination. The *People's Daily* lavished praise on him under the heading 'The Spirit of Opposition to the Current'. Had not Mao said that 'to rebel is right'? The good old spirit of the Red Guards had returned. This was the Revolutionary Line of Chairman Mao.[23] How far this was from the voice of Zhou Peiyuan, pleading a year earlier for the reintroduction of the teaching of basic science!

At the end of 1973 another young hero emerged, a peasant boy from the Northeast who had joined the University in Shanghai though he had had no secondary education, a genuine 'rebel', who organised political meetings to reform the University. It is the task of the worker-peasant-soldier students, he said in a speech, to make their way into universities and to manage and reform them. His speech was recorded and published with a laudatory editorial note in the two Shanghai newspapers.

He complained indignantly that the universities in Shanghai were awarding degrees to the proletarian students after two years and then dismissing them, while retaining others, without publishing their names, for further studies. (The Shanghai schools were sabotaging the 'rebel' trend.) The Party praised the revolutionary spirit of such fine proletarian youngsters, and they were supported by Party leaders in Shanghai and in the Northeast. Shanghai was run by Jiang Qing's men, Wang Hongwen, Zhang Chunqiao and Yao Wenyuan. In the Northeast, Mao Yuanxin, Mao's nephew, was a man of power.[24]

In September 1973, a month after the Tenth Party Congress, a major campaign was begun against Confucius, of whom Lin Biao was declared to be a student. In China Confucius has always been a living force. In the 1920s, China wanted to modernise and break with the old Confucianist ethics. Under the People's Republic, Confucianism made a surprising comeback in the 1960s, when the universities exalted Confucianist morality, the very opposite of class struggle. This was a symptom of protest against Communist rule. However, in 1973 Jiang Qing's radicals rejected Confucius, declaring him no better than a murderer. This was a ridiculous assertion, and it deceived nobody. Nevertheless there was a spate of articles about 'Confucius the murderer'. Simultaneously, there was glorification of Qin Shi Huang, known as the First Emperor (second century BC), the man who, as every Chinese knew, burnt the Confucianist classics and buried Confucianist scholars alive. Throughout 2,000 years of Chinese history, the name of this man had been recalled with horror.

Mao Zedong, however, had always admired the First Emperor, — with good reason, for he was the first man to unite the country and set up an administrative system, a system that has lasted until the present day. This, however, was not what moved the 1973 radicals. In September of that year the *People's Daily* commented: 'Bourgeois ambitionists, conspirators, counter-revolutionary double-dealers, renegades and traitors, Lin Biao and his dead party used to talk about the burning of books and the burying of scholars to attack our great Party and the socialist system of proletarian dictatorship.'[25]

In January of the following year, 1974, mass meetings were held throughout the country to 'mobilise the masses for the criticism of Lin Biao and of Confucius'. A ferocious new campaign was introduced under the title 'Criticise Lin Biao, Criticise Confucius'. 'A large-scale movement of criticism of Lin Biao and of Confucius is sweeping the country,' a *People's Daily* editorial said. Yet there was no intention of returning to the ways of the Cultural Revolution. It was ordered that the campaign should not divide the revolutionaries into factions. On the other hand, it was laid down that those who criticised the Cultural Revolution and those who slandered or sabotaged the criticism of Lin Biao and Confucius were counter-revolutionaries. Provincial Party leaders took part personally in the shouting against Lin Biao and Confucius at the mass meetings.[26]

All this seemed irrational, but the real purpose was not opposition to Confucius but opposition to Zhou Enlai and his colleagues, who represented the old regime, as opposed to the radicals. Zhou Enlai was Confucius and Confucius was Zhou Enlai. The crucial question posed was: What do you think about the Cultural Revolution and the 'new-born things', the achievements of Jiang Qing? 'A small clique of class enemies in the country and outside is attacking the great proletarian Cultural Revolution,' said the New Year joint editorial of the Peking papers in 1974. Not all were enthusiastic followers of the new craze. As the newspaper of Hubei province put it in February 1974, there were Party organisations which were 'halting deeper penetration and development of the criticism of Lin Biao and of Confucius'.[27] And a radio broadcast in Hunan province commented: 'How is it possible that today, eight years after the Cultural Revolution, and following two years of the criticism of Lin Biao, there are still comrades who do not understand what this is all about?'

Army men themselves became wary of all the changes. A political commissar of a regiment was quoted as having said: 'For twenty years there have been many battles within the Party. I thought that the Ninth Party Congress, held after the great victory of the great proletarian Cultural Revolution [the Party Congress that made Lin Biao the heir-designate], was like a red line marking the end. After that, I thought, it would be possible to live in peace.' Referring to Zhou Enlai's words in his Report to the Tenth Party Congress of August 1973, the man said: 'Some comrades have wondered when there will be an end to this struggle of the Lines. They want to keep out of the struggle. When something happens, they do not take sides, and when they bump into difficulties, they make a detour and walk away.' They saw that the battle at the top had not yet ended; these men in the middle ranks were cautious, eager to avoid all pitfalls by not taking sides.

The village cadres wondered even more why they should be involved in these purges. 'Some of the comrades did not understand this whole business of criticism of Lin Biao, least of all, why it had to reach down to the village Party cadres. The villagers, they thought, do well enough if they work and hand over grain to the state. Why involve them in the criticism of Confucius?'[28]

In Peking the anger and frenzy of Jiang Qing knew no bounds. In January 1974, a Literature and Art Festival was held in Peking. It consisted solely of plays written in imitation of her *Model Plays*. The festival, the *People's Daily* said, was a victory for the proletarian revolutionary literary line of Chairman Mao, and it was a criticism of Lin Biao and of Confucius. A month later, however, it was discovered that one of the plays performed at the festival was evil, that it was 'a counterrevolutionary plot'. The play, *Three Visits to Peach Peak*, was a simple story about a village that cheated another village, the Peach Peak great brigade, by selling it a sick horse: when the Party secretary of the first village discovered this he went three times to the Peach Peak to apologise. The *People's Daily* thought it a terrible story. There was no class struggle in it but only a sanctimonious man who apologised and forgave — Confucianist loyalty and forgiveness, repayment of injustice with virtue.

It was recalled that in the early 1960s Wang Guangmei, Liu Shaoqi's wife, led the socialist educational campaign in a place called Peach Garden. In 1965 the Chairman condemned her work there. Yet Wang Guangmei sent Peach Garden a horse, and a stone stele with the inscription 'To the undying memory of the work of Wang Guangmei' was erected there. Worse still, the story was set in 1959. That was the time of the Communes and the Great Leap, which was criticised by Liu Shaoqi. In the play it was said that the horse's sickness was due to violent handling, and it was described as a 'disease of the brain', words which had been used in criticism of the Leap by Deng Tuo, then editor of the *People's Daily*. The horse in the play 'could not stand such violent driving, its body was covered with sweat, its four legs trembled.' It died, and from this, the play said, 'the lesson must be learnt.' With incredible audacity the author had called the heroine of the play Qing Lan, and one of the songs in the plays quoted an old proverb: 'Green (*qing*) emerged from the blue (*lan*), and blue was victorious.'

Jiang Qing must have been furious. Everybody knew that in her young days when she was a film starlet in Shanghai her screen name was Lan Ping (Blue Apple).

The story of this play about the horse was blown up into an issue of national importance. Province after province, even the *Tibetan Daily*, thundered against *Three Visits to Peach Peak*.[29] There was more to come. In the province of Hunan a play, *The Song of the Gardener*, was sung in the traditional Hunanese sing-song opera style. However the plot was politically unsound — the teachers in the play did not appreciate the revolutionary spirit of a recalcitrant student and gave him bad marks. This of course was entirely against the rebel spirit as existed during the Cultural Revolution, when ignorant proletarians were sent to the schools. After the fall of Lin Biao initial steps were taken towards a return to normal education but the radicals could not tolerate this.

Then came the case of Antonioni, the world-famous Italian film director who in 1972 made a television documentary called *China*, which was shown in many countries. Two years later, when the Jiang Qing fury got the upper hand, all China learnt the name of Antonioni, the wicked man who showed the dark sides of life in China, 'old people, exhausted draught animals, dilapidated houses, poor hygiene, humans pulling carts, and an old woman with bound feet'. Antonioni, the *People's Daily* said in horrified amazement, did not shoot a single scene from the *Revolutionary Model Plays*! Worse still, an aria from one of the *Model Plays* served as background music to a pig wagging its head — 'a deliberate slander on our *Revolutionary Model Plays*'. The Chinese ambassador to Italy was recalled for consultations.

After the Peach Peak horse and Antonioni's pig, the next animal in the menagerie was a cockerel. The Shanghai Export Corporation published an album of Chinese paintings. Instead of showing the glorious mountains and rivers of China, there were pictures of barren hills and menacing waters. This immediately reminded the public of Antonioni's film, which had only shown unpleasant scenes of China. One painting in the album was called 'To Welcome Spring'. What did it show? It showed a cockerel with its feathers and tail pointing up to heaven and with ferocity in its face, as if it were about to attack somebody. Interpretation was easy: 'Obviously this expressed discontent with the great proletarian Cultural Revolution and hatred of it.'[30] All this sounded puerile, but nobody dared to say so. All applauded the emperor's new clothes.

Jiang Qing and the army

Jiang Qing's interference in the army was a much more serious cause for concern. In January 1974 the Party's central authorities published a selection of documents, one of which was a letter from a military company in Zhejiang province to Jiang Qing, thanking her for her letter to them, which had been delivered by two comrades, Chi Qun and Xie Jingyi. Chi Qun was a member of the no. 8341 Troop, Mao's personal guard, which was being held up as a model for the organisation of the Party. Xie Jingyi was a female Party secretary of Peking city. Both had been Red Guard organisers in the Peking universities in the early days of the Cultural Revolution.

Another of these documents came from the Nanjing Troops (the military command of three provinces — Jiangsu, Anhui, Zhejiang — and Shanghai city). The document mentioned a letter from Jiang Qing and went on to thank Comrade Jiang Qing and Chairman Mao for the interest they showed in the Troops and promised that Comrade Jiang Qing's letter would be studied by the army. Both the letter and the document were dated January 1974.[31] The newly-appointed commander of the Nanjing Troops was Ding Sheng. A month earlier, at the end of December 1973, the commanders of the Great Military Areas had been reshuffled. This was a shrewd move because the generals had to leave their own troops and this lessened their power and influence over them.

Xu Shiyou had been in command of the Nanjing Troops since the early 1950s until he was transferred abruptly to Canton. Such an order could have come only from Mao. Since the disappearance of Lin Biao the army had had no other supreme commander. The inspiration for the move, however, must have come from Jiang Qing and her radicals. General Xu was not one of Jing Qing's devotees. In Nanjing he was in the awkward position of having had two of his subordinates in the army, the Shanghai pair, elevated above him: Wang Hongwen, who was the political commissar of the Shanghai garrison, had become Vice-Chairman of the Party, and Zhang Chunqiao, the first political commissar of the Nanjing Troops, was high up in Peking.[32] Ding Sheng, who had been transferred to Nanjing, was more obliging. He was one of the few of Lin Biao's generals who had not been purged after Lin's fall. He joined Jiang Qing's group, probably to save his skin, but miscalculated badly. Two years later, after Mao's death and the arrest of Jiang Qing and company, Ding Sheng also fell. At the critical moment of the fall of Jiang Qing and her friends, Xu Shiyou was brought back to his old troops in Nanjing to ensure that Shanghai, the stronghold of the Jiang Qing radicals, should not cause trouble.[33]

Thus in 1974 Jiang Qing had direct influence, or indirect influence through Mao, on the army.

Militia

The fear that Shanghai might cause trouble at the time of the arrest of Jiang Qing and company was not unfounded. The newly-organised Shanghai urban militia had become the model for the whole country. Organisation began in earnest in September 1973, a month after the Tenth Party Congress which had made the young Shanghai radical, Wang Hongwen, a Vice-Chairman of the Party. On September 29, 1973, the *People's Daily* and the army newspaper stated jointly that the urban militia's purpose was 'future city fighting' against imperialism and against a sudden attack by the Soviet Union. In fact it was meant to be the fighting wing of the Jiang Qing radicals.

Two months later Peking reported that there were 400,000 militiamen in the city. In Shenyang in the Northeast there were 450,000. The *People's Daily* printed photographs of worker-militiamen, small teams of men and women patrolling the cities with fixed bayonets.[34] The militia was supposed to help the army and the security forces to screen the population and to search houses. In the Shanghai lanes the search went on for hidden illegal elements, particularly youths in hiding: many of the students sent to the villages had returned illegally to the cities. The Peking city militia was said to have been organised on the Shanghai model. When it was established, the only Politbureau members present were the two from Shanghai, Zhang Chunqiao and Yao Wenyuan.

A number of provinces held militia conferences, and all swore to imitate Shanghai. But progress in organising the militia in the cities was slow. A year later, in 1974, only half-a-dozen cities had their urban militia, and only lip-service was being paid to Shanghai. The Peking press stopped publishing news about progress in the provinces so as to conceal the poor response to the call of the radicals. The trouble was that the militia was trained by and dependent on the army, and the army generals were not all enthusiastic about this new development. The command of the Wuhan Troops, which ruled two provinces, used the workers' militia to keep order in the factories and 'to serve as an example of unity', the last thing the Shanghai pair wanted. They had hoped that the urban militia would join in the criticism of Lin Biao and Confucius, i.e. Zhou Enlai.

When planning their own armed forces, the radicals may have wanted to imitate Zulfiqar Ali Bhutto, who at that time in Pakistan was organising an armed security organisation independent of the army. This could not be done in China. The army commands were dutifully chanting 'Learn the Shanghai experience,' but the militia remained under their control. Separation of the militia from the army proved impossible. The urban militia of armed workers was to patrol the streets and maintain public order and protect State property. (During the Cultural Revolution the urban militia was attacked first by student Red Guards, and later by other workers which had split into rival fighting units.) Fresh disorder erupted. In the important coal mines in Anhui province, fighting between groups of workers brought production to a halt. The worst-hit sector of the economy was the railways. Strikes on the railways affected wide sections of the country in the Northwestern and Southwestern provinces. Militiamen were ordered to unload goods from the trains, and the highest provincial authorities made symbolic gestures, going personally to load and unload the trains.

In September 1974 the first anniversary of the establishment of the urban militia was celebrated in many places. On the second anniversary, in 1975, there was silence. Ni Zhifu, one of the Party's rising stars, alternate-member of the Politbureau, Party secretary and head of the workers of Peking city, remained conspicuously absent from everything connected with the urban militia.[35] In doing this Ni Zhifu, who was only forty-one, acted wisely. He survived the fall of Jiang Qing in 1976 and in the 1980s he became head of the national Trade Union.

Deng at the United Nations

These years witnessed extraordinary contrasts. Two currents, the radicals of Jiang Qing and the men of Zhou Enlai, were running in opposite directions. While the radicals were clenching their fists against Confucius, Deng Xiaoping was sent to New York to represent China in April 1974 at the special session of the United Nations. There he exposed Mao's new doctrine on Three Worlds. The United States and the Soviet Union make up the First World; the developing countries in Asia, Africa, Latin America and China make up the Third World. The developed countries between the two, like those in Western Europe, make up the Second World. This was a revised version of an old idea of Mao's. Ever since the Yan'an days in the 1940s, he had liked to divide the world into zones. The division changed with the changing world. What Deng put forward was Mao's most recent classification.

Sick Zhou

Zhou Enlai should have gone to the UN meeting; but he was not well.

In May 1974 when foreign guests arrived, it was Deng, not Zhou, who received them at the airport; Zhou met them in the city guest-house. When Zulfiqar Ali Bhutto of Pakistan arrived, Zhou said to him: 'I am not very well; I am old.' In those days nobody knew whether Zhou was really sick or was making a diplomatic retreat. Not even his radical opponents knew for certain.

On April 26, 1974, the English-language *Peking Review* published a translation of an article from the November 1973 issued of *Red Flag*. It dealt with an historical figure of the second century BC named Fan Sui. The article was an historical allegory. 'Although Fan Sui became Prime Minister,' it said, 'he was actually sitting on top of a volcano that could erupt any time. The influence of the old aristocrats at the time was still powerful. But the class struggle was strong and Fan Sui was asked to return the seal of prime minister because of illness.' The parallel with Zhou Enlai was unmistakable.[36]

Zhou Enlai was indeed ill. From early summer 1974 to September 1975 he received foreign dignitaries, before or after they met Mao, as the communiqué said, 'in hospital'. Deng Xiaoping was giving state banquets 'in the name of Premier Zhou', and it was he and Li Xiannian, never Wang Hongwen, who were present when Mao received foreign guests. The last time Zhou appeared 'in hospital' was when he received a Romanian delegation on September 7, 1975. He died of cancer in January 1976.

Zhou's last grand act

A year before he died, in January 1975, unprecedented public homage was paid to Zhou — already a sick man — at the People's Congress. After an interruption of ten years, he had succeeded in getting together a session of the People's Congress. Before it met, a three day Central Committee Plenum was held on January 8–10, the second C.C. Plenum since the 1973 Party Congress. That a meeting had taken place was announced a week later, in a six-line statement, with no mention of who had taken part in it or whether Mao had been present. The announcement did say, however, that 'the conference elected Comrade Deng Xiaoping a Vice-Chairman of the Party Central Committee and a member of the Standing Committee of the C.C. Politbureau.'

Mao was certainly not present at the People's Congress. His customary place at the centre of the official photograph was taken by Zhou Enlai. At the Congress Zhou delivered the usual government report. It was the shortest report he ever produced at a People's Congress. He was obviously a sick man, and he was warmly applauded.

Though sick, Zhou had lost nothing of his mental acumen. He began his report with praise of the *Revolutionary Model Plays* and the 'New Born Things', the achievements of Jiang Qing, without mentioning her by name.

Divided

The People's Congress elected twelve Vice-Premiers. The second, after Deng, was the radical Zhang Chunqiao.

There was an uneasy truce. The ministries dealing with the economy were taken by Zhou's men, those handling ideology and the mass media by the radicals. In the army Deng Xiaoping was Chief-of-Staff and Zhang Chunqiao was the new head of the General Political Department of the army. Ye Jianying became minister of defence.

The press in Shanghai, Zhang Chunqiao's city, interpreted the new State Constitution enacted by the People's Congress as supporting the radicals. From the 1973 Party Charter it retained the revolutionary phrases known as the 'Four Great': 'Great noise, Great release, Great character posters and Great debate', which in the radicals' interpretation meant Opposing the Current, i.e. opposing the old guard.

After the People's Congress, Jiang Qing and her achievements were exalted even more highly than before. Her latest, a village near Tianjin called Xiao Jin Zhuang, was declared 'a model of the criticism of Lin Biao and Confucius campaign' and was held up for imitation by the whole country. Imitated it was, leading officials in the provinces took up the praises of Xiao Jin Zhuang. The Shenyang Military Command, commanding the three provinces of the Northeast (commander, Li Desheng), ordered study of Xiao Jin Zhuang, which had been set up as a model village in 1974. It was Jiang Qing's pride and joy. In September 1974 she brought the first lady of the Philippines, Imelda Marcos, to visit it.[37]

Despite these pleasantries the atmosphere in 1975 was charged with gunpowder.

January–February

At the January 1975 People's Congress, Zhou Enlai promised wonders. By 1980 China would have built 'an independent and relatively comprehensive industrial and economic system', and by the end of the century 'there will be a comprehensive modernisation of agriculture, industry, national defence, science and technology' — the 'Four Modernisations' — 'so that our national economy will be in the front ranks of the world.'

Zhou always excelled in projecting a bright future. At the time of the oil crisis in 1973, he promptly announced that China was a great petroleum producer — which was far from the truth — and the world was amazed. Yet Zhou, ever careful not to provoke the radicals, added that great attention should be paid to the socialist revolution, to class struggle and to the struggle of the Lines. 'Only if the revolution is carried on can production progress.'

A month later, in February, the radicals set up an entirely different goal for the national economy. The *People's Daily* and the army newspaper published three pages of quotations from Marx, Engels and Lenin on proletarian dictatorship, and asked: Is China going towards final Communism or sliding back to bourgeois capitalism? On February 9 the *People's Daily* editorial quoted Mao as saying: 'It would be easy for people like Lin Biao to seize power and bring in a capitalist system.' He did not say Lin Biao but 'people like Lin Biao'. The quotations from Marx-Engels-Lenin were carefully chosen. They dealt with revolution to the very end; and the need for violence for overthrowing the existing social system. They cited Lenin on prevention of the development of bourgeois habits among Soviet officials and 'bourgeois rights' (remnants of capitalism — commerce and money — still remaining after the abolition of private ownership of the means of production). They spoke about the possibility that a new bourgeois class might emerge, the danger that free trading might lead to capitalism, and so on. These were radical statements selected from the holy writ to prove that the radicals were the real Marxists.

The revised State Constitution introduced relative moderation and some freedom in the economic activities of the people. Article 9 said: 'The state protects the citizens' rights to ownership of their income from work, their savings, their houses and their other means of livelihood,' and the Constitution allowed 'individual labour of nonagricultural individual labourers'. In the eyes of the radicals these were evil concessions of 'bourgeois rights'. The attacks on 'bourgeois rights' began in February. It was the struggle of Jiang Qing's radicals against the moderate policies of the men in charge of the economy.

In the March 1975 issue of *Red Flag*, Yao Wenyuan wrote a ferocious article, which was broadcast on all radio stations several times that day. It may be recalled that it was an article of Yao's in November 1965 that heralded the Cultural Revolution. Now, his article started with a saying of Mao's: 'It would be easy for people like Lin Biao to seize power and bring in a capitalist system.' If bourgeois rights are not restricted, Yao wrote, the men who praise material incentives will encourage theft, embezzlement, corruption, speculation and capitalist wealth, and a new class of bourgeois parvenus will arise. 'If the new bourgeois class wins power, it will carry out a bloody repression.'

Yao quoted an old story about the wolf that was saved by a man. That wolf turned on the man and ate him. The implication was that the wicked old guard who had been rejected and then forgiven and taken back had turned against their benefactors.

Yao ended by quoting a passage from Mao's 1966 letter to Jiang Qing in which Mao spoke about the danger of the rightists' seizing power.[38]

Jiang Qing and foreign affairs

In the year 1975, Jiang Qing's power grew to terrifying dimensions. She was in command of literature and art; through her model village Xiao Jin Zhuang, she was in command of life in the villages; she held sway over the army, or at least part of it; she even had a voice in foreign affairs. An inner-Party document revealed that in March 1975 she delivered a directive to all Chinese embassies around the world. Speaking, so she said, in the name of Mao, she outlined the aim of China's foreign policy: realisation of Communism in the world and incitement of revolution in the Third World countries, a revolution by stages. She quoted Mao: 'The states must be independent; nations must be liberated; people must revolt.' Since her directive was meant for internal consumption only, what she said about the leaders of Third World countries was very different from what Peking officials said when they met these leaders. She called them 'the black friends, the small friends, the poor friends'. She quoted Mao's famous saying that 'political power comes from the barrel of a gun', and said that Mao had said to Prince Sihanouk of Cambodia: 'If you want arms, buy them. If you have no money we can give them to you free. There is only one condition, revolution.' She also revealed what Peking thought of Henry Kissinger: he was 'an adventurer and a defeatist'. Kissinger when in Peking, she said, revealed that the United

States intended to abandon the Asian theatre of the Pacific. This, she said, was an ostrich policy.

She then went on to speak about the Chinese embassies abroad. They were meant to carry out the United Front policy, and work for the disintegration of the enemy from within; but many embassies were not doing so. They were not interested in politics; their cables to Peking were all about trade. A number of embassies in Eastern and Central Africa were neglecting the study of politics completely. The Party secretaries in the embassies — the real bosses — should see to it that the political issues, the criticism of Lin Biao and Confucius, were studied seriously. Embassy personnel were permitted to send in complaints about their local superiors. In Peking the Foreign Ministry and the Party Central Committee's Foreign Liaison Department (which is superior to the Foreign Ministry) should take a firmer grip on political work in the embassies.[39]

Jiang Qing spoke in authoritative tones, but it is probable that the Central Committee's Foreign Liaison Department at home, and the Chinese embassies abroad, shelved the first lady's directives and ignored them. Deng Xiaoping, who, owing to the illness of Zhou Enlai, was running foreign affairs, certainly ignored them. According to the 1982 *Record of Major Events*, on May 3, 1975, Mao put Deng Xiaoping in charge of the affairs of the Politbureau during Zhou Enlai's illness.[40] In the same month, Peking established relations with the European Economic Community, and Deng visited Paris.[41]

Deng's programme

In the summer of 1975, when the radicals' attacks were becoming ever louder, Deng and his men began work on an important document, 'A General Programme for All the Work of the Party and of the Country'. This document dealt with the reorganisation of the whole economy, of education and culture and, above all, of scientific work. It has never been published, not even in the 1980s when Deng, by now the leader, started putting into practice what he had planned in 1975. The Programme was known only from the ferocious attacks made on it by the radicals in April 1976. They published extracts from it, and according to these, the Programme quoted selected words of Mao to give the impression that science and technology must be promoted. Deng's assistants were working on the Programme and one (unnamed) assistant was visiting the research institutes to explain it. He was quoted as having said: 'If the

Party secretary of an institute does not understand the problem, he should be honest enough to say: "Director, I follow, you lead." ' The Programme insisted on learning technology from abroad, establishing permanent trade contacts and buying modern equipment, for which China was to pay with coal and petroleum.

Deng himself was quoted as having said: 'It is wrong to practice egalitarianism, denying differences in remuneration' and 'It is very wrong to have no regard for the difficulties the masses experience in living.' Deng also said that Marxism-Leninism and Mao Zedong Thought should be studied, but that techniques and trades should be studied at the same time.[42]

The 1976 attack on this 1975 Programme did not give the names of those who had helped Deng draw it up, but the 1982 *Records of Major Events* said the Programme for the reform of scientific institutes had been drawn up by Hu Yaobang, who had been leader of the Academy of Science in 1973, when Guo Moruo, the President of the Academy, had fallen ill (he died in 1978).[43]

Deng's group planned to publish a review to propagate their ideas. The review never appeared.[44] The mass media were not in their hands. Domination of the mass media has always been a matter of importance in the People's Republic. There may be powerful organisations at work throughout the nation which never get a mention in the press. What one hears and reads in the news rarely conveys a complete picture of power relations.

End of 1975

According to an inner-Party publication of 1981, in the autumn of 1975 Mao, under the influence of his nephew Mao Yuanxin, who was his liaison man in the Northeast, turned against Deng Xiaoping and against the rehabilitation of the old guard.[45]

Jiang Qing's radicals were jubilant. At the end of October 1975, having control of the film industry, they released a film entitled *Spring Sprout*, shot in 1969 after the Ninth Party Congress. It told the story of a rebellious young woman, a bare-footed doctor named Spring Sprout, who revolts against the bourgeois in the rural health service. The film opened on a violent note. Spring Sprout, having noticed the signboard of a doctor who was working for money, seizes the signboard, breaks it and throws it away. The rest of the film continued in the same vein.[46]

Deng saw the film and did not like it. In the March 1976 issue of *Red*

Flag — Deng having vanished from the political scene — one of Jiang Qing's professional scribes wrote about 'that unrepentent man on the capitalist road' who for ten years had refused to watch the *Revolutionary Model Plays* (of Jiang Qing). 'He came to see the film *Spring Sprout*. In the middle, he flicked his sleeves and walked out, saying it was "ultra-left".' Unrepentent bourgeois of this kind, the article went on, say that 'class struggle is not something absolute', that 'in ordinary life class struggle is not everything', that 'insistence on the Revolutionary Model Plays keeps the creative spirit in bonds', and so on.[47]

The December 1975 issue of *Red Flag* accused the Peking universities of having 'reversed the verdict', and said that bourgeois class education had come back to the schools. The *People's Daily* published on its first page a note of protest against bourgeois education written by the young hero Zhang Tiesheng, the man who in 1973 had handed in a blank examination paper.[48] The December 1975 issue of *Red Flag* laid down the norm of true Marxism: 'Support or opposition to the Socialist New-Born Things is the criterion for distinguishing true from sham Marxism.'

Mao's role

With Zhou Enlai out of circulation and dying in hospital, and Mao ailing — though in December 1975 he was still able to receive President Ford and in February 1976 Richard Nixon — it may be asked: what was Mao's role in this bitter infighting between Jiang Qing's radicals and the old guard? The radicals' attack was now directed against Deng Xiaoping. Deng was perhaps too rough; he did not have the smoothness and grace of Zhou Enlai.

What did Mao himself want? He had failed to find a successor. Lin Biao's name had been put into the Party Charter at the Ninth Party Congress in 1969, but he had proved a disappointment. At the Tenth Party Congress in 1973, out of the blue, a young worker, Wang Hongwen, who had distinguished himself in Shanghai during the Cultural Revolution, became one of the five Vice-Chairmen of the Central Committee. Wang looked like a possible successor-designate, but after May 1975 he was no longer visible in Peking on important occasions. He had fallen out of favour with Mao.[49] After the death of Zhou Enlai in January 1976, Mao named not Wang but Hua Guofeng, who was not even a Vice-Chairman of the Party, as successor to Zhou Enlai.

Was Mao in 1975 still at the old game, playing one group against another? Or was he at a loss what to do? Or was he already senile and easily influenced by the radicals, whose radicalism touched a sensitive chord in the heart of the old rebel?

The radical craze certainly got hold of him. In August 1975 he made a pronouncement condemning an ancient novel, *Water Margin*. This was a story of noble bandits and disgraced officials who lived high up on a mountain. For centuries the exploits of the heroes of this novel had been sung on the stage and retold by story-tellers in the villages and in city market-places. It was, as everybody knew, one of Mao's favourite books (he considered himself a rebel bandit). In 1973 books on classical literature were still quoting Mao's praise of *Water Margin*. Now everything was reversed. Mao himself said that the book was a bad book, and that though its hero, a government official named Song Jiang, had fled with others to the mountains, he had in the end surrendered to the Emperor. Here the Emperor was not Mao but Deng Xiaoping and his companions, the old guard who had kept the old traditions.

The September 1975 issue of *Red Flag* elaborated on the evils of *Water Margin* in violent terms. Writers who had earlier praised the book because Mao had done so now published apologies. Song Jiang, the hero of the novel, was not a rebel, but an abject Confucianist. He had even asked: 'If a man rebels against heaven, opposes his own father and does not observe loyalty and filial piety, what use is such a man to this world?' This showed that Song Jiang was a Confucianist loyalist — he was not a rebel.

In the November issue of *Red Flag*, one of the radical scribes wrote: 'The criticism of *Water Margin*, which is now beginning, is an integral part of the theory of Proletarian Dictatorship.' The analysis of *Water Margin* is very useful 'for learning how to distinguish true from sham Marxism, the revolutionary group from the surrendering clique'. The spirit of the 'rebels' of the early stage of the Cultural Revolution was revived. The response in the country was, however, anaemic. Few provinces got excited about this curious new campaign.[50]

After Zhou's death

1976 was a dramatic year in the history of the People's Republic. Zhou Enlai's death on January 8 did not come as a surprise, but it changed the political situation. Zhou's funeral, even as heard over the radio, was a moving event. There was, one felt, genuine sadness in the air. Deng

Xiaoping, who a year earlier had become one of the Vice-Premiers, delivered the funeral oration on January 15: he did not omit praise for the New Born Things, the achievements of Jiang Qing. Zhou's body was cremated, and in accordance with his wishes, his ashes were strewn over the country. Perhaps he had been thinking of earlier Party leaders whose graves were desecrated by the rebels in the Cultural Revolution.

Mao, who was suffering from Parkinson's disease, still had a clear mind. When condemning *Water Margin* he had shown himself to be the old rebel, but when it came to choosing a successor to Zhou, he struck a balance between the polarised extremes, the old guard led by Deng, and the followers of his own radical wife. To avoid trouble, he chose, against all expectations, the man who was the First Party secretary of his province, Hunan, and since 1974 had been minister of security in Peking. This man was Hua Guofeng. He was then fifty-six, the age at which Mao had become leader of the country in 1949. He was not a widely-informed man — he had joined the Red Army at the age of fifteen. In 1949 he was only a county leader, and six years before the death of Zhou Enlai was still only a Party secretary of Hunan province. In the early 1970s he was summoned to Peking, where, according to a *People's Daily* report in 1972, he was employed in preparing documents for Zhou Enlai. The Ninth Party Congress in 1969 made him a member of the Central Committee, the Tenth in 1973 elected him to the Politbureau, and in January 1975 he became the sixth Vice-Premier in Zhou's Cabinet.

This, it was announced on February 3, was the man whom Mao had selected to be Acting Premier and to take charge of the daily work of the Party Central Committee. The appointment came as a surprise. Hua had done nothing to qualify himself to become a leader. Unlike Liu Shaoqi, he had not contributed any writings to the formation of the Party. Unlike Lin Biao, he had created no doctrine of his own. He had not a shadow of Zhou Enlai's prestige. He had, however, been the man in charge of security after the great disorders of the Cultural Revolution. People could scarcely guess whether he was on the side of the old guard or of the radicals. He seemed neutral. What forces were backing him? Lin Biao had had the backing of the army; Deng had the backing of the old guard who had regained power. Who was backing Hua Guofeng?[51]

The radicals may have been disappointed that it was not one of their own men who had become Zhou's successor. They probably had two reasons for acquiescing in the choice. First, Huo Guofeng was a light-weight, easy to knock off. Secondly, and this counted for much, Hua's promotion meant the demotion by Mao of their chief enemy, Deng Xiaoping. After delivering Zhou's funeral oration on January 15, Deng vanished. The criticisms of Confucius and of *Water Margin* were turned against him and his colleagues. On February 3, 1976, the *People's Daily*, in an article headed 'The Criticism of Confucius Must Continue', said that as soon as the modern Confucianists (the old guard) regained power, they favoured the bourgeois intellectuals, wanted scientific research — accusations aimed at Deng's 1975 reform programme — and wished to put an end to class struggle. *Red Flag* in its February 1976 issue spoke similarly against those who were over-emphasising education, science, the study of basic theories and research, thus belittling the role of politics. An article in the *People's Daily* in February was menacing: 'If you want to go on your own way, then the waves of the revolutionary masses will smash you.' It added: 'It is a fantastic lie to say that we do not want production and the Four Modernisations.'[52]

On March 28, 1976, the *People's Daily* quoted what it called 'the most recent instruction of Chairman Mao': 'That man [Deng] is not interested in class struggle . . . He spoke of white and black cats. For him it matters little whether it is Imperialism or Marxism.' Deng's famous saying, published in earlier years in anti-Deng Red Guard tabloids, was that for him it did not matter whether a cat was black or white. So long as it caught the mice it was a good cat.

Deng disappeared. The radicals were in their element. At the highest level of the Party, the Politbureau Standing Committee, Zhou Enlai, Kang Sheng and Dong Biwu were dead. There remained Mao Zedong, the nonagenarian Zhu De (he died a few months later in July), Ye Jianying — and two radicals, Wang Hongwen and Zhang Chunqiao. In the Cabinet, with Deng gone, the first of the remaining eleven Vice-Premiers was Zhang Chunqiao. The radicals were therefore on top in both Party and government. The unanswered questions were: would they gain recognition from the Party leaders around the country, particularly those who had been rejected by the Cultural Revolution and reinstated by Zhou Enlai or Deng Xiaoping, and would Jiang Qing's radicals be able to survive the disappearance of Mao?

A nationwide movement was started to condemn 'the men on the capitalist road', but responses from the provinces were slow in coming. All the provinces held meetings of some sort, but only four of the provincial First Party secretaries joined the chorus personally.[53]

Zhou's supporters

In April came a decisive event, the great traditional Qing Ming Festival, when the Chinese visit their ancestors' graves and honour the dead. In the first days of the month, foreign correspondents noticed that people were bringing wreaths to the Monument of the People's Heroes in the centre of the immense Tian An Men Square in Peking. Many of the wreaths bore a picture of Zhou Enlai or the words 'In Memory of Zhou Enlai'. By April 4 the wreaths had been piled up to a height of 60 feet around the monument. One of the wreaths was dedicated to Yang Kaihui; another had the inscription 'Hail Chairman Mao! Beat down Empress Ci Xi [Tz'u Hsi]!' Yang Kaihui was Mao's second wife, executed by the Nationalist government in the early days of the revolution; Tz'u Hsi was the Empress in the final days of the Manchu dynasty. Both women's names were direct affronts to Jiang Qing. No such spontaneous manifestation, with wreaths from factories and schools all over Peking, had hitherto been heard of in the People's Republic.[54]

After Zhou's death in January, his memory was buried in silence: the mass media were in the hands of the radicals. Deng Xiaoping, who should have succeeded Zhou, had been eliminated — by what means has never been revealed. Zhou Enlai's memory was to be obliterated. The reaction in April came as a surprise, and it was not confined to Peking alone — there were similar manifestations of respect for Zhou in provincial capitals.[55] After the event, the June 1976 issue of *Red Flag* said that the whole manifestation was the work of an underground nationwide organisation set up by Deng Xiaoping. 'Only a short period elapsed between Deng Xiaoping's return to office and his fall, but [in that short period] he worked out a programme, influenced public opinion and set up an organisation.'[56] This was probably true. The mass media may be in the hands of a single group, but another powerful organised network may exist without access to newspapers.

It was revealed, but not till five years later, in an inner-Party document, that on April 4 the Politbureau held a meeting — there was no mention of how many Politbureau members took part — to discuss what was going on in Tian An Men Square. Hua Guofeng condemned the demonstration. Wu De, the boss of Peking, said — and this was published later in the June issue of *Red Flag* quoted above — that it was the work of Deng Xiaoping's forces. It was, he said, a counter-revolutionary incident. Mao Yuanxin, Mao Zedong's nephew, described it as 'the activity of a planned underground organisation'.

In the evening of the same day the wreaths were cleared off the plaza 'with the permission of Mao Zedong'. The next day, on April 5, the masses protested but their protests were suppressed.[57] Three days later the *People's Daily* described the events of that day as follows: 100,000 people gathered in the square. A dozen young persons and several policemen were beaten up. Five cars and some military barracks were set on fire. At 6.30 p.m. Wu De broadcast a speech and three hours later tens of thousands of militia, police and soldiers went into action, detaining the criminals.

Eye-witnesses saw only a quiet crowd of people watching burning cars; it was not possible to find out who had set them on fire. Throughout the day, groups of militiamen were sitting quietly at the end of the square and there were soldiers stationed in the nearby former British embassy building. The violence looked like an operation planned by the authorities.

The Two Resolutions

Two days later, on April 7, 1976, a double decision of the Politbureau was announced: 'On the proposal of our great leader Chairman Mao, the Politbureau unanimously agrees to dismiss Deng Xiaoping from all posts both inside and outside the Party while allowing him to keep his Party membership so as to see how he will behave in the future.' Hua Guofeng was named first Vice-Chairman of the Central Committee (Mao was the Chairman) and Prime Minister. The two decisions, called The Two Resolutions, were printed on the same page of the *People's Daily*.[58] This was the document that was to seal the fate of Hua Guofeng a few years later.

The nation was shocked: a radical writer in *Red Flag* found himself obliged to answer objections. People were saying: 'It used to be thought that the Communist Party was pure', or 'It seems that the struggle within the Party is not an objective struggle but a struggle between people.' Such questions were answered, but the shock of seeing the fall, one after another, of Mao's former close allies and advisers had obviously shaken the credibility of the Party.

Peking has never been able to understand why so much fuss was made in the United States about so trifling an affair as Watergate. In February Nixon visited China as ex-President, was received with honour and met

Mao Zedong — Zhou Enlai was dead, and Deng was already out of favour.

On July 1, 1976, the official birthday of the Party, the joint editorial of the Peking papers announced a Party purge designed to rid the Party of Deng's followers and so maintain in power those who 'study Marxism-Leninism and Mao Zedong Thought and support the New-Born Things', i.e. the supporters of Jiang Qing's radical group.[59] The purge was hard to carry out, for a number of the prominent old Party members rehabilitated by Deng were still in power, and there was fear that young hotheads might seize the opportunity to cause trouble. At the start the radicals talked about 'suppression of counter-revolutionaries', but later these words were rarely heard. Instead accusations levelled against Deng were repeated with the persistence of a Tibetan lama's prayer wheel. Even the most sensational accusations become monotonous if they are repeated daily.[60]

Mao's health was declining. The last time he received a foreign visitor was on May 27, when he met Zulfiqar Ali Bhutto, Prime Minister of Pakistan.[61]

Inexplicably, the Two Resolutions, the dismissal of Deng and the elevation of Hua, evoked a widespread response from provincial leaders. Tens or hundreds of thousands of people were gathered to acclaim the Two Resolutions, and regional military leaders appeared in person to approve them. Among these were Qin Jiwei, commander of the Peking Troops who, before and after this time, seemed to be one of Deng's confidants, and Xu Shiyou, commander of the Canton Troops, certainly no friend of the radicals. Yang Dezhi did not appear in person at a mass gathering; he was ill, but he telephoned from hospital to express his support. (In the 1980s, under Deng, he became Chief-of-Staff.)[62] In August 1976, Jiang Qing issued three documents; one on the economy, one on industry and one on science and technology, as a repudiation of the programme Deng worked out a year earlier.[63]

Mao's death

At ten minutes after midnight on September 9, Mao Zedong died. In typical Communist style, the morning news said nothing. People went to work, government offices opened, business went on as usual. The news was broadcast in the afternoon and mourning began at once and lasted till the memorial service in Tian An Men Square on September 18. In rather bad taste, the announcement to the nation of Mao's death was accompanied by criticism of Soviet revisionism and of

Deng and the 'rightists', and by support for the New Born Things and for the restriction of 'bourgeois rights'.

On September 11 – 17 the body lay in state and the leaders received the condolences of foreigners. On the 18th a million people gathered in Tian An Men Square for a memorial meeting, at which Hua Guofeng delivered the funeral oration, garnished with praise of the New-Born Things. He made no mention of what a joint editorial in the Peking papers two days earlier had described as a hitherto unknown phrase of Mao's: 'Abide by the set directives.'[64] This phrase was to make history: it was the phrase on which Jiang Qing and company based their right of succession. After the arrest of the Gang, Hua Guofeng invoked another phrase of Mao's to justify his own succession.[65]

Let us examine the sequence of events. The joyful celebrations for the National Day, October 1, were cancelled. Instead, discussion meetings were held the day before, on the roof of the Tian An Men, the gateway to the Forbidden City. An official photograph of these discussions was published, in which Hua Guofeng stood not in the centre, but on the left, at the end of the row. On his right were the young Wang Hongwen, the aged Ye Jianying, and then the special trio, Zhang Chunqiao, Jiang Qing and Yao Wenyuan. They were so arranged that Zhang Chunqiao and Yao Wenyuan were seen to be one step behind Jiang Qing. Thus although all were standing in the correct order according to rank, Jiang Qing was in the centre of the picture published in the *People's Daily*.

On the following morning, October 1, the October issue of *Red Flag* repeated the words 'Abide by the set directives' and referred to Marx and Engels. When Marx died in 1883, Engels, who shared his ideals, remained to carry on his work. In the same issue of *Red Flag*, the Jiang Qing revolutionaries of Peking University wrote: 'The bourgeois within the Party may launch a counter-revolutionary armed coup. This would raise the Red Flag [meaning a false red flag] against the Red Flag and alter the Marxist-Leninist Line of the Party . . . Before launching a counter-revolutionary coup, they will try to prepare a counter-revolutionary public opinion.'

Part Three: 1976 – 1985

CHAPTER XIX

AFTER MAO, 1976 – 1977

The coup

The *coup* was not delayed for the preparation of public opinion.[1] Six days later, on October 6, the four, Jiang Qing, Wang Hongwen, Zhang Chunqiao and Yao Wenyuan, were arrested. There is no impartial report on how this happened. Much later the *People's Daily* reported that Yao Wenyuan was busy collecting compromising data on the life of Zhou Enlai and that he worked on this 'until the afternoon of October 6'. The four were therefore arrested in the evening of October 6. Who arrested them is not clear; a 1981 inner-Party document said that on October 6, 1976, Hua Guofeng, Ye Jianying and Li Xiannian, carrying out the wish of the Politbureau (of which Jiang Qing and the other three were members), 'isolated Jiang Qing, Zhang Chunqiao, Yao Wenyuan and Wang Hongwen for investigation.'[2]

On October 24, when Hua Guofeng was solemnly inaugurated as the new Chairman at the Tian An Men, Wu De said that he had become Chairman on October 7 (the day after the *coup*) and that this had been done in accordance with the wishes of Chairman Mao, who had written in his own hand to Comrade Hua Guofeng the words 'With you in charge, I am at ease.'[3] October 6, 1976, was a momentous day in the history of the People's Republic. In a speech two months later, Hua Guofeng said bluntly that if the Four had succeeded in winning power, it would have meant civil war.

It can hardly be doubted that the radicals had their supporters in the provinces, former Red Guards, the former rebels who a few years earlier had arrested the Party leaders whom Zhou Enlai and Deng later released and put in responsible posts.

At the end of 1976, several provinces denounced supporters of the radicals, calling them 'black hands'. A 'black hand' in Henan province, it was said, had declared after the death of Mao: 'Preparations must be made for the great act. The matter will be settled in October, all must be ready to give their blood.' Another 'black hand', Zhang Tiesheng, the young man who had handed in a blank paper at an examination and been honoured by the radicals for this fine act, was agitating in Shanxi province. The 'black hands' in Hubei province had been raiding offices for personal dossiers and saying that soon after the death of Mao it would be announced that Jiang Qing was the new Chairman. The 'black hands' included a member of the provincial Party committee, and a deputy head of the provincial revolutionary committee. These two had their own armed militia and their influence reached to the counties. After Mao's death these rebels in Hubei wrote a letter expressing their loyalty to Jiang Qing.

In those days Zhao Ziyang was the first Party secretary of Sichuan province. On November 20, 1976, at a meeting attended by 20,000 people, he said: 'The Gang of Four erected a bourgeois stronghold . . . they established their own organisations . . . they intended to overthrow the provincial Party committee.'[4]

Rumour had it that on October 6 the radicals were on the point of arresting their enemies, and that they themselves were arrested only half an hour before they were to have gone into action. Whether this is true, whether they were ready for a *coup*, is not certain. They were certainly in a bellicose mood. On October 4, two days before they were seized, one of their writers wrote: 'When Marx died, Engels took over leadership; but after the death of Stalin, the renegade clique of Khrushchev and then of Brezhnev promoted counter-revolutionary revisionism. In China too, some revisionist leaders want to manipulate the set directives to castrate the revolutionary soul.' The 'set directives' was a reference to Mao's alleged dictum, 'Abide by the set directives', words the radicals intended to use to take over the leadership. They were, quite certainly, closer to Mao than the others. A year later, when a dossier of accusations against Jiang Qing and company was being compiled, one passage said that at the bedside of the dying Mao were Jiang Qing and her companions, but none of the others.

The new leaders, Hua Guofeng and others, interpreted the radicals' October 4 article as 'a counter-revolutionary call for mobilisation, the point of which was aimed directly at the Party Central headed by Comrade Hua Guofeng'.[5]

If . . .

It is tempting to speculate on what would have happened to China if the *coup* had gone the other way. It is of course merely a matter of speculation, but certain probabilities stand out. Probably Hua Guofeng, who was opposed by the Shanghai and Northeast supporters of Jiang Qing, would have gone, and the Four would have taken the leading posts in Party and government and old Chen Boda, for thirty years Mao's Marxist assistant, would have been freed from the prison into which he was put after the Lushan meeting in 1970. A younger generation would have led the country. They were already at hand. Probably a number of the old cadres would have been reinstated, but not in top jobs. Jiang Qing could have become the leader of the Party — but, without Mao for how long? The supporters of Zhou and Deng would have gone to labour camps — as the supporters of the Gang went when Deng achieved power. The Deng regime said later that under the Gang of Four, China was closed to foreign trade; but this was not true. In 1976–7 the American company Kellogg was building modern fertiliser plants in Manchuria. Foreign policy would not have changed much; the recognition of China by the United States, Japan and then many other countries was the work of Zhou, but it flattered the national pride of all. In 1973 at Jiang Qing's request the Philadelphia Philharmonic Orchestra under Eugene Ormandy played Beethoven's 6th Symphony in Peking, although the newspapers had declared Beethoven and Schubert reactionary.[6] What trend would have taken the upper hand if her group had gained power? Would they have given up their ultra-radical policies? Would the temperamental lady have quietened down? Her previous performances did not augur well. When the Four were arrested, many in the Party ranks — but not the younger generation, which was imbued with the rebel spirit — took a deep breath.

The new Chairman

The arrest of Jiang Qing and the other three was not announced to the party organisations until October 18, twelve days after the event. It was said that between September 8 and 15, Shanghai, the radicals' main bastion, was ready for an uprising.[7] Contemporary rumour had it that Xu Shiyou had returned from Canton to his former military command in Nanjing and had seen to it that there would be no disturbances in Shanghai. It is certain that Ding Sheng, the commander of the Nanjing Area, to which Shanghai belongs, disappeared, and that Xu was hailed as the hero of the hour.[8]

Hua Guofeng took over the leadership on October 7, the day after the Four were arrested. On October 9, it was announced that a Mao mausoleum, the Memorial Hall, was to be built in Peking, that the fifth volume of Mao's *Selected Writings* would be published soon, that more volumes would follow, and that at a later date the *Complete Works of Mao Zedong* would be published 'under the direct guidance of the Politbureau headed by Hua Guofeng'. (Vol. V, a selection of Mao's writing up to November 1957, was published in May the following year; vol. VI has not appeared.)[9]

At the end of October 1976 a four-day celebration was organised at the Tian An Men in Peking. The headlines in the Peking newspapers were printed in red, and Hua Guofeng's titles — Chairman of the Party Central Committee and Chairman of the Military Committee of the C.C. — were officially announced by Wu De, the Party boss of Peking city. Wu De declared that Hua had become Chairman on October 7 and that he had been selected by Mao himself, with the words: 'With you in charge, I am at ease.' It was Hua, he said, who uncovered the clique of the Four. On the following day the Peking newspapers reported that Comrade Hua Guofeng had taken 'resolute measures against the anti-Party Gang of Four, smashed their plot and saved the revolution and the Party'. The cult of the new leader began at once. The commanders of the Military Areas sent congratulatory cables, and provincial newspapers wrote about the great happiness of the people.

'Rotten eggs'

A smear campaign against Jiang Qing was begun. She was described as 'the rotten egg'. When she visited her own model village, Xiao Jing Zhuang, she would not eat the local food but brought her own Western-style food with her, and even a sofa-like lavatory. When she visited Dazhai, the model village created by Mao, she arrrived with a retinue of 100 people and four riding horses; when she visited Hainan island at the southern end of the country, she ordered her three horses to be brought there by plane; when she swam in the sea, the navy had to encircle the whole harbour. She had compared herself to an empress in the Han dynasty who had ruled the country. That she behaved like an empress was confirmed by Professor Roxane Witke of Boston, whom she invited to China in 1972 and talked to for sixty hours in the hope that her guest would become her biographer, as Edgar Snow had been Mao's.[10]

It was also said that Jiang Qing wanted to destroy documents that would have revealed her life as a young film star in Shanghai. Rumour has it that in 1934 she was arrested by the Kuomintang and confessed. In 1964 she asked two men in the Shanghai police to look for the compromising documents, and during the Cultural Revolution she had both of them arrested, so that no trace might be found of her enquiry: one of them died in prison.

She also sent men to raid the home of the woman who had been her servant in the 1930s. The woman was arrested and spent seven years in prison. All who knew anything about her past were eliminated.[11]

Photographs

The fall of the Gang of Four had an extraordinary photographic history. The November 1976 issue of *China Pictorial*, a large-size Peking pictorial monthly, published after a four-month delay in March 1977, carried photographs of Mao's memorial services in September 1976 and showed the leaders lined up in a row to receive the condolences of foreign diplomats. In these reproductions the Gang of Four were nowhere to be seen. In the photograph of foreigners shaking hands with the Chinese leaders, the Four had been taken out and the figures of the others had been pushed together. In the picture of Mao's memorial service of September 18, not even this much was done. The row of leaders was shown, but the Four had simply been cut out of the picture and the space left blank. This photograph was not a forgery; it simply showed that the Four had become non-entities and had disappeared from public life. The same pictures, with the Four in them, were published in the *People's Daily* immediately after the funeral. Thus it was easy to compare earlier editions with the March 1977 *China Pictorial* versions. On October 1, 1976, the picture of the leaders with Jiang Qing standing prominently in the middle was also published — this was not reproduced in March 1977.

After all this, on March 25, 1977, the *People's Daily* had the impudence to accuse the Gang of Four of having falsified photographs and said that those taken at the Tenth Party Congress in August 1973 were forgeries. One picture showed Mao with Jiang Qing and Zhou Enlai. Jiang Qing, the *People's Daily* alleged, ordered that Wang Hongwen should be added to the photo. Another showed Jiang Qing herself with General Xu Shiyou; she ordered Xu to be cut out and one of her men, Zhang Chunqiao, put in his place. It was also asserted that on the eve of National Day the leaders had not stood in the order shown in the picture published at the time, with Jiang Qing in the middle; the photo had been rearranged.[12] This particular accusation of forgery may not be true; it may have been put forward to save the reputation of Hua Guofeng, who was also in the picture.

Persecution

When a leader falls, it is usual to publish documentation of his crimes and start a purge to eliminate his followers. A collection of the crimes of the Gang of Four was published — extracts from personal diaries, depositions of witnesses, and so on. A purge with the usual criticism and self-criticism was to start 'to expose and criticise the Gang of Four and to purify the ranks of the Party'. To begin with, it did not get very far. Some local leaders were 'afraid that they themselves would become involved'. 'There are persons who are afraid to beat the snake lest they be bitten by it. Some of the followers of the Gang are resisting stubbornly, some are spreading rumours in an effort to change the direction of the purge.'[13]

The pursuit of the followers of the Gang of Four went ahead, however. Mass organisations that had been formed during the Cultural Revolution and suppressed by Lin Biao had revived under the rule of Jiang Qing's radicals and caused trouble. Some, using guerilla methods, halted and robbed freight trains and caused stoppages and strikes in factories. Mass meetings in the provinces, gatherings of 100,000 to 200,000 people, were urged to act against these trouble-makers. Four million people listened in Jiangxi province to a broadcast of a mass accusation meeting which condemned those who had committed atrocities during the Cultural Revolution.[14] Some provincial leaders who had supported the radicals were condemned, and the names of some regional leaders were published. General Song Peizhang, First Party secretary of Anhui province, was an ardent supporter of the radicals' Shanghai-type militia organisation. In the summer of 1976, just before the death of Mao, he attempted to remove the militia from the control of the army. He promoted young people to positions of leadership and removed old Party men. His main crime was that he was opposed to Deng. He was present at the March 1977 Work Session of the Party Central which discussed the rehabilitation of Deng; but as soon as he was back in his province, he spoke against Deng.

The First Party secretary of Gansu province, General Xian Henghan, was removed from his post in May 1977. The charge against him was that on November 2, 1976, twenty-six days after the arrest of Jiang Qing and company, he had quoted in public 'Abide by the set directives', the words, allegedly from Mao, with which Jiang Qing intended to prove the legitimacy of her power.

Deng up again

The new regime of Hua Guofeng did not upset the old system. The Gang of Four and their followers were denounced, but the Cultural Revolution was still being praised. Soldier-Party-secretaries were still running a number of provinces. When the death of Mao was announced in September, the message included praise of the New Born Things and of the restriction of bourgeois rights, and criticism of Deng Xiaoping.[15] But at the end of October 1976, at the inauguration of Hua Guofeng at the Tian An Men, pictures of Zhou Enlai were carried in the demonstration, and in the November 8 issue of the army newspaper, Liu Shaoqi and Lin Biao were condemned but not Deng Xiaoping.[16]

Hua's situation *vis-à-vis* Deng was, to say the least, awkward, for the condemnation of Deng and the elevation of Hua had been published on the same page of the April 7, 1976, issue of the *People's Daily*. In the following year Deng was rehabilitated.

In March 1977 Deng wrote two letters, one to Hua Guofeng and one to Ye Jianying. In the same month at a Work Conference of the Central Committee, the rehabilitation of Deng Xiaoping was decided upon. It was not stated who was present at this conference.[17] Inner-Party documents published in 1981 revealed that Deng spoke and praised the 'system' of the Thoughts of Mao.[18] (A few years later Deng explained that 'system' implied that not all Mao's words need to be taken literally, but the system must be accepted.)

On July 16–21, 1977, the Third Plenum of the C.C. (the third after the Tenth Party Congress of 1973), met in Peking without, of course, the radicals. The Plenum reinstated Deng in the posts he had previously held: Vice-Chairman of the C.C., member of the Politbureau and of the Politbureau's Standing Committee, Vice-Premier, and chief of the general staff of the army.

The Plenum announced the convocation of a Party Congress, the Eleventh since 1921, to approve a revision — one more revision — of the Party Charter and to elect a new Central Committee. As usual, everything was arranged in advance, to be served up to the Party Congress when it opened three weeks later. The number of C.C. members present at the Plenum was not disclosed. At the Congress (August 12–18, 1977), 114 of the previous 319 C.C. members were dropped on suspicion of having been followers of Jiang Qing and company. Obviously the 114 were not present at the C.C. Plenum that prepared the documents and the nomenclature of the Congress.[19]

The Eleventh Party Congress, 1977

The Party Congress listened to three major speeches, one from Hua Guofeng, the Chairman of the Party, one from Ye Jianying explaining the revision of the Party Charter, and a short concluding address by the newly re-emerging Deng Xiaoping. The 1,510 delegates had only to say 'Amen'. The 1,510, it was said, represented 35 million Party members, 7 million more than in 1973, the time of the preceding Party Congress. Of the 35 million Party members, half had entered the Party since the time of the Cultural Revolution, i.e. since 1966.

Hua Guofeng's speech followed the Mao Line. He spoke about the inevitability of a world war, described the United States and the Soviet Union as paper tigers, and said that the newly improved relations with the United States were 'temporary, vacillating, unstable, unreliable and conditional'. He still spoke of 'continued revolution under the dictatorship of the proletariat' and of 'bourgeois rights', which he said had been misinterpreted by the Gang of Four. He still praised Dazhai and Daqing, the agricultural and industrial models created by Mao. He spoke of class enemies — 'landlords, kulaks, reactionary capitalists, murderers, arsonists, hooligan organisations, those who beat, smash and loot, and bad elements who seriously disturb public order'. Yet he also spoke about the reinstatement of discarded old Party officials in their posts, and said that the livelihood of the people should be improved through increased production. Speaking about educated people, he said that those who were not opposed to Marxism and Socialism should be employed. In support of this, he quoted a saying attributed to Mao on 'doing away with the mistaken metaphysical notion that gold must be pure and that man must be perfect'.

The revised Party Charter followed the old lines. The highest ruling organ, as before, was the Politbureau Standing Committee, consisting of the Chairman and the Vice-Chairmen. The Chairman was Hua Guofeng. The four Vice-Chairmen were Ye Jianying, Deng Xiaoping, Li Xiannian and, surprisingly, Wang Dongxing, who was head of the General Office of the C.C. and commander of the no. 8341 Troop of the army. He was an obscure figure who rarely appeared in public, one of Mao's henchmen — and apparently the man who took the leading role in the arrest of Jiang Qing and the others. Only this last act can explain why he got such a high post in the Party.

The other sensation of the Congress was the fact that Deng delivered the concluding speech. He started with the words 'presided over by our wise leader Comrade Hua Guofeng'. (Three years later Deng was to squeeze Hua out of the Premiership and, after another year, out of the Chairmanship of the Party.) 'Our Congress has been a Congress adhering to Chairman Mao's proletarian revolutionary line,' he went on, and he even used the formulas 'We must hold high and defend the great banner of Chairman Mao . . . and continue the revolution under the dictatorship of the proletariat . . . hold to the principal link, class struggle and [repeating] consolidate the dictatorship of the proletariat' — sayings and policies he flatly repudiated later.[20]

Wang Dongxing

How did Wang Dongxing become a Vice-Chairman of the Party? He had been with Mao since the Yan'an days. A booklet published in 1965 recounted the events of 1947–8 when the Nationalist troops took Yan'an and the Communists had to leave. It depicted Wang Dongxing as a man of great courage and total loyalty to Mao, and said that he led a crack troop to explore the situation round Yan'an. In 1971 a revised version of this booklet appeared with added passages about Jiang Qing as an important leader. It may be concluded, not only that Wang was in Mao's intimate entourage in Yan'an, but also that he was on good terms with Jiang Qing, certainly in 1971.

When the People's Republic was established in 1949, Wang was commander of the C.C. Secretariat guard. In that year he accompanied Mao to Moscow as his bodyguard. In 1966, in the same capacity, he accompanied Liu Shaoqi on his visit to South Asian countries. From 1955 to 1958 he was Vice-Minister of Security. Then he was sent off to Jiangxi province, where he established a much-praised Communist University. In 1960 he was back in Peking in his old post. On the eve of the Cultural Revolution, in November 1965, while remaining commander of Mao's guard, he also became head of the General Office of the C.C., replacing an old C.C. leader, Yang Shangkun. In 1969 the Ninth Party Congress, the Congress of Lin Biao, made him an alternate-member of the Politbureau. The Tenth Party Congress in 1973, the Congress of the radicals, made him a full Politbureau member. At the Eleventh Party Congress in 1977, he became a Vice-Chairman, ranked after Ye Jianying, Deng and Li Xiannian in seniority.

On the first anniversary of Mao's death, September 8, 1977, three weeks after the Eleventh Party Congress, an article filling two pages was published in the People's Daily, not by Wang Dongxing, but under the name of his General Office of the C.C.

The article — introduced by a large picture of Mao standing in front of Wang's No. 8341 Troop — seemed to explain why Wang had got so high in the Party leadership. 'The 8341 Troop, under the personal leadership of Chairman Hua and Vice-Chairman Ye Jianying, resolutely carried out the order of the Party Central, dealing a devastating blow to the Gang of Four.' This implies that Wang and his men were responsible for the arrest of Jiang Qing and company.

Why Wang turned against Jiang Qing is not very clear. Possibly he had never been happy with her imperial manners. The *People's Daily* article said that after the disappearance of Lin Biao on September 13, 1971, Jiang Qing tried to abolish the No. 8341 Troop, but Mao had said: 'If it were not for the 8341, Lin Biao would have done harm to me.' After the Tenth Party Congress, in August 1973, the Gang of Four wanted to seize power in the Party and the army and also in the Central Committee's General Office, but this was prevented by Chairman Mao. After the death of the Chairman, the Gang of Four wanted to take over the C.C.'s General Office headed by Wang.

All this is probably true, but it does not explain adequately why Mao's chief guard turned against his old master's wife. Possibly he did not see much future for the ambitions of Jiang Qing after Mao's death. The article gave some glimpses from the thirty year-history of relations between Mao and his guard, revealing aspects of Mao and his way of ruling the country not seen elsewhere.

The guard was not simply Mao's bodyguard. Its men were also his secret informers — and probably more than that. In 1955, at the time of the collectivisation of the land, Mao instructed his guard to recruit members from each 'special district' — there were some 200 of these administrative units, between the size of a county and a province. When these men had been trained, they were to be sent back to the villages they had come from to investigate the situation there. When they returned, Mao listened to them for three consecutive days and read their reports carefully, even correcting their style, and told them to write home every second month to keep in touch with the situation. In December 1965 Mao emphasised that it was the duty of the guard to protect the Party's secrets.

In 1967 when Mao sent the army to impose order on the turbulent Cultural Revolution, he assigned to the guard certain factories and schools in Peking in which they should take action. At the time of the reconstitution of the Communist Party in 1970, the whole country had to study how the 8341 Troop had reconstituted the Party in Peking.

Wang was acutely aware of the importance of the C.C.'s General Office, of which he was the head. Liu Shaoqi, Lin Biao and the Gang of Four all intrigued to gain control of the General Office in order to seize supreme power in the country, the article said. The General Office struggled against all of them.

Wang Dongxing may have been one of Mao's faithful guards, but he was not a skillful politician. A year later on September 11, 1978, the 8341 Troop was still able to have published in the *People's Daily* an article recalling how Mao had cared for the education of soldiers in the guard and how highly he appreciated the Jiangxi Communist University, the creation of Wang Dongxing. By the end of the year, however, the writing was literally on the wall: Wang's name appeared in the wallposters of Peking accusing him of having opposed Deng Xiaoping and Deng's rehabilitation. The wallposters were not put up by Red Guards: their time was over — this was an official warning. In February 1980, Wang Dongxing 'resigned' from the Vice-Chairmanship and from the Politbureau.[21] On December 25, 1978, a Politbureau meeting dismissed Wang from the General Office of the C.C.[22] That was the end of his power. At the Twelfth Party Congress in September 1982, he was listed among the alternate-members of the C.C. only, which meant that he no longer even had the right to vote.

Wang Dongxing, who undoubtedly took an active part in the arrest of Jiang Qing and company, had to go because the whole network of Mao's secret police was being demolished.

Mao's nephew

Not until 1977 did it become visible what an important man Mao's nephew Mao Yuanxin was. He was the son of Mao's brother, who was killed in Xinjiang in 1942 when his son was three years old. During the Cultural Revolution Mao Yuanxin led a fierce radical group in the Northeast. This explains the close connection between the Northeast and the Jiang Qing radicals in Shanghai, which formed a formidable radical axis. The Northeast and Shanghai were the most intensely industrialised parts of China.

During the Cultural Revolution, Mao Yuanxin became vice-chairman of the revolutionary committee of Liaoning province in the Northeast, and when the provincial party committee was set up in January 1971, he became its deputy secretary. His authority extended beyond his own province. In the summer of 1976, before Mao's death, he stayed in Peking. When in 1977 he was openly condemned (though not by name — Mao's nephew could not be condemned by name) he was described as 'the sworn follower of the Gang of Four in Liaoning'. Everybody knew who the 'sworn follower' was. Only then was it revealed that his power in the country was widespread. He was in full control of the ministry of metallurgy in Peking, where the minister was his man, a soldier from Liaoning province. After the fall of the Gang of Four the minister disappeared from the scene.

Mao Yuanxin was accused of having closed village markets and prevented the broadcasting of news he did not like.[23] The May 1977 issue of *Red Flag* compared 'the sworn follower' with Gao Gang, the ruler of the Northeast, purged in 1954. It accused him of being behind the rebel student Zhang Tiesheng, who had handed in a blank examination paper and so become a hero.

It may perhaps be said that Mao Yuanxin — who since his childhood had been close to his uncle and who had wielded such great power as long as the old Mao was still in the saddle — represented the best (or worst) ideas of Mao Zedong, his dreams of a revolutionary, proletarian 'New China'. Mao did not choose his nephew as his successor. Neither did he choose his wife Jiang Qing; he chose Hua Guofeng, rejecting Deng Xiaoping and Deng's liberal ideas.

Mao Yuanxin disappeared from the political scene and it is not known whether he is in prison, has been executed or is still alive in some remote corner of China.

Purge

After the Eleventh Party Congress of August 1977, the pursuit of the followers of the radicals intensified. More mass meetings were held in the provinces to denounce the enemies. In one province, Guizhou, 360,000 people were trained to carry out the purge. Yet resistance was strong and there was confusion in finding out who were and who were not the enemy. It could not be asserted that all those who had taken part in the Cultural Revolution had been wrong. The Cultural Revolution had been launched by Mao, and Mao's reputation was still unimpaired. It proved necessary to resort to tortuous arguments. The *People's Daily* reported on January 19, 1978: 'It cannot be denied that the great Cultural Revolution produced enormous results. But it was manipulated by Lin Biao and the Gang of Four, who sabotaged the strategic arrangements of Chairman Mao and savagely opposed Chairman Mao's policy, harming and oppressing a great many old cadres who were the leaders on all levels . . . Many were called renegades, spies, incorrigible men on the capitalist road.'

Fang Yi, a member of the Politbureau and deputy president of the Academy of Science, who had been in charge of the economy for many years, said that the purge should not reach back to the early years of the Cultural Revolution. It was hard to know how to judge the Cultural Revolution now when the radicals were being persecuted and a number of the old guard who had suffered it had been reinstated. The army newspaper urged strong action against opportunists who changed with the wind, and 'sliders whose feet are smeared with oil and look you straight in the face pretending to be the greatest enemies of the Gang of Four'.

This purge eliminated a number of Party leaders. One notable removal was that a soldier named Guo Yufeng, who had been head of the Organisation Department of the Central Committee. He was replaced in 1978 by Hu Yaobang, then said to be sixty-five.

Liu Xingyuan, one of Lin Biao's leading generals, had become the First Party secretary of Guangdong province under Lin Biao, taking the place of the purged Zhao Ziyang. In 1973, two years after the fall of Lin Biao, Zhao Ziyang returned to Guangdong. Liu, however, was not purged — not yet. He was transferred to Sichuan to be the First Party secretary of that important province. He was also commander of the military in Sichuan province and in Tibet. At the Tenth Party Congress in 1973 Liu was still a C.C. member. Two years later, in 1975, Zhao Ziyang left Guangdong province to take Liu's place as First Party secretary of Sichuan province. Liu remained in command of the troops, and two years later, in 1977, Liu was still a C.C. member at the Eleventh Party Congress; but in that year he lost his military post and in 1978 was accused of having been a follower of the Jiang Qing radicals, the Gang of Four.[24]

Hu Yaobang and Zhao Ziyang were Deng's men. Deng therefore already had an important voice in nominations. In 1980 Zhao Ziyang became Prime Minister, and in 1981 Hu Yaobang took over the Party leadership from Hua Guofeng.

The purge was aimed primarily at the followers of the radicals, but it was extended to corruption in the Party. Some famous cases were publicised: the First Party secretary of the city of Luda in the Northeast was accused of waste; he had built twenty-one clubs for local Party men, each with seating for over 1,000, plus seven guest-houses, and a huge club for the military occupying half of a park in the centre of the city. All the work was done by people condemned to forced labour. The Party leader of a machine factory in a city in Gansu province in the Northwest was accused of having established his own prison where those caught were beaten and tied up. In Jilin province in the Northeast, the Party leader of a scientific research institute had given rough treatment to the scientists. He accused 166 people, researchers and research assistants, of being spies — the proof was that they had radios or cameras at home, or that they could speak a foreign language. This man set up his own court and exposed the accused to torture. Some of them committed suicide. The man who had done all this not merely went unpunished; he was promoted to be a Party secretary of the provincial science and technology office.

The First Party secretary of Jilin province was a soldier, Wang Huaixiang. In 1977 he was sent back to the barracks and his post in Jilin was taken by Wang Enmao, who had been leader of Xinjiang from the 1950s to the Cultural Revolution, in which he was purged. (In 1981 he was back in his old post in Xinjiang.)

An odd accusation was made against the Party head of a chemical industry plant: that he cared too much for the workers. He had set up a hospital for them, with a swimming pool and an artificial waterfall — an unnecessary luxury. His factory engaged in bartering steel products for timber and other building materials, disregarding state plans. He was also accused of wanting to avoid the purge of the followers of the Gang of Four, and of having accused others to cover himself.[25]

CHAPTER XX

DENG UP, 1978

People's Congress

At the end of February 1, 1978, after a three-year delay, a National People's Congress was held. The People's Congress is a government, not a Party affair, but the role of the Party leaders in the government is important. Hua Guofeng, as Prime Minister and head of the State Council, presented the usual Report on Government Work. Ye Jianying left the ministry of defence to become head of the People's Congress Standing Committee, which was the highest government post. Deng Xiaoping became pre-eminent among the thirteen Vice-Premiers.

The Chinese People's Political Consultative Conference also met, simultaneously with the People's Congress. Nominally this is a gathering of non-Party members but it too is dominated by Party leaders. Zhou Enlai had formerly been head of this gathering, but now Deng Xiaoping stepped into his shoes. This was a big step forward for Deng; but he was not yet the chief figure in Party and government (Hua Guofeng was still head of both). In his Government Report Hua introduced an ambitious ten-year (1976–85) development plan: 120 large industrial units were to be set up, including ten large iron and steel plants, ten new oil and gas fields, thirty large power stations, six trunk railway lines and large industrial bases in fourteen geographically favourable areas. The country was to be divided into six great economic areas — the same six which until 1954 had been known as the Great Administrative Areas. Hua also spoke about the introduction of reforms in many fields. A new wage system was to be published, and industry premiums proportionate to piece-work were to be added to the basic salary. In agriculture also, work was to be paid at piece-rates. The growth of population was to be reduced to below one per cent within three years. Twelve large grain-producing regions were to be developed. (A year later, when Deng had reached the top, these ambitious plans were scrapped as unsound and unrealistic.)[1]

Science

Deng's policy was introduced gradually during 1978. A few weeks after the People's Congress, a congress on science was held. Both Hua and

Deng addressed the meeting, but they did not say the same things. Hua insisted on a better understanding of Marxism: as soon as the scientists have mastered the proletarian Communist world outlook, 'We shall be speaking the same language, not only the language of patriotism but the common language of the Communist world outlook'. Hua also insisted on the popularisation of science: 'Should the modernisation of science and technology be left to a few people in research institutes or universities?' he asked. He spoke of the need for having 'red-and-expert scientists and technicians'. Deng had entirely different things to say. 'A warm helping hand' should be held out to scientists, he said. What is red and what is white? 'White is a political concept, only reactionaries who oppose the Party and socialism should be called white. How can you label as "white" a man who studies hard to improve his knowledge and skill? . . . If someone works seven days and seven nights on end to meet the needs of science or production, that shows a lofty spirit of selfless devotion to the cause of socialism.'

In the Communist world, not just in China, the intellectuals and scientists are called a stratum, not a class. Deng was here introducing a revolutionary change. 'Are people engaged in scientific and technological work workers or not?' he asked. 'The overwhelming majority of them are part of the proletariat. The difference between them and manual workers lies only in a different role in the social division of labour.'

Deng went even further. A scientific institute was normally under a director, who himself was under the leadership of the Party committee of the institute. Deng had a different idea: 'The primary duty of the Party committee in scientific institutes is to guarantee services and supplies and to provide the necessary working conditions'. Turning to the scientists present at the Congress, he said: 'I am willing to be the director of the logistics department, at your service'.

Hua and Deng laid down diametrically opposite policies. Hua spoke about scientists in accordance with correct Marxist ideology, Deng thanked the scientists and said that they belonged to the working class and promised that he and the Party would serve them.

Education

A few weeks later, on April 22, a conference on education was held. Only two top leaders of the Party, Li Xiannian and Deng, took part. Two major reports were delivered, one by Deng and one by the minister of education. Deng repeated what Hua had already said in his report at the People's Congress, that preferential schools, pilot institutions, were to be developed from primary to university level. He insisted on proper education and on a search for and development of talented youth. A year earlier, instructions had been issued on the introduction of educational reforms and on not bringing into universities ignorant proletarians with no previous education.

Army meeting

A few days later a third major conference was held, the Political Work conference of the army. This was a highly important meeting. Hua, the Party Chairman, and two of the four Vice-Chairmen, Deng and Ye Jianying, and the head of the army's General Political Department, Wei Guoqing, were there. Hua produced the old Maoist platitudes, speaking of the contradiction between the proletariat and the bourgeoisie, saying that 'politics is the soul of everything', prophesying war between the United States and the Soviet Union and asserting that the Cultural Revolution, which he said had lasted eleven years, was a 'great political revolution'. Ye Jianying supported Hua and quoted from his speech to the science congress the words: 'Far from being weakened, political and ideological work should be strengthened.'

Deng began with compliments to Hua and Ye. Having said that he agreed with everything they had said, he ingeniously twisted their arguments and, by quoting selected words of Mao, made mincemeat of rigid adherence to Marxist theories and to Mao's Thoughts. 'Chairman Mao', he said, 'warned the comrades of the Party not to take Marxist theories as rigid dogmas and not to regard individual phrases in Marxist-Leninist books as miracle-working medicine . . . Chairman Mao pointed out that there is only one true theory in the world, the theory that derives from objective reality and is verified by objective reality . . . There are comrades', he said, 'who think that it is enough to parrot the words of Marx, Lenin and Chairman Mao, and that anyone who does not do that is opposed to Marxism-Leninism, to Mao Zedong Thought and to the spirit of the Party Central. This is no minor matter, it is the problem of how Marxism-Leninism and Mao Zedong Thought should be regarded.'

No less subtly Deng condemned the Cultural Revolution. Yes, he said, 'the great proletarian Cultural Revolution, launched and guided by Chairman Mao himself' was a good thing, but 'Lin Biao and the clique of the Gang of Four conspired from the early days to wreck the great proletarian Cultural Revolution.' The Gang of Four should have criticised Lin Biao; instead they criticised Zhou Enlai and Ye Jianying. No one should be afraid of bringing up crimes committed during the Cultural Revolution. 'Some say that this would mean a denial of the value of the Cultural Revolution, and that digging up historical debts [old crimes] might affect the unity [of the Party]. This is not true.'

In summary, what he said at these three meetings of scientists, educationalists and the army combined to form the basis of Deng's new doctrine:

1. Intellectuals, scientists, teachers *et al.* belong to the proletariat. Thus at one blow he destroyed the doctrine of Mao and of Hua Guofeng that the proletariat consists only of workers, peasants and soldiers.
2. Party men should not pretend to understand science; rather they should assist scientists and meet their material needs.
3. Scientists and their like should get on with their work and not be bothered with Marxist indoctrination. A scientist is 'white' only if he opposes the regime.
4. In schools, study should come first; in admission to universities, children of the proletariat should not get preference.
5. It is ridiculous to keep on for ever quoting words of Marx and Mao.
6. Marxism is not an immutable doctrine.
7. Those who committed crimes during the Cultural Revolution should be punished.[2]

What Deng said in 1978 was what he had proposed in 1975 when Zhou Enlai was still alive. In those days Deng's words were not even published in the press (till a year later when his doctrine was refuted and Deng himself was dismissed). Now he was up again, and he had the guts to say such things in public at important meetings in the presence of the dyed-in-the-wool old Maoists.

Revenge or not?

When Deng spoke of 'historical debts' he was touching on an interminable issue that has frequently agitated the Communist Party. A good Communist must have a clean history. Whenever friction arises within the Party, a major question always is: who betrayed the Party in the past and, in particular, who betrayed his comrades in the prisons of the Nationalist Government?

The 'historical debt' is therefore a highly sensitive subject, one that quickly arouses passion, hatred and vengeance.

The question in 1978 was: how had people behaved during the Cultural Revolution, and should the crimes committed then be punished? Opinions varied widely. Under the rule of Hua all had to say that the Cultural Revolution 'launched and guided by Chairman Mao' was a good thing but was misused by Lin Biao's criminals and Jiang Qing's radicals. What was to be done? Not thousands but hundreds of thousands, indeed millions, had been involved in the violent acts of the Cultural Revolution. Should old 'debts' be dug up? Fang Yi, as quoted above, said no. Deng Xiaoping was all for revenge, all for making a clean sweep. The Party leadership was divided.

The *Liberation Army Daily* was for revenge, but acknowledged that there was no unanimous view on this question. 'Some say', it said, 'that conditions in those days were as they were, and conditions today are as they are. What happened then was correct then, what is happening today is correct also. This is wrong; it implies that in those days the oppression of cadres was legal.'

A month later in August an article appeared in the same army paper under the heading 'The Old Accounts of the Lin Biao Line Must be Settled'. It is true, it said, that Chairman Mao said that 'entanglement in historical "old accounts" may easily get out of control' — that revenge awakes revenge and violence awakes violence. Indeed the evoking of old historical accounts brought trouble when Lin Biao and the Gang of Four accused old cadres of imaginary past crimes. All this is true, but Chairman Mao also said, in 1959, that if all historical debts were discounted it would be impossible to appease the anger of the masses. He himself at the time of the 1942–5 Party Rectification in Yan'an condemned Wang Ming (his rival) for what he had been doing ten years earlier. The army paper next quoted Deng: 'Some people committed errors which they have not yet admitted and have not yet confessed. Should these errors be called "old accounts" and so not be counted?'

This was one view. Those who opposed it were afraid that a campaign of revenge would lead to interminable trouble and would divide the Party. They were also afraid of resistance from strong groups which might cause further trouble. An important article in the September 1978 issue of *Red Flag* was headed 'Strengthen the Unity of the Party'. There are still many obstacles to unity, it said, and the pursuit of followers of the Gang of Four is meeting with considerable resistance. These people may cause an earthquake that will split the Party. In many places the evil-doing of the past is still being covered up, and false reports and false accusations are appearing. There should be wide discussion in a democratic spirit, criticism but not punishment. A revision of the condemnation of cadres must be undertaken and those wrongly condemned should be rehabilitated, but 'leading cadres should have the right attitude towards the great Cultural Revolution. They should not become entangled in historical old accounts.' Then a saying from the time of the Cultural Revolution was quoted: 'Say no words, do no deeds which impede unity.'

The two sides of the argument had been clearly exposed. According to Deng, the culprits of the Cultural Revolution should be punished. Only then could the political atmosphere be clarified and genuine unity be established within the Party and the army. *Red Flag*, on the other hand, representing another view in the highest leadership, believed that reopening old wounds could only create new problems and would harm Party unity, which at that time, 1978, was precarious and fragile. One false step and the Party might split. This was a warning from cautious men against Deng's daring moves.

Ye Jianying sided with the moderate view. As head of the People's Congress Standing Committee, he spoke in the middle of September of 'stability and unity', and repeated the saying quoted in *Red Flag*: 'Say no words, do no deeds which impede unity.' Unity, he said, is necessary for the modernisation of agriculture, of industry, of defence and of science — the Four Modernisations.

The *People's Daily* editorial published on National Day, October 1, seemed to combine the two views. It quoted 'Say no words, do no deeds which impede unity', but it also defended Deng's plan for a clean sweep and said that the purge of the followers of the Gang of Four would have to continue since there were places where past crimes were being covered up, and unjustly condemned cadres were not being released. Speaking about the Gang of Four, the *People's Daily* editorial left open the question whether the crimes committed before the death of Mao, during the hectic days of the Cultural Revolution, should be punished.

All agreed that Party leaders who had been discarded during the past years should be rehabilitated. Many were still suffering in dark corners. But there was a sharp division on the question of 'historical accounts'; on whether the heroes of the Cultural Revolution — the 'rebels', the 'revolutionary small generals' as they were called in the days of their triumph — should be condemned.

With such divergent opinions at the top, the provinces did not know clearly what to do. Wang Enmao, the pre-Cultural Revolution boss of Xinjiang — himself heavily purged —, who in 1977 had taken over the leadership of Jilin province in the Northeast from the radicals following General Wang Huaixiang, toured his province and found that in many places those who had taken part in 'beating, smashing, looting' during the Cultural Revolution were still in leading positions, and that local Party leaders who had suffered at their hands did not dare to open their mouths. Higher regional leaders now in charge were afraid to touch the question, lest they should be accused of taking revenge. Wang Enmao introduced radical measures to eliminate the old heroes of the Cultural Revolution from responsible posts. The major criminals, those who had killed or taken part in armed robbery or committed rape, were to be punished (which meant execution), but the ordinary beating-smashing-looting crowds should be treated leniently, and the majority were not to be prosecuted.

The same policy was followed in Sichuan province, where it was said that 'those whose hands were dripping with blood', counter-revolutionaries, must be arrested and punished in accordance with the law — which in such cases always meant execution. But it should be remembered that during the Cultural Revolution many people were deceived. Many of those who had taken part in armed fights, encouraged by Jiang Qing, had later expressed regret. Of those who had committed violent acts, beating, smashing and looting, only the main protagonists should be punished.

In Hubei province the provincial Party newspapers spoke with hesitation. The Cultural Revolution and its inventions, the New Born Things, and the entry of the army to help the leftist rebels cannot be condemned, but many acts committed during those years were wrong. Today many people do not dare to talk. They think in one way and speak in another, afraid that they will be accused of having denied the Cultural Revolution altogether. People should feel free to talk, but they do not. 'When two persons meet, they may tell the truth; when three persons meet they tell lies; when four meet they say nothing, merely exchanging polite jokes.'[3] In that year, 1978, Hua Guofeng was still Chairman but Deng's policies were begining to make an impact.

Deng's revenge

With the emergence of Deng the whole stage-setting changed. In October 1978 came Deng's revenge for his April 1976 condemnation. In those days (1976) when silent crowds were piling up thousands of wreaths round the heroes monument at the Tian An Men in memory of Zhou Enlai, and their silent tribute was being answered with violent incidents provoked by the authorities, the voice of Wu De, the Party boss of the city, could be heard from the loudspeaker and the leaders of the demonstration were being arrested. That tribute to the memory of Zhou was staged simultaneously in several major cities. The whole popular movement had been set in motion by Deng and his colleagues through an underground organisation.

Wu De was the speaker at the four-day celebration for the new Chairman Hua Guofeng at the end of October 1976. He remained First Party secretary and mayor of Peking for two more years, but at the end of October 1978 he lost both posts. A week later the meaning of the Tian An Men events was reversed. The people at the Tian An Men, the *Guang Ming Daily* of Peking said on October 28, 1978, were crowds 'who were mourning Premier Zhou, showing their anger against the Gang of Four, and supporting the struggle of Deng Xiaoping'. They wrote, it said, one of the most brilliant pages of the history of the revolution in China.[4]

The 388 persons arrested in 1976 were released, and it was stated that not a single counter-revolutionary, not a single bad person, had been found among them. The April 5, 1976, happenings at the Tian An Men became a legend, a monument marking the beginning of a new era. During the demonstration, poems were laid down at the foot of Monument of the Heroes praising Zhou and attacking Jiang Qing. The poems and photographs of what was happening have now become holy relics, and those who were arrested have become heroes. An album with 500 photographs was prepared for publication.

Hua Guofeng, who was elevated on the very day on which Deng was condemned — Mao was still alive —, had to make a humble act of reparation: he had to write with his own hand the title of the book containing poems celebrating the Tian An Men events. This was an apology and an act of surrender to Deng.

The style of rule in China had not changed. The legend of the April 5, 1976, events at the Tian An Men was not unlike the legends of Dazhai, of Jiang Qing's model village Xiao Jin Zhuang or of her theatre plays. A new play, *A Place of Silence*, was produced, this time to glorify the Tian An Men events. It was about an evil man and his good daughter who fell in love with a young man who was on the right side at the Tian An Men — Deng's side.

Wallposters appeared in Peking and were left untouched for many days. They castigated Deng's enemies, men who had been involved in the Tian An Men events. One poster attacked Wu De and the leaders of the security office of Peking city who had arrested Deng's men. Another made a violent attack on Wang Dongxing, the head of Mao's guard who had become Vice-Chairman of the Party. Some posters were even directed against Mao himself: it was he who had made Lin Biao his successor and who had been behind the Gang of Four; he must have consented to the condemnation of Deng.

One poster said that an Investigation Team had been set up to investigate the Tian An Men incident. The team included, according to the poster, Zhao Ziyang, then First Party secretary of Sichuan province, Wan Li, First Party secretary of Anhui, and Hu Yaobang, then head of the Organisation Department of the C.C., all of them close to Deng.[5]

Those posters were not put up by rebel youngsters, nor were they torn down by the authorities. 'In those days — the second half of 1978 — it looked as if Deng and his followers were ready to liquidate Mao's memory.

The triumph of Deng

From December 18–22, 1978, the Central Committee held its Third Plenum, the third since the Eleventh Party Congress in August 1977. Most of the C.C. members had been in Peking since the middle of November, taking part in a month-long discussion. The inner story of this four-week discussion was not revealed. The holding of the C.C. Plenum itself was not announced till it was over.

In the period of preparation, the campaign against Deng's enemies continued. At the time, it looked as if these men might lose their posts at the coming C.C. Plenum. They did not in fact lose them, but it was made clear that their position in the Party leadership was precarious. Deng's position was immensely strengthened. He was not Chairman of the Party — he was only one of the Vice-Chairmen — but he was the leader. For the first time in the history of communism, it was not the number one but the number three man (as Vice-Chairman he came behind Ye Jianying) who wielded real power. He had worked his way up gradually. In the first half of 1978 he spoke as a leader at the conferences on science, education and the army. Towards the end of the year, through the reassessment of the 1976 Tian An Men incident, he annulled the April 7, 1976, decree which had dismissed him, and elevated Hua.

The disappearance of Lin Biao and of Jiang Qing's radicals heralded the end of the era of Mao radicalism and a return to the situation of twenty years earlier when, at the Eighth Party Congress in 1956, Mao had been put under some restraint. The other top leaders of those days, Liu Shaoqi, Zhou Enlai, Zhu De, were dead — only Deng remained. As General Secretary of the Party before the Cultural Revolution he had built up a wide-ranging network of supporters among the veteran Party men who had been rehabilitated one by one and had gained leading posts. The C.C. Plenum posthumously rehabilitated the memories of two men, Marshal Peng Dehuai and Tao Zhu, who at the start of the Cultural Revolution became head of Party propaganda, and, having been purged soon after, was accused of being the man behind organised resistance to Mao and Lin Biao.

At this December 1978 C.C. Plenum, four additions were made to the twenty-three-member Politbureau: Deng Yingchao, widow of Zhou Enlai; Chen Yun, a highly respected old Party leader; Wang Zhen, whose intervention with Mao had brought Deng back to Peking; and Hu Yaobang, the leader of the Youth Corps till March 1965.

Nine new members were added to the Central Committee to be confirmed by the coming Twelfth Party Congress. (The C.C. has the power to elect Politbureau members but not C.C. members.) Eight of the nine new C.C. members had been purged, like Deng himself, during the Cultural Revolution. The ninth, Huang Kecheng, had been discarded by Mao back in 1959 when Marshal Peng Dehuai was condemned as a 'rightist opportunist' (Huang Kecheng had been Chief-of-Staff in 1959). Among the nine new C.C. members were Hu Qiaomu, a close collaborator of Mao's for many years and author of the quasi-official history of the Communist Party published in 1951; Wang Renzhong, the First Party secretary of Hubei province whose story of swimming with Mao in the Yangze had made him famous and who at the beginning of the Cultural Revolution was called to Peking to be deputy head of Party propaganda under Tao Zhu, but was quickly purged; and Xi Zhongxun, who, having been secretary-general of the Cabinet before the Cultural Revolution, had not been seen for thirteen years until December 1978, when he became First Party secretary of Guang-dong province. The meeting rehabilitated Bo Yibo, the former head of the State Economic Commission, and Yang Shangkun, whom the Red Guards accused of having bugged Mao and Jiang Qing's bedroom.

It was not stated at the Plenum that Mao had been responsible for the purging of such good men; their reinstatement was to prove eloquent enough. It was a condemnation of Mao and of the Cultural Revolution, although no summary judgement was passed on it. That, the communiqué released by the Plenum said, was to come later when the time was ripe. A cryptic sentence in the communiqué condemned Mao's secret intelligence network, and thus by implication three men, Kang Sheng, Xie Fuzhi and Wang Dongxing. (Kang Sheng had been Mao's henchman ever since the Yan'an era. Xie Fuzhi was made minister of security and head of the Politico-Legal Bureau of the Cabinet in 1959. During the Cultural Revolution Kang Sheng was adviser to the Central Cultural Revolution Team and Xie Fuzhi was its deputy head — Chen Boda was head. Kang Sheng died in December 1975, a month before Zhou Enlai. He had been one of the five Vice-Chairmen of the C.C. since the Tenth Party Congress of 1973; at the Eleventh Party Congress in August 1977, Hua Guofeng listed him among the most venerated of the dead Party leaders, but then a few months later his name ceased to be mentioned. He joined the ranks of world Communist leaders whose memories were purged after their deaths. Xie Fuzhi had died earlier, in March 1972. The third man involved in Mao's secret service, Wang Dongxing, was still a member of the C.C. at this meeting, but was no longer a Vice-Chairman.)

The cryptic sentence in the communiqué of the Plenum was: 'The conference held that the formerly used methods of setting up special investigative units to investigate cadres, without the supervision of the Party and of the Masses, had many defects and must be abolished for ever.' It was not stated whether these organs were *ad hoc* teams for checking the cases of one or more cadres, or permanent organisations. *Ad hoc* investigation organs were still active. One was investigating the case of Lin Biao and another the 1976 Tian An Men incident, which had led to the condemnation of Deng. The condemnation of Mao's chief secret agents, dead or alive, was an indication that this cryptic sentence was aimed at Mao's secret intelligence network.

The C.C. Plenum took one more mighty step. There were to be no more 'large-scale storm-like mass class struggles', although proletarian dictatorship was not to be weakened. China therefore was no longer to be ruled, as it had been for thirty years under Mao, by shattering political campaigns.

While all this was happening at the December 1978 C.C. Plenum, mass trials of political culprits were being held in some provinces and broadcast to the whole country. In contrast with the time of Khrush chev's condemnation of Stalin, the forced labour camps were not closed — only the inmates changed.

This Plenum — dominated by Deng — outlined the coming economic policies. The outline was a blueprint of what he wanted to introduce: extreme centralisation of economic management was to go; the ever-growing bureaucratic organisations were to be reduced; and the distinction between Party and government was to be made clear. The Party was no longer to take the place of the government, nor the government the place of enterprise managements. Regions and enterprises were to be given a larger right to self-determination, and two regulations on agriculture were to be sent to provinces for discussion and trial. The price paid by the state for grain purchases was to be increased by 20 per cent. The amount to be paid for grain purchased beyond the target was to be increased by 50 per cent. The provision of foodgrain for the consumer was to be subsidised, and the price was not to be raised.[6]

Freeing the outcasts

Soon after the December 1978 C.C. Plenum, a radical change in the social fabric of the People's Republic was announced — probably this had been decided upon at the Plenum. The social outcasts, classified as 'landlords, kulaks, counter-revolutionaries and bad elements', were to be liberated. For many, many years there had been no real landlords or kulaks in China, but the families and descendants of former landlords were branded with these titles. They were outcasts from society, along with counter-revolutionaries and the ill-defined group of 'bad elements'. They had to work unpaid in labour camps, farms or factories, segregated from other people who were afraid to touch them, let alone inter-marry with them; they were not members of the People. The freeing of these slaves was Deng's great act. At the end of 1979 it was announced:

Taking into account the fact that since the land reform and collectivisation of the land, the landlord and kulak elements have undergone correction by labour from 20 to 30 years, and that the great majority of them are now earning their living, it is time to remove their landlord and kulak 'caps' and to solve the problem of the social status of their children. Apart from the very few who persist in their reactionary attitude and have not reformed, the caps of all landlords, kulaks and counter-revolutionaries and bad elements should be taken off, as soon as the approval of the county authorities has been given.

The ministry for security ordered that the list of the rehabilitated should be made public, and that no fixed quotas should be adhered to in the rehabilitation process. (This referred to the system used in political campaigns in which a predetermined percentage of the people were to be condemned.) Those who had not reformed were to continue to live under surveillance.

Not all the outcasts were released. The instruction of the ministry for security said: 'Class struggle should not be amplified, but it should not disappear. There are still counter-revolutionaries who are enemies and saboteurs of the socialist modernisation . . . There are still uncorrected landlords, kulaks, counter-revolutionaries and bad elements. There is still class struggle and proletarian dictatorship.'

Besides the four categories of outcasts — landlords, kulaks, counter-revolutionaries and bad elements — there was a fifth, the 'rightists', whose origin went back to 1957, the time when the criticism of the Party asked for by Mao had gone too far. Mao then imposed a clampdown. Millions were sent by simple administrative decree to a new type of forced-labour camp euphemistically called 'labour education'. Theoretically these camps were different from the labour camps for counter-revolutionaries; in fact both the condemned groups worked together in the same camps. The 'labour education' inmates were supposed to be kept in the camps for only three years, but most of them were kept much longer. Others were sent to work under surveillance in villages and factories. If they were dismissed from their jobs they received no salary and lived on a pittance. A small number of them were restored to normal life in the years 1959–64, but the majority remained in their deprived state for twenty-one years — a long period in a person's life. When in 1979 they were released, the best part of their lives lay behind them.

It was not stated that their condemnation had been unjust. It could not be admitted that an institution started by Mao which had lasted twenty-one years had been a complete error. When the Party leadership decided to release them, the following statement was issued: 'The value of the 1957 anti-rightist struggle cannot be denied. In those days the rightists were attacking us. They wanted to take our place and were shouting "Kill the Communists". They wanted to overthrow the Communist Party and socialism. We counteracted in time. This was necessary and correct.'

All that was admitted was that the campaign had gone to excess and that many innocent people had been condemned. Accordingly the majority of the rightists were to be released. Those who had been expelled from the Party were to get back their Party cards and their old jobs and be reinstated in the salary scale they had enjoyed before; but salaries for the intervening years were not paid, as they had been in the cases of the rehabilitation of victims of the Cultural Revolution.

In spite of all these limitations, the release of the rightists was a great and important event. It meant the end of a craze in which a word spoken against Mao would be enough to send a man to a labour camp. 'Some erroneous words were taken as anti-Party and anti-socialist; friends discussing things among themselves were branded as an ''anti-Party clique''; an expression of criticism of the leading comrade of the Party [Mao] was taken as an attack on the central leadership.' People were condemned not only for what they had done, but for what they had said or had been accused of saying. A word that could be interpreted as criticism of Mao or of the regime could send the man and his family to misery. By 1979 Mao was no longer the idol. A new idol was slowly emerging, and those who criticised Deng's new regime took the places vacated by the rightists of 1957.[7]

Deng's Marxism

The radical changes introduced by Deng changed the face of Marxism in China. Deng chose the word Realism. When he spoke to the army's Political Work conference on June 2, 1978, he had harsh words for those 'who parrot the words of Marx, Lenin and Chairman Mao'. 'There is only one true theory in the world,' he said, 'the theory that derives from objective reality and is verified by objective reality.'

In the same month, June 1978, the army newspaper had a long article on 'The Most Fundamental Principle of Marxism'. The article was translated into English and appeared in subsequent issues of *Peking Review*. It quoted Deng's words of June 2 with admiration, 'How right! how profound! how well said!'. The article went on to explain that Marxism had been revised constantly:

We all know how Marx and Engels revised certain principles in *The Communist Manifesto*. There are innumerable similar examples in the history of Marxism, not excluding Stalin. Stalin in his *The Economic Problems of Socialism in the USSR* said that the treatment of some questions in the past was not correct and was no longer valid. To sum up, truth is developing. The development of Marxism and of Mao Zedong Thought undoubtedly involves the revision of some outmoded principles; but this is not revisionism.

(It was, of course, blatant revisionism. From that time onward, the Russian Communists, who for some fifteen years had been dubbed revisionists by Peking, were spared this epithet.) The article in the army paper quoted Mao's saying that Marxism is held to be true, not because it was scientifically formulated by Marx, Engels, Lenin and Stalin, but because it has been verified in the subsequent practice of revolutionary class struggle. It also quoted Engels: 'Marx's thought is not a doctrine, but a method.' Lin Biao and the Gang of Four did not see that Marxism and Mao's Thought constituted a science; they made an absolute out of it, a religion. Their propaganda said that every word of it is true, that it is the peak, an 'absolute authority', and so on.

On July 1, 1978, Party Day, a speech delivered by Mao sixteen years earlier, on January 30, 1962, was made known to the public for the very first time. However, this speech was not completely unknown; it had been published in the collection of Mao's speeches compiled by the Red Guards, but the general public now saw it for the first time, after a sixteen-year delay. It was published to show that Mao was not omniscient. He was speaking in 1962, after the failure of the Great Leap. He accepted responsibility for the mistakes and explained that in 1960, speaking to Edgar Snow, he had said: 'When it comes to socialist construction, we have not done it in the past, and we still have no experience . . . Snow wanted me to say something about China's long-term plans for construction. I said, "I do not know." He said: "You are being too cautious." I replied, "It is not a question of being cautious. I really do not know; we simply lack experience . . . There are many problems in the work of economic construction which I still do not understand. I know very little about industry and commerce for instance." '

About the Commune and the Great Leap, Mao said: 'We had not the time to work out a complete set of specific principles, policies and measures . . . We could not conceivably have had genuine unity between knowledge and action. This became possible only after a period of time, after we had suffered some setbacks and acquired both positive and negative experience . . .'

This speech of Mao's was useful for proving both of Deng's theses, that experience is the norm of Marxism, and that Mao was not an infallible leader.

In the same month, June 1978, the review *Philosophical Research* organised discussions in which academicians, journalists and people from the ministries took part. Zhou Yang, who twenty years earlier had been the terrifying scourge of the cultural world, was there to explain the new thesis that 'practice is the sole norm for the verification of truth'. He was still the terrifying Zhou Yang of old. He explained that this was not merely a theoretical thesis; it was a political question. (In the People's Republic 'political question' is a frightening phrase, evoking visions of handcuffs, forced labour, or worse.) 'There are people', Zhou Yang said, 'who still do not admit that practice is the sole norm of truth.' He added that the search for the followers of Lin Biao and the Gang of Four was still going on; the ghosts of those evils were still around. 'The poison must be washed away and the ghosts dispersed; otherwise the new tasks of new times cannot be carried out.' Zhou Yang added, however: 'The Party will not repress free scientific discussion.' The 160 participants in the discussion were so satisfactorily intimidated that the report on the discussions was able to say: 'All were of one mind about the norm of verification of truth.' Apparently some participants did propose some modest queries. The report on the discussion said that certain problems — how to square the thesis with the laws of logic, how to verify the value of practice — would be discussed later.

All these people, Party members, had been told since their youth that the basic tenets of Marxism were Dialectical Materialism and Historical Materialism; they regarded Marxism as an unshakable compact edifice, a guide to life and to action. Now the edifice had begun to shake.

Several provinces responded to the new order. No mass meetings were held; ordinary Party members would not have understood what the whole thing was about. But leaders of political work in the military, the provincial propaganda and the social science research institutes held meetings in many places to profess that 'practice is the sole norm of truth'.[8]

The professional students of Marxism in the inner Party circles must have been exhilarated by this discovery of Deng's. They were familiar with the history of Marxism and must have known that the Lenin and Stalin brand of Marxism was a distortion of what Marx and Engels had taught. They knew there were many divergent schools of Marxism, from Lassalle to Gramsci and Althusser, although they had not been allowed to write about them. Marxism in China seemed to present the front of a monolithic system elaborated in the USSR. That Marxist theories had been given many and often contradictory explanations — that it is difficult to say what Marxism is — was not stated openly even at this time, in 1978. Nevertheless the campaign was an iconoclastic one and it aroused interesting controversies among Marxist theoreticians. They could now say things that had been taboo till then.

One of them published his views in the *People's Daily*, agreeing, of course, with Deng's doctrine. 'The doctrines of Marx or Engels and the development of Marxism by Lenin, Stalin and Mao Zedong cannot be proved from the doctrine itself,' he wrote, 'but must be proved through practice.' He enumerated some of the mistakes in the predictions of old masters, starting from Marx and Engels, who in 1848 thought that the revolution of that year was the beginning of the victorious proletarian revolution. The worst mistakes, naturally, were those of Lin Biao and the Gang of Four, who wanted to build up a superstitious religious worship of Mao. The man who wrote this, Song Zhenting, knew from experience — as did Deng — what exaggerated worship of Mao could do. Song had been the propaganda chief in a province, but was purged, like Deng, by the Cultural Revolution. He regained his old post after it, and became a leading member of the Central Committee's Party School in Peking.

Another article quoted Stalin as saying that Marx had pinned his revolutionary hopes on England. Engels revised this and said that the revolution would start in France and come to fulfilment in Germany. Was Engels a revisionist? Marx and Engels considered the Paris Commune (the Paris uprising in 1871) a form of proletarian dictatorship; but Lenin said that the Paris Commune had not been led by Marxists. Was Lenin a revisionist? Yet today people still say that not a single word of the canons should be changed.

These articles were written in October and November 1978. In December the C.C. held a Plenum, which turned out to be a momentous victory for Deng and his doctrine. The official communiqué of the C.C. Plenum said: 'The whole conference expressed its high appreciation of the discussion on 'Practice is the Only Norm of Truth', which helps to liberate the minds of the comrades . . . an event of far-reaching historical significance.' In 1979 the New Year editorial in the *People's Daily* started with the words: 'Comrade Mao Zedong said: ''We should not believe anything except science. In other words, we should not believe in superstitions.'' '

Then for some time the newspapers stopped writing about this revolutionary doctrine of Deng's. This was the time of effervescence among students and young workers, who suddenly felt 'liberated' from the shackles of doctrinaire guidance and started putting up posters on the walls of Peking. Yet the discussions continued in the inner circle of Marxist philosophers. The doctrine of 'practice being the only norm of truth' raised many eyebrows. The question had to be faced: was there any difference between this and the American Pragmatism of John Dewey, which had had an overwhelming influence in China since the 1920s? The March 1979 issue of *Philosophical Research* explained the difference. Pragmatism, it said, looks at the individual; but the Marxist Practice is 'the production struggle, class struggle and scientific experiment of the masses' — these words were Mao's. The first view, the article said, is certainly wrong. Suppose a person finds that the belief in God has helped him: then he is a pragmatist. Belief in God is objectively harmful.

Then too it was necessary to explain the difference between questioning the validity of the Marxist canons and scepticism. The answer appeared in the February issue of *Philosophical Research*. Scepticism denies objective truth; Marxism does not; but the truth must be proved by practice. To say that Marxist principles can be revised in the light of new experiences 'is neither scepticism nor an abandonment of the revolutionary banner of Marxism-Leninism'. Is the doctrine of Practice then not the same thing as utilitarianism? This was answered by a quotation from Mao's 1942 'Talk on Literature and Art': 'Nothing in the world is outside utilitarianism. In a class society, if it is not the utilitarianism of this class, then it is the utilitarianism of the other. We are the utilitarians of the proletarian revolution . . .' Mao was being very frank when he said this. What he said had been true of Marxism, ever since Marx. Practice as the norm of truth was not invented by Deng or by Mao — it goes back to the origins. But it hardly squares with other tenets of Marxism or with the impressive edifice of a comprehensive but rigid ideology elaborated in Stalin's Soviet Union.

Another controversy also arose in China during 1978–9, a controversy about the class character of truth. The standard teaching was that only the proletarian class can know the truth, and that this truth is expressed by the vanguard of the proletarian class, the Communist Party and its leaders. In this controversy also, Mao was quoted: 'In a class society everybody lives in a certain class and inevitably bears the mark of that class.' Some queried the validity of this. One Marxist philosopher wrote in *Philosophical Research*: 'It is absurd to say that the laws of society have a class character. The objective laws of development of society are independent of human will and cannot be altered by the will of a class.'

An article in a Peking newspaper made a subtle distinction between truth and thought, i.e. truth and an ideological system. An ideological system has class character. As Engels said, every social class has its own class morality. Truth itself, however, has no class character. The discovery of Copernicus had no class character, the measuring of the speed of a satellite has no class character.

This was the old Marxist discussion about natural sciences, whether or not nature and human society follow the same rules. It is an old controversy and it is still being argued over.

What is certain is that the way Deng brought up the old Marxist axiom that practice is the norm of truth, without adding that Marxism, as it had been taught until that time, was a fixed system of doctrine valid for ever had the effect of a time-bomb. It raised doubts about the ideological system and queries about what Marxism was.[9]

CHAPTER XXI

TWO CAMPS, 1979 – 1984

Deng under fire

The two years after the death of Mao, with the arrest of the Mao radicals and then Deng's revolutionary new doctrine at the end of 1978, brought about many changes and filled many minds with confusion. The *People's Daily* said on March 8, 1979, that higher Party leaders would have to show understanding of the difficulties of lower-grade Party comrades.

When Deng launched his 'revolution', young people were encouraged to express their opinions. On January 22, 1979, the *People's Daily* said to them: 'We believe in you, therefore we grant you democracy.' At the end of January, Deng went on a visit to Washington. With the democratic wave at home, Washington was under the impression that China had become a democratic state. Whether the trip was engineered for that purpose is difficult to say. Probably it was not, but his visit to the world-centre of democracy was suggestive. That visit lasted from January 29 to February 8. Two weeks after Deng's return home, Chinese troops began attacking the northern border of Vietnam, only to withdraw two months later.

It is not certain that there was any connection between the details of external policy and the new trend inside the country. There were no mass demonstrations in the Chinese cities in support of what was called the 'glorious self-defensive counter-attack' against Vietnam. The cities were busy quelling restless crowds demanding more democracy.

Disturbances began in December 1978 (they were believed to have been started by the gangs formed during the Cultural Revolution). The radio news in northern Heilongjiang province spoke of those who 'commit murders, hold up trains, rob, rape women, organise criminal gangs'. Thousands of miles away in the southern province of Sichuan there were 'hooligan gangs, murder, arson, robbery and rape'. In Hunan young workers and students danced in the main streets throughout the night; fights broke out, fortune-tellers were active and illegal publications were sold in public. Crowds in Shanghai, the *People's Daily* said, 'halted traffic in the heart of the city, stopped trains, damaged public property, attacked public offices, beat up officials'. Many young Shanghai workers employed in other regions resigned from their jobs and returned to Shanghai to take part in these exhilarating events. When some gang leaders were arrested the crowds shouted 'Give back our comrades-in-arms!'

On March 16, Deng asked for strong measures to stop the excesses of popular activity inside the country. His words were not published in Peking, but were quoted in the provinces. Orders were issued, so the radio of Anhui province said on April 1, 1979, forbidding 'travelling on trains without a ticket, robbing freight trains and putting up wallposters in places other than those assigned by the authorities'.[1] All could see that the reforms introduced by Deng had caused trouble.

The dismantling of Maoist China had begun under Hua Guofeng. With Deng the change took a brusque turn. Every word of Marx and Mao had previously been sacrosant; now they had become problematical. Formerly, farmers had been told to work out of enthusiasm, not for money; intellectuals had been the underdogs; the economy had been subject to comprehensive central planning. To make money had been considered capitalistic. All this had changed; what had been a sin had become a virtue and what had been a virtue had become a sin.

The youth thought that the time of freedom and democracy had arrived. The Party-*apparatchiks* were shocked. As an important article in the *People's Daily* said on December 14, 1979:

We are facing mountains of problems, mountains of difficulties, mountains of trouble. On one side anarchy and excessive individualism, on the other side bureaucracy and the privileges of bureaucrats, who do not change. Two or three years [since the death of Mao] have not been enough to get rid of the poison and the unhealthy influence of the ultra-left line of Lin Biao and the Gang of Four.[2]

Under pressure from both the unruly youth and the Maoists, Deng was forced to retreat.

The Party leaders held a lengthy discussion in Peking from January 18 to April 3, 1979. News of the holding of this discussion was not published till 1981, and then only in an inner-Party publication.[3] From January 29 to February 8, Deng was unavoidably absent (he was visiting Washington and Tokyo). On March 30, he spoke. Clever politician that he was, he adopted as his own the objections of his enemies, while continuing to push his own reforms. His speech was given in his *Selected Writings*, published years later, in 1983, perhaps in the original form, perhaps polished up — there is no way of knowing.

Deng started with the need for modernisation. He followed by exposing what was called the 'Four Basic Principles', Socialism, Proletarian Dictatorship, Leadership by the Party and Marxism-Leninism and Mao Zedong Thought.

Even under Socialism, he said, there are counter-revolutionaries, there are spies, there are saboteurs, embezzlers, speculators and other bad elements. On Marxism and Mao Thoughts, he said that it is necessary to maintain the 'scientific system consisting of their basic principles, omitting their errors which do not belong to the scientific system of the basic principles of Marxism-Leninism and Mao Zedong Thought'.

In earlier speeches Deng had not mentioned the 'Four Basic Principles'. The sudden stress he placed on them was the concession he had to make to the Maoists. He made a distinction, however. A selection should be made from the words of Marx and Mao, taking what is wanted, leaving the rest. This was not what a good Maoist understood by the 'Four Basic Principles'. 'Scientific Socialism', Deng said, 'is not Utopian Socialism; Marxism cannot remain on the level on which it was a hundred years ago.' He repeated that 'The norm of truth is practice.' Deng, well aware of the disorder caused by the eruption of his liberal ideas, said some tough things:

In recent times in some places some people have caused disorder . . . The masses were incited to attacks on and occupation of Party and government offices, to sit-in hunger strikes, to disruption of traffic, of public order and of production . . . Some brought up such slogans as 'human rights', organised demonstrations and contacted foreigners that their words might be brought to the outside world. Wallposters appeared over the name of 'China's Human Rights Group', asking the President of the United States to protect human rights in China. Could we allow people to ask a foreigner in public to interfere in Chinese internal affairs?

Deng also spoke of 'secret or half-secret organisations' with links throughout the country — though he had said earlier in his speech that only a few people were following such wrong lines. Then he spoke of misguided youth 'who admire capitalist countries, some of them even having contacts with foreigners, abasing the dignity of their own national feelings'.[4]

Deng did not think much of human rights. In China the monitoring of human rights was quelled before it could even start. He accepted the tough Maoist 'Four Basic Principles' as a concession to reality and a compromise with his enemies.

Two women

The compromise was visible in the story of two women. In the spring and summer of 1979, a new heroine appeared, much publicised in the press. This was Zhang Zhixin, a young employee in the propaganda department of Liaoning province in the Northeast. During the Cultural Revolution, in September 1969, she was arrested and severely tortured and in April 1975 she was executed. In March 1979 her memory was rehabilitated by the Party committee of Liaoning province, and she was extolled as an indomitable fighter against the radicals. Her rehabilitation was described as a notable act of defence of the Third C.C. Plenum of December 1978. It had happened, a Peking newspaper said, at the very time, March 1979, when the radicals were denying the value of the Third Plenum, i.e. of Deng's reforms. The unnamed culprit, the man responsible for the fate of the woman, was referred to as 'the deadly enemy of the Party in Liaoning province', a description applied constantly to Mao Yuanxin, Mao's nephew. The culprit, the article said, would not escape punishment.[5]

The whole country was worked up to worship the new heroine. Her writings, genuine or faked, were published in the *People's Daily,* and province after province celebrated the memory of the 'martyr'. Photographs of her were published, painters glorified her with their brushes. Zhang Zhixin became a new saint in the Party's pantheon. She was extolled as the embodiment of Deng's resistance to the radicals.

The cult of Zhang Zhixin did not last long; by the end of 1979 it was over and her name was rarely mentioned. This silence was probably part of Deng's retreat in the face of his enemies. The memory of Zhang Zhixin the martyr was almost forgotten, but not quite. Her name cropped up occasionally; in 1985 the 'tenth anniversary of the sacrifice of martyr Zhang Zhixin' was celebrated by the provincial Party committee of Liaoning province,[6] but only by them. The case of this woman's death is not yet closed, and what happened to Mao Yuanxin has never been made public.

The other woman who appeared and disappeared was Mao's second wife, Yang Kaihui, who had been arrested and executed by the Nationalists in 1931.

One of the wreaths laid at the monument of the Heroes of the Revolution during the April 1976 Dengite-orchestrated demonstration at the Tian An Men was dedicated to Yang Kaihui. This was a direct affront to Jiang Qing, Mao's wife, who in those days was dominating the political scene. Two years later in late 1978, when Deng was taking revenge for the suppression of the Tian An Men demonstration, Yang Kaihui's name was extolled. She had become a heroine. Her glory was proclaimed in a theatrical performance showing martyr Yang Kaihui amid angelic figures lifted up beyond the clouds.

This was not to the taste of the Maoist radicals, who did not want to see Jiang Qing's image smeared. At the end of 1979 a very old lady named He Zizhen appeared in Peking. She had been Mao's third wife, a revolutionary leader in Yan'an whom Mao had dismissed when he fell in love with Jiang Qing. She had been living quietly for years near Shanghai, and her appearance in Peking put an end to the legend of Yang Kaihui.[7] This was another defeat for Deng.

Fourth Central Committee Plenum

In September 1979 the Fourth C.C. Plenum, the fourth since the 1977 Eleventh Party Congress, was held. It was a dull meeting, with none of the sparkling lustre that had graced the Third Plenum held in December 1978, the Plenum at which the new ideas of Deng had shone. This 1979 meeting merely approved a document which was presented to the public by Ye Jianying on the day after the Plenum, September 29, two days before the National Day. This was a long speech containing nothing new. Ye spoke highly of the work of Hua Guofeng (he always did). He also spoke highly of Mao Zedong without Deng's abrasive distinctions. He spoke of the need for 'lifting high the Thoughts of Mao Zedong'. There was, however, a remarkable passage in what he said about the Thoughts of Mao: 'What we call Mao Zedong Thought . . . is not the product of Mao Zedong's personal wisdom alone; it is the product of the wisdom of Mao and his comrades-in-arms . . . it is the crystallisation of the collective wisdom of the Chinese Communist Party.'

Deng could not halt this praise of Mao and of Hua Kuofeng. He did, however, succeed in putting his men into the highest leading positions. More old cadres were rehabilitated or promoted. Zhao Ziyang was promoted from alternate membership of the Politbureau to regular membership. Twelve formerly powerful Party leaders who had been out of favour during the years of the Cultural Revolution were reinstated in the C.C. Among these were Yang Shangkun, who later, in the C.C.'s Military Committee, became a powerful leader of the army; Bo Yibo, in earlier years head of the State Economic Commission, later to become the man in charge of the Party purge, and Peng Zhen, who became a member of the Politbureau and head of the People's Congress Legal Commission, and, a few years later head of the People's Congress.[8]

Security and the army

The rowdy youngsters did not quieten down, but the time of freedom and democracy was over. There was one young man, Wei Jingsheng — said to be the son of a high-ranking official — who at the time of the liberal jamboree had expressed his ideas freely. In October 1979 he was arrested and received a fifteen-year sentence. Wei held that Marxist socialism did not suit China, and he criticised Deng.[9]

Who ordered the arrest and condemnation of Wei? It may have been the new head of the Legal Commission of the People's Congress, Peng Zhen, who was also taking over a much more important job, leadership of the Politico-Legal Committee in the Party C.C., with the task of restoring order in security organs and the police, both of which were in disarray.

Xie Fuzhi, minister of security and head of the Politico-Legal Bureau of the Cabinet since 1959, died in March 1972 and his name was no longer mentioned. He had collaborated with the notorious Kang Sheng, who had died in December 1975 — and been buried with honours. Both were righthand men to Mao and Lin Biao. Even their memories were rejected in the years after Mao. There were rumours that both Xie Fuzhi and Li Zhen, his successor as head of the ministry of security, had been assassinated. (Such news circulates in rumours only, never in the press.) The powerful Luo Ruiqing, head of security before 1959 and then Chief-of-Staff of the army, who had been badly mauled by the Cultural Revolution but reappeared with honour after it, died in 1978.

After the disappearance of these leaders, the security organs began to disintegrate. On September 1, 1979, a *People's Daily* article revealed that the men in the security forces and the police did not agree with Deng's rehabilitation of 'landlords, kulaks, counter-revolutionaries and bad elements', and were calling this a 'denial of the class line', a departure from genuine Marxism and Mao Zedong Thought. Sixty-three leading members of the security forces who had been condemned as rightists in the late 1950s were rehabilitated. The old gang in the security forces called this 'smearing the face of Comrade Luo Ruiqing' — who had purged the sixty-three. There was grumbling among the comrades in the security forces about the low reputation they now enjoyed: 'The Party newspapers depict the security organs in pitch black, as executioners of the Gang of Four. This is unjust and untrue.'

The Cultural Revolution left deep wounds in those who had been arrested and tortured by the security men. The injured did not forget what had happened to them.

A national conference on security in the cities was held at the end of November 1979, and addressed by Peng Zhen in his capacity as head of the Legal Commission of the People's Congress Standing Committee. The conference was told that the military would take part in restoring public order. This was a strange come-back for the military, which made itself unpopular during the Cultural Revolution when Mao, in February 1967, ordered them to enter the political scene to 'aid the leftists'. They entered in a big way, helping rebel organisations which were supporting Lin Biao and suppressing the rest. On December 23, 1979, an editorial in the *People's Daily* praised the action of the military during the Cultural Revolution:

In those grave circumstances, Chairman Mao and Premier Zhou ordered the army to carry out this 'three-aid' 'two-military' task. [The 'three-aid' meant 'aid leftists, aid industry, aid agriculture'; the 'two-military' meant military administration and training.] It played an important role in stabilising the situation and on the whole the results were good. Problems arose only from interference by Lin Biao and the Gang of Four.

This was an effort to whitewash the army, but the rough handling the soldiers had given to Party leaders was not forgotten. The same *People's Daily* article said that the armed troops should approach the civilian regional leaders and the 'masses' in the spirit of self-criticism, and that the civilian regional leaders should show sympathetic understanding. The army was ordered to hand back to the civilian government the land and houses taken away during the Cultural Revolution and to make good the injustices done to various people.

Nevertheless veteran Party leaders, in higher and lower posts, remembered how during the Cultural Revolution they had been set aside and humiliated, and had seen their comrades being tortured to death. Fourteen years had passed but the scars remained. As this *People's Daily* article said: 'There are comrades who are lukewarm towards the movement for supporting the army. There are people who see only defects in the army and forget that without the armed troops the Chinese revolution would not have succeeded.'

At the end of 1979 the General Political Department of the army ordered the reform of abuses in the army. The army should assist the civilian local authorities in maintaining public order, and help in the modernisation of the country. The armed forces sent soldiers to the universities to give the students military training; to factories, ports, bus stations and the streets to keep order; and to the countryside to establish

permanent contact with the villages – – to maintain public order and to
aid socialist construction.

In the effort to re-establish public order, in November 1979 (four
months after the enacting of a relatively civilised Criminal Law by the
People's Congress), the Standing Committee (Peng Zhen was head of
the Legal Commission) passed a Supplementary Regulation reiterating
the 1957 Regulation on forced labour, called 'Labour Education', which
was imposed not by the courts but by administrative measures. The same
session of the Standing Committee determined that all laws and decrees
promulgated since 1949 should remain valid, including the infamous
1951 Regulation on suppression of counter-revolutionaries — the murderous suppression led in Peking in those years by Peng Zhen.[10]

The Fifth Central Committee Plenum

The year 1980 saw two opposing movements. In the top leadership of
the Party, Deng strengthened his position; but he was unable to discard
his opponents.

The Fifth Plenum of the Central Committee was held on February
22–29. Hua Guofeng presided as Chairman of the Party. One of the
Vice-Chairmen, the notorious Wang Dongxing, and three members of
the Politbureau, all Hua's men, were dismissed or, as it was more
politely put, had their resignations approved. The three Politbureau
members were Wu De, who as Party boss of Peking had delivered the
inaugural speech in October 1976 when Hua Guofeng was officially
acknowledged as Chairman; Ji Dengkui, a minor provincial official
during the Cultural Revolution who, having been brought to Peking by
Mao, had become head of the Politico-Legal Team of the C.C. in
1978–9; and General Chen Xilian, commander of the Peking Great
Military Area, who had been removed from command a few days before
this C.C. Plenum.

Wang Dongxing and Chen Xilian remained in the C.C., but Ji
Dengkui disappeared. Deng's two main supporters, Hu Yaobang and
Zhao Ziyang, were promoted to the highest policy-making body of the
Party, the Standing Committee of the Politbureau, joining Ye Jianying,
Deng Xiaoping, Li Xiannian and Chen Yun.

The C.C. Plenum made another important move. It re-established the
C.C. Secretariat, with Hu Yaobang as its head. The Secretariat ranks
below the Standing Committee of the Politbureau, but it is a powerful

body, since it has charge of the normal daily running of Party affairs. The Secretariat was suppressed during the Cultural Revolution and was not re-established by the Tenth Party Congress in 1973 or by the Eleventh of 1977. Now in 1980 it was re-established. Including Hu Yaobang, it had eleven members.

Under attack

All this was a renewed triumph for Deng. Two months later, however, in April 1980, the armed forces held a Political Work Conference under the chairmanship of Hua Guofeng, who was both Party Chairman and — as Mao had been in his day — Chairman of the C.C. Military Committee. His appearance there came as a surprise. The dismissal in February of the four former associates of the Gang of Four, in particular the sacking of Wu De, seemed to have swept the ground from under his feet, and all that seemed lacking was an occasion for removing him gently from office.

A month earlier the Chinese People's Political Consultative Conference, with Deng as its Chairman, had held a meeting. The report on this meeting did not even mention Hua, though he had been present and had spoken. Under the rules of official Peking etiquette, this was a blatant insult to the man who was Chairman of the Party and Prime Minister. Accordingly, Hua's prominence at the April Political Conference of the armed forces came as a surprise.

This conference was one of considerable importance for the heads of the political departments of all central branches of the army and of all the Great Military Areas took part. In the report on the conference it was noted that Ye Jianying had been present, and had paid great attention to the proceedings. He had always been a supporter of Hua Guofeng. Wei Guoqing, the head of the political department of the army, and Geng Biao, the Secretary-General of the C.C. Military Committee, addressed the conference.

The speeches did not accord with the doctrine of Deng. Deng held that there were no longer any classes of landlords and of kulaks, or a capitalist class; though he had indeed said that class struggle must go on. At this conference however, both Hua and Wei Guoqing came out with an old slogan from the radical times: 'Exalt the proletariat and exterminate the bourgeoisie.' This can also be translated as 'Exalt the proletarian and exterminate the bourgeois.' Hua spoke in the latter sense. 'We communists exalt proletarian ideology,' he said. 'Marxism-Leninism and Mao

Zedong Thought will overcome the bourgeois ideology and the ideology of the exploiting class.' What he was saying was a repetition of what he had said at the People's Congress in 1979: 'We must continue to wage class struggle so that it may be impossible for the bourgeoisie to exist, or for a new bourgeoisie to arise.'

Such words were not passing remarks, uttered lightly. In the month in which this military conference was held, April 1980, *Red Flag* had an article by a military man which said that the phrase 'exterminating the bourgeois' had a respectable history. It comes from Marx, the article said; it was used by Deng Xiaoping himself in a speech in 1957 and by Zhou Enlai in 1964. It is contained in the 'Four Basic Principles' which were formulated after the December 1978 Third C.C. Plenum. The article ended by saying: 'We continue to purge the poison left by Lin Biao and the Gang of Four, but this does not mean that we are abandoning the correct slogan "Exterminating the bourgeois and exalting the proletariat" simply because Lin Biao and the Gang used it.'

A month later an article in the Peking *Guang Ming Daily*, Deng's mouthpiece, launched an attack on what it called the wrong interpretation of the 'Four Basic Principles'. 'Are there not people', it asked, 'who under the pretext of adhering to the Four Basic Principles oppose the liberation of minds? [Deng's motto]. They say that liberation of the mind has gone too far and has brought disorder. They question the Third C.C. Plenum and resist it. Some are still angrily grinding their teeth.'

Controversial Liu

In May 1980, a month after the military conference at which Hua Guofeng and Wei Guoqing spoke of the extermination of the bourgeois, a solemn memorial service was held to commemorate Liu Shaoqi. Till the Cultural Revolution Liu had been number two in the Party and Head of State. He had been dismissed by Mao in 1966 and had died in disgrace in prison in 1969. His rehabilitation was decided upon at the February 1980 Fifth C.C. Plenum. Why the memorial service was delayed for three months was not explained. Apparently the Party leadership was not united on that issue. In the course of his long history in the Party Liu Shaoqi had made many enemies, and moreover his rehabilitation was a direct repudiation of Mao. Ye Jianying and Li Xiannian, both Vice-Chairmen of the C.C., absented themselves from the memorial service. Ye spent that day in South China and did not care to go to

Peking for the occasion. Li Xiannian, just returned from his visit to Australia, was back in China already, though not in Peking. Their absence from Liu's memorial service was conspicuous. Deng Xiaoping attended and made a short memorial speech. He said little about Mao and laid the blame for Liu's misfortunes on Lin Biao and the Gang of Four.

On the occasion of the memorial service the *People's Daily* said: 'The rehabilitation of Comrade Liu Shaoqi is bound to cause a certain amount of shock and misinterpretation.' It added that Mao himself had admitted that a leader can be wrong. When Party leaders were condemned during the Cultural Revolution 'Comrade Mao Zedong nodded, but when he saw that the cases had been wrongly judged he was indignant and corrected the misdeeds. The cases that Comrade Mao Zedong did not solve or could not solve, we must solve.'

Two days later the *People's Daily* carried another article, headed 'A Revolutionary Must Learn from Mistakes', which said:

At the time of the Cultural Revolution the Party made deplorably grave mistakes . . . though we may liquidate Lin Biao and the Gang of Four, we cannot ascribe all the mistakes of ten years to them alone . . . We must see for which mistakes the whole collectivity, the whole Party, must be held responsible, and for which mistakes the leader [Mao] must be held responsible . . . In the course of the past years we have made many mistakes and some of these have not been corrected . . . Some comrades have developed a passive, pessimistic outlook, and they now have doubts about the Four Modernisations . . . We should not rush to draw quick conclusions. History and the next generation will be able to do that.[11]

(The Party proved unable to wait for the judgement of history. In the following year, 1981, an important Party document laid down what had been right and what wrong in Party activity since the establishment of the People's Republic in 1949.)

The circumstances of the rehabilitation of Liu Shaoqi, a man so central to the history of the Party and of the Cultural Revolution, provides an insight into the passions and the anger that smouldered among the Party leaders. Many had not forgotten that when the Japanese began penetrating into North China in 1935, and the Communists in South Hebei province were ready to attack them, Liu Shaoqi said no, and ordered instead resistance through guerilla penetration. Similarly, in the same year, when the Peking students revolted against the Nationalist general in charge of the city, it was Liu who, together with Peng Zhen, dissuaded them from violence, preferring quiet underground Communist propaganda (see Chapter VIII, pp. 108ff.). Liu was of course right in both instances, but the hot-headed revolutionaries still resented what he had done. Their objections were raised thirty years later during the Cultural Revolution when Liu was condemned. Another grievance, which had been brought up several times, was that when prominent leaders of the Party were arrested by the Nationalists in the early 1930s, it was Liu who sent instructions ordering them to make a fake surrender so that they should be liberated (see p. 282). A Communist must never surrender, the accusers said. And there was the case of a Party leader, Li Qingyu, who opposed Liu in 1937, when working under him. Liu did not forget. Twenty-three years later, in 1960, he expelled Li from the Party, and during the Cultural Revolution Li came forward with accusations against Liu. After the death of Lin Biao, Li was arrested and he died under persecution. He was posthumously rehabilitated in July 1979 — seven months before the rehabilitation of Liu.[12] (In studying the inner history of the Party leaders, one gets lost in baffling labyrinths.)

Hua — out

On August 18–23, 1980, there was a secret Politbureau meeting, announced only in inner-Party papers. Deng, yielding to the Maoists, spoke against the dangers of an irruption of bourgeois thoughts; but he also spoke about changing the system of excessive economic centralisation, rejuvenating the cadres and abolishing the system of life-long service.[13]

In early September 1980, at the yearly People's Congress, Hua Guofeng resigned the Premiership. This was done gently. Hua himself spoke, saying that the highest Party authorities (was he not the Chairman of the Party?) had decided that veteran Party leaders — Li Xiannian, Chen Yun and Deng himself — should not continue to be Vice-Premiers and that 'the Party Central was now proposing that Comrade Zhou Ziyang should be the Premier'. He did not say that he himself had wished to give up that post.

Hua was accused by Deng's group of having proposed unrealistically high targets for the economy at the 1978 People's Congress. In his Congress speech of resignation, Hua admitted that the projects had been ambitious, but he pointed out in justification that at that time, in 1978, 'we were all intent on making good the damage done by ten years of confusion.'[14]

Maoists attack

From November 10 till December 5, 1980, the Politbureau was locked in another unpublicised meeting. This meeting eliminated Hua Guofeng from the Chairmanship of the Party and put Hu Yaobang in his place as Chairman, and Deng as head of the C.C.'s Military Committee. Thus for the first time since Yan'an the two posts, Chairman of the Party and head of the Military Committee, were separated. Hu Yaobang obviously did not have much backing among the generals. Hua Guofeng was retained as Vice-Chairman. Since the Politbureau has no power to make such decisions, these changes were put forward as proposals for the next Plenum of the Central Committee — which was not held for another seven months.

A few days later the C.C. was summoned, not for an official Plenum, but for a discussion that lasted from December 16–25.[15] This meeting reversed the policy laid down by the Third C.C. Plenum held exactly two years earlier in December 1978. The Maoists, Deng's enemies, brought up against him the political and economic damage his policies had caused. The conference reasserted the Maoist doctrine and the strict interpretation of the conservative 'Four Basic Principles'. It laid down that there must be an intensification of discipline in Party, government and army, in the economy, in the schools and in all organisations. Everyone must observe strict vigilance and must hit out at the counter-revolutionaries and ordinary criminals. There must be no toleration of those who were clamouring for greater freedom. The *People's Daily* editorial published on February 8, 1981, said that:

There is a small number of people who say they are fighting for democracy and freedom. They use the methods of the Cultural Revolution, great discussions and wallposters. They want, so they say, to kick out the Party committees and to set up democracy. They are building up blocs, producing manifestos and starting strikes in factories and schools. They want to create democracy; but this is bound to lead to disorder. Using the pretext that the Party has many defects and has made mistakes, they want to get rid of the Party leadership.

The December 1980 discussion itself, and even the fact that it had been held, were not made public for some time. However, the January 1981 *People's Daily* editorial, which defended Deng, revealed indirectly what had been discussed in December. (The press was in the hands of Deng's men.) 'Some ask, does this all mean that the direction of the policies of the Third Plenum has been changed?. . . . They remember how many changes have occurred in the past. As the proverb says, "Once bitten by a snake, one is afraid of a moving string." ' The answer was that nothing had changed, 'merely some concrete measures have been altered and wrong interpretations of the decisions have been corrected.'

Deng's enemies could certainly point to the economic harm done by his policies. The newspapers admitted in January 1981 that during the two years since the introduction of Deng's policies, the output of energy and of the machine industry had declined, that enterprises which had been allowed to work out their own gains and losses had refused to hand over their profits to the state and that this had led to a deficit in the state budget: too much was being spent on capital construction, and prices had risen unreasonably. The following remedies were prescribed: investment and foreign currency were to be strictly controlled; industrial development was to rely on more skilful utilisation of existing equipment; wages were to be raised only when there had been a rise in labour efficiency; the people's standard of living was to be raised only if production and labour efficiency had improved; taxation was to be strictly centralised and all profits were to go to the central treasury, except those of certain enterprises which had permission to experiment with the self-management system, though no more enterprises were to be assigned to this category. In direct opposition to Deng's policy, it was laid down that the state must centralise industry and that the economy must be run by administrative measures. Blame for the impoverishment of the state treasury and for the destabilising of the economy was laid on the policy, introduced two years earlier, of raising the prices paid to the farmers for agricultural products.[16]

On the last day of the working session, December 25, 1980, Deng himself spoke. His speech was published three years later in the *Selected Writings of Deng Xiaoping*. He defended his economic policies, but he admitted that in the two years since their introduction the adjustment of the economy had not been carried out properly, that too much capital construction had been undertaken, that too many banknotes had been printed, and that the state budget had shown a serious deficit. He attributed all this to the lack of understanding of his policies. He also admitted that disorders had followed his liberalisation. 'A small clique of people who wanted only disorder had made evil use of the policies of the Cultural Revolution. Some were even calling for a second "Great Cultural Revolution". Young people 'had caused trouble, set up illegal organs, published illegal publications, spread pamphlets against the Party and against Socialism, . . . committed murder and arson, caused explosion, theft and robbery, and raped women . . .' He called these troublemakers counter-revolutionaries. 'In some places the situation may be very grave,' he said. If necessary, it is allowable to proclaim martial law, after careful consideration, and to move troops in to restore order.

'Some people may complain that the direction given by the Third Plenum [of two years earlier] has been changed and Liberalisation has turned into Restriction.' This he denied. All we want to do is to act against counter-revolutionaries and against ordinary criminals. Regrettably, the newspapers and magazines had not fought the evil trends, and they had neglected the ideological struggle. Deng praised the Thoughts of Mao and said that criticism of the errors of Mao's late years should not overshadow their validity.

Deng went far in this retreat. He said that the Party's propaganda work was not forceful enough in proclaiming the 'Four Basic Principles' (socialism, proletarian dictatorship, Party guidance and Marx-Mao). 'The Four Basic Principles', he said, should not hinder the liberation of minds — which he had proclaimed two years earlier. He insisted on discipline and what he called 'spiritual civilisation'. By this, he said, he meant Marxist ideology, 'Marxist thought, Marxist faith, morality, discipline and revolutionary stance'. The real revolutionary, he said, has the spirit of 'not to fear hardship, not to fear death'.[17]

By taking this huge backward step Deng ensured his survival. He went very far when he quoted the saying, 'Not to be afraid of hardship, not to be afraid of death', for this had been the battle cry of the radicals at the time of the Cultural Revolution.

In January, a few days after the December 1980 discussion, the army newspaper said: 'Not to be afraid of hardship, not to be afraid of death is the glorious tradition of our Party, and of our army, which led the long revolutionary struggle. Today the Four Modernisations still need this revolutionary spirit.'

Two months later the same army newspaper asked: 'Will not strict discipline stand in the way of democracy?' It answered: 'Democracy must come under the guidance of centralism', and it invoked the memory of Lei Feng, a young soldier who died in 1962 and was exalted by Mao in 1963, Lei Feng the hero of obedience, 'the cog in the machine', as he was called. On March 1981 the youth of Peking were ordered to spend their Sundays sweeping the streets, helping to direct traffic and propagating 'spiritual civilisation', thus 'imitating Lei Feng'.

All this was a manifestation of the Maoists' reaction against liberalisation. On February 7, 1980, the *Wen Hui Bao*, a

Shanghai newspaper, had published a letter from a Shanghai youth asking: 'Should we learn from Lei Feng in the 1980s? Lei Feng was the hero of the bitter struggle in the 1960s. We are now in the 1980s in the time of modernisation.' Moreover, in 1980 the press dared to air the view of the younger generation, which held that 'we are in the era of natural sciences and technology, not of Marxism-Leninism', and it admitted that many youngsters had become cynical. When a soldier jumped into a lake in Peking to save a student who had fallen into the water, some youngsters who were watching jeered and said: 'He has a good chance of gaining merit and becoming a Party member.' The prestige of the Communist Party was at a low ebb. The press spoke of a 'crisis of faith'.

The Mao radicals had had enough of this. They thought the spirit of the nation was disintegrating. It probably was. They wanted to re-establish Maoist discipline and Marxist faith, and Deng had to go along with this.

The question has often been asked, whether Deng's liberalisation policy in 1978 was genuine or tactical. In other words, did Deng and his colleagues hold that the Maoist system was not working and perhaps that Marxism itself did not suit China? Or was Deng still what he had been throughout his life, a hardline Marxist, and had he proposed his liberal doctrines merely as a manoeuvre to gain power?

The history of the two-year period, 1979–1980, between the Third Central Committee Plenum and the December 1980 C.C. Working Session seems to point to the first answer, and suggests that if it had depended on Deng, Maoism and perhaps Marxism itself would have been dispensed with in China, but that this proved impossible in face of the continuing resistance of those who could not think in any terms except those of Marx and Mao.

In the second half of January 1981, barely a month after that momentous discussion in December 1980, the General Political Department of the army held another conference. This was in many ways a triumph for the Maoists in the army. The conference was addressed by Geng Biao and Wei Guoqing, and also by Hu Yaobang — though it was not Hu but Wei Guoqing, head of the General Political Department, who carried the day. He spoke, as he had spoken a year earlier, against the worship of capitalism and of liberal bourgeois tendencies. The whole conference praised Marx and Mao without reservation, and extolled the 'Four Basic Principles' and the saying 'Not to be afraid of hardship, not to be afraid of death'.

The military, however, were not a united force that could have stood in solid opposition to Deng.

The trial of the Gang

All this time, the turn of the years 1980–1, the trial of Jiang Qing and company had been going on. It was a trial that cut deep into the flesh of the army. The indictment included among the sixty criminals not only Lin Biao's four major-generals but also twenty-eight other army men and a member of the air force. Among these was Ding Sheng, who as commander of the Nanjing Troops commanded three provinces and Shanghai city, and other prominent army leaders.[18] The head of the court that judged Lin Biao's chief generals was himself an army man, Wu Xiuchuan, once a vice-foreign-minister and at the time of the trial deputy Chief-of-Staff. Lin Biao's chief lieutenants were condemned. Huang Yongsheng, the Chief-of-Staff, got eighteen years; Wu Faxian, commander of the air force, and Li Zuopeng, first political commissar of the navy, were both sentenced to seventeen years; and Qiu Huizuo, head of army logistics, got sixteen years. The five years they had already spent in prison were to be counted. Thus they should be freed in 1992–4.

The televised trial was a tragi-comedy. The indictment was directed not only against the living but also against the dead — Lin Biao, his wife and his son, Kang Sheng and Xie Fuzhi. A long passage in the indictment dealt with the persecution of Deng. The trial was his revenge. The decision to try them must have been taken by a higher Party meeting, but it was not said when. On this point at least China's leaders, victims of the Cultural Revolution, could agree.

It was alleged that in the army 80,000 people had been persecuted, of whom 1,169 had died, and that in literary and artistic circles 2,600 had been falsely charged. It was also alleged that 142,000 people involved in education and 53,000 involved in science and technology had been persecuted, and so on.

A curious undercurrent of doubt ran beneath the trial. On December 29, 1980, a Peking newspaper, the *Guang Ming Daily*, brought up the question: why were the acts of Lin Biao and the Jiang Qing clique called counter-revolutionary? After all, they were the highest Party and government authority at the time. The answer was that they had seized the highest authority to give legal form to their counter-revolutionary activities.

Lin Biao was dead, so the star at the trial was Jiang Qing; and she, as everybody saw on television, said that she had acted on instructions from Mao. 'Arresting and trying me affect Chairman Mao,' she said. In a later hysterical outburst she said: 'In purging me you are condemning the Red Guards and the small red soldiers of the time of the great Cultural Revolution.'[19]

The trial was an emotional drama throughout. Three years later Wu Xiuquan, who had been head of the Second Court of the trial, described it in an article in the *Wen Hui Bao*. When he pronounced the death sentence on Jiang Qing, Wu Xiuquan said, he was so perturbed by her violent reaction that he forgot to add the second part of the sentence, 'with two years' suspension of execution'.[20]

The battle goes on

The trial of Jiang Qing and her associates was a major event but it was unrelated to the main issue, the tension between Deng's group and the Maoists.

Deng had numerous people on his side. Most of the media were in the hands of his men, although the *People's Daily*, as the organ of the C.C., had to publish polemics from various sides in the top leadership. Another Peking newspaper, the *Guang Ming Daily*, was entirely Deng's. On April 9, 1981, it asserted that Deng's reforms had met serious resistance in ideology, politics and organisation. (The word 'organisation' meant the Party ranks.) The policies of the Third Plenum (1978) had not been implemented, it said, and some still believed that it was better to be leftist (radical) than to be rightist. The article did not mince its words. It quoted Mao as having said 'Which do you think are more intelligent, men or pigs? Pigs, because when they bump into something they turn back. There are men who refuse to budge.' It is not true, it went on, that the decisions of the Third Plenum were wrong or that the Work Conference of December 1980 corrected them. Such people say 'You admit that they [Deng's men] had to give in and even they are now talking about political indoctrination and hard struggle.' The answer was: No, the 'Four Basic Principles' (the Maoist doctrine) have been upheld ever since the Third Plenum.

On May 1, 1981, Labour Day, Hua Guofeng — already expelled from his post as Chairman of the Party, though this had not yet been sanctioned by an official C.C. Plenum — appeared in Peking accompanied by China's two most powerful military figures, two old marshals, Xu Xiangqian and Nie Rongzhen, together with Li Xiannian and Peng

Zhen, none of them Deng liberals. Zhao Ziyang was present, but Hu Yaobang preferred to stay away and to celebrate the occasion in a provincial city; Deng was nowhere to be seen. The December 1980 Work Conference, which had made adjustments in the economic and political programme he had proposed two years earlier, must have left a bad taste in his mouth.

The army generals themselves were obviously split on the issue. The few generals clearly on Deng's side criticised those in the army who believed that the Party leadership (Deng, Hu etc.) was rightist. In March 1981 at a conference of the Army's Logistics, its political commissar, General Wang Ping, a Deng man, spoke against those who were still talking the language of the Cultural Revolution and saying 'Kick out the Party committees and start a revolution', and spreading rumours in the hope that 'the spear would be turned against those high up'. General Qin Jiwei, whom Deng had summoned to Peking from Sichuan in 1975 and who was commander of the Peking area (commanding two provinces and the city of Peking), said that the country had been suffering from leftist, radical deviations for thirty years. He condemned the 'three-aid two-military' — the active intervention of the army during the Cultural Revolution — 'which had done great harm to the army'.

On the other side, Wei Guoqing, still head of the General Political Department of the army, speaking in Nanjing in April 1981, fiercely defended the Maoist 'Four Basic Principles'. He paid a compliment to Deng, but added: 'We should not neglect correcting rightist and other errors.' Some other generals, among them Zhang Tingfa, commander of the air force, spoke against both left and right.[21]

On June 22, 1981, the *People's Daily* published a full-page article by Wei Guoqing, ostensibly written in commemoration of the sixtieth anniversary of the Communist Party. From beginning to end he praised Mao but he also spoke highly of the 'emancipation of the minds', a phrase favoured by Deng. Yet he added a direct attack on Deng: 'It is imperative to avoid using the emancipation of the minds as a pretext for denying the basic principles of Marxism-Leninism, Mao Zedong Thought and the socialist system, and so trying to put an end to the great achievements of thirty-two years' construction of the country. (The thirty-two years included periods when Mao's radical policies were being imposed, doing harm, and were repudiated by the school of Deng.) The article praised the liberal policy of the 'blooming of the Hundred Schools', but added: 'There must be no confusing of the Hundred Schools with bourgeois class liberalism.'

These words meant what the Maoists kept on saying all the time, that Deng's liberal policies would destroy the Marxist tradition of the Party.

There appeared at that time in Hong Kong a short-lived pro-Communist daily paper, the *Cheng Ming Daily*, a fierce defender of Deng's policies. The wind of change in Peking soon forced it to close down. This paper gave the following interpretation of Wei Guoqing's article. 'From this lengthy article by Wei Guoqing it is evident that a fierce duel is being fought between the remnants of the extreme-left, represented by Hua Guofeng, and the party of Deng and Hu.' Hua Guofeng, it said, still had a great deal of support in the country among regional leaders.

In the background of the controversy was a story, *Bitter Love*, written by Bai Hua, a member of the Cultural Revolution Team in the army. A film was made based on the story but was shown only within Party circles. The story and the film were severely attacked by the army newspaper on April 20. The pro-Communist Hong Kong newspaper said that the condemnation of the film in the *Liberation Army Daily* had been approved by Wei Guoqing. The story dealt with a scientist who returned to China, was exposed to persecution and, when dying in the Mongolian snowfields, wrote on the snow a huge question-mark, of which the dot was to be his dead body. One phrase in the story became famous: 'I love the Fatherland, but the Fatherland does not love me.'

The *Liberation Army Daily's* attack was rejected by Deng's group. The *Guang Ming Daily* said: 'It is not right to pick out a phrase or two and make a great fuss about them . . . Critics should not fall upon anyone like a wasp's nest; they should not be one-sided; they should not force their views on others.'[22]

The Sixth Central Committee Plenum

It was in this atmosphere of acrimonious debate that the June 27–29, 1981, Sixth Plenum of the C.C., the sixth since the 1977 Eleventh Party Congress, was held: It was preceded by two weeks of discussion, about which nothing was made public. Wei Guoqing's June 22 *People's Daily* article against Deng (mentioned earlier) was published during the preparatory discussions. It must have reflected the fierce debate that was going on behind closed doors. Deng was ready to make concessions, to retreat — as he had been doing ever since March 1979. He made concessions so as to be able to insert his own men into the top leadership.

What had been decided at the November-December 1980 Work Conference was sanctioned at the Plenum of the C.C. Hu Yaobang became Chairman of the Party. Hua Guofeng, who could not be ousted altogether, became one of the Vice-Chairmen of the C.C. and thus a member — though he was ranked last on the list — of the highest ruling body of the Party, the Politbureau's Standing Committee. This then consisted of Hu Yaobang as Chairman, Ye Jianying, Deng Yinchao, Zhao Ziyang, Li Xiannian, Chen Yun and Hua Guofeng.

The earlier days when Mao was the supreme leader had gone. It was obvious that the real power lay with the number two Vice-Chairman, Deng Xiaoping. He, not Chairman Hua, became Chairman of the C.C.'s Military Committee. The general situation was still hazy. The Third Plenum in December 1978 set up a Disciplinary Investigation Committee, headed by Chen Yun; but after two years the Committee had not yet established branches in all the provinces, not even in Shanghai.

Party history

The profound disunity of the C.C. Plenum meant that little could be achieved. Yet it succeeded, as an act of compromise, in publishing an odd document on Party history, the *Resolution on Some Historical Questions of the Party since the Establishment of the Country* — i.e. since the establishment of the People's Republic in 1949. This document had been under preparation for more than two years. The Third Plenum of December 1978 discussed it and said it would take time to reach a consensus. The consensus apparently has been reached. It was a compromise document, asserting both Deng's achievements and the radicals' views on Marxism and Mao. The Cultural Revolution, it said, had been 'the error of a great leader of proletarian revolution'.

The document was not history in the normal sense of the word. It was not unlike the previous official history of the Party, written in 1945 when Mao had just become head of the Party. We saw in the section on 1921–49, in Chapter III, what kind of document that was and how after the death of Mao old Party leaders uncovered the bias it contained. The prototype of such historiography was Stalin's *History of the Communist Party in the Soviet Union*. All such 'histories' are Party directives, prescribing what is to be said about history. The new document said that Mao Zedong had had more merits than faults, and long passages praised him and his Thoughts. Mao was retained as a source of wisdom, in politics, in the economy, in military affairs, in administration, even in philosophy. The establishment of the Communes and the Great Leap of 1958 were errors, but Mao himself had corrected the excesses. The famine in the years following the Communes was called nothing worse than 'serious difficulties'.

Not much good could be said about the Cultural Revolution, which had purged many of the leaders who were writing this document. This was 'the error of a great proletarian revolutionary', which had been used by Lin Biao and Jiang Qing for their counter-revolutionary purposes. Neither the Red Guards nor the devastation were mentioned, and the Cultural Revolution was presented merely as a fierce internal battle within the Party leadership. The causes of the Cultural Revolution were explained in a new way. First, the Marxist doctrines had been misunderstood. Secondly, the polemics in the early 1960s between Peking and Moscow had given rise to an anti-revisionist campaign in China, and to intensified class struggle. Both of these developments were wrong. 'The Party found it difficult to resist the leftist ideas of Mao Zedong and other comrades . . . This led to the eruption of the Cultural Revolution.' Mao was not the only one responsible. 'The Party Central also bears a certain responsibility . . . not a single person and not a group of persons but the whole Party.' (Thus it should not be said that those closest to Mao, Liu Shaoqi, Zhou Enlai and Deng Xiaoping, were responsible for not having stopped Mao.)

Yet even during the Cultural Revolution not everything went wrong. Mao's foreign policy was right. There was economic progress: new railway lines, hydrogen bombs, satellites and hybrid rice were developed. (This differed from the view, widely held in 1979–80, that the Cultural Revolution had brought the economy to the verge of collapse.)

A considerable part of the document dealt with the history of the preceding two years. Hua Guofeng, it said, continued the earlier leftist error, though he gained merit by smashing the Gang of Four. He created a personality cult for himself and he offered opposition to Practice as the only Norm of Truth (i.e. Deng). The December 1978 Third C.C. Plenum (Deng's) was described as a turning-point in China, which ushered in the rehabilitation of the unjustly condemned, the emancipation of minds, the declaration that there were no longer any exploiting classes — though class struggle and people's dictatorship still remained because destructive activities in politics, ideology, culture and in the economy had not yet come to an end. The slogan 'Continue the revolution under proletarian dictatorship' was wrong, but its condemnation did not mean that the revolution had ended and that the revolutionary struggle should not be continued until classes had disappeared and the final stage of Communism had arrived. The December 1980 C.C. Work Conference was mentioned: it strengthened political ideology, prescribed 'socialist spiritual civilisation' and criticised opposition to the 'Four Basic Principles'.[23]

This was indeed a compromise document, sorting out the cards evenly. It justified Deng, although he in fact had had to make far-reaching concessions to the Maoists.

Deng for discipline

The Sixth C.C. Plenum of June 1981 may have reached a compromise between Deng and the Maoists; but there was another enemy lurking in the background — not the Maoists but liberal public opinion, expressing itself in novels, films and the theatre. This was sapping the foundations of the Marxist regime and undermining the prestige of the Party. It could not be tolerated. But how was it to be suppressed without resort to the old Maoist tactics of brutal suppression? This was the question Deng had to face.

On July 17, 1981, three weeks after the C.C. Plenum, Deng spoke to the leaders of the propaganda department of the Party. After that, in August, the department held a discussion, attended by all those in charge of propaganda in the provinces and in the army. Deng was not present, but Hu Yaobang repeated Deng's July speech. The subject of the discussion was 'the ideological battlefront', how to cure the party's 'laxity and weakness' in controlling ideology — Party leaders permitting the publication of literature critical of the Party and of Socialism.

Deng may not have thought much of Mao, or perhaps even of Marx; but the power of the Party, and his own power, had to be defended. He must have seen with regret that the seeds of freedom he had sown three years earlier had found all too fertile soil.

Deng's July speech was published two years later in his selected speeches. 'I told Comrade Hu Yaobang', it began, 'that I wanted to talk to the propaganda department about the problem of the ideological battlefront, particularly in literature and art . . . I think there is laxity and weakness and no courage to criticise wrong tendencies; moreover, once a man is criticised he claims he is being beaten by a stick.' [. . .] 'Before the Sixth Plenum', Deng went on, 'the novel *Bitter Love* was criticised by the *Liberation Army Daily*. That was right, but the critique was poorly written. It would have been better to publish such criticism in the magazine *Literature*, criticism moreover of a higher literary standard.' (A film, *The Sun and Man,* was made from the story of *Bitter Love*.) 'I went to see it. The impression that film gives is that the Party is bad and Socialism is wrong. If this film were to be shown to the public what impression would it give? There are people who say that not loving Socialism does not mean not loving the country. Is the love of the Fatherland an abstract notion? If you do not love the Socialism of the New China led by the Communist Party, what do you love?'

Other things have also happened. In the Teachers Training University, Peking, a young poet recited her poems. 'With this all the effects of the ideological training of the students were blown away. Yet the Party committee of the school has done nothing about it.' This recalls the rightists of 1957. The criticism of the rightists was excessive, but criticising the rightists was correct. 'The essence of the "Four Basic Principles" is leadership by the Communist Party. If the Communist Party does not lead, chaos will follow. . . . Today some people under the banner of defending Comrade Hua Guofeng intend to overthrow this or that person.'

'The present situation is the result of the preceding ten years of disorder and the irruption of bourgeois ideology from abroad. The difficulty is that we do not react with strength; our reaction is lax and weak. To handle these questions we must learn the lessons of the past. We cannot launch a political campaign. Each case must he handled on its own merits. But ideological work must go on and criticism and self-criticism must not be neglected.'[24]

This was Deng's speech that was presented again at the August 1981 meeting of the propaganda department, chaired by Wang Renzhong, head of Party propaganda and a member of the C.C. Secretatriat.[25] (A year later Wang lost both posts.)

The tough Peng Zhen

A department of the Central Committee has great power, but it is subordinate to the Politbureau, to the Standing Committee of the Politbureau and to the Secretariat of the C.C. Wang Renzhong's propaganda department was such a department. There was also another C.C. department that had emerged as a strong power-base. This was the Politico-Legal Committee of the C.C., which, though it is rarely mentioned in public, directs all organs of political repression. At its head was Peng Zhen.

Peng Zhen, purged in spring 1966 when he was sixty-three, re-emerged from the obscurity of the Cultural Revolution in February 1979, thus missing the Third C.C. Plenum held in December 1978. Peng Zhen's rehabilitation was not Deng's work. Peng had a more illustrous Party history behind him than Deng himself.

Until his reappearance, the C.C. had only a small Politico-Legal Team, headed by Ji Dengkui, a nonentity promoted during the Cultural Revolution. The security organs were still in a state of turmoil (as described earlier). Then Peng Zhen stepped in. He took over from Ji Dengkui the work of the C.C. Politico-Legal Team, which was renamed a Committee (no longer a mere Team). On the government side he became the head of the Legal Commission of the People's Congress. In November 1979 he addressed a conference of the security organs. In the same month (see above) the Standing Committee of the People's Congress regulated Labour Education, a type of forced labour first introduced in 1957, and decreed that all previous legal acts, including the most repressive, were still in force.

In May 1981, a month before the Sixth Plenum of the C.C., the Politico-Legal Committee held a national conference. The holding of this conference was not announced publicly till three months later. The conference decided to increase the severity of sanctions and to speed up legal procedures. This decision was legalised a month later, in June, by the People's Congress Standing Committee, which prescribed that the courts must impose sanctions one grade higher than the maximum prescribed in the Criminal Law. If, for example, the maximum sanction was fifteen years, a life sentence must be imposed; if the maximum was a life sentence, capital punishment must be imposed. The security organs, police, prosecution offices and the courts are, it proclaimed, 'the state organs of dictatorship and must remain strictly under the guidance of the Party committee'. All these organs came under the authority of the Politico-Legal Committee of the C.C.

These orders were carried out promptly though not without some grumbling from legal experts. Public executions began in front of crowds in sports stadiums and other public places, and photographs of these mass meetings were published in the newspapers, beginning in June 1981, the month of the Sixth Plenum of the C.C.[26]

At the time it was difficult to say whether Peng Zhen's Politico-Legal Committee, with its ruthless policy, was supporting Deng's group by quelling disorder and eliminating Deng's enemies, or was supporting the anti-Deng Maoists who believed that Deng's policies had conceded too much freedom and so undermined Marxist discipline. Peng Zhen, though he was only head of one department of the C.C., seemed to be quite independent of Deng's group. These, however, could not be displeased to see some order re-established. The Maoists too were probably applauding Peng Zhen. Now there seemed to be not two but three rival forces: Deng's group, the Maoists and Peng Zhen's set-up. The leadership was split into different sectors which agreed on some points and disagreed on others.

Low standards in the Party

In January 1979, a month after its establishment, the Disciplinary Investigation Committee of the C.C., headed by Chen Yun, drew up a twelve-point directive on the Standard of Political Life Within the Party. It was published in February 1980 by the Fifth Plenum of the C.C. This twelve-point rule of Party life was designed to normalise discipline in the Party after the abnormal times of the Cultural Revolution. The first eight points insisted on discipline and what is called Party democracy. Within the Party, the directive went on, members may hold divergent opinions, appeal to higher organs, and retain their dissenting opinions. But they must tell the truth and keep Party secrets, even at home with their families. Those who hold opinions contrary to decisions should not be persecuted. No cliques or factions must be formed in the Party. Elections in the Party are held by secret ballots at Party congresses or Party conferences, but elections are to be preceded by careful consultations and tentative pre-elections. When no Party Congress is being held or when the higher authorities so wish, the authorities can bypass elections and name the man to be put in charge.

The rules in the second part were less gentle. They prescribed an obligation to denounce evil trends and evil people in the Party. They also prescribed 'struggle' to get rid of evil men, 'tearing off their skin'. No reactionary trends were to be tolerated, but physical torture was not to be used. When a Party member was expelled, he might be 'handed over to the legal organs for sanctions'. (In the traditional view of the Party, 'Law' meant: repression, death, prison or labour camp. That a court might acquit an accused person was inconceivable. A Party member, so long as he was in the Party, enjoyed immunity from legal prosecution.) The last two points stated that in the Party all are equal and nobody should enjoy any privilege — a principle that, as all knew, had never been observed. The very last point spoke of the Four Modernisations, the 'Four Basic Principles' of Marxism, and the need for educated Party members and of being both 'red and expert'.[27] This was a description of what a good Party member should be. The reality was described two and a half months later on Party Day, July 1, 1980, when the *People's Daily* meditated on the low moral standards of the Party. The cause of this decadence, it said, may be that after the glorious fighting of the old days, the Party has become the ruling body of the country, and the puritan proletarian ideology has rusted away. 'There are feudalist features in the system: people are holding life-long posts and this results in dictatorial manners, bureaucracy and privileges.' The article also mentioned 'female influence', whatever this may have meant — perhaps a reference to Jiang Qing. Yet the spirit of the Party will be reformed, it said.

Newspaper publication of some scandals in the Party was ordered as a means of educating others. Among the abuses exposed was the easy life of local Party bosses, who were dining and entertaining at public expense, and obtaining cigarettes, wine, tea, free theatre shows and many other things by cultivating personal relations. There were great numbers of official guest houses in big and small cities and in towns around the country, where Party leaders were entertained at nominal prices. The children of Party leaders were being appointed to jobs they were not qualified for. A gang of youngsters whose parents were Party members had terrorised the city of Changchun in the Northeast for many years. They had raped ninety-two girls and held up people with knives. Ultimately they were arrested and the gang leader was executed. Their fathers cared nothing at all about it. Such people believe, a commentary in the *Chinese Youth Daily* of Peking said, that law is for commoners, not for princes. Many Party and state secrets were being leaked by the children of Party leaders. A Party member should not show secret documents to his children and friends. General nepotism prevailed and relatives were enjoying special privileges: entry to schools, entry to the Party, promotion in the ranks, moves from villages to the cities, permits to travel abroad. The privileged were even protected when committing crimes.

Peking had urged that those who had been wrongly condemned should be rehabilitated, but in many regions this was not done. Cliques and factions within the Party protected their own members and ostracised others. Some refused to obey orders transferring them to new posts — a form of insubordination unknown till then. They did not want to move from cities to villages, or to places far away from their families. A circular issued by the Party committee of Shanghai spoke of 'factionalism, secret manipulation, open fights for higher posts, presents given as bribes, divulging of inner-office secrets'.[28]

On July 15, 1981, the Cabinet issued a circular, published two days later in the *People's Daily*, about collective corruption in state-run enterprises, all run by Party members. These enterprises, the Circular said, acquire raw materials and sell products illegally, paying illegal commissions to their purchasing agents. It said that clandestine agreements, illegal transfer of bank credits, and speculation — selling things they do not own — are not uncommon.

The Disciplinary Investigation Committee discovered a scandal involving leading Party members in Yunnan province, an area that grows high-quality tobacco. The tobacco was being sold at a huge profit to leading personalities in other provinces and to the military. The committee publishing these added: 'This is a universal practice, everywhere, in all trades.' An ingrained abuse aired by the same Disciplinary Committee was the illegal building or occupation of houses by Party leaders of counties and communes, who 'occupy public land and use public money, public building material, transport and manpower, in order to build houses for themselves or their children'.

On September 7, 1981, the *People's Daily* said that there were Party members who 'ridicule, insult, slander, ostracise and isolate those who stick to their principles, those who have the courage to resist corrupt comrades'. Another *People's Daily* article spoke of 'three kinds of people who are isolated':

1. those who firmly support the Party Central are ostracised and isolated;
2. those who work hard and make an effort to do their work properly are exposed to sneers and isolation;
3. those who dare to tell the truth suffer and are isolated.[29]

On March 8, 1982, the People's Congress Standing Committee revised the Criminal Law of 1979, imposing heavy penalties, including the death sentence, life imprisonment and long prison terms, on those engaged in speculative gains, theft, or the smuggling of cultural relics. A week later the *People's Daily* commented that the main threat to the Party 'comes not from outside but from within the Party'. It compared the situation then (1982) with the *San-fan* anti-corruption campaign of 1952, thirty years earlier. It recalled Mao as having said in 1938 that if 100 or 200 Party leaders were good Marxist-Leninist comrades, then the Party had sufficient fighting spirit. Today (1982), it said, if we have 10,000 or 20,000 who stand firm in Marxism, then we can do the job; but if the middle-level and higher-level Party leaders are corrupt and this trend cannot be halted, then we are facing trouble. The trouble it spoke of was described as 'peaceful transformation'.

In the March 1, 1982, issue of *Red Flag*, Wang Renzhong, then a member of the C.C. Secretariat and head of Party propaganda, wrote:

There are those, though their number is small, who believe that our Party is degenerate and without hope, that it must be overthrown and a new dynasty must start [in China people always think in terms of dynasties]. They want a two-party system like that of the United States, one coming up and the other going down, the two ruling alternately. . . . These people, he said, organise illegal organisations and publish illegal publications. . . . There are people among the young, muddle-headed young people, who have no faith in our Party.

Red Flag, on March 16, 1982, struck a more pessimistic note, saying that if the Party were not reformed, 'not only will modernisation fail; the Party and the state may also perish.' The official newspaper of Zhejiang province, the *Zhejiang Daily*, saw the danger of 'peaceful transformation' in the spread of religious beliefs among young people who were going to temples to worship. 'Such things, together with pornography and gambling [religion is always listed with these two] must be extirpated by class struggle.'

The general complaint was that the children of leading cadres had been infected by bourgeois habits. 'This opened up a breach in the younger generation, bringing forward the threat of peaceful transformation,' said a leader of Jiangxi province. On April 10, 1982, the C.C. Disciplinary Committee said: 'The behaviour of the children of some of the higher cadres and their disregard for discipline and law have reached unbearable proportions.'[30]

Marxism, 1980–1982

The August 1981 meeting on ideological correctness had had little effect. Deng's speech, delivered a month before that meeting, was not even published. Peng Zhen's organisation cracked down on irregularities and crimes, but did not change people's minds. People learnt from Deng's doctrine that 'practice is the only norm of truth' and that Marx and Lenin were not infallible. Above all, expanding contacts with the 'bourgeois' West had revealed another world.

To counteract this, the *People's Daily* dilated on the hardships of the unemployed in the West — unemployment which brings with it 'isolation, hopelessness, drunkenness, drugs, sex abuse and religious superstition' (religion is always considered a social evil). The workers' wages have increased, it said, and their living conditions have improved, but these things never keep pace with the gains of the capitalists. The opposition between the two never vanishes, and discontent brings people closer to Marxism.

But on the very next day, September 23, 1980, a Shanghai newspaper gave the information that in the West the majority of workers have their own cars and television sets, and many own their own houses. This renders some of Marx's theses obsolete, it said. Marx stated that in capitalist countries the workers lose everything essential to human life, and Engels said that the number of proletarians would increase and they would turn to revolution. The Shanghai paper commented: 'Can one repeat this today, when workers have their own cars, television sets and refrigerators? Yes, the unemployed do have a difficult time, but social security safeguards their basic needs. [It drew the conclusion that Marx's theory is not immutable.] Marx looked forward to the time when the difference between city and village, between manual and mental labour, would disappear. In developed capitalist countries, backward villages no longer exist, and agriculture has been industrialised. Therefore we can no longer speak of Marx's theory of impoverishment of the proletariat, and we have to think of a new formulation of Marxism.'[31]

Between September and the end of 1980, the *People's Daily* and other newspapers published sweeping articles against old-fashioned Marxist dogmas. On November 11 an article in the *People's Daily* was headed 'Crisis of Faith, What Does It Mean?' ('Crisis of faith' meant crisis of faith in Marxism.) 'Today we are on the threshold of a new era and we are searching for a way of combining Marxism with this new era. No answer to this has yet appeared, or if it has appeared it has not yet been recognised. It is not recognised as the Marxist answer; it is called heresy and revisionism.'

The search for a new Marxism is found in the doctrine of Deng, the article went on. Our leadership is leading the liberation of minds, but is meeting with serious resistance from people who label the discussion of the Norm of Truth a crime, a hauling-down of the banner of Marxism. Comrade Deng Xiaoping is resolutely dealing with the resistance and is supporting this discussion.

The masses, particularly the youth, have doubts about Marxism, and in consequence 'the crisis of faith has arisen,' another *People's Daily* article said. 'Conditions have changed, and the old theses cannot be applied today. Marxism has always held that practice is the only norm of truth. Yet this phrase as proposed in the first half of 1978 [by Deng] has a new meaning.'

Another article stated: 'For twenty years we have been using sayings of Lenin, but many of Lenin's sayings cannot be understood without understanding the peculiar circumstances of his time in Russia.'

'Thirty years ago', another article said, 'our Marxism — dialectical materialism, historical materialism — came from the Soviet Union. Unfortunately, with time these phrases have become empty formulas. Yet the doctrine itself must be upheld.'

In that year, 1980, Eurocommunism blossomed as a promising revision of old Marxism. In the spring of 1980 the then Italian Communist leader Enrico Berlinguer received a warm reception in Peking. In November the leader of the Spanish Communists, Santiago Carillo, who had rejected the doctrine of proletarian dictatorship, was also there. Eurocommunism — short-lived as it was — looked in those days like an ally for Deng's revisionist doctrines.

However, Carillo, in a lecture in Peking University, introduced an idea that displeased his hosts: the need for a multi-party system. Soon afterwards Feng Wenbin, deputy dead of the C.C.'s Party School, wrote in the *People's Daily* that some people in China had also proposed a two-party system. He rejected the idea: the Chinese Communist Party represented the whole people.[32] Santiago Carillo's visit was remembered for a long time. In April 1981 a long study in the *People's Daily* recalled Carillo's saying that not all problems are solved merely because a party has gained political power. Since this has never been asserted in China, the article said, it is necessary to explain the meaning of Socialism in Marxism. Marx and Engels themselves scarcely distinguished between Socialism and Communism. In some of his writings, however, Marx did speak of two stages of Communism, an initial stage and a second — full Communism — under which the axiom 'From each according to his ability, to each according to his needs' (that nebulous phrase that has bedevilled social revolutionary thought for a hundred years) becomes reality. It was Lenin, the *People's Daily* article went on, who called the initial stage of Communism socialism. But experience has shown that things are not so simple. 'The development of the world has not responded to the predictions of Marx and Engels. The revolution led by the proletariat (where has there been a Communist revolution not led by intellectuals?) succeeded, not in countries where production had progressed and capitalism had developed, as the Marxist doctrine taught, but in countries where production was backward and capitalism undeveloped. We in China also have established Socialism, calling it "ownership by the whole people"; in fact it is State ownership. Most of the financial transactions are arranged by transfer of accounts between State organs, and the market mechanism is ignored. There is also collective ownership, but this collectivised economy also relies on the State. Land was collectivised and then communised abruptly. This system had proved impracticable not only in China but in most socialist countries. The socialist countries have begun to realise that one cannot simply follow the Marxist canon. The economy cannot be planned totally, and elements of market economy must be introduced.'

This study went further, proposing what in the West was called the 'convergence theory', the closer convergence of the capitalist and the socialist system. The *People's Daily* went one step further, saying that both ways will lead to final Communism. 'Human society will ultimately reach communism, but it will do so in two different ways. Capitalism will reach a high degree of socialisation. Socialism will develop a commodity economy, and thus the material foundation for communism will be laid. This is how countries which had a backward economy but in which, for historical reasons, the revolution first achieved victory, will reach Communism.'

(The underlying thought was that there cannot be 'distribution according to needs' without plenty. Why plenty would lead to Communism was not explained.)

What this article was voicing was the thesis Deng had proposed at the celebrated C.C. Plenum in December 1978. It had suffered a severe setback at the December 1980 Work Conference and at the C.C. Plenum in June 1981; but Deng's party continued to expound their views.[33]

Orthodox Marxism, however, returned. In the early 1980s, 353 books were published (91 million copies in all) to popularise orthodox Marxism in an easily understandable form. This was done, as a press article said, to combat 'disbelief in the value of Socialism and the widespread view that the Marxist axiom that capitalism leads to impoverishment of the proletariat was not true, and to explain what human rights and democracy meant in the Marxist system'. It was admitted that these books did not sell well, while ancient Chinese adventure stories were being bought by the million. Even a five-volume edition of Sherlock Holmes in Chinese sold 950,000 copies.

In April 1982 a *Peking Daily* article admitted that over 90 per cent of the youth did not have an inkling of what Marxism was. Moreover, they knew nothing about modern Chinese history. This was the 'crisis of faith' in Marxism.

A former Vice-President of the Central Committee Party School, Fan Ruoyu, who was still teaching Scientific Socialism in the school, explained what was plaguing Marxism in China. Until the 1960s, he said, the classic Soviet books were studied in China — *Fundamentals of Marxism-Leninism* by Stalin, and the *History of the Communist Party of the Soviet Union (Bolsheviks), Short Course*. These were the main texts in the C.C. Party School. Later the Soviet Union rewrote its Party history. By then we were no longer following them. In the second half of 1957 we, like Moscow, stopped studying *The Fundamentals of Marxism-Leninism*, but nothing took its place, until 1977 when comrade Hu Yaobang, who was then running the C.C. Party School, proposed the introduction of a course on Scientific Socialism.

What Professor Fan said was tantamount to an admission that the study of Marxism was neglected for the twenty years that followed China's abandoning of the Russian model. This neglect, Professor Fan wrote, had a devastating effect. 'Many comrades do not care for the study of theories, saying that theories change, theories are useless'. Professor Fan himself believed that Marxism was not changing; it was developing in the light of new revolutionary experiences. As Deng Xiaoping was saying, 'practice is the only norm of truth'.

(Professor Fan mentioned the role of Hu Yaobang in the C.C. Party School in 1977. In that year Hua Guofeng, as well as being Chairman of the Party, was also head of the C.C. Party School and Hu Yaobang was one of the Vice-Presidents. It was Hu who proposed that a special chair should be established for teaching Scientific Socialism. Professor Fan was the first holder of the chair.)

Scientific Socialism did not mean a return to rigid Stalinist theories. The freedom to reinterpret Marx initiated by Deng was warmly welcomed by professional Marxist scholars, and resulted in writings that shook the foundations of the traditional doctrine. It seemed that the traditional teaching of Marxism, propagated in popular books on Marxism, had become 'the opium for the masses'. The Marxist experts themselves indulged in the new freedom. Theses which had been held unshakably for thirty years were now questioned.

Marxist textbooks had always followed the doctrine of Engels that 'man was created by labour', i.e., transformed from ape into man through the constantly improving use of the hands, and that this was followed by the development of speech. The Marxist scholars now found this untenable in the light of modern biology. The doctrine that society had developed in stages, from primitive society to slavery, from slavery to feudalism, from feudalism to capitalism and then to the present stage of socialism, which would lead to final Communism, had been considered a sacrosanct thesis in Marxism. It was still being taught in popular Marxist books. But Marxist scholars asserted that neither Marx, Engels nor Lenin had taught this, and that the five periods of historical development had been invented by Stalin in his *Dialectical Materialism and Historical Materialism*. The histories of many countries contradict Stalin's theory, they said.

Marxist experts were saying these things in scientific journals, but *Red Flag*, the organ of the C.C., in its March 16, 1982, issue, was still talking about the five periods of historical development. Indeed, if the five periods were rejected, all the Marxist literature published in China would have to be rewritten, and Party members who could not think of history, Chinese or foreign, in any other terms would be deeply perturbed. (In the Soviet Union the theory of five periods was not abandoned. Indeed in the 1980s the Russian edition of one of the *Oxford Dictionaries* adopted this formula under the headings 'Capitalism' and 'Socialism'.)

Another fundamental thesis of Mao's China was that China had had a feudal system for 2,000 years, and that this had turned into a semi-feudal regime in the middle of the nineteenth century. Some Marxist scholars now had the guts to contradict this and to state that China had never had a feudal system, and that land in China had been owned by small independent farmers. These theses were too revolutionary to be accepted by the Party cadres, and Chinese history continued to be described as 2,000 years of feudal history.

In esoteric Marxist circles, even the basic notion of the nature of matter was freely discussed. An article published in March 1982 in the *People's Daily* said: 'Modern physics explores the composition of matter, and today we know that the atom and the nucleus are more complex than was thought before. Marxism must find an answer.'[34]

Humanism was discussed towards the end of 1981 and in early 1982 in connection with *Man, Oh Man!*, a novel about university life written by a woman Party member. *Man, Oh Man!* portrayed a wide range of characters. There was a heartless Party secretary. There was a man who, having entered the party at the age of eighteen and been condemned in 1957 as a 'rightist', had led a life of misery; he then wrote a book on

Marxism and Humanism. He was presented as a good man who was kind to everybody. There was also a woman — a self-portrait of the author — who was a Party branch secretary in the department of Chinese literature. She lost all ideals, but rediscovered Mao through the writer of the book about humanism. The postscript to the book said: 'I believe that Marxism and humanism are the same, are identical. Even if one does not find the theoretical basis for this in the [Marxist] canons, I do not wish to suppress the deep call I feel in my heart.' The critics were divided: some were sympathetic. Others condemned the book, saying that in his early days, in 1844, Marx had defended humanism under the influence of Feuerbach. Soon, however, he repudiated both humanism and all people who treated Communism as a doctrine of morality and substituted some sort of human solidarity for class struggle. The book *Man, Oh Man!* does not square with Marxism, these critics said.

Humanism was a delicate subject. In 1942, in his much-lauded 'Talk on Literature and Art', Mao had declared that there is no human nature, only class nature. In 1980 the Vice-Director of the Philosophy Research Institute of the Academy of Social Sciences wrote that Marx was fundamentally a humanist and that there was no break between the young and the mature Marx — a point that had been much debated among Marxist scholars in the West. This article was prominently printed in the *People's Daily* on August 15, 1980; but a year later this thesis was challenged by those who believed that Marxism and humanism were incompatible.[35]

In 1981 a Shanghai newspaper carried a unique piece of writing, the only article in thirty or so years in the Communist press that raised the question: did not Marxism, and the internal struggle it brought to China, do harm to the country? The article, published in the Shanghai *Wen Hui Bao* on July 22, 1981, was headed 'Without the Communist Party the Chinese People Would Not Have Been Liberated'. It was an answer to those who had doubts. The article recalled the attacks that the Nationalist theoretician Ye Qing had made on the Communists in the early 1930s. Ye studied with Zhou Enlai and others in France and later was in Moscow in the 1920s, but he left the Communists in 1927, became a leader in the Kuomintang and attacked the Communists mercilessly, calling them 'warlords who split the unity of the country'. 'Should Marxism-Leninism lead the Chinese revolution?' was the focus of discussion in the 1930s. Ye Qing said no. His argument was: Communism is a European product, an imported foreign commodity. The Communists' reply was that Marxism is the universal truth about mankind, which transforms the world. The Shanghai article quoted from Chiang Kai Shek's famous book *The Destiny of China* the words: 'The harm done to the revolution by the internal disorder [the civil war between the Nationalists and the Communists] had a baneful influence on foreign relations; without the internal disorder foreign invasion would not have taken place.' This meant that if the Japanese had not seen an internally torn and thus greatly weakened China, they would have had second thoughts about their military invasion of the country.

Bringing up such old objections in 1981 was a serious matter. This article appeared a month after the Sixth C.C. Plenum, held in June 1981, which had exposed the grave mistakes of Mao, though not those of his early years. Readers in China may well have been stunned by the questions raised: Had the whole Communist movement in China not done harm to the country? — and would the Japanese have invaded if the Communists had not divided the country by civil war? At a time when the prestige of the Party was low and people had many doubts, these questions had to be answered.

These doubts were not mere youthful questionings. The young had no memories of those early days. The questioning must have arisen in the minds of those who had fought for the cause all their lives, and now, on thinking back, were wondering whether the struggle had been worth the trouble, whether the Communist revolution had been beneficial or harmful to the country. They had fought against the Nationalist Government which they had regarded as degenerate and corrupt, and now they saw the Party leaders engaged in a desperate struggle against the same type of corruption. Would the country not have fared better if it had remained united, under any government, and not been torn apart by civil strife for over twenty years?[36] It was in this atmosphere that the Twelfth Party Congress was held.

The Twelfth Party Congress

The Twelfth Party Congress was held from September 1 to September 11, 1982. The opening speech, delivered by Deng, showed who was the boss. Looking back at past Party Congresses, he extolled the importance of the Seventh, held in Yan'an in 1945. The Eighth Party Congress — first session held in 1956 — had acted correctly, he said, but what it decided was not put in practice; he did not say that this was because of the resistance of Mao. It was at that Congress session in 1956 that he himself, as Secretary-General of the Party, had condemned the cult of personality; that Congress had sought, without success, to reduce the figure of Mao to manageable proportions. Deng did not even mention Party Congresses later than the Eighth, but said simply that 'the quarter-century of tortuous development of our socialist revolution after the Eighth Congress taught the whole Party profound lessons' — until the December 1978 C.C. Plenum, his own Plenum, at which 'our Party restored correct policies'. He simply dismissed the Ninth Party Congress held in 1969, which had made Lin Biao heir-designate to Mao; the Tenth, in 1973, which had raised Jiang Qing's group to the highest leadership; and the Eleventh, in 1977, which had been held under the chairmanship of Hua Guofeng.

Hu Yaobang delivered the main report to the Congress — he, not Deng, was the Chairman. He asserted that the Eleventh Congress, the most recent, had been wrong in its 'theories, policies and slogans'.

This blotting out of the memory of twenty-six years of the Party's history and of three Congresses was an almost unparalleled innovation. The only comparable event was Khrushchev's denunciation of Stalin in 1956. Deng and Hu did not denounce Mao by name; but Hu said that the Party

had subjected comrade Mao Zedong's mistakes in his later years to scientific analysis and criticism, while firmly safeguarding the scientific truth of Mao Zedong Thought and affirming Comrade Mao Zedong's historical role.[. . .] Beginning in the late 1950s, the personality cult appeared and gradually developed, and political life in the Party and in the state, and particularly in the Central Committee, grew more and more abnormal, leading eventually to the decade of domestic turmoil.

Hu admitted the low standard of Party life, and said that though the Party leadership and the Disciplinary Committee were working to uphold Party discipline, 'they had met with considerable, and in some cases shocking, obstruction in their work.' He explained: 'A few Party members and cadres have sunk to corruption, embezzlement and other malpractices, committing serious economic crimes. There is also a small remnant of the followers of the Lin Biao and Jiang Qing counter-revolutionary cliques. They still hold some leading positions and are waiting for a chance to stir up trouble.'

Hu had a lot to say about 'socialist spiritual civilisation', the latest invention of the Party, which was to be added to 'material civilisation'. 'Spiritual civilisation', Hu said, meant culture — education, science, art, literature, public health, libraries and so on — and ideology, Communist ideology. Hu and the other old Party leaders may not have understood that for the young generation civilisation meant either a Western style of life; or a search for the meaning of life in religious belief. Perhaps Hu did know. He quoted Mao's old words to prove that those who think that Communism is a 'vague airy mirage' or that 'Communism has not been proved by practice' are wrong — Deng had said that practice is the norm of truth.

The Party Congress published a revised Party Charter. The titles of Chairman and Vice-Chairman were abolished. Instead, as in the Soviet Union and elsewhere, the Party head was to be known as the General-Secretary. It was laid down that he was not the leader but a member of the Politbureau Standing Committee; however, he was to direct the C.C. Secretariat, which has charge of the daily work of the Party leadership. This job-description was tailored for Hu Yaobang. The Politbureau Standing Committee, consisting of six members, was elected at the first C.C. Plenum, held immediately after the Congress. It was composed of very old men indeed.

(One never knows the exact age of Peking's leaders. When the Sixth C.C. Plenum re-established the Party Secretariat in 1980, a Hong Kong Communist newspaper published short biographies of its members, indicating their ages. On the following day, March 2, 1980, the *People's Daily* did the same. The *People's Daily*, however, docked the ages of the leaders by a few years each. In the Hong Kong paper Hu Qiaomu was seventy-five, and in the *People's Daily* sixty-eight; Wan Li was seventy, and in the *People's Daily* sixty-four; Wang Renzhong was seventy-six, and in the *People's Daily* sixty-three; and so on. Hu Yaobang was sixty-seven, and in the *People's Daily* sixty-five.)

At the preceding Eleventh Party Congress (1977) the supreme ruling body, the Politbureau Standing Committee, had consisted of the then Chairman Hua Guofeng, Ye Jianying, Deng Xiaoping, Li Xiannian and Wang Dongxing, who was ousted at the Fifth Plenum in 1980. Hua Guofeng resigned at the Sixth Plenum in 1981. Chen Yun became a member of the Politbureau Standing Committee at the Third Plenum in December 1978. Hu Yaobang and Zhao Ziyang became members at the Fifth in 1980. No changes were made at this Twelfth Congress. Thus it came about that there was an even number at the top. If two triumvirates take opposite views, no majority decision can be reached. The six Politbureau Standing Committee members were Ye Jianying, aged about eighty-five; Chen Yun, Deng Xiaoping and Li Xiannian, close to eighty, Hu Yaobang aged sixty-five and Zhao Ziyang aged sixty-three. Hu and Zhao, both promoted by Deng, would certainly vote with

Deng, but the veterans Ye Jianying and Li Xiannian had nothing to thank Deng for, and were closer to the Maoists. On many points Chen Yun agreed with these two.

This Party Congress introduced an innovation unknown in other Communist parties. It established an Advisory Commission for meritorious old Party leaders. According to the Charter, members of the Advisory Commission must have been Party members for forty years or more. Also according to the Party Charter, the General Secretary (Hu Yaobang), the Chairman of the Advisory Commission (Deng) and the Chairman of the Military Committee (Deng) must be members of the C.C. Standing Committee. The other four members also held important posts in Party or government. Chen Yun had been head of the Party's Disciplinary Investigation Committee since December 1978; Ye Jianying was head of the Standing Committee of the People's Congress, which at that time was the highest government post; Zhao Ziyang was Prime Minister; and Li Xiannian became the President of the Republic (a restored title) in 1983.

Not Peng Zhen

A seventh member of the Politbureau Standing Committee might have been expected. This was Peng Zhen, born in 1902, who had entered the Party in 1923 and been a distinguished leader throughout the history of the Party. He had been a member of the Politbureau since 1945, except during the Cultural Revolution and the reign of the Jiang Qing radicals.

In the very days when the Party Congress was in session he — quite surprisingly for the secretary of the C.C.'s Politico-Legal Committee — was holding a Working Conference for legal work. A month earlier in August 1982, a *People's Daily* editorial had said that this Politico-Legal Committee was in control of the security organs in cities and villages. It had charge of the police, security, the courts, the procuratorates and — a new, powerful body — the People's Armed Police: at the end of 1982 a section of the army was relieved of its duties and given new uniforms, a new function and a new name: People's Armed Police Troops.

When Ye Jianying — now old and sick — retired in 1983, Peng Zhen became the head of the Standing Committee of the People's Congress (not of the Party), which was superior to the Cabinet. In 1982 the statute of the Standing Committee of the People's Congress was revised. Till then laws had been enacted only by plenary sessions of the People's

Congress, which were convened once a year. The 1982 session, held in December, gave the power of enacting laws to the Standing Committee, which was to be convened every second month. With these two functions — head of the C.C. Politico-Legal Committee of the Party and head of the People's Congress — Peng Zhen wielded considerable power. Yet he was not made a member of the Standing Committee of the Politbureau, whereas Zhao Ziyang, a minor Party leader till the 1960s, was a member of the Standing Committee of the Politbureau.

Deng — Peng Zhen

The Twelfth Party Congress made some important personnel changes. Five former Politbureau members were no longer members. Hua Guofeng, though out of power, remained a member of the C.C., but Chen Yonggui (hero of the famous Dazhai village, a fake model created by Mao to illustrate how with willpower one can work miracles) was nowhere to be seen. The days of Chen Yonggui and Dazhai were over. Marshal Liu Bocheng was no longer on the list of the Politbureau members, but he was very old, about ninety, and in bad health. He had been Deng's protecting symbol: as a commander during the civil war, he had had Deng as his political commissar. Saifudin, an alternate-member of the outgoing Politbureau, was also dropped. The sensation of the day — though the Chinese press of course never speaks of 'sensation' — was that Geng Biao and Peng Chong were no longer in the Politbureau. Geng Biao was a distinguished member of the Party. He had been an ambassador from the 1950s to 1970 except for a five-year interruption during the Cultural Revolution. From 1971 to 1979 he was head of the Foreign Liaison Department of the C.C., a post higher than that of foreign minister. From 1979 to 1981 he was Secretary-General of the Military Committee of the C.C. In the spring of 1981 he became minister of defence, and held that post till November 1982 when, two months after the Twelfth Party Congress, he was replaced by General Zhang Aiping. At the same Congress, Geng Biao was appointed to the C.C.'s Advisory Commission. He was of course not young, being well over seventy years old, but others in the Politbureau were even older. In the following year, 1983, he became head of the Foreign Affairs Committee (not in the Party organisations but in the People's Congress) under Peng Zhen. It seemed to all intents and purposes as if Peng Zhen was collecting distinguished people discarded by Deng.

Peng Chong, the other man dropped in 1982 from the Politbureau, had had an odd career. He was First Party secretary of Jiangsu province in 1975. After the death of Mao and the arrest of the Jiang Qing clique he was moved to Shanghai: in 1979 he became First Party secretary of that city and Party leader of the Shanghai garrison. The Eleventh Party Congress in 1977 made him a member of the Politbureau, and in 1980 he became a member of the C.C. Secretariat. He was one of the up-and-coming 'younger' men in the Party. Said to have been born in 1915, he was sixty-seven, about the same age as Zhao Ziyang. After being dropped by Deng in 1982, he became a deputy head of the People's Congress Standing Committee.

The third important person dropped by Deng was Wang Renzhong. He was not a member of the Politbureau but was in the 1980 C.C. Secretariat. He was, it may be remembered, the man who went swimming with Mao in the Yangze in 1966. He was then First Party secretary of Hubei province. At the beginning of the Cultural Revolution he was called to Peking to be the deputy head of propaganda (under Tao Zhu), but he soon disappeared under the waves of the Cultural Revolution. Deng's December 1978 C.C. Plenum made him a member of the C.C. In 1979 and 1980 he seemed to be a very important person. Early in 1979 — already in the Deng Xiaoping era — Wang Renzhong became the head of a new organ called the State Agricultural Commission, which gave him seniority over the ministries dealing with agriculture. He was then seventy-three. He also became one of the Vice-Premiers. He was very much in the limelight when he became a member of the C.C. Secretariat in March 1980 and was made head of the Party's propaganda — a very important post. Then, in the spring of 1982, five months before the Twelfth Party Congress, he lost his post as head of propaganda to Deng Lichun. At the Twelfth Party Congress he was dropped from the C.C. Secretariat and for some time one was left wondering what had happened to Wang Renzhong.

He also was picked up by Peng Zhen. In 1983, when Peng became head of the People's Congress, Wang became deputy head of the Standing Committee and head of the Finance and Economic Commission of the People's Congress. All this sounded very odd, as if Peng Zhen was deliberately taking in men who were no longer trusted by Deng.

Deng could not eliminate all his opponents at once. Wei Guoqing, as head of the Army's Political Department, was the most outspoken of the critics of the new reforms. At the Twelfth Congress in 1982, he remained a member of the Politbureau, but ceased to be head of the Army's Political Department. (This post was taken over by Yu Qiuli, a confidant of Deng's and, it may be remembered, one of Deng's companions at the card table.)[37]

Deng had certainly strengthened his position, but his opponents had not been completely eliminated. Of the twenty-seven members of the Politbureau, seven were active in the military. Their number included three marshals who were not necessarily on his side — Ye Jianying, Ne Rongzhen and Xu Xiangqian.

The army and Deng

On August 28, 1982, a few days before the opening of the Twelfth Party Congress, an article in *Liberation Army Daily*, the army newspaper, created a furore. On reading it out of context, one finds it hard to guess why. The article said that a distinction must be made between bourgeois civilisation and Communist civilisation. On the surface, it said, the two may seem similar, but the civilisation of the bourgeois class is false and deceptive, a cover for the struggle for profit, and a conveyor-belt sucking the blood of the proletariat. We do not reject the advanced technology of the capitalist countries and we study the cultural heritage of the outside world, but we must not transplant these wholesale. Our Party promotes socialist spiritual civilisation. The article then praised Deng for having said that 'All must have ideals, morality and discipline'.

This is the right Party spirit, the right spirit of the Yan'an times, it said. This means education, science, culture, art, sports, public health and so on. This is the meaning of Deng's three words 'ideals, morality and discipline', three words that promote the 'Four Modernisations'. Culture should be distinguished from ideology. The Communist heroes, such as Lei Feng, had no high cultural standard, yet they were outstanding examples for our comrades.

'The threat from bourgeois-class liberal trends should not be underestimated . . . Some responsible comrades in literature and culture and in news services have supported and propagated bourgeois liberal errors opposed to the Four Basic Principles . . .'

Why did this article seem controversial? Why did it create a furore? Hu Yaobang in his Party Congress report had spoken of the state of mind of Party leaders in no less sombre tones. The rejection of bourgeois liberalism was not new, it had been loudly proclaimed in the middle of the previous year. Yet a month after the appearance of this article in the

Liberation Army Daily, that paper had to publish an apology — an apology for what?

The article quoted a phrase of Deng's that the great man had used when talking to foreign visitors on August 6 — what he said then had never been published for the general public. Deng's words were: 'We want our people to have idealism, morality, culture and discipline.' The *Liberation Army Daily* article had left out 'culture'! It had extolled Communist ideology as if Marxist ideology could exist without culture and education! This was a sensitive point. The party leadership was striving to raise the educational standard of its leaders. On October 14, 1982, the front-page article of the *People's Daily* said that a number of people in the central organisations of the Party and government had only received primary education and that this must change. Yet the *Liberation Army Daily* article had left out the word 'culture'. By this, the criticism said, it expressed doubts about and opposition to the Third Plenum of the Eleventh C.C., i.e. the reforms introduced by Deng.

To anyone used to the slapdash journalism common in the West, the omission of one word may seem a trivial matter. Things are otherwise in China, where no important article appears without meticulous preliminary scrutiny. The fact that an article in the *Liberation Army Daily* had left out a word of Deng's meant that important figures in the army were defending the Maoist position and were opposed to Deng. It had become necessary for some prominent regional army leaders on Deng's side to display their Dengist colours and manifest their loyalty by quoting Deng's four words — without leaving out 'culture'.

The critical article had other implications. On the very day when the army newspaper published it, it was reprinted in the *Liberation Daily,* the official Party newspaper of the Shanghai Party Committee. At the head of the Shanghai Committee's propaganda department was Chen Yi (not to be confused with his apparent namesake the late Marshal Chen Yi), who was known for his radical Maoist stance. The *Liberation Daily* had to reprint the *Liberation Army Daily*'s apology, but it did not apologise for having reprinted the erring article. Within two years Chen Yi had lost his job; at the end of 1984 another person appeared in his post. It is not impossible that Peng Chong lost the First Party secretaryship of Shanghai because of the opposition of his propaganda chief to Deng.[38] The lesson to be learnt from this odd incident is that in the second half of 1982 the Maoists still had a voice in the army and were opposed to Deng.

The army had had no single powerful leader since the death of Lin Biao in 1971, twelve years earlier. Deng, who had become head of the

C.C. Military Committee and had gathered round him a few of his faithful friends, exerted great pressure to subdue the army's resistance to his policies. The army budget was reduced, and in February 1983 the C.C. Military Committee ordered an investigation into the finances of the armed forces. About 100,000 of those working in the offices of the army were despatched to survey lower units. Industries serving the army exclusively were ordered to produce goods for civilian purposes — to this there was resistance, reflected in the official reports, based on fears that this would affect the production of goods needed for the army. The ministry in charge of producing weapons was accused of irregularity in finances, including illegal expenditure and supplementary payments to its staff.[39]

Ten of the eleven commanders of regional commands, the Great Military Areas, were changed. Only Li Desheng, commander of the Northeast, remained in his post. There was some manifest nervousness behind the changes, especially as the commanders of six military regions had already been changed since 1979. Now they were changed again. In the Wuhan Great Military Area, commanding Hubei and Henan provinces, the commander, Yang Dezhi, was moved to another region in 1979 and promoted to Chief-of-Staff in Peking in 1980. His successor in Wuhan, Wang Bicheng, who had been transferred there from another Great Military Area, lasted only one year. He was then replaced by General Zhang Caiqian. In 1982 General Zhang was retired and replaced by one of his deputy commanders, Zhou Shizhong. Most of the provincial military leaders were also changed. It was not known, however, who was responsible for the new nominations. Theoretically, Deng's men should have been responsible, but that was not certain. The discordant voice in the *Liberation Army Daily* in the middle of 1982 was the tip of the iceberg. Deep down, many generals were not satisfied — how could they be? — with the changed situation and the humiliation of the armed forces that was taking place.

There were definite signs that not all Great Military Area leaders were Deng's nominees. In January 1983 Zheng Weishan was made commander of the Lanzhou Great Military Area. During the Cultural Revolution he was the acting commander of Peking and he became a C.C. member in 1969 at the Ninth Party Congress, Lin Biao's Congress. After Lin Biao's death in 1971 he disappeared from the scene. Zheng Weishan was obviously a Lin Biao man, yet he was named commander of the very important Northwest area responsible for four provinces.

The loyalty of Jiang Yonghui, the new commander of the Fuzhou

Great Military Area in the sensitive region facing Taiwan, also seemed questionable. He too had become a member of the C.C. in 1969. Before 1949, he had been in Lin Biao's Fourth Route Army. The army leadership of the Northeast was also ambiguous. In February 1983 Liu Zhenhua became the political commissar of the Great Military Area of Shenyang in the Northeast. He also was a Lin Biao man.

The Shenyang Great Military Area was commanded by Li Desheng, who was promoted from a provincial job to become one of the Vice-Chairmen of the Party in 1973, in the period of Jiang Qing's rule; but a few months later he was relegated to Shenyang, where he became the commander under Deng. In many press articles Li Desheng proclaimed his utter loyalty to Deng in terms too warm to be credible.

These were cases, particularly that of Zheng Weishan, which raised doubts about Deng's power over the army. It was not even clear whether Yang Dezhi, the Chief-of-Staff, was an ardent Deng supporter. He had been a C.C. member through all the troubled years since 1956, and a commander of the Wuhan Great Military Area since 1976. He joined the chorus condemning Deng when he fell from power before the death of Mao. In 1979 he was transferred to command the Kunming Great Military Area in the Southwest, and in the following year, 1980, he became Chief-of-Staff. He may or may not have changed his personal views and his loyalties.

Armed Police Troops

The central command of the People's Armed Police Troops was not officially established in Peking till April 1983, but it had been set up before that date. At the end of 1982 a provincial command was announced in Jiangsu province, and it was stated that the Armed Police Troops were not under the control of the army but under the ministry of security. The border defence, the armed militia in the counties, and the fire brigades were merged with the Armed Police Troops. Their main purpose was 'the maintenance of public order and the protection of the Party and of the government'.

In January 1983 the Armed Police Troops were established in Shanghai. In February a *People's Daily* article confirmed that the judiciary and the security organs (together with the Armed Police Troops) were under the Politico-Legal Committee of the C.C., headed by Peng Zhen. The Armed Police Troops were rapidly established in the provinces, and in April, after the official establishment of the overall command, a national conference of these troops was held in Peking under the leadership of Chen Pixian, who appeared under the title Party secretary of the C.C. Politico-Legal Committee.[40]

People's Congress of 1983

In June 1983 the newly-elected People's Congress, the sixth since 1954, held its first yearly session. It promoted to very high posts two men who were not from Deng's circle. The new State Constitution, adopted a year earlier, had re-established the post of Chairman (President) of the Republic. Li Xiannian now became President. Peng Zhen became head of the People's Congress Standing Committee, i.e. of the People's Congress. With three exceptions the twenty deputy-heads of the People's Congress were all new.

It was at this time that Peng Zhen took in those who a year earlier had been ousted from their posts by Deng. The maneouvre was too obvious to escape notice.

The Standing Committee also established six sub-committees, four of them headed by men who had lost their posts under Deng. Peng Chong became the head of the Legal Commission (a post previously held by Peng Zhen). Wang Renzhong became head of the Finance and Economic Commission, Geng Biao of the Foreign Affairs Commission, and Ye Fei of the Overseas Chinese Commission.

(One should never ask the ages of Peking leaders. A Peking booklet published in 1983 to present the documents of the People's Congress also carried photographs of and brief biographical notes on the new leaders of the People's Congress. As in 1980 [see p. 456], many of them were rejuvenated in the 1983 booklet. Li Xiannian, said to have been born in 1909, lost four years; Wei Guoqing, born in 1913, lost seven years; Wang Renzhong, born in 1917, lost eleven years, and so on.)

Deng's book

On the other side of the picture, Deng attained extreme prominence through the publication of his writings, put on sale on July 1, Party Day, 1983. The title was *Selected Writings of Deng Xiaoping, 1975–82*. It contained a number of speeches never published before, but none made before 1975, the year when he first proposed (though not yet publicly) his great reform programme. All his earlier speeches, those made under Mao, were to be blotted out from memory. The booklet was hailed as Mao's used to be in the old days, and was published both in Peking and in the provinces: the provincial authorities held meetings to acclaim the great event, and innumerable articles analysed the profound meaning of Deng's words. Within three months 40 million copies were issued,[41] quite an achievement, though not comparable to the hundreds of millions of copies of Mao's writings issued during the Cultural Revolution. The book was acclaimed in some provinces, but the acclamation was not comparable to the frenzy that had greeted the pronouncements of Mao and Lin Biao in earlier times. It was particularly noticeable that, among the generals, only the few in Deng's immediate entourage echoed the sentiments in his book. The sixth volume of *Mao's Selected Works,* promised by Hua Guofeng when he was in power, did not appear, and nothing was heard of the preparation of the complete works of Mao, similarly promised. The new doctrine was that of Deng.

Fake photographs

The exaltation of Deng was accompanied by a repetition of the chicanery with photographs that had been employed several times in the past. The front page of the first issue of *Red Flag* in 1983 showed an old group photo of Mao, Zhou Enlai, Liu Shaoqi, Zhu De, Chen Yun and Deng, with Chen Yun reaching out his hand to shake Mao's. No explanation accompanied the photograph. This picture of the leaders had appeared — also without any explanation — on July 1, 1962, in two Peking papers, but not in the *People's Daily*. The readers of those days viewed the photograph as a sign of reconciliation between Mao and Chen Yun, who had criticised the Great Leap in 1959. In 1962 the photograph had also shown a seventh person, Lin Biao. In the 1982 version in *Red Flag* Lin Biao had been cut out.

In 1983 the photo was reprinted in the provinces, 2 million copies in one province alone.[42] A report said that a printing press in a single county had printed 20,000 copies and that the photo was hanging in the homes of the peasants who were celebrating the good harvest.[43] It was not said, though it was implied, that all should thank the leaders for the good harvest, as in the old days when Mao used to be thanked for all earthly blessings.

In September 1983 a photograph of the seventy-nine-year-old Deng swimming in the sea was published, with the comment that he was so fit that he could swim 1,000 m. in 90 minutes every day.[44] Who can have failed to recall the photograph of Mao swimming in the Yangze in

1966, an event that was commemorated year after year. To add oddity to oddity, the issue of the official Party monthly that published the photograph of Deng's head sticking out from the water, published a similar photo of Peng Zhen in the water, with an accompanying text to explain that the eighty-one-year-old Peng was accustomed to swim 400 metres in 45 minutes in the sea and to walk for 40 minutes a day. This was published to show how the leaders were keeping themselves fit. (Premier Zhou Ziyang was said to jog for 40 minutes and Hu Yaobang to walk a regular 10,000 steps every day.)

Another photograph of the 1962 gathering of the supreme leaders was published on December 15, 1983, in commemoration of the ninetieth birthday of the late Mao Zedong. The photo showed Mao, Liu Shaoqi, Zhou Enlai, Chen Yun and Deng, but in the place Lin Biao had occupied in the 1962 photo stood Peng Zhen, who in 1962 was not one of the Vice-Chairmen of the Party, or its Secretary-General, as Deng then was, but merely a Politbureau member.

Severity

In 1983, two years after the condemnation of Jiang Qing and her colleagues, other leaders of the Cultural Revolution were brought to trial. One of these was Nie Yuanzi, by then a sixty-year-old woman. In 1966, when she was Party branch secretary in the philosophy department of Peking University, Mao had praised her for having put up the first wall-posters of the Cultural Revolution. Her condemnation was a condemnation of Mao himself. As a student, Kuai Dafu had been another famous personality of the Cultural Revolution. It was he who organised the fight in Qinghua University, Peking. In 1983, then aged thirty-seven, he was accused of counter-revolutionary murders. Both he and Nie Yuanzi were condemned at a mass trial, refused to admit guilt and were sentenced to seventeen years in prison.[45]

The June 1983 yearly session of the People's Congress added a new ministry to the Cabinet. There was already a ministry of security. Now there was also a ministry of state security, officially designated as an organ for preventing external espionage. The Chinese name of the ministry is the exact equivalent of the KGB in the Soviet Union. The minister, Ling Yun, was a vice-minister of public security. The need for a new ministry, detached from the former one, arose from the rapidly increasing contact with the outside world. China was opening up economically, but wanted to close its gates, not only against external spies, but also against the penetration of Western ideas. All security came under the Politico-Legal Department of the C.C., and thus under Peng Zhen.

The impression given was that Deng and his men were working for the opening up of China, and Peng Zhen and his apparatus for protection against the corrupting influence of Western political and mental poison. The highest leaders may have agreed on the basic lines of an economic policy designed to make the country more efficient, but there was a division on politics. Deng's men were in charge of the mass media; but the organs of repression, internal security and state security, rarely mentioned in the press, were in the hands of Peng Zhen.

Second Central Committee Plenum

The conflict between the two trends became apparent at the second Central Committee Plenum held on 11–12 October, 1983. Deng and Chen Yun spoke, but their speeches were not published. The official communiqué said only that Deng Xiaoping had brought up the question of 'ideological battle', which would be discussed at a special meeting either in the winter or the spring. The Plenum published one document only, about Party reform — no document was published about the 'ideological battle'. Obviously it had proved impossible to reach agreement at the Plenum. The promised special meeting was never held. Nevertheless, immediately after the Plenum, the ideological battle, renamed 'spiritual pollution', sent a shock-wave through the nation.

The Party Reform

The Plenum decided that the Party Reform was to start immediately and last three years. A powerful committee was established to guide the Reform. It was headed by Hu Yaobang and it included none of the men ousted by Deng in 1982. The evils that had made the Party Reform necessary were described: there were in the Party three types of evil people left over from the Cultural Revolution: the rebels, the factionalists, and those who had taken part in violent action. There were Party members who had lost the spirit of the Party and were working for their own personal profit. There were those who had turned criminal. There were Party members who had turned against Marxism and were declaring this publicly. Above all 'it was necessary to resist the influx of rotten capitalist ideology and the remnants of the feudalist way of thinking.'

The state of the Party was painted in gloomy colours. Party policy, it was said, was not being implemented. Marxist criticism and self-criticism were not popular; criticism was evoking revenge.

The Party had 40 million members. Immediately after the Twelfth Party Congress, on October 29, 1982, the *People's Daily* reported 39 million Party members, and published percentages for the end of 1981 indicating the party-age of the members: 6.8 per cent had entered the Party before 1949; 38.6 per cent between 1949 and the Cultural Revolution (the middle of 1966); 40.6 per cent — a considerable proportion — during the Cultural Revolution (which in Party parlance meant the years 1966–76), and 14 per cent after the Cultural Revolution, i.e. between 1976 and the end of 1981. The Party purge aimed at sorting out, above all, the 40.6 per cent, 15.8 million, who had entered during the Cultural Revolution.

The purge was to be carried out in two stages: first the central organs and provincial Party committees in 1983–4, then the lower echelons in 1984–5. The Party Reform in the army was to be carried out alongside that of the civilian party.

As usual, a purge was to start with study of prescribed Party documents, accompanied by criticism and self-criticism. The whole process was to end with the re-registration of Party members. More Party members should be enlisted from the field of the economy, and there should be more young people, more peasants and students, more educated people, more women and more from the national minorities.[46]

Spiritual pollution

Ten days after the C.C. Plenum, an informal five-day meeting was held to discuss 'ideological battle' and 'spiritual pollution', about which the document of the C.C. Plenum had said little. This was unprecedented. Never before had any kind of supplementary meeting been held after a solemn C.C. Plenum. Seven leading members of the Politbureau took part. In addition, old non-party members and prominent members of the People's Congress and other organisations were invited. The main speaker was Peng Zhen, himself not a member of the Politbureau's Standing Committee. Hu Yaobang, the head of the Party, was present but did not speak. Peng Zhen praised the document on Party Reform, but said that it needed to be complemented by a document on spiritual pollution, a matter that was to be discussed at a coming Party conference. (No conference was held, and no complementary document ever appeared.) Peng Zhen spoke against spiritual pollution in contemporary literature and art. 'Such things must stop,' he said.[47]

The other main speaker was Wang Zhen, who spoke about deviations in Marxism. Wang Zhen was the President of the C.C. Party School, which is the watchdog of Marxist purity. Unfortunately, he said, the writings and speeches of many comrades do not observe the basic principles of Marxism, the 'Four Basic Principles'. Some even hold that our country is not a socialist country. Others speak of alienation — a Hegelian term used by Marx in his earlier writings. Wang Zhen was shocked to learn that some Marxist writers had found alienation in the system of socialism itself. 'When we criticise "bourgeois liberalism", people say we are turning back to the old days of leftist radicalism, hitting people on their heads with a stick. If anyone propagates Marxism, people laugh and say that these are big empty words. We are not leftist, but we cannot give up criticising spiritual pollution.'[48]

An important article in the *People's Daily* said that at the C.C. Plenum Deng had proposed to combat spiritual pollution. Combatting it should be on the permanent agenda of the Party organisations, the *People's Daily* said. Not only leftist but rightist deviations should be combatted, though spiritual pollution should be treated not as a crime but as an error to be corrected.[49] Another *People's Daily* article said that what Deng and Chen Yun had said at the C.C. Plenum about spiritual pollution was aimed particularly at writers who were 'the engineers of souls' (one of Mao's phrases). Today writings appear which 'propagate sex and religion', distort the history of the revolution and deviate from the thinking of the Party.[50]

After this, most prominent writers wrote articles attacking literary works which contained spiritual pollution and criticising literary magazines which printed such articles. A number of literary works were mentioned as belonging to that evil category. All this was a stunning blow for writers and producers. The ridiculous accusations of the past seemed to be returning. Short stories were scrutinised to find traces of spiritual pollution. A Peking literary monthly published in its March 1983 issue a story describing the frustration caused by irregularities and disorder during a wait at a bus station. The conclusion was drawn that this story sought to defame the whole Chinese system. A story in another magazine suggested that this world is all a dream — a very evil thing to suggest in writing. Love stories which did not speak of love of Socialism were exposed. Other writings were damned for expressing worship of modern Western literature.[51]

The Party Committee of the Chinese Writers' Association held a meeting on November 4, 1983, attended by all the distinguished Communist writers. At this meeting it was pointed out that the Party had criticised the influence of bourgeois liberalism as long ago as 1981.[52] In fact, earlier still, in February 1980, Hu Yaobang, then head of Party propaganda, had made a six-hour speech discussing literature, in particular the play *If I Were Truly*, which ridiculed the privileges of the children of Party leaders. He referred to Deng: 'Deng Xiaoping had declared that no one should any longer say that literature must serve politics; yet this does not mean that literature can be detached from politics.' He added menacingly: 'We are marching along rugged mountain paths, with storms above our heads and precipices under our feet . . . Will some fall away, will some desert the ranks?' These warnings of Hu Yaobang sounded frightening, but they were largely ignored and his speech did not appear in print until a year later, in 1981. In that same year, Deng spoke against ideological disorder, defending Marxism and Socialism from erosion by writers. This speech was published after a delay, this time of two years, when it appeared in the *Selected Writings of Deng*.

At the C.C. Plenum in October 1983 the problem was brought forward, but it was not solved. The speech Deng made at the Plenum was not published. Immediately after the Plenum, Peng Zhen, no friend of Deng's, brought 'spiritual pollution' into the arena, and this was followed by a nationwide witch-hunt. People naturally wondered what had really happened at the C.C. Plenum and what attitude Deng and his men had taken. At the time no straightforward answer could be found. A few months later the whole spiritual pollution affair fizzled out — though not completely.

In December 1983, two months after the C.C. Plenum, the State Science and Technological Committee held a meeting at which it was declared that in matters of natural science and technology spiritual pollution should not be brought up, and that free scientific discussion should not be described as 'not keeping in line with the Party'. Fang Yi, the head of the Committee, said bluntly: 'One certainly cannot use philosophical categories [i.e. Marxism] to replace scientific research.'[53]

In the same month the propaganda head, Deng Lichun, declared that the question of spiritual pollution should not be raised in the villages. Obviously he was afraid that it would upset the liberal reforms introduced in the countryside. Neither should it be applied to the way people dress or use cosmetics, he said.[54] The range of the spiritual pollution was narrowed to two fields: culture — including literature, theatre and film — and Marxist philosophy.

Pollution in literature

The witch-hunt for spiritual pollution in literature continued for some months. In March 1984 a young poet made an apology, saying that he had published his poems at a time when such restrictions had not been imposed.[55] In the second half of 1984 the situation changed. In August the *People's Daily* said that stories with no political themes or implications were welcome. Early in December a fierce attack on restrictions on literature was published:

Our Party leadership had spent much energy on criticising and opposing leftism [radicalism] in the field of the economy. In the field of literature and culture, however, we do not oppose leftism. It is not logical to oppose the left in the economy and to oppose the right in literature and art. It is all very well to say, that those who deviate will not be hit on the head; but the sound of the whip whirling above one's head is enough to make one feel paralysed.

These were blunt words. Yet this article then made a 180-degree turn and said: 'Recently the Party leadership has been emphasising that all should combat wrong ideology in literature and art . . . If serious problems are found they must be criticised and the authors must be helped, though not hit on the head.' On the same page of the *People's Daily* there was high praise for a film which propagated the proper Communist ideology, and illustrated the correct way of carrying out the Party Reform[56] — certainly not an apolitical piece of art.

The year 1984 ended on a dubious note. On December 29 the Chinese Writers' Association held its Fourth Congress, the fourth since 1949. It was honoured by the presence of Hu Yaobang and other leaders and was addressed by Hu Qili, not a writer but a member of the C.C. Secretariat. He did not mention 'spiritual pollution', indeed he harped on about the 'freedom' of writing, supposing however that 'our writers will make an effort to write about real life basing themselves on dialectical materialism and historical materialism'.[57] This speech and the meeting at which it was made were greeted by many writers as a great concession to freedom in writing.

Polluted Marxism

The other terrain where spiritual pollution was found was Marxism. The point at issue may have seemed to be a mere theoretical question, one that had been discussed for years among Western scholars. The question was whether the theories of the 'mature Marx' contradicted the humanist 'young Marx' found in his 1844 writings, which had been discovered only in the 1930s. In other words, and this was the crucial point, should a Marxist in China favour humanism? It was necessary to dispel the apparently widespread view that Marxism and the Communist regime had exploited people and alienated man from society, leading to the personal cult and absolute rule of a single person, Mao.

Free discussion of the fundamental tenets of Marxism flourished in the years 1980–2 and then came to an end. After the October 1983 C.C. Plenum a spate of articles appeared condemning the theory of 'alienation'. The *People's Daily* commented: 'Recently some comrades among the theoreticians have written that there is alienation under a socialist system.' According to them 'socialism ties man down, makes man a slave, lowers the value of man.' These comrades point to some aspects of life in a socialist country, to bureaucratism, to the cult of personality, to the absence of democracy — remnants of this kind from the old society — and ask: what, then, is the difference between socialism and capitalism? They are wrong because socialism prepares the final stage of Communism and deliverance from alienation. A number of articles explained that such erroneous theories were only reactions against the abuses of the Cultural Revolution. Those days, however, were gone.

Wu Liping, an elderly Marxist theoretician from Yan'an days, argued that there had been no break in the thoughts of Marx. Marx began with the theory of alienation and then developed it to that of surplus value and exploitation. Comrade Deng Xiaoping, he wrote, had admitted that there are still many defects in our society, but this does not mean that the system of socialism is wrong.[58]

However, an outstanding Party propaganda leader from the old days had to publish an apology. This was Zhou Yang, the head of literature in the propaganda department before the Cultural Revolution who in 1983 was the head of the Federation of Literature and Art. He expressed regret for what he had said at a meeting of Marxist theoreticians. As reported on March 16, 1983, in the *People's Daily*, he made a humble apology, admitting that for seventeen years before the Cultural Revolution humanism had been persecuted in literature and art. 'In the past, my articles and speeches in this respect were incorrect or partially incorrect.' Speaking of alienation, he denied that there was a break between the young Marx, who in 1844 was under the influence of Hegel and Feuerbach, and Marx after 1845, when he was teaching about the exploitation of the working class. In our society, Zhou Yang said, there is still alienation — abuse of power by Party men, which is political alienation — but since the reform of December 1978 (of Deng) and through the Party Reform, things have been improving.

In November, a month after the Second C.C. Plenum, Zhou Yang apologised again for what he had said in his March apology, when he had not realised that what he was saying about alienation might be distorted and lead to lack of faith in socialism and in future Communism. His intention in March was to criticise the left; he had neglected criticism of rightist tendencies. He did not realise that spiritual pollution may do great harm. Concerning humanism, Zhou Yang said, he supported Deng Xiaoping who had said that under socialism class struggle still continues.[59]

In November 1983 a meeting of theoreticians was convoked by the *Economic Daily* of Peking to condemn the theory that Socialism is exploitation and that China had no alternative to developing capitalism.[60] While this discussion was held by the *Economic Daily*, which did not have much to do with philosophy, the official review on philosophy, *Philosophical Research*, remained silent. Only in April 1984 did a study on alienation appear in that review. Thus while the daily press and the reviews were filled with articles about spiritual pollution in Marxist philosophy, the professional Marxist philosophers kept silent.

Humanism

The problem of alienation and particularly of humanism remained alive, however. On January 27, 1984, four of the eight pages of the *People's Daily* were filled by a study on humanism and alienation, written by Hu Qiaomu, a member of the Politbureau. Hu was an authority on theory and on Party affairs. In 1945 he formulated the official version of Party history, and in 1951 he wrote a pamphlet on the subject. He disappeared during the Cultural Revolution. When the Academy of Social Sciences was set up in 1978, he was its first President, and he was the author of the new version of Party history covering the years since 1949, promulgated in 1981.

Hu Qiaomu did not think much of brave young Marxist scholars who re-examined the Marxist doctrine; some of them, he wrote, are victims of wrong trends coming from Marxist scholars in the West who play up Marx's 1844 writings: 'Some of our comrades dealing with ideology are under their influence. What they write about Marxism has influenced our literary world. Comrades working on the ideological front should study what Comrade Deng Xiaoping said at the Second Plenum about spiritual pollution.' (What Deng said was not published.)

Hu Qiaomu did not think much of Liberty, Equality and Fraternity. In their day, during the French Revolution, such sayings had a function, he said, but they deal with an abstract idea of man. The comrades who say that 'Man is the starting point of Marxism' are wrong. Marxism teaches that 'the history of mankind is primarily the history of production methods . . . and not of abstract human nature.' Those who say that socialism is a system of exploitation fall far away from dialectical materialism. In socialism all labour serves the interests of the people; the thesis that labour under socialism is exploitation, that 'man is being used as a tool', is untenable.

Hu Qiaomu repeated the classic Marxist dogma, explained in Mao's famous 1942 'Talk on Literature and Art', that there was no such thing as human nature, only class nature. This article of Hu's was reprinted in _Red Flag_, the official organ of the Central Committee; but how many Party members cared to read it? In July 1984 a short comment in the _People's Daily_ said that books which are supposed to be compulsory Marxist reading are found in obscure corners covered with dust.[61]

What worried the Dengist reformers was the widespread doubt surrounding the reforms.

There are many people who do not understand, have doubts about, do not follow, do not approve of the line, the direction, the basic policies followed since the Third C.C. Plenum [of 1978], and wonder whether this is genuine Marxism. There are people who, on seeing some defects and some unhealthy phenomena, on seeing abuses and crimes in the economy, wonder whether the Party policy of opening towards the outside world is correct. There are people who admit the good results of development of the economy, but worry that the Party line may become too rightist.[62]

Such nagging objections were reflected in the official press. Ever since the beginning of the reforms, Deng had been encouraging people to become rich. 'To become rich by one's labour corresponds to Socialism and Communism'; yet 'not all agree, and some are afraid that this may lead to polarisation of wealth, that some will become rich, and will live a life of luxury and lose their moral standards, while others will remain poor.'[63] The mass media did their best to dispel such thoughts; but if these doubts had not been widespread it would not have been necessary to dispel them. People worried, not without reason, about what would happen if, as in the old days, some became rich and others remained poor. What social consequences would this have?

Blot out the Cultural Revolution

Whether Deng was really opposed to what was called rightist deviation, spiritual pollution, was not clear. But he was vehemently opposed to what was called the 'left', the old guard of the old Maoist bastion. The Party Reform was meant to uproot the men who had been active in the Cultural Revolution and had survived and were still holding positions in the Party or in the government.

On April 23, 1984, a short commentary in the *People's Daily* was headed 'Reject the Cultural Revolution Totally'. A week later, *Red Flag* thundered against what it called factionalism originating from the time of the Cultural Revolution. In those days (1967) the country was divided into fighting groups, each pretending to be more revolutionary than the other, *Red Flag* said. Then Comrade Mao Zedong sent in the troops to 'aid the left'. These troops protected one faction against the other. The suppressed factions, however, did not disappear and kept on struggling. The Third C.C. Plenum (December 1978) put an end to this; but the sole result was that the factions submerged and 'continued their ghost-like existence'. The comradeship between the former members of the factions still existed. There were many ways of expressing solidarity, by giving preference in wages, promotion, allotting housing and a thousand other things. Even if a person had been removed from his original post, the secret solidarity was still there as a 'protecting umbrella', resisting investigation, covering up past crimes — in total contradiction of the genuine Party spirit.[64] The pursuit of the Cultural Revolution rebels was a difficult task. Many of them had disappeared from the public eye; some had changed their names, were good workers, were protected by their superiors and had even got on the list for promotion.[65]

Some cases were described. One man had been leader of a rebel group during the Cultural Revolution. He became Party secretary of a commune and later deputy Party secretary of a county. He was a protégé of a man who was himself a protégé of Chen Yonggui, the hero of the famous, or infamous, Dazhai village — the village which Mao turned into the model for the whole country. In 1980 this man was denounced at the Organisation Department of the C.C. in Peking, but instead of being punished, he was promoted to be deputy head of the administration of the Yellow River. He had a whole network of Party members on his side, and some leading party members of the province gave false testimony to protect him against accusations. Three years later, in 1983, Peking sent Liu Liying, a woman member of the Disciplinary Investigation Committee of the C.C., to investigate the case. She was an energetic person, and had been on the board at the trial of Jiang Qing. In 1984 the man was arrested.[66]

Another case was that of a former leader of a rebel gang, a worker. After 1978 he had a job in a city in Heilongjiang province. He did not go to work for six years, yet he regularly received his wages and promotion and bonuses. He had some sympathisers in the Party committee of the city and a gang of thirty who were claiming their rights (what the rights were was not made clear). In 1981 they caused bedlam in the city court when demanding the release of some of their colleagues. In April 1983 they broke into the city Party committee during a meeting, accusing the wife of one of the leaders of having slapped one of their men. In October 1983 the leader was arrested.

In Baotou, a city in the North, one of the rebels from the time of the Cultural Revolution died in June 1984. He was certified as having died of cancer and his body was to be cremated; but his wife said that he had died as a result of the investigation he had been subjected to. The man's friends, ex-rebels and Party members, came to the house and insisted that the case should be investigated and the dead man's memory rehabilitated. Things went so far that what had been two hostile factions at the time of the Cultural Revolution came together to protest against the decision of the Party leadership and against the Peking decision on 'totally rejecting the Cultural Revolution'. When the authorities forbade the holding of a funeral service for the dead man, the factionalists insisted on holding it, and sent wreaths and demanded justice. The story ended with these men being expelled from the Party by the city Party committee.[67]

From a county in Henan province in the centre of China, there came a curious story about a man called Wang Xunren. According to the story, Wang had been condemned in 1951 for embezzlement and sentenced to six months' 'labour education'. (The People's Daily article made a slip here. In 1951 there were no 'labour education' camps, only 'corrective labour' camps. 'Labour education' camps were established in

1957.) In 1970 Wang was working in his own county, and yielded again to temptation. The county's Party head of finance denounced him for embezzlement and Wang was dismissed from his job. He paid back the amount embezzled, and eleven years later, in 1981, was rehabilitated, on the ground that the decision of the Third C.C. Plenum of December 1978 (which had proclaimed the milder policies of Deng) should be implemented. The man who had denounced Wang eleven years earlier protested, his protest was not well received and he was dismissed for having opposed the new policies of Peking. The story did not end there. In 1983 the Disciplinary Investigation Committee of the C.C. sent an investigation team, which was joined by men from the provincial authorities and the Area Party Committee. The joint team rehabilitated the man who had denounced Wang, but the county Party committee took Wang's side. The deputy Party secretary of the county was a man who during the Cultural Revolution had led a Red Guard group in a university in Peking. He called upon the Party members of the county to side with Wang and the county Party committee. The highest Party secretary of the county declared that if the C.C. Investigation Committee sent another team he would disarm them by entertaining them with the best *mao-tai* wine. A deputy secretary in the Area, the unit between a county and province in size, supported the county Party committee, quoting Peking's policy that 'though class struggle still exists, today it is not the main issue'. In the spring of 1984 the Disciplinary Investigation Committee sent another team, joined by men from the province and the area, but the county Party committee did not yield. With this the *People's Daily* story ends.[68]

This particular story is a perfect illustration of the powerlessness of the highest authorities, even the C.C. Disciplinary Investigation Committee itself, in the face of resistance from local Party bosses, even from so small a body as the Party committee of one of the 2,000 counties. It shows too how the new policies of Peking were being interpreted, or misinterpreted, at lower levels — Peking's milder policy, Peking's axiom on class struggle, and the rest. It also throws light on the play of personal animosities — one man denouncing another and being punished for denouncing someone who was protected by his cronies and this man then appealing to the highest disciplinary body of the Party — in a case of minor embezzlement. It is striking to find no mention of law or courts in the report, though Peking documents insist on observance of the law and legal proceedings. The *People's Daily* report on the case of Wang and his county was published only to show that 'rebels' of the Cultural Revolution were still in responsible posts, and that they should be 'totally rejected'.

Total rejection of all who took part in any faction in the Cultural Revolution was a tall order, and it would not be easy to implement. Millions had been involved in their younger days in one or other of the fighting rebel groups during the Cultural Revolution, and many of them later became leaders of Party organisations. One article in the *People's Daily* said that it was no excuse to say that what had been done during the Cultural Revolution was done under orders. The Cultural Revolution must be totally rejected. No one should plead that what he did was done out of deep affection for Chairman Mao. It is true that at the beginning of the Cultural Revolution many people joined out of idealism; but when the great gangs were formed and began fighting each other, no one could say that this originated from ardent love of Mao or of the Party. Nevertheless, it added, total rejection of the Cultural Revolution does not mean that the economic, scientific and technological triumphs achieved during that period should be denied, or that the Party itself should be rejected.[69]

The original fierce statement on the Cultural Revolution had therefore to be somewhat modified. It is enough, another *People's Daily* statement said, if those who took part come to understand that the Cultural Revolution and all factional fights were wrong. There is no need to go any further.[70] This was written in July 1984, three months after the clarion call for 'total rejection'. A further three months passed, and in October the tone became even more conciliatory. It was simply impossible to reject everybody totally, the many millions who took part in the fights of the Cultural Revolution.

'Rejecting the Cultural Revolution' — a first-page commentary in the *People's Daily* stated in October — 'in the cases of the majority of the comrades means merely a lesson to be learnt, means a better understanding of the question and certainly not the rejection of all who took part in the Cultural Revolution, much less the rejection of the wide masses who were involved. To say that the Cultural Revolution was wrong does not mean that all those who took part in it are evil people.'[71]

Two months later, on December 21, 1984, Bo Yibo, the man in charge of the Party Reform, spoke in his report on the first year of the Reform about those who had committed violent acts, attacked people, ransacked houses and so on. Some of them, he said, had sneaked into the Party and were on the list of men to be promoted to leading positions. They must be removed and punished; but not all of them. 'Those who have reformed and admitted what they did should be excused and re-employed, though not in leading Party positions'.[72] This was a far cry from the stiff order of April for 'totally rejecting' those who had taken any part in the Cultural Revolution.

The astonishing fact was — the newspapers did not discuss it — that in 1984, after so many years, the Cultural Revolution was still a major issue. The fierce rebels, the 'revolutionary small generals', students and workers, were in the fifteen-to-twenty-five age bracket in 1967. In 1984, seventeen years later, they were men and women aged between thirty-two and forty-two. Many had retained their allegiance to their groups. What kept these groups together through the years? Together-ness such as they had known in perilous situations during the Cultural Revolution, fighting side by side in one's young days, does form a lasting bond. Moreover, when their days of glory ended and they them-selves were exiled to the villages, they found the schools closed and no education available; they could scarcely have succeeded in life without mutual help.

Much personal animosity lingered on from the time of the Cultural Revolution, and a desire for revenge was in the air. It was not easy to for-get that men of the opposite faction had persecuted, perhaps killed, members of one's family or friends, or plunged oneself into prison or into misery for ten years or more. A *People's Daily* report quoted the omi-nous sayings of ex-rebels who in 1984 were still in humble positions: 'A movement has its ups and downs. Today you are dealing with me; later I will deal with you.'[73]

In the 1980s the forced labour camps were filled, not as in the old days with ex-Kuomintang people and anti-Mao rebels, but with young people, the children of proletarian families. This was openly admitted in many reports. Heaven alone knows what these youngsters were plan-ning for the future in their hearts. A lot of what was going on among young people and young workers was not reported but only hinted at. In 1984 it was common knowledge in China that Shanghai was out of step with Peking, that Shanghai was still 'leftist', though no clear expla-nation of the difference was offered. At the end of the year the *People's Daily* did state that old rebels, indeed some under whose hands Party lea-ders had died, were still in important positions in the communications system of that city, and that an 'anarchic situation' existed among Shanghai port workers. When the Executive Committee of the National Trade Union held a meeting at the end of 1984, it was noted with laconic brevity that not all traces of the poison of the Cultural

Revolution had been washed off the young workers.[74] Who were the 'young workers'? Young eighteen-to-twenty-year-old workers could not have had any personal recollection of the days of the Cultural Revolution; but many young people were apparently bored by the monotony of life. In September 1984 the *People's Daily* first-page commentary dealt with this problem under the heading 'The Rebel Temperament Must Be Rejected'. 'Notice must be taken', it said, 'of the fact that there are young people, who at the time of the Cultural Revolution were little babies and are now all for the rebel spirit. They did not know how much damage and devastation it had caused. Education therefore for the total rejection of the Cultural Revolution is of great importance.'[75]

Total rejection meant two things. First it meant making sure that the heroic stories the ex-Red Guards could tell about the days when they were ruling many parts of China should not captivate the imagination of the young. Secondly, it meant making sure that the really savage men of the Cultural Revolution should not be left in leading positions in the Party. The Party Reform was to see to it that this did not happen.

The hectic days of the Cultural Revolution ended in 1969. Yet fifteen years later the furrows it had cut were still open and this was causing anxiety in the highest circles. In Chinese society, and particularly under this authoritarian regime, what is visible on the surface and proclaimed by the well-controlled mass media is one thing; what remains hidden until it unexpectedly surfaces is quite another. This was the case with the secret societies in imperial times, with the Communist underground under the Nationalist government, with Lin Biao in the 1960s before the Cultural Revolution, and indeed with Deng's group of supporters at the time of his condemnation in the first months of 1976. It can perhaps be said that even in 1984 the Cultural Revolution had not yet ended.

The Party Reform goes on

The screening of 40 million Party members was an enormous undertaking, and it was carried out with little imagination. In the 1980s, many things in China and in the Party were not what they had been earlier, but the old methods of Party reform were used as if nothing had changed since Yan'an days, the time of the Party Reform learnt from Stalin. The main weapon remained the good old Stalinist method of 'criticism and self-criticism'. The difference was that the purge was now aimed primarily at those who had behaved badly during the Cultural Revolution.

Times had changed, and it was not easy to induce Party members to criticise each other publicly or to reveal their own failings. The rough scenes of the past had not been forgotten. 'Among a great number of Party members', it was said in March 1984, 'criticism and self-criticism is not getting off the ground. There are comrades who do not want to hear criticism and do not want to criticise others . . . Instead people remain polite and deferential.' The reason was that 'people remember the political campaigns of the past, particularly the ten years of disorder during which the Party rectification turned into violent condemnations. In the proper way of carrying out criticism, all should be allowed to answer criticism and to reserve their own opinions.'[76]

In December 1983 the Party Reform Leading Team sent teams to guide the reform in the provinces and in the highest Party and government organisations. It was explicitly stated that the leaders of the teams were the most experienced Party men, some of them reactivated from retirement. The provinces and the central offices also established Party reform teams.[77]

The list of the veteran Party men who were to lead the reform was not published; they must have been old men in their seventies. Bo Yibo, the leader of the reform, was seventy-six or seventy-seven. The presence of these old men was added proof that the Party leaders, in spite of the endeavours to rejuvenate the Party and take in larger numbers of educated persons, were not prepared to introduce major changes for the adjustment of the Party to the new times. The Party Reform was designed to adjust the Party to the old ways, to try to remodel the Party in the 1980s into the shape known to these veterans in the 1940s.

In March 1984 the Permanent Secretary in the C.C. Disciplinary Investigation Committee, Wang Heshou — in the Yan'an days a member of the Party organisation's secret agents (then called the Social Department) — reported that the Party Reform had already begun in counties and areas. He was still talking about spiritual pollution in literature and art and he said that those infected should be re-educated and in serious cases be given Party sanctions. He also said that the Party Reform would be finished within three years and that after five years, by 1988, the Party spirit would be sound again.[78]

In August 1984 Bo Yibo, the man in charge of Party Reform, was in the Northeastern city of Dairen. There he found Party veterans who, because of the active part they had taken in the Cultural Revolution, still had accusations hanging over them. He ordered the release of Party veterans who, despite their errors in those years, had won great merit in the Party in earlier years. He warned, however, against accepting younger men who had taken an active part in the Cultural Revolution, saying that if they succeeded in worming their way into leading positions in the Party now, trouble might come later. This, he said, had happened in the case of Chen Boda and Zhang Chunqiao, who had been traitors to the Party from within since the 1930s.[79]

This was an incredible accusation. In the 1930s, Zhang Chunqiao was an anonymous Party member whereas Chen Boda had been close to Mao since Yan'an times. He was Mao's confidant; for over thirty years he was the principal interpreter of Mao's thoughts and policies, and in 1958 was the founder and chief editor of *Red Flag*, the organ of the C.C. To describe him as an enemy infiltrated into the Party in the 1930s was nonsense. It was a statement made by biased, angry old men who could not forget, much less forgive, what had happened to them during the Cultural Revolution. Such feelings of irrational hatred explain why the Party Reform was to 'reject the Cultural Revolution totally'. The Standard of Political Life in the Party (see p. 444), which had been formulated under Deng in 1979–80, may have rejected the violent methods of the Cultural Revolution; but the Communist Party was still racked by mutual suspicion, rivalry and hatred.

At the end of 1984, Bo Yibo spoke again about the Party Reform. This time he did not mention Chen Boda, but he repeated that those who had infiltrated the Party should be removed. The Party purge, he said, in contrast with past practices, was now using gentle methods, 'heart-to-heart talks', just as was done in the Party Rectification in Yan'an. (Bo Yibo forgot what had been revealed only two or three years earlier, namely that the 1942–4 Yan'an Party Rectification was a harsh affair in which many were tortured and some died. He also forgot that when private industrialists had to hand over their factories to the state in the 1950s, this had been done in street processions under the banner 'We give our hearts to the Party'.)

About the Party Reform, Bo Yibo said that, since its inception in October 1983, the Party leadership of the provinces and of the Party Central organisations (388,000 persons in all) had been checked, and that now, at the end of 1984, the Reform was beginning in the Party committees of areas and counties. This would involve checking a total of 13 million Party members, not including those in the army. The whole Party Reform was designed, he said, the better to carry out the Four Modernisations. Repeating what had often been said before, he declared: 'The Four Modernisations is a most important political task.'[80]

In the provinces

In the Fujian provincial offices, sixteen Party members were exposed who had taken part in violence during the Cultural Revolution, ransacking homes and beating people up. Others had been leaders of rebel factions. The accused were ordered to apologise personally to those they had harmed. In Shandong province, in the North, cases were brought up of men who had been falsely accused during the Cultural Revolution and in 1984 had not yet been rehabilitated. In Henan province 476 members of Party provincial offices were living in illegally appropriated houses; they were told to move out. 260 people had to return to the former owners goods taken at the time of the ransacking of houses during the Cultural Revolution. In that province the second phase of the Party Reform — in areas and counties, major factories and universities — had just begun and was supposed to end at the beginning of 1986.[81]

The election of the new provincial Party leadership proved difficult. Of the twenty-six units (twenty-one provinces and five autonomous areas), ten had received new Party leaders before October 1983, the date when the Party Reform was announced. Six of these were appointed from above without the summoning of a provincial Party Congress. In the four provinces which held provincial Party Congresses, the head of the provincial Party, appointed earlier by Peking, was retained. The re-election of the provincial Party heads was carried out, in accordance with the new rule, after long consultations and deliberations, with tentative pre-elections and further consultations. This was called the 'democratic mode of election'.

In Shaanxi province in the Northwest, the county Party secretaries and others, 300 persons in all, were gathered for lengthy discussions on electing the provincial Party leaders, who, they were told, should be aged between fifty and sixty. Ultimately, six names were presented, and of these one was chosen. His name was presented to the outgoing Party committee and put forward for approval to Peking. The new leader was a man who was already on the Standing Committee of the Party committee and was governor of the province.[82] It was not explained why the new leadership was not elected by a provincial Party Congress, as prescribed in the Party Charter of 1982.

There were certain anomalies in the titles of the provincial Party leaders. The Party Charter of 1982 prescribed that the Party Congresses, on all levels, should elect Party secretaries and deputy secretaries. In 1983 and 1984, however, the new provincial leaders had a variety of titles. Several former First Party secretaries retained their titles. In some provinces there were two, three or four Party secretaries. In others again there was a First Party secretary and a few Party secretaries; or a First Party secretary and only deputy secretaries below him. Such a divergence of responsibility was unknown in the provincial Party structures of the old days. One was left wondering whether the change meant that greater freedom was being granted to the provinces, or whether Peking had to some extent lost its grip. In itself it was a meaningless division.

According to schedule, the Party Reform in the counties should not have started till the winter of 1984–5 and should have ended a year later. In fact the C.C. Propaganda Department announced at the beginning of October 1984 that the county leadership over the whole country had already been renewed and that the new leaders were younger — average age forty-five — and better educated than the outgoing ones.[83] Although this was never said, all appearances suggested that the Party leaders of counties and provinces had not been screened by the normal process of the Party Reform. The routine Party Reform — the screening of Party members — was only meant for ordinary members of the Party, the 388,000 in the provinces and the central organs, and the 1.3 million in 'area' and county offices mentioned earlier.

Age and education

The rejuvenation of the whole Party was an urgent priority. In 1950 26.6 per cent of the Party members were below the age of twenty-five (minimum age eighteen); in 1983 only 3.34 per cent were under twenty-five, and only 2.25 per cent in the Shanghai region. There was no rush among the young to enter the Party.

Another great issue was the raising of the standard of education and of the number of educated people in the Party. It was stated that in the past only 11 per cent of county leaders had had any higher education; in the renewed leadership the percentage was raised to 45 per cent.[84] Much was written about resistance on the local level to accepting educated people into the Party. According to the Party Charter, a Party member is accepted by the Party branch with the approval of the Party organisation one grade higher, i.e. the Party committee immediately above that of the branch. If therefore the Party cell of a factory refused to accept a particular person, not much could be done about it. This reluctance to accept educated people was understandable: the educated newcomers might soon have authority over Party members who had toiled in the Party for twenty or thirty years. Another question also hung in the balance: how would the Party's image be affected if the educated middle class took over the jobs? (The example of the Soviet Union could have shown that it would mean little change.)

Peng Zhen in 1984

The Party Reform sought to eliminate factionalism from the Party but in practice it meant that Deng's faction was to have overall power. Resistance to Deng appeared from an unexpected quarter in 1984.

In May, Peng Zhen presided over the yearly session of the Congress. In a Communist country the parliament, which is what the People's Congress is, has a secondary role, subservient to the Party. The People's Congress holds a ceremonial annual meeting, but the government is run by the State Council (the Cabinet) which is staffed by top Party leaders. In 1982, as we saw above, the new State Constitution, introduced by Peng Zhen, gave legislative power to the Standing Committee of the People's Congress — which was to meet every two months.

The May 1984 People's Congress was to make some unprecedented comments. Four weeks before it opened, Peng Zhen spoke to journalists. We have gone through two periods, he said — revolution and construction. During the revolution, Party policy was the guide. When any problem had to be faced, people asked: what is the Party policy? The Party policy was correct and we won. We had some laws in those days, but they were few and simple; in the revolution there was no need for more. That was the way of acting our comrades were trained in. In the second period, since the establishment of the regime in 1949, at first we had a temporary Common Programme. In 1954 we had the first State Constitution and some other laws, but we must admit that we did not bother much about observing them. Even now we have few legislative acts. 'The policy of the Party must pass through the State to become the policy of the State.' Some comrades are not used to this and think that it is too troublesome and that the Party policy is sufficient. The policy must be laid down in the form of legislation, and everybody should know and observe the laws. It is incumbent upon the journalists to help to publicise the importance of legality, particularly among the younger generation. The newspapers should discuss legislation, compare our laws with laws in other countries and discuss the eventual need for the revision of laws.[85]

A week before the opening of the People's Congress, Peng Zhen addressed a meeting of the Security Ministry. Among those present was Chen Pixian, a member of the C.C. Secretariat who bore the title of Secretary of the C.C. Politico-Legal Committee, and ranked first among the deputy heads of the People's Congress.[86] At the Congress he explained that the Standing Committee of the People's Congress is above the Government, i.e. the State Council. The Standing Committee of the People's Congress is 'the organ of State power; the government [the Cabinet] is its executive organ. The Standing Committee supervises the work of the Cabinet. The Standing Committee of the People's Congress must be a strong body. It also must have a growing role in China's international relations, sending delegations to foreign countries and receiving them.'[87]

While the People's Congress was in session, Peng Zhen and Chen Pixian held an informal discussion with the leaders of the Standing Committees of the provincial People's Congresses. This took place on May 28, 1984, three days after a televised speech on the future of Hong Kong in which Deng had publicly repudiated what Geng Biao and Huang Hua had said on that subject. This was an unprecedented public insult. Geng Biao, as we saw earlier, had guided foreign policy in the C.C. for many years, and until November 1982 he had been minister of defence. Huang Hua was foreign minister until November 1982. In 1984 both were deputy heads of the Standing Committee of the People's Congress under Peng Zhen and both figured prominently at the May 28 discussion. The repudiation of their statements was an extraordinary public demonstration of the friction between Deng and Peng Zhen. Towards the end of the People's Congress, both Peng Zhen and Chen Pixian spoke.[88]

Chen Pixian repeated that the Standing Committee of the People's Congress is the highest state organ and that the Cabinet is only an executive body supervised by the Standing Committee. About the international activities of the Congress, he reported that in 1984 Huang Hua had led a delegation to New Delhi and that Geng Biao had led one to Geneva — the two men publicly repudiated by Deng — and that the Standing Committee was discussing how to expand its international activities. He said that a national discussion with the provincial congress leaders would be held every three months. The Congress, he said, had listened to the reports of the ministries of culture and of education on spiritual pollution; but the Standing Committee had had no time to make up its mind on what spiritual pollution meant. The Congress decided to set up a new ministry of state security, distinct from the ministry of security. The new ministry would deal specifically with espionage cases and have the power of investigation, arrest and detention.[89]

At the beginning of a yearly Congress session, the Premier presents the yearly Government Report, which is then discussed and approved by those present. This time Zhao Ziyang presented the Report, but what he said was largely ignored by the delegates. They spoke about the legal vacuum, alleging that forty aspects of national life needed legislative regulation. They also aired many grievances. It was alleged that the standard of higher education was low; many schools were being run, not by the ministry of education, but by other ministries, and these cared little about the schools and were supplying little financial support for them. The heads of the scientific institutes had no power over personnel or funds, and could only get things as personal favours.

Concerning the economy, several spoke of cumbersome red-tape hindering foreign trade; it could take years to sign a contract. Some people were worried about the opening of the country to the outside world. Cities, though now opened to outside contact, were unable to make use of the new opportunities. A man from Gansu province said that his province was rich in mineral deposits and coal, and had hydro-electric potential, but did not have enough technicians. A man from Tibet complained that while outsiders were being sent to Tibet to help construction, local people were not being trained, and little emphasis was being laid on the Tibetan language in schools.[90] The impression created by the speeches at the Congress was that in spite of constant talk about reform, many things remained as they had been before.

Reaction of the Deng group

Deng's group could not be happy about such a development. Deng could hardly have welcomed the People's Congress' claim to supreme authority. In the past it had been the unwritten rule that the Central Committee of the Party should hold a meeting before the annual People's Congress session, and carefully prepare what was to be served up to the Congress. No such Party meeting had been held before a

Congress session since 1982, when its Standing Committee, under the influence of Peng Zhen, had given itself greater power.

The power of the two Congress leaders, Peng Zhen and Chen Pixian, had grown formidably. They were not only in charge of legislation — which was supposed to bind the Party together — they were also the leaders of the C.C. Politico-Legal Committee whose responsibilities included all the organs of repression — security, courts, police, the Armed Police Troops, and apparently the newly-established ministry of state security.

Deng's group could not look upon this development with favour. They could hardly eliminate Peng Zhen, who had had a more distinguished career in the Party than Deng himself; but they could do something about Chen Pixian, who a few years earlier had only been one of the provincial Party secretaries. A week after the Congress, Chen Pixian was the major speaker at the security conference. After this his name did not appear again. Had be been ousted by Deng?

Third Central Committee Plenum, October 20, 1984

Six months after the People's Congress, the C.C. gathered for its third annual meeting, the third since the 1982 Party Congress. It was, however, an odd C.C. Plenum, no less odd than the Second Plenum, held a year earlier, which had got bogged down in the problem of spiritual pollution. This 1984 meeting was held in the afternoon of October 20, 1984, and lasted in total for only an hour and a half. There was just enough time for a show of hands to approve a motion for the holding of a Party conference in September 1985, and one approving a long document on structural changes in the economy.

What is a Party conference? A Party conference is not a Party Congress. The members of a Party Congress are elected by the provincial Party Congresses; the members of a Party conference are selected and invited by the Party leaders. Only one earlier national Party conference had been held, that of March 1955, at which Deng listed the crimes of Gao Gang.[91]

The possibility of a Party conference had been foreseen in only one Party Charter, that of 1945, drawn up in Yan'an at the Seventh Party Congress. There was no mention of a Party conference in the following Party Charters, those of the Eighth, Ninth, Tenth and Eleventh Party Congresses, in 1958, 1969, 1973 and 1977. The Party Charter of the 1982 Party Congress brought back Party conferences 'in county and above', but made no specific mention of a national Party conference.

This decision of the 1984 C.C. Plenum laid down that the 1985 conference should elect a new Central Committee. No such power was given to a Party conference in the 1982 Party Charter. It was a tacit admission that the Party leaders, Deng and company, did not want provincial Party congresses to elect the members of a national body. They wanted an *ad hoc* meeting, a Party conference whose members would be invited by themselves. It was plain to everybody that the leadership did not trust the bulk of the Party, and that the opposition within the Party was such as to make the convocation of a regular Party Congress a risky undertaking. A regular Party Congress was due in 1987. A Party conference, invested with extraordinary powers, could arrange things so that the coming Party Congress should be in line with Deng's policies.

This October 1984 C.C. Plenum was preceded by a six-day preparatory meeting, but there was no announcement of what had been discussed at it or who had taken part. At the same time the Party leadership held discussions with members of the small satellite political parties and a number of highly educated people. They were all well advanced in years; many of them had been prominent in pre-Communist times. They emphasised one thing: no modernisation would be possible without the promotion of education. In his speech Hu Yaobang said that the country did not have enough money to promote education. Unfortunately, he added, many people in the Party do not recognise the importance of education and look down on educated people.[92] During that brief afternoon meeting a long document was passed on Structural Reform of the Economy. China would have a 'planned commodity economy, not a market economy'. The market economy would be 'confined to certain farm and side-line products and small articles of daily use and services and repair trades'. It did not mention that this programme had already been carried out in some East European Communist countries. The economic reform was to create a 'Chinese way of Socialism'. There would be mandatory planning in banking, railways and the like, and in 'products which have a direct bearing on the national economy and the people's livelihood and which have to be allocated and distributed by the state. Government organs will formulate the strategy, plans, principles and policies for economic and social development . . . co-ordinate development plans of localities, departments or enterprises . . . work out economic regulations and ordinances and supervise their execution, appoint and remove cadres, administer matters related to external economic and technological exchanges and co-operation, etc.'

Deng

On October 30, 1984, three days after the C.C. Plenum, Deng addressed the Advisory Committee of the C.C. — that gathering of aged leaders, many of them still active in Party work. His speech, published on January 1, 1985, said that some foreigners he had spoken to had expressed doubts about the stability of the governing system in China. 'They were wrong,' he said. 'Here are Comrades Hu Yaobang, who is sixty-nine years of age, and Zhao Ziyang, sixty-five. Both will soon be seventy. Under these two, and under the coming generation, the policy will not change, because if it were changed, people's livelihood would suffer. The life of the 800 million peasants has improved and the lot of the tens of millions of peasants who have still not enough food [an unexpected admission of a sad reality] will be improved.'

Deng expressed his feelings about Taiwan. 'The Hong Kong question has been solved through the agreement with Britain,' he said, 'but Chiang Ching Kuo [President of Taiwan] wants a united country based on the Three Principles [of Sun Yat Sen]. What did the Three Principles contribute to China under the Nationalist regime from 1927 to 1949?' He then spoke about the great improvement expected by the end of the century, when the country's gross output value is estimated to $US1,000 billion.[93]

It was not a brilliant speech. Nor did the long document on restructuring the economy produced by the Plenum convince everybody. Six days after the Plenum, the *People's Daily* published a commentary: 'There are some people in whose eyes protecting the purity of socialism means the maintenance of the old system with all its defects, and for whom employing the price mechanism in developing socialist commodities is capitalism.'[94]

Peng Zhen and Chen

On October 24, four days after the C.C. Plenum, Peng Zhen spoke to an informal meeting of members of the People's Congress. This meeting discussed, not the decision on holding a Party conference in 1985, for that was strictly a Party affair, but the proposals for economic reform. He repeated the uncompromising pronouncement he had made at the May 1984 People's Congress, that Party policy becomes law — i.e. has binding force — only if 'examined and proved correct by legislative procedure'.

Peng Zhen's speech was not welcomed in some quarters. That

is the only explanation of why the *People's Daily* only reported it after a three-week delay.[95]

What had happened to Chen Pixian? He seemed to have been eliminated from Peking. In December he appeared at functions unconnected with either the People's Congress or the C.C. Politico-Legal Committee. Meanwhile, two other men's names had appeared in November bearing the title of deputy secretary of the Politico-Legal Committee. One was Liu Fuzhi, minister of security; the other was Chen Weida, who had resigned from his job as Party boss of Tianjin city.[96] One wondered whether Chen Pixian had been ousted from his important post — that is, till January 1985, when he reappeared at an important gathering of the leaders of the Armed Police Troops, surveyed by Peng Zhen.[97] The two who joined Peng Zhen's important Politico-Legal Committee might have been infiltrated into it by Deng, but this was not the case. Both were known to be close to Marshal Ye, who, though ailing, still had many followers, and was a force to be reckoned with — and not one of Deng's supporters.

A January 1985 meeting of the Standing Committee of the People's Congress discussed the new economic policy and decided that the situation was muddled and fluid, not yet ripe for legislative acts.[98]

CHAPTER XXII

1985: CHAOS AND THE PARTY CONFERENCE

Shock

The optimistic forecast for the economy announced at the Third Central Committee Plenum in October 1984 was followed by a setback at the beginning of 1985. The economy had become overheated and inflation had risen. There were not enough funds and not enough material or fuel for the rapidly growing investments in capital construction, and too much money had been printed. There was a feeling of alarm. Repeated warnings were issued, and steps were taken to slow down the economy. Banks were ordered to restrict credit; factories were ordered to pay lower wages and bonuses; excessive imports of foreign goods were discouraged. These warnings went mostly unheeded. In July 1985 the Statistical Office was still complaining that the unplanned surge of the economy was continuing at an excessive and harmful speed.[1] The dash for quick achievements was compared with the illusory speed attained during the Great Leap of 1958.[2] Deng Xiaoping himself, when talking to foreign visitors, admitted that the speedy development had been harmful.[3]

General lawlessness in the economy could not be halted. In September it was candidly admitted that no blueprint for economic reform existed and that no such blueprint was even under preparation.[4] Many local leaders of the economy were changed, but the new ones often used their new powers for personal gain.[5] The press repeatedly complained that the quality of products was declining. General lawlessness, faked products and harmful drugs were widespread.

Party Reform

All this had a direct effect on the Party Reform. The second phase of the Party Reform, as we saw earlier, started at the turn of 1984–5. The reform of the economy meant that the enterprises were to be run not by the administration but by newly-established business firms. In December 1984 the 'Party Central and the Cabinet' forbade public servants, Party or government officials, to run these firms. This prohibition was ignored. Many government departments were running businesses for personal profit. In February 1985 a press report spoke of a regional administration in Hebei province, comprising several counties, in which 150 industrial and commercial firms, dealing in steel, timber, cement, trucks and tractors, were run by the former administration, mostly Party members, who divided the profits among themselves.[6] In April 1985 the Committee in charge of the Party Reform spoke of what was called a widespread 'new trend of irregularities', which meant disregard for instructions, and corruption.[7] In June the Party Reform Committee was still facing the same problems, regretting that the 'trend of irregularities' was persisting even in higher organs that had been purged in the first phase of the reform. People were out to make more money. The children of Party leaders were still living privileged lives. When Party men were forbidden to engage in business, their children took over and became deeply involved in irregular speculative business transactions, making profits with no goods in hand. 'Bourgeois freedom', including pornographic publications and videotapes ('spiritual pollution'), was widespread.[8] A month later, in July, the second phase of the Party Reform was discussed again. More irregularities were raised: collective corruption of the Party members of a whole government department, or of a region, who were using the restructuring of the economy as a means of making illegal profits.[9]

The fact that many such cases were reported in the press was a sure sign that corruption was not a rare, isolated ill. Here are some examples. Food departments in six counties in Gansu province were involved in corporate corruption; bribery was detected in the rail transport administration in Hunan province and in Peking itself; speculation in buying and selling trucks by provincial government officials took place with the support of an old retired (unnamed) leader from Peking; 1,000 tons of pseudo-aluminium were sold in one place; cars were assembled with faulty spare parts and sold at high prices in another place; forty-two government cadres gave official permits to swindlers and made 10 million yuan on the deals; government officials engaged in the illegal buying and selling of steel in Wuhan city, with the help of an (unnamed) official in Peking; railway wagons were sold illegally; in Hainan island some 57,000 cars were imported and sold around the country without permits; groups of Party leaders' children organised a national exhibition of quality products which turned out to be a complete swindle.[10]

Party membership

In a Party Reform, which is a euphemism for a Party purge, a certain number of Party members should be expelled and new ones should be brought in. No figures for such changes have been published. The Party in China has never revealed how many have given up their Party cards voluntarily, though the number is probably not very high. Party membership involves few burdens, apart from the payment of a minimal membership fee, and it is a ticket for promotion.

Under Mao there was only a sprinkling of educated people in the Party. The Yan'an guerillas had an innate dislike of people who thought too much. Twenty years later the Cultural Revolution dealt a savage blow to intellectuals both inside and outside the Party. Under Deng, increasing contact with the outside world brought the realisation that without the promotion of educated people, China could not be modernised. To make sure that educated people would follow the Party Line, a number of them were given Party cards. No precise numbers appeared, and only fragmentary data has become available. In Henan province (population 76 million) in 1984, 20,000 'intellectuals' — a term which includes those with rudimentary secondary education — entered the Party. This was 31 per cent of the new Party members of that year — i.e. 69 per cent of the new members were recruited from among uneducated peasants.[11] In Inner Mongolia (population 19 million) in 1984, 15,000 joined the Party, and half of this number were 'intellectuals'.[12]

The Party was said to have some 42 million members.[13] The exact number was probably not known, for the villages did not keep proper registers of membership, and the great bulk of Party members live in the villages.[14] The number of educated Party members is still small. In March 1985 only 4 per cent of the 42 million Party members had 'university education'. (This does not mean that they had graduated, for they may only have taken short courses in schools of higher education.) Of all Party members, 13.8 per cent had studied in higher secondary schools, 42.2 per cent had only been to primary schools and 10.1 per cent were illiterate.[15] (Nothing was said about the remaining 30 per cent.) The picture was different if one considered, not the 42 million Party members, but the 20 million 'cadres', a term that covers those on the government payroll — government workers, doctors and teachers, but not industrial workers or peasants. The majority of the 'cadres', but not all, were Party members. Of the 20 million cadres two-thirds were educated; 21

per cent of the 20 million had had higher education and 42 per cent secondary education. The proportion of educated persons among the cadres, therefore, was much higher than among Party members as a whole. But this may be an optical illusion. The educated persons were, of necessity, concentrated in offices where their presence was indispensable. A sample survey carried out at the end of 1983 revealed that '70 per cent of cadres heading organisations on all levels had only primary school education or were illiterate.'[16] Those 'heading organisations on all levels' were Party comrades.

In the Soviet Union in 1983 no Party secretary, high or low, had primary education only; 35.3 per cent had secondary education; 60.3 per cent had finished university; 3.1 per cent had studied but had not finished university education. Of all Party members (18.1 million in 1983) 29.5 per cent had finished and 2.2 per cent had not finished their university education, and 43 per cent had full secondary education.[17]

The contrast between the two countries, and between the educational levels of the two Communist parties, was striking. In China it was not easy for an educated person to join the Party; the old reluctance to take educated people into the fold still lingered on. The Organisation Department of the Party reported that many local Party units were opposed to taking in educated people: 'They refuse to admit [what Deng had decreed] that intellectuals are part of the working class.' These old Party units considered the intellectuals to be proud and unacceptable people, having their own independent views, unfit by their nature to obey the Party. 'They [the Party units] dig out old records of the applicants, look at their family origins — whether they come from proletarian families — and examine their friends and social relations [to make it hard for them to enter the Party].'[18]

This was one side of the picture. The other was that in 1985 it took some courage to apply for Party membership. By applying, one risked alienating one's friends: it was not a popular thing to do. The *People's Daily* itself said that people dared not send in their applications for acceptance into the Party, fearing that people would laugh at them, call them 'ambitious', and perhaps even do them harm. Peking television broadcast a story about a man who expressed interest in public affairs. His colleagues jeered at him, saying he wanted to show off.[19] Thus the prospective Party men found themselves caught between two evils. They might advance their careers by joining the Party but in doing so they might lose their friends.

The Party realised that the modernisation of the country demanded better-educated people. To preserve its power, it wanted them under its control, inside the Party. This was not easy to bring about. A great effort was made to promote educated people to leading positions, but this was not enough. More is needed than just to have an élite at the top. The 20 million 'cadres', the local leaders, the whole Party of 40 million would have to be changed. Could this be done in one generation?

Changes of leadership

1985 saw a brusque change of leaders in all quarters — in the army, in the government, and in the Party. It is hard to explain why the changes followed so quickly one after the other: in May 1985 in the army, in June in the provincial leadership and in September in the Party. These were all changes in the Party leadership: army, government and Party are not separate entities. The supreme command of the army lies with the Central Committee's Military Committee, headed by Deng Xiaoping at the time of writing. There is no head of a provincial government who is not also a member of the Party leadership of the province. Even the small satellite political parties which profess to be distinct from the Communist Party are led by Communist Party members. There is no organisation in China which is not run by Party men.

The army

There was a time, in the second half of the 1960s and the first half of the 1970s, when the whole administration of the country was in the hands of the army, or rather of the Party organisations in the armed forces, under the supreme command of Marshal Lin Biao. The army has never recovered from the shock of Lin Biao's sensational death in 1971. For over forty years the army, and with it the Party, has been sharply divided on the lines of allegiances in the old Field Armies. Under Mao and with his blessing, Lin Biao, through his Fourth Field Army generals, succeeded in ruling the whole army. Since his fall the army has had no single ruler. The generals of the Fourth Field Army were fatally compromised by the fall of Lin Biao, and Deng has promoted his old comrades in the Second Field Army to leading Party posts.

The army had been a state within a state. It had its own industry, its own universities, and the best hospitals in the country. Under Deng, orders were given for the opening of these facilities to the civilian population. To humiliate the soldiers, army financial scandals were aired in public.

In May–June 1985, the Military Committee, having met under Deng's chairmanship, announced that the regional commands were to be reorganised and that within two years the armed forces would be reduced by one million men.[20] In fact, even before this announcement the army had already been reduced by probably more than a million. In 1984 the Railway Troops, numbering some 170,000 men who had built new railroads, were put under the authority of the ministry of railways, and the Engineering Troops, numbering some 450,000 men, under various ministries dealing with industry. In 1982–4 a large section of the army — estimated at 500,000 men — was formed into the People's Armed Police Troops, with the duty of watching over security in the whole country including the border areas. They wear a special uniform and come under the ministry of security,

The eleven regional Great Military Areas were reduced to seven, corresponding roughly to the Military Areas of the early 1950s. The most noticeable change was the abolition of the separate command for the territory of Xinjiang, which is as large as Western Europe. This gigantic territory was now put under the command of Lanzhou Military Area. Was this done to preclude the rise of separatist tendencies in Xinjiang, which borders the Soviet Union?

This decision involved a change in the regional military leadership. Three of the seven commanders came from Deng's Second Field Army. Li Desheng, also from the Second Field Army, lost his job as commander of the Northeast (Manchuria), and was named deputy head of the Liberation Army Defence University, a newly organised supreme training school for the armed forces. Of the eleven leading political commissars, two already held a regional military post and retained it, but five new men were brought in from various places and from different streams of the army. The degree of their political loyalty to Deng was difficult to ascertain.

The provinces

The provincial Party and government leaders (all the latter, as mentioned earlier, members of the provincial Party leadership) were changed in the same abrupt manner. Some provinces held provincial Party congresses and 'elected' the new leadership; others did not go through such formalities. Peking announced with satisfaction that two-thirds of the top provincial Party leaders were under the age of sixty, and that ten of these were under fifty.[21] To the men in their seventies or eighties who were still at the top of the Party, a man of fifty seemed very young. These Nestors seemed to have forgotten that when they themselves were leading the Party in the revolution they were in their twenties or thirties, and that when they took over the whole country few of them were over forty or forty-five.

The changes did indeed reduce the average age of the provincial leadership; but the reshuffle of leaders did not involve a major change. In most cases, the persons promoted to leading posts already belonged to the province. Only three provincial or special-city Party leaders were brought in from outside. Even the men who lost their jobs were not retired from leadership; eighty-seven of them were simply transferred to the provincial Party Advisory Committee, the provincial People's Congress or the provincial People's Consultative Conference, where they would still wield considerable power.

The Party conference

In accordance with an announcement made a year earlier (see p. 488), a Party conference was held on September 18–23, preceded by a Central Committee Plenum on September 16 (the fourth since the 1982 Party Congress) and followed by another Central Committee Plenum, the fifth, on September 24. The agenda for these meetings contained two points: change of personnel and a proposal for the coming seventh Five Year Plan (1986–90).

This change of leaders was spectacular: sixty-five comrades 'asked to be withdrawn' from the Central Committee. However they were not withdrawn from active service: thirty-eight joined the Central Committee Advisory Committee, headed by Deng, and another twenty-two retained their leading posts in Party, army and government. Only five seemed to disappear from the political scene, and two of these, Ye Jianying and Huang Kecheng, both sick and incapacitated, were specially honoured by the conference.

Thirty-seven members of the Advisory Committee resigned and thirty of the Disciplinary Investigation Committee gave up their membership. The conference added fifty-six regular and thirty-five alternate members to the Central Committee, fifty-six to the Advisory Committee, and thirty-one to the Disciplinary Investigation Committee. This was a massive change in the leadership. (Nobody seems to have pointed out that according to the Party Charter, a Party Conference — only one had been held since 1949, that of 1955 — has no right to elect a new Central Committee.) The Fifth Central Committee Plenum, held the day after the end of the Conference, added six new members to the Politbureau and five to the Central Committee Secretariat.[22]

Major policies are not determined by the large, 343-strong Central Committee. They are determined by the Politbureau, which at this time had twenty-two members, six less than before. Of the twenty-eight members elected in 1982, one had died. Ten now resigned and only five new members were added. The old guard held on to the reins of power at the top, where it matters. There were seventeen old members and only five new ones in the Politbureau.

At the very top, in the Standing Committee of the Politbureau, there were no new men at all. In 1982 there were six members. Apart from Ye Jianying, who was sick, there were three old men — Deng, Chen Yun and Li Xiannian — and two 'young' men who had joined the Politbureau in 1980, Hu Yaobang and Zhao Ziyang. How did these five rule? Whose was the decisive voice? Since there were only five members, and since Hu and Zhao were promoted by Deng, there were three against two in his favour.

On September 28 the newspapers carried photographs of the top leaders. The publication of photographs, as we have seen, is a sensitive issue in Communist countries, and in China photographs had been manipulated many times in the past. This time the Peking newspapers carried a picture of the five members of the Politbureau Standing Committee. In the middle stood not Hu Yaobang or Deng, but Chen Yun. This picture, however, was not to be found in the *People's Daily*, the official newspaper of the Central Committee — another of the mysteries of the People's Republic.

A few months earlier Hu Yaobang had been quoted as saying: 'I am old, Hu Qili [one of the new members of the Politbureau] is middle-aged. There are men still younger. These three generations belong to three historical periods.'[23] The impression given was that he might not last long in his office. Hu has hardly any backing in the armed forces, which, in spite of all their troubles, are still very influential.

There were no signs of a reshuffle in the Military Committee, either in the Party or in the government (the same people are found in both).

Two marshals, Xu Xiangqian and Nie Rongzhen, who had been made deputy heads in 1982 under Deng, and resigned from the Central Committee in 1985, did not resign from the Military Committee.

The split

The four major speeches at the Party conference were delivered by four members of the Politbureau Standing Committee. The speeches followed two opposing directions. At the opening of the conference Hu Yaobang delivered a colourless speech. He did reveal, however, that the selection of those who were to resign or to be elected to the leadership had been made by a seven-man team which had discussed the matter for months. Five of the seven were old leaders, the sixth was Hu Yaobang himself, and the seventh was Qiao Shi, at sixty-one an up-and-coming 'young' man.[24] Hu did not mention that the meeting was held at Beidaihe, the coastal resort where Deng spent his vacation.

The bombshells came on the last day of the conference, September 23, when Deng, Chen Yun and Li Xiannian spoke. Deng kept on talking about economic reform, saying that it had been successful in the villages and was now being tackled in the cities. He repeated his well-worn phrase that some regions or some people should become rich first; but he added — a concession to his critics — that 'all should become rich together'. He also spoke of his cherished 'Socialism peculiar to China' (what this means has never been defined). But in another concession to his opponents he said that Marxist theories should be studied.

Chen Yun's speech was very different. He spoke first of the importance of promoting younger men — which implied that not only Deng but he and other veterans had had a say in the choice. Chen Yun then went on the attack. For some time, he said, peasants who became rich, '10,000-yuan households', as they were called, had been lavishly publicised in the press. This was a departure from reality. In fact, the number of peasants who had become rich was very small. Chen Yun then insisted on the importance of growing foodstuffs — which the peasants, in their enthusiasm for making money, were neglecting. The 1,000 million people of China need above all, he said, food and clothing. Lack of food might lead to political disturbances.

He approved of the economic reforms, but he warned that economic reforms in the cities — which meant in the state enterprises — would have to be carried out with caution. He repeated what he had been saying for years, that planned economy comes first and market economy second — a market economy without a plan could lead to chaos. He quoted what Deng had said earlier, that the economy was developing at an unhealthy speed. This was a judicious quotation to use. He went on to say that gross output had increased by 14 per cent in 1984. In this year, 1985, from January to July, it had increased by 22.8 per cent over the gross output for the same period in 1984. It would be impossible to maintain such a high speed. The available energy, transport and raw materials could not meet the current need. It is necessary to proceed at a steady pace.

Chen Yun is an authority on the economy. He is also head of the Party Disciplinary Investigation Committee. Large numbers of Party members and even old Party members are abusing their authority, he said. Even now, in the middle of the present Party Reform, there is widespread sale of adulterated drugs and wine. Party members should take care that their children do not live privileged lives or seek only power and money. Today many Party members are disregarding the interests of the country and seek only financial gain. There is corruption. There is bribery. There are illegal incomes. All this is happening because political ideology has been neglected. These harsh words implied that the policies of the flamboyant Deng Xiaoping had done harm.

Li Xiannian's address to the conference was in a similar vein. 'In the past few years', he said, 'we have neglected ideological political work. Bourgeois liberal ideology must be resisted, in particular the craze for chasing money.'[25] The day after the close of the Party conference, Chen Yun spoke to the Disciplinary Investigation Committee, stressing the importance of morality, the 'spiritual civilisation', of Party members, and expressing his indignation that grown-up children of Party leaders had set up no less than 20,000 firms, making money in legal and illegal ways.[26]

The bombardment of Deng had been going on for some time. A speech that Peng Zhen had delivered in June was published in the *People's Daily*, obviously with some reluctance, two months later. This was a direct attack. Deng had said earlier that Marx and Engels were unaware of the needs of the present time; his motto is 'Practice is the Norm of Truth.' In a direct attack on Deng, Peng Zhen said: 'The Norm of Truth? Is it social practice or something else? This is a fundamental question that can be solved only by making clear the fundamental principles of Marxism and Leninism.' Having insisted on the importance of Marxist theories, he repeated what he had said at earlier meetings of the People's Congress, that Party policies must be expressed in the form of law, and that not all Party policies can be made law overnight. 'Law cannot be changed at a whim to fit in with the changing views of the leaders.'[27]

On the eve of National Day (October 1), Peng Zhen told leaders of the People's Congress that 'socialist construction must be guided by Marxist theories; otherwise things may go wrong.'[28] On October 1, National Day, the photograph of only one leader appeared in the press, that of the fifty-six-year-old Hu Qili, the up-and-coming new leader. Ten days later the Central Committee's Advisory Committee held a meeting at which the speaker was not the head of the Committee, Deng Xiaoping, but another old man, Bo Yibo. He spoke about studying the documents of the Party conference, and insisted on one point, 'stability and unity',[29] a phrase much used in earlier days at times of crisis, during the Cultural Revolution and after the fall of Lin Biao, when the stability and unity of the Party were threatened. The Party conference had opened great gaps, or rather had made them known to the public. There was uncertainty in the air. The next conference, the Thirteenth Party Congress, was to be held in two years'time, in 1987. How many of the octogenarians would still be there? Which of the new, younger members of the Politbureau (in their fifties) would have come to the top? There were six of these younger men in the new Politbureau. Hu Qili's star was high. Li Peng and Tian Jiyun were both Vice-Premiers in the government. Qiao Shi had moved from one post to another — head of the Foreign Liaison Department in 1982, head of the Central Committee's Office in 1983-4, and Party secretary of the Central Committee's Political-Legal Department in 1985. (On September 20, 1985, his picture appeared in the *People's Daily* with Peng Zhen — a sign that he had not been brought into the Politbureau by Deng, against Peng Zhen's wishes.) There was also the sixty-four-year-old Wu Xueqian, minister of foreign affairs, and the mysterious Ni Zhifu, just over fifty, who had been high in Jiang Qing's regime and a member of the Politbureau since 1973.

Many of the new men in their fifties were trained thirty years ago in the Soviet Union. Li Peng himself studied for years in the University of Moscow at the time when Gorbachev was a student there. Perhaps not surprisingly, 1985 saw a rapid revival of cultural contacts with the Soviet

Union. Russian books, Russian ballet, important delegations reappeared on Chinese soil after an absence of twenty-five years.

Looking back

It was far from clear what the future would bring for the Communist Party in China. In August the *People's Daily* carried an article by a remarkable Party man, Gao Yang (seventy-five years of age, one of the few educated Party leaders, a minister for the chemical industry in the 1960s, a minister again in 1979 and in 1982–5 First Party secretary of Hebei province). In 1984 he recalled that the Marshallian economics he had studied in his young days — the theory of money, the theory of foreign currencies and so on — had proved useless under the Soviet economic system introduced into China. That is why the present generation completely lacks the understanding of modern business that is needed for the present reforms, he wrote.[30] In August 1985, a month before the Party conference, he wrote in the *People's Daily* about himself and about the country, giving the reflections of a man who knows what Communism has done to China:

When I was young, I was not taught the Four Books of Confucius as was the practice in the old days. My village had a modern school. Yet a nation cannot slough off its cultural tradition. The school was a modern-type school, but the education insisted on respect for parents and teachers, and we were taught to be polite and humble in speech. We learnt to write properly, to sit properly, to hold the brush properly. We had to learn to write big and small characters, copying the calligraphy of ancient masters. We learned classic texts by heart. I still remember poems I learned in higher middle school. In primary school we had military exercises and sang military songs and wore certain military uniforms. In the 1920s, under battling warlords, the country was not united, but education in the universities was orderly. At university I studied law and economics, using English textbooks. The education followed the capitalist model, but we Communist students refused to accept capitalist ideas.

I would not dare to say whether education under the New China [the Communist regime] was right. The emphasis was on class struggle and natural sciences. The young people I meet now have little knowledge, cannot write Chinese properly and cannot think logically. Moreover, their behaviour has become savage. It is said that this comes from the Cultural Revolution, but young people who were hardly born in those days also behave in a savage way.

Our cadres, elderly cadres included, did not receive proper training. They are rude and do not know how to express themselves, how to write a proper report, how to carry on a discussion.[31]

Gao Yang knew what he was talking about. He had spent some fifty years in the Party, and succeeded in making a career though he never reached the top. He must have suffered on seeing the old culture and the traditional good manners of China being destroyed, and on seeing Chinese behaviour become what he himself called 'barbarous', with uneducated people who could not even write good Chinese leading the country. He obviously expected that this would change, but he did not say so.

Marxism in 1983–1985

China is the first Marxist-ruled country in which the validity of some basic Marxist tenets has been openly challenged. When Deng Xiaoping proclaimed in 1978 that 'Practice is the Sole Norm of Truth', he seemed to be on solid Marxist ground. Ever since Marx, practice — action and revolutionary action — has counted for more than mere theories. Yet what Deng meant was rather — as his policies in the ensuing years have shown — 'Be practical and forget empty theorising.'

We have seen the daring views put forward by Marxist theoreticians in the years 1980–2 (pp. 447ff.) That trend, however, met with strong opposition. A whole generation of Party members felt that if the Stalinist Marxism on which they had been brought up and nurtured was to be repudiated, the ground would crumble beneath their feet and the whole country would be destabilised. Expert Marxist scholars wrote — we quoted them earlier — that the doctrine of historical determinism, the doctrine of development from primitive society through slavery, then feudalism and capitalism, leading to socialism, had been invented by Stalin and had not been taught by Marx. The bulk of Party leaders, however, did not accept this discovery, and they have continued to talk about the set periods of historical development.

In 1983 provincial Party organs published several books, textbooks on Marxism, which ignored the recent discoveries of top Marxist theoreticians. A typical example was *The Philosophical Principles of Marxism*, a book of 396 pages, designed as teaching material for Party members and published by the Party School of Peking city.[32] This book does not mention Stalin — it only quotes Lenin — but Stalin's doctrine on development of historical periods is presented as irrefutable truth. As in the Stalinist-style books of the 1950s, philosophical doctrines are sorted out into materialist and idealist. The origin of man is taught as in the

1950s: the ape became human by labour, moving its hands in making tools, and this was followed by the emergence of speech. The book also taught the old doctrine of quantitative growth leaping into qualitative change, and the doctrine of superstructures, that everything produced by the human mind is built upon the base, the production system. Following Engels, the book also states that thought and the revolutionary will in turn influence the production system. This, it says, is what happened in China. Study of Marxist thought in the early stage led to the establishment of the new production system under Marxist rule. The book asserts that among the various superstructures, change of political rule is easier than change of inveterate 'feudal' habits. Feudal superstitions and religious beliefs are slow to change. Religion is the ally of idealism and the great enemy of scientific socialism.

All these are well-worn theses of Marxism — Marxism as it was taught in China for thirty years. To give a gloss of up-to-date news, the new policies of Deng Xiaoping are added almost as an appendix: class struggle, essential in Marxism, should not be the main motive power of social life, though it may re-emerge in a sharp struggle. The whole liberal economic policy of Deng Xiaoping is thrust in, badly as it fits into this manual of old Marxism. Real life has overtaken the Marxist theory of the book. As was only proper, this manual of Marxism put forward the abolition of private ownership of the means of production as the cornerstone of the Marxist socialist order; but the print on the book was not yet dry when sale and purchase of means of production — machines etc. — was permitted.

This and similar books published for the indoctrination of Party officials repeats the old Stalinist doctrine parrot-fashion. Obviously some of the Party leaders did not agree with the reformist Marxist scholars working in the highest research centres of Marxist studies. In June 1984 the Central Committee's Propaganda Department ordered compulsory study of Marxism for all, to be concluded before the year 1990. Marxist philosophy, political economy and the history of the Chinese revolution should be constantly studied, and three months should be devoted in every three-year period to the full-time study of these subjects.[33]

There is no mistaking the discord between the old guard who still teach the old Marxism and the Marxist scholars who support Deng Xiaoping's forward-looking thinking. The Marxist scholars did not retreat. On December 7, 1984, the *People's Daily* 'Commentator' warned the 'propaganda comrades' that they must face reality and not lag behind; neither Marx nor Engels nor Lenin could have answers to our present problems. Mao Zedong himself condemned bookish learning. A few words taken from the old Marxist canons were cited as proof.

All this was not new. Zhao Ziyang himself had said it years earlier. The world press, however, misunderstood and took it as an open rejection of Marxism by Peking. On the following day the *People's Daily* felt obliged to publish a three-line correction. The statement that Marx-Engels-Lenin could not solve 'our problems' should have read 'all our problems'.

On December 21 the *People's Daily* returned to the same subject. Another 'commentary', quoting the authority of Deng Xiaoping, said that the words of the Marxist masters should not be taken literally. Lenin and Stalin corrected Marx, and Mao Zedong reinterpreted Marx for China. Mao introduced the new concept of 'villages surrounding the cities' (this is far from the truth — see p. 33). Marx's theory that under socialism there would be no commerce or money was altogether unrealistic.

This *People's Daily* 'commentary' made it clear that Deng Xiaoping was on the side of the Marxist scholars who were dissecting the traditionally-held Marxism — or rather that the scholars dared to speak openly because they were backed by Deng Xiaoping. Yet many still defended the old Marxism. The two opposite views were plainly to be seen in the pages of the *People's Daily*, the organ of the highest Party leadership. This meant that the latter were divided into conservatives and modernisers. They seemed to agree, however, on one point — that the general public had lost all interest in Marxist theories, whatever trend they might represent. In May 1985 a provincial Party secretary wrote: 'Today political work has no market; people are looking for money.' He believed that the way Marxism was taught in the 1950s was still the best way to train Party members.[34]

A different view was expressed by Li Shu, a leading Marxist scholar and for twenty years chief editor of the magazine *Historical Research*, the mouthpiece of the Party on historical questions — i.e. on the application of political norms to history. Li Shu wrote a preface to a book about Hu Shi, who in the 1920s had been the father of the modernisation of Chinese culture. The changing appreciation of Hu Shi is itself a sign of the new wind. Hu Shi, the pragmatist pupil of John Dewey and in his later years the Taiwanese ambassador to the United States, was attacked mercilessly under Mao. The book to which Li Shu wrote the preface found that Hu Shi, a materialist though an anti-Communist, had said some things worth saying.

This, however, was not the main point of Li Shu's preface. We have completely misinterpreted Marxism, he wrote. For many years we thought that its core was to be found in criticism and revolution, that the revolutionary spirit should guide scientific work, and that writing history should serve the cause of the Chinese revolution. Detached, objective historical writing was not possible. Throughout those years only the historians trained in the Yan'an days were accepted as true historians in China. On looking back, Li Shu says, we find that these men did not learn Marxism properly and, having had no access to libraries in remote Yan'an, were not equipped to write history. Li Shu mentioned by name Jian Bozang — one of the three leading and greatly honoured historians of the Mao regime. In his later years, Li Shu wrote, Jian himself was well aware of all this, as were other Party-member historians.[35]

This was written by a veteran historian of the Mao school. How the world had changed! The younger generation might be expected to criticise the Mao era, but this came from a man who for almost half a century had followed the Party line. Li Shu, like many of his colleagues, was giving expression to long-standing frustration and disappointment with the regime he had served. These men had had time to think about their life, and about the regime, during the years of the Cultural Revolution and the ensuing reign of the ultra-radicals, when they were purged and pushed aside and suffered many difficulties. Their feelings of frustration were not shared by the bulk of middle-rank uneducated Party men whose minds had been conditioned during the Stalin-Mao era.

What Li Shu said was also said — at the same time, in the middle of 1985 — by a professor at Wuhan University. This man's article first appeared in the journal of that University, but it was reprinted in the *People's Daily*. 'We were brought up', he said, 'in an extremely abnormal political and cultural period in the history of our country. The present structure of our thought is totally inadequate to the needs of modernisation. There are still many comrades whose brains move within the old fixed framework. It is futile to imagine that the present young generation of the 1980s would accept their theories.' In the eyes of these comrades, he went on, the present economic policy is wrong; it is sheer revisionism. They believe that every word of the old Marxist doctrine must be obeyed absolutely. However, there are others who say that today we must get on with the job, setting philosophy aside. Lenin said this was wrong: one should not go from one extreme to another.

Marxist philosophy remains very important for the modernising of the country, but it cannot be the Marxism we were taught: 'The teaching of Marxist philosophy today [1985] still mirrors, both in content and in the mode of presentation, what Soviet and Chinese scholars were teaching in the old days. Some new material, some more up-to-date examples, have been added, but what is being taught fits ill with modern science and contemporary social life. . . . We are still teaching the class-character of philosophy as if the classes had nothing in common. We still follow Zhdanov, saying that the history of philosophy is nothing but the history of the struggle between idealism and materialism.' (Few people in Western Communist parties now remember the name of Zhdanov, the terror of Marxist philosophers in the Soviet Union after the Second World War. In China his name is still mentioned without comment.)

The result, the article went on, is that all the many schools of idealism, except Hegelianism, are condemned *en bloc*; not a single thing worth mentioning is found in non-Marxist writings, and only a distorted caricature is given of the 2000-year tradition of Chinese philosophy. We are teaching a world outlook based on an antiquated knowledge of the world. We are circumventing the basic principle of philosophy, the principle of Identity, and hold that S may be P and not be P at the same time. This, we say, is dialectics; the principle of Identity is 'metaphysics'.

If we use such methods, how can we train our present young students? Can we use the methods of the 1950s to make our students believe in Marxism?[36]

Such daringly outspoken articles appear in university journals, and are only read by an élite; the reprinting of this article in the country's leading newspaper was a startling novelty. The article described the situation of Marxism in 1985, nine years after the death of Mao, and in the sixth year of the reign of Deng Xiaoping. Nevertheless the official teaching of Marxism in the Party schools has not changed. We saw an example of this in the Marxist textbook of the Party school of Peking city drawn up for training Party members.

If the old way is to be abandoned, what should be taught? The school of Deng has loudly rejected the old Stalin-Mao brand of Marxism; but it has nothing positive to put in its place. Everybody is fully conscious that the young are not interested in any form of 'ism'. They cannot be harnessed any longer to the old discipline. What is to come next?

CHAPTER XXIII

WHAT MARXISM HAS DONE TO CHINA

Marxism came to China almost by accident. Veteran Party leaders admitted in the 1980s that they were, first and foremost, revolutionary patriots who, after the collapse of the Qing dynasty, dreamed of a new revolutionary China. The October Revolution in Russia served as a spark, an inspiration for the establishment of a new, revolutionary order. The Chinese Communist Party was organised, in its modest beginnings, by emissaries from the Comintern in Moscow. Very few Chinese knew anything — very few know anything even today — about the earlier history of Marxism in Europe, about the First International — that amorphous international association of people founded in London in 1864, which collapsed in 1876 during Marx's lifetime — or about the Second International, set up in 1889 in Paris, which was hardly more than an advisory body grouping European socialists together. This too collapsed in 1914, when German socialists came out in support of the war. What the first Chinese revolutionaries learned about was the Third International, organised by Lenin in 1919. They did not make their acquaintance with Marxist theories until sixteen years after the establishment of the Party, in Yan'an, and then from the official Stalinist textbooks. The comrades scarcely knew that there were many divergent schools of Marxism in Europe and in Russia itself. To them the Marxism of Lenin, interpreted by Stalin, was the truth, and all other theories were heretical deviations. They can hardly have known that what they learnt as Marxism was an oversimplification of Marx. When, for example, the Chinese comrades studied the criticism passed by Marx on the Gotha Programme in 1875, how could they understand that Marx was arguing against a draft programme drawn up by German socialists — Bebel, Liebknecht and Lassalle? Who in China knew who those gentlemen were? When they read Engels' book that is commonly called *Anti-Dühring* (1878), but was originally known as *Herrn Eugen Dühring's Umwälzung der Wissenschaft*, what could they make of Engels' arguments against an obscure Berlin professor of philosophy?

Marxism, whether in the original German controversies or in the disputes in Russia, was alien to China and had no points of contact with Chinese thought and tradition. It may be thought — some scholars have held this view — that Marxism in its closed, compact, Stalinist form fitted China well and replaced the similarly compact Confucianist understanding of the world and society. It can be argued that, just as the old Confucianist system had a homogeneous outlook on life and on the world, so also, in a different way, had Marxism when it was presented as a monolithic, all-comprehending *Weltanschauung* (world philosophy). The differences, however, were enormous. Chinese society, under the influence of ancient Chinese philosophies and of Buddhism, had created a social consensus of harmony and a spontaneous acceptance of an ethical code. Law and order in a nation can hardly exist without at least a minimal underlying consensus on basic moral values.

Traditional social values, gracious courtesy and respect, were wiped away by the crude Stalinist practice of mutual denunciation, class hatred that divided husband from wife and parents from children, and the recurring political campaigns which landed millions in prison and in forced-labour camps.

Chinese Communists, when adopting Marxism from Russia, did not advert to the fact that the Marxism adopted by Russia could hardly find a deep echo in China. In China such a man as Lunacharsky could never have emerged. Lunacharsky (born in 1875) belonged, as did Berdiaev, to a group of Russians living outside Russia who dreamed of an ideal post-Christian society. After his return to the Soviet Union in 1917, he compared Lenin to the saints, prophets and martyrs of Russia. For Lunacharsky socialism was the perfect religion which creates the Superman. The Trinity meant: Production force — Proletariat — Scientific Socialism. For him religion had developed from early myths into the philosophical religion of Spinoza and Hegel, and was to culminate in Scientific Socialism. For him Marx was the greatest prophet after such prophets as Isaac, Jesus Christ, Paul of Tarsus and Spinoza.

In 1908 both he and Berdiaev dreamed of a new religion in Russia that would save the world, but soon after this their ways parted. Berdiaev, who taught philosophy at Moscow University after the October Revolution, became a great Christian writer. Lunacharsky was Commissar for Education from the October Revolution until 1929, and promoted a bloody persecution of Christian denominations. Lenin did not think much of either of them. In a letter to Gorky in 1913 he wrote disparagingly of those 'who are in search for God' (the school of Berdiaev), and the 'constructors of God' (Lunacharsky). Berdiaev was expelled from the Soviet Union in 1922; Lunacharsky was condemned by Stalin in 1929, and died in France in 1933.[37] For Lenin and Stalin, socialism was not a religion, yet the Russian religious spirit was not dead. The new religion had its bible, its ritual and its almighty Pastor. The old messianic Russia, the saviour of the world, became Russia the promoter of world revolution. Stalin found many admirers and followers in many countries.

Few Chinese are even aware of the fact that the first step in the development of Marx's ideas — before he came into contact with the French social radicals who first formulated the world 'Communism' — was his rejection of Christian faith under the influence of the Hegelian German theologians, Bruno Bauer and David Friedrich Strauss, or that Feuerbach interpreted God and the Bible in the Hegelian sense, exalting the 'autoconscience of Man', or that Marx himself wrote about Luther and Strauss.[38] China got its Marxism served up ready-made, tailored by Stalin and his theoreticians. Worldwide agitation was part of it. China joined in. But for China this agitation had a political aim only. When Peking turned against Moscow, China's agitation in Africa and Latin America was aimed against Moscow.

Marxism in China has had a battered history. In Yan'an times, and later during the Communist rule of the country, the enemies of Mao were dubbed enemies of Marxism. During the Cultural Revolution the Party's outstanding Marxist theoreticians were sent to prisons and labour camps. Those at the top, Lin Biao and Jiang Qing, were the only true Marxists; their enemies were 'sham Marxists'. As soon as Lin Biao and Jiang Qing had been toppled, they in turn became 'sham Marxists'. How could the average Party man not lose his faith in Marxism?

The economic theses of Marx — accumulation of wealth, impoverishment of the proletariat, exploitation — were rarely mentioned. The state was the only employer. What resulted was state ownership of all means of production. All economic power was concentrated in the hands of the leaders. The doctrines of historical materialism and dialectical materialism were essential courses in Party schools. Belief in a future ideal Communist society of plenty was taught. During the Great Leap in 1958 the immediate coming of final Communism was preached. That mirage was later moved to a remote future.

In grim fact, Marxism meant the unlimited rule of the Party, including strict control of thoughts and words. For the people at large, the state monopoly of the economy, the compulsory purchase of agrarian products, the rural communes and the absolute power of local Party bosses, were all seen as essential elements of Marxism.

The reforms of Deng Xiaoping meant a revolution. Millions of big and small Party men saw the end of communes. The peasants were no longer remunerated in proportion to 'work-points' allotted by the local Party men; the means of production, industrial equipment and raw materials were up for sale; individuals were encouraged to start their own businesses. How much remained of what people had thought of as genuine Marxism?

Deng Xiaoping's Marxist theoreticians were sapping the foundations of what had seemed to be a monolithic *Weltanschauung*. The teaching of historical materialism, it was now said, impeded the objective study of history; dialectics led to muddled thinking; perpetual talk about class brought on quarrels, jealousies, fights and disruption of the nation's life. Inciting children to denounce their parents destroyed the family. The Deng regime described the family as the basic cell of society. What would good old Marx have thought of all this? Lenin might have been less dissatisfied: the Leninist rule of the Party — strict materialism, and imposition of discipline — remained.

The question 'What is Man?' remained unresolved.

Hu Qiaomu's lengthy article in January 1984 reasserted the old Marxist doctrine that there is no 'abstract human nature', no man in the full sense of the word, but only class-man, with class struggle leading to the extinction of the exploiting class. He wrote in opposition to the widespread view inside the Party that the system had ignored the values of man and that Marxism should be interpreted in a humanistic way. Hu Qiaomu was a respected Party theoretician who had formulated two widely-known documents on the history of the Party, those of 1945 and of 1981.

At the end of 1984 a long article appeared in the *People's Daily* signed by no less a person than the crippled son of Deng Xiaoping. This son, Deng Bufang, had been disabled during the violence of the Cultural Revolution. He wrote his article after a visit, in a wheelchair, to Hong Kong, where he had inspected the work done for disabled people. On his return to China he established a Foundation for the Disabled. In Hong Kong, young Deng wrote, he had witnessed genuine humanistic service inspired by a Christian spirit. During the last 100 years humanism had spread widely in Western bourgeois society. We must admit, he wrote, that the criticism of humanism after Liberation (i.e. after the establishment of the regime) was harmful. We have cadres who despise disabled persons. In social welfare we fall well behind the capitalist countries and also behind the Soviet Union. We must recognise that in relieving the hardships of people we cannot rely merely on the government. 'Nuns in capitalist countries, urged by Christian propaganda, sacrifice their lives [to aid the disabled]; can we Party members, armed with dialectical and historical materialism, fall behind?'[39]

APPENDIX

PARTY RULES

In 1983 the Organisation Department of the Communist Party published in Peking a 299-page book entitled *Questions and Answers on the Work of the Party Organisation*. In 250 questions and answers this book explains the rules of the Party under the regime of Deng Xiaoping. One learns from it things one hardly knew before.

Archives and dossiers

The Party pays special attention to its archives and personal dossiers. One man is designated to work full-time or part-time on keeping the dossiers of every 1,000 Party members. This means that in 1983, when the Party had 40 million members, 40,000 were busy writing and filing the dossiers on their comrades. The Party committee of every county is responsible for keeping its archives safe from robbery, fire, humidity and insects. Every six months the dossiers must be checked and errors must be corrected. Special arrangements have been made for the dossiers dealing with the turbulent years of the Cultural Revolution. People who were unjustly accused may get back compromising documents or may ask that they be destroyed. Documents containing unjust accusations are to be destroyed. The destruction must be witnessed by two witnesses and before the documents are destroyed they must be registered. (All this means of course that many documents implicating Party leaders are lost to historians.)

The Organisation Department of the Central Committee is responsible for the dossiers of persons of the rank that includes vice-ministers and deputy heads of provincial organisations. (We are not told what happens to the dossiers of people who hold the rank of minister or above.) The dossiers of prominent non-Party-members are kept by the United Front Department of the C.C. Five years after an individual's death, his or her dossier is transferred to the C.C. Dossier Hall for perpetual preservation. The dossiers of lower-ranking Party members are kept by the Personnel Departments, and five years after their deaths are transferred to the C.C. or the archives of the appropriate province.

Deng's reform has broken with the Stalinist-Maoist tradition qualifying people according to family origin. In a person's dossier, however, this entry is retained, together with 'qualification of the person', recording the person's past history. In August 1980 a regulation on the statistics of Party members ordered that the local Party organisation departments should send in their figures before February 15 each year.

The Party rules all

The term 'cadre' signifies a civil servant, who may be a high Party official or a non-Party-member village teacher. A cadre is a person employed and paid by the state. Out of the 40 million Party members 17 million are 'cadres'; the total number of cadres is about 20 million. The Party rule book makes it clear that all cadres come under the direction of the Party. It also makes it clear that there are Party committees within non-Party organisations. This is not stated in so many words in the book; but to the question as to which Party organs control the cadres of which offices, the answer is that the highest leadership of the Party controls the cadres in the Party's central offices and those in the central government organs; the provincial Party leadership controls the cadres in the provincial and county Party and government organs, i.e. both cadres in Party organisations and those in government organs. The boundary therefore between Party and government is tenuous, though in official parlance they are separate.

The Party's role within the economic organisations is defined. The leaders of the enterprises act on their own. The Party committee within the enterprise does not assume the daily running of business, but it 'decides the basic principles [of the enterprise] and entrusts the implementation of the decision to the management. It also checks the implementation.' It 'guides' the operation but does not 'direct' it. It also 'checks the life of Party members and sees to it that they carry out the policy of the Party'.

Membership fee

Party members pay a membership fee. The size of the fee is determined by a system resembling progressive taxation. Those who earn less than 100 yuan a month pay 0.5 per cent of their monthly wages. The highest fee is paid by those who earn over 600 yuan a month: they pay 3 per cent of their wages. Extra income, bonuses etc. are not counted. Peasants, fishermen and the like pay 5 cents a month.

Resignation

Party sanctions, from admonition to expulsion, have been defined in the Party Charters. The Party Charter of 1982 defined that those who take no part in Party meetings for six months, do not pay their membership fee, or refuse to do Party work are considered to have left the Party. This will be checked at Party meetings; the Party member concerned may present his counter-arguments. A Party member who, having gone legitimately abroad or to Hong Kong or Macau and overstayed his leave for less than half a year, should be exposed to criticism. If he repents he should be allowed to continue his normal Party life. If he does not return for over a year he is considered to have left the Party.

Retirement

The retirement and pensioning of Party and government cadres are subject to detailed regulations applying to all cadres whether they work for the Party or for the government. According to a Cabinet regulation, Cabinet ministers, vice-ministers, Party secretaries of provinces *et al.* retire at the age of sixty-five; all others (men) retire at the age of sixty, and women at fifty-five. Those above the eighteenth grade (there are twenty-three or twenty-four grades; the higher the number the lower the category) receive a full year's salary plus a yearly allotment proportionate to the number of years' service they have completed. The years of service count from the time they entered the Party or the Youth Corps, going back to the earliest days of the Party. This applies also to those who served incognito in underground Party work in the Nationalist government's area, but not to those who merely rendered occasional service 'carrying letters, putting up posters, taking part in anti-Chiang Kai Shek demonstrations'. Officers in the Nationalist army who joined the Communists are included in the system. The time Party members spent in Nationalist prisons (if they did not betray the cause) is also counted. Special allowances are given to those who worked for years in places over 4,500 m. above sea-level. The 'political treatment' of the retired Party members is unchanged. 'Political treatment' means the right to attend meetings, listen to reports and read inner-Party documents.

Suicide

A special answer deals with those who commit suicide. Each case is to be examined. Some Party members or cadres were exposed to severe mass criticism and could not bear the humiliation. Some were tortured. Some made mistakes and were afraid to reveal them. Some committed suicide because of illness. Therefore not all who committed suicide should be excluded from the Party. Those, however, who committed suicide because they were afraid of punishment for crimes should be excluded. Those who committed suicide during the Cultural Revolution (a great number) should not be counted as suicides.

'Comrade'

The rules lay down that Party members of all ranks should be called simply 'comrade' and not by the title of any office, such as 'Party secretary'. Reference is made to an order of Mao in 1959, and instructions of the Party in 1965 and December 1978. This, like many other regulations, has never been observed in practice.

PREFACE TO THE 2018 EDITION

Laszlo Ladany's valuable work, *The Communist Party of China and Marxism 1921–1985* is now coming out in a new edition. For some four decades, Ladany closely monitored the press of the People's Republic of China. His work thus explores all the important events since the founding of the Communist Party of China in 1921, that affected greatly the later development of the Party and what happened to the People's Republic of China. No other non-Chinese scholar ever amassed and analysed such a vast collection of first hand material from Chinese communist documents and the press.

Many Western scholars have tried to master as much first hand material as possible to form a reliable description of what happened to China and the Chinese people under the communist regime. Several of Roderick MacFarquhar's books and Frank Dikötter's *Mao's Great Famine* are among those. Though great efforts have been made to seek the truth, those Chinese scholars who have been brought up with limited historical knowledge and who insist on the principle of the Party spirit still mistrust the source of the material collected by Western scholars. Many even allege that the stories cited by them are not fact but have been fabricated by 'Western hostile forces'. Thus it remains very difficult for many Chinese scholars to discuss the Party's historical development with their counterparts in an atmosphere of honest dialogue.

As for Laszlo Ladany, though the material he collected from the People's Republic of China touches very lightly on many important historical facts, for example, the great famine during the Great Leap Forward, which claimed the lives of more than 35 million people, yet what he mastered is sufficient to demonstrate what he wanted to expound.

The significance of this book by Laszlo Ladany for contemporary academic research lies in the possibility that even those Chinese scholars who believe firmly in the principle of the Party spirit will accept all his citations as from reliable sources, even while they may remain critical of the conclusions he draws from them. Yet Ladany bases his understanding of the political situation under the communist regime on rationality, humanism and universal values that are open to debate and mutual correction. Reminiscent of the Chinese saying 'using your own spear to pierce your own shield,' Ladany uses the mutually contradictory documents that appeared in different media or at different times to expose many lies. Once we can agree on the reliability of the sources, then we can have a useful discussion whether, in fact, they really were lies and who is responsible for them. Using the same sources to identify lies may become an effective way to convince those who never trust in sources other than their own.

Another significant aspect of this book lies in its philosophical and historical perspective. It will help provoke consideration of the real problems that hinder political reforms in China. The Chinese communists learned a great deal from the Stalinist administration in the Soviet Union when they overthrew Chiang Kai-shek's Nationalist government and tried to found a new state. Though Mao stoutly resisted Soviet influence, and even in some sense during the Cultural Revolution smashed the political system copied from the Soviet Union, still he did not change fundamentally the Stalinist model. Deng Xiaoping restored some of what was cast aside by Mao, but basically did not touch the model, such that it has survived all the political changes in China since 1949. But the Soviet Union existed for about seventy years, during which all kinds of problems increasingly accumulated, increasingly until finally becoming unmanageable.

Now the People's Republic of China — where because of the Great Leap Forward, and the Cultural Revolution, even more problems accumulated than in the Soviet Union — is approaching its seventieth birthday. The main difference is that China today has a rapidly developing economy, on which both the Chinese communists and the vast Chinese population pin their Chinese dream. While almost all of them fear that their peaceful and rapidly improving life would be greatly affected by any instability emerging from a political reform carried out without care, the Chinese dream nevertheless includes a political reform that will yield a genuine commitment to the 24-character socialist core values. The nations of the West and their governments also share the hope for a socially stable and economically prosperous China, because an unstable Chinese society or any decline in Chinese economic progress will have dangerous consequences, even though they continue to insist on their dislike of dictatorship in all its forms. Thus, as it approaches its seventieth birthday, China has many more advantages than its Soviet 'elder brother.' Its present leader Xi Jinping may have good reasons to say that he will not become another Gorbachev.

But just as in the Soviet Union, the forces that destroyed communist rule came from within the Soviet Communist Party, those threatening communist rule in China cannot but come from within the Party as well in the present political situation. The public or clandestine power struggle within the Party, as well as the unprecedented scale of corruption, are the most serious factors contributing to instability and unrest. For the present leadership, it would be wise to push forward political reforms, thus making it easier to enforce effectively all its lines and policies, without worrying about being attacked by those who hide in the shadows during or even after their time in office.

Laszlo Ladany was more insightful than many Western scholars in seeing through the reason why the Chinese communist leadership always lags behind in their efforts to carry out political reform. A party that has seized political power through violence will be unable to solve the challenge of a peaceful hand-over of power. Marx did not agree with the idea that socialism would triumph wherever capitalism was not well developed. A country without developed capitalism would remain in a political system more or less of dictatorship, where the tradition of democracy still has not yet formed. Though Marx also talked about the possibility of proletarian dictatorship in the area of developed capitalism, he contended that it would be only a short-term transition. Lenin, however, ran counter to Marx's idea that socialism can only be built on the basis of developed capitalism, trying instead to found a socialist state upon a proletarian dictatorship, which became his tool to wipe out his enemies and political rivals. Stalin brought Lenin's dictatorship to its fullest expression. It is precisely the Stalinist political model that affected the Chinese Communist Party the most at the key moment of its development. What happened to the Soviet Union might also happen to China. In order to avoid such an outcome, political reforms to change the Stalinist political model are unavoidable.

Now the question becomes whether to change the Stalinist political model back to Marxism or to something other than Marxism? According to Ladany, Marxism as the theory guiding the industrial working class did not match the practice of peasant uprisings headed by Mao in China. After being transformed by Lenin and Stalin, the Marxism that came to China actually became a political tool, transformed by Party scholars to meet the needs of the Chinese communist leaders. So it makes little sense simply to revert to a name. Moreover, Marxism places too much stress on class struggle, especially conflicts between capital and labour during an industrial era based mainly on manufacturing. Now we are in a society based mainly on service and information, facing many new questions that should be answered with integrity and social responsibility so that harmony can be achieved for all. In this sense,

Confucianism and traditional Chinese ethics may be more effective in holding the Chinese together and urging them to strive hard in a common effort for the Chinese dream.

Now we come to a very important consideration pointed out by Laszlo Ladany that remains a very difficult obstacle to substantial political reforms in China. Ladany described that obstacle as communist attitudes to the history of the Party. He mentions the two resolutions of the Chinese Communist Party on a number of historical issues, the first passed in 1945, the second in 1981. Normally, historical issues should be explored by historians and scholars based on their investigation into the historical facts. If a politician or a party wishes to cover up some of their political behaviour or is eager to embellish the roles they play in some important events, then it is reasonable to conclude that they are primarily interested in preserving their own reputations or careers. Mao made use of the first resolution to change many historical facts to his own benefit. The second resolution was largely based on the first one, though it criticises Mao for making mistakes during the Cultural Revolution, yet protects Mao from being rejected by the Chinese people in order to keep the Party's position intact. But this kind of resolution was not Mao's own invention. He was inspired by what Stalin did in the *History of the Communist Party of the Soviet Union (Bolsheviks), Short Course*. But to expose some core secrets of the Communist Party to the light is never easy. Khrushchev only made public the secrets of Stalin within a small circle, and he was punished with house arrest for life. Gorbachev called for openness to push forward political reforms in the Soviet Union, but finally he had to declare the dissolution of the Soviet Communist Party. So the present Chinese leader has to tread warily. On the one hand, he has to continue the economic reforms initiated by Deng Xiaoping; on the other hand, he should be very careful about political reforms. But no matter how careful he is with the Party's history, how unwilling he is to make public a reliable history of the Party, and how dangerous it is to tell the truth about the Party's past, it will prove impossible to turn that history into something that meets the political needs of the Party. Only when this distorted history is set right, will China have signalled the beginning of genuine political reform.

Friedrich Young
July 2017

Dabbru 'al-Lev Yerusalim
'Speaking to the Heart of Jerusalem' (Is 40:2)

LADANY THE PROPHET ADDRESSES
THE PEOPLE OF CHINA

Rev. Fr. Laszlo Ladany SJ (1914–1990) was the most outstanding commentator on mainland Chinese affairs in the twentieth century. His trenchant *China News Analysis* gave the most accurate portrait of communism in China at the time, not without a characteristic irony.

Ladany's father's surname was Hoffenreich. He was a Hungarian Jew. In 1881 he changed the family name from the Germanic Hoffenreich into the Hungarian Ladany. By 1908, when his father was thirty-one, half of all Hungarian lawyers and doctors were Jewish, so it is no surprise to learn that his father was the local doctor. In that year, like many Jews of the time, he converted to Christianity. Hence when Laszlo was born the family had been Catholic for nearly six years, but in studying law Laszlo still kept to a familiar Hungarian Jewish tradition. He registered at university in Budapest in 1931 and graduated on 6 June 1935. Simultaneously he also studied the violin under Bela Bartok at the Liszt Music Academy from 1932–35. On completing his studies he joined the Society of Jesus, or Jesuit order, and was sent to China in 1940.

As Communism took over China, Ladany moved south and installed himself first in Guangzhou and then, from 22 January 1949, in Hong Kong, where he started to listen to refugees' stories, and so began what became his life's work, *China News Analysis. CNA* was published between 1953 and 1998 with the exception of 1983. Initially it came out every week, but then every two weeks before settling into the rhythm of twice a month. Ladany was responsible for it until the end of 1982. Although Ladany was responsible for overall publication, it was not solely his work. His faithful secretary, Helen Lee, worked for over twenty years without ever taking any time off, even on Christmas Day. Mr Pei went on until 1994 reading every issue of the *People's Daily* (*Renmin Ribao*) with a devotion that probably exceeded that of the most ardent communist. Various people helped with the English editing of CNA, especially the Irish Jesuits, Alan Birmingham and Jerry

McCarthy, in Hong Kong. Ladany would also invite guest writers in particular for issues on North Vietnam (Patrick J. Honey) and Mongolia.

On retirement from publishing *China News Analysis*, Ladany gathered his thoughts to write his history of the Communist Party (1921–1985), first published in 1988 and now republished here.[1] He also gathered materials for a book on law in China since this reflected his early studies in Budapest. The book was published posthumously. These two works were to be completed by a third on religion. His manuscript notes had a few drafts for chapters, which I have consulted, but it would have been difficult to expand those into a book manuscript. This was partly because in his last years he was very critical of any attempt to open up to Communist China and work with the official representatives of its 'Catholic' Church. To be a Catholic, for him, meant unswerving loyalty to the Pope, no truck with Communism in any form, and martyrdom: this at a time when seminaries, albeit under government supervision, were beginning to allow foreigners, including Chinese who were not PRC citizens, to come and lecture. Coming from a persecuted people he identified with those persecuted under Communism.

If we turn to Hungarian Judaism at the time of Ladany's birth, we find that in 1906 Budapest had 39 daily papers compared to 24 in Vienna, 25 in London and 36 in Berlin.[2] In 1910 over 40 per cent of journalists were Jewish, this out of a population where Jews numbered only 5 per cent of the total.[3] It is my feeling that Ladany saw himself as a successor to these Hungarian Jewish journalists, a form of prophet, speaking out to the people about the iniquities of the times. The prophetic mantle fitted him even more in that when he was writing about China, he did so against a background of authors who hailed Mao's new China as a paradise on earth. Even Chinese Jesuit theologians wrote books comparing the New China with the redemption from Egypt and the New Man of St Paul.[4] Ladany was often seen by his contemporary China-watchers as backward and an arch-conservative. He himself would see them as false prophets, and like Jeremiah, set himself to proclaim the real facts and pull down illusions. In the end, he was proved right.[5]

Ladany was passionately interested in the details of China and earned his reputation by noticing slight shifts of emphasis in the Chinese daily press: whose photo appeared or did not appear; who was praised or not. It was from these obscure details that he learnt to work out what was going on inside a closed regime. Hence *CNA* often reads a bit like a detective novel, as the author attempts to work out what is going on and who are the villains behind the latest political witch-hunt.

Chinese communism, however, is not the same as its Russian counterpart. In 1957 Ladany described the Chinese form as one with 'fluid truth'. He notes how the Chinese honour capitalists and intellectuals and encourage them to join non-Communist Parties, but how at the same time they are called on to toe the Party line. While Russians suppressed religion, the Chinese support it and put into prison only those who object to their religious policy for their 'imperialism or some such secular error' (*CNA* 173:2). The result is that people are confused, or to put it more poetically, 'muddying the water to improve the fishing has been raised to the level of a fine art.'

The real evil of the time lay in the moral destruction wrought on the people: "this is a generation that grew up without fundamental norms of behaviour, without value judgements, without knowing what it is to be Chinese".[6] From this we can see that what he attacks in Chinese Marxism is the destructive effects it has had on people's souls and their culture.

Ladany was not given to expressing his religion in public but in his private writings we can see that he always retained a sense of the holiness of God that is the hallmark of Jewish faith. Take these words he wrote in January 1989: 'God and us, he the eternal, we ephemeral; he the almighty, we feeble nothing; he the Immaculate, we full of dirt and sin. But does it not remind one of the history of God's people in the Old Testament? Is it not the history of a sinful people, and the ever recurring love of God?' (Doc 31: 28, 4 Jan 1989)[7]

His criticism of contemporary China was born out of a love for the people and their culture. In recent years we find many Chinese intellectuals who share his concern over the moral vacuum that blights Chinese society. Ultimately, though, Ladany's vision is one of hope. God will not fail to send his prophets to restore his people. Similarly, the ancient culture of China, suitably renewed for the present era, will rise again to offer meaning and hope to millions.

Edmund Ryden, SJ
Law Department, Fu Jen Catholic University

Notes

1. Ladany sets his history of the Party according to the theme that the Chinese knew very little about Marx and that essentially they imbibed Stalinism. Indeed, he notes that no Communist regime was ever based on Marxism: "All Communist regimes are based on these three factors: dialectical materialism, the power of the

Party, and a secret police. No Communist regime is based on pre-Lenin Marxism." (Ladany, *The Communist Party*, 8).

2. Paul Lendvai, *Die Ungarn*, München: Goldmann, 2001, 371.
3. Paul Lendvai, *Die Ungarn*, 370–1.
4. The following quotation comes from Michael Chu SJ, writing about Maoist China, "Here, if ever, we have an instance of 'salvation outside the Church', a salvation in which it would seem the Church played no role at all." (M. Chu (ed.), *The New China: A Catholic Response*, 1977). When Fr Chu was able to visit his relatives in Shanghai, many of whom had suffered in labour camps, he wept and regretted ever writing such things. Ladany was right.
5. His obituary in *The Times* (28 Sept 1990) reads, in part, "The exactitude with which he compiled his reports was accompanied by a certain sceptical wit that poured cold water on any attempt to add lustre to the new promise of Mao's revolution."
6. Laszlo Ladany, *Law and Legality in China*, London: C. Hurst, 1992, 31.
7. Ladany's papers are kept in the archives of the Chinese Province of the Society of Jesus in Taipei. I refer to them by number of document (if there is one), page and date.

EPILOGUE

Thirty years after its first publication, Laszlo Ladany's *The Communist Party of China* may now be ready for a wider public that can appreciate its significance. The book presents itself as a *Self-Portrait*, as it attempts to come to grips with how the Party has portrayed itself from its founding in 1921 through a number of tumultuous periods up to 1985. When Ladany was analyzing media reports from China he was particularly focused on the development of Chinese society in all its complexity. Why, he was asking over the years, would a particular photo of government officials include certain figures, and then, all of a sudden, someone would disappear from the scene? Very early Ladany drew the attention of his readers to Deng Xiaoping who after a bumpy career up and down the Party hierarchy would end up as the chief architect of the so called 'open door' policy: ('*gaige kaifang*'). Deng's pragmatic argument that it does not matter whether a cat is white or black so long as it catches mice indicated a radical departure from the ideological madness that culminated in the Cultural Revolution (1966 – 1976). While it is tacitly acknowledged by the Party that the period of the 'Great Proletarian Revolution' was a unique disaster involving the large-scale destruction of culture, religion and basic human decency, it is still taboo nowadays in China to analyze the historical facts of this uniquely Chinese holocaust.

Emerging from the ashes of the Gang of Four's hysterical outbursts of ideological madness, China under Deng Xiaoping set out on a path of "modernization" focused exclusively on economic development. It remains its historical achievement that millions of people have been lifted out of poverty. While Ladany's *Self-Portrait* indicates that the Party never abandoned the rhetoric of Marxism, he consistently points out the irony that the comrades who harassed and killed people they considered as 'counter-revolutionaries' supposedly under the banner of Karl Marx and Friedrich Engels hardly understood even the basics of Marxism. The enigmatic catch-all phrase indicating the supposedly 'Chinese Characteristics' of Marxism in fact masked the founding of another Dynasty in China focused on its founding father Chairman Mao. Without ever admitting it, the Communist Party constructed a modern form of slavery by maintaining a rigid system of household registration, the so-called *hukou*, which made it impossible for migrants who constitute roughly a third of the population in the great cities of China to have the same access to education as their city counterparts. Only recently has the rigidly imposed one child policy been adjusted as the flaws of a growing gender imbalance bordering on "gendercide" became obvious. Despite a highly publicized anti-corruption campaign corruption is still deeply engrained in Chinese society and actually, according to the respected measurements of the Berlin based "Transparency International," has dramatically worsened in the last three years.

The Self-Portrait painted by Ladany by no means should provoke sentiments of self-complacency or cultural chauvinism. It was never intended as a form of "China bashing." On the contrary, Ladany's analyses reveal a profound appreciation and love of Chinese people and their cultures. One of its underlying messages is that only with an honest confrontation with the truth about recent history may genuine reform gradually emerge. The Chinese people have every reason to be proud about their great cultures. However, remaining prisoners of the Maoist dynasty with all its deadly ghosts is more and more proving to be an obstacle to progress. Ladany trusts that China may bring about a genuine reform that truly honors the basic "Communist" commitment to "serve the people". Instead of remaining a hostage held by an oligarchy emerging from the circles around Chairman Mao, it is hoped that China may find its unique way, certainly in many ways different from other cultures, to respect the basic human dignity of each one of its citizens. The writings of Ladany neither support the idea that reform can only happen within the framework of Western democracy nor, of course, that it should come about with violence. Nevertheless, the present ecological disaster emerging from air, water and soil pollution is just a strong reminder that a system that fails to give enough voice to its civil society may not only prove to be a catastrophe for its own people but also for the rest of the world. Therefore we may be surprised to discover an impressive message of hope in this 'Self-Portrait' that China, looking through a mirror at the period between 1921 – 1985, may be able one day to find ways to seek the historic truth and ultimately to rediscover its own rich treasure of wisdom and moral values which have hardly been destroyed by the events of this period.

Peter Hoffenreich
19 January 2017

NOTES

Abbreviations applicable to Notes

BD (Jap)　　Biographical Dictionary of Contemporary China （現代中國人名辭典）(in Japanese), published by the Japanese Foreign Ministry, Tokyo, 1982.

Biographies　Biographies of Personalities in Party History (Zhong-gong dang-shi ren-wu zhuan 中共黨史人物傳), 30 vols, Shaanxi, 1980–6, edited by the CCP History Research Association (editor-in-chief, Hu Hua) 胡華主編 .

CCP　　Chinese Communist Party

Ci Hai　　(Dictionary), separate volume on Contemporary History of China （ 辭海中國現代史), Shanghai, 1980.

CNA　　China News Analysis, Hong Kong.

GMD　　Guang Ming Daily （光明日報), Peking.

Klein-Clark　Biographical Dictionary of Chinese Communism, 1921–1965, edited by Donald W. Klein and Anne B. Clark, Cambridge, Mass., 1971.

LD　　Liberation Daily (Jiefang Ri-bao 解放日報), Shanghai.

List　　List of Important Meetings of the CCP (Zhong-guo gong-chan-dang li-ci zhong-yao hui-yi-ji中國共產黨歷次重要會議集), vol. 1, Shanghai, 1982.

MHS　　Modern History Studies (Jin-dai shi yan-jiu 近代史研究), quarterly, Peking.

MZJ (Jap)　Collected Works of Mao Zedong (Mao Zedong Ji 毛澤東集), edited by Takeuchi Minoru, 10 vols, Tokyo, 1972.

PD　　People's Daily (Ren-min Ri-bao 人民日報), Peking.

Record　　Record of Major Events in China's Modern and Contemporary History (Zhong-guo jin-xian-dai shi da-shi-ji 中國近現代史大事記), 1982, Shanghai.

RR　　Reminiscences on the Revolution (Ge-ming hui-yi-lu 革命回憶錄), a series of booklets published in the early 1980s by the People's Publishing House, Peking.

Chapter I. How China became Communist

1. Quoted in *World Marxist Review: Problems of Peace and Socialism*, no. 8, Prague, 1982, p. 17.
2. Stephan Possony, *Lenin*, Stanford: Hoover Institution Press, 1964, p. 19.
3. *MHS*, no. 1, 1983, pp. 7–36.
4. 'On the People's Democratic Dictatorship', June 30, 1949, in *Selected Works of Mao Zedong*, vol. IV (English edn), Peking, 1961, vol. IV, p. 413.
5. *GMD*, May 9, 1978.
6. *Social Sciences (She-hui ke-xue* 社會科學), Shanghai, no. 4, 1982, p. 67.
7. *Social Sciences Quarterly (She-hui ke-xue ji-kan* 社會科學季刊), no. 2, Shenyang, 1983, pp. 45–7.
8. *Social Sciences*, 北京日報 , no. 8, 1982, pp. 21–3.
9. Ibid.
10. *Philosophical Research (Zhe-xue Yan-jiu* 哲學研究), monthly, no. 11/12, Peking,1959, p. 26.
11. *PD* March 25, 1983, p. 5.
12. Helmut Dahm, *Der Gescheiterte Ausbruch. Entideologisierung und Ideologische Gegenreformation in Osteuropa (1960–1980)*, Baden-Baden, 1982, pp. 267–76.
13. *GMD*, June 22, 1983.
14. *Liaoning University Journal (Liao-ning da-xue xue-bao* 遼寧大學學報), no. 4, 1981, p. 15.
15. *PD*, March 16, 1983, p. 4.

Chapter II. Before Mao

1. Witold S. Sworakowski (ed.), *World Communism: A Handbook, 1918–1965*, Stanford: Hoover Institution Press, 1973.
2. *Wen Hui Bao*, 文滙報（上海）, Shanghai, June 21, 1981.
3. Branko Lazitch, *Biographical Dictionary of the Comintern*, Stanford: Hoover Institution Press, 1973, see under 'Joffe'.
4. Li Chien-nung, *The Last Hundred Years' Political History of China (Zhongguo jin-bai-nian zheng-zhi-shi* 李劍農：中國近百年政治史), Taipei, 1957 (preface 1942), vol. II, p. 610.
5. Milorad M. Drachkovitch (ed.), *The Revolutionary Internationals, 1864–1943*, Stanford: Hoover Institution Press, 1966, p. 170.
6. *PD*, Oct. 6, 1980, p. 5. Biographical notes on Comintern emissaries in China are to be found in Branko Lazitch, *Biographical Dictionary of the Comintern*, Stanford: Hoover Institution Press, 1973; in *Biographical Dictionary of Foreigners in China in Recent Times (Jin-dai lai-hua wai-guo-ren ming-ci-dian* 近代來華外國人名辭典), Peking: Translation Bureau of Modern History Research, Institute of Chinese Academy of Social Sciences, 1981. There are many discrepancies in the sources.
7. *Before and After the First Congress ('Yi-da' qian-hou* "一大"前後), Peking, 1980 (inner-Party publication).
8. *MHS*, no. 2, 1984, pp. 300–5.

9. *Documents of the Comintern concerning the Chinese Revolution (Gongchan guo-ji you-guan di wen-xian zi-liao* 共產國際有關的文獻資料), Peking, 1981, vol. I, pp. 76–7.

10. Ibid., pp. 78–80.

11. *Historical Research (Lishi Yan-jiu* 歷史研究), Peking, no. 2, 1983,pp. 178–92.

12. *List*, pp. 64, 70–1.

13. *Biographical Dictionary of the Comintern*, see under 'Pavel Mif'.

14. *Documents of the Comintern concerning the Chinese Revolution*, pp. 263–71.

15. Ibid., pp. 175–98.

16. *Biographical Dictionary of the Comintern*, see under 'Tan Pingshan'; *Ci Hai* (History), pp. 146–7.

17. *Documents of the Comintern concerning the Chinese Revolution*, pp. 281–2.

18. *Historical Research*.

19. Ibid.

20. *Record*, pp. 100–1.

21. *List*, pp. 73–8.

22. *List*, pp. 80–1; *Record*, p. 102.

23. *Documents of the Comintern concerning the Chinese Revolution*, p. 338.

24. *Before the Sixth Congress: Documents of Party History (Liu-da yi-qian: dang di li-shi cai-liao* "六大"以前一黨的歷史材料), comp. by the Party Central Committee Secretariat, Peking, 1980, 994 pp., pp. 850 ff.

25. *MHS*, no. 2, 1980, pp. 66–7.

26. *MHS*, no. 1, 1983, p. 135.

27. Leon Trotsky, *The History of the Russian Revolution*, vol.I, New York, 1933, p. 314.

28. *List*, pp. 80–90.

29. *List*, p. 91; *Record*, p. 103.

30. *List*, pp. 91–7.

31. *Biographical Dictionary of the Comintern*, p. 235.

32. Richard C. Thornton, 'The Emergence of a New Comintern Strategy for China, 1928' in M.M. Drachkovitch and Branko Lazitch (eds), *The Comintern: Historical Highlights*, Stanford: Hoover Institution Press, 1966, pp. 66–110.

33. *Documents of the Comintern concerning the Chinese Revolution*, pp. 350–3.

34. *List*, p. 97.

35. *MHS*, no. 4, 1980, pp. 1–14.

36. *Biographical Dictionary of the Comintern*, see under 'Hsiang Chung-fa'.

37. Benjamin I. Schwartz, *Chinese Communism and the Rise of Mao*, Cambridge, Mass., 1952, pp. 122 ff.; Karl A. Wittfogel, *Oriental Despotism*, New Haven, 1957, p. 405; Richard C. Thornton, 'The Emergence of a New Comintern Strategy for China, 1928'.

38. *Selected Works of Mao Zedong* (English edn), Peking, 1965, vol. III, p. 165.

39. Ibid., pp. 182–3.

40. *Before the Sixth Congress: Documents of Party History*, p. 864.

41. *Selected Works of Mao Zedong*, vol. III, p. 175.

42. *List*, pp. 102–4.

43. *List*, pp. 107–33.

44. *MHS*, no. 1, 1983, p. 142.

45. *List*, pp. 122–31.

46. *List*, p. 133.

47. Tso Liang Hsiao, *Power Relations within the Chinese Communist Movement*,

1930-1934: A Study of Documents, Seattle, 1961, pp. 25-6.

48. *MHS*, no. 1, 1983, pp. 135-42.
49. *GMD*, March 12, 1978.
50. *Biographical Dictionary of the Comintern*, see under 'Ch'en Shao-yu'; see also Donald W. Klein and Anne B. Clark (eds), *Biographical Dictionary of Chinese Communism 1921-1965*, 2 vols, Cambridge, Mass., 1971.
51. *Selected Works of Mao Zedong*, (English edn), vol. III, p. 190.
52. *MHS*, no. 3, 1983, pp. 249-50.
53. *MHS*, no. 1, 1983, p. 139.
54. *List*, p. 146.
55. Reminiscences by Wu Xiuzhuan in *Worker's Daily (Gong-ren Ri-bao* 伍修權 工人日報), Peking, Nov. 18, 1984, repr. in *Xinhua Digest (Xinhua wenzhe* 新華文摘), Peking, no. 1, 1985, pp. 163-5.
56. *Ci Hai* (History), 1980, p. 44.
57. *List*, p. 62.
58. *Selected Works of Mao Zedong* (English edn), vol. III, pp. 184-5, 191.
59. *Biographies of Personalities in the Party History of the CCP*, Shaanxi: CCP History Research Association, vol. III, pp. 1-65.
60. *Commemorating the Sixtieth Anniversary of the CCP (Zhonggong liu-shi-nian ji-nian wen-xuan* 中共六十年紀念文選), Peking, 1982, pp. 389-400.
61. *Peng Dehuai's Own Narration (Peng Dehuai Zi-zhu* 彭德懷自述), 1981, Peking.
62. *Ci Hai* (History), pp. 26-31; *Biographical Dictionary of Chinese Communism*, see under 'He Long'; *Biographies of Personalities in the Party History of the CCP*, vol. II, Shaanxi, 1981.

Chapter III. From Jing Gang Shan to Yan'an

1. *MHS*, no. 1, 1983, pp. 121-3.
2. Wang Jianmin, *History of the Chinese Communist Party (Zhong-guo gong-chan-dang shi-gao* 王健民：中國共產黨史稿), 3 vols, Taipei, 1965, vol. I, pp. 105, 143.
3. *List*, pp. 96, 137.
4. Gong Chu, *The Red Army and I (Hong Jun Yu Wo* 龔楚：我與紅軍), Hong Kong, 1954, pp. 119-22.
5. *PD*, July 30, 1965, p. 5.
6. *Ci Hai* (History), p. 107; *Peng Dehuai's Narration (Peng Dehuai Zi-shu* 彭德懷自述), Peking, 1981, pp. 143-4.
7. *Selected Works of Zhou Enlai (Zhou Enlai xuan-ji* 周思來選集), vol. I, Peking, 1980, p. 179.
8. *Selected Works of Mao Zedong* (Chinese edn), Peking, 1952, p. 106.
9. *MHS*, no. 1, 1983, p. 134; *List*, p. 137.
10. *List*, p. 147.
11. *MHS*, no. 1, 1983, p. 139.
12. *List*, p. 150.
13. *Record*, p. 110.
14. Tso-liang Hsiao, *Power Relations Within the Chinese Communist Movement, 1930-1934*, Seattle, 1961, pp. 98 ff.
15. *Reports on a Conference on Party History (Dang-shi hui-yi bao-gao ji* 黨史會議報告集（內部）), published by the Central Committee's Party School

(inner-Party publication), 1982, p. 263.

16. Cai Xiaoqian, *Reminiscences on the Jiangxi Soviet Area and The Flight to the West of the Red Army (Jiangxi Su-qu, Hong-jun xi-cuan hui-yi* 蔡孝乾，江西蘇區，紅軍西竄回憶'), 1970, Taipei, pp. 55–7.

17. *RR*, no. 8, 1983, p. 3.

18. *MHS*, no. 1, 1983, p. 139.

19. Ibid.

20. *Documents of the Comintern concerning the Chinese Revolution (Gongchan guo-ji you guan di wen-xian zi-liao* 共產國際有關的文獻資料), Peking, vol. II, 1982, pp. 145 ff; *Power Relations Within the Chinese Communist Movement, 1930–1934*, pp. 155–7.

21. *List*, pp. 146–50.

22. *Selected Works of Mao Zedong* (English edn), vol. III, pp. 187–92.

23. *Nanfang Daily* (南方日報), Canton, June 19, 1981.

24. *Power Relations Within The Chinese Communist Movement, 1930–1934*, pp. 240–1; *MZD* (Jap.), vol. III, pp. 299–301.

25. *PD*, July 14, 1983, p. 8.

26. *MZJ*, vol. IV, pp. 219–94 (see quotation on p. 284).

27. *MZJ*, vol. III, pp. 47–52.

28. *MZJ*, vol. IV, p. 250.

29. *Study Dictionary (Xue-xi ci-dian* 學習辭典), Peking, 1951, p. 31.

30. *Chinese Youth Daily (Zhongguo qing-nian bao* 中國青年報), Peking, June 23, 1981.

31. *Liaowang*, 瞭望 (fortnightly), no. 10, Peking, 1984, pp. 40–2.

32. *List*, pp. 208, 214.

33. *Peking Daily* (北京日報), June 26, 1981.

34. *List*, p. 164.

35. *Biographies of Personalities in the Party History of the CCP*, vol. X, 1983, p. 27; *Selection of Studies on Party History (Zhong-gong dang-shi yan-jiu lun-wen-xuan* 中共黨史研究論文選), Hunan: People's Publishing House, 1984, vol. II, p. 7; *PD*, April 4, 1984, p. 5.

36. Agnes Smedley, *The Great Road: The Life and Times of Chu Teh*, New York, 1956, p. 332.

37. *MHS*, no. 1, 1980.

38. *Workers Daily (Gong-ren Ri-bao* 工人日報), Peking, Feb. 4, 1980.

39. *MHS*, no. 1, 1983.

40. *PD*, Oct. 16, 1979, p. 3.

41. *Biographies of the Generals of the Liberation Army (Jie-fang-jun jiang-ling zhuan* 解放軍將領傳), 1st series, Peking, 1984, pp. 327, 495.

42. *Biographical Dictionary of Contemporary China*, Tokyo, 1982.

43. *Memoirs of Nie Rongzhen (Nie Rongzhen hui-yi-lu* 聶榮臻回憶錄), vol. I, Peking, 1983, pp. 303–14; *Peng Dehuai's Narration (Peng Dehuai Zi-shu* 彭德懷自述), Peking, 1981; *Biographies of the Generals of the Liberation Army (Jie-fang-jun Jiang-ling zhuan* 解放軍將領傳), 1st series, 1984, Peking.

44. *Party History Studies (Dang-shi yan-jiu* 黨史研究), no. 6, 1981, repr. in *Selection of Studies on Party History (Zhonggong dang-shi yan-jiu lun-wen xuan* 中共黨史研究論文選), 3 vols, Hunan: People's Publishing House, 1983, vol. II, p. 726.

45. *Peng Dehuai's Narration*, Peking, 1981; *Memoirs of Nie Rongzhen (Nie Rongzhen hui-yi-lu)*, vol. I, Peking, 1983, pp. 314 ff; *Biographies of the Generals of the Liberation*

Army, first series, Peking, 1984; *Selection of Studies on Party History*, vol. II, p. 726.

46. *Peng Dehuai's Narration*, pp. 217–8.
47. *Philosophical Research (Zhe-xue yan-jiu* 哲學研究), Peking, no. 11, 1979.
48. *Chronological Table of CCP History (Zhonggong dang-shi da-shi nian-biao* 中共黨史大事年表（內部）), 1981, published by the CCP Central Committee Party History Research Bureau, p. 48 (inner-Party publication).
49. *Liaowang* 瞭望 (monthly), Peking, no. 10, 1983, p. 43.
50. *List*, p. 192.

Chapter IV. In Yan'an, 1937–1948

1. *List*, pp. 196–8.
 2. Ibid, pp. 214–20.
 3. *RR*, no. 9, 1983; *PD*, April 20, 1984, p. 3; May 23, 1984, p. 5.
 4. *List*, pp. 230–1.
 5. P. Vladimir, *The Vladimir Diaries, Yan'an, China, 1942–48*, Moscow, 1975.
 6. *PD*, Mar. 23, 1985.
 7. *Reminiscences on Yan'an Central Research Academy (Yan'an zhong-yang yan-jiu-yuan hui-yi-lu* 延安中央研究院回憶錄), published jointly by the Chinese Academy of Social Science and Hunan People's Publishing House, 1984.
 8. Ibid.
 9. 'Rectify the Party's Style of Work' in *Selected Works of Mao Zedong* (English edn), vol. III; *The Great Victory of the First Party Reform (Zhongguo gong-chan-dang di-yi-ci zheng-feng yun-dong di wei-da sheng-li* 中國共產黨第一次整風運動的偉大勝利), Kirin, 1957, 40 pp.
10. 'Some Questions Concerning Methods of Leadership' in *Selected Works of Mao Zedong* (English edn), vol. III, pp. 117–22.
11. *Peking Daily*, 北京日報 , June 26, 1981.
12. Ibid.
13. *PD*, July 4, 1981, p. 3; *Nanfang Daily*, Canton, June 19, 1981.
14. *Outline of Chinese Contemporary History (1919–1949) (Zhongguo xian-dai shi-gao* 中國現代史稿（1919—1949）), 2 vols., Harbin, 1981, vol. II, pp. 188–91.
15. *RR*, no. 9, 1983, pp. 167–70.
16. *Reminiscences on Yan'an Central Research Academy*.
17. *Selected Works of Mao Zedong* (English edn), vol. III.
18. *PD*, Aug. 22, 1980, p. 5.
19. *MHS*, no. 1, 1982, pp. 13–28.
20. *Collection of Reports at a Conference on Party History (Dang-shi hui-yi bao-gao-ji* 黨史會議報告集（內部）), 1982 (inner-Party publication).

Chapter V. The Secret of Mao's Success

1. *PD*, June 10, 1982, p. 5.
 2. *PD*, Sept. 5, 1981, p. 7.
 3. *World Communism, A Handbook, 1918–1965*, pp. 87, 90.

4. *PD*, Apr. 4, 1984, p. 5.
5. *PD*, Jan. 27, 1985, p. 5.
6. *Party History Research Materials (Dang-shi yan-jiu zi-liao* 黨史研究資料（內部）), first series, Sichuan People's Publishing House, 1980 (inner-Party publication), pp. 410–14. For a detailed account of the Xi'an Incident see Tien-wei Wu, *The Sian Incident: A Pivotal Point in Modern Chinese History*, Ann Arbor, 1976, Michigan Papers in Chinese Studies, no. 26.

Chapter VI. The Japanese War, 1937–1945

1. Wan Ya-kang, *Simple History of the Chinese Communist Party*, Taipei-Hong Kong, 1951.
2. *RR*, no. 3, 1981, pp. 95–109.
3. *Wen Hui Bao*, 文滙報（上海）, Shanghai, Aug. 15, 1983.
4. *MHS*, no. 3, 1983, pp. 27–43.
5. David D. Barrett, *Dixie Mission: The US Army Observer Group in Yenan, 1944*, Berkeley, 1970, p. 82; *Introduction to the Amerasia Papers*, US Government Printing Office, Washington, DC, 1970, p. 90.
6. Tang Tsou, *America's Failure in China, 1941–50*, Chicago, 1963, pp. 233–5.
7. *Dixie Mission: The US Army Observer Group in Yenan, 1944*.
8. *Selected Works of Mao Zedong* (English edn), vol. III.
9. Ibid.
10. Cf. Jürgen Domes, *Vertagte Revolution: Die Politik der Kuomintang in China 1923–1937*, Berlin, 1969.
11. *Xinhua Monthly*, 新華月報, no. 7, 1951, p. 579.
12. *List*, p. 235.
13. Xu Yuandong, *et al.*, *Talk on the History of the Chinese Communist Party (Zhongguo gong-chan-dang li-shi jiang-hua* 徐元冬等：中國共產黨歷史講話), Chinese Youth Publishing House, 1962, revised edn, 1981, p. 396.
14. *MHS*, no. 2, 1985, p. 155.
15. *Selected Works of Mao Zedong* (English edn), vol.IV, Peking, 1965, p. 55.
16. Jacques Guillermaz, *Histoire du Parti Communiste Chinois 1921–1949*, Paris, 1968, p. 374; *Monthly Account of the Events of the 3rd Internal Revolutionary War (Di-san-ci guo-nei ge-ming zhan-zheng da-shi yue-biao* 第三次國內革命戰爭大事月表), Peking, 1961, pp. 9–10.
17. *Histoire du Parti Communiste Chinois 1921–1949*, p. 382.

Chapter VII. Marxism in Yan'an

1. *GMD*, Sept. 1, 1979.
2. *MHS*, no. 2, 1979, p. 119.
3. Cf. *Biographical Dictionary of Chinese Communism 1921–1965*, under 'Yeh Ting'.
4. *Selected Works of Mao Zedong* (English edn), vol. III, Peking, 1965, p. 38.
5. Ibid., pp. 63–5.
6. Ibid., pp. 69–98.

7. *PD*, Mar. 8, 1982, p. 5; *GMD*, Apr. 10 and July 3, 1982; *CNA*, no. 1242, pp. 6–7.

8. *GMD*, Dec. 28, 1982; *CNA*, no. 1242, p. 6.

9. *China Quarterly*, no. 9, London, July/Sept.1964.

10. Stuart R. Schram, *The Political Thought of Mao Tse-tung*, New York, 1963, pp. 120–35.

11. Raymond F. Wylie, 'Ch'en Po-ta and the Sinification of Marxism, 1936–1938', *China Quarterly*, no. 79 (Sept. 1979).

12. Nick Knight, 'Mao Zedong's On Contradiction and On Practice: Pre-Liberation texts', *China Quarterly*, no. 84 (Dec. 1980).

13. *GMD*, Feb. 14, 1982.

14. *Bulletin of Library Science (Tu-shu-guan xue tong-xun)*, no. 4, Peking, 1983, p. 35.

15. Karl A. Wittfogel, 'Some Remarks on Mao's Handling of Concepts and Problems of Dialectics' in *Studies of Soviet Thought*, vol. IV (Dec. 1963), Dordrecht, pp. 251–77.

16. *MZJ* (Jap.), vol. VI, pp. 265–304.

17. *Philosophical Research (Zhe-xue yan-jiu* 哲學研究 *)*, no. 6, Peking, 1983, p. 12.

18. Gustav A. Wetter, *Dialectical Materiali.m*, transl. from German with the author's additions, London, 1958, p. 212.

19. Ibid., pp. 128–76.

20. *Commemorating the 60th Anniversary of the CCP (Zhong-gong liu-shi-nian ji-nian wen-xuan* 中共六十年紀念文選 *)*, Peking, 1982, p. 369.

21. *GMD*, Feb. 14, 1982.

22. *History of the Communist Party of the Soviet Union (Bolsheviks), Short Course*, Moscow, 1951, p. 172.

23. Ibid., pp. 171–2.

24. M.B. Mitin, *Dictionary of Dialectical Materialism (Bian-zheng-fa wei-wu-lun ci-dian* 辯證法唯物論辭典 *)*, 4th edn, Shanghai-Zhongqing, 1947, preface to 1939 Chinese translation, p. 22.

25. Gustav A. Wetter, *Dialectical Materialism*, pp. 218–9.

26. Quoted in M.M. Rozental, *Materialist Dialectics (Wei-wu bian-zheng-fa* 唯物辯證法 *)*, Hong Kong, 1949, p. 119. This is a translation of the 2nd Russian edn of 1941. The Chinese translation's preface is dated Shanghai, 1946.

27. *Selected Works of Mao Zedong* (English edn), vol. V, Peking, 1977, pp. 367–9.

28. Ibid., vol. III, p. 90.

29. *PD*, May 26, 1981, p. 1.

30. *PD*, Nov. 19, 1981, p. 5.

31. *PD*, Jan. 12, 1982, p. 5.

Chapter VIII. Underground Party Workers

1. *PD*, Jan. 24, 1979, p. 2.

2. *Wen Hui Bao*, 文滙報（上海）, Shanghai, Apr. 28, 1979.

3. *LD*, 解放日報 , Shanghai, Apr. 9, 1980.

4. *PD*, Mar. 25, 1980, p. 4.

5. *PD*, Oct. 12, 1983, p. 5.

6. *MHS*, no. 1, 1983, pp. 131–3, 147–8. Biographical notes are taken from *Ci Hai* (History).

7. *LD*, Shanghai, Apr. 9, 1980.

8. *PD*, Aug. 8, 1979, p. 6.

9. See *Biographical Dictionary of Chinese Communism*, under 'Hu Yu-chih'.

10. *Wen Hui Bao*, Shanghai, June 17, 1983.

11. *Ci Hai* (History), see under 'Du Zhongyuan' 杜重遠..

12. *PD*, Dec. 9, 1980, p. 4.

13. *Ci Hai* (History), see under 'Liu Shaoqı' 劉少奇.

14. *Ci Hai*, 1979 edn, vol. I, p. 418.

15. *PD*, Dec. 27, 1958, p. 1.

16. *GMD*, Nov. 4, 1983.

17. *Literary Criticism (Wen-xue pin-lun* 文學評論), no. 2, 1980 (repr. in *PD*, Mar. 5, 1980, p. 5).

18. *PD*, Mar. 12, 1980, p. 5.

19. *PD*, Feb. 20, 1983, p. 3.

20. *PD*, Mar. 1, 1980, p. 5.

21. Ibid.

22. *PD*, Apr. 1, 1981, p. 1.

23. *Literary Criticism*, no. 1, 1980, pp. 92–101.

24. *Literary Criticism*, no. 3, 1978, pp. 10–33.

25. Su Hsueh-lin, 'Present-day Fiction and Drama in China' in Joseph Schyns, *1,500 Modern Novels and Plays*, Peking, 1948.

26. *PD*, Oct. 14, 1981, p. 4.

27. *Biographies Under the Republic (Ming-guo ren-wu-zhuan* 民國人物傳), vol. I, Peking, 1978, under 'Ma Xiangbo' 馬相伯.

28. *Wen Hui Bao*, Shanghai, Dec. 9, 1980; *Social Sciences (She-hui ke-xue* 社會科學（上海）   ), no. 4, Shanghai, 1983, pp. 87–91; *Record*, p. 119.

29. *PD*, May 22, 1981, p. 4.

30. *Wen Hui Bao*, Shanghai, Feb. 2, 1983.

31. *PD*, Sept. 1, 1985, p. 5.

32. *PD*, May 22, 1981, p. 4.

33. *PD*, May 30, 1981, p. 1; May 17, p. 1; May 15, p. 1.

34. *PD*, June 2, 1981, p. 3.

35. *PD*, July 14 and 15, 1983, p. 8.

36. *Selected Works of Zhou Enlai (Zhou Enlai xuan-ji* 周思來選集), vol. I, Peking, 1980, p. 415.

37. *Wen Hui Bao*, Shanghai, March 1, 1983.

38. *Wen Hui Bao*, Shanghai, Feb. 10, 1983.

39. *PD*, Feb. 4, 1983, p. 8.

40. *PD*, Mar. 7, 1983, p. 8.

41. *Social Sciences (She-hui ke-xue* 社會科學（上海）), Shanghai, no. 1, 1985, pp. 69–72.

42. *PD*, Mar. 21, 1985, p. 4.

43. *Reminiscences on Xinhua Daily (Xinhua Ri-bao di hui-yi* 新華日報的回憶), 2nd series, Sichuan People's Publishing House, 1983, pp. 17–23.

44. *PD*, Mar. 21, 1984, p. 5.

45. *PD*, Jan. 24, 1979, p. 2.

46. *Peking Daily*, Sept. 9, 1981.
47. *LD* 解放日報 (上海), May 9, 1979.
48. *PD*, Apr. 27, 1979, p. 1.
49. Emily Hahn, *The Soong Sisters*, London, 1941, p. 211.
50. *Ci Hai* (History), p. 137.
51. *PD*, Mar. 26, 1980, p. 4; Mar. 21, 1983, p. 4.
52. *Xinhua Daily* 新華日報 (南京), Nanjing, June 25, 1981.
53. *PD*, Feb. 13, 1981, p. 5.
54. *RR*, no. 9, 1983, p. 171.
55. *Nanfang Daily* 南方日報 , Canton, June 29, 1983.
56. *PD*, Jan. 24, 1979, p. 2.
57. *China Handbook*, New York, 1950, p. 276.
58. *PD*, Feb. 12, Mar. 6, 1985.
59. *PD*, Apr. 27, 1979, p. 1.
60. *PD*, Sept. 10, 1983, p. 4.

Chapter IX. Conquest of the Country, 1947–1949

1. *Why Was the Mainland Lost (Wei-shen-mo shi-qu da-lu* 為什麼失去大陸), Taipei, 1964, vol. II, pp. 411–31 (8th vol. of *Second Series of Modern Chinese History Materials*).
2. *Monthly Account of the Events of the Third Internal Revolutionary War in China (Di san-ci quo-nei ge-ming zhan-zheng da-shi yue-biao* 第三次國內革命戰爭大事月表), Peking, 1961.
3. Ibid., pp. 52–3; *List*, pp. 248–52.
4. *Selected Works of Mao Zedong*, vol. IV (English edn), Peking, 1961, pp. 197–9.
5. *Collection of Japanese Materials on New China* 新中國資料集成 , Tokyo, 1964, vol. II, p. 43.
6. *List*, pp. 265–73.

Chapter X. Dirty Linen

1. *PD*, Aug. 31, 1978, p. 2.
2. *Nanfang Daily* 南方日報 , Canton, Nov. 11, 1981.
3. *List*, p. 138–45.
4. *Frontline of the Social Sciences (She-kui ke-xue zhan-xian* 社會科學戰線) (quarterly), no. 3, Jilin, 1980, pp. 6–11.
5. *PD*, June 6, 1979, p. 1; *Da Gong Bao*, 大公報 (香港), Hong Kong, June 15, 1979.
6. *Frontline of the Social Sciences*, no. 3, Jilin, 1980, pp. 6–11.
7. *Ci Hai* (History), p. 137.
8. *PD*, Aug. 14, 1983, p. 5.
9. *Party History Study Materials (Dang-shi yan-jiu zi-liao* 黨史研究資料 (內部)), first series, Sichuan People's Publishing House, 1980.
10. *Collection of Reports at a Conference on Party History (Dang-shi hui-yi bao-gao-ji* 黨史會議報告集 (內部)), Peking, 1982, p. 102.

11. Tso-liang Hsiao, *Power Relations Within the Chinese Communist Movement 1930–1934. A Study of Documents*, Seattle, 1961, p. 146.
12. *Biographical Dictionary of Chinese Communism*, see under 'Ch'in Pang-hsien'.
13. *Power Relations Within the Chinese Communist Movement, 1930–1934, A Study of Documents*, p. 146.
14. *Biographies of Personalities in the Party History of the CCP*, vol. VI, p. 45.
15. *GMD*, Mar. 12, 1978.
16. *LD* 解放日報, Dec. 9 and 10, 1979; *PD*, Jan. 23, 1981, p. 5.
17. *Selected Works of Mao Zedong*, vol. III (English edn), p. 190.
18. Kong Yongsong and Lin Tianyi, 'The World of Fujian and Jiangxi — the Battles of the Red Army in Fujian and Jiangxi and the Struggle to set up the West-Fujian Base' ('Min-gan lu qian-li — hong-jun zhuan-zhan min-gan yu chuang-zao min-xi gen-ju-di di dou-zheng' 孔永松・林天乙：閩贛路千里—紅軍轉戰閩贛與創建閩西根據地的門爭), passage repr. in *MHS*, no. 3, 1983, pp. 244–7.
19. Ibid., pp. 244–5.
20. *PD*, Aug. 2, 1978, p. 2.
21. Published in the August 1969 Red Guard edition of Mao's unedited speeches, entitled *Long Live the Mao Zedong Thought (Mao Zedong si-xiang wan-sui* 毛澤東思想萬歲), pp. 476–7; *CNA*, no. 1001, p. 6.
22. *PD*, Aug. 2, 1978, p. 2; *MHS*, no. 1, 1980.
23. *Biographies of Personalities in the Party History of the CCP*, vol. II, pp. 126–62.
24. *BD* (Jap.).
25. *Wen Hui Bao* 文滙報(上海) , Shanghai, July 1, 1980.
26. *PD*, Jan. 22, 1983, p. 4.
27. *Masses Daily (Qun-zhong ri-bao* 羣眾日報), Jinan, May 20, 1980.
28. *PD*, Dec. 29, 1980, p. 5.
29. *GMD*, Mar. 20, 1980.
30. *PD*, Feb. 10, 1983, p. 5.
31. *Wen Hui Bao* 文滙報(上海) , Shanghai, Mar. 9, 1980.

Chapter XI. Ruling the Country

1. *Record.* 中國近現代史大事記
2. See ch. IX of the present work, p. 184.
3. Helmut Dahm, 'Das ideologische Führungsamt', unpubl. research paper, Bundesinstitut für ostwissenschaftliche und internationale Studien, Cologne, 1983.
4. *Xinhua Monthly*, 新華日報 , July 1950, pp. 498–500.
5. *Chang Jiang Daily* 長江日報 , Wuhan, Sept. 4, 1951.
6. Ibid., Dec. 9, 1951.
7. *PD*, May 3, 1951.
8. *Chang Jiang Daily*, Wuhan, Nov. 15, 1951.
9. *LD* 解放日報, Nov. 29, 1951.
10. *CNA*, no. 1224, p. 3.

11. *LD*, Mar. 16, 1951.
12. *PD* (editorial), Dec. 29, 1950; Xinhua News Agency, Peking, Dec. 28, 1950.
13. *PD*, Sept. 19, 1951.
14. *PD*, Feb. 22, 1951.
15. Ibid.
16. *PD*, Feb. 24, 1951.
17. *PD*, Apr. 20, 1951.
18. *LD*, Apr. 30, 1951.
19. *Xinhua Monthly* , Apr., 1951, pp. 1241–3.
20. Ibid., pp. 1238–40.
21. *LD*, Apr. 4, 1951 (reprint of a *PD* editorial).
22. *PD*, May 31, 1951, reprinted in *Xinhua Monthly*, June 1951, pp. 261–2.
23. *Xinhua Monthly*, June 1951, p. 259.
24. *PD*, July 12, 1951.
25. *PD*, Aug. 23, 1951.
26. *PD*, Oct. 1, 1951.
27. *PD*, Sept. 14, 1956, p. 1.
28. *Xinhua Monthly*, June 1951, pp. 267–8.
29. Ibid., pp. 269–70.
30. *Xinhua Monthly*, 1951, pp. 1245–6.
31. *Selected Works of Mao Zedong* (English edn), vol. IV, pp. 417–8. Emphasis added.
32. *Xinhua Monthly*, Jan. 1952, p. 15.
33. Ibid., p. 5.
34. *Chang Jiang Daily*, Wuhan, Jan. 11, 1952, p. 1.
35. *PD*, Dec. 27, 1951, p .4.
36. *PD*, Dec. 16, 1951, reprinted in *Xinhua Monthly*, Jan. 1952, pp. 7–8.
37. *Xinhua Monthly*, Dec. 1951, pp. 13–17.
38. *Xinhua Monthly*, Jan. 1952, p. 15.
39. *PD*, Feb. 13, 1952.
40. *PD*, Mar. 12, 1952.
41. *PD*, Mar. 31, 1952.
42. *PD*, Feb. 2, 1952.
43. *PD*, Mar. 8, 1952.
44. *PD*, Sept. 13, 1951.
45. *PD*, Jan. 1, 1952.
46. *PD*, Feb. 10, 1953.
47. *PD*, May 19, 1957; *CNA*, no. 184, p. 3.
48. *Teaching Material on the History of the CCP (Zhongguo Gongchandang Lishi Jiangyi* 中國共產黨歷史講義), Shanghai, 1981, vol. II, p. 6.
49. Zhao Han, *Talking about the Zheng Feng Movement of the CCP (Tan-tan Zhongguo Gongchandang Zhengfeng Yundong)*, 談談中國共產黨的整風運動·趙漢著 , Chinese Youth Publishing House, 1975.
50. *Xinhua Monthly*, July, 1950, pp. 505–6.
51. *CNA*, no. 13.
52. *Xinhua Monthly*, July, 1951, p. 579.
53. *CNA*, no. 12, pp.2–4.
54. *PD*, Feb. 10, 1953.
55. *Chang Jiang Daily*, June 24, 1952.

56. *South Sichuan Daily*, 川南日報 , Oct. 23, 1952.
57. *Chang Jiang Daily*, Aug. 7, 1952.
58. *CNA*, no. 13.
59. *PD*, Jan. 12, 1952.
60. *PD*, May 25, 1953.
61. *PD*, July 13, 1952.
62. *Chang Jiang Daily*, Sept. 1, 1952.
63. *PD*, Nov. 2, 1953, editorial.
64. *PD*, Mar. 21, 1954.
65. *PD*, May 1, 1954.
66. *PD*, June 30, 1954.
67. *PD*, July 2, 1954.
68. *Xinhua Fortnightly*, 新華半月刊 , no. 2, 1956, p. 19.
69. *CNA*, no. 14, p. 6.
70. *CNA*, nos. 20, 65.
71. *CNA*, nos. 60, 68.
72. *CNA*, nos. 68, 89.
73. *GMD*, Peking, July 26, 1955.
74. *PD*, July 27, 1955.
75. *CNA*, no. 43, p. 3.
76. *Xinhua Monthly*, no. 21, July 25, 1951, p. 579.
77. *PD*, Feb. 18, 1954; *CNA*, no. 34.
78. *CNA*, no. 80.
79. *PD*, June 24, 1956, p. 5.
80. *PD*, Sept. 20, 1956, p. 4.
81. *Xue Xi Monthly*, 學習月刊 , no. 1, Peking, 1958 (quoted in *CNA*, no. 214).

Chapter XII. Mao and the Party, 1956–1958

1. *CNA*, no. 106; *PD*, Oct. 16, 1955.
2. *CNA*, no. 105.
3. *CNA*, no. 96, p. 4; 69.
4. *CNA*, no. 120.
5. *CNA*, no. 138.
6. *CNA*, nos. 155, 156.
7. *CNA*, no. 127.
8. *CNA*, no. 131.
9. *CNA*, nos. 102, 132.
10. *CNA*, no. 146.
11. *PD*, May 19, 1955, editorial.
12. *CNA*, no. 146.
13. *PD*, Jan. 18, 1956, editorial.
14. *CNA*, no. 146.
15. Figures for 1956 in *Ten Great Years* (statistical tables 偉大的十年), Peking, 1959.
16. *PD*, Sept. 15, 1956, p. 1; *CNA* no. 151, p. 1.
17. *1950 People's Yearbook (1950 Renmin Nianjian* 人民年鑑 · 香港大公報出版   ), Hong Kong: *Da Gong Bao*.

18. *Xinhua Fortnightly*, no. 20, 1956, p. 171.
19. *CNA*, no. 9, p. 6.
20. *CNA*, no. 743, p. 2.
21. *CNA*, no. 757, p. 3.
22. *CNA*, no. 152.
23. *CNA*, nos. 156, p. 3; 163, p. 2.
24. *CNA*, no. 163.
25. *CNA*, no. 205, p. 2.
26. *CNA*, no. 202, pp. 2–3.
27. *CNA*, no. 205, p. 7.
28. *CNA*, no. 485, p. 3.
29. *CNA*, no. 205, p. 7.
30. *CNA*, no. 485, p. 5.
31. *CNA*, no. 205, p. 3
32. *CNA*, no. 205.
33. *Khrushchev Remembers*, London, 1971, pp. 424, 438.

Chapter XIII. 1957: The Trap

1. *PD*, June 19, 1957; *Xinhua Fortnightly*, no. 13, 1957; *CNA*, no. 187.
2. *PD*, March 5, 1957; *CNA*, no. 173.
3. *PD*, May 1, 1957; *Xinhua Fortnightly*, no. 10, 1957; *CNA*, no. 181, p. 5.
4. *CNA*, nos. 168, 177.
5. *CNA*, no. 195.
6. *CNA*, no. 181.
7. *CNA*, no. 182.
8. *CNA*, nos. 182, 183.
9. *PD*, June 8, 1957, editorial.
10. *CNA*, no. 187.
11. *CNA*, no. 194.
12. *CNA*, no. 185.
13. *Wen Hui Bao*, Hong Kong, 香港文滙報, Dec. 23, 1982.
14. *CNA*, nos. 184, 185, 187, 193.
15. *CNA*, no. 193.
16. *PD*, July, 1957, editorial; reprinted in *Selected Works of Mao Zedong*, vol. V.
17. *CNA*, no. 203.
18. *CNA*, no. 231; *Xinhua Fortnightly*, no. 15, 1958, pp. 64–73.
19. *CNA*, no. 216; *Xinhua Fortnightly*, no. 7, 1958, pp. 40–1.
20. *Selected Works of Mao Zedong*, vol. V, 1977 (English edn), pp. 483–97.
21. *PD*, Oct. 19, 1957; *Xinhua Fortnightly*, no. 22, 1957.
22. *CNA*, no. 235, p. 4.
23. *Peking Daily (Beijing Ribao)*, Feb. 7, 1979; Henan Radio broadcast, Mar. 28, 1979; *Da Gong Bao*, Hong Kong, May 19, 1978; *LD*, Shanghai, Oct. 26, 1980.
24. *PD*, Aug. 18, 1980, p. 1.

Chapter XIV. Shock to Marxism

1. *Philosophical Research (Zhexue Yanjiu* 哲學研究), Peking, no. 4, 1958, p. 14.
2. Ibid., no. 3, 1958, p. 1.
3. Ibid., no. 6, 1957, p. 6.
4. Ibid.
5. *Chinese Social Sciences (Zhong-guo she-hui ke-xue* 中國社會科學), no. 5, 1981.
6. *CNA*, no. 191.
7. 'On the Correct Handling of Contradictions among the People', in *Selected Works of Mao Zedong*, vol. V., Peking, 1977.
8. *CNA*, no. 217, p. 4.

Chapter XV. 1958–1959: The Leap

1. *Teaching Material on the History of the CCP*, Shanghai, 1981, vol. II, p. 69.
2. *PD*, Feb. 3, 1958; reprinted in *Xinhua Fortnightly*, no. 5, 1958.
3. *Teaching Material on the History of the CCP*, vol. II, p. 69.
4. *CNA*, no. 231; *Xinhua Fortnightly*, no. 11, 1958.
5. *CNA*, no. 231; *Xinhua Fortnightly*, no. 11, 1958, p. 19.
6. *CNA*, no. 246.
7. *Xinhua Fortnightly*, no. 9, 1958.
8. *PD*, Aug. 11, 12, 13, 1958; *Xinhua Fortnightly*, no. 16, 1958.
9. *GMD* 光明日報 , Aug. 4, 1958; *Xinhua Fortnightly*, no. 16, 1958.
10. *CNA*, no. 278.
11. *Xinhua Fortnightly*, no. 18, 1958, p. 1.
12. *CNA*, no. 254, p. 4.
13. *CNA*, no. 1153, p. 2.
14. *CNA*, no. 258; *Xinhua Fortnightly*, no. 24, 1958.
15. *PD*, Apr. 8, 1959; *Xinhua Fortnightly*, no. 8, 1959.
16. *Xinhua Fortnightly*, no. 9, 1959.
17. *Selected Writings of Deng Xiaoping (Deng Xiaoping Wenxuan* 鄧小平文選), Peking 1983, p. 260.
18. *CNA*, no. 293, p. 4.
19. *CNA*, no. 294, p. 2.
20. *CNA*, no. 685.
21. *PD*, Mar. 25, 1982, p. 5; Aug. 13, 1981, p. 5.
22. *CNA*, no. 1145, pp. 4–5.
23. *CNA*, nos. 1148, p. 3; 1153, p. 2.
24. *Peng Dehuai's Narration (Peng Dehuai Zi-shu* 彭德懷自述), Peking, 1981, pp. 265–89 (2.7 million copies were published).
25. *Record*, p. 163.
26. *CNA*, no. 1153, p. 2n.
27. *PD*, Dec. 31, 1981, p. 5.
28. Ibid.
29. *Xinhua Fortnightly*, no. 16, 1958, p. 1.
30. *CNA*, no. 249, p. 6.
31. *CNA*, no. 297.

32. *CNA*, no. 279.
33. *CNA*, no. 485, p. 3.
34. *CNA*, no. 278, pp. 4–5.
35. *CNA*, no. 279.
36. Karl Marx, Friedrich Engels, *Ausgewählte Werke*, vol. IV, Berlin, 1972.
37. V.I. Lenin, *The State and Revolution*, Moscow, 1952; *CNA*, no. 278, pp. 2–3.
38. *Politische Ökonomie, Lehrbuch*, Berlin, 1955, first published as *Politicheskaya Economiya*, Moscow, 1954.
39. *PD*, Jan. 29, 1959; *Xinhua Fortnightly*, no. 4, 1959, pp. 50–3.
40. *CNA*, nos. 271, p. 6; 279, p.6.
41. *CNA*, no. 638, p. 7.
42. C.D. Kernig (ed.), *Marxism, Communism and Western Socialism: A Comparative Encyclopaedia*, vol. II, New York, 1972, pp. 78–9.
43. *CNA*, no. 278, p. 5.
44. *CNA*, no. 279, p. 5.

Chapter XVI. The Years 1960–1965

1. *PD*, Nov. 21, p. 7; Dec. 9, 1960 p.7; *CNA*, no. 357, pp. 3–4.
2. *CNA*, no. 331, p. 6.
3. *CNA*, no. 364.
4. *CNA*, no. 365, p. 4.
5. *CNA*, no. 404, p. 4.
6. *CNA*, nos. 364, 382.
7. *CNA*, nos. 1182, p. 7; 1187, p. 3.
8. *CNA*, no. 1153, p. 2.
9. *Sociology (She Hui* 社會), no. 3, Shanghai, 1984, p. 19.
10. *Statistical Yearbook of China (Zhongguo Tongji Nianjian* 中國統計年鑑), Peking 1984, p. 83.
11. *CNA*, no. 367.
12. *CNA*, no. 358, p. 7.
13. *CNA*, no. 357, p. 7.
14. *Hail Mao Zedong Thought (Mao Zedong Sixiang wansui* 毛澤東思想萬歲), Peking, 1967, p. 258 ff.
15. *CNA*, nos. 399; 537.
16. *CNA*, no. 371, p. 2.
17. *Statistical Yearbook of China*, 1981.
18. *CNA*, nos. 395, p. 5; 404, p. 3; 377, p. 6; 372, p. 6.
19. *CNA*, no. 393.
20. Ibid.
21. *CNA*, nos. 441; 457.
22. *Hail Mao Zedong Thought*, 1969, pp. 430–6.
23. *CNA*, nos. 441, p. 3n; 1177, p. 2.
24. *CNA*, no. 432, pp. 6–7.
25. *Selection of Writings of Comrade Chen Yun (Chen Yun Tong-zhi wen-gao xuan-bian* 陳雲同志文稿選編（內部）), 1956–62, Peking, 1980 (inner-Party publication).
26. *CNA*, no. 639, p. 7.

27. *CNA*, nos. 395, p. 2; 459, p. 7.
28. *CNA*, no. 452.
29. *CNA*, no. 474.
30. *CNA*, no. 812, p. 5.
31. *CNA*, no. 479, pp. 3–4.
32. *CNA*, no. 542.
33. *CNA*, no. 567.
34. *CNA*, no. 545; *Record*, pp. 172–3.
35. *CNA*, no. 574.
36. *CNA*, no. 592.
37. *CNA*, nos. 560, p. 7; 519, pp. 3–4.
38. *CNA*, no. 607.
39. *CNA*, no. 620, pp. 2–3.
40. *CNA*, nos. 436; 578, p. 3.
41. *CNA*, no. 538.
42. *CNA*, no. 537, p. 6.
43. *CNA*, no. 581.
44. *CNA*, no. 557.
45. *Selected Readings of the Works of Mao Zedong (Mao Zedong Zhu-zuo xuan-du* 毛澤東著作選讀), Peking, 1965.
46. *CNA*, no. 635, p. 4.
47. *CNA*, no. 428.
48. *Collection of the Original Documents Concerning the Lin Biao Affair (Lin Biao Shijian Yuanshi Wenjian Huibian* 中國革命史250題解答), China Mainland Research Institute, Taipei, 1973.
49. *CNA*, no. 518.
50. *CNA*, no. 518, p. 6.
51. *CNA*, no. 535.
52. *250 Questions and Answers on the History of the Chinese Revolution (Zhongguo Gemingshi 250 ti jieda* 林彪事件原始文件彙編), by the Marxist-Leninist teaching staff at the Shanghai Jiaotong University, Shanghai, 1983, p. 244.
53. *CNA*, no. 622, p. 4.
54. *CNA*, no. 683.
55. *CNA*, nos. 529, p. 7; 557, pp. 5–7.
56. *CNA*, no. 559.
57. *CNA*, no. 523.
58. *CNA*, no. 643.
59. *CNA*, nos. 563; 720.
60. *CNA*, no. 1156, p. 2.
61. Li Weihan, *The Question of the United Front and Nationalities (Tongyi Zhanxian Wenti yu Minzu Wenti* 統一戰線問題與民族問題‧李維漢著), Peking, 1981; *CNA*, no. 1222.
62. *CNA*, nos. 506; 507.
63. *CNA*, no. 561, p. 3.
64. *CNA*, nos. 663, p. 4; 432, p. 7.
65. *Record*, pp. 169–71.
66. *Source Material on the Question of Liu Shaoqi (Liu Shaoqi Wenti Ziliao Zhuanji* 劉少奇問題資料專輯), Taipei, 1970, p. 624.

67. *Record*, pp. 172–3.
68. *CNA*, no. 632.
69. *CNA*, no. 570, p. 6.
70. *CNA*, no. 954, p. 6.
71. *CNA*, no. 756, p. 4.

Chapter XVII. The Cultural Revolution and Lin Biao, 1966–1971

1. *CNA*, no. 557.
2. *CNA*, no. 607, pp. 6–7.
3. *CNA*, no. 609, pp. 4–5.
4. *Record*, pp. 174–5.
5. *CNA*, no. 597.
6. *Record*, p. 175.
7. *Record*, p. 175.
8. *CNA*, nos. 664, p. 6; 789, pp. 3–4.
9. *250 Questions on the History of the Chinese Revolution*, Shanghai, 1983, pp. 244–5.
10. Ibid., p. 243.
11. *CNA*, no. 664, p. 6.
12. *CNA*, no. 615.
13. *CNA*, no. 633.
14. *Red Flag (Hong-qi 红旗)*, Peking, no. 13, 1967.
15. *CNA*, no. 626.
16. Ibid.
17. *CNA*, no. 629; *Peking Review*, no. 37, Sept. 9, 1966.
18. *CNA*, no. 661, p. 3.
19. *CNA*, nos. 629; 627, p. 7.
20. *CNA*, no. 642, pp. 1–2.
21. *Record*, p. 177.
22. *CNA*, nos. 642, p. 4; 637, p. 4.
23. *CNA*, no. 642, pp. 3–4.
24. *CNA*, nos. 644; 645.
25. *CNA*, no. 646.
26. *CNA*, no. 681, p. 3.
27. *CNA*, no. 663, pp. 1–2.
28. *CNA*, no. 655, p. 3.
29. *CNA*, no. 664, p. 4.
30. *CNA*, nos. 653; 654; 682.
31. *Xinhua Digest (Xinhua Wenzhai 新华文摘月刊)*, monthly, Peking, no. 12, 1984, p. 151 ff.
32. *Record*, pp. 178–9.
33. *CNA*, no. 671, p. 5.
34. *CNA*, no. 671.
35. *CNA*, no. 727, p. 3.
36. *CNA*, nos. 728, p. 1; 724, p. 6.
37. *CNA*, no. 961, p. 2.
38. *CNA*, no. 688, p. 5.

39. *Red Flag*, no. 3, 1967, p. 17; *CNA*, no. 682, p. 6.
40. *PD*, Feb. 26, 1979, p. 2; *CNA*, no. 1153, p. 8.
41. *CNA*, no. 680, pp. 3–4; *Red Flag*, no. 14, 1967.
42. *PD*, Sept. 3, 1967, p. 1.
43. *CNA*, no. 690, p. 3.
44. *CNA*, no. 684, p. 6.
45. *Collection of Secret Documents of the CCP (Zhonggong Jimi Wenjian Huibian* 中共機密文件彙編), Political International Relations Research Center, Taipei, 1978.
46. *PD*, Apr. 9, 1968, p. 3; *Reminiscences on Xinhua Daily (Xinhua Ribao di Hui-yi* 新華日報的回憶), 2nd series, Sichuan: People's Publishing Press, 1983, pp. 3–16.
47. *CNA*, no. 862, pp. 4–5.
48. *CNA*, no. 680, p. 1.
49. Record, p. 179; *CNA*, nos. 609, p. 4; 706, p. 4.
50. *CNA*, no. 681; *Red Flag*, no. 14, 1967, p. 16.
51. *CNA*, nos. 684, p. 2; 688, pp. 2–3.
52. *CNA*, no. 661.
53. Ibid.
54. *CNA*, no. 690, p. 3.
55. *Yearbook on Chinese Communism (Zhonggong Nianbao* 中共年報), Taipei, 1969, Section 7, pp. 45–8.
56. *CNA*, no. 690, p. 3.
57. *CNA*, no. 642, p. 2.
58. *CNA*, no. 690, p. 3.
59. *CNA*, nos. 688, p. 1; 662.
60. *CNA*, no. 840.
61. *CNA*, no. 711, pp. 1–2.
62. *Yearbook on Chinese Communism (Zhonggong Nianbao)*, Taipei, 1968, pp. 165–6.
63. *CNA*, no. 699.
64. *CNA*, no. 742.
65. *CNA*, nos. 703, p. 7; 707, p. 5.
66. *Yearbook on Chinese Communism (Zhonggong Nianbao)*, Taipei, 1968, Section 3, p. 9.
67. *Xinhua Digest (Xinhua Wenzhai)*, monthly, Peking, no. 12, 1984, p. 151 ff.
68. *CNA*, no. 707, p. 1.
69. *CNA*, no. 730.
70. *CNA*, nos. 729, p. 6; 739, pp. 3–4.
71. *CNA*, no. 710.
72. *CNA*, no. 731, p. 4.
73. *PD*, Feb. 8, 1983, p. 1.
74. *PD*, Aug. 2, 1984, p. 1.
75. *CNA*, no. 751, pp. 5–6.
76. *CNA*, nos. 705; 710.
77. *CNA*, no. 739, p. 6.
78. *CNA*, nos. 732, 743; p. 2.
79. *CNA*, no. 746.
80. *CNA*, no. 756.
81. *CNA*, no. 757.

82. *CNA*, no. 758.
83. *CNA*, no. 763.
84. *CNA*, no. 754, p. 5.
85. *CNA*, nos. 730; 754.
86. *CNA*, no. 745, p. 5.
87. *CNA*, no. 1199, p. 5.
88. *CNA*, nos. 768, p. 2; 797, p. 4.
89. *CNA*, no. 743.
90. *CNA*, no. 813.
91. *CNA*, no. 768.
92. *CNA*, no. 814.
93. *CNA*, nos. 817, p. 4; 821, p. 2.
94. *CNA*, no. 817.
95. *CNA*, nos. 851; 848; 849, p. 2.
96. *CNA*, no. 1199.
97. *CNA*, no. 838, p. 4.
98. *CNA*, no. 839.
99. *CNA*, no. 380.
100. *CNA*, no. 848.
101. *CNA*, no. 852, p. 3.
102. *CNA*, no. 857, p. 5.
103. *CNA*, nos. 857; 862, p. 5.
104. *CNA*, nos. 862; 866.
105. *Collection of the Original Documents Concerning the Lin Biao Affair*, Taipei, 1973.
106. *CNA*, no. 857, p. 4.
107. *CNA*, nos. 934, p. 5; 896, p. 3n.
108. *CNA*, no. 823.
109. *CNA*, no. 793, p. 5.
110. *CNA*, no. 830.
111. *CNA*, no. 896.
112. *250 Questions on the History of the Chinese Revolution*, Shanghai, 1983, p. 262.
113. *CNA*, nos. 896, p. 6; 871.
114. *PD*, May 1, 1966, p. 1.
115. *CNA*, no. 862, p. 5.
116. *CNA*, no. 897.
117. *CNA*, nos. 876, p. 7; 921; 924, p. 5.
118. *CNA*, no. 924, p. 5.
119. *CNA*, no. 870.
120. *CNA*, no. 756, p. 7.
121. *CNA*, no. 840.
122. *CNA*, no. 690, p. 4.
123. *CNA*, no. 719, p. 4.
124. *CNA*, no. 790, p. 4.
125. *CNA*, no. 790.
126. *CNA*, nos. 797; 833.
127. *Yearbook on Chinese Communism*, Taipei, 1972, Section 2, p. 18.

128. *CNA*, no. 859, p. 7.
129. *CNA*, no. 686.
130. Wang Chien-min, *History of the CCP (Wang Jianmin: Zhong-guo Gong-chan-dang shi-gao* 中國共產黨史稿·王健民著), Taipei, vol. II, pp. 119 ff.
131. *Teaching Material on the History of the CCP*, Shanghai, 1981, vol. II, p. 69.
132. *Xinhua Fortnightly*, no. 11, 1958, p. 6.
133. *CNA*, no. 768.
134. *China Quarterly*, London, no. 46, p. 243.
135. *CNA*, no. 635, pp. 6–7.
136. *CNA*, no. 598, pp. 2, 4.
137. *CNA*, no. 635, p. 4.
138. *CNA*, nos. 768, p. 5; 814, p. 6.
139. *CNA*, no. 768.
140. *CNA*, no. 795, p. 1n.

Chapter XVIII. The Last Years of Mao, 1972–1976

1. *CNA*, no. 927, p. 2.
2. *CNA*, no. 872, p. 5.
3. *CNA*, no. 927, p. 2.
4. *CNA*, no. 892, pp. 5–6.
5. *CNA*, no. 927, pp. 3–4.
6. *CNA*, no. 870, p. 7.
7. *CNA*, nos. 872, p. 5; 927, p. 2.
8. *CNA*, no. 893, p. 7.
9. *CNA*, no. 877.
10. *CNA*, no. 905, p. 7.
11. *CNA*, no. 887, pp. 3–4.
12. *PD*, Oct. 14, 1972.
13. *Chronological Table of Major Events of the CCP (Zhonggong Dangshi Dashi Nianbiao* 中共黨史大事年報（內部）), Peking, 1981 (inner-Party publication).
14. *CNA*, nos. 911, p. 5; 912, p. 5.
15. *CNA*, no. 906, p. 5; *Chronological Table of Major Events of the CCP*.
16. Ibid.
17. *Red Flag*, no. 3, 1973; *CNA* nos. 911; 924.
18. *CNA*, no. 932.
19. *CNA*, no. 907, p. 7.
20. *CNA*, nos. 934; 907, p. 7.
21. *Record*, p. 187; *CNA* no. 1057, p. 2.
22. *PD*, Aug. 22, 1984.
23. *CNA*, no. 937.
24. *CNA*, no. 945.
25. *CNA*, no. 939.
26. *CNA*, nos. 951; 954.
27. *CNA*, no. 951, p. 6.
28. *CNA*, no. 946, pp. 3–5.
29. *CNA*, no. 954.

30. *CNA*, nos. 961; 955.
31. *CNA*, no. 974.
32. *CNA*, no. 948, p .3.
33. *CNA*, nos. 1096, p. 3; 1085, p. 7.
34. *CNA*, no. 940.
35. *CNA*, nos. 859; 868; 878, p. 5; 981; 1010; 1019.
36. *CNA*, no. 963.
37. *CNA*, nos. 989; 990; 991; 997.
38. *CNA*, no. 993.
39. *CNA*, no. 1004.
40. *Record*.
41. *CNA*, no. 1002, p. 5.
42. *CNA*, no. 1044.
43. *Record, BD* (Jap). *Biographical Dictionary of Contemporary China (Xiandai Zhongguo Renmin Cidian* 現代中國人名辭典), Foreign Office, Tokyo, 1982.
44. *CNA*, no. 1044.
45. *Chronological Table*, pp. 171–2.
46. *CNA*, no. 1041.
47. *CNA*, no. 1035, pp. 2–3.
48. *CNA*, no. 1028, pp. 2–3.
49. *CNA*, nos. 1019, p. 3; 1058, p. 5.
50. *CNA*, no. 1022.
51. *CNA*, nos. 1032, p. 3; 1039, p. 3; 1065, p. 7; *Chronological Table*.
52. *CNA*, no. 1032, p. 5.
53. *CNA*, no. 1035, pp. 5–6.
54. *CNA*, no. 1039.
55. *CNA*, no. 1043.
56. *CNA*, no. 1040, p. 3.
57. *Chronological Table*.
58. *CNA*, no. 1030.
59. *CNA*, no. 1040.
60. *CNA*, nos. 1052; 1054, p. 2.
61. *CNA*, no. 1058, p. 6.
62. *CNA*, no. 1040.
63. *Chronological Table*.
64. *CNA*, nos. 1055; 1059; 1076.
65. *CNA*, no. 1065, p. 5.

Chapter XIX. After Mao, 1976–1977

1. *CNA*, no. 1050, p. 7.
2. *CNA*, no. 1070, pp. 2–3; *Chronological Table*.
3. *CNA*, nos. 1060, p. 5; 1067.
4. *CNA*, no. 1067.
5. *CNA*, nos. 1065, p. 4; 1099, p. 6.
6. *CNA*, nos. 1062, pp. 2–3; 1060, p. 6.
7. *Chronological Table*, ch. XVII, p. 13.

8. *CNA*, no. 1085, p. 7.
9. *CNA*, nos. 1057, p. 1; 1081, p. 1.
10. *CNA*, nos. 1060, p. 5; 1066.
11. *CNA*, no. 1085, p. 3.
12. *CNA*, no. 1076.
13. *CNA*, nos. 1099; 1071.
14. *CNA*, no. 1086.
15. *CNA*, no. 1050, p. 6.
16. *CNA*, no. 1061, p. 5.
17. *CNA*, nos. 1090, p. 1; 1091, p. 6; 1095, p. 3.
18. *Chronological Table*.
19. *CNA*, no. 1095, p. 3.
20. *CNA*, no. 1095; *Documents of the Eleventh National Congress of the CCP*, Peking, 1977.
21. *CNA*, no. 1177, p. 4.
22. *Chronological Table*.
23. *CNA*, no. 1091.
24. *CNA*, nos. 1110, p. 2; 1118, p. 3.
25. *CNA*, no. 1121.

Chapter XX. Deng Up, 1978

1. *CNA*, nos. 1114; 1157.
2. *CNA*, no. 1128.
3. *CNA*, no. 1137.
4. *CNA*, no. 1142, p. 5.
5. *CNA*, no. 1142.
6. *CNA*, no. 1146.
7. *CNA*, no. 1152.
8. *CNA*, no. 1134.
9. *CNA*, no. 1155.

Chapter XXI. Two Camps, 1979–1984

1. *CNA*, no. 1153.
2. *CNA*, no. 1171, p. 2.
3. *Chronological Table*.
4. *Selected Writings of Deng Xiaoping*, Peking, 1983.
5. *PD*, May 25, 1979; *GMD*, Peking, June 24, 1979.
6. *PD*, Mar. 9, 1985, p. 3; *CNA* no. 1171, p. 6n.
7. *CNA*, nos. 1039, p. 4; 1142, p. 3; 1171, p. 1.
8. *CNA*, nos. 1168, p. 2; 1177.
9. *CNA*, no. 1168, p. 6.
10. *CNA*, nos. 1146; 1176; 1180.
11. *CNA*, nos. 1177; 1183.
12. *Yearbook on Chinese Communism*, Taipei, 1968, pp. 802 ff.

13. *Chronological Table.*
14. *CNA*, no. 1191.
15. *Chronological Table.*
16. *CNA*, no. 1201.
17. *Selected Writings of Deng Xiaoping*, Peking, 1983, pp. 313–33.
18. *CNA*, nos. 1185; 1189; 1203.
19. *CNA*, no. 1199.
20. *Wen Hui Bao*, Hong Kong, Oct. 11, 1984.
21. *CNA*, no. 1207.
22. *CNA*, nos. 1211, p. 3; 1219, p. 6.
23. *CNA*, no. 1211.
24. *Selected Writings of Deng Xiaoping*, Peking, 1983.
25. *CNA*, no. 1219, pp. 6–7.
26. *CNA*, no. 1215.
27. *PD*, Mar. 15, 1980.
28. *CNA*, nos. 1183, p. 4; 1185.
29. *CNA*, nos. 1218; 1220, p. 6.
30. *CNA*, no. 1232.
31. *CNA*, no. 1193.
32. *CNA*, no. 1195.
33. *CNA*, no. 1214.
34. *CNA*, no. 1242.
35. *CNA*, no. 1231.
36. *CNA*, no. 1214.
37. *CNA*, nos. 1177; 1243; 1164.
38. *CNA*, no. 1245.
39. *PD*, Sept. 19, 1983, p. 4; *Sichuan Daily* 四川日报, Apr. 17, 1983; *PD*, Nov. 20, 1983, p. 4.
40. *PD*, Apr. 6, 1983, p. 1; *Xinhua Daily* 新華日報 (南京), Nanjing, Dec. 29, 1983; *Wen Hui Bao* 文滙報 (上海), Shanghai, Jan. 15, 1983; *PD*, Feb. 28, p. 1; Nov. 22, p. 8, 1983.
41. *PD*, Oct. 10, 1983, p. 1.
42. *Xinhua Daily*, Nanjing, Jan. 15, 1983.
43. *Zhejiang Daily* 浙江日报, Feb. 1, 1983.
44. *Liaowang* 瞭望月刊, monthly, no. 9, Peking, 1983.
45. *Peking Daily*, Mar. 17, 1983.
46. *PD*, Oct. 13, 1983.
47. *PD*, Oct. 24, 1983, p. 1.
48. *PD*, Oct. 25, 1983, p. 1.
49. *PD*, Nov. 4, 1983, p. 1.
50. *PD*, Oct. 31, 1983, p. 1.
51. *Fei Tian Yue Kan* 飛天月刊 monthly, no. 6, Lanzhou, 1984; quoted in *New China Digest (Xinhua Wen-zhai)*, monthly, Peking, no. 8, 1984, pp. 163 ff.
52. *PD*, Nov. 1, p. 3; Nov. 2, p. 3; Nov. 5, p. 1, 1983.
53. *PD*, Dec. 18, 1983, p. 1.
54. *PD*, Dec. 10, 1983, p. 1.
55. *PD*, Mar. 5, 1983, p. 7.
56. *PD*, Dec. 10, 1984, p. 7.

57. *PD*, Dec. 30, 1984, p. 1.
58. *GMD*, Peking, Oct. 15, 1983; *PD*, Dec. 5, 1983, p. 5.
59. *PD*, Mar. 16, pp. 4–5; Nov. 6, p. 1, 1983.
60. *Economic Daily (Jinji Ribao* 經濟日報), Peking, Nov. 14, 1983.
61. *PD*, July 10, 1984, p. 1.
62. *PD*, May 18, 1984, p. 5.
63. *PD*, Aug. 3, 1984, p. 5.
64. *Red Flag*, no. 9, 1984; *PD*, Apr. 23, 1984, p. 1.
65. *PD*, June 8, 1984, p. 4.
66. *PD*, Mar. 21, 1984, p. 8.
67. *PD*, July 10, p. 4; July 20, p. 4, 1984.
68. *PD*, July 23, 1984, p. 4.
69. *PD*, Aug. 14, 1984, p. 5.
70. *PD*, July 14, 1984, p. 4.
71. *PD*, Oct. 17, 1984, p. 1.
72. *PD*, Dec. 23, 1984.
73. *PD*, Feb. 9, 1984, p. 3.
74. *PD*, Dec. 27, p. 4; Dec. 28, p. 1, 1984.
75. *PD*, Sept. 22, 1984, p. 1.
76. *PD*, Mar. 25, 1984, p. 1.
77. *PD*, Dec. 12, 20, 23, 1983.
78. *PD*, Apr. 22, 1984, p. 1.
79. *PD*, Aug. 15, 1984, p. 1.
80. *PD*, Dec. 23, 1984.
81. *PD*, Oct. 16, 1984, pp. 4, 5.
82. *PD*, Nov. 13, 1984, p. 1.
83. *PD*, Oct. 5, 1984.
84. *PD*, Aug. 27, p. 1; Oct. 5, 1984.
85. *PD*, May 12, 1984, p. 4.
86. *PD*, May 11, 1984, p. 1.
87. *PD*, May 27, 1984, p. 2.
88. *PD*, May 29, p. 1; May 31, p. 3, 1984.
89. *PD*, June 6, 1984, p. 2.
90. *PD*, May 20, 1984, p. 2.
91. *CNA*, no. 272, p. 2.
92. *PD*, Oct. 22, 1984, p. 1.
93. *PD*, Jan. 1, 1985.
94. *PD*, Oct. 26, 1984, p. 1.
95. *PD*, Nov. 16, 1984, p. 1.
96. *PD*, Nov. 2, and 5, 1984.
97. *PD*, Jan. 11, 1985, pp. 1, 4.
98. *PD*, Jan. 14, 1985.

Chapter XXII. 1985, Chaos and the Party Conference

1. *PD*, July 31, 1985, p. 1.
2. *PD*, Mar. 12, p. 8; Mar. 29, p. 5, 1985.

3. *PD*, Aug. 3, 1985, p. 1.
4. *PD*, Sept. 9, 1985, p. 5.
5. *PD*, June 14, 1985, p. 5.
6. *PD*, Feb. 26, 1985, p. 5.
7. *PD*, Apr. 13, 1985, p. 1.
8. *PD*, June 30, 1985, p. 1.
9. *PD*, July 15, 1985, p. 1.
10. *PD*, Sept. 12, p. 3; June 15, p. 5; Sept. 15, p. 2; Sept. 24, p. 5; Sept. 29, p. 4; June 24, p. 2; June 29, p. 1; June 18, p. 5; Aug. 26, p. 1; Sept. 13, p. 2; Sept. 27, p. 1.
11. *PD*, Feb. 14, 1985, p. 3.
12. *PD*, Feb. 23, 1985, p. 4.
13. *PD*, Oct. 16, 1985, p. 2.
14. *PD*, Aug. 18, 1985, p. 4.
15. *PD*, Mar. 15, 1985, p. 1.
16. *PD*, June 5, 1985, p. 8.
17. Boris Meissner, 'Das Soziale Gefüge der KPDSU am Ausgang der Breshnew-Ära', *Osteuropa*, no. 7/8, 1985.
18. *PD*, Mar. 15, 1985, p. 1.
19. *PD*, Mar. 21, 1985, pp. 5, 8.
20. *PD*, June 11 and 12, 1985.
21. *PD*, Sept. 9, 1985, p. 1.
22. *PD*, Sept. 17, 19 24 and 25, 1985.
23. *PD*, May 2, 1985, p. 1.
24. *PD*, Sept. 19, 1985, p. 1.
25. *PD*, Sept. 24, 1985.
26. *PD*, Sept, 27, 1985, p. 1.
27. *PD*, Aug. 16, 1985, p. 1.
28. *PD*, Oct. 1, 1985, p. 1.
29. *PD*, Oct. 11, 1985, p. 1.
30. *PD*, July 13, 1984, p. 5.
31. *PD*, Aug. 15, 1985, p. 4.
32. *Cadres' Teaching Material (Makesi zhu-yi zhe-xueh yuan-li* 馬克思主義哲學原理 （幹部教材）), Peking, 1983, 396 pp.
33. *PD*, June 28, 1984, p. 3.
34. *PD*, May 23, 1985, p. 4.
35. *PD*, May 3, 1985, p. 5.
36. *PD*, July 5, 1985.
37. Jutta Scherer, 'L'intelligentsia russe: sa goute de la "vérité réligieuse du socialisme" ' in *Le Temps de la réflexion, vol. II: La réligion de la Politique*, Paris 1981.
38. *Biografia intellectuale di Marx*, Florence, 1968 (An Italian translation of *Genesis des historischen Materialismus* by Paul Kägi, Vienna, 1965.
39. *PD*, Dec. 7, 1984, p. 5.

SELECT BIBLIOGRAPHY

This is a selection, by its nature incomplete, of Chinese and non-Chinese-language books and reviews dealing with the Chinese Communist Party and Marxism. Chinese-language and non-Chinese-language books are listed separately. The English translations of the titles of Chinese books may give those who do not read Chinese some idea of the subjects treated. For those who do read Chinese, authors and titles in Chinese characters have been included.

The Chinese-language books are divided roughly into four classes; viz. those
1. published before or at the beginning of the establishment of the regime (1949);
2. of the 1950s and 1960s, until the Cultural Revolution;
3. published in the period of the Cultural Revolution and the years of the ultra-radicals; and
4. published since the death of Mao in 1976.

Books published in China follow the Party Line. Those which attempted to express personal opinions — a book by the economist Ma Yinchu, the writings of Liang Shuming (both non-Party members) and those of Party-member Hu Feng — were condemned in the mid-1950s and became targets of nationwide smear campaigns. In the second half of the 1950s the writings of leading Party intellectuals were rejected in political campaigns. Under Deng the policy changed and so did the writers; but their fears have not yet been dispelled. No great independent writers have emerged. The Party Line, the ever-changing Party Line, is still being followed. One does not hear of manuscripts by great writers being smuggled out for publication in the West, as has happened in Eastern Europe.

Serious studies published in Taiwan — not listed separately — prove more objective than might have been expected (they are not sold to the public in Taiwan).

Books written abroad, whether by sinologists or by Chinese scholars who have lived abroad for many years, are of great value, although — or because — they represent various schools of thought. Some writers, one must admit, confound their affection for China with affection for the ruling regime. Some of them change their judgment of things Chinese according to the changing winds in the People's Republic. Some books on Party history use only materials published under the Maoist regime; others go deeper, using independent sources. An impressive number of scholars have published writings of lasting value. Some of these have been translated by Peking, strictly for inner-Party circulation.

The English-language periodicals which publish articles on the Communist Party and Marxism are well known: *China Quarterly, Asian Survey,* the *Journal of Asian Studies, Problems of Communism* (published by the USIA, United

States Government), and the weekly *Far Eastern Economic Review*, Hong Kong. Among the English-language periodicals published in China, *Beijing Weekly*, once known as the *Peking Review*, is meant for foreign consumption. It is useful since it carries the texts of some major documents. *World Marxist Review: Problems of Peace and Socialism*, the monthly of the pro-Moscow Communist world, says little about China, but is useful for comparing the systems.

A few Chinese periodicals have been included, but only those which deal with the history of the Party or of Marxism. *Red Flag (Hong Qi)*, the organ of the Party Central Committee, was founded in the year of the Leap, 1958, and was transformed into a fortnightly in 1980. Its contents mirror changes in Party policy through the years. There was a time, from November 1959 on, when *Red Flag* was the only magazine allowed to leave the country.

Some of the reviews published in the 1950s were suspended during the hectic days of the Cultural Revolution and resumed publication under Deng Xiaoping. Under the regime of the Jiang Qing radicals, which lasted till the arrest of the 'Gang of Four' in 1976, three ultra-radical Marxist reviews appeared in Shanghai.

Under Deng a number of new periodicals were launched. The monthly *Liaowang*, founded in 1981, is regarded as the organ of the Central Committee Secretariat. In January 1984 it became a weekly. This was followed by a decline in the standard of its contents. *Fortnightly Talk (Ban-yue-tan)* is addressed to less educated Party officials. New periodicals have appeared for the study of Party history. The quarterly *Modern History Studies* published important articles in 1979–82, years of relative freedom. *Party History Research* is published for inner-Party circulation only.

The journals of universities are important. They are written for a selected audience, and are more outspoken than other publications. There are numerous new reviews on what is called 'social sciences', which means Marxism and connected subjects.

Mention should be made of periodicals published in Taiwan dealing with mainland China. These contain objective studies with a minimal propagandist slant.

New reviews published by the Central Committee Party School need separate notice. These are written in the tone of the old Stalinist Marxism of the 1950s, in striking contrast with the new liberal publications of Deng's group.

NON-CHINESE BOOKS AND ARTICLES

Barnett, A. Doak, *Communist China and Asia: A Challenge to American Policy*, New York, 1960.

——, *Communist China: The Early Years, 1959–1955*, London, 1964.

Barrett, David D., *Dixie Mission: The United States Army Observer Group in Yenan, 1944*, Berkeley, 1970.

Bartke, Wolfgang, *Who's Who in the People's Republic of China*, Brighton, England, 1981.

Baum, Richard, and Frederick C. Teiwes, *Left in Form, Right in Essence: The Rural Socialist Education Campaign and the Crimes of Liu Shao-ch'i*, Hong Kong, 1967.

Beal, John Robinson, *Marshall in China: Account of the 11th Hour Mission that Almost Changed the Course of History*, New York and Toronto, 1970.

Beloff, Max, *Soviet Policy in the Far East, 1944–1951*, Oxford University Press, 1953.

Bennett, Gordon, *Yundong: Mass Campaigns in Chinese Communist Leadership*. Berkeley, 1976,

Bernstein, Richard, *From the Center of the Earth*, Boston, 1983.

Biographical Dictionary of Contemporary China, published by the Japanese Foreign Office (in Japanese), Tokyo, 1982.

Bisson, T.A., *Yenan in June 1937: Talks with the Communist Leaders*, Berkeley, 1973.

Bonavia, David, *Verdict in Peking: The Trial of the Gang of Four*, New York, 1984.

Boorman, Howard L. (ed.), *Biographical Dictionary of Republican China*, 3 vols, New York, 1967.

Brandt, Conrad, *Stalin's Failure in China, 1924–1927*, Cambridge, Mass., 1958.

Brandt, Benjamin Schwartz, and John K. Fairbank (eds), *A Documentary History of Chinese Communism*, London, 1952.

Brière, O., 'Les 24 ans du Parti Communiste Chinois (1921–1946)', *Bulletin de l'Université l'Aurore*, 1946.

Bush, Richard C., S.M. Goldstein and K. Sears, *People's Republic of China: A Basic Handbook*, New York, 1981.

Butterfield, Fox, *China: Alive in the Bitter Sea*, New York, 1982.

Chai, Winburg, *The Search for a New China: A Capsule History, Ideology and Leadership of the Chinese Communist Party, 1921–1974, with Selected Documents*, New York, 1975.

Chang, Parris H., *Élite Conflict in the Post-Mao China*, rev. edn, University of Maryland, 1983.

Chang Kuo-t'ao, *The Rise of the Chinese Communist Party*, Kansas, vol. I: 1921–1927, vol. II: 1928–1938.

Chassin, Lionel Max, *The Communist Conquest of China: A History of the Civil War 1945–1949*, Cambridge, Mass., 1965.

Chen Po-ta, *On the Ten-Year Civil War (1927–1937)*, Peking, 1966.

——, *Mao Tse-tung on the Chinese Revolution*, Peking, 1953.

Ch'en, Jerome, *Mao Papers: Anthology and Bibliography*, Oxford University Press, 1970.

——, *Mao and the Chinese Revolution*, London, 1965.

Chiang Kai Shek, Generalissimo, *Resistances and Reconstructions: Messages During China's Six Years of War, 1937–1943*, New York and London, 1943.

Chiu, Hungdah, and Shao-Chun Leng (eds), *China Seventy Years after the 1911 Hsin-hai Revolution*, Charlottesville, 1984.

Copper, John F., Franz Michael and Wu Yuan-li, *Human Rights in Post-Mao China*, Boulder, Colorado, 1985.

Dahm, Helmut, 'Das Ideologische Führungsamt', unpubl. research paper, Cologne: Bundesinstitut für ostwissentschaftliche und internationale Studien, 1983.

Das, Naranarayan, *China's Hundred Weeds: A Study of the Anti-Rightist Campaign in China*, Calcutta, 1979.

Domes, Jürgen, *China after the Cultural Revolution: Politics between Two Party Congresses*, London, 1976.

——, *Vertagte Revolution. Die Politik der Kuomintang in China, 1923–1937*, Berlin, 1969.

——, *The Internal Politics of China, 1949–1972*, London, 1973.

Drachkovitch, Milorad M., and Branko Lazitch (eds), *The Comintern: Historical Highlights*, Stanford, 1966.

Eighth National Congress of the Communist Party of China, vol. I: *Documents*, and vol. II: *Speeches*, Peking, 1956.

Elegant, Robert S., *China's Red Leaders: Political Biographies of the Chinese Communist Leaders*, London, 1952.

From Emperor to Citizen: The Autobiography of Aisin-Gioro Pu Yi, 2 vols, Peking, vol. I, 1964; vol. II, 1965.

Galbiati, Fernando, *P'eng P'ai and the Hai-Lu-Feng Soviet*, Stanford, 1985.

Guillermaz, Jacques, *The Chinese Communist Party in Power, 1949–1976*, Boulder, Colorado, 1976 (transl. from French).

——, *History of the Chinese Communist Party 1921–1949*, New York, 1972 (transl. from French).

Hahn, Emily, *The Soong Sisters*, London, 1941.

Harrison, James Pinckney, *The Long March to Power: A History of the Chinese Communist Party, 1921–1972*, New York, 1972.

Hatano, Ken'ichi, *Chugoku Kyosanto Shi* (History of the Chinese Communist Party) (7 vols) Tokyo, 1932.

Heinzig, Dieter, *Mao Tse-tung Weg zur Macht 1931 bis 1935 und die Otto-Braun-Memoiren*, Cologne: Bundesinstitut für ostwissenschaftliche und internationale Studien, no. 52, 1970.

Ho Kan Chih, *A History of the Modern Chinese Revolution*, Peking: Foreign Languages Press, 1959, 627pp.

Hong Yung Lee, *The Politics of the Chinese Cultural Revolution: A Case Study*, Berkeley, 1978, 369pp.

Hsiao Tso-Liang, *Chinese Communism in 1927: City Versus Countryside*, Hong Kong, 1970.

——, *Power Relations Within the Chinese Communist Movement, 1930–1934: A Study of Documents*, Seattle, 1961.

Hsü, Immanuel C.Y., *The Rise of Modern China*, 2nd edn, New York, 1975.

Hsüeh Chün-tu, *The Chinese Communist Movement, 1921–1937*. An annotated bibliography of selected materials in the Chinese collection of the Hoover Institution on War, Revolution and Peace, Stanford, 1960.

——, *The Chinese Communist Movement, 1937–1949*, Stanford, 1962. 312pp.

Hu Chiao-mu, *Thirty Years of the Communist Party of China*, Peking: Foreign Languages Press, 1951.

Huang, Philip C.C., et al., *Chinese Communists and Rural Society, 1927–1934*, Berkeley, 1973.

Isaacs, Harold R., *Re-encounters in China: Notes of a Journey in a Time Capsule*, New York, 1985.

——, *The Tragedy of the Chinese Revolution*, 2nd edn, Stanford, 1951.

Joffe, Ellis, *The Chinese Red Army: Growth of Professionalism and Party-Army Relations, 1949–1963*, Cambridge, Mass., 1963.

Jones, F.C., *Manchuria Since 1931*, London, 1949.

Kallgren, Joyce K. (ed.), *The People's Republic of China After Thirty Years: An Overview*, Berkeley, 1970.

Karnow, Stanley, *Mao and China: from Revolution to Revolution*, intro. by John K. Fairbank, London, 1972.

Ken Ling, *The Revenge of Heaven: Journal of a Young Chinese*, New York, 1972.

Kernig, C.D. (ed.), *Communism and Western Socialism: A Comparative Encyclopaedia*, 8 vols, New York, 1972.

Khrushchev Remembers, tr. Strobe Talbot, intro., commentary and notes by Edward Crankshaw, London, 1971.

Kim, Ilpyong, J., *The Politics of Chinese Communism: Kiangsi under the Soviets*, Berkeley, 1973.

Klein, Donald W., and Anne B. Clark (eds), *Biographic Dictionary of Chinese Communism 1921–1965*, 2 vols, Cambridge, Mass., 1971.

Kleinknecht, Günter, *Die kommunistische Taktik in China 1921–1927. Die Komintern, die koloniale Frage und die Politik der KPCh.*, Cologne, 1980.

Kubek, Anthony, *Introduction to the Amerasia Papers: A Clue to the Catastrophe of China*, repr. by the Committee of One Million, Washington, D.C., 1970.

Leonhard, Wolfgang, *Three Faces of Materialism: The Political Concepts of Soviet Ideology, Maoism, and Humanist Marxism*, New York, 1965.

Leys, Simon, *The Chairman's New Clothes: Mao and the Cultural Revolution* (transl. from French), London, 1977.

——, *Images Brisées: Confucius, Lin Piao, Chou En-lai, Mao Tse-tung, et Li Yi-che*, Paris, 1976.

Lieberthal, Kenneth, *A Research Guide to Central Party and Government Meetings in China, 1949–1975*, New York, 1976.

——, *Central Documents and Politbureau Politics in China*, Ann Arbor, 1978.

Lin Piao, *Long Live the Victory of People's War! In commemoration of the twentieth anniversary of victory in the Chinese People's War of Resistance against Japan*, Peking, 1967.

Liu Shao-chi, *How to be a Good Communist*, Peking: Foreign Languages Press, 1951.

——, *On The Party*, Peking, 1951.

——, *Long Live Leninism*, Peking, 1960.

MacFarquhar, Roderick, *The Hundred Flowers*, Paris, 1960.

——, *The Origins of the Cultural Revolution*, vol. 2: *The Great Leap Forward, 1958–1960*, Oxford University Press, 1983.

Magnenoz, Robert, *De Confucius à Lénine. La Montée au Pouvoir du Parti Communiste Chinois*, Saigon, 1951.

Marxism-Leninism and our Time, Prague, 1973.

Meisner, Maurice, *Marxism, Maoism and Utopianism: Eight Essays*, Madison, 1982.

——, *Li Ta-chao and the Origins of Chinese Marxism*, Cambridge, Mass., 1967.

Melis, Giorgio, *Cina: Rivoluzione/Restaurazione*, Milano, 1976.

North, Robert C., *Moscow and Chinese Communists*, 2nd edn, Stanford, 1968.

——, and Xenia J. Eudin, *M. N. Roy's Mission to China: The Communist-Kuomintang Split of 1927*, Berkeley, 1963.

Onate, Andres D., *Chairman Mao and the Chinese Communist Party*, Chicago, 1979.

Pepper, Suzanne, *Civil War in China: The Political Struggle, 1945–1949*, Berkeley, 1978.

Polemic on the General Line of the International Communist Movement, Peking, 1965.

Pye, Lucian, *The Dynamics of Chinese Politics*, Cambridge, Mass., 1981.

——, *Warlord Politics*, New York, 1971.

Robinson, Thomas W., *The Sino-Soviet Border Dispute: Background Development, and the March 1969 Clashes*, Santa Monica, 1970.

Rue, John A., *Mao Tse-tung in Opposition, 1927–1935*, Stanford, 1966.

Scalapino, Robert A. (ed.), *Élites in the People's Republic of China*, Seattle, 1972.

Schram, Stuart R., *Mao Tse-tung*, New York, 1967.

——, *The Political Thought of Mao Tse-tung*, New York, 1963.

Schurmann, Franz, *Ideology and Organisation in Communist China*, Berkeley, 1970.

Schwartz, Benjamin I., *Chinese Communism and the Rise of Mao*, Cambridge, Mass., 1952.

Seagrave, Sterling, *The Soong Dynasty*, New York, 1985.

Smedley, Agnes, *The Great Road: The Life and Times of Chu Teh* , New York, 1956.

Snow, Edgar, *Random Notes on Red China, 1936–1945*, Cambridge, Mass., 1957.

——, *Red Star Over China*, New York, 1938.

——, *The Other Side of the River*, New York, 1961.

Solomon, Richard S., *Mao's Revolution and Chinese Political Culture*, Berkeley, 1971.

Sworakowski, Witold S. (ed.), *World Communism: A Handbook, 1918–1965*, Stanford, 1973.

T'ang Leang-Li (ed.), *Suppressing Communist Banditry in China, 1941–1950*, Shanghai, 1934.

Tang Tsou, *America's Failure in China, 1941–1950* (2 vols), Chicago, 1963.

Teiwes, Frederick C., *Leadership Legitimacy and Conflict in China: From a Charismatic Mao to the Politics of Succession*, London, 1984.

——, *Provincial Party Personnel in Mainland China, 1956– 1966*, New York, 1967.

Terrill, Ross, *Mao: A Biography*, New York, 1980.

'The Indictment Against Lin Biao-Jiang Qing Cliques', *Ta Kung Pao* (English supplement), Hong Kong, Nov., 1980.

Thornton, Richard C., *China, the Struggle for Power, 1917–1972*, Bloomington, 1973.

——, *The Comintern and the Chinese Communists, 1928–1931*, Seattle, 1969.

Ting Wang, *Chairman Hua: Leader of the Chinese Communists*, London, 1980.

Trager, F.N., and William Henderson (eds), *Communist China, 1949–1969: A Twenty-Year Appraisal*, New York, 1970.

Vogel, Ezra, *Canton Under Communism: Programs and Politics in a Provincial Capital, 1949–1966*, Cambridge, Mass., 1969.

Wah Yah-Kang, *The Rise of Communism in China, 1920–1950*, Hong Kong, 1952.

Waller, Derek J., *The Kiangsi Soviet Republic: Mao and the National Congresses of 1931 and 1934*, Berkeley, 1973.

Wedemeyer, Albert C., *Wedemeyer Reports*, New York, 1958.

Wetter, Gustav A., *Dialectical Materialism: A historical and systematic survey of philosophy in the Soviet Union*, New York, 1958.

——, *Sowjet-Ideologie Heute. Dialektischer and historischer Materialismus.* Frankfurt/Main, 1962.

Whiting, Allen, *Soviet Politics in China, 1917–1924*, New York, 1954.

Whitson, William W., and Chen-Hsia Huang, *The Chinese High Command: A*

History of Communist Military Politics, 1927– 1971, New York, 1973.

Wilbur, Martin C. *The Nationalist Revolution in China, 1923–1928*, Cambridge University Press, 1983.

——, and Julie L. How (eds), *Documents on Communism, Nationalism and Soviet Advisers in China 1918–1927: Papers seized in the 1927 Peking raid*, New York, 1972.

Wilson, Dick, *Chou: The Story of Zhou Enlai, 1896–1976*, London, 1984.

Witke, Roxane, *Comrade Chiang Ch'ing*, Boston, 1977.

Wittfogel, Karl A., 'Some Remarks on Mao's Handling of Concepts and Problems of Dialectics', in *Studies in Soviet Thought*, Fribourg, 1963.

——'A Short History of Chinese Communism', unpubl. paper, 1964.

Wolfe, Bertram D., *Marxism: 100 Years in the Life of a Doctrine*, New York, 1965.

Wu Tien-wei, *Lin Biao and the Gang of Four*, Carbondale, Illinois, 1983.

——, *The Kiangsi Soviet Republic, 1931–1934: A Selected and Annotated Bibliography of the Ch'en Ch'eng Collection*, Cambridge, Mass., 1981.

——, *The Sian Incident: A Pivotal Point in Modern Chinese History*, University of Michigan Papers in Chinese Studies, no. 26, 1976.

Wylie, Raymond F., *The Emergence of Maoism: Mao Tse-tung, Ch'en Po-ta, and the Search for Chinese Theory, 1935–1945*, Stanford, 1980.

Yakhontoff, Victor A., *The Chinese Soviets*, New York, 1934.

CHINESE BOOKS

1921–1950

Ai Siqi, *Da-zhong zhe-xue* 艾思奇：大衆哲學 (Philosophy of the Masses), Hong Kong, 1936, 233pp.

Bo Gu, *Bian-zheng wei-wu-lun yu li-shi wei-wu-lu ji-ben wen-ti* 博　古：辯證唯物論與歷史唯物論基本問題 (Basic Questions of Dialectical Materialism and Historical Materialism), 4 vols, Peking, 1949, 1322pp.

Chen Congyi, *Wan-nan shi-bian qian hou* 陳從一：皖南事變前後 (Before and After the South Anhui Incident), Shanghai, 1st edn, 1950, 15th edn, 1957, 74pp.

Chen Yun, *Zen-yang zuo yi-ge cong-chan-dang-yuan* 陳　雲：怎樣做一個共產黨員 (How to Be a Good Communist), Canton, 1950, 32pp.

Deng Chumin, *She-hui ke-xue chang-shi jiang-hua* 鄧初民：社會科學常識講話 (Lecture on Basic Notions of Social Science), Shanghai, 1949, 220pp.

Feng Ding, *Ping-fan di zhen-li* 馮　定：平凡的真理 (The Ordinary Truth), Dairen, 1949, 239pp.

Feng Xuefeng, *Lun min-zhu ge-ming di wen-yi yun-dong* 馮雪峯：論民主革命的文藝運動 (On the Literary Movement of the Democratic Revolution), Shanghai: Writers Studio, 1946, 136pp.

Feng Ziyou, *Zhongguo ge-ming yun-dong er-shi liu-nian zu-zhi-shi* 馮自由：中國革命運動二十六年組織史(26 Years' History of the Organisation of the Chinese Revolutionary Movement), Shanghai: Commercial Press, 1948, 299pp.

Gong-chan-dang-yuan ke-ben 共產黨員課本 (Textbook of Party Members), Central-South Bureau of the CCP, Hankou: Propaganda Dept., 1950, 72pp.

Hua Yingshen (ed.), *Zhong-guo gong-chan-dang lie-shi zhuan* 華應申：中國共產黨烈士傳 (Martyrs of the CCP), Hong Kong, 1949, 324pp.

Luo-xun-ta-er (Rozental). *Wei-wu bian-zheng-fa* 羅遜塔爾：唯物辯證法 (Materialist Dialectic), (transl. from Russian), Hong Kong, 1949, 196pp.

Ma-En-Lie-Si si-xiang fang-fa-lun 馬恩列斯思想方法論 (Ideological Method in Marx-Engels-Lenin-Stalin), Shanghai, 1950, 446pp.

Mu-qian xing-shi he wo-men di ren-wu — 1947 nian yi-lai zhong-guo gong-chan-dang zhong-yao wen-jian-ji 目前形勢和我們的任務——一九四七年以來中國共產黨重要文件集(Present Situation and Our Tasks — Collection of CCP Important Documents Since 1947), Hong Kong, 1949, 202pp.

Wu Liping, *She-hui zhu-yi shi* 吳黎平：社會主義史 (History of Socialism), Shanghai, 1950, 332pp.

——, and Ai Siqi, *Ke-xue li-shi-guan jiao-cheng* 吳黎平、艾思奇：科學歷史觀教程 (Teaching Materials of Scientific Concept of History), 1939, 268pp.

Yi-jiu-si-jiu-nian yi-lai zhong-guo gong-chan-dang zhong-yao wen-jian-ji, 1949年以來中國共產黨重要文件集 (Collection of Important Documents Concerning the CCP since 1949), Hong Kong, 1949, 148pp.

Zhong-hua-ren-min gong-he-guo kai-guo wen-xian 中華人民共和國開國文獻 (Documents on the Beginning of the Chinese People's Republic), Hong Kong, 1949, 311pp.

1951–1965

Ai Siqi, *Li-shi wei-wu-lun — she-hui fa-zhan-shi* 艾思奇：歷史唯物論—社會發展史 (Historical Materialism — History of Development of Society), Peking, 1951, 270pp.

Bi Zhiqian, *Zhong-guo gong-chan-dang di yi-ci zheng-fen yun-dong di wei-da sheng-li* 畢植蒨：中國共產黨第一次整風運動的偉大勝利 (The Great Victory of the First Rectification Campaign of the CCP), Changchun, 1957, 40pp.

Cai Xiaoqian, *Jiangxi su-qu: Hong-jun xi-cuan hui-yi* 蔡孝乾：江西蘇區・紅軍西竄回憶 (Reminiscences on the Flight of the Red Army in the Jiangxi Soviet Area), Taipei, 1960, 414pp.

Chen Boda, *Lun Mao Zedong si-xiang — Ma-ke-si Lie-ning zhu-yi yu Zhong-guo ge-ming di jie-he* 陳伯達：論毛澤東思想—馬克思列寧主義與中國革命的結合 (Mao Zedong Thought — Combining Marxism with the Chinese Revolution), Peking, 1951, 58pp.

Di-san-ci guo-nei ge-ming zhan-zheng da-shi yue-biao 第三次國內革命戰爭大事月表 (Chronology of the 3rd Internal Revolutionary War), Peking, 1961, 100pp.

Di-yi-ci guo-nei ge-ming zhan-zheng shi-qi di nong-min yun-dong 第一次國內革命戰爭時期的農民運動 (Peasant Movement during the First Internal Revolution), Peking, 1953, 439pp.

Ding Shouhe, Yin Xuyi, and Zhang Bozhao, *Shi-yue ge-ming dui zhong-guo ge-ming di ying-xiang* 丁守和、殷敘彝、張伯昭：十月革命對中國革命的影響 (The Influence of the October Revolution on China), Peking, 1957, 180pp.

Gong Chu, *Wo yu hong-jun* 龔楚：我與紅軍 (The Red Army and I), Hong Kong, 1954, 454pp.

Hu Hua (ed.), *Zhong-guo ge-ming-shi jiang-yi* 胡 華：中國革命史講義 (Lectures on the History of China's Revolution), Peking: Chinese People's Univ. Publishing House, 2nd edn, 1962, 569pp.

——, *Zhong-guo xin-min-zhu zhu-yi ge-ming-shi xiu-ding-ben* 胡 華：中國新民主主義革命史修訂本 *(History of the New Democratic Revolution)*, 3rd edn, Peking, 1953, 270pp.

Hu Qiaomu, *Zhong-guo gong-chan-dang di san-shi-nian* 胡喬木：中國共產黨的三十年 (Thirty years of the CCP), Peking, 1951, 94pp.

Huang He (ed.), *Zhong-guo gong-chan-dang san-shi-wu nian jian-shi* 黃 河：中國共產黨三十五年簡史 (Simple History of 45 Years of the CCP), Peking, 1957, 96pp.

Jiang Qinfeng, *Zai Mao-zhu-xi zhou-wei* 蔣秦峯：在毛主席周圍 (Around Chairman Mao), Peking, 1958, 86pp.

Kang-ri-zhan-zheng shi-qi jie-fang-qu gai-kuang 抗日戰爭時期解放區概況 (The Situation in the Liberated Areas During the Resistance War), Peking: Contemporary Chinese History Publications, 1953, 132pp.

Li Da, *Shi-jian lun jie-shuo* 李 達：實踐論解說 (commentary to 'On Practice'), Peking, 1951, 181pp.

Li Jiannong, *Wu-xu yi-hou san-shi-nian zhong-guo zheng-zhi-shi* 李劍農：戊戌以後三十年中國政治史 (30 Years Political History of China Since the Time of the Wu-xu), Peking, 1965, 388pp.

Liang Hanbing, *Zhong-guo xian-dai ge-ming shi jiao-xue can-kuo ti-gang* 梁寒冰：中國現代革命史教學參考提綱 (Outline of Teaching Material on the History of Chinese Contemporary Revolution), Tianjin, 1955, 206pp.

Lie-ning zhu-yi wan-sui 列寧主義萬歲 (Hail Leninism), Hong Kong, 1960, 150pp.

Mao Zedong xuan-ji 毛澤東選集 (Selected Writings of Mao Zedong), 5 vols., vols. 1 and 2, 1952, vol. 3, 1953, vol. 4, 1960, vol. 5, 1977.

Mao Zedong zhu-zuo jie-shao 毛澤東著作介紹 (Introduction to the Works of Mao Zedong), Peking, 1962, 314pp.

Mao Zedong zhu-zuo xuan-du 毛澤東著作選讀 (Selected Readings of Mao Zedong), 2 vols., Peking, 1964, 520pp.

Miao Min, *Fang Zhimin zhan-duo di yi-sheng* 繆 敏：方志敏戰鬥的一生 (The Lifelong Struggle of Fang Zhimin), Peking, 1958, 110pp.

Nanjing-lu-shang hao-ba-lian 南京路上好八連 (The Nanjing Road Good Eighth Company) Peking: Liberation Army Culture Section, 1963, 126pp.

Shaan-gan-ning bian-qu can-yi-hui wen-xian hui-ji 陝甘寧邊區參議會文獻彙輯 (Collection of Documents of the Shanxi-Gansu-Ningxia Area Consultative Conference), Peking, 1958, 379pp.

She-hui zhu-yi jiao-yu ke-cheng di yue-du wen-jiang hui-bian 社會主義教育課程的閱讀文件彙編 (Collection of Documents to be Read on Socialist Education),

Peking, 3 vols, vol. I, 1957, 1123pp; vols II & III, 1958, 1112pp., & 430pp.

Shen Yunlong, *Zhong-guo gong-chan-dang zhi lai-yuan* 沈雲龍：中國共產黨之來源 (The Origin of the CCP), Taipei, 1959, 92pp.

Wan Yagang, *Zhong-guo gong-chan-dang jian-shi* 萬亞剛：中國共產黨簡史 (Brief History of the CCP), Hong Kong, 1951, 86pp.

Wang Jianmin, *Zhong-guo gong-chan-dang shi-guo* 王健民：中國共產黨史稿 (Outline of the History of the CCP) Taipei, 1965, 3 vols., vol. I, 591pp.; vol. II, 742pp.; vol. III, 728pp.

Wang Shi (ed.), *Zhong-guo gong-chan-dang li-shi jian-bian* 王　實：中國共產黨歷史 簡編 (Brief Description of the History of the CCP), Shanghai, 1958, 302pp.

Xiao Mu, *Zhong-gong zen-yang gao pu-xuan* 蕭　牧：中共怎樣搞普選 (How Chinese Communism Carries on Universal Suffrage), Hong Kong, 1954, 74pp.

Xue-xi Ma-ke-si En-ge-si Lie-ning Si-da-lin guan-yu gong-chan zhu-yi di li-lun 學習馬克思恩格斯列寧斯大林關於共產主義的理論 (Study Theory of Communism in Marx-Engels-Lenin-Stalin), Peking, 1959, 232pp.

Xin Zhong-guo zi-liao ji-cheng 新中國資料集成 (Collection of Materials on New China), in Japanese, Tokyo, 2 vols, vol. I 1945–47, 675pp.; vol. II 1948–49, 693pp.

Xu Yuandong (ed.), *Zhong-guo gong-chan-dang li-shi jiang-hua* 徐元冬：中國共 產黨歷史講話 (Lectures on the History of the CCP), Peking: Chinese Youth Publishing House, 2nd edn, 1981, 408pp.

Yi Chongguang, *Dang tian-xia yu dang guo-jia* 易重光：黨天下與黨國家 ('Criteria of Party and State'), Hong Kong, 1958, 2 vols., 239pp.

Zhang Cixi, *Li Dazhao xian-sheng zhuan* 張次溪：李大釗先生傳 (The Life of Li Dazhao), 1951, 114pp.

Zhang Ruxin, *Mao Zedong tong-zhi dui Ma-ke-si Lie-ning zhu-yi wei-wu-lun di gong-xian* 張如心：毛澤東同志對馬克思列寧主義唯物論的貢獻 (Contribution of Comrade Mao Zedong to the Materialism of Marxism-Leninism), Peking, 1954, 97pp.

Zhao Han, *Tan-tan Zhong-guo gong-chan-dang di-zheng-fen yun-dong* 趙　漢：談談中國共產黨的整風運動 (Talking About the Rectification Campaign of the CCP), Peking, 1957, 75pp.

Zhong-guo gong-chan-dang cheng-li san-shi zhou-nian ji-nian zhuan-ji 中國共產黨 成立三十週年紀念專輯 (Special Edition on the 30th Anniversary of the Establishment of the CCP), comp. by the CCP Central Committee South-China Branch Office, Canton, 1951, 146pp.

Zhong-guo gong-chan-dang jian-shi 中國共產黨簡史 (Brief History of the CCP), Peking: Study (*Xue-xi*) Review Publishing House, 1951, 52pp.

Zhou Yuanbing, *et al.*, *Zen-yang cheng-que ren-shi he chu-li ren-min nei-bu mao-dun*

周原冰等：怎樣正確認識和處理人民內部矛盾 (How to Know and How to Handle Contradictions Within the People), Shanghai, 1957, 64pp.

1966–1977

Cao Boyi, *Jiangxi su-wei-ai zhi jian-li ji qi beng-kui, 1931–1934* 曹伯一：江西蘇維埃之建立及其崩潰 (The Establishment and Collapse of the Jianxi Soviet, 1931–1934), Taipei, 1969, 690pp.

Chen Changfeng, *Gen-sui Mao-zhu-xi chang-zheng* 陳昌奉：跟隨毛主席長征 (In the Steps of Chairman Mao During the Long March), Hong Kong, 1971, 69pp.

Cheng Fangwu, *Chang-zheng hui-yi-lu* 成仿吾：長征回憶錄 (Reminiscences on the Long March), Peking, 1977, 196pp.

Ding Wang, *Zhong-gong wen-ge yun-dong zhong di zu-zhi yu ren-shi wen-ti, 1965–1970* 丁望：中共"文革"運動中的組織與人事問題 (Questions of Organisation and Persons during the Cultural Revolution of the CCP, 1965–1970), Hong Kong, 1970, 264pp.

——, *Zhong-gong wen-hua-da-ge-ming zi-liao hui-bian* 丁望：中共文化大革命資料 (Materials of the Great Cultural Revolution of the CCP), *Ming Bao Monthly*, Hong Kong, vol. I, 1967, 717pp.; vol. II, 1969, 582pp; vol. III, 1969, 510pp.; vol. IV, 1970, 750pp.; vol. V, 1970, 681pp.; vol. VI, 1972, 733pp.

Fung Yulan, *Lun Kong-qiu* 馮友蘭：論孔丘 (On Confucius), Peking, 1975, 123pp.

Gao Chongyan, *Zhong-gong ren-shi bian-dong, 1959–1969* 高崇岩：中共人事變動 (Personnel Changes in the CCP, 1959–1969), Hong Kong, 1970, 915pp.

Ge-ming zai fa-zhan ren-min zai qian-jin 革命在發展 人民在前進 (Revolution Develops, People Advance), Study Material no. 1, Hong Kong: Sanlian, 1970, 126pp.

Hai Feng, *Guan-zhou di-qu wen-ge li-cheng shu-lüe* 海楓：廣州地區文革歷程述略 (Narration of the Cultural Revolution Events in the Canton Region), Hong Kong, 1971, 450pp.

Hua-zhu-xi shi wo-men di hao ling-xiu 華主席是我們的好領袖 (Chairman Hua is Our Good Leader), Peking, 1977, 131pp.

Jiang Qing tong-zhi jiang-hua xuan-bian, 1966–1968, 江青同志講話選編 (Selection of Speeches of Comrade Jiang Qing, Feb. 1966-Sept. 1968 [inner-Party publication]), Hebei: People's Publishing House, 1969, 85pp.

Ma-ke-si En-ge-si Lie-ning Si-da-lin fan chao-liu di guang-hui shi-li 馬克思恩格斯列寧斯大林反潮流的光輝事例 (The Shining Examples of Marx, Engels, Lenin and Stalin, Opposing the Trend), Peking, 1975, 95pp.

Mao Zedong si-xiang wan-sui 毛澤東思想萬歲 (Hail Mao Zedong Thought), Red Guard unofficial publication, 4 vols, vol. I, 1969; vols II-IV, 1967.

Mao-zhu-xi yong-yuan huo zai wo-men xin-zhong 毛主席永遠活在我們心中 (Chairman Mao Lives For Ever in Our Hearts), Peking: People's Literature Publishing House, 1977, 408pp.

Ru Xin, *et al.*, *Ou-zhou zhe-xue-shi-shang di xian-yan-lun he ren-xing lun pi-pan* 汝信：歐洲哲學史上的先驗論和人性論批判（論文集） (Criticism of Apriorism and of the Doctrine of Human Nature in the History of European Philosophy), Peking, 1974, 165pp.

Wei-da di li-cheng; hui-yi zhan-zheng nian-dai di Mao-zhu-xi 偉大的歷程（回憶戰爭年代的毛主席） (Great History Remembering Chairman Mao in the War Years), Peking, 1977, 321pp.

Wei Wen (ed.), *Han-ying ci-hui shou-ce* 蔚 文：漢英詞滙手冊 (Handbook of Chinese-English Vocabulary), Peking, 1970, 1618pp.

Yuan Yue, *Lin Biao shi-jian yuan-shi wen-jian hui-bian* 袁 悅：林彪事件原始文件彙編 (Collection of Original Documents on the Case of Lin Biao), Taipei, 1973, 154pp.

Zhong-guo gong-chan-dang fa-qi-ren fen-lie shi-liao 中國共產黨發起人分裂史料 (Materials on the History of Ruptures among Founders of the CCP), Hong Kong: Long-wen Bookstore, 1968, 199pp.

1978–1985

Chen Xulu (ed.), *Zhong-guo jin-dai-shi ci-dian* 陳旭麓：中國近代史詞典 (Dictionary of Modern Chinese History), Shanghai, 1982, 863pp.

Chen Yun tong-zhi wen-gao xuan-bian, 1956–1962 陳雲同志文稿選編 (Compilation of Selected Writings of Comrade Chen Yun 1956–1962 [inner-Party publication]) Peking, 1980, 216pp.

Chen Zhiling, *Xin-bian di-yi-ci guo-nei ge-ming zhan-zheng shi-gao* 陳志凌：新編第一次國內革命戰爭史稿 (Outline of the First Internal Revolutionary War), Shaanxi: People's Publishing House, 1981, 291pp.

Chen Zhirang, *Jun-shen zheng-quan — jin-dai zhong-guo di jun-fa shi-qi* 陳志讓：軍紳政權—近代中國的軍閥時期 (The Period of Warlords in Modern China — Military Political Power), Hong Kong, 1970, 174pp.

Ci Hai jun-shi fen-ce 辭 海（軍事分冊） (Ci Hai Dictionary: Articles on Military Affairs), Shanghai, 1980, 179pp.

Ci Hai li-shi fen-ce: zhong-guo xian-dai shi 辭 海（歷史分冊，中國現代史） (Ci

Hai Dictionary: Contemporary History of China), Shanghai, 1980, 203pp.

Da-lu di-xia kan-wu hui-bian 大陸地下刊物彙編 Mainland Underground Publications), Taipei, vol. I, 334pp.; vol. II, 338pp (1980); vol. III, 330pp., vol. IV, 334pp (1981).

Dai Weisen zhu, and Lian Xinghuo yi, *Tuo-luo-ci-ji-zhu-yi fen-xi* 戴維森著、連星火譯：托洛茨基主義分析 (Analysis of Trotskyism), *Seventies* magazine, Hong Kong, 1979, 90pp.

Dang di zu-zhi gong-zuo wen-da 黨的組織工作問答 (Questions and Answers on the Party's Organization Work), Peking, 1983, 299pp). (comp. by the CCP Central Committee Organization Dept. Research Bureau and Organization Office).

Dang-shi yan-jiu zi-liao Zhong-guo ge-ming bo-wu-guan dang-shi yan-jiu shi-bian 黨史研究資料 (Research Material on Party History), comp. by the Museum of Chinese Revolution Party History Research Bureau, vol. I, Chengdu, 1980, 502pp.

Fan Zhimin zhuan 方志敏傳 (The Life of Fan Zhimin), Jiangxi: People's Publishing House, 1982, 302pp.

Gao Song, *et al.*, *Ma-ke-si zhu-yi lai-yuan yan-jiu lun-cong* 高崧：馬克思主義來源研究論叢 (Research Papers on the Origin of Marxism), Peking: Commercial Press, 1983, 435pp.

Ge-ming hui-yi-lu 革命回憶錄 (Revolutionary Reminiscences), Peking: People's Publishing House, 1980.

Gong-chan-guo-ji yu guan zhong-guo ge-ming di wen-xian zi-liao, 1929–1936 共產國際有關中國革命的文獻資料 (Documents of the Comintern Concerning the Chinese Revolution), Peking: Chinese Academy of Social Sciences Publishing House, 2 vols, vol. I, 1981, 610pp.; vol. II, 1982, 481pp.

Hu Hua zhu-bian. Zhong-gong dang-shi ren-wu-zhuan 胡華主編：中共黨史人物傳 (Biographies of Persons in Chinese Communist Party History Series), comp. by the Research Society of Personalities in CCP History, Shaanxi: People's Publishing House (series began in 1980).

Hua Shijun, and Hu Yumin, *Yan'an zheng-feng shi-mo* 華世俊、胡育民：延安整風始末 (Story of the Yan'an Rectification), Shanghai, 1985, 96pp.

Hui-yi Pan Hannian 回憶潘漢年 (Remembering Pan Hannian), Jiangsu: People's Publishing House, 1985, 259pp.

Hui-yi Wang Jiaxiang 回憶王稼祥 (Remembering Wang Jiaxiang) Peking: People's Publishing House, 237pp.

Jian-ming guo-ji gong-chan zhu-yi yun-dong-shi ci-dian 簡明國際共產主義運動史辭典 (Simple Dictionary of the International Communist Movement), comp. by the Zheng-zhou, Anhui, Hubei, Suzhou and Beijing Universities, Anhui: People's Publishing House, 1985, 709pp.

Jie-fang-jun jiang-ling-zhuan 解放軍將領傳 (Biographies of Generals of the Liberation Army), vol. I, Peking: Liberation Army Publishing House, 1984, 569pp.

Li Dazhao zhuan 李大釗傳 (The Life of Li Dazhao), Peking, 1979, 265pp.

Li Weihan, *Tong-yi-zhan-xian wen-ti yu min-zu wen-ti* 李維漢：統一戰線問題與民族問題 (The Question of United Front and Nationalities), Peking, 1981, 677pp.

Li Xin, *et al.*, *Min-guo ren-wu zhuan* 李新等：民國人物傳 (Biographies of Personalities of the Republic), Peking, vol. I, 1978, 408pp.; vol. II, 1980, 418pp.; vol. III, 1981, 398pp.

Liao Gailong, *Quan-guo jie-fang zhan-zheng jian-shi* 廖蓋隆：全國解放戰爭簡史 (Brief History of the War of Liberation of the Whole Country), Shanghai, 1984, 264pp.

Lin Daizhao, and Pan Guohua, *Ma-ke-si zhu-yi zai zhong-guo — cong ying-xiang di zhuan-ru dao zhuan-bo* 林代昭，潘國華：馬克思主義在中國—從影響的傳入到傳播 (Marxism in China from its Beginning to its Propagation), Peking: Qinghua University Publishing House, 1983, vol. I, 426pp.; vol. II, 589pp.

Liu-da yi-qian — dang di li-shi cai-liao 六大以前—黨的歷史材料 (Before the Sixth Party Congress — Material for Party History), Peking, 1980, 994pp.

Ma-ke-si En-ge-si Lie-ning Si-da-lin Mao Zedong lun zheng-que dui-dai Ma-ke-si zhu-yi 馬克思恩格斯列寧斯大林毛澤東論正確對待馬克思主義 (Marx, Engels, Lenin, Stalin and Mao Zedong on Correct Treatment of Marxism), Peking: CCP Central Committee Marx-Engels-Lenin-Stalin's Works Translation Office, 1979, 141pp.

Ma-ke-si zhu-yi di san-ge lai-yuan 馬克思主義的三個來源 (The Triple Origin of Marxism), comp. by the Theory Section of the no. 1116 Troops of the Liberation Army and the Philosophy Research Institute, Western Philosophy Section, of the Chinese Academy of Social Science, Peking, 1978, 313pp.

Ma-ke-si zhu-yi zhe-xue yuan-li (gan-bu jiao-cai) 馬克思主義哲學原理（幹部教材）(The Principles of Marxist Philosophy [materials for cadres]), Peking: Peking City Party Committee's Party School, Teaching of Philosophy Research Bureau, and the Chinese Academy of Social Sciences Publishing House, 1983, 396pp.

Ma-ke-si zhu-yi zai zhong-guo 馬克思主義在中國 (Marxism in China), Peking: Qinghua University Publishing House, 1983.

Ma-ke-si zhu-yi zai zhong-guo di fa-zhan 馬克思主義在中國的發展 (Development of Marxism in China), Peking: Red Flag Publishing House, 1983.

Mao Zedong tong-zhi ba-shi-wu dan-chen ji-nian wen-xuan 毛澤東同志八十五誕辰紀念文選 (Selection of Writings for the 85th Birthday of Comrade Mao Zedong), Peking: People's Publishing House, 1979, 301pp.

Nan-chang qi-yi zi-liao 南昌起義資料 (Materials on the Nanchang Uprising), comp. by the Research Bureau of Chinese Contemporary Revolutionary History of the Chinese Academy of Social Sciences, Peking, 1979, 462pp.

Nie Rongzhen hui-yi-lu 聶榮臻回憶錄 (Reminiscences of Nie Rongzhen), Peking: Soldier Publishing House, vol. I, 1983, 335pp.; vol. II, 1984, 585pp.

Peng Dehuai zi-shu 彭德懷自述 (Peng Dehuai's Narration), Peking, 1981, 300pp.

Ren Bishi 任弼時 (Ren Bishi), Hunan: People's Publishing House, 1979, 295pp.

Shi-jian shi jian-yan zhen-li di wei-yi biao-zhun wen-ti tao-lun ji 實踐是檢驗真理的唯一標準問題討論集 (Collection of Papers on the Question of Practice, the Sole Criterion of Truth), comp. by the Editorial Board of *Philosophical Research*, Peking: Chinese Academy of Social Sciences Publishing House, 1979, vol. I, 366pp.; vol. II, 371pp.

Su Shuangbi, and Wang Hongzhi, *Wu Han zhuan* 蘇雙碧・王宏志：吳晗傳 (The Life of Wu Han), Peking, 1984, 368pp.

Wang Kuixi, *et al.*, *Jin-dai dong-bei ren-min ge-ming dou-zheng shi* 王魁喜等：近代東北人民革命鬥爭史 (History of the Revolutionary Struggle in the Northeast), Jilin, 1984, 206pp.

Wei Hongyun (ed.), *Zhong-guo xian-dai shi-gao, 1919–1949* 魏宏運：中國現代史稿 (Outline of Contemporary Chinese History, 1919–1949), Heilongjiang, 1980, vol. I, 550pp.; vol. II, 459pp.

Wen Jize (ed.), *Yan-an zhong-yang yan-jiu-yuan hui-yi-lu* 溫濟澤：延安中央研究院回憶錄 (Reminiscences on Central Research Yuan in Yan'an), Hunan: People's Publishing House, 1984, 295pp.

Wuhan di-xia dou-zheng hui-yi-lu 武漢地下鬥爭回憶錄 (Reminiscences on the Underground Struggle in Wuhan), Hubei: People's Publishing House, 1981, 390pp.

Wu Yuzhang hui-yi-lu 吳玉章回憶錄 (Memoirs of Wu Yuzhang), Peking, 1978, 252pp.

Xiao Xiaoqin (ed.), *Dang-shi hui-yi bao-gao-ji* 蕭效欽：黨史會議報告集 (Collection of Reports on Party Meetings), Peking: CCP Central Committee Party School Publishing House, 1982, 404pp.

Xinhua ri-biao di hui-yi 新華日報的回憶 (Remembering *Xinhua Daily*), Sichuan Publishing House, vol. I, 1979, 470pp.; vol. II, 1983, 504pp.

Xin-shi-dai; Hunan ge-ming shi-liao xuan-ji 新時代（湖南革命史料選輯） (New generation: Selection of historical materials on the revolution in Hunan), Zhangsha, 1980, 384pp.

Xin-si-jun di wu-shi kang-zhan li-cheng 新四軍第五師抗戰歷程 (History of the 5th Regiment of the 4th Route Army), Hubei Publishing House, 1985, 286pp.

Xue-xi li-shi jue-yi zhuan-ji 學習歷史決議專輯 (Study the Decision on History), Peking, CCP Central Committee Party School Publishing House, 1982, 198pp.

'Yi-da' qian-hou — *Zhong-guo gong-chan-dang di-yi-ci dai-biao da-hui qian-hou zi-liao xuan-bian* "一大"前後—中國共產黨第一次代表大會前後資料選編 (Before and After the 1st Party Congress — Selection of Materials), comp. by the Contemporary History Bureau of the Chinese Academy of Social Sciences and the Party History Research Bureau of the Museum of the Chinese Revolution, Peking, vol. I, 1980, 452pp.

Yu Jinan, *Zhang Guotao he 'Wo di hui-yi'* 于吉楠：張國燾和《我的回憶》 (Zhang Guotao and His 'Memoirs'), Sichuan People's Publishing House, 1982, 313pp.

Zhong-gong dang-shi bai-ti jie-da 中共黨史百題解答 (One Hundred Questions and Answers Concerning the History of the CCP), Jiangxi People's Publishing House, 1979, 318pp.

Zhong-gong dang-shi can-kao zi-liao — di-san-ci uo-nei ge-ming zhan-zheng shi-qi 中共黨史參考資料（第三次國內革命戰爭時期）(Materials on the History of the CCP: the Period of the 3rd Internal Revolutionary War), comp. by the CCP Central Committee Party School Teaching Party History Research Bureau, Peking, 1979, 548pp.

Zhong-gong dang-shi can-kao zi-liao — guo-min jing-ji hui-fu shi-qi 中共黨史參考資料（國民經濟恢復時期）(Materials on the History of the CCP: The Period of Restoration of the National Economy), comp. by the CCP Central Committee Party School Teaching Party History Research Bureau, Peking, 1980, 260pp.

Zhong-gong dang-shi shi-jian ren-wu-lu 中共黨史事件人物錄 (Records of Events and People in CCP History), Shanghai, 1983, 759pp.

Zhong-gong liu-shi-nian ji-nian wen-xuan 中共六十年紀念文選 (Selected Articles on the 60th Anniversary of the CCP), comp. by the Reading Materials Bureau of the CCP Central Party History Research Bureau, Peking: CCP Central Committee Party School Publishing House, 1982, 589pp.

Zhong-gong ji-mi wen-jian hui-bian 中共機密文件彙編 (Collection of Secret Documents of the CCP), Taipei, 1978, 579pp.

Zhong-guo ge-ming-shi 250 ti jie-da 中國革命史250題解答 (250 Questions and Answers Concerning the History of the Revolution in China), comp. by the Marxism-Leninism Research Bureau of Jiaotong University, Shanghai. Peking: Soldiers' Publishing House, 1983, 371pp.

Zhong-guo gong-chan-dang li-ci dai-biao da-hui 中國共產黨歷次代表大會 (The Congresses of the CCP), comp. by the Contemporary History Research Bureau of the Academy of Social Sciences. Peking: CCP Central Committee Publishing House, 1982, 196pp.

Zhong-guo gong-chan-dang li-ci zhong-yao hui-yi-ji 中國共產黨歷次重要會議集 (Important meetings of the CCP), comp. by the Teaching of Party History Research Bureau, Materials Section of the CCP Central Committee Party School, Shanghai: People's Publishing House, 1982, 273pp.

Zhong-guo gang-chan-dan li-shi jiang-yi 中國共產黨歷史講義 (Lectures on the History of the CCP), 4th enlarged edn, Zhejiang, 1982, 169pp.

Zhong-guo gong-chan-dang li-shi jiang-yi 中國共產黨歷史講義 (Lectures on the History of the CCP), Shanghai, vol. II, 1981 1st edn; 2nd edn, 1982, 200pp.

Zhong-guo jin-dai-shi zhi-shi shou-ce 中國近代史知識手冊 (Manual of Knowledge of Modern Chinese History), Peking: Zhonghua Bookstore, 1980, 300pp.

Zhong-guo xian-dai-shi 中國現代史 (Contemporary Chinese History), Peking: Teachers University Publishing House, 1983, vol. I, 471pp; vol. II, 406pp.

Zhu Min, *Hui-yi wo-di fu-qin Zhu De wei-yuan-zhang* 朱敏：回憶我的父親朱德 (Remembering My Father, Committee Chairman Zhu De), Peking, 1978, 130pp.

CHINESE PERIODICALS

Ban-yue-tan 半月談 (Fortnightly Talk), Peking.

Beijing da-xue xue-bao 北京大學學報 (Journal of Peking University).

Dang-shi yan-jiu 黨史研究 (Party-history Research), published every two months by the Central Party School.

Dang-shi yan-jiu 黨史研究 (Party History Research), published by the review's editorial board (inner-Party publication).

Fei-qing yan-jiu 匪情研究 (Bandits' Conditions Research), see *Zhong-gong yan-jiu*.

Fei-qing yue-bao 匪情月報 (Bandits' Conditions Monthly) see *Zhong-guo da-lu yan-jiu*.

Fu-dan xue-bao 復旦學報 (Journal of Fudan University), Shanghai, published every two months.

Hong-qi 紅旗 (Red Flag), the Central Committee's organ.

Jin-dai-shi yan-jiu 近代史研究 (Modern History Studies), quarterly, started in Sept. 1979, Peking: Chinese Academy of Social Sciences Publishing House.

Jin-dai-shi zi-liao 近代史資料 (Modern History Materials), Chinese Academy of Social Sciences Publishing House, no. 46, Apr. 1982; no. 47, Mar. 1982.

Lan-zhou da-xue xue-bao 蘭州大學學報 (Journal of Lanzhou University).

Li-lun yue-kan 理論月刊 (Theory Monthly), Central Party School.

Li-shi yan-jiu 歷史研究 (Historical Research), monthly, Peking: Chinese Academy of Social Sciences Publishing House.

Liao Wang 瞭望 (Outlook), Xinhua News Agency, Peking, monthly (Apr. 1981-Dec. 1983); weekly from Jan. 1984.

Nanjing da-xue xue-bao 南京大學學報 (Journal of Nanjing University), quarterly.

Renwu 人物 (Personalities), fortnightly, Peking.

She-hui 社會 (Society), Shanghai University (dept. of Literature).

She-hui ke-xue 社會科學 (Social Sciences), monthly, Shanghai: People's Publishing House.

She-hui ke-xue ji-kan 社會科學輯刊 (Social Sciences Quarterly), Liaoning Academy of Social Sciences.

She-hui ke-xue yan-jiu 社會科學研究 (Social Sciences Research), Chengdu.

She-hui ke-xue zhan-xian 社會科學戰線 (Frontline of Social Sciences), quarterly, Jilin People's Publishing House.

Tu-shu-guan-xue tong-xun 圖書館學通訊 (Correspondence on Library Science), quarterly, Peking: Wen-wu Publishing House.

Wen Shi Zhe 文史哲 (Literature, History, Philosophy), published every two months, by Shandong University.

Wen-wu tian-di 文物天地 (Cultural Relics), published every two months, Peking.

Wen-xue ping-lun 文學評論 (Literary Criticism), published every two months, Peking.

Wen-yi bao 文藝報 (Literature), fortnightly, Peking.

Wuhan da-xue xue-bao 武漢大學學報 (Journal of Wuhan University).

Xinhua wen-zhe 新華文摘 (Xinhua Digest), Peking.

Xinhua yue-bao 新華月報 (Xinhua Monthly), Peking.

Xue-shu yue-kan 學術月刊 (Learning Monthly), Shanghai.

Xue-xi 學習 (Study), monthly.

Xue-xi yu pi-pan 學習與批判 (Study and Criticism), monthly, Shanghai (Journal of the 'Gang of Four').

Xue-xi yu si-kao 學習與思考 (Study and Reflection), published every two months, Peking: Chinese Academy of Social Sciences, Graduate School.

Xue-xi yu tan-suo 學習與探索 (Study and Search), published every two months, Heilongjiang: Academy of Social Sciences.

Zhao-xia 朝霞 (Zhao-xia), Shanghai (literary magazine of the 'Gang of Four').

Zhe-xue yan-jiu 哲學研究 (Philosophical Research), Peking.

Zheng-zhi-xue yan-jiu 政治學研究 (Political Science Research), published every two months, Academy of Social Sciences.

Zhong-gong nian-biao 中共年報 (Yearbook on Chinese Communism), Taipei.

Zhong-gong yan-jiu 中共研究 (Studies on Chinese Communism), monthly, Taipei (formerly known as Bandits' Condition Research).

Zhong-guo da-lu yan-jiu 中國大陸研究 (Mainland China Research), monthly, Taipei (formerly known as Bandits' Condition Monthly).

Zhong-guo she-hui ke-xue 中國社會科學 (Chinese Social Sciences), published every two months, Peking.

Zhong-guo she-hui ke-xue-yuan yan-jiu-sheng-yuan xue-bao 中國社會科學院研究生院學報 (Journal of Chinese Academy of Social Sciences, Graduate School), published every two months, Peking.

Zhong-shan da-xue xue-bao 中山大學學報 (Journal of Zhong-shan University), quarterly, Canton.

Zhong-yang min-zu xue-yuan xue-bao 中央民族學院學報 (Journal of Central College of Nationalities), quarterly, Peking.

Zi-ran bian-zheng-fa za-zhi 自然辯證法雜誌 (Review of Natural Dialectic), quarterly, Shanghai (Journal of the 'Gang of Four').

CHRONOLOGY
of the Chinese Communist Party, 1921–1985

1921 *July*. First Party Congress, in the presence of a Comintern agent, held in Shanghai.

1922 *January*. Chinese representatives present at a meeting in Moscow.
July. Second Party Congress in Shanghai elects Chen Duxiu as leader. The Party officially joins the Comintern.

1923 *June*. Third Party Congress in Canton decides to join, as individuals, the Nationalist Party (Kuomintang).
October. Borodin in Canton.

1924 *January*. First Congress of the Kuomintang in Canton, Communists in the Kuomintang Executive Committee.
May. Whampoa Military Academy set up, with Soviet help. Head of School: Chiang Kai Shek. Head of political department: Zhou Enlai.

1925 *January*. Fourth Party Congress, in Shanghai.
March. Sun Yat Sen dies.

1926 *January*. Kuomintang holds Second Congress. Seven Communists in the thirty-six-member Executive Committee.
March. Chiang Kai Shek accuses Communists of violent revolt.
June. Nationalists start Northern Expedition for the conquest of China.

1927 The Fifth Party Congress. Chiang Kai Shek in Nanjing.
July. Comintern Executive Committee condemns Chen Duxiu. A provisional Politbureau is set up.
August. Abortive Communist occupation of Nanchang; disarray among Communist ranks. The 'Eight-Seven' (August 7) meeting.
September. Party headquarters moved from Wuhan to Shanghai.
October. Mao to Jing Gang Shan.
November. Party meeting in Shanghai criticises Mao's action.
December. Abortive Canton uprising.
End of year. Hubei-Henan-Anhui corner base established by Xu Xiangqian and Zhang Guotao. Xu Haidong establishes a base. He Long sets up a base in Hubei.

1928 *January*. Zhu De and Chen Yi set up a soviet government in South Hunan.
March. He Long leads uprising in Hunan-Hubei border.
April. Liu Zhidan's uprising in Shaanxi province.
May. Fang Zhimin's revolutionary base to the east of Jiangxi province set up.
June–July. Sixth Chinese Communist Party Congress held in Moscow: Xiang Zhongfa Secretary-General. Peng Dehuai organises troops in Hunan.
June. Zhang Zuolin killed by Japanese agents. Nationalist troops occupy Peking.
October. Nationalist government organised in Nanjing.

December. Peng Dehuai to Jing Gang Shan. Western countries recognise the Nationalist Nanjing government.

1929 *January*. Mao moves to Ruijin.
September. Peng Dehuai returns to Hunan-Hubei-Jiangxi border.
November. Chen Duxiu expelled from the Party.

1930 *June*. Li Lisan's radical policies. Hunan-Hubei-Jiangxi base under Peng Dehuai.
September. Instruction of Comintern; Li Lisan eliminated from leadership.
December. Futian Incident.
End of year. Mao carries out a violent purge.

1931 Fourth Plenum of Sixth Central Committee. 'Returned students' Wang Ming and Bo Gu in leadership.
September. The Japanese occupation of Manchuria.
November. Mao censured in Ruijin.
December. Zhou Enlai arrives in Ruijin.

1932 *January*. Unsuccessful Japanese attack on Shanghai.
October. Mao criticised at a Party meeting.
End of year. Xu Xiangqian's 'long march' to the west (arriving in 1934).

1933 *January*. Party leadership moves from Shanghai to Ruijin.
February. Luo Ming affair.
November. Short-lived revolt of Nationalist troops in Fujian.

1934 *January*. Fifth Plenum of Sixth Central Committee held in Ruijin. Bo Gu Secretary-General. The Ruijin soviet government's second Congress addressed by Mao.
October. Long March begins.

1935 *January*. Zunyi Conference.
August. Anti-Japanese Manifesto, following decision of the Seventh Congress of the Comintern.
October. Arrival in north Shaanxi.
End of year. 'Long March' of Xu Haidong to the west (arriving in August).

1936 *December*. Xi'an Incident.

1937 *January*. Party headquarters move to Yan'an.
March. Zhang Guotao criticised.
May. Yan'an conference on underground Party work.
July. Japanese attack near Peking. Start of the Japanese war. Common Front with Nationalist forces.
August. Establishment of the Eighth Route Army.
September. Lin Biao's victory at Ping Xing Guan.

1938 *January*. New Fourth Army established. *Xinhua Daily* starts publication in Hankow.
September. Sixth Plenum of Sixth Central Committee. Mao establishes his authority over Wang Ming.

October. Japanese troops occupy Canton.

December. Wang Jing Wei leaves Zhongqing.

1939 *January*. Zhou Enlai sets up South China Bureau in Zhongqing.

September. War starts in Europe.

1941 *January*. Clash between Nationalist and Communist troops, known as the South Anhui Incident.

May. *Liberation Daily* starts publication in Yan'an. Party's Central-China Bureau set up under Liu Shaoqi.

1942 *February*. Beginning of Party Rectification in Yan'an.

March. General Stilwell appointed Chief-of-Staff of the China Theatre.

1943 *November*. Chiang Kai Shek present at the Cairo Conference with Roosevelt and Churchill.

1944 *May*. Central Committee's Seventh Plenum (Seventh after the 1928 Sixth Party Congress), lasting a year, concludes the Rectification.

June. Zhangsha, capital of Hunan province, taken by the Japanese.

October. General Wedemeyer replaces General Stilwell.

November. Guilin, in Guangxi province, taken by the Japanese.

1945 *January*. General Patrick Hurley named as United States ambassador to China. Dong Biwu takes part in the San Francisco United Nations conference.

April. Seventh Party Congress. Mao now supreme ruler. Mao's 'On Coalition Government'.

May. Germany surrenders.

June. Nationalist government's foreign minister T.V. Soong visits Moscow.

August. Japan surrenders. Soviet friendship treaty with Nationalist government — Mao arrives in Zhongqing.

October. Mao returns to Yan'an.

December. George Marshall arrives in Zhongqing.

1946 *January*. Marshall Mission: tripartite (American-Nationalist-Communist) peace negotiations. Political Consultative Conference established. China recognises independence of Mongolian Republic.

June. Mass anti-American demonstrations.

August. Stalin urges Chinese Communists to avoid civil war.

December. Anti-American demonstrations.

1947 *January*. General Marshall leaves China.

March. Nationalist troops occupy Yan'an.

September. Land reform announced.

1948 *June*. *People's Daily* starts publishing as organ of the Party's North China Bureau.

September. Lin Biao leads the battle of Shenyang.

November. Re-organisation of the army into First, Second, Third and Fourth Field Armies and North-China Field Army.

1949 *January*. Surrender of Peking.

March. Second Plenum of Seventh Central Committee, near Peking.

April. Fall of Nanjing.

May. Fall of Shanghai.

July. Mao's 'On People's Democratic Dictatorship'.

September. People's Political Consultative Conference.

October 1. Official establishment of the Chinese People's Republic. Canton taken.

December. Mao goes to Moscow.

1950 *March*. Mao returns from Moscow. Suppression of counter-revolutionaries.

May. New Party reform.

June. Third Plenum of Seventh Central Committee, on the economy and land reform.

October. China enters Korean war.

1951 *May*. Occupation of Tibet.

December. Anti-corruption campaign starts.

1954 *February*. Fourth Plenum of Seventh Central Committee, condemns Gao Gang.

September. First People's Congress. Mao Chairman of the State.

October. Khrushchev in Peking.

1955 *March*. National Party Conference condemns Gao Gang.

April. Fifth Plenum of Seventh Central Committee. Lin Biao and Deng Xiaoping become Politbureau members. Zhou Enlai at Bandung Conference.

May. Hu Feng condemned.

July. Mao announces collectivisation of land.

October. Socialisation of private business.

1956 *January*. Zhou Enlai encourages intellectuals.

February. Twentieth Party Congress in the Soviet Union. Khrushchev denounces Stalin.

May. Mao speaks of Hundred Flowers, freedom of expression.

September. Eighth Party Congress.

1957 *February*. Mao's speech 'On Contradictions within the People'. In the following months free criticism of the Party is allowed.

June. Critics called 'rightists'.

September. Second Plenum of Eighth Central Committee. Mao criticises Eighth Party Congress.

November. Mao's second visit to the Soviet Union.

1958 *January–March*. At regional meetings Mao encourages speedy development.

May. Supplementary meeting of Eighth Party Congress. Fifth Plenum of Eighth Central Committee, Lin Biao elected Vice-Chairman.

June. *Red Flag* starts publication.

July. Khrushchev in Peking.

August. Establishment of Communes.

November. Sixth Plenum of Eighth Central Committee; Mao to give up post as Head of State.

1959 *March.* Revolt in Tibet.

April. Seventh Plenum of Eighth Central Committee. People's Congress elects Liu Shaoqi as Head of State.

August. Eighth Plenum of Eighth Central Committee at Lushan, Peng Dehuai condemned.

September. Lin Biao named minister of defence.

1960 *April.* *Red Flag* publishes 'Hail Leninism!'

May. Instruction concerning food shortages.

June. Peng Zhen leads delegation to Bucharest International Communist Conference.

July. Soviet experts withdrawn from China.

September. Liu Shaoqi and Deng Xiaoping at International Communist Conference in Moscow. Establishment of Central Committee Regional Bureaus.

1961 *January.* Ninth Plenum of Eighth Central Committee, moderate economic policy.

October. Zhou Enlai at Twenty-second Party Congress of the Soviet Union; he departs abruptly.

1962 *September.* Tenth Plenum of Eighth Central Committee, Mao's radical insistence on class struggle.

October. Military intervention in Assam, India.

1963 *March.* Mao cites the soldier Lei Feng as model of total obedience.

May – September. Contradictory instructions on purge in the villages (called the Socialist Education Campaign, or Four Cleansing).

September. Public controversy with Moscow.

December. Zhou Enlai's efforts to unite Asian and African countries.

1964 *May.* *Little Red Book* (Sayings of Chairman Mao) published for the general public.

June. Mao chastises the world of art.

October. First atom bomb exploded.

November. Zhou Enlai visits new Soviet leader Leonid Brezhnev in Moscow.

1965 *September.* Mao warns of revisionism inside Party.

November. Wang Dongxing, head of Mao's bodyguard, becomes head of the Office of the Central Committee. Yao Wenyuan's article against a play entitled *Dismissal of Hairui* interpreted as criticism of Mao.

December. Luo Ruiqing, Chief-of-Staff, dismissed.

1966 *May.* Original Cultural Revolution team (Peng Zhen, Luo Ruiqing, Lu Dingyi, Yang Shangkun) dismissed. Radical new team (Chen Boda, Jiang Qing, Kang Sheng) set up.

June. 'Rebels' organised in universities in Peking.

August. Eleventh Plenum of Eighth Central Committee. Lin Biao sole Vice-Chairman. Liu Shaoqi becomes number eight in Party hierarchy. Mass parades of Red Guards begin. Vandalism in private homes and religious buildings.

March. Writers of *People's Daily* dismissed.

1967 *January*. Liu Shaoqi humiliated. 'Rebels' take over leadership in provinces. Army enters the political arena (called '3-aid 2-military').

February. Veteran Party leaders (Tan Zhenlin, etc.) resist and are condemned.

April. Liu Shaoqi condemned.

June. First H-bomb exploded.

July. Peking's emissaries Wang Li and Xie Fuzhi are resisted in Wuhan.

August. Police and security and foreign ministry taken over by 'rebels'. British Embassy burnt down. Radical Wang Li dismissed.

1968 *March*. Leading generals dismissed.

July. Mao sends workers' teams to restore order in schools.

September. Revolutionary Committees established in all provinces.

October. Cadres locked in 'May 7 Schools'. Twelfth Plenum of Eighth Central Committee, Liu Shaoqi expelled from Party.

December. Red Guards dismissed, sent to villages.

1969 *March*. Military conflict with Soviet troops at Ussuri River.

April. Ninth Party Congress. Lin Biao designated successor to Mao.

1970 *June*. Universities re-open.

August. Second Plenum of Ninth Central Committee. Mao's conflict with Lin Biao and Chen Boda. Reorganisation of Party.

1971 *July*. Kissinger's first visit to Peking.

August. Mao in South China.

September. Lin Biao dies under mysterious circumstances, his generals are arrested.

October. United Nations votes for admission of PRC.

1972 *February*. President Nixon visits Peking.

September. Prime Minister Tanaka of Japan visits Peking.

1973 *March*. Deng Xiaoping reappears.

August. Tenth Party Congress. Jiang Qing's followers in highest leadership. Criticism of Confucius and Lin Biao.

1974 *January*. Lin Biao condemned not as 'leftist' but as 'rightist'.

April. Campaign against Zhou Enlai begins, without mention of his name. Deng Xiaoping speaks at UN about Mao's division into three worlds.

1975 *January*. Second Plenum of Tenth Central Committee. Deng elected Vice-Chairman. Sick Zhou Enlai at People's Congress.

February. The radicals assert Marxism.

March. New attacks on Zhou Enlai.

April. Chiang Kai Shek dies in Taiwan.

August. Mao criticises renowned novel *All Men Are Brothers*, apparently aiming at Zhou Enlai and Deng Xiaoping.

September. Dazhai conference. Deng's plan for restoring scientific work.

1976 *January*. Zhou Enlai dies. Mao names Hua Guofeng Acting Premier.

April. Tian An Men incident. Hua Guofeng named First Vice-Chairman of Party and Premier; Deng Xiaoping dismissed from all his posts.

July. Zhu De dies. Earthquake at Tangshan.

September. Mao dies.

October. Jiang Qing and her companions, the 'Gang of Four', arrested. Hua Guofeng declared Chairman of the Party.

1977 *July*. Third Plenum of Tenth Central Committee. Deng reinstated.

August. Eleventh Party Congress, led by Hua Guofeng. Vice-Chairmen: Ye Jianying, Deng Xiaoping, Li Xiannian, Wang Dongxing.

December. Hu Yaobang named head of the Party's organisation department.

1978 *February*. Deng becomes head of Political Consultative Conference.

April. Deng Xiaoping criticises literary interpretation of Mao's sayings.

November. 1976 Tian An Men incident reinterpreted.

December. Diplomatic relations with United States. Third Plenum of Eleventh Central Committee introduces Deng Xiaoping's policies, sets up Disciplinary Investigation Committee (Chen Yun). Commemoration of Peng Dehuai and Tao Zhu, victims of Cultural Revolution. Politbureau makes Hu Yaobang Secretary-General and relieves Wang Dongxing from post of head of Office of Central Committee.

1979 *January*. The outcasts — 'landlords, kulaks, counter-revolutionaries and bad elements' — mostly rehabilitated. Commemoration of some Party-leader victims of the Cultural Revolution. Deng visits the United States (January 29–February 5)

February. Military action against Vietnam.

June. Criminal Law published.

July. Memory of Zhang Wentian rehabilitated. More victims of Cultural Revolution commemorated.

September. Fourth Plenum of Eleventh Central Committee. Zhao Ziyang and Peng Zhen become members of Politbureau.

1980 *February*. Fifth Plenum of Eleventh Central Committee; Hu Yaobang and Zhao Ziyang become Politbureau Standing Committee members. Rehabilitation of Liu Shaoqi decided, Wang Dongxing dismissed.

March. Li Lisan commemorated.

May. Liu Shaoqi (died 1969) commemorated.

September. Zhao Ziyang replaces Hua Guofeng as Premier.

October. Kang Sheng and Xie Fuzhi expelled from Party posthumously.

November. Trial of Jiang Qing and companions begins.

December. Propaganda Department reintroduces ideological training.

1981 *January.* *Rules for Political Life of the Party* published. Jiang Qing and companions sentenced, Jiang Qing sentenced to death (suspended for two years).

February. Rules for polite behaviour published.

June. Sixth Plenum of Eleventh Central Committee. Resolution on Party history since 1949; Hu Yaobang elected Chairman of the Party. Politbureau Standing Committee consists of Hu Yaobang, Ye Jianying, Deng Xiaoping, Zhao Ziyang, Li Xiannian, Chen Yun, Hua Guofeng.

August. Propaganda Department discusses ideology, called 'Question of Ideological Frontline'.

1982 *March.* Month of March declared month of courtesy. People's Congress Standing Committee orders courts to impose severe sentences on criminals.

April. Party leadership and Cabinet order severe punishment for economic crimes.

July. Census held.

September. Twelfth Party Congress. Title of Party Chairman abolished. Hu Yaobang elected General Secretary, Deng Xiaoping head of Military Committee. Politbureau Standing Committee consists of Hu Yaobang, Ye Jianying, Deng Xiaoping, Zhao Ziyang, Li Hsiennian, Chen Yun.

December. People's Congress Standing Committee passes new State Constitution.

1983. *February.* Disciplinary Investigation Committee orders Party leaders to hand back illegally occupied houses.

June. Peng Zhen elected head of People's Congress Standing Committee.

1984 *April. People's Daily* article on 'total rejection of the Cultural Revolution'.

May. Peng Zhen states that Party policy becomes law only when passed through People's Congress. Deng Xiaoping criticises Geng Biao and Huang Hua.

October. Third Plenum of Twelfth Central Committee orders holding of Party conference and structural changes in economy.

1985. *May-June.* Army reform.

September. National Party Conference.

SUBJECT INDEX

WADE GILES-PINYIN KEY TO SURNAMES

Wade-Giles	Pinyin	Wade-Giles	Pinyin
Chang	Zhang	Jen	Ren
Chao	Zhao	Kao	Gao
Ch'en	Chen	Ke	Ge
Cheng	Zheng	Keng	Geng
Chi	Ji	K'o	Ke
Ch'i	Qi	Ku	Gu
Chia	Jia	Kuan	Guan
Chiang	Jiang	Kung	Gong
Ch'iao	Qiao	Kuo	Guo
Chien	Jian	Lo	Luo
Ch'ih	Chi	Pa	Ba
Ch'in	Qin	Pai	Bai
Ch'iu	Qiu	Po	Bo
Chou	Zhou	Pu	Bu
Chu	Zhu	Shih	Shi
Ch'ü	Qu	Sung	Song
Chung	Zhong	Teng	Deng
Ho	He	T'ien	Tian
Hsi	Xi	Ting	Ding
Hsia	Xia	Ts'ai	Cai
Hsiang	Xiang	Ts'ao	Cao
Hsiao	Xiao	Tseng	Zeng
Hsieh	Xie	Tu	Du
Hsien	Xian	Tung	Dong
Hsing	Xing	Yen	Yan
Hsü	Xu	Yü	Yu
Jao	Rao		

NAME INDEX

591